T0336844

Handbook of Research on Emerging Developments in Data Privacy

Manish Gupta
State University of New York at Buffalo, USA

A volume in the Advances in Information Security, Privacy, and Ethics (AISPE) Book Series

An Imprint of IGI Global

Managing Director: Lindsay Johnston
Managing Editor: Austin DeMarco
Director of Intellectual Property & Contracts: Jan Travers
Acquisitions Editor: Kayla Wolfe
Production Editor: Christina Henning
Typesetter: Amanda Smith
Cover Design: Jason Mull

Published in the United States of America by
Information Science Reference (an imprint of IGI Global)
701 E. Chocolate Avenue
Hershey PA, USA 17033
Tel: 717-533-8845
Fax: 717-533-8661
E-mail: cust@igi-global.com
Web site: http://www.igi-global.com

Library of Congress Cataloging-in-Publication Data

Handbook of research on emerging developments in data privacy / Manish Gupta, editor.
  Summary: "This book brings together new ideas on how to deal with potential leaks of valuable customer information, highlighting the legal aspects of identity protection, trust and security, and detection techniques"-- Provided by publisher.
  ISBN 978-1-4666-7381-6 (hardcover) -- ISBN 978-1-4666-7382-3 (ebook) -- ISBN 978-1-4666-7384-7 (print & perpetual access) 1. Data protection. 2. Data protection--Law and legislation. 3. Computer security. 4. Online identity theft. 5. Data encryption (Computer science) I. Gupta, Manish, 1978-HF5548.37.H37 2015 005.8--dc23
  2015003713

This book is published in the IGI Global book series Advances in Information Security, Privacy, and Ethics (AISPE) (ISSN: 1948-9730; eISSN: 1948-9749)

British Cataloguing in Publication Data
A Cataloguing in Publication record for this book is available from the British Library.

For electronic access to this publication, please contact: eresources@igi-global.com.

Advances in Information Security, Privacy, and Ethics (AISPE) Book Series

ISSN: 1948-9730
EISSN: 1948-9749

MISSION

As digital technologies become more pervasive in everyday life and the Internet is utilized in ever increasing ways by both private and public entities, concern over digital threats becomes more prevalent.

The **Advances in Information Security, Privacy, & Ethics (AISPE) Book Series** provides cutting-edge research on the protection and misuse of information and technology across various industries and settings. Comprised of scholarly research on topics such as identity management, cryptography, system security, authentication, and data protection, this book series is ideal for reference by IT professionals, academicians, and upper-level students.

COVERAGE

- Electronic Mail Security
- Device Fingerprinting
- Privacy Issues of Social Networking
- Access Control
- Internet Governance
- IT Risk
- Computer ethics
- Telecommunications Regulations
- Information Security Standards
- Privacy-Enhancing Technologies

IGI Global is currently accepting manuscripts for publication within this series. To submit a proposal for a volume in this series, please contact our Acquisition Editors at Acquisitions@igi-global.com or visit: http://www.igi-global.com/publish/.

Titles in this Series

For a list of additional titles in this series, please visit: www.igi-global.com

Handbook of Research on Securing Cloud-Based Databases with Biometric Applications
Ganesh Chandra Deka (Ministry of Labour and Employment, India) and Sambit Bakshi (National Institute of Technology Rourkela, India)
Information Science Reference • copyright 2015 • 434pp • H/C (ISBN: 9781466665590) • US $335.00 (our price)

Handbook of Research on Threat Detection and Countermeasures in Network Security
Alaa Hussein Al-Hamami (Amman Arab University, Jordan) and Ghossoon M. Waleed al-Saadoon (Applied Sciences University, Kingdom of Bahrain)
Information Science Reference • copyright 2015 • 450pp • H/C (ISBN: 9781466665835) • US $325.00 (our price)

Information Security in Diverse Computing Environments
Anne Kayem (Department of Computer Science, University of Cape Town, South Africa) and Christoph Meinel (Hasso-Plattner-Institute for IT Systems Engineering, University of Potsdam, Potsdam, Germany)
Information Science Reference • copyright 2014 • 354pp • H/C (ISBN: 9781466661585) • US $245.00 (our price)

Network Topology in Command and Control Organization, Operation, and Evolution
T. J. Grant (R-BAR, The Netherlands) R. H. P. Janssen (Netherlands Defence Academy, The Netherlands) and H. Monsuur (Netherlands Defence Academy, The Netherlands)
Information Science Reference • copyright 2014 • 320pp • H/C (ISBN: 9781466660588) • US $215.00 (our price)

Cases on Research and Knowledge Discovery Homeland Security Centers of Excellence
Cecelia Wright Brown (University of Baltimore, USA) Kevin A. Peters (Morgan State University, USA) and Kofi Adofo Nyarko (Morgan State University, USA)
Information Science Reference • copyright 2014 • 357pp • H/C (ISBN: 9781466659469) • US $215.00 (our price)

Multidisciplinary Perspectives in Cryptology and Information Security
Sattar B. Sadkhan Al Maliky (University of Babylon, Iraq) and Nidaa A. Abbas (University of Babylon, Iraq)
Information Science Reference • copyright 2014 • 443pp • H/C (ISBN: 9781466658080) • US $245.00 (our price)

Analyzing Security, Trust, and Crime in the Digital World
Hamid R. Nemati (The University of North Carolina at Greensboro, USA)
Information Science Reference • copyright 2014 • 281pp • H/C (ISBN: 9781466648562) • US $195.00 (our price)

Research Developments in Biometrics and Video Processing Techniques
Rajeev Srivastava (Indian Institute of Technology (BHU), India) S.K. Singh (Indian Institute of Technology (BHU), India) and K.K. Shukla (Indian Institute of Technology (BHU), India)

www.igi-global.com

701 E. Chocolate Ave., Hershey, PA 17033
Order online at www.igi-global.com or call 717-533-8845 x100
To place a standing order for titles released in this series, contact: cust@igi-global.com
Mon-Fri 8:00 am - 5:00 pm (est) or fax 24 hours a day 717-533-8661

List of Contributors

Table of Contents

Detailed Table of Contents

Section 1
Legal Aspects

Concerns about government snooping in the wake of revelations by whistle blower Edward Snowden have deterred enterprises and IT professionals from keeping sensitive data in the clouds. Moving towards cloud-based computing has emerged and has gained acceptance as a solution to the tasks related to the processing of information. However, cloud computing carries serious risks to business information. The questions around risk and compliance are still largely unknown and need to be ironed out. Cloud computing opens numerous legal, privacy, and security implications, such as copyright, data loss, destruction of data, identity theft, third-party contractual limitations, e-discovery, risk/insurance allocation, and jurisdictional issues. This chapter discusses the associated legal risks inherent in cloud computing, in particular the international data transfer between EU and non-EU states.

This chapter provides an analysis of the data protection rules in EU law, focusing on the constitutional and legal developments after the entry into force of the Lisbon Treaty. It examines the jurisprudence of the Court of Justice of the EU on data protection issues, including the recent decisions of the Court on metadata retention and the new right to be forgotten. It concludes with a critical comment on the possibilities and limitations of the EU to provide for effective and comprehensive data protection.

In cyberspace, copyright enforcement and privacy rights have become two clashing realities. In fact, with the arrival of digital technology, especially the Internet, right holders, facing massive online infringements to their reproduction or distribution exclusive rights, mainly by file-sharers on Peer-to-Peer (P2P) systems or Cloud storage systems clients, started developing more and more intrusive new enforcement strategies in electronic communications as a means to identify the infringers and the committed infractions. The goal of the chapter is to study how the boundaries between what is public or private become fainter, whether the use of tracking software is consistent with personal data protection legislation, and whether it is possible to reconcile these two human rights, proposing a reflection on a possible extension of the use of levies in order to compensate right holders for private copies originating from unlawful sources.

The work environment is changing in response to market pressures, and the psychological contract that previously typified many employer and employee work relationships is coming under distinct threat as pervasive Internet-based technologies now enable management to monitor employees' email, computer interactions, and general work productivity. Although in some cases management may have legitimate reasons to monitor employees' actions, it is becoming increasingly evident that the use of these technologies has the potential to negatively impact employee productivity and morale, and in some cases employee health and wellbeing. This chapter outlines some of the emerging issues relating to workplace surveillance from the employees' perspective, as well as the motivation behind management's decision to employ technologies in order monitor their employees.

Healthcare employees generally have access to view hospital patient's medical records. This access can be simply viewing their chart or reviewing information on a computer screen. With this type of accessibly, hospital employees have the opportunity to view diagnosis, personal medical histories, as well as demographic information such as age and gender. Social engineers can use methods such as familiarity with co-workers for instance to obtain this information from unsuspecting health care workers. In addition, weak password selection can provide opportunities for a wealth of information to be stolen. In this chapter, current security legislation that addresses the security of patient's health care records, social engineering tactics, and passwords are explored.

Section 2
Identity Protection

Over the last few years, there has been emerging interest in authenticating users through the medium of music. Historically, developers of alternate modality systems have focused on image- and haptic-based techniques, instinctively shying away from music. This might be due to the inherently temporal nature of the listening task and the belief that this would be impractical and frustrating for users. In this chapter, the authors discuss and present new research in this field that, to the contrary, indicates that the "enjoyability factor" means users may be more willing to spend additional time authenticating with music than they would with other techniques. Although undeniably not the optimal solution in time-critical contexts, for many other pursuits music-based authentication could feasibly replace passwords, easing the number of secure strings the average user is expected to remember. Music may also offer a better solution for those suffering memory or cognitive impairments. This chapter incorporates discussion on recent advances in the field of authentication research within the context of a changing threat landscape. A prototype musical password system is presented and a summary of results from online user testing and a lab-based controlled experiment are presented which further reinforce the importance of accounting for "enjoyability" in the assessment of recognition-based authentication schemes.

Chapter 7

Guillermo A. Francia III, Jacksonville State University, USA
Frances Shannon Hutchinson, ITEL Laboratories, USA
Xavier Paris Francia, Jacksonville State University, USA

The proliferation of the Internet has intensified the privacy protection and identity theft crises. A December 2013 report by the U.S. Department of Justice indicates that 16.6 million persons were victims of identity theft with direct and indirect losses amounting to almost \$24.7 billion in 2012 (Harrell & Langton, 2013). These startling and apparently persistent statistics have prompted the United States and other foreign governments to initiate strategic plans and to enact several regulations in order to curb the crisis. This chapter surveys recently enacted national and international laws pertaining to identity theft and privacy issues. Further, it discusses the interplay between privacy and security, the various incentives and deterrence for privacy protection, and the prospects for the simulation of the social and behavioral aspects of privacy using the agent-based modeling.

Chapter 8

Reema Bhatt, State University of New York – Buffalo, USA
Manish Gupta, State University of New York – Buffalo, USA
Raj Sharman, State University of New York – Buffalo, USA

Identity management is the administration of an individual's access rights and privileges in the form of authentication and authorization within or across systems and organizations. An Identity Management system (IdM) helps manage an individual's credentials through the establishment, maintenance, and eventual destruction of their digital identity. Numerous products, applications, and platforms exist to address the privacy requirements of individuals and organizations. This chapter highlights the importance of IdM systems in the highly vulnerable security scenario that we live in. It defines and elaborates on the attributes and requirements of an effective identity management system. The chapter helps in establishing an understanding of frameworks that IdM systems follow while helping the reader contrast between different IdM architecture models. The latter part of this chapter elaborates on some of today's most popular IdM solutions.

The ease and convenience of Internet Banking or e-banking has made it the most preferred way for customers as well as the banking industry alike. The fact that e-banking enables remote accessibility of a customer's account translates to round-the-clock service from the bank and has made this mode of operation a success in every sense. The starting and most important point for which would be the authentication to customer's financial data. This chapter sheds light on the different authentication mechanisms that could be followed as per the situational demands taking into consideration the various threat environments and possible vulnerabilities in the system. The advantages and disadvantages arising out of different authentication mechanisms are presented with the possible attack scenarios enumerated. An overview of the personal computer environ and the mobile environ are discussed. The chapter will be invaluable for managers and professionals in understanding the current authentication landscape.

Section 3
Trust and Security

Security requirements engineering identifies security risks in software in the early stages of the development cycle. In this chapter, the authors present the SQUARE security requirements method. They integrate privacy requirements into SQUARE to identify privacy risks in addition to security risks. They then present a privacy elicitation technique and subsequently combine security risk assessment techniques with privacy risk assessment techniques. The authors discuss prototype tools that have been developed to support SQUARE for security and privacy as well as recent workshops that have focused on additional results in the security and privacy requirements area. Finally, the authors suggest future research and case studies needed to further contribute to early lifecycle activities that will address security and privacy-related issues.

The importance of data privacy, information availability, and integrity is increasingly recognized. Sharpened legal requirements and increasing data leakages have further promoted data privacy. In order to implement the different requirements in an effective, efficient, and sustainable way, the authors integrate different governance frameworks to their holistic information security and data privacy model. More than 1.5 million organizations worldwide are implementing a standard-based management system. In order to promote the integration of different standards, the International Standard Organization (ISO) released a common structure. ISO/IEC 27001 for information security management was changed accordingly in October 2013. The holistic model fulfills all requirements of the new version. Its implementation in several organizations and the study's results are described. In that way data privacy and security are part of all strategic, tactical, and operational business processes, promote corporate governance and living security, as well as the fulfillment of all standard requirements.

Chapter 12

Cyril Onwubiko, Research Series Limited, UK

Health IT is the use of Information Technology (IT) in healthcare to improve patients' experience, enable quality care, efficiency, speed, and security of the collection, exchange, sharing, and storage of sensitive personal information. But Health IT faces a number of notable challenges ranging from privacy risks to trust and confidence in the use of EHRs. In this chapter, a framework for conducting Privacy Impact Assessment (PIA) of Health IT projects is discussed. Privacy impact assessment is a process through which privacy risks are assessed. The chapter includes recommendations for mitigating identified risks and ensuring compliance to policy and processes for handling and processing of highly sensitive and Personally Identifiable Information (PII).

Chapter 13

Wolfgang Boehmer, Technische Universität Darmstadt, Germany

The importance of personal data and managing them is increasing worldwide. However first, one must be able to distinguish between data, information, and knowledge, before one turns to protecting them. Furthermore, it must be considered that, in open systems, security is a relative term and can be characterized only with the term risk. This suggests that security is not a state in open and dynamic systems but can only be maintained on a pre-defined level (conservation status) with a security management system. Data privacy therefore requires security management systems to ensure sustainable protection at a previously defined level. Pure guidelines and policies are just not sufficient for the protection of data in open systems, as is typical in companies.

Chapter 14

Qing Zou, McGill University, Canada
Eun G. Park, McGill University, Canada

This is the networked age, when people participate in various virtual communities through a platform or network of communities. Members of the communities communicate in faster and more simultaneous interactions in invisible ways. Since the importance of trust in virtual communities has been widely recognized, trust as a complex, multi-faceted, and context-dependent concept has been examined by many researchers in several disciplines. In this chapter, the authors aim to examine the definitions and characteristics of trust in the context of virtual communities and discuss terms relevant to the concept and types of trust. Relevant issues on trust and trust building in virtual communities are discussed, and future research directions are suggested for further study.

Chapter 15

M. J. Warren, Deakin University, Australia
S. Leitch, RMIT, Australia

The chapter investigates the security and ethical issues relating to privacy and security. This chapter also examines the ethical issues of new forms of bullying that are being played out weekly in the media: cyber bulling, specifically on SNS such as Facebook. The traditional and direct forms of bullying are being replaced by consistent abuse via SNS due to the ease and accessibility of these new forms of communications.

Section 4
Detection Techniques

Chapter 16

Ulf Larson, Ericsson AB, Sweden
Erland Jonsson, Chalmers University of Technology, Sweden
Stefan Lindskog, Karlstad University, Sweden

This chapter aims at providing a clear and concise picture of data collection for intrusion detection. It provides a detailed explanation of generic data collection mechanism components and the interaction with the environment, from initial triggering to output of log data records. Taxonomies of mechanism characteristics and deployment considerations are provided and discussed. Furthermore, guidelines and hints for mechanism selection and deployment are provided. Finally, this chapter presents a set of strategies for determining what data to collect, and it also discusses some of the challenges in the field. An appendix providing a classification of 50 studied mechanisms is also provided. This chapter aims at assisting intrusion detection system developers, designers, and operators in selecting mechanisms for resource-efficient data collection.

Chapter 17

Nana K. Ampah, Jacobs Engineering Group, USA
Cajetan M. Akujuobi, Prairie View A&M University, USA

Designing, planning, and managing telecommunication, industrial control, and enterprise networks with special emphasis on effectiveness, efficiency, and reliability without considering security planning, management, and constraints have made them vulnerable. They have become more vulnerable due to their recent connectivity to open networks with the intention of establishing decentralized management and remote control. Existing Intrusion Prevention and Detection Systems (IPS and IDS) do not guarantee absolute security. The new IDS, which employs both signature-based and anomaly detection as its analysis strategies, will be able to detect both known and unknown attacks and further isolate them. Auto-reclosing techniques used on long rural power lines and multi-resolution techniques were used in developing this IDS, which will help update existing IPSs. It should effectively block Distributed Denial of Service attack (DDoS) based on SNY-flood attacks and help eliminate four out of the five major limitations of existing IDSs and IPSs.

A great deal of research attention has been paid to data mining on data streams in recent years. In this chapter, the authors carry out a case study of anomaly detection in large and high-dimensional network connection data streams using Stream Projected Outlier deTector (SPOT) that is proposed in Zhang et al. (2009) to detect anomalies from data streams using subspace analysis. SPOT is deployed on 1999 KDD CUP anomaly detection application. Innovative approaches for training data generation, anomaly classification, false positive reduction, and adoptive detection subspace generation are proposed in this chapter as well. Experimental results demonstrate that SPOT is effective and efficient in detecting anomalies from network data streams and outperforms existing anomaly detection methods.

The detection of bots and botnets in the network may be improved if the analysis is done on the traffic of one bot alone. While a botnet may be detected by correlating the behavior of several bots in a large amount of traffic, one bot alone can be detected by analyzing its unique trends in less traffic. The algorithms to differentiate the traffic of one bot from the normal traffic of one computer may take advantage of these differences. The authors propose to detect bots in the network by analyzing the relationships between flow features in a time window. The technique is based on the Expectation-Maximization clustering algorithm. To verify the method they designed test-beds and obtained a dataset of six different captures. The results are encouraging, showing a true positive error rate of 99.08% with a false positive error rate of 0.7%.

Preface

In an increasingly competitive landscape, recent years have witnessed a large amount of data collected by organizations to assist them with providing quality and personalized services to their customers and to bolster return on investment to the stakeholders. This is more and more becoming a practice that is very much needed to just keep pace with changing and increasing customer expectations. This is raising serious concerns about privacy protection. There are many dimensions to the privacy problem that this situation is creating. The failure around privacy protection can be caused by many factors including accidental disclosure and intentional and deliberate breach by individuals and organizations. In addition to the causal factors, there could be a potentially wide range of impact from identity theft to legal actions to reputational damage. To address these concerns, the issue around data privacy has been approached from various angles including identity protection, privacy-enhancing techniques and technologies, legal frameworks, and security and trust issues. The book covers these areas in four sections: "Legal Aspects," "Identity Protection," "Trust and Security," and "Detection Techniques."

Data privacy generally refers to the concepts around how much leverage one has on controlling practices used for collecting and using one's personal information (Stone et al., 1983; Westin, 1967). Even though conceptually it appears to be a phenomenon which should be easy to understand, there are a lot of aspects of data privacy that create ambiguity and confusion. It has been studied and analyzed from various disciplinary angles including economics, sociology, psychology, technology, and legal, amongst others. Hence, it has been mostly agreed that implications of privacy is contingent on the investigative discipline, such as it means individual rights or corporate practices in legal field (Warren & Brandeis, 1890) and means ability to control collection and use in most social sciences including technology-related fields (Culnan, 1993; Westin, 1967).

The available technologies are providing ways for organizations to collect and innovatively use personal information that were not imaginable a decade ago. This is not only helping companies, but it is also helping individuals. However, recent increase in privacy breaches and resulting impacts have shown that the firms are required to ensure adequate privacy protection (Miller & Tucker, 2009). While individuals express their privacy concerns, they are also open to sharing personal information if they perceive economic benefits (Acquisti & Grossklas, 2005; Bennett, 1995). However, their concerns are only validated with due time because of agency problems of adverse selection, where they don't have complete information on either the protection practices that will be used to safeguard their information or how the information could be used. The onus is on the companies to not only disclose their practices on how they collect and use information but also to provide sufficient protection to the information. Several legal precedents are showing that transparent and reasonable processes also need to be employed to gain an individual's consent.

The book covers different contemporary dimensions of data privacy. The book is organized into four sections, each focusing on emerging developments in an important aspect of data privacy. The coverage of the book is detailed and provides latest advancements in the data privacy space in areas of law, security, identity protection, and technology. The book can serve as a reference on data privacy, which is undeniably one of the most pressing challenges in the digital world. The book provides insights into how data (personal information) is collected, stored, and used. Each chapter provides an in-depth discussion on most relevant topics on data privacy including cloud computing, emerging data protection laws and their impact, copyright issues, surveillance, identity protection, detection technologies, and trust and security management. The 19 chapters in the book are contributed by leading data privacy researchers and practitioners from around the world. The chapters cover research into issues and problems of privacy protection within organizations, while providing contributions on technological, legal, policy-based, and trust-based approaches for enhancing privacy protection.

LEGAL ASPECTS

In wake of the amount of data collected by private companies and government agencies, many countries around the world are adopting data protection laws that are geared towards information privacy protection of collected sensitive data. There have been numerous cases where failure to protect data privacy has led to many lawsuits warranting government investigations and tremendous monetary and reputational losses to companies. The legal protection provided to individuals around data privacy differs vastly around the world. With recent uptick in formulation of privacy laws around world, today over 80 countries and independent territories have adopted comprehensive data protection laws, most notably in Europe. The US has been facing criticism for not adopting a comprehensive information privacy legal framework, but rather supporting limited sectoral laws in few areas (Greenleaf, 2014). The US laws have been focusing on health care (HIPPA) or credit card companies (PCI).

It has been more than four decades since the first national data privacy law called Data Act of 1973 was adopted in 1973 by Sweden. The US did adopt US Privacy Act of 1974, but that was applicable only to federal agencies. Since then, while the U.S. has been relying on sectoral legislation for data privacy protection, the European Union has adopted a rather comprehensive privacy legislative framework.

In order to bridge these different privacy approaches and provide a streamlined means for U.S. organizations to comply with the Directive, the U.S. Department of Commerce in consultation with the European Commission developed a "safe harbor" framework. The safe harbor—approved by the EU in July 2000—is a way for U.S. companies to comply with European privacy laws (Safe Harbor, 2014).

Despite this, reconciling the trans-Atlantic divide in scope and scale of data privacy laws, is an enormous task since organizations are challenged by efforts that are needed to track changes to and comply with regulations in the domain of information privacy. Examples of one of these changes in legal framework include impacts of Lisbon Treaty on data protection laws in EU and non-EU states, which one of the chapters covers in the book. In addition, 46 US states have data breach notification acts to inform customers of a potential breach so they can take steps to reduce the adverse impact from consequences of security and privacy breaches.

In Chapter 1 titled "Cloud State Surveillance: Dark Octopus Tentacle Clouds from the Atlantic," Dr. Sylvia Kierkegaard (of International Association of IT Lawyers, Denmark) asserts that cloud computing opens numerous legal, privacy, and security implications, such as copyright, data loss, destruction of data, identity theft, third-party contractual limitations, e-discovery, risk/insurance allocation, and jurisdictional issues, and discusses the associated legal risks inherent in cloud computing, in particular the international data transfer between the EU and non-EU states.

In Chapter 2, "Data Protection in EU Law after Lisbon: Challenges, Developments, and Limitations," the author (Dr. Maria Tzanou, Keele University,UK) provides an analysis of the data protection rules in EU law, focusing on the constitutional and legal developments after the entry into force of the Lisbon Treaty. It examines the jurisprudence of the Court of Justice of the EU on data protection issues, including the recent decisions of the Court on metadata retention and the new right to be forgotten. It concludes with a critical comment on the possibilities and limitations of the EU to provide for effective and comprehensive data protection.

In Chapter 3, "File-Sharing of Copyrighted Works, P2P, and the Cloud: Reconciling Copyright and Privacy Rights," the author (Pedro Pina, Polytechnic Institute of Coimbra, Portugal) studies how increasingly the distinction between public and private is becoming weaker. The chapter analyzes whether the use of tracking software is consistent with personal data protection legislation and investigates extension of the use of levies in order to compensate rightholders for private copies originating from unlawful sources.

In Chapter 4, "Dataveillance in the Workplace: Privacy Threat or Market Imperative?" the author (Regina Connolly, Dublin City University, Ireland) outlines some of the emerging issues relating to workplace surveillance from the employee perspective, as well as the motivation behind management's decision to employ technologies in order monitor employees.

In Chapter 5, "Social Engineering Techniques, Password Selection, and Health Care Legislation: A Health Care Setting," the authors (B. Dawn Medlin, Appalachian State University, USA, and Joseph A. Cazier, Appalachian State University, USA) discuss current security legislation that addresses the security of patient's health care records, associated social engineering tactics, and issues with passwords.

IDENTITY PROTECTION

In general, identity and access management to information systems lay the foundation for effective security and privacy management. Implementing a privacy-aware identity management system is critical for any organization's risk management because such systems provide the first layer of defense for most information assets and hence serve as a foundation for privacy protection. These have been long treated as a commonly available and most used Privacy Enhancing Technology (PET). Privacy-Enhancing Technologies (PET) have considered the technological defense against social and legal privacy problems. PETs not only provide tools to manage personal data so that security and privacy requirements are effectively met but also tools manage access to such data. Modern Identity and Access Management systems provide users with the capabilities to control their own individual and group digital identities, which indirectly affect their ability to control access to their information. However, "[most] existing commercially available Identity Management Systems (IMS) do not yet provide privacy-enhancing functionality" (Hansen, et al., 2008, p. 39). The book includes a few chapters in these areas that provide more insights into recent trends and offerings of identity management systems, which are increasingly becoming important for privacy management. With the advent of big data and exploding data available on social networking sites, companies have started to re-focus their efforts on privacy issues by empowering individuals and organizations alike to manage access to their information, which puts more controlling powers in their hands. Recent evolutionary trend towards user-centric identity management systems have put "individuals in charge of when, where, how, and to whom they disclose their personal information" (Hansen et al., 2008, p. 39).

Along with PETs, practices and principles also play a vital role in privacy protection. One the most widely accepted set of such principles is the Fair Information Practice Principles (FIPPs). These principles lay the foundation for and provide guidance to companies on how to collect, process, store, and disseminate information. There are many variants of these sets of principles adopted by different organizations. For example, Federal Trade Commission (FTC) sets forth four privacy practice principles for protecting personal information, which include:

1. **Transparency:** To ensure that there is a hidden data collection process and also to provide information on collection of personal data, so users can make an informed decision,
2. **Choice:** To give choices on how the collected information will be used,
3. **Information Review and Correction:** To provide the ability to be able to review and if needed correct collected information,
4. **Information Protection:** To require data collecting entities to provide sufficient protection around the data.

In Chapter 6, "*Play That Funky Password!* Recent Advances in Authentication with Music," the authors (Marcia Gibson, University of Bedfordshire, UK, Karen Renaud, University of Glasgow, UK, Marc Conrad, University of Bedfordshire, UK, and Carsten Maple, University of Bedfordshire, UK) discuss and present new research in the field of music-based authentication. This chapter incorporates discussion on recent advances in the field of authentication research within the context of a changing threat landscape. A prototype musical password system is presented and a summary of results from online user testing and a lab-based controlled experiment are presented suggesting the importance of "enjoyability" in assessment of recognition-based authentication schemes.

In Chapter 7, "Privacy, Security, and Identity Theft Protection: Advances and Trends," the authors (Guillermo A. Francia, III, Jacksonville State University, USA, Frances Shannon Hutchinson, ITEL Laboratories, USA, and Xavier Paris Francia, Jacksonville State University, USA) survey recently enacted national and international laws pertaining to identity theft and privacy issues. Further, the chapter discusses the interplay between privacy and security, the various incentives and deterrence for privacy protection, and the prospects for the simulation of the social and behavioral aspects of privacy using agent-based modeling.

In Chapter 8, "Identity Management Systems: Models, Standards, and COTS Offerings," the authors (Reema Bhatt, State University of New York – Buffalo, USA, Manish Gupta, State University of New York – Buffalo, USA, and Raj Sharman, State University of New York – Buffalo, USA) highlight the importance of IdM systems in protecting today's highly vulnerable information assets. The chapter establishes an understanding of the frameworks that IdM systems follow while at the same time helping the reader contrast between different IdM architecture models. The latter part of this chapter elaborates on and discusses some of today's popular IdM solutions.

In Chapter 9, "How Private Is Your Financial Data? Survey of Authentication Methods in Web and Mobile Banking," the authors (Vidya Mulukutla, State University of New York – Buffalo, USA, Manish Gupta, State University of New York – Buffalo, USA, and H. R. Rao, State University of New York – Buffalo, USA) survey different Web and mobile banking authentication mechanisms while suggesting considerations to follow per situational demands of various threat environments and possible vulnerabilities in the system.

TRUST AND SECURITY

Trust and security issues play vital roles in assurance for privacy protection effectiveness at all levels. Individuals, in the context of privacy, want to ensure that they control what and how information related to them is collected and have the rights to be able to decide what can be collected and how it is used. Trust is important for individuals when they make such decisions. They are also concerned with how the information will be protected from unintentional disclosure to parties from both inside and outside of the organization. Security breaches have been shown to negatively impact reputation, and hence trust, of the victim organization. For corporations, they are concerned with security of the personal information they collect, store, and use for their business sustenance. They need to institute processes and technologies to enforce laws, policies, and standards to secure personal data from unauthorized disclosure. To assist corporations with securing the information and infrastructure, security models and frameworks provide guidance on how to design the security program for most effectiveness and tailor it to meet their requirements. This also lends them credence on their efforts and initiatives. Chapters in the book discuss implementation of ISO 27001 security model and a framework to manage privacy impact assessment. Other relevant topics include security management systems, security and privacy requirements engineering, and trust building.

In Chapter 10, "Security and Privacy Requirements Engineering," the authors (Nancy R. Mead, Carnegie Mellon University, USA, and Saeed Abu-Nimeh, Damballa Inc., USA) present a SQUARE security requirements approach that integrates privacy requirements into SQUARE to identify privacy risks in addition to security risks. They present a privacy elicitation technique and then combine security risk assessment techniques with privacy risk assessment techniques.

In Chapter 11, "An Information Security Model for Implementing the New ISO 27001," the author (Margareth Stoll, Italy) presents a holistic information security and data privacy model that fulfills all requirements of ISO/IEC 27001:2013, which was published in October 2013 to promote integration of other extant standards. Details of implementation of the suggested holistic model in several organizations and the case studies results are described. The model enables data privacy and information security to be part of strategic, tactical, and operational business processes while promoting corporate governance.

In Chapter 12, "Health IT: A Framework for Managing Privacy Impact Assessment of Personally Identifiable Data," the author (Cyril Onwubiko, Research Series Limited, UK) proposes and discusses a framework for conducting privacy impact assessment of Health IT projects. The chapter provides guidance on how to assess privacy risks of both new and in-service projects and discusses lessons learned from managing privacy risks that result from aggregation, collection, sharing, handling, and transportation of personally identifiable information.

In Chapter 13, "Do We Need Security Management Systems for Data Privacy?" the author (Wolfgang Boehmer, Technische Universität Darmstadt, Germany) presents possible uses of corporate and security policies for management systems, including privacy management systems, and identifies their potential applications. Furthermore, the chapter presents a field study, which highlights the advantages of management systems in practice. Moreover, this chapter shows how a formal description of an information security management system can be created by means of discrete-event systems theory and how an objective function for management systems can be defined.

In Chapter 14, "Trust and Trust Building of Virtual Communities in the Networked Age," the authors (Qing Zou, McGill University, Canada, and Eun G. Park, McGill University, Canada) examine the definitions and characteristics of trust in the context of virtual communities and discuss terms relevant to the concept and types of trust. Relevant issues on trust and trust building in virtual communities are discussed and future research directions are suggested for further study.

In Chapter 15, "The Security, Privacy, and Ethical Implications of Social Networking Sites," the authors (M. J. Warren, Deakin University, Australia, and S. Leitch, RMIT, Australia) investigate the security, privacy, and ethical issues arising from widespread use of global social networking sites and its impact on prevalent social problems. This chapter also examines the ethical issues of new forms of bullying that are being played out weekly in the media: that of cyber bulling, specifically on SNS such as Facebook.

DETECTION TECHNIQUES

A recent survey (Poneman, 2012) done in the healthcare sector shows that 94% of respondent organizations had at least one data breach in last two years. Important and revealing information from the survey was that more than half of the organizations reported little or no confidence in their organization's ability to detect all data loss or theft. This shows how critical monitoring and detection is in managing data loss and prevention. Failing to detect data breach and ensuing notification can put tremendous burden and loss to companies. Another survey (Javelin, 2013) shows a strong correlation between data breaches and identity theft. The survey shows that individuals who received a data breach notification in 2012 had an identity theft incidence rate of 22.5 percent, which is more than four times the 5.3 percent rate for all adults.

Forty-six states in the US have adopted breach notification laws. Thirty-six of these states require notification to be done on a prioritized basis without unreasonable delay. Similar initiatives in EU (Directive 2002/58/EC and Regulation 611/2013) require that authorities be notified within 24 hours of the detection of the personal data breach (or within 72 hours in some cases). A "personal data breach" is defined by Directive 2002/58/EC as

... a breach of security leading to the accidental or unlawful destruction, loss, alteration, unauthorized disclosure of, or access to, personal data transmitted, stored, or otherwise processed in connection with the provision of a publicly available electronic communications service in the community. (DPWP, 2014, pp. 3)

This highlights the importance of timely detection and response to privacy and security breaches to minimize the negative impact and provide early warning signals for potential damages.

In Chapter 16, "Guidance for Selecting Data Collection Mechanisms for Intrusion Detection," the authors (Ulf Larson, Ericsson AB, Sweden, Erland Jonsson, Chalmers University of Technology, Sweden, and Stefan Lindskog, Karlstad University, Sweden) provide a detailed explanation of generic data collection mechanism components and the interaction with the environment, from initial triggering to output of log data records. The chapter also presents taxonomies of mechanism characteristics and deployment considerations while suggesting guidelines and hints for mechanism selection and deployment.

In Chapter 17, "An Auto-Reclosing-Based Intrusion Detection Technique for Enterprise Networks," the authors (Nana K. Ampah, Jacobs Engineering Group, USA, and Cajetan M. Akujuobi, Prairie View A&M University, USA) propose a new and unique IDS that employs both signature-based and anomaly detection as its analysis strategies and will be able to detect both known and unknown attacks and further isolate them. The proposed IDS uses auto-reclosing technique that is used on long rural power lines.

The authors assert that the IDS method should effectively block SYN-flood attacks, Distributed Denial of Service attacks (DDoS) based on SNY-flood attacks, and help eliminate four out of the five major limitations of existing IDSs and IPSs.

In Chapter 18, "A Dynamic Subspace Anomaly Detection Method Using Generic Algorithm for Streaming Network Data," the author (Ji Zhang, University of Southern Queensland, Australia) presents a case study of anomaly detection in large and high-dimensional network connection data streams using Stream Projected Outlier deTector (SPOT) technique. The chapter also introduces innovative approaches for training data generation, anomaly classification, false positive reduction, and adoptive detection subspace generation. The experimental results demonstrate that the technique proposed in the chapter is effective and efficient in detecting anomalies from network data streams and outperforms existing anomaly detection methods.

In Chapter 19, "Detecting Botnet Traffic from a Single Host," the authors (Sebastián García, Universidad Nacional del Centro, Argentina & Czech Technical University, Czech Republic, Alejandro Zunino, Universidad Nacional del Centro, Argentina, and Marcelo Campo, Universidad Nacional del Centro, Argentina) propose a unique method to analyze trends and behavior of one bot alone to detect bots and botnets. They propose to detect bots in the network traffic by analyzing the relationships between flow features in a time window, based on the Expectation-Maximization clustering algorithm. The result of their study is encouraging, showing a true positive error rate of 99.08% with a false positive error rate of 0.7%.

Manish Gupta
State University of New York – Buffalo, USA

REFERENCES

Acquisti, A., & Grossklags, J. (2005). Privacy and rationality in individual decision making. *IEEE Security and Privacy*, *3*(1), 26–33.

Bennett, C. J. (1995). *The political economy of privacy: A review of the literature*. Hackensack, NJ: Center for Social and Legal Research.

Culnan, M. (1993). How did they get my name? An exploratory investigation of consumer attitudes toward secondary information use. *Management Information Systems Quarterly*, *17*(3), 341–363.

DPWP. (2014). *Opinion 03/2014 on personal data breach notification, article 29 data protection working party, 693/14/EN, 25 March 2014*. Retrieved from http://www.ec.europa.eu/justice/data-protection/article-29%2Fdocumentation/opinion-recommendation/files/2014/wp213_en.pdf

Greenleaf, G. (2012). Global data privacy laws: 89 countries, and accelerating (February 6, 2012). *Privacy Laws & Business International Report*, (115). Available at SSRN: http://ssrn.com/abstract=2000034

Hansen, M., Schwartz, A., & Cooper, A. (2008, March/April). Privacy and identity management. *IEEE Security and Privacy*.

Javelin. (2013). *2013 identity fraud report: Data breaches becoming a treasure trove for fraudsters*. Available at http://www.javelinstrategy.com

Miller, A. R., & Tucker, C. (2009). Privacy protection and technology diffusion: The case of electronic medical records. *Management Science*, *55*(7), 1077–1093.

Poneman. (2012). *Study on patient privacy & data security*. Ponemon Institute. Retrieved from http://www2.idexpertscorp.com/ponemon2012/

Safe Harbor. (2014). *Information privacy law*. Wikipedia Article. Retrieved online from http://en.wikipedia.org/wiki/Information_privacy_law#cite_note-1

Stone, E., Gardner, D., Gueutal, H., & McClure, S. (1983). A field experiment comparing information privacy values, beliefs, and attitudes across several types of organizations. *The Journal of Applied Psychology*, *68*(3), 459–468.

Warren, S. D., & Brandeis, D. L. (1890). The right to privacy. *Harvard Law Review*, *4*(5), 193–220.

Westin, A. (1967). *Privacy and freedom*. New York: Atheneum.

Section 1
Legal Aspects

Chapter 1
Cloud State Surveillance:
Dark Octopus Tentacle Clouds from the Atlantic

Sylvia Kierkegaard
International Association of IT Lawyers, Denmark

ABSTRACT

Concerns about government snooping in the wake of revelations by whistle blower Edward Snowden have deterred enterprises and IT professionals from keeping sensitive data in the clouds. Moving towards cloud-based computing has emerged and has gained acceptance as a solution to the tasks related to the processing of information. However, cloud computing carries serious risks to business information. The questions around risk and compliance are still largely unknown and need to be ironed out. Cloud computing opens numerous legal, privacy, and security implications, such as copyright, data loss, destruction of data, identity theft, third-party contractual limitations, e-discovery, risk/insurance allocation, and jurisdictional issues. This chapter discusses the associated legal risks inherent in cloud computing, in particular the international data transfer between EU and non-EU states.

1. INTRODUCTION

Information is the heart and soul of many businesses. The information that companies generate and share are generating a wealth of benefits. E-mail, social media, mobile phones, drop boxes, increased internet devices and broadband connections have enabled businesses and consumers to exchange high data volumes and files everywhere and over vast networks with high speed communication.

Information is now available and shared to an extent almost unimaginable 10 years ago due to the increasing digitization and modern technology. At the same, it has caused organizations to struggle with the high volumes and diversities of information and seek solutions to manage the information and to reduce cost through effective information governance.

Information Governance (Info Governance) is the specification of decision rights and an accountability framework to encourage desirable

DOI: 10.4018/978-1-4666-7381-6.ch001

behaviour in the valuation, creation, storage, usage, archiving and deletion of information. It includes the processes, roles, standards and metrics that ensure the effective and efficient use of information to enable an organization to achieve its goals. (Logan, 2009) These include the management of information securely, efficiently and effectively—what information is retained, where and for how long, and how it is retained (e.g., protected, replicated and secured), who has access to it and how the polices are enforced. They encompass not only suitable policies, accountability, and procedures but also the technology to create a solid governance framework. Unmanaged and inconsistently managed information increases risk and cost.

Information technology officers are looking for technologies that will help them focus more on the benefits to the organization, which can bring institutional agility, flexibility and cost saving. Moving towards cloud-based computing has emerged and gained is acceptance as a solution to the tasks related to the processing of information. The IT industry has witnessed a rapid adoption of the public cloud and many have migrated enterprise applications to the cloud. Cloud promises a single portal view to better manage email, archiving, and records retention (etc). Since web 2.0, "cloud computing" has been the buzz word in the IT industry. Cloud advocates argue that implementing any form of IT or information governance is far easier and far more effective in a fully-virtualized private cloud model than in the traditional, physical IT world.

The promise of a utility-based IT service delivery model is well understood and highly desirable. The greatest gain for business is that cloud services can create advantage cutting out hardware costs and reducing their costs per unit as demand increases while for enterprise customers, it enables information to be accessible from any device that is connected to the Internet.

However while cloud computing certainly brings efficiencies, it is still immature and carries serious risks to business information. Many companies are still hesitant to move their core business applications into the cloud until cloud providers address several main concerns, including security, control, customization, and complexity. The questions around risk and compliance are still largely unknown and need to be ironed out. As the adoption of cloud computing continues to grow across the world, security, privacy and regulation of data in the cloud is becoming more prominent and relevant.

A survey, which was carried out at RSA Conference 2014 in San Francisco, looked at the attitudes of nearly 280 IT security professionals towards cloud security. A third of IT security professionals do not keep corporate data in the cloud because of fears of government snooping. In the same survey conducted in 2012, 48% of respondents were discouraged from using the cloud because of fear of government snooping, while 86% preferred to keep more sensitive data on their own premises (Ahford, 1014).

The European Union is addressing the challenges concerning the threat to information security specific to cloud computing through several measures. While businesses and governments wax lyrical about the benefits of cloud computing, EU regulators have been more wary, as further take-up of cloud systems would mean a large swathe of public and commercial data would migrate to servers possibly located outside national borders or even on other continents.

Despite the EU's best efforts, laws to protect and store data are outdated and cannot cope with the legal problems presented by cloud computing, such as determining who owns data which is no longer handled in situ. This article will provide an overview of cloud computing and discuss the current and legal risks for businesses using cloud computing, especially state surveillance on private citizens.

2. CLOUD COMPUTING: ONCE UPON A TIME

"Cloud" is a metaphor for the Internet. Thus, cloud computing is the usage of the Internet as a computing infrastructure and resource. Cloud Computing describes a whole range of infrastructure, software, data or applications residing in the 'cloud' – that is to say, off your own premises and accessed via the Internet. The idea of computation being delivered in public space was proposed by computer scientist John MacCarthy who proposed the idea of computation being delivered in public space. In 2006, Eric Schmidt of Google described their approach to Software as Service (SaaS) as cloud computing at the Search Engine Strategies Conference. (Google Press Center, 2006) Amazon included the word "cloud" in EC2 (Elastic Compute Cloud) when it was launched a few weeks later.

Cloud Computing found its origin in the success of server virtualization and the possibilities to run IT more efficiently through server consolidation. Soon, visionaries came up with idea to bring virtualization to a next level by implementing some early storage and network virtualization techniques and thus making abstraction of the hardware in the entire data centre. Add to this self-provisioning and auto scaling, and cloud computing was born. (Leyden, 2009) The most important contribution to cloud computing has been the emergence of "killer apps" that provided access to large bodies of map data. In 2009, as Web 2.0 hit its stride, Google and Microsoft, among others, formalized the Application Programming Interfaces (APIs). Mashups exploded and everyone sat up and took notice of the opportunities for innovation bootstrapped upon the shared capabilities of Google's code and servers, and the underlying data licensed by Google (Miller, 2008).

The key aspect of cloud computing is that the users do not have or need to have the knowledge, control or ownership of the computer and network infrastructure. The users just simply access the software or service they require to use and pay for what they use. Therefore, "in cloud-service engagements, buyers [users] only need to care about the service [level or quality] without worrying about its implementation. (Khan, 2009) Because cloud computing services are available at all times, they solve the problem of intermittent availability of applications. Cloud computing services allow users to store their data and their applications on networked servers rather than on local computers and data centres. They do not require software that sits on a PC or laptop, other than an Internet connection and a Web browser. These companies are finding that cloud computing can provide power, low costs, functionality and flexibility. Mobility workers can access their applications and data from multiple locations, such as offices, home computers, client sites, airports, and smart phones. (Stroh, et al, 2009) Cloud computing, virtualization and mobility all entered the limelight because of the net savings they represent.

2.1 Cloud Computing Defined

With an ever-growing list of cloud computing service providers and emerging applications, there abounds so many definitions flying around that it has been a struggle to find a common definition of cloud computing. How does one define this infrastructural paradigm shift that is sweeping across the enterprise IT world?

Cloud computing is loosely defined as an Internet – based development and use of computer technology. As its name suggests, data is stored in "the clouds" and the programs that run it are in the "cloud" (or the Internet). The concept is not new - Active Server Pages (ASPs), outsourcing, Web site hosting and browser-based applications are all forms of cloud computing What probably differ are the strata of services that cloud computing offers and that the data and the programs no longer live on the computer. The main philosophy of cloud computing is to provide every required things as a service.

Cloud Computing is a paradigm that is composed of several strata of services. These include services like Infrastructure as a Service, Storage as a Service, Platform as a Service and Software as a Service. The main goal of cloud computing is to provide ICT services with shared infrastructure and the collection of many systems. Not all cloud providers are the same. Some cloud providers are both providers and users, offering services to their own customers/end-users built on other providers' services. In cloud computing every facility is provided in terms of service in the cloud, which can be perceived as a layer of architecture offering numerous resources in different layers. It assumes that the hardware, software and data storage are stored in cyberspace (cloud) instead of residing on desktop or internal servers. The objective of outsourcing in the clouds is to free up company resources, and minimize costs. Companies pay only for the amount of services they use.

In cloud computing, the Internet is used to provide utility computing services and platforms, as well as a collection of computing software and services that can be accessed via the Internet. These ICT services include data storage, software applications, and email and file exchanges with shared infrastructure and the collection of many systems.

'Cloud computing' in simplified terms can be understood as the storing, processing and use of data on remotely located computers accessed over the internet. The European Union defines cloud as an "elastic execution environment of resources involving multiple stakeholders and providing a metered service at multiple granularities for a specified level of quality (of service)." (Information Age, 2010) The Report also states that clouds do not refer to a specific technology, but to a general provisioning paradigm with enhanced capabilities. Among the functional characteristics of a compute cloud, as identified by the report, are 'elasticity', 'reliability' and 'availability'.

Cloud computing has a range of defining features (which make a general definition elusive) as follow (European Commission, 2012)

- Hardware (computers, storage devices) is owned by the cloud computing provider, and not by the user who interacts with it via the Internet;
- The use of hardware is dynamically optimised across a network of computers, so that the exact location of data or processes, as well as the information which piece of hardware is actually serving a particular user at a given moment does not in principle have to concern the user, even though it may have an important bearing on the applicable legal environment;
- Cloud providers often move their users' workloads around (e.g. from one computer to another or from one data centre to another) to optimise the use of available hardware;
- The remote hardware stores and processes data and makes it available, e.g. through applications (so that a company could use its cloud-based computing in just the same way as consumers already today use their webmail accounts);
- Organisations and individuals can access their content, and use their software when and where they need it, e.g. on desktop computers, laptops, tablets and smartphones;
- A cloud set-up consists of layers: hardware, middleware or platform, and application software. Standardisation is important especially at the middle layer because it enables developers to address a wide range of potential customers and gives users choice;
- Users normally pay by usage, avoiding the large upfront and fixed costs necessary to set up and operate sophisticated computing equipment;
- At the same time, users can very easily modify the amount of hardware they use (e.g. bring new storage capacity online in a matter of seconds with a few mouse clicks).

The US National Institute of Standards and Technology (Mell and Grance, 2009) offers a more specific and lengthy definition. It defines cloud computing as:

Cloud computing is a model for enabling convenient, on-demand network access to a shared pool of configurable computing resources (e.g., networks, servers, storage, applications, and services) that can be rapidly provisioned and released with minimal management effort or service provider interaction. This cloud model promotes availability and is composed of five essential characteristics, three service models, and four deployment models.

The NIST describes the characteristics as follow:

Essential Characteristics

- **On-Demand Self-Service:** A consumer can unilaterally provision computing capabilities, such as server time and network storage, as needed automatically without requiring human interaction with each service's provider.
- **Broad Network Access:** Capabilities are available over the network and accessed through standard mechanisms that promote use by heterogeneous thin or thick client platforms (e.g., mobile phones, laptops, and PDAs).
- **Resource Pooling:** The provider's computing resources are pooled to serve multiple consumers using a multi-tenant model, with different physical and virtual resources dynamically assigned and reassigned according to consumer demand. There is a sense of location independence in that the customer generally has no control or knowledge over the exact location of the provided resources but may be able to specify location at a higher level of abstraction (e.g., country, state, or data center). Examples of resources include storage, processing, memory, network bandwidth, and virtual machines.
- **Rapid Elasticity:** Capabilities can be rapidly and elastically provisioned, in some cases automatically, to quickly scale out and rapidly released to quickly scale in. To the consumer, the capabilities available for provisioning often appear to be unlimited and can be purchased in any quantity at any time.
- **Measured Service:** Cloud systems automatically control and optimize resource use by leveraging a metering capability at some level of abstraction appropriate to the type of service (e.g., storage, processing, bandwidth, and active user accounts). Resource usage can be monitored, controlled, and reported providing transparency for both the provider and consumer of the utilized service.

Service Models

Cloud computing activities are often described in terms of three service models (Mell P. and Grance,T. 2011):

- **Cloud Software as a Service (SaaS):** The capability provided to the consumer is to use the provider's applications running on a cloud infrastructure. The applications are accessible from various client devices through a thin client interface such as a web browser (e.g., web-based email). The consumer does not manage or control the underlying cloud infrastructure including network, servers, operating systems, storage, or even individual application capabilities, with the possible exception of limited user-specific application configuration settings.

- **Cloud Platform as a Service (PaaS):** The capability provided to the consumer is to deploy onto the cloud infrastructure consumer-created or acquired applications created using programming languages and tools supported by the provider. The consumer does not manage or control the underlying cloud infrastructure including network, servers, operating systems, or storage, but has control over the deployed applications and possibly application hosting environment configurations.

- **Cloud Infrastructure as a Service (IaaS):** The capability provided to the consumer is to provision processing, storage, networks, and other fundamental computing resources where the consumer is able to deploy and run arbitrary software, which can include operating systems and applications. The consumer does not manage or control the underlying cloud infrastructure but has control over operating systems, storage, deployed applications and possibly limited control of select networking components (e.g., host firewalls).

Deployment Models

- **Private Cloud:** The cloud infrastructure is operated solely for an organization. It may be managed by the organization or a third party and may exist on premise or off premise. Private cloud (internal enterprise) is a cloud computing-like environment within the boundaries of an organization and typically for its exclusive usage.

- **Community Cloud:** The cloud infrastructure is shared by several organizations and supports a specific community that has shared concerns (e.g., mission, security requirements, policy, and compliance considerations). It may be managed by the organizations or a third party and may exist on premise or off premise.

- **Public Cloud:** The cloud infrastructure is made available to the general public or a large industry group and is owned by an organization selling cloud services. Public cloud (services offered over the internet) is a cloud computing environment that is open for use to the general public, whether individuals, corporations or other types of organizations. Amazon Web Services are an example of a public cloud.

- **Hybrid Cloud:** The cloud infrastructure is a composition of two or more clouds (private, community, or public) that remain unique entities but are bound together by standardized or proprietary technology that enables data and application portability (e.g., cloud bursting for load-balancing between clouds). Hybrid cloud (a mix of both) is a computing environment combining both private (internal) and public (external) cloud computing environments. May either be on a continuous basis or in the form of a 'cloudburst'.

3. LEGAL RISKS

Cloud computing generally refers to providing access to computer software through an Internet browser, with the software and data stored at a remote location at a "data centre" or "server farm," instead of residing on the computers' hard drive or on a server located on the user's premises. Basically, the data created and managed by these services are stored offsite, in the "cloud and managed by private firms that provide remote access through web-based device. Although the cost benefits of moving from traditional IT structures to the cloud are often clear, there are issues that corporations need to consider when making the switch to the cloud model. Cloud computing opens numerous legal, privacy and security implications, such as copyright, data loss, destruction of data, identity theft, third-party contractual limitations, e-discovery, risk/insurance allocation and jurisdictional issues. For example, the data which is the subject of litigation may not be accessible by the provider, leading to spoliation of evidence. Some of the key security issues in cloud computing are:

- Who has access to facilities to data.
- What happens to data in the event of a disaster and intrusion.
- What happens to data if company goes bankrupt.
- Insurance or liability coverage- will they handle claims of privacy breaches and hacking?
- What restrictions on cross border data transfer?
- Where will the data be stored?
- Where are the servers?
- What kind of data will be in the cloud?
- Where do the data subjects reside?
- Where will the data be stored?

Other important issues arise from the anticompetitive actions of giant provider with dominant position, controlling and retaining billions of personal/sensitive data (Economist, 2009).

3.1 Contract Issues

Cloud computing services generally provide the users a standard contract with weak obligations. Many of them are one sided contracts, which disclaim liability, offer no warranties and impose responsibility on the users for issues like data location or disaster recovery. Some of the contracts often lack contingency plans for what would happen if one or more of the companies involved suffer a disruption or data breach. The language is often ambiguous and does not define how data will be handled and encrypted. In some cloud agreements, a vendor's maximum liability is relatively small, frequently limited to fees paid in a one- or two-month subscription period or none at all. For example, the terms of service for Google Apps are:

Google and partners do not warrant that

1. *Google services will meet your requirements,*
2. *Google services will be uninterrupted, timely, secure, or error-free,*
3. *The results that may be obtained from the use of google services will be accurate or reliable,*
4. *The quality of any products, services, information, or other material purchased or obtained by you through google services will meet your expectations ()* (Source: http://www.google.com/apps/intl/en/terms/user_terms.html).

These disclaimers are actually ineffective against statutory liabilities, especially when they are not in conformity with consumer protection or product liability. Even in a business-to-business context, cloud providers may not be able to exclude all risk relating to service interruptions or data loss. Liability arises for negligence and other forms of product liability. The complexity and uncertainty of the legal framework for cloud services providers mean that they often use complex contracts or service level agreements with extensive disclaimers. The use of "take-it-or-leave-it" standard contracts might be cost-saving for the provider but is often undesirable for the user, including the final consumer. Such contracts may also impose the choice of applicable law or inhibit data recovery. Even larger companies have little negotiation power and contracts often do not provide for liability for data integrity, confidentiality or service continuity.

Under international law, specifically Article 35 of the UN Convention on International Sales of Goods (CISG)," sellers are liable for any lack of conformity of the goods with the contract." The "as is" warranties in the imposed standard form can be challenged under the EU Unfair Contract Terms Directive 93/13/EEC, which imposes limits in the kind of terms and conditions particularly in relations to exclusions of liability. "As is" warranties are services/goods provided as they are without any promise of being suitable or attaining a certain level of performance. In the US, such onerous contractual terms could be considered "unconscionable."

Aside from the default position contained in the standard form, cloud agreements fail to include terms relating to compliance with export of personal data to other countries, privacy laws, back-up schedules, vendor's disaster recovery plan and data recovery responsibilities. A jungle of standards generates confusion by, on one hand, a proliferation of standards and on the other hand a lack of certainty as to which standards provide adequate levels of interoperability of data formats to permit portability; the extent to which safeguards (European Commission, 2012).

Other limitations include the following:

- Customer unable to decrease the number of users during a subscription term;
- Remedies for breach of a limited warranty restricted to termination and refund of pre-paid unused fees;
- Supplier to delete all customer data after 30 days after termination, unless a request for such data is made within such time period by the customer.

Although existing EU legislation protects users of cloud services, consumers are often unaware of their relevant rights especially including the applicable law and jurisdiction in civil and commercial matters, notably when it comes to contract law questions.[1]

3.2 Data Protection

Problems with contracts were related to worries over data access and portability, change control and ownership of the data. For example there are concerns over how liability for service failures such as downtime or loss of data will be compensated, user rights in relation to system upgrades decided unilaterally by the provider, ownership of data created in cloud applications or how disputes will be resolved.

In a cloud agreement, the vendor normally provides the hardware infrastructure, operating system, application, and the backup service. Hardware and software are no longer procured and operated by users themselves but obtained as services. Documents, e-mails and other data will be stored on-line, "in the cloud", making them accessible from any PC or mobile device. To provide these resources, providers often rely on other cloud providers for storage or computer capacity. This means that many third parties may access the data across a number of jurisdictions. In many instances, the storage location of the data is not disclosed and the consumer is not aware where the processing takes place. The co-location and virtual software segregation of resources raise serious concerns about data leakage due to misconfiguration, software failure or exploited hypervisor vulnerabilities where virtualized (Gorniak et al., 2010).

When users release the data in the cloud, they might "not even "own them unless it has been stipulated in the Service Agreements. The client cedes control of his documents. In many cases, the cloud provider does not provide sufficient and adequate information on their data handling practices. Cloud providers have tended to forgo strong security solutions. In cases where there are multiple transfers of data, the data protection risk is exacerbated. By submitting personal data to the systems managed by a cloud provider, cloud clients may no longer be in exclusive control of this data. This means that they may not be able to deploy the technical and organisational measures necessary to ensure for example the availability and confidentiality of data, for which the user of cloud computing services remains legally responsible under EU law. Consumers, once they have released their data "in the cloud", as opposed to the current practice to store them in the comfort of their personal PCs, or their servers, may not technically "own" them, possibly being left at the whim of cloud computing services providers and/or to lock-in arrangements, and/or possible failures by the telecommunication systems, needed to retrieve their personal data.

In addition, insufficient information about a cloud service's processing operations poses a risk to data controllers as well as to data subjects, because they might not be aware of potential threats and risks and thus cannot take measures they deem appropriate to mitigate those risks.

The security risk is further aggravated when the provider is changed. Cloud services are frequently offered through third-party providers that may have little ability or leverage to alter the security practices of the data centers from whom they are acquiring cloud resources, and are therefore unable to offer similar protections to their customers (Bennet, 2010).

Since data generally has to be unencrypted at the point of processing, this means that if it is processed using cloud computing, it will generally be present in unencrypted form on a machine in the service provider's or subcontractor's network. There is therefore a risk of data security breaches, data loss and destruction, as well as dangers of theft or sabotage by a rogue employee of the service provider or subcontractor (Mowbray, 2009). Data stored in the cloud may not be safe; data security breaches and data loss/destruction are ever more

becoming consumers' main concern –and, in the US, the focus of practically all legislative and regulatory effort, at both federal and state levels.

Because most cloud services on a given server are shared between multiple organizations, full or timely deletion of data may be impossible because the disk to be destroyed also store data from other clients. In some instances, extra copies of data may not be available. For users who subscribe to cloud providers without effective encryption, the security risk is higher.

Compounding the problem is the lack of harmonized data retention period in different jurisdictions. How long are certain data being kept? Countries that are part of the European Union are bound by EC Directives, but their interpretation of these rules is often inconsistent. In the European Union, the Data Retention Directive 2006/24/EC allows the member states to retain data between 6 and 24 months. Under the Directive, authorities can request access to details such as IP address and time of use of every e-mail, phone call and text message sent or received. Member States have different retention times with Italy having the shortest retention period. Legislation also imposes different retention period for different types of data - employment records, tax records, health and safety files-posing more problems for the companies.

On April 8, 2014, he European Court of Justice in a land mark ruling declared the EU directive imposing data retention obligations on electronic communications services, such as telecoms operators or Internet access providers, as no longer valid. The Court underlined that "the declaration of invalidity takes effect from the date on which the directive entered into force," and not simply from the moment the judgment was made. The directive was adopted in November 2006. According to the Court in Digital Rights Ireland Ltd (*C-293/12- Minister for Communications, Marine and Natural Resources, v. Minister for Justice, Equality and Law Reform, Commissioner of the Garda Síochána, Ireland*), the Directive imposed "a wide-ranging and particularly serious interference with the fundamental rights to respect for private life and to the protection of personal data, without that interference being limited to what is strictly necessary." (Electronic Privacy Information Center, 2014) The Court of Justice held that the directive falls foul of the EU's Charter of Fundamental Rights because of the potential to restrict a person's privacy. The court found that the data retained could allow the authorities to identify the person using the telecoms service, and how often they use it. Furthermore, the data may provide "very precise information on the private lives of the persons whose data are retained, such as the habits of everyday life, permanent or temporary places of residence, daily or other movements, activities carried out, social relationships and the social environments frequented". As a result the directive "interferes in a particularly serious manner with the fundamental rights to respect for private life and to the protection of personal data." The ruling continues: "The fact that data are retained and subsequently used without the subscriber or registered user being informed is likely to generate in the persons concerned a feeling that their private lives are the subject of constant surveillance. The court acknowledges that the content of the communications is not scrutinised, and that the directive carries "certain principles of data protection and data security. It also acknowledges the "general interest" in retaining data in order to fight serious crime and terrorism. However, the Court ruled that the European Commission, in adopting the new directive had "exceeded the limits imposed by compliance with the principle of proportionality. In particular the directive was indiscriminate in that it affected "all individuals, all means of electronic communication and all traffic data without any differentiation, limitation or exception being made in the light of the objective of fighting against serious crime. The court found

that the directive lacked "any objective criterion" or procedural conditions which would ensure that data was only being used for preventing, detecting or prosecuting serious crime. The court also found that the directive did not safeguard against the misuse of the data for unlawful purposes, and that it was vague as to which categories of data could be held the longest (Judgement of the Court in Digital rights Ireland, April 2014).

The judges also condemned the fact that the directive allows law enforcement agencies to use personal data without the need of clearly specifying that they can be used "only for the purposes of prevention, detection or criminal prosecutions offences that may be considered to be sufficiently serious to justify such an interference." In other words, there are no sufficient safeguards against possible abuses. The Court also laments the fact that the directive does not include provisions to prevent personal data of EU citizens from being used by third countries - a clear reference to the ongoing debate sparked by Edward Snowden's revelations of the spying activities of the US National Security Agency. "The Court states that the directive does not require that the data be retained within the EU. Therefore, the directive does not fully ensure the control of compliance with the requirements of protection and security by an independent authority, as is explicitly required by the Charter" of fundamental rights (Ibid).

Data located in particular jurisdictions may be subject to disclosure through extensive government surveillance. For example, US Federal District Court Judge Michael Mosman ruled on June 23, 2009 (Nos. 08-9131-MC, 08-9147-MC) that e-mail should not be afforded the same protection against unlawful searches and seizures under the Fourth Amendment. Mosman declared that people who send emails cannot expect to have the same level of privacy as when one sends a regular piece of mail through the post office. Thus, the police can serve the ISP providers with a search warrant and get the information turned over without notifying an e-mail account holder. Mosman reasoned that when we send e-mails and instant messages, they travel from computer to computer and are "stored "by ISP providers. Therefore, when the government obtains the e-mail of the account holder and reads it, it does not have to inform the user that it has done this. It has only to tell the internet service provider - that a search and seizure of the "papers and effects" has taken place. The lack of adequate data protection in many countries and the intrusion powers of government agencies threaten the confidentiality and privacy of data stored in the clouds. Cloud users do not have the confidence that as their data moves from the desktop to the cloud, it will stay private and secure.

Not all cloud services are created equal. Some are more robust than the others. If a cloud vendor goes bankrupt, there is a serious possibility that the customer will lose access to the IT resources – hardware and software and copy of their data, especially when the cloud provider did not have adequate backup procedures.

3.3 Transborder Transfer in the EU

Cloud computing allows the constant flow of data between the user's computer and multiple cloud servers located around the world creating conflicting legal obligations. Most likely, personal data may be sent to multiple servers worldwide. From a legal standpoint, different legal rules will apply depending on where the data is or has been and what country has jurisdiction over these data.

The European Data Protection Directive 95/46 regulates the processing of personal data within the European Union and imposes wide ranging obligations regarding the collection, storage and use of personal information. The Directive primarily regulates data controllers. A controller is defined in Article 2 of the Directive as the natural or legal person or public agency that "alone or jointly with others" determines "the purposes and means of processing" personal data. A processor is a natural or legal person or agency that processes data on behalf of a controller. "Processing" is defined very broadly in the Directive to include collection, use, storage, manipulation, disclosure, disposal, and virtually any other action with personal data.

The Directive applies to a cloud provider established in the EU or acting as processor for a controller established in the EU, as well as a provider which uses equipment (such as servers) in an EU Member State or acting as processor for a controller using such equipment. Under Article 17 of the EU Data Protection Directive 95/46, data controllers must implement appropriate technical and organizational measures to protect personal data against

1. Accidental or unlawful destruction or loss;
2. Unauthorized alteration, disclosure or access (in particular where the processing involves the transmission of data over a network); and
3. All other unlawful forms of processing.

The Directive applies to all personal data that fall within the scope of EU jurisdiction regardless of where the data are processed. Article 6 of the Directive requires data controllers to process personal data for purposes compatible with those for which it was initially collected. In the context of cloud computing, this should deter controllers from using information for incompatible purposes.

However, Article 3 excludes from the scope of application of the Directive data processing carried out "by natural persons in the course of a purely personal or household activity" (the 'household exception'). If the information uploaded to the cloud is not covered by the Directive because it is information of a personal nature, then the processing activities that are carried out on behalf of the individuals involved might not be covered either. Therefore cloud providing services will not be caught by the Directive if the processing service is carried out on behalf of end users acting in their personal capacity.

The Directive also imposes an obligation on companies not to transfer personal data from their operations within the European Economic

Area (EEA) in the United States (and other places outside the EEA) unless the recipient in the non-EEA country provides "an adequate level of protection".

Under Article 25(1) the Directive permits the transfer of personal data outside of the EU:

The Member States shall provide that the transfer to a third country of personal data which are undergoing processing or are intended for processing after transfer may take place only if, without prejudice to compliance with the national provisions adopted pursuant to the other provisions of this Directive, the third country in question ensures an adequate level of protection.

The transfer of data to a country that is considered not adequate maybe authorized provided that the data controller obtains the consent of the data subject. However, obtaining freely given, specific and informed consent from each data subject would be burdensome. Furthermore, individuals have a fundamental right under European Union data protection law to access, block, rectify or delete their personal data. It may be difficult to effectively manage this right in a cloud computing infrastructure.

If the importing country does not ensure an adequate level of protection, the Directive contemplates further means by which personal data may be transferred aside from the data subject's consent. These means include the derogations in Article 26.

1. The transfer is necessary for the performance of a contract between the data subject and the controller or the implementation of precontractual measures taken in response to the data subject's request; or
2. The transfer is necessary for the conclusion or performance of a contract concluded in the interest of the data subject between the controller and a third party; or
3. The transfer is necessary or legally required on important public interest grounds, or for the establishment, exercise or defence of legal claims; or
4. The transfer is necessary in order to protect the vital interests of the data subject; or
5. The transfer is made from a register which according to laws or regulations is intended to provide information to the public and which is open to consultation either by the public in general or by any person who can demonstrate legitimate interest, to the extent that the conditions laid down in law for consultation are fulfilled in the particular case.

These exceptions are mandatory.

The transfer of personal data to a third country that does not ensure an adequate level of protection requires an authorisation by the Commissioner. In order to approve the transfer, the Commissioner must at least be satisfied that the controller has provided adequate safeguards, particularly by means of appropriate contractual provisions in accordance with the proviso of Article 28(3) of the Data Protection Act.

However, the data protection authority of the German federal state of Schleswig-Holstein is of the opinion that " clouds located outside the European Union are *per se* unlawful, even if the EU Commission has issued an adequacy decision in favour of the foreign country in question (for example, Switzerland, Canada or Argentina). A Commission adequacy decision does not confer "agent" status, which normally would privilege such transfers, on entities located in the adequate jurisdiction. The recipient entities remain "third parties" which means that a transfer in the legal sense takes place and therefore a legal basis is required. The potential legal basis, for example, under German law ("fulfilment of contract" or "balancing of interests test") requires that the transfer is also "necessary." The DPA is of the opinion that there are no arguments that the use of a cloud located outside the EU is compulsory (European Commission, 2010).

The current Data Protection Directive has resulted in each EU country adopting its own interpretation or implementing into national laws the Data Protection Directive. Each country adopted its own interpretation of the principles set forth in the directive, which created a patchwork that lacked the expected uniformity and consistency. To resolve this legal uncertainty, the EU Parliament has adopted the EU Commissions' proposal for Data Protection Reform. With the new EU data protection regulation, there will be one single rule: The countries will not have the freedom to make choices. As soon as the regulation is passed, each of its provisions will become part of the national legal system of each EEA Member State, "as is."

European Parliament Vote

Article 3: Territorial Scope

1. This Regulation applies to the processing of personal data in the context of the activities of an establishment of a controller or a processor in the Union, whether the processing takes place in the Union or not.
2. This Regulation applies to the processing of personal data of data subjects in the Union by a controller or processor not established in the Union, where the processing activities are related to:
   a. The offering of goods or services, irrespective of whether a payment of the data subject is required, to such data subjects in the Union; or
   b. The monitoring of such data subjects.

The EU regulation thus applies on the processing of personal data in the context of activities of an establishment of a controller or a processor in the EU. It also applies on the processing of personal data of data subjects residing in the EU by controllers not established in the EU, where the processing activities are related to:

- The offering of goods or services to such data subjects in the EU,
- The monitoring of their behaviour.

According to Article 73, data subject shall have the right to lodge a complaint with a supervisory authority in any Member State if they consider that the processing of personal data relating to them does not comply with this Regulation. Unlawful processing of data, Loss, destruction of data, identity theft, retaliation on consumers, grounded on unfairly strong bargaining positions of the cloud computing service providers should not only constitute very serious administrative and/or criminal violations, directly prosecutable in the consumers' jurisdiction – for instance, through a mandatory-legal-representative mechanism, for purposes of ensuring enforcement" - but also actionable at law and in equity (injunctions and "cease-and-desist" orders) through class-action-like procedural devices and expansive cross-border recognition/enforcement tools (European Privacy Association, 2009).

The security provisions of the proposed data protection regulation are also much more extensive than previously under Directive 95/46/EC and more stringent than what is usually found under U.S. law.

Safe Harbor Certification

Data controller can adduce safeguards through the following:

1. International Safe Harbor Certification,
2. Binding Corporate Rules,
3. Model contracts.

US companies may comply either by participating in the Safe Harbor scheme administered by the US Department of Commerce. US companies that participate in the International Safe Harbor Certification, which allows data transfer from the EU to the US (but not from the EU to other countries), are considered as offering adequate data protection and data flows to those companies will continue. An EU organization can ensure that it is sending information to a U.S. organization participating in the safe harbor by viewing the public list of safe harbor organizations posted on https://www.export.gov/safehrbr/list.aspx. Claims brought by European citizens against U.S. companies will be heard in the U.S. subject to limited exceptions.

To qualify for the safe harbor, an organization can:

1. Join a self-regulatory privacy program that adheres to the safe harbor's requirements; or
2. Develop its own self-regulatory privacy policy that conforms to the safe harbor.

Organizations must comply with the seven safe harbor principles:

- **Notice:** Organizations must notify individuals about the purposes for which they collect and use information about them.
- **Choice:** Organizations must give individuals the opportunity to choose (opt out) whether their personal information will be disclosed to a third party or used for a purpose incompatible with the purpose for which it was originally collected or subsequently authorized by the individual.
- **Onward Transfer:** To disclose information to a third party, organizations must apply the notice and choice principles.
- **Access:** Individuals must have access to personal information about them that an organization holds and be able to correct, amend, or delete that information where it is inaccurate, except where the burden or expense of providing access would be disproportionate to the risks to the individual's privacy in the case in question, or where the rights of persons other than the individual would be violated.

- **Security:** Organizations must take reasonable precautions to protect personal information from loss, misuse and unauthorized access, disclosure, alteration and destruction.
- **Data Integrity:** Personal information must be relevant for the purposes for which it is to be used. An organization should take reasonable steps to ensure that data is reliable for its intended use, accurate, complete, and current.'
- **Enforcement:** In order to ensure compliance with the safe harbor principles, there must be
    ◦ Readily available and affordable independent recourse mechanisms so that each individual's complaints and disputes can be investigated and resolved and damages awarded where the applicable law or private sector initiatives so provide;
    ◦ Procedures for verifying that the commitments companies make to adhere to the safe harbor principles have been implemented; and
    ◦ Obligations to remedy problems arising out of a failure to comply with the principles.

However, the Data Protection Authority (DPA) issued a recent opinion on June 18, 2010 that even self-certification to the U.S. Department of Commerce's Safe Harbor framework alone does not provide an adequate level of protection in the cloud context. Accordingly, reliance on certification to the Safe Harbor should not be used to circumvent the more strict EU legal requirements applicable to cloud computing. In addition, the DPA indicated that, because SAS 70 Type II Certificates used by some cloud providers do not contemplate the material and procedural interests of data subjects, such certifications offer only partial compliance with German legal requirements for commissioned data processing. (Ibid)

In Opinion 05/2012 on Cloud Computing, the Article 29 Working Party analyses the applicable data protection laws and obligations for companies providing or using cloud computing services in the EU. The Opinion identifies data protection risks that are likely to result from the use of cloud computing services, such as lack of control over personal data and lack of information about how, where, and by whom the data are being processed or sub-processed in the cloud. It also stresses the importance of informing data subjects about who processes their data, for what purposes, and in which locations, and how they can exercise the rights afforded to them in this respect when their data are hosted or processed in the cloud. It also examines the issues associated with the sharing of resources with other parties, the lack of transparency of outsourcing chains with multiple cloud processors and subcontractors, and the transfer of personal data to cloud providers established out of the EEA. In this regard, the most significant aspect of the Opinion is its negative evaluation of the ability of the Safe Harbor self-certification to meet the requirements of the national laws implementing the 1995 European Union Data Protection Directive. The Article 29 Working Party thinks that the loss of governance, insufficient audit trails, insecure or incomplete data deletion are not sufficiently addressed in the existing Safe Harbor principles to provide adequate assurance that the necessary security measures are met (Gilbert, 2012).

In June 2013, the existence of a number of U.S. surveillance programmes involving the large-scale collection and processing of personal data was revealed. The programmes concern in particular the collection of personal data from U.S. internet and telecommunication service providers and the monitoring of data flows inside and outside the U.S. Taking into account the political importance of the Safe Harbor authorities by EU organizations, the current discussions on the revelations on mass State surveillance by US security authorities, improvements to Safe Harbor have become highly necessary. Recent revelations about U.S. intelligence collection programmes have negatively affected the trust on which this cooperation is based. Google regularly receives requests from governments and courts around the world to hand over user data. The company received 20,938 requests for user data in the first half of 2012, up from 18,257 requests in the second half of 2011. The United States accounted for 7,969 requests in the 2012 report. And of these requests, Google provided user data to the US government in 90% of the cases. (Transparency report, 2014)

In February of 2014, the FTC announced enforcement action against 12 companies who also falsely claimed to be Safe Habor certified. Most recently the FTC announced that it had settled with a gaming company that falsely claimed to be certified under the US Safe Harbor. This a new sign on the willingness of FTC to enforce the safe harbor agreement in the light of the public concern among European consumers that their data may be at risk if it is held in the US or by US companies.

The European Commission has set out the actions that need to be taken to restore trust in data flows between the EU and the U.S., following deep concerns about revelations of large-scale U.S. intelligence collection programmes have had a negative impact on the transatlantic relationship. Cecilia Malmström, European Commissioner for Home Affairs (European Commission, 2013) commented on the US spying:

European citizens' trust has been shaken by the Snowden case, and serious concerns still remain following the allegations of widespread access by U.S. intelligence agencies to personal data. Today, we put forward a clear agenda for how the U.S. can work with the EU to rebuild trust, and reassure EU citizens that their data will be protected. Everyone from Internet users to authorities on both sides of the Atlantic stand to gain from cooperation, based on strong legal safeguards and trust that these safeguards will be respected.

The EU Commission's proposal for a swift adoption of the EU's data protection reform with clear rules that are enforceable also in situations when data is transferred and processed abroad is, more than ever, a necessity. The Commission made the made 13 recommendations to improve the functioning of the Safe Harbour scheme, after an analysis found the functioning of the scheme deficient in several respects made 13 recommendations to improve the functioning of the Safe Harbour scheme, after an analysis finds the functioning of the scheme deficient in several respects. The 13 Recommendations (European Commission, 2013) are:

Transparency

1. Self-certified companies should publicly disclose their privacy policies.
2. Privacy policies of self-certified companies' websites should always include a link to the Department of Commerce Safe Harbour website which lists all the 'current' members of the scheme.
3. Self-certified companies should publish privacy conditions of any contracts they conclude with subcontractors, e.g. cloud computing services.
4. Clearly flag on the website of the Department of Commerce all companies which are not current members of the scheme.

Redress

5. The privacy policies on companies' websites should include a link to the alternative dispute resolution (ADR) provider.
6. ADR should be readily available and affordable.
7. The Department of Commerce should monitor more systematically ADR providers regarding the transparency and accessibility of information they provide concerning the procedure they use and the follow-up they give to complaints.

Enforcement

8. Following the certification or recertification of companies under Safe Harbour, a certain percentage of these companies should be subject to ex officio investigations of effective compliance of their privacy policies (going beyond control of compliance with formal requirements).
9. Whenever there has been a finding of non-compliance, following a complaint or an investigation, the company should be subject to follow-up specific investigation after 1 year.
10. In case of doubts about a company's compliance or pending complaints, the Department of Commerce should inform the competent EU data protection authority.
11. False claims of Safe Harbour adherence should continue to be investigated

Access by US Authorities

12. Privacy policies of self-certified companies should include information on the extent to which US law allows public authorities to collect and process data transferred under the Safe Harbour. In particular companies should be encouraged to indicate in their privacy policies when they apply exceptions to the Principles to meet national security, public interest or law enforcement requirements.
13. It is important that the national security exception foreseen by the Safe Harbour Decision is used only to an extent that is strictly necessary or proportionate.

The recommendations proposed by the EU beef up requirements in relation to transparency, redress, enforcement and, access by US law enforcement agencies. It is difficult to see how the recommendation that companies state in their privacy policies that they may disclose data for the purposes of national security and law enforcement, will qualify really for legitimate purposes since it is doubtful will truthfully inform the company the truth about the specific request.

The European Parliament on its resolution of 12 March 2014 on the US NSA surveillance program, surveillance bodies in various Member States and their impact on EU citizens' fundamental rights and on transatlantic cooperation in Justice and Home Affairs (2013/2188(INI)), supports the idea that under the current circumstances, the possibility for Safe Harbor to provide adequate protection for EU citizens is questionable. The resolution notes that the companies identified by media revelations as being involved in the large-scale mass surveillance of EU data subjects by the US NSA are companies that have self-certified their adherence to the Safe Harbour, and that the Safe Harbour is the legal instrument used for the transfer of EU personal data to the US (examples being Google, Microsoft, Yahoo!, Facebook, Apple and LinkedIn). The European legislators expressed its concerns that these organisations have not encrypted information and communications flowing between their data centres, thereby enabling intelligence services to intercept information. The Resolution (European Parliament, 2014) calls for action to the following:

- Considers that large-scale access by US intelligence agencies to EU personal data processed by Safe Harbour does not meet the criteria for derogation under 'national security';
- Takes the view that, as under the current circumstances the Safe Harbour principles do not provide adequate protection for EU citizens, these transfers should be carried out under other instruments, such as contractual

clauses or BCRs, provided these instruments set out specific safeguards and protections and are not circumvented by other legal frameworks;

- Takes the view that the Commission has failed to act to remedy the well-known deficiencies of the current implementation of Safe Harbour;
- Calls on the Commission to present measures providing for the immediate suspension of Commission Decision 2000/520/EC, which declared the adequacy of the Safe Harbour privacy principles, and of the related FAQs issued by the US Department of Commerce; calls on the US authorities, therefore, to put forward a proposal for a new framework for transfers of personal data from the EU to the US which meets Union law data protection requirements and provides for the required adequate level of protection;
- Calls on Member States' competent authorities, in particular the data protection authorities, to make use of their existing powers and immediately suspend data flows to any organisation that has self-certified its adherence to the US Safe Harbour Principles, and to require that such data flows are only carried out under other instruments and provided they contain the necessary safeguards and guarantees with respect to the protection of the privacy and fundamental rights and freedoms of individuals;
- Calls on the Commission to present, by December 2014, a comprehensive assessment of the US privacy framework covering commercial, law enforcement and intelligence activities, and concrete recommendations based on the absence of a general data protection law in the US; encourages the Commission to engage with the US administration in order to establish a

legal framework providing for a high level of protection of individuals with regard to the protection of their personal data when transferred to the US and ensure the equivalence of EU and US privacy frameworks.

The parliament also stressed that the level of data protection in a cloud computing environment must not be inferior to that required in any other data-processing context. The Resolution also noted that the data protection law, since it is technologically neutral, already applies fully to cloud computing services operating in the EU. The mass surveillance activities give intelligence agencies access to personal data stored or otherwise processed by EU individuals under cloud services agreements with major US cloud providers such as Yahoo and Google. institutions has also been accessed by intelligence authorities; The access to personal data constitutes a violation of international obligations and of European fundamental rights standards including the right to private and family life, the confidentiality of communications, the presumption of innocence, freedom of expression, freedom of information, freedom of assembly and association and the freedom to conduct business. The persistent illegal access of the US government to private data of EU citizens have made it harder for non-European businesses to sell into the European market without setting up European servers or an EU cloud.

Binding Corporate Rules

Binding Corporate Rules (BCRs) are legally binding internal corporate data privacy rules that establish a corporation's practices regarding the transfer of personal information within the corporate group. Binding corporate rules are also an appropriate tool for companies seeking to implement a cloud solution. Under this route, transfers can be made where the organization demonstrates adequate safeguards with respect to the protection of personal data. BCR ensure that all transfers are made within a group benefit from an adequate level of protection. This is an alternative to the company having to sign standard contractual clauses each time it needs to transfer data to a member of its group and may be preferable where it becomes burdensome to sign contractual clauses for each transfer made within a group. Once approved under the EU cooperation procedure, BCR provide a sufficient level of protection to companies to get authorisation of transfers by national data protection authorities ("DPA"). It should be noted that the BCR does not provide a basis for transfers made outside the group.

A coordinated European procedure has been introduced enabling multinationals to apply to a national authority (which in this case takes the lead at European level) that will then contact the other European authorities involved to conduct a common study of the draft code of conduct. The idea is to come to coherent decisions of the various data protection authorities (Commission for the Protection of Privacy, n.d.). The BCR must contain in particular: Privacy principles (transparency, data quality, security, etc.), tools of effectiveness (audit, training, complaint handling system, etc.), and an element proving that BCR are binding.

The Article 29 EU Working Group document effectively endorses this route in principle, whilst also setting out guidance, both as to the content of the binding corporate rules and the procedures for organizations to adopt them. The BCRs are designed for a multinational company and therefore may not function well for cloud provider relationships. In March 2009, the Article 29 working group issued an opinion to update the standard controller-to-processor contract clauses. It identifies controllers as the entities that decide to have some personal data processed for their own purposes. It recognizes that multiple parties (such as a parent company and its affiliates or business partners) may collectively decide which data elements are needed and how they will be handled. They need not have equal voices in those decisions, and their respective responsibility and liability may be limited to their own decisions.

While standard contractual clauses appear to be efficient to frame non-massive transfers made by a data exporter located in the EU to a data importer located outside the EU, the outsourcing industry has been constant in its request for a new legal instrument that would allow for a global approach to data protection in the outsourcing business and officially recognize internal rules organisations may have implemented.

In the context of outsourcings and other service arrangements (e.g., the purchase of cloud computing services), BCRs have not previously been used by data processor service providers as a means to transfer personal data outside of the EEA because, prior to January 1, 2013, they were only available to data controllers in relation to internal transfers of their own data. Instead data processor service providers transferring data from the EEA had to rely on other mechanisms to ensure transfers were adequate, including the use of Model Clauses or a U.S. service provider's Safe Harbor membership. The Article 29 Working Party adopted in the course of December 2012 a working document setting up a table with the elements and principles to be found in BCR for Processors and an application form for submitting binding corporate rules for Processors.

BCR for Processors are a safeguard for international transfers provided by a Processor to its client (Controller) and it is the Controller that is primarily liable towards Data Protection Authorities and data subjects for ensuring that personal data transferred outside the EU are protected. As such, BCR for Processors shall be made binding toward the Controller through a specific reference to it in the Service Agreement. In addition to this and in order for the BCR for Processors to be unambiguously linked to the Service Agreement signed with each client (Controller), it is important to make sure in the Service Agreement that:

- The Controller shall commit that if the transfer involves special categories of data, data subjects have been informed or will be informed before the transfer that their data could be transmitted to a third country not providing adequate protection;

- The Controller shall also commit to inform data subjects about the existence of Processors based outside of EU and of the BCR for Processors. The Controller shall make available to data subjects upon request a copy of the BCR for Processors and of the Service Agreement (without any sensitive and confidential commercial information);

EU Standard Contract Clauses

Where a third country does not ensure an adequate level of protection, Directive 95/46/EC provides that the European Commission may decide that certain standard contractual clauses (SCCS) offer sufficient safeguards for transfers of personal data for the data. Model contracts or EU standard contract clauses (SCCs) allow data transfer from the EU to non-US countries. Unlike the safe harbor, data transfers under SCCs require notification to the data protection authorities in many European countries for each transfer to a country (point to point) where the legal framework is not adequate, as well as a prior approval by the local Data Protection Authorities (DPA).

In practice this is very difficult to implement in cloud computing, which entails the continuous transfer of personal data. Cloud providers are reluctant to make any contractual offer because in many cases they cannot say which countries the data will be transferred to or from. To address this problem, the EU recommends the use of Model Contracts or SCCs.

In 2002, the European Commission passed Decision 2002/87/EU which approved three sets of contractual clauses: two of these sets apply to transfers from data controllers to other data controllers, while the third set has been drafted for transfers from data controllers to recipients who act as data processors only. However, they do not always work well with multi-tiered vendor relationships. As more and more organizations are transferring personal data to a "processor" but also to one or more "sub-processors" outside the EU/EEA, the original standard contractual clauses were no longer suitable to deal with these complex onward transfers.

On 5 February 2010, the European Commission repealed the 2002 "controller to processor" standard contractual clauses to take account of the expansion of processing activities and new business models of companies for international processing of personal data. Guaranteeing a continuously adequate level of protection with the use of available tools for framing international data transfers, as described above, is proving difficult, which is mainly due to the increasing number and complexity of international data transfers (resulting from e.g. Cloud computing,, social networks, etc.). This was implemented on May 15, 2010 when the European Union adopted a new set of SCCs through Commission Decision 2010/87/EU of 5 February 2010 on standard contractual clause for transfers between Controllers and Processors under Directive 95/46/EC, which deals with data transfers outside the corporate group or directly from Europe to vendors outside the United States. Under these standard contractual clauses, an EU company exporting data (controller) should instruct its processor established in a third country to treat the data with full respect to the EU data protection requirements and should guarantee that appropriate technical and security measures are in place in the destination country.

While standard contractual clauses appear to be efficient to frame non-massive transfers made by a data exporter located in the EU to a data importer located outside the EU, the outsourcing industry has been constant in its request for a new legal instrument that would allow for a global approach to data protection in the outsourcing business and officially recognize internal rules organisations may have implemented. The Article 29 Working Party adopted in the course of December 2012 a working document setting up a table with the elements and principles to be found in BCR for Processors and an application form for submitting binding corporate rules for Processors (Article 29 Working Party, 2013).

Neither Safe Harbor, nor Standard Contractual Clauses, nor BCRs could serve as a legal basis to justify the transfer of personal data to a third country authority for the purpose of massive and indiscriminate surveillance. In fact, the exceptions included in these instruments are limited in scope and should be interpreted restrictively. They should never be implemented to the detriment of the level of protection guaranteed by EU rules and instruments governing transfers.

4. CONCLUSION

The cloud computing model is a wonderful system when it works and a nightmare when it fails. The most worrying aspect of the dark cloud is the numerous legal, privacy and security implications. There is currently little on offer in the way of tools, procedures or standard data formats or services interfaces that could guarantee 100% data protection. It is difficult to determine whether the cloud provider is processing and storing the data lawfully, especially in the case of multiple transfers of data. Not only is there a risk of data security breaches, but cloud customers also lose control of the data processed by the cloud provider.

Regulatory bodies are grappling with the privacy and data security implications of cloud computing. Given the rapidly-evolving legal landscape, venturing into the cloud is a risky matter. The large volume of data transfers carried out on a daily basis, increased outsourcing and the emergence of new business models have opened a Pandora box of security nightmares: how to facilitate easier movement of data across borders while maintaining legal protection for consumers. The European Union is trying to close security loopholes and offer best-practice solutions and guidance on governance, standards and compliance. It is trying to develop more balanced and predictable rules to enhance legal certainty. The proposed Data Protection Regulation takes account of the expansion of processing activities and international processing of personal data, increased outsourcing and cloud computing. It is intended to provide a legitimate and efficient means to transfer personal data.

In contrast, the United States seems to take a lax approach to the principles of privacy and contractual liability. US District Court Judge Michael Mossman ruling as stated below reflects the US government's approach to privacy- the right of government law agencies to read all of the private email stored on the Internet server with only a notice to the Internet/Cloud Service Provider:

A person uses the Internet, however, the user's actions are no longer in his or her physical home; in fact he or she is not truly acting in private space at all.

The Snowden revelations of mass surveillance by the US government have exposed the existence of so many different surveillance programmes run by intelligence services which able to collect data about virtually everyone. US intelligence services use of personal data of European citizens is pervasive and underlines the need to set limits on the scale of surveillance. The conditions for international transfers of personal data set out in directive 95/46/EC need to be respected: this means above all that the recipient ensures an adequate level of protection and that transfers need to be in line with the original purpose for which the data were collected. Transfers must also comply with the need to have the appropriate legal basis for a fair and lawful processing. None of the instruments available that can be used as an alternative basis to transfer personal data to countries that have not been found adequate (Safe Harbor, Standard Contractual Clauses and BCRs) allow for third country public authorities for the purpose of indiscriminate, massive surveillance to gain access to personal data transferred on the basis of these instruments (Article 29 Working Party Opinion on Surveillance of electronic communications for intelligence and national security purposes, 2014).

Companies seeking to implement cloud computing solutions should proceed with caution and closely monitor global developments. The challenge to companies seeking to implement cloud computing is determining what assurances should be in the contracts and how much risk and liability are being assumed when a service is moved to the 'cloud'. As the adage goes, "caveat emptor."

REFERENCES

Article 29 Working Party: Explanatory Document on the Processor Binding Corporate Rules. (2013). Retrieved from http://www.dsb.gv.at/DocView.axd?CobId=53536

Article 29 Working Party Opinion on Surveillance of Electronic Communications for Intelligence and National Security Purpose. (2014). Retrieved from http://ec.europa.eu/justice/data-protection/article-29/documentation/opinion-recommendation/files/2014/wp215_en.pdf

Ashford, W. (2014, March). State surveillance keeping a third of firms from the cloud. *Computer Weekly.* Retrieved from http://www.computerweekly.com/news/2240217011/State-surveillance-keeping-a-third-of-firms-from-the-cloud

Battle of the Clouds. (2009, October 15). *The Economist.* Retrieved from http://www.economist.com/node/14644393

Bennet, M. (2010, November). Negotiating cloud computing agreements. *Law Technology News.* Retrieved from http://www.lawtechnologynews.com/id=1202446025928?slreturn=20140923072606

Commission for the Protection of Privacy. (n.d.). *Binding corporate rules.* Retrieved from http://www.privacycommission.be/en/transfers-outside-the-eu-without-adequate-protection/bcr

Electronic Privacy Information Center. (n.d.). *Data retention*. Retrieved May 19, 2014, from http://epic.org/privacy/intl/data_retention.html

European Comission. (2013). *European Commission calls on the U.S. to restore trust in EU-U.S. data flows.* [Press Release]. Retrieved from http://europa.eu/rapid/press-release_IP-13-1166_en.htm

European Commission. (2010). *Opinion 1/2010 on the concepts of "controller" and "processor"*. Retrieved from http://ec.europa. eu/justice/policies/privacy/docs/wpdocs/2010/ wp169_en.pdf

European Commission. (2012). *COM (2012)529 - Unleashing the Potential of cloud computing in Europe*. Retrieved from http://eur-lex.europa. eu/LexUriServ/LexUriServ.do?uri=COM:201 2:0529:FIN:EN:PDF

European Parliament. (2014). *Report on US NSA surveillance programme, surveillance bodies in various member states and their impact on EU citizens' fundamental rights and on transatlantic cooperation in justice and home affairs (2013/2188(INI))*. Retrieved from http://www.europarl.europa.eu/sides/getDoc. do?type=REPORT&reference=A7-2014-0139&language=EN

European Privacy Association. (2009). *New challenges for privacy: Advanced technologies, effective legal frameworks and active responsibility*. Retrieved from http://ec.europa.eu/ justice/news/consulting_public/0003/contributions/organisations/european_privacy_association_en.pdf

European Union Defines Cloud Computing. (2010). *Information Age*. Retrieved on from http://www. information-age.com/technology/data-centre-and-it-infrastructure/1147048/european-union-defines-cloud-computing

Gilbert, F. (2012, July). Article 29 working party cloud computing opinion: Blow to safe harbor? *TechTarget*. Retrieved from http://searchcloud-security.techtarget.com/tip/Article-29-Working-Party-cloud-computing-opinion-Blow-to-Safe-Harbor

Google Press Center. (2006). Conversation with Eric Schmidt hosted by Danny Sullivan. *Search Engine Strategies Conference*. Retrieved from http://www.google.com/press/podium/ses2006. html

Google Terms of Service. (n.d.). Retrieved from http://www.google.com/apps/intl/en/terms/ user_terms.htm

Gorniak, S., Ikonomou, D., Saragiotis, S., Askoxylakis, I., Belimpasakis, P., Bencsath, B., … Vishik, C. (2010, April). Report priorities for research on current and emerging network technologies. *Enisa*. Retrieved from https://www. enisa.europa.eu/activities/identity-and-trust/ library/deliverables/procent

Jefferey, K., & Neidecker-Lutz, B. (Eds.). (2010). Expert group report: The future of cloud computing. *European Commission: Information Society and Media*. Retrieved from http://cordis.europa. eu/fp7/ict/ssai/docs/cloud-report-final.pdf

Judgement of the Court in Digital Rights Ireland. (2014). *InfoCuria - Case-law of the Court of Justice*. Retrieved from http://curia.europa.eu/juris/ document/document.jsf;jsessionid=9ea7d0f130d 686ae333e76e448e28720eb03f4442ff1.e34Kaxi Lc3eQc40LaxqMbN4OaNiLe0?text=&docid=1 50642&pageIndex=0&doclang=en&mode=req &dir=&occ=first&part=1&cid=30149

Khan, I. (2009). Cloud computing set to go mainstream. *Outsourcing*, *13*, 30–31.

Leyden, T. (2009, October). A brief history of cloud computing. *Sys-Con Media*. Retrieved from https://tleyden.sys-con.com/node/1150011

Logan, D. (2009). Hype cycle for legal and regulatory information governance. *Gartner*. Retrieved from http://www.gartner.com/DisplayDocument?doc_cd=208630&ref=g_rss

Mell, P., & Grance, T. (2009). *The NIST definition of cloud computing*. National Institute of Standards and Technology. Retrieved from http://www.nist.gov/itl/cloud/upload/cloud-def-v15.pdf

Mell, P., & Grance, T. (2011, September). *The NIST definition of cloud computing*. NIST Special Publication 800-145 National Institute of Standards and Technology Gaithersburg. Retrieved from http://csrc.nist.gov/publications/nistpubs/800-145/SP800-145.pdf

Miller, P. (2008, August). Everywhere I look I see clouds. *ZDNET*. Retrieved from http://www.zdnet.com/blog/semantic-web/everywhere-i-look-i-see-clouds/179

Mowbray, M. (2009). *The fog over the Grimpen Mire: Cloud computing and the law*. HP Laboratory. Retrieved from http://www.hpl.hp.com/techreports/2009/HPL-2009-99.pdf

Transparency Report. (n.d.) Retrieved from http://www.google.com/transparencyreport/userdatarequests/

Restoring Trust in EU-US Data Flows - Frequently Asked Questions. (2013, November 27). Retrieved from http://europa.eu/rapid/press-release_MEMO-13-1059_en.htm

Stroh, S., Acker, O., & Kunar, A. (2009, June). *Why cloud computing is gaining strength in the IT marketplace*. Retrieved from http://www.strategy-business.com/article/li00131?gko=c331a

ENDNOTE

[1] The Brussels I Regulation on jurisdiction and the enforcement of judgments in civil and commercial matters (Regulation 44/2001/EC) has been recast. Regulation 1215/2012 h on jurisdiction and the enforcement of judgments, will come into force in January 2015. The basic jurisdictional rules in the recast Regulation remain the same as in the existing Regulation. The starting point is the domicile of the defendant (article 4(1)), though there are potentially additional jurisdictions (e.g. in matters relating to contract, the courts for the place of performance of the obligation in question (article 7(1)(a)) or jurisdictions that override domicile (e.g. proceedings that have as their object rights in rem in immoveable property (article 24(1)) or where the parties have agreed to the exclusive jurisdiction of particular courts (article 25)). Regulation (EC) No 864/2007 of the European Parliament and of the Council of 11 July 2007 on the law applicable to non-contractual obligations (Rome II) defines the law applicable to non-contractual obligations in situations involving a conflict of laws; it does not harmonise the substantive law of the Member States. It covers civil and commercial matters with certain exceptions, notably family relationships and the liability of the State, and will apply in all EU Member States, except Denmark, from 2009.

Chapter 2
Data Protection in EU Law after Lisbon:
Challenges, Developments, and Limitations

Maria Tzanou
Keele University, UK

ABSTRACT

This chapter provides an analysis of the data protection rules in EU law, focusing on the constitutional and legal developments after the entry into force of the Lisbon Treaty. It examines the jurisprudence of the Court of Justice of the EU on data protection issues, including the recent decisions of the Court on metadata retention and the new right to be forgotten. It concludes with a critical comment on the possibilities and limitations of the EU to provide for effective and comprehensive data protection.

1. INTRODUCTION

The rapid expansion of the Internet, the development of new technologies which make possible the use of big data and the fight against terrorism and serious crime have led to an unprecedented need for exchange of personal data. Data protection in Europe was born out of the concerns raised in the 1970s about the establishment of huge data banks and the increasingly centralized processing of personal data. In the EU, the first data protection legal instrument, the Data Protection Directive was adopted in 1995. Since then data protection has gone a long way culminating to its constitutional recognition as a fundamental right next to privacy in the EU Charter of Fundamental Rights.

The present chapter provides an analysis of the data protection rules in EU law, focusing on the constitutional and legal developments after the entry into force of the Lisbon Treaty. It examines the jurisprudence of the Court of Justice of the EU on data protection issues, including the recent decisions of the Court on metadata retention and the new right to be forgotten. It concludes with a critical comment on the possibilities and limitations of the EU to provide for effective and comprehensive data protection.

DOI: 10.4018/978-1-4666-7381-6.ch002

2. THE EU DATA PROTECTION REGIME AFTER THE LISBON TREATY

2.1 The Lisbon Treaty and Constitutional Developments in the EU

In 2004, two failed referendums in France and the Netherlands marked the early end of the ambitious EU Constitutional Treaty (or the Treaty establishing a Constitution for Europe). Not very long after this, the Lisbon Treaty was signed on December 13, 2007 and entered into force on December 1st 2009. The Lisbon Treaty was presented by its authors –the EU Member States- as an amending Treaty of the founding Treaties of the EU that aimed to introduce only an 'incremental change' (Cremona, 2012, p. 40) and not the complete new legal framework that the Constitutional Treaty proposed. However, the Lisbon Treaty represents an important new departure for the EU (Berman, 2012, p. 3) and marked a new era for the EU constitutional and human rights framework in general and the right to data protection in particular.

The pre-Lisbon EU constitutional framework was built-up on the so-called three –pillar system: the first encompassed the European Community (EC) Treaty and Euratom (and formerly the Coal and Steel Community); the second the provisions on Common Foreign and Security Policy (CFSP); and the third the provisions on Police and Judicial Cooperation in Criminal Matters (PJC). The pillar structure was considered very problematic as the different pillars were comprised of different rules concerning institutions, decision-making instruments and procedures, decision-making powers, judiciary competences and the protection of human rights and fundamental freedoms (Dougan, 2007, p. 617). The Lisbon Treaty abolished the pillar system of the EU. It amended the Treaty on the European Union (TEU) and the EC Treaty by renaming the latter the Treaty on the Functioning

of the EU (TFEU). Essentially, the provisions of the former first and third pillars are now found in the TFEU, while the 'distinctive' rules relating to the CFSP are found in the TEU. These amendments have major implications for the right to data protection that will be discussed in detail below.

At this point before the analysis moves on to discuss data protection in the post-Lisbon era, one further major development introduced by the Lisbon Treaty should be mentioned. The EU Charter of Fundamental Rights (EUCFR) was given legal force by the Lisbon Treaty and is now incorporated into European constitutional law (Anderson & Murphy, 2012, p. 155). The Charter, which constitutes the EU's own written bill of rights, enjoys now the same legal value as the Treaties. In fact, the Lisbon Treaty recognizes in Article 6 TEU three formal sources for EU human rights law: the first is the EUCFR, the second is the accession of the EU to the European Convention for the Protection of Human Rights and Fundamental Freedoms (ECHR), and the third is the protection of fundamental rights as 'general principles of EU law' that have been developed by the European Court of Justice (ECJ) (now: Court of Justice of the EU (CJEU) over the years.

2.2 The Constitutional Framework for the EU Data Protection Regime

The current constitutional legal base for measures concerning data protection within the EU is Article 16 TFEU. The substantive part of this provision stipulates that "[e]veryone has the right to the protection of personal data concerning them" (paragraph 1). Article 16 TFEU, which replaces Article 286 EC, applies both to the former first and third pillars and provides for the use of the ordinary legislative procedure (Peers, 2011, p. 874) when rules "relating to the protection of individuals with regard to the processing of personal data by Union institutions, bodies, offices and agencies, and by the Member States when carrying out activities which fall within the scope of Union law", or "rules relating to the free movement of data" are adopted (paragraph 2). Furthermore, the Article provides that compliance with data protection rules will be subject to the control of independent authorities (paragraph 2).

It should be noted that Article 16 is included in Title II of the TFEU under 'Provisions having general application' among other important principles, such as the consistency of EU law (Article 7 TFEU), combating discrimination (Articles 8 and 10 TFEU), environmental protection (Article 11 TFEU), consumer protection (Article 12 TFEU) and good governance and public access to documents (Article 15 TFEU). The most important ramification of Article 16 TFEU is that it applies to the processing of personal data in the area of police and judicial cooperation attempting, therefore, to solve many of the deficiencies of the fragmented pillar system and the inequalities in protection found in the former third pillar (Hijmans and Scirocco, 2009, p. 1515).

That being said, Article 16 TFEU does not apply to the former second pillar. As the Article itself stipulates in 16 (2) TFEU "the rules adopted on the basis of this Article shall be without prejudice to the specific rules laid down in Article 39 of the Treaty on European Union." This means essentially that the similar provision regarding Common Foreign and Security Policy is found in Article 39 TEU which is drafted as a derogation from Article 16 TFEU. The main difference between the two provisions is that Article 39 TEU excludes the use of the ordinary legislative procedure with the involvement of the European Parliament for the adoption of data protection rules in the context of the CFSP, where the Council is still (even in the post-Lisbon era) considered as the main legislator.

2.3 Data Protection as a New Fundamental Right Next to Privacy in the EU Legal Order?

The entry into force of the Lisbon Treaty marked a historic moment for data protection in Europe: the right, besides figuring in the EU Treaties, was elevated in the EU Charter of Fundamental Rights to the status of a fundamental right within the EU legal order, alongside the right to privacy (Tzanou, 2013a, p. 88). In particular, Article 7 of the EUCFR recognizes 'the right to private and family life, home and communications', which is also found in Article 8 ECHR. In addition to this, Article 8 EUCFR provides for the right to protection of personal data, according which: "Everyone has the right to the protection of personal data concerning him or her (paragraph 1). Such data must be processed fairly for specified purposes and on the basis of the consent of the person concerned or some other legitimate basis laid down by law. Everyone has the right of access to data which has been collected concerning him or her, and the right to have it rectified (paragraph 2). Compliance with these rules shall be subject to control by an independent authority (paragraph 3)."

But, what is the relationship between privacy and data protection? Is data protection a separate or an autonomous fundamental right, distinct from the right to privacy, or is it a mere aspect of privacy? This debate, which is alive among European scholars is not only theoretical, but it can also have practical implications.

In this respect, the first point that should be made is that privacy and data protection are not identical rights. At a first glance, data protection seems to fall in this aspect of privacy that is known as 'informational privacy' or 'control over personal information'. In his seminal work, Alan Westin (1970, pp. 31-32) defined privacy as "the claim of individuals, groups, or institutions to determine for when, how, and to what extent information about them is communicated to others." Along the same lines, Charles Fried (1968, pp. 482-483) pointed out that "privacy is not simply an absence of information about what is in the minds of others; rather it is the *control* we have over information about ourselves." However, what privacy protects is "irreducible to personal information" (Rouvroy and Poullet, 2009, p. 70). Privacy is a much broader concept that embodies a range of rights and values, such as non interference or the right to be let alone (Warren and Brandeis, 1890, p. 193) limited access to oneself (Solove, 2008, p.18), intimacy (Inness, 1996, p. 56), personhood (Reiman, 1976, p. 314), and so on according to the various definitions proposed by scholars (Tzanou, 2013b, p. 26).

Furthermore, not all personal data (which is defined as information related to an identified or identifiable person) are necessarily "private" or, to put it differently, not all of them are capable of intimately affecting the individual's private sphere. As the Court of First Instance (CFI) (now: General Court) rightly noted in *Bavarian Lager*, "[i]t should be emphasized that the fact that the concept of 'private life' is a broad one, in accordance with the case-law of the European Court of Human Rights, and that the right to the protection of personal data may constitute one of the aspects of the right to respect for private life, does not mean that all personal data necessarily fall within the concept of 'private life.' A fortiori, not all personal data are by their nature capable of undermining the private life of the person concerned" (paras. 118-119).

Finally, data protection is more than informational privacy itself because it serves other, further fundamental rights and values besides privacy, such as transparency in the processing, due process rights for the data subject, data quality, data security, accountability of the data controller, non-discrimination, and proportionality (Tzanou, 2013a, p. 91).

That being said, does it really matter if privacy and data protection are seen as the same or different rights? It has been argued elsewhere by the present author that in the EU legal context it does since the EUCFR recognizes both rights. However, the CJEU has adopted a different approach so far. While the Court in *Promusicae* identified data protection as an autonomous fundamental right found in Article 8 of the EUCFR, even before the EUCFR had became legally binding (Tzanou, 2011, p. 275), in the subsequent *Schecke* case, it confusingly saw the two rights together in what it called "the right to respect for private life with regard to the processing of personal data, recognized by Articles 7 and 8 of the Charter." In this regard, the Court then proceeded to analyze the permissible limitations to the right to data protection on the basis of the right to privacy, using Article 8(2) ECHR and ignoring entirely the right to data protection in Article 8 EUCFR.

I submit that this approach of the CJEU is problematic because by seeing only data protection though the lens of privacy it ends up denying individuals the specific safeguards they are provided with by the data protection information principles (data quality, data security, transparency, due process, accountability, non-discrimination, and proportionality) and which do not form part of the right to privacy (Tzanou 2013a, p. 94; Tzanou, 2013b, p.27).

2.4 The Current Legislative Framework: Shortcomings and Challenges

2.4.1 The Data Protection Directive

Besides the EU primary law discussed above, a rather extensive EU legislation on data protection also exists: On the one hand, within the scope of the former first pillar (Community law), there is the Data Protection Directive; the ePrivacy Directive, the Data Protection Regulation; and the Data Retention Directive that was presented as a modification of EC data protection legislation. On the other hand, within the scope of the former third pillar, there is only one general instrument applying to the processing of data in the area of Police and Judicial Cooperation in Criminal matters (PJC), the relevant Framework Decision. This is supplemented by several data protection rules in further specific third pillar instruments, which concern the processing of personal data for different purposes.

Even though the Treaty of Lisbon has repealed the former Title VI of the TEU and abolished the distinction between the first and the third pillar (Guild and Carrera, 2010, p.4) the data protection rules adopted within the framework of the former third pillar will remain valid until they are amended (Peers, 2011, pp. 883-884), due to the Treaty's transitional provisions.

On 25 January 2012, the Commission put forward a proposal for a new legal framework for data protection in the EU. Despite the expectations for a consolidated regime, the Commission's proposal package includes two separate instruments: A Regulation –aimed to replace the Data Protection Directive- setting out a general framework for data protection, and a Directive –aimed to replace the Data Protection Framework Decision- laying down rules on the protection of personal data processed for the purposes of prevention, detection, investigation or prosecution of criminal offences and related judicial activities. The discussion will turn to the two proposed data protection instruments in the following chapter after it discusses the current legal framework.

The Data Protection Directive (Directive 95/46/EC) constitutes the central legislative measure of the EU data protection regime (Tzanou, 2011, p. 276). Adopted in October 1995, the Directive was the first piece of data protection legislation in the EU legal order. The aim of the Directive is twofold: on the hand, protect privacy with respect to the processing of personal data,

on the other hand, ensure the free movement of personal data in the EU. The Directive defines 'personal data' as "any information relating to an identified or identifiable natural person ('data subject') and 'processing' as "any operation or set of operations which is performed upon personal data, whether or not by automatic means."

The Directive sets out a number of principles concerning the legitimate processing of personal data, normally referred to as 'data protection' or 'fair information principles'. It is the obligation of the so-called 'controller' to comply with these principles. 'Controller' is, according to the Directive, "the natural or legal person, public authority, agency or any other body which alone or jointly with other determines the purposes and means of the processing of personal data." The data protection principles found in the Directive include the fair and lawful processing (Article 6 (1) (a)); the purpose specification and limitation principle according to which, data collected for specified, explicit and legitimate purposes, may not be further processed in a way incompatible to those purposes (Article 6 (1) (b)); the data quality and the proportionality principle (Article 6 (1) (c) and (d)). The Directive provides for increased protection for 'sensitive data' that reveal "racial or ethnic origin, political opinions, religious or philosophical beliefs, trade-union membership, and data concerning sex or health life" (Article 8 (1)).

Furthermore, the Data Protection Directive lays down a number of rights of the data subject, which are primarily procedural. The data subject has a right to information (Article 10), a right of access (Article 12) and a right to object (Article 14) to the processing of their data. In addition, the Directive imposes a number of further obligations to controllers: confidentiality of processing (Article 16), security of processing (Article 17), and the obligation to notify the supervisory authority before carrying out any processing operation (Article 18).

Compliance of the controllers with the Directive is ensured by independent authorities in the territory of each Member State (the National Data Protection Authorities (NDPAs)). The National Data Protection Authorities are endowed with investigative powers, powers of intervention, the power to engage in legal proceedings where the national data protection law implementing the Directive has been violated, they can hear claims concerning data protection issues lodged by individuals or associations and issue public reports on their activities.

Alongside the NDPAs, the Directive establishes also an independent EU Advisory Body on the protection of individuals with regard to the processing of personal data, normally referred to as the 'Article 29 Working Party' or the 'Working Party'. The Working Party is composed of representatives of national data protection authorities, the European Data Protection Supervisor, and the Commission. Its main tasks, which are laid down in Article 30 of the Directive, consist in examining any question covering the application of the national measures adopted under the Directive in order to contribute to the uniform application of such measures; in providing expert opinions from member state level to the Commission on questions of data protection; in advising the Commission on any proposed measures affecting data protection rights; and in making recommendations on its own initiative on matters relating to the protection of persons with regard to the processing of personal data in the Community. Even though the Working Party has only advisory competences, it has played an important role in promoting data protection issues within the EU, and has produced a significant number of reports, recommendations and opinions on privacy matters.

If one attempts an evaluation of the Data Protection Directive, it can be argued without any doubt that this has been the centerpiece and the foundation of data protection in Europe. However, one cannot deny that the Directive, a piece of legislation adopted nineteen years ago, cannot respond adequately to the challenges posed by the rapid technological developments in the era of the Internet and the big data. It is worth noting that it was not until 2003 in the *Lindqvist* case that the ECJ recognized that the Data Protection Directive applies to the Internet. The Data Protection Directive has fulfilled its role, but now new more robust legislation is needed in order to provide for effective protection of privacy and personal data in the digital era.

2.4.2 The E-Privacy Directive

The e-Privacy Directive (Directive 2002/58/EC) concerning the processing of personal data and the protection of privacy in the electronic communications sector was adopted on July 12, 2002. The e-Privacy Directive aims at harmonizing the different national provisions on the protection of the right to privacy, with respect to the processing of personal data in the electronic communications sector while ensuring the free movement of such data and of electronic communications equipment and services in the Community (Article 1 (1)). In essence, it particularizes and complements the provisions of the Data Protection Directive with respect to the processing of personal data of natural persons in the electronic communications sector. However, it goes beyond Directive 95/46/EC in many respects, and offers a new approach to the protection of privacy in the information society. First of all, unlike Directive 95/46/EC, which applies only to the processing of data of individuals, the e-Privacy Directive also includes in its scope the protection of legal persons (Article 1 (2)). Furthermore, it contains provisions regarding unsolicited communications. According to Article 13 of the Directive, the use of automatic calling machines, fax or electronic mail for the purposes of direct marketing may only be allowed in respect of subscribers who have given their prior consent. In addition, the Directive takes into account a number of particularities of the Internet environment such as cookies, spyware, web bugs, hidden identifiers and other similar devices that may seriously intrude upon the privacy of users by entering their terminal without their knowledge in order to gain access to information, to store hidden information or to trace their activities (Recitals 6, 7, 8, 24 and 25). It allows the use of such devises only for legitimate purposes, with the knowledge of the users concerned.

According to Article 5 (1) of the e-Privacy Directive, Member States shall ensure the confidentiality of communications and the related traffic data through national legislation. In particular, they shall prohibit listening, tapping, storage or other kinds of interception or surveillance of communications and the related traffic data by persons other than users, without the consent of the users concerned, except when legally authorized to do so. Furthermore, traffic data relating to subscribers and users processed and stored by the provider of a public communications network must be erased or made anonymous when it is no longer needed for the purpose of the transmission of a communication (Article 6). However, Article 15 enables Member States to adopt legislative measures to restrict the scope of the rights provided for in the Directive 'when such restriction constitutes a necessary, appropriate and proportionate measure within a democratic society to safeguard national security (i.e. State security), defence, public security, and the prevention, investigation, detection and prosecution of criminal offences or of unauthorised use of the electronic communication system.'

The e-Privacy Directive was amended on 19 December 2009 by Directive 2009/136/EC. Under the new regime, communications service providers are required to notify national data protection authorities and consumers of security breaches (Article 4 (3)); legal remedies are provided to natural and legal persons adversely affected by infringements concerning unsolicited communications (Article 13 (6)); enhanced penalties (with the possibility of adoption of criminal sanctions) are laid down for infringements of the Directive (Article 15a (1)); and national data protection authorities receive new enforcement and investigative powers (Article 15a (2, 3, 4)).

2.4.3 Regulation 45/2001/EC

The Data Protection and the e-Privacy Directive are addressed to the Member States and, accordingly, they do not apply as such to the EU institutions and bodies. Regulation 45/2001/EC on the protection of individuals with regard to the processing of personal data by the institutions and bodies of the Community and on the free movement of such data is the legal instrument that lays down the data protection rules for the EU institutions.

The Regulation which is based on Article 286 EC, aims at protecting the fundamental rights and freedoms of natural persons, and in particular their right to privacy with respect to the processing of personal data (Article 2). It applies to the processing of such data by all Community institutions and bodies insofar as such processing is carried out in the exercise of activities all or part of which fall within the scope of Community law (Article 3). Regulation 45/2001 specifies the data processing obligations of the controllers within the Community institutions and bodies (Articles 5-12), sets out the rights of the data subject (Articles 13-19), provides the individuals with judicial remedies (Article 32) and establishes an independent supervisory authority, the European Data Protection Supervisor (Articles 41-48).

The European Data Protection Supervisor (EDPS) aims to promote a "data protection culture" in Community (now Union) institutions and bodies. He is the independent authority that ensures at the EU level that the fundamental rights and freedoms of natural persons, and in particular their right to privacy, are respected by the EU institutions and bodies. His tasks consist in supervising personal data processing by the institutions or bodies of the Union, in examining the data protection and privacy impact of proposed new legislation, and in cooperating with other data protection authorities, mainly within the platform of the Article 29 Working Party, in order to ensure consistency in the protection of personal data.

Insofar as his supervisory role is concerned, the EDPS undertakes prior checks on the processing of data by Union institutions and bodies and carries out inquiries on complaints received from EU staff members or from other people that allege that their data has been mishandled. Furthermore, the EDPS advises the EU institutions and bodies on data protection issues in a range of policy areas. His consultative role relates to proposals for new legislation as well as soft law instruments like communications that affect personal data protection in the EU. He also monitors new technologies that may have an impact on data protection. Overall, the contribution of the European Data Protection Supervisor in the establishment of a high level of protection of personal data can be characterized as significant (Hijmans, 2006, p. 1341).

2.4.4 The Data Retention Directive

In the aftermath of the Madrid train bombings, the European Council adopted on 25 March 2004 a Declaration on Combating Terrorism, in which it instructed the Council, among others, to examine measures for establishing rules on the retention of communications traffic data by service providers. One month later, on 28 April 2004, France, Ireland, Sweden and the UK presented a proposal for a 'Draft Framework Decision on the Retention of Data Processed and Stored in Connection with the Provision of Publicly Available Electronic Communications Services or Data on Public Communications Networks for the Purpose of Prevention, Investigation, Detection and Prosecution of Crime and Criminal Offences Including Terrorism' to be adopted by the Council under the framework of police and judicial cooperation in criminal matters (the former third pillar). The Draft Framework decision covered data processed and stored by providers of a public communications network or publicly available electronic communications services and provided that these would be retained for a period of at least 12 months and no more than 36 months following their generation. The Article

29 Working Party criticized heavily this proposal and stated that "the mandatory retention of all types of data on every use of telecommunication services for public order purposes, under the conditions provided in the draft framework decision, is not acceptable within the legal framework set in Article 8 ECHR." The Draft Framework decision was also challenged by the European Parliament, which contended that it contained measures that came both under the first and the third pillar.

Almost a year later and after many debates on whether the measure fell under the first or the third pillar, the Commission presented on 21 September 2005 a proposal for a directive on the retention of data processed in connection with the provision of public electronic communication services. After long negotiations between the Commission, the European Parliament and the Council the Directive was finally passed on 15 March 2006.

The Data Retention Directive (Directive 2006/24/EC) aims to harmonize Member States' provisions concerning the obligations of the providers of publicly available electronic communications services or of public communications networks with respect to the retention of certain data which are generated or processed by them, in order to ensure that the data are available for the purpose of the investigation, detection and prosecution of serious crime, as defined by each Member State in its national law (Article 1 (1)). It applies to traffic and location data on both legal entities and natural persons and to the related data necessary to identify the subscriber or registered user, but does not apply to the content of electronic communications (Article 1 (2)).

The Directive does not include within its regulatory framework the prevention of crimes, but it requires the retention of data only for the purpose of the "investigation, detection and prosecution of serious crime." For this reason, Member States are obliged to ensure that the data retained and any other necessary information relating to such data can be transmitted upon request to the competent authorities without "undue delay" (Article

8). The lack of a definition of what constitutes 'serious crime' could prove to be problematic. The choice not to define the notion of 'serious crime' is to be criticized because it can result to an excessive broadening of the scope of the Directive, and therefore of the retention of data, for any crime that is to be characterized as 'serious' by each Member State. To prevent such a risk, the Council urged the Member States to "have due regard" to the crimes listed in Article 2 (2) of the Framework Decision on the European Arrest Warrant and crime involving telecommunication when they implement the Directive to national law. However, this is not enough to alleviate the fear that data retention will be required for an extensive list of crimes according to the legislation of each Member State.

The Commission's Evaluation Report of the Data Protection Directive proves that this fear is not unsubstantiated. In particular, ten Member States have defined in their national legislation 'serious crime', with reference to a minimum prison sentence, to the possibility of a custodial sentence being imposed, or to a list of criminal offences defined elsewhere in national legislation; eight Member States require data to be retained "not only for investigation, detection and prosecution in relation to serious crime, but also in relation to all criminal offences and for crime prevention, or on general grounds of national or state and/or public security"; and finally, four Member States do not define 'serious crime' at all.

The Directive lays down the obligation of the Member States to retain metadata; in the terminology used by the Directive 'traffic' and 'location' data as well as any other related data necessary to identify the subscriber or user. 'Traffic data' means any data processed for the purpose of the conveyance of a communication on an electronic communications network or for the billing thereof (Article 2 (b) of Directive 2002/58/EC); 'location data' is understood as any data processed in an electronic communications network, indicating the geographic position of the terminal equipment

of a user of a publicly available electronic communications service (Article 2 (c) of Directive 2002/58/EC).

However, the Data Retention Directive explicitly provides that no data revealing the content of the communication may be retained (Article 5 (2)). This distinction drawn by the Directive between metadata on the one hand, and content data on the other, is certainly important because it safeguards the confidentiality of communications. Nevertheless, it is submitted that this distinction is not always so clear (Tzanou, 2013b, p. 29). Whereas in the context of the traditional telephone communications it is rather easy to separate content from traffic data, this is not always the case in the modern digital networks (Goemans and Dumortier, 2003, p. 4). This is because, in practice, in the Internet environment content and metadata are generated simultaneously. The example frequently used is that of a request operated with a search engine, such as Google. For instance, if we want to make a search on 'terrorism', our request will give the following result: 'https://www.google.com/search ?q=terrorism&oq=terrorism&aqs=chrome.0.69i 59j69i65l3j0l2.2669j0j7&sourceid=chrome&es_ sm=93&ie=UTF-8'. This information, however, which reveals already our interests, combined with our IP address constitutes information "relating to an identified or an identifiable natural person" in the words of the Data Protection Directive, and thus personal data. This conclusion, however, cannot be left unqualified. It has to be examined, further, whether IP addresses are personal data. The general position of the Article 29 Working Party on the issue is that: "... unless the Internet Service Provider is in a position to distinguish with absolute certainty that the data correspond to users that cannot be identified, it will have to treat all IP information as personal data, to be on the safe side." However, this general statement is not without problems, in particular because IP addresses are normally dynamic, namely they may change for each session. Even dynamic IP addresses can be considered as data relating to an identifiable person. This contribution argues that dynamic IP addresses can be considered personal data when Internet access providers utilize different methods (recording of logs in, keeping of logbooks, e-mail accounts opened) to link the IP address assigned to a computer to a specific Internet user. This requires, however, a case-by-case analysis and rejects a general, unqualified assumption that all dynamic IP addresses constitute personal data.

The categories of data to be retained are laid down in Article 5 of the Directive. They consist of: data necessary to

1. Trace and identify the source of a communication;
2. Identify the destination of a communication;
3. Identify the date, time and duration of a communication;
4. Identify the type of communication;
5. Identify users' communication equipment or what purports to be their equipment; and
6. Identify the location of mobile communication equipment.

The Directive stipulates that the retention period will be between six months and two years starting from the date of the communication (Article 6). However, a Member State facing particular circumstances may request an extension of the maximum retention period. In this case, it is obliged to notify the Commission and inform the other Member States of the measures taken and state the grounds for introducing them (Article 12). It is puzzling that the Directive does not set a specific period for data retention but allows Member States for variations. This raises questions as to the level of harmonization that it aims to achieve, in that it cannot be excluded that a data retention period of six months in one Member State and of two years in another, might affect the competition between the service providers in the common market. According to the Commission's Evaluation Report the retention period stipulated in national laws varies from two years

(one Member State), 1.5 years (one Member State), one year (ten Member States) six months (three Member States), to different retention periods for different categories of data (six Member States). In this respect, the Commission admits that "the Directive provides only limited legal certainty and foreseeability across the EU for operators operating in more than one Member State and for citizens whose communications data may be stored in different Member States."

Data Retention and the Rights to Privacy and Data Protection

The Data Retention Directive raises serious concerns regarding its compliance with fundamental rights requirements. The discussion has focused mainly on its implications on the right to privacy, the right to data protection, freedom of expression and the right to property (Breyer, 2005, p. 375). Regarding the rights to privacy and data protection, the paradox of the Data Retention Directive is remarkable: while it is listed as a modification of EU data protection legislation; the Directive itself seems to violate the rights to privacy and data protection (Tzanou, 2011, p. 282).

As seen above, the Directive requires the retention of metadata, namely data revealing the source, the destination, the date, time, duration, the type and the location of the communication, alongside with any other related data necessary to identify the subscriber or user of electronic telecommunication services. Metadata interfere with the confidentiality of the communications as they can reveal the location of individuals, their movements, the persons to whom they talk, the time and duration of their communications, the web sites that they are visiting, and information on the e-mails they sent, such as the time, the addressee and the size of possible attached files (Rauhofer, 2006, p. 323). The issue posed, therefore, by the Data Retention Directive is, above all, a privacy problem (Breyer, 2005, p. 366). The right to privacy is enshrined in Article 7 EUCFR which essentially repeats the relevant provision of Article 8 (1) ECHR (de Hert and Gutwirth, 2006, p. 81): "Everyone has the right to respect for his or her private and family life, home and communications."

In the present case, it is the privacy of individuals' communications that is at stake (communications' privacy). The fact that metadata are merely 'envelope' data and they do not touch upon the content of the communications is not crucial. 'Envelope' data can reveal an extensive amount of information about the individuals, concerning, for instance, among others, political activities, health condition, ideological, religious, and philosophical beliefs, and sexual preferences. Therefore, they interfere with the confidentiality of personal communications, even if they do not apply to their exact content. It would be mistaken, hence, to restrict the protection of confidentiality of communications merely in the content of these communications and exclude 'envelope' data. This is not only because 'envelop' data reveal already a lot about the individuals. It is because it introduces a very narrow understanding of the concept of personal privacy as secrecy. Notwithstanding this, as mentioned above, in the context of the Internet, there is no clear distinction between 'envelope' and 'content' data, as the 'envelope' reveals much of the content.

What about the fundamental right to data protection? Are there any data protection issues raised by the Data Retention Directive? Leaving aside the common misconception, according to which, when privacy is interfered with, then there is an interference with data protection as well; the answer to this question is trickier, because it has to be established first, before assessing any potential interferences with data protection principles, whether 'traffic' and 'location' data are 'personal data'. 'Traffic' data may, *inter alia*, consist of data referring to "the routing, duration, time or volume of a communication, to the protocol used, to the location of the terminal equipment of the sender or recipient, to the network on which

the communication originates or terminates, to the beginning, end or duration of a connection", and to "the format in which the communication is conveyed by the network" (Recital 15 of Directive 2002/58/EC). 'Location' data may refer to "the latitude, longitude and altitude of the user's terminal equipment, to the direction of travel, to the level of accuracy of the location information, to the identification of the network cell in which the terminal equipment is located at a certain point in time and to the time the location information was recorded" (Recital 14 of Directive 2002/58/EC).

These definitions are not enough to prove that 'traffic' and 'location' data constitute information relating to any identified or identifiable natural person, according to Article 2 (a) of the Data Protection Directive. However, a closer look to the Data Retention Directive leaves no doubts: it mandates the retention of 'traffic' and 'location' data, as well as "the related data necessary to identify the subscriber or user" (Article 2 (2) (a)) of the electronic communications network or service. The combination of these data, to the extent that it relates to an identified and identifiable person, it can be considered as personal data.

Having established that 'traffic' and 'location' data combined with any related data necessary to identify the subscriber or user constitute personal data and that their retention by the telecommunications' providers constitutes 'processing', it is time to investigate now, whether this is interfering with any data protection principles. The 'fair information principles' potentially affected by the Directive are purpose limitation, data security, and data minimization. Further problems could be also be raised concerning the duration of the data retention period.

The period of retention of the communications is a data protection issue, to the extent that Article 6 (1) (e) of the Data Protection Directive stipulates that personal data should be kept "for no longer than is necessary for the purposes for which the data were collected or for which they are further processed." This constitutes an important fair information principle, as it expresses the proportionality value. That being said, it is very difficult to see how this principle can be violated to its essence, unless retention of data for many years is at stake. The duration of the retention of the data has, therefore, to be judged alongside with other fair information principles to determine whether it is proportionate. Insofar as the Data Retention Directive is concerned, a retention period of 6 months to 2 years can be deemed considerable.

Data security is a further fair information principle that the Data Retention Directive might have an impact upon. The importance of the protection of the stored data from accidental loss or unauthorized access cannot be overemphasized. For this reason, the Data Direction Directive contains a number of provisions on the security of personal data. Article 7 requires that the providers of electronic communications services respect, as a minimum, the following data security principles:

1. The retained data should be of the same quality and subject to the same security and protection as those data on the network;
2. Appropriate technical and organizational measures to protect the data against accidental or unlawful destruction, accidental loss or alteration, or unauthorized or unlawful storage, processing, access or disclosure should be in place;
3. The data should be subject to appropriate technical and organizational measures to ensure that they can be accessed by specially authorized personnel only; and
4. The data, except those that have been accessed and preserved, should be destroyed at the end of the period of retention.

The Directive, further, envisages that the application of the above mentioned provisions regarding the security of the stored data should be monitored by independent authorities within each Member State. There is no reason to consider that these provisions are inadequate to ensure data security. On the contrary, it seems that the Directive takes this data information principle very seriously into account. There is, however, one small (at first sight) detail here that should not go unmentioned. The data security requirements of the Directive might impose a "considerable financial burden" (Tsiftsoglou & Flogaitis, 2011, p. 20) on the service providers. This is confirmed in the Evaluation Report where the Commission mentions that five major industry associations stated that the economic impact of the Directive was "substantial" or "enormous" for "smaller service providers", because the Directive leaves "broad room for manoeuvre." The question is who will bear this burden. The issue might appear unimportant from a data protection point of view, but it seems at least ironic that EU citizens might be possibly called upon to "pay for their own surveillance" (Kaifa-Gbanti, 2010, p. 43).

Finally, data retention interferes with the purpose limitation principle. This requires that personal information should be collected for specified, explicit and legitimate purposes and not further processed in a way incompatible with those purposes. The use of communications data for law enforcement reasons is a purpose incompatible with their retention, initially foreseen solely for reasons directly related to the communication itself, such as for instance billing purposes.

Metadata Retention before the Courts

As seen above, the Data Retention Directive interferes seriously with fundamental rights. For this reason, the Directive and its implementing laws in the Member States have been challenged several times before the European and national courts.

The first challenge of the Data Protection Directive was brought in front of the ECJ in 2006. Ireland supported by Slovakia asked the Court to annul the Directive on the ground that Article 95 EC (now 114 TFEU), which has as its object the establishment and the functioning of the internal matter, was not the appropriate legal basis, because the main aim of the Data Retention Directive is to facilitate the investigation, detection and prosecution of serious crime, including terrorism, and thus it should have been adopted under the (then) third pillar. The Court in its judgment disagreed and held that the Directive was adopted on the appropriate legal basis, since both its aim and its content fell under Article 95 EC. It started by noting that after the Madrid and London terrorist attacks, several Member States, "realising that data relating to electronic communications constitute an effective means for the detection and prevention of crimes, including terrorism, adopted measures with a view to imposing obligations on service providers concerning the retention of such data" (para 67). These measures, not only "have significant economic implications for service providers in so far as they may involve substantial investment and operating costs" (para 68), but they also "differed substantially particularly in respect of the nature of the data retained and the periods of data retention" (para 69). The legislative and technical disparities between the national provisions governing the retention of data by service providers, were liable, according to the Court of Justice, to have "a direct impact on the functioning of the internal market" (para 71), and, thus, justified the adoption of harmonised rules by the Community legislature. The Court clarified that Article 95 EC was the correct legal basis for the adoption of these rules, since "the provisions of Directive 2006/24 are essentially limited to the activities of service providers and do not govern access to data or the use thereof by the police or judicial authorities of the Member States" (para 80). As the Data Retention Directive does not harmonise the issue of access to data by the competent national law-enforcement authorities neither the use and exchange of those data between those authorities, it does not fall under the framework of police cooperation in criminal matters (former third pillar) (para 83), but under the Community

(former first pillar). It is worth noting that the Court of Justice did not refer to the human rights dimension of the Directive. The examination of this was dismissed with a short statement that "the action brought by Ireland relates solely to the choice of legal basis and not to any possible infringement of fundamental rights arising from interference with the exercise of the right to privacy contained in Directive 2006/24" (para 57).

Following this uninspiring decision by the ECJ, the implementing national laws of the Data Retention Directive were challenged in the national courts of many Member States. In particular, proceedings regarding the national laws transposing the Data Protection Directive have been brought in Bulgaria, Romania, Germany, Cyprus, the Czech Republic, Hungary, Poland and Slovakia (Kosta, 2013, p. 345). The present analysis will focus on the decisions of the German, the Romanian and the Czech Constitutional courts.

In its seminal decision on the law transposing the Data Retention Directive in Germany, the German Constitutional Court declared this unconstitutional because it did not guarantee adequate data security or an adequate restriction of the purposes of use of the data, and it did not satisfy, in every respect, the constitutional requirements of transparency and legal protection.

The Constitutional Court started its analysis by rejecting the need to submit a referral to the Court of Justice, since "a potential priority of Community law" was not relevant in this case. After this –not unquestionable- assertion, the Court went on to discuss the possible constitutional problems that the transposing law – not the Directive- raised in the Federal Republic of Germany. The Court, based, rightly, its analysis on the right to secrecy of telecommunications, enshrined in Article 10.1 of the German Constitution. In this respect, it distinguished between the storage of telecommunications by service providers and their subsequent access and use by law enforcement authorities. The Court opined that "the storage of telecommunications traffic data without occasion for six months for strictly limited uses in the course of prosecution, the warding off of danger and intelligence service duties is not in itself incompatible with Article 10 of the Basic Law." Nevertheless, such storage constitutes "a particularly serious encroachment with an effect broader that anything in the legal system to date." This is because, according to the Court: "Even though the storage does not extend to the contents of the communications, these data may be used to draw content-related conclusions that extend into the users' private sphere. In combination, the recipients, dates, time and place of telephone conversations, if they are observed over a long period of time, permit detailed information to be obtained on social or political affiliations and on personal preferences, inclinations and weaknesses. Depending on the use of the telecommunication, such storage can make it possible to create meaningful personality profiles of virtually all citizens and track their movements. It also increases the risk of citizens to be exposed to further investigations without themselves having given occasion for this. In addition, the possibilities of abuse that are associated with such a collection of data aggravate its burdensome effect. In particular since the storage and use of data are not noticed, the storage of telecommunications traffic data without occasion is capable of creating a diffusely threatening feeling of being watched which can impair a free exercise of fundamental rights in many areas."

That being said, the German Constitutional Court went on to recognize, surprisingly enough, that there are certain factors that make such retention of data acceptable under the Constitution. The first is that the storage "is realized not directly by the state, but by imposing a duty on the private service providers. In this way, the data are not yet combined at the point of storage itself, but remain distributed over many individual enterprises and are not directly available to the state as a conglomerate." The second, and more dubious one is that "precautionary storage of telecommunications traffic data considerably reduces the latitude for

further data collections without occasion, including collections by way of European Union law."

In any case, such storage, according to the Court, is compatible with Article 10.1 of the Basic Law only if its formulation satisfies particular constitutional requirements on data security, purpose limitation, transparency and legal protection. The Court provided detailed guidance on all these issues to the legislator. Concerning the use of data pro-actively, in order to prevent criminal activity, the Court accepted that this may only be permitted, according to the principle of proportionality, "if there is a sufficiently evidenced concrete danger to the life, limb or freedom of a person, to the existence or the security of the Federal Government or of a *Land* or to ward off a common danger." The principle of proportionality also requires that: "there should be a fundamental prohibition of transmission of data, at least for a narrowly defined group of telecommunications connections which rely on particular confidentiality. These might include, for example, connections to persons, authorities and organizations in the social or ecclesiastical fields which offer advice in situations of emotional or social need, completely or predominantly by telephone, to callers who normally remain anonymous, where these organizations themselves or their staff are subject to other obligations of confidentiality in this respect."

The Romanian Constitutional Court in its decision on the law transposing the Directive into the Romanian legal order, noted that "the continuous retention of personal data transforms the exception from the principle of effective protection of privacy right and freedom of expression, into an absolute rule." In this respect, the users of electronic communication services or networks, are made "permanent subjects to intrusions into their exercise of their private rights to correspondence and freedom of expression, without the possibility of a free, uncensored manifestation, except for direct communication, thus excluding the main communication means used nowadays."

Moreover, the Romanian Court focused on a further aspect of the data retention regime: that fact that it has an effect not only on the person that performs the communication, by sending for instance a message, but also on the receiver of that information. The called person is thus exposed, according to the Court, to the retention of the data connected to his private life, irrespective of his own act or a manifestation of will but only based on the behavior of another person – of the caller- whose actions he cannot control to protect himself against bad faith or intent of blackmail, harassment etc. Even though he is a passive subject in the intercommunication relationship, the called person can become, despite his will, suspect in front of the law enforcement authorities. This intrusion in private life of third individuals was deemed by the Romanian Court as excessive.

On 22 March 2011 the Czech Constitutional court delivered its decision on the national law implementing the Data Retention Directive in the Czech Republic. Following the judgments of the German and the Romanian Constitutional courts, it also declared the implementing law unconstitutional.

The Court had, first, to decide whether it should submit a preliminary reference question to the ECJ on the validity of the Directive. Employing a similar argument with the German Court, it rejected this possibility on the basis that the content of the Data Retention Directive provided the Czech Republic with sufficient space to implement it in conformity with the constitutional order, since its individual provisions in fact only define the obligation to retain data. The legislator had certainly to respect the objective of the Directive when transposing it in national law, but the challenged provisions concerned "an expression of the will of the Czech legislator, which may vary to some extent as far as the choice of relevant means is concerned, while observing the Directive's objective, yet when making such choice, the legislator was at the same time bound to the constitutional order" (para 25).

The Czech Constitutional Court assessed the implementing law of the Directive on the basis of "the individual's fundamental right to privacy in the form of the right to informational self-determination" (para 37). The Court noted that although the obligation to retain traffic and location data does not apply to the content of individual messages "the data on the users, addresses, precise time, dates, places, and forms of telecommunication connection, provided that monitoring takes place over an extended period of time and when combined together, allows compiling detailed information on social or political membership, as well as personal interests, inclinations or weaknesses of individual persons" (para 44).

As *obiter dictum* the Constitutional Court expressed its doubts on whether an instrument of global and preventive retention of location and traffic data on almost all electronic communications "may be deemed necessary and adequate from the perspective of the intensity of the intervention to the private sphere of an indefinite number of participants to electronic communications", (para 55) and whether "it is at all desirable that private persons (service providers in the area of the Internet, telephone and mobile communication, i.e. in particular, mobile operators and commercial enterprises providing Internet access) should be entitled to retain all data on the communication provided by them" (para 57). This is indeed a very valuable comment that should not go unnoticed in the context of the discussion of the Data Retention Directive.

Following the severely critical decisions of the national courts, the question was what would be the response of the EU judiciary regarding data retention. The Court of Justice of the EU had a second opportunity to consider the validity of the Data Retention Directive, this time through the preliminary reference procedure. More particularly, the High Court in Ireland and the Austrian Constitutional Court asked the CJEU to consider the validity of the Data Retention Directive in the light of Articles 7 (privacy), 8 (data protection) and 11 (freedom of expression) of the EU Charter of Fundamental Rights.

The CJEU in its decision in Joined Cases C-293/12 and C-594/12 *Digital Rights Ireland and Seitlinger and others*, delivered on 8th April 2014 focused on the interference of the Directive on the rights to privacy and data protection. It started its analysis by noting that metadata make it possible to know the identity of the person with whom a subscriber or registered user has communicated and by what means, and to identify the time of the communication as well as the place from which that communication took place. They also make it possible to know the frequency of the communications of the subscriber or registered user with certain persons during a given period. Such data, taken as a whole, may allow "very precise conclusions to be drawn concerning the private lives of the persons whose data has been retained, such as the habits of everyday life, permanent or temporary places of residence, daily or other movements, the activities carried out, the social relationships of those persons and the social environments frequented by them" (para 27). The Court, therefore, pointed out that it is not important that the content of the communications is not retained because even the retention of metadata might have a chilling effect on the use of the means of communication covered by the Directive.

The Court went on to discuss the potential interference of metadata retention with the rights to privacy and data protection. It found that the obligation imposed by the Directive on providers of electronic communications services to retain data relating to a person's private life and to his communications constitutes in itself an interference with the right to privacy. Furthermore, the access of the competent national authorities to the data constitutes, according to the Court, a further interference with privacy. Also, the Data Retention Directive interferes with the right to data protection because it provides for the processing of personal data. The Court characterized these interferences "particularly serious" as they are "likely to generate in the minds of the persons concerned the feeling that their private lives are the subject of constant surveillance" (para 37).

The CJEU then focused its decision on the proportionality of the Directive. It started by pointing out that the interference caused by metadata retention is not limited to what is strictly necessary because it applies to all communications concerning fixed telephony, mobile telephony, Internet access, Internet e-mail and Internet telephony and it covers all subscribers and registered users. In essence, for the Court this means that the Directive entails an interference with the fundamental rights of "practically the entire European population" (para 56). The CJEU went even further by noting that the Directive affects in a comprehensive manner all persons using electronic communications services, but without the persons whose data are retained being, even indirectly, in a situation which is liable to give rise to criminal prosecutions. It therefore applies even to persons for whom there is no evidence capable of suggesting that their conduct might have a link, even an indirect or remote one, with serious crime (para 58). Further problems regarding the proportionality of the measure have to do with the fact that the Directive does not contain any specific provisions posing limits to the access of the competent national authorities to the data and their subsequent use for the purposes of prevention, detection of serious crime, and there is no EU definition of 'serious crime', but that is left to the discretion of each Member State (para 60). The Directive is also problematic, according to the Court because it does not make the access by the competent national authorities to the data retained dependent on any requirements of prior review carried out by a court or by an independent administrative body (para 62).

The Court also had issues with the retention period required by the Directive, which does not make any distinction between the categories of data retained "on the basis of their possible usefulness for the purposes of the objective pursued or according to the persons concerned" (para

63). Finally, the Court was concerned about data security as the Directive does not provide for sufficient safeguards against the risk of abuse and against any unlawful access and use of the data (para 66). For these reasons, the Court of Justice ended the data retention saga by declaring the Data Retention Directive invalid.

2.4.5 The Framework Decision on Data Protection in the Area of Police and Judicial Cooperation in Criminal Matters (Former Third Pillar)

The adoption of a data protection measure in the area of police and judicial cooperation in criminal matters (former third pillar) took three years of vigorous discussions. The Commission submitted its proposal in October 2005 and the Council adopted finally the framework decision in its meeting on 27-29 November 2008. The European Parliament was consulted twice on the data protection framework decision: once in September 2006 and a second time in June 2007. The European Data Protection Supervisor issued three Opinions in which while he welcomed the importance of the proposal as a considerable step forwards for the protection of personal data in an important area, he expressed his concerns that developments in the negotiations in the Council were leading towards a level of protection of personal data not only below the standards laid down in the Data Protection Directive, but also incompatible with the more generally formulated Council of Europe Convention No 108.

The purpose of Framework Decision 2008/977/JHA is to "ensure a high level of protection of the fundamental rights and freedoms of natural persons, and in particular their right to privacy, with respect to the processing of personal data in the framework of police and judicial cooperation in criminal matters..., while guaranteeing a high level of public safety" (Article 1 (1)). It applies to personal data that are exchanged within the framework of police and judicial cooperation for the purpose of the prevention, investigation, detection or prosecution of criminal offences or the execution of criminal penalties. The Framework Decision allows the Member States to provide for higher-level safeguards for protecting personal data than those established in this instrument.

The scope of application of the Framework Decision is limited. First, it applies only to trans-border flows of data between the law enforcement authorities of the Member States, and does not cover the collection and processing of personal data at national level. Second, it does not affect the relevant set of sector-specific data protection regimes found in the acts governing the functioning of Europol, Eurojust, the Schengen Information System (SIS) and the Customs Information System (CIS). Third, the Framework Decision applies "without prejudice to essential national security interests and specific intelligence activities in the field of national security" (Article 1 (4)). Forth, it is also "without prejudice to any obligations and commitments incumbent upon Member States or upon the Union by virtue of bilateral and/or multilateral agreements with third States" existing at the time of its adoption (Article 26).

Most of the substantive provisions of the Framework Decision seek to mirror the data protection safeguards stipulated in the Data Protection Directive. The Decision provides for the principles of lawfulness, proportionality and purpose limitation (Article 3); the rectification, erasure and blocking of data (Article 4); the right of information (Article 16), the right of access (Article 17), the right to rectification, erasure or blocking (Article 18), the right to compensation (Article 19); judicial remedies (Article 20); and, the establishment of national supervisory authorities, responsible for advising and monitoring the application of the Framework Decision within the territory of each Member State (Article 25).

The safeguards may be there, but they are fraught with exceptions or their content is significantly different from that found in the provisions of the Data Protection Directive. For instance, while the Framework Decision establishes that "personal data may be collected by the competent authorities only for specified, explicit and legitimate purposes in the framework of their tasks and may be processed only for the same purpose for which data were collected" (Article 3 (1)); the second paragraph of the same Article comes to introduce several exceptions, where further processing for another purpose shall be permitted. The same applies to the rights of the data subjects. In this respect, the right of access can be restricted for reasons such as obstruction of official or legal inquiries, investigations or procedures, public security, national security, and the protection of the data subject or the rights and freedoms of others (Article 17 (2)). Numerous other provisions of the Framework Decision suffer from the same problem. Exceptions to data principles are too many and too often.

Concerning sensitive data, the Framework Decision stipulates that their processing "shall be permitted only when this is strictly necessary and when the national law provides adequate safeguards." This, of course, contradicts the in-principle prohibition rule laid down both by Article 8 of the Data Protection Directive and by Article 6 of Convention 108, pursuant to which sensitive data may not be processed unless in certain cases provided specifically by the law and respecting a number of safeguards. The same applies to the rule of prohibition of the automated processing of data found in Article 15 of the Data Protection Directive. In this respect, the Framework Decision provides that automated processing "shall be permitted if authorized by a law" (Article 7).

While on the one hand, data protection principles are "emptied" (de Hert & Papakonstantinou, 2009, p. 411) of their essential core through a number of exceptions, on the other hand, the Framework Decision includes an innovative provision on the sharing of information with the private sector, creating, thus, public-private partnerships to fight crime (Article 14).

The regulation of the transfer of data to third states or international bodies is found in Article 13 of the Framework Decision. According to this, personal data transmitted or made available by the competent authority of another Member State may be transferred to third States or international bodies, only if:

1. It is necessary for the prevention, investigation, detection or prosecution of criminal offences or the execution of criminal penalties;
2. The receiving authority in the third State or receiving international body is responsible for the prevention, investigation, detection or prosecution of criminal offences or the execution of criminal penalties;
3. The Member State from which the data were obtained has given its consent to transfer in compliance with its national law; and
4. The third State or international body concerned ensures an adequate level of protection for the intended data processing.

However, prior consent is not needed when the transfer of the data is essential for the prevention of an immediate and serious threat to public security of a Member State or a third State or to essential interests of a Member State and it cannot be obtained in good time. In this case, the authority responsible for giving consent should be informed without delay (Article 13 (2)).

The Framework Decision provides for a number of derogations, whereby personal data can be transferred to third countries even if these do not ensure an adequate level of protection. This may happen if:

1. The national law of the Member State transferring the data so provides because of:
   a. Legitimate specific interests of the data subject; or
   b. Legitimate prevailing interests, especially important public interests; or
2. The third State or receiving international body provides safeguards which are deemed adequate by the Member State concerned according to its national law (Article 13 (3).

Once again the provisions of the Framework Decision seem to fall short the relevant stipulations of the Data Protection Directive under the former first pillar. Although the Decision provides that transborder data flows should take place when the third State or the international body concerned ensures an adequate level of protection, the adequacy decision is not taken in this case under the centralized model of the Data Protection Directive. Instead, the absence of a harmonized system means that each Member State will assess at its own discretion the level of adequacy provided for by the third country or international organization. As a consequence, the list of adequate countries and international organizations to which a transfer is allowed will considerably vary from Member State to Member State.

2.5 The Case-Law of the Court of Justice on Data Protection

Since the adoption of the Data Protection Directive the Court of Justice of the EU has been called upon several times to rule on questions of interpretation and application of the Directive. If we attempt a comment of the Court's reading of the Data Protection Directive, this would be that the Court, in essence, has interpreted an internal market harmonisation instrument (the Directive) in a manner that fosters the protection of a fundamental right within the Community (Tzanou, 2011, p. 284).

The Court has adopted an expansive reading of the protective scope of the Directive, which goes beyond the exercise of economic activities (*Österreichischer Rundfunk*), and a restrictive one concerning the exemptions not covered by it (*Lindqvist*). The ECJ clarified that the exception of Article 3 (2) applies only to the activities which are expressly listed there. As a result, the Data Protection Directive applies to all the other activities regardless of their connection with the internal market. Thus, it applied to the charitable and

religious activities carried out by Mrs Lindqvist, who worked as a volunteer catechist in a parish of the Swedish Protestant Church. Mrs Lindqvist had published on her internet site personal data on a number of people working with her and the ECJ found this activity to fall within the scope of the Data Protection Directive.

Furthermore, the Court has held that the processing of personal data files which contain solely, and in unaltered form, material that has already been published in the media, falls within the scope of application of the Data Protection Directive (*Satakunnan Markkinapörssi and Satamedia*). In this regard, the ECJ stressed that a general derogation from the application of the directive in respect of published information would largely deprive it of its effect. It would be sufficient for the Member States to publish data in order for those data to cease to enjoy the protection afforded by the Directive.

The flexible interpretation adopted by the Court has also opened the way to apply the guarantees offered by the Directive to new technological developments, and in particular the Internet (*Lindqvist*). In this respect, in the same case the Court ruled that information published on a website containing the name, telephone number and the working conditions or hobbies of specified people, was covered by the definition of 'personal data' of Article 2 (a) of the Directive. Furthermore, the placing of this information in the Internet constituted 'processing of personal data wholly or partly by automatic means'.

When the rights of the Union citizens have been at issue, the ECJ has proved to be even more cautious in its analysis based on the central for the EU legal system principle of non-discrimination on the ground of nationality, and has found suspicious every national measure discriminating against Union citizens from other Member States (*Huber v Bundesrepublik Deutschland*). In this case, its scrutiny of the national legislation has been stricter, and it has not hesitated to strike down such legislation as incompatible with primary Community law, even though the Member State at issue invoked the argument of the fight against crime which falls outside the scope of the Data Protection Directive.

Moreover, the Court has stressed the need for independence of the national data protection supervisory authorities. The Court has interpreted the notion of "independence" broadly. In this context, it has emphasized that independence precludes not only any influence exercised by the supervised bodies, but also any directions or any other external influence, whether direct or indirect, which could call into question the performance of their tasks (*Commission v. Germany* and *Commission v. Hungary*).

Concerning the interpretation of the right of access to personal data found in Article 12 of the Data Protection Directive, the Court stated that this right is necessary, on the one hand, to enable the data subject to exercise a number of other rights, such as the rights of rectification, erasure or blockage of data; and on the other hand, to enable the data subject to exercise his right to object to his personal data being processed or his right of action where he suffers damage. Thus, Article 12 (a) requires Member States to ensure a right of access to information not only in respect of the present but also in respect of the past (*Rijkeboer*).

The Court has been asked several times to balance the right to data protection with other fundamental rights and freedoms protected within the EC legal order (*Promusicae*). While it has normally noted the importance of all the fundamental rights at issue, it has avoided pronouncing on the final outcome of this reconciliation. Instead, it has left the final decision on the matter to the (referring) national court. This is because, according to the Court, a balance must be found between the rights and interests involved at the stage of the application at national level of the legislation implementing the Data Protection Directive in individual cases. However, it has sought to provide guidance to the national court by stressing the importance of the principle of proportionality. In this regard, certain measures have been found inacceptable by the Court. For instance, it has held that the adoption of a court injunction requiring an Internet Service Provider (ISP) to install a filtering system that monitors, without any limitation in time, all the electronic communications made through the network of the ISP in the interests of copyright rightholders, would not be respecting the requirement that a fair balance be struck between the right to intellectual property, on the one hand, and the freedom to conduct business, the right to protection of personal data and the freedom to receive or impart information, on the other, and therefore is precluded from the relevant EU legislation (*Scarlet Extended*).

The Court has also ruled in favor of the disclosure of the names of the representatives in the Commission meeting according to the fundamental right to access to the EU documents (*Bavarian Lager II*). The Court has stressed, however, that no automatic priority can be conferred on the objective of transparency over the right to protection of personal data, even if important economic interests are at stake (*Schecke*).

The ECJ has shown itself to be very sensitive in cases that concern the balancing between the freedom of expression, and more particularly, journalism, on the one hand, and data protection on the other (*Satakunnan Markkinapörssi and Satamedia*). In these cases, it seemed ready to accept an exception from data protection rules.

Finally, the Court has ruled on which pillar different types of processing fall. More particularly, it has held that the transfer of airline passenger data to the US law enforcement authorities falls outside the scope of the Data Protection Directive (*European Parliament v. Council and Commission (PNR)*).

2.6 The Commission Proposals for a New Data Protection Framework

2.6.1 The Proposal for a Data Protection Regulation

In its Explanatory Memorandum, the Commission justified its proposals for a new data protection framework on the basis of two main reasons: First, the need to better respond to the challenges posed by the rapid development of new technologies and increasing globalization while maintaining technological neutrality of the legal framework. Second, the current data protection framework in the EU is very fragmented, since even after the entry into force of the Lisbon Treaty, different rules exist regarding the processing of personal data for commercial and law enforcement purposes. This goes clearly against legal certainty and new rules harmonizing data protection are required.

As mentioned above, despite the call for harmonization of the new data protection legal framework, the Commission proposed two –instead of one- measures. This chapter will consider the main provisions of the proposed Data Protection Regulation, which aims to replace the Data Protection Directive.

The first point that should be made concerns the legal instrument selected this time for data protection: a Regulation instead of a Directive. The advantages of such a choice are obvious: a Regulation is directly applicable, according to Article 288 TFEU in all national legal orders and it, therefore, eliminates national discretion and fragmentation and by ensuring harmonization it provides greater legal certainty.

The proposed Regulation contains eleven chapters. The first Chapter defines the subject matter of the Regulation, determines its material and territorial scope and, sets out its two objectives. It then contains the definitions of terms used in the Regulation, such as 'data subject', 'personal data', 'processing', etc. Some definitions are the same as those provided for in the Directive ('personal data', 'processing', 'controller', 'processor'), but others are modified in order to be made clearer or newly introduced (for instance, 'personal data breach', 'genetic data', 'biometric data', etc.).

Chapter II sets out the data protection or fair information principles. All the data protection principles found in the Data Retention Directive are preserved, but new principles are added as well. The new elements added included the transparency principle, the clarification of the data minimization principle and the establishment of a comprehensive responsibility and liability of the controller.

Chapter III is entitled 'Rights of the data subject' and contains five sections. The first section introduces the obligation on controllers to provide transparent and easily accessible and understandable information, inspired by the Madrid Resolution on international standards on the protection of personal data and privacy. Furthermore, it lays down obligations for the controller to provide procedures and mechanism for exercising the data subject's rights. The second section is dedicated to the data subject's right to information and access to her data; the third to the data subject's right to rectification and erasure of her personal data; and, the fourth to the right to object. The final section clarifies the empowerment for the EU and the Member States to maintain or introduce restrictions of the fair information principles and the data subject's rights.

The third section of this Chapter contains two new rights: the right to be forgotten (Article 17) and the right to data portability (Article 18). The much welcome in Europe Article 17 reads as follows:

1.   "The data subject shall have the right to obtain from the controller the erasure of personal data relating to them and the abstention from further dissemination of such data, especially in relation to personal data which are made available by the data subject while he or she was a child, where one of the following grounds applies:

a. The data are no longer necessary in relation to the purposes for which they were collected or otherwise processed;

b. The data subject withdraws consent on which the processing is based … or when the storage period consented to has expired, and where there is no other legal ground for the processing of the data; the data subject objects to the processing of personal data…;

c. The processing of the data does not comply with this Regulation for other reasons.

2. Where the controller referred to in paragraph 1 has made the personal data public, it shall take all reasonable steps, including technical measures, in relation to data for the publication of which the controller is responsible, to inform third parties which are processing such data, that a data subject requests them to erase any links to, or copy or replication of that personal data. Where the controller has authorized a third party publication of personal data, the controller shall be considered responsible for that publication.

3. The controller shall carry out the erasure without delay, except to the extent that the retention of the personal data is necessary:

a. For exercising the right of freedom of expression…;

b. For reasons of public interest in the area of public health…;

c. For historical, statistical and scientific research purposes…;

d. For compliance with a legal obligation to retain the personal data by Union or Member State law to which the controller is subject; Member State laws shall meet an objective of public interest, respect the essence of the right to the protection of personal data and be proportionate to the legitimate aim pursued;

e. In the cases referred to in paragraph 4.

4. Instead of erasure, the controller shall restrict processing of personal data where:

a. Their accuracy is contested by the data subject, for a period enabling the controller to verify the accuracy of the data;

b. The controller no longer needs the personal data for the accomplishment of its task but they have to be maintained for purposes of proof;

c. The processing is unlawful and the data subject opposes their erasure and requests the restriction of their use instead;

d. The data subject requests to transmit the personal data into another automated processing system...

5. Personal data referred to in paragraph 4 may, with the exception of storage, only be processed for purposes of proof, or with the data subject's consent, or for the protection of the rights of another natural or legal person or for an objective of public interest.

6. Where processing of personal data is restricted pursuant to paragraph 4, the controller shall inform the data subject before lifting the restriction on processing.

7. The controller shall implement mechanisms to ensure that the time limits established for the erasure of personal data and/or for a periodic review of the need for the storage of the data are observed.

8. Where the erasure is carried out, the controller shall not otherwise process such personal data…"

The right to be forgotten, although much celebrated in Europe, has been controversial because it does not seem to strike a fair balance with freedom of speech (Rosen, 2012, p. 88). In the recently decided case C-131/12 *Google Spain v. Agencia Española de Protección de Datos (AEPD) and Mario Costeja González*, the Court of Justice of the EU upheld the right to be forgotten and ordered Google Spain to remove from its list of results links to web pages published by third parties (in this case a newspaper) containing information relating to a person, even when the publication in itself on those pages is lawful. This decision of the CJEU, which chose not to follow the Opinion of the Advocate General raises concerns regarding the obligations of search engines as 'controllers' of personal data and freedom of speech in the Internet.

Article 1 introduces the data subject's right to data portability, namely her right to transfer data from one electronic processing system to and into another, without being prevented from doing so by the controller. As a precondition and in order to further improve access of individuals to their personal data, it provides the right to obtain from the controller those data in a structured and commonly used electronic format.

Chapter IV sets out the general obligations of 'controllers' and 'processors' of personal data; Chapter V regulates the transfer of personal data to third countries or international organizations; Chapter VI lays down the rules on the establishment and the duties of the national supervisory authorities; Chapter VII, which is entitled 'Co-operation and Consistency', introduces rules on mutual assistance of national supervisory authorities; and, Chapter VIII provides the remedies available to the data subject and the liability and sanctions for unlawful processing.

Chapter 9 sets out a number of different rules concerning specific data processing situations. In this respect, Article 80 obliges Member States to adopt exemptions and derogations from specific provisions of the Regulation where necessary to reconcile the right to the protection of personal data with the right of freedom of expression. Article 81 obliges Member States to ensure specific safeguards for processing data for health purposes. Article 82 empowers Member States to adopt specific laws for processing personal data in the employment context. Article 83 provides for specific conditions for processing personal data for historical, statistical and scientific research purposes.

2.6.2 The Proposal for a Data Protection Directive with Regard to the Processing of Data for Criminal Matters

As explained above, the current Framework Decision 2008/977/JHA has a limited scope of application, since it only applies to cross-border data processing and not to processing activities by the police and judiciary authorities at the national level. Also, its substantive provisions provide for less protection of personal data processed for law enforcement purposes than the one provided by the Data Protection Directive. For these reasons, following the entry into force of the Lisbon Treaty and on the basis of Article 16 TFEU, the Commission introduced a proposal for the adoption of a Directive relating to the protection of individuals with regard to the processing of personal data in the areas of police and judicial co-operation in criminal matters. Of course, the Commission can be criticized on the basis of Article 16 TFEU for proposing different legal instruments on data protection, a Regulation for commercial processing and a Directive for law enforcement processing as this still maintains the fragmentation of data protection rules in the detriment of legal certainty. In its Explanatory Memorandum to the Directive, the Commission justified this choice on the basis of the specific nature of the field of police and judicial co-operation in criminal matters that requires specific rules on the protection of personal data and the free movement of such data.

The proposed Directive's objective is twofold: it aims, on the one hand, to protect the right to personal data protection, and, on the other hand, to ensure the exchange of personal data between competent authorities within the EU. The scope of the proposed Directive is not limited as the Framework Decision to cross-border data processing but applies to all processing activities carried out by the competent law enforcement authorities.

The Directive is structured in a similar way to the proposed Regulation. Chapter II sets out the fair information principles, Chapter III the rights of the data subject, Chapter IV the obligations of controllers and processors, Chapter V regulates the transfer of personal data to third countries or international organizations in the context of police and judicial co-operation in criminal matters, Chapter VI obliges the Member States to establish supervisory authorities, Chapter VII introduces rules on mandatory co-operation and, Chapter VIII provides for the remedies of the data subject.

3. CONCLUSION

The entry into force of the Lisbon Treaty has brought forward significant developments with regard to the right to data protection. Data protection is now constitutionally entrenched as a new fundamental right in the EU Charter next to privacy and there is a general legal basis for data protection measures to be found in Article 16 TFEU. The abolition of the pillar system meant that new data protection legislation is necessary to address the fragmentation of the current rules.

The Commission's proposals in this respect are certainly welcome, although a single measure covering processing for commercial and law enforcement purposes instead of two would have been preferable. The right to be forgotten in the digital age is one of the most important innovations of the Commission's proposed Regulation and has already received the approval of the Court of Justice of the EU in its controversial *Google Spain* judgment. However, it still remains to be seen whether a right to be forgotten can be enforced in the Internet context while striking a fair balance with freedom of expression.

The most important jurisdictional development with regard to data protection that has taken place in the EU is without doubt the CJEU's decision to declare invalid the Data Retention Directive because it interferes disproportionately with the rights to privacy and data protection. Given the recent revelations of the secret retention of telephony metadata by the NSA, such a judgment is certainly a cause for optimism.

REFERENCES

Anderson, D., & Murphy, C. (2012). The charter of fundamental rights. In A. Biondi, P. Eeckhout, & S. Ripley (Eds.), *EU law after Lisbon* (pp. 155–179). Oxford, UK: Oxford University Press.

Berman, P. (2012). From Laeken to Lisbon: The origins and negotiation of the Lisbon Treaty. In A. Biondi, P. Eeckhout, & S. Ripley (Eds.), *EU law after Lisbon* (pp. 3–39). Oxford, UK: Oxford University Press. doi:10.1093/acprof:oso/9780199644322.003.0001

Breyer, P. (2005). Telecommunications data retention and human rights: The compatibility of blanket traffic data retention with the ECHR. *European Law Journal*, *11*(3), 365–375. doi:10.1111/j.1468-0386.2005.00264.x

Cremona, M. (2012). The two (or three) treaty solution: The new treaty structure of the EU. In A. Biondi, P. Eeckhout, & S. Ripley (Eds.), *EU law after Lisbon* (pp. 40–61). Oxford, UK: Oxford University Press. doi:10.1093/acprof:oso/9780199644322.003.0002

De Hert, P., & Gutwirth, S. (2006). Privacy, data protection and law enforcement: Opacity of the individual and transparency of power. In E. Claes, A. Duff, & S. Gutwirth (Eds.), *Privacy and the criminal law* (pp. 61–104). Oxford, UK: Intersentia.

De Hert, P., & Papakonstantinou, V. (2009). The data protection framework decision of 27 November 2008 regarding police and judicial cooperation in criminal matters – A modest achievement however not the improvement some have hoped for. *Computer Law & Security Report*, *25*(5), 403–414. doi:10.1016/j.clsr.2009.07.008

Dougan, M. (2007). The Treaty of Lisbon 2007: Winning minds, not hearts. *Common Market Law Review*, *45*, 617–703.

Fried, C. (1968). Privacy. *The Yale Law Journal*, *77*(3), 475–493. doi:10.2307/794941

Goemans, C., & Dumortier, J. (2003). Enforcement issues - Mandatory retention of traffic data in the EU: Possible impact on privacy and on-line anonymity. In C. Nicoll, J. E. J. Prins, & M. J. M. Van Dellen (Eds.), *Digital anonymity and the law: Tensions and dimensions* (pp. 161–183). The Hague, The Netherlands: T.M.C. Asser Press. doi:10.1007/978-90-6704-579-7_8

Guild, E., & Carrera, S. (2010). The European Union's area of freedom, security and justice ten years on. In E. Guild, S. Carrera, & A. Eggenschwiler (Eds.), *The area of freedom, security and justice ten years on: Successes and future challenges under the Stockholm Programme* (pp. 1–12). CEPS.

Hijmans, H., & Scirocco, A. (2009). Shortcomings in EU data protection in the third and the second pillars: Can the Lisbon Treaty be expected to help? *Common Market Law Review*, 46, 1485–1525.

Inness, J. (1996). *Privacy, intimacy and isolation*. Oxford, UK: Oxford University Press. doi:10.1093/0195104609.001.0001

Kaifa-Gbanti, M. (2010). *Surveillance models in the security state & fair criminal trial*. Athens, Greece: Nomiki Vivliothiki. (in Greek)

Kosta, E. (2013). The way to Luxemburg: National court decisions on the compatibility of the data retention directive with the rights to privacy and data protection. *SCRIPT-ed*, 10(3), 339–363. doi:10.2966/scrip.100313.339

Peers, S. (2011). *EU justice and home affairs law*. Oxford, UK: Oxford University Press.

Rauhofer, J. (2006). Just because you're paranoid, doesn't mean they're not after you: Legislative developments in relation to the mandatory retention of communications data in the European Union. SCRIPT-ed, 322-343.

Reiman, J. (1976). Privacy, intimacy, and personhood. *Philosophy & Public Affairs*, 6, 26–44.

Rosen, J. (2012). The right to be forgotten. *Stanford Law Review Online*, 64, 88–92.

Rouvroy, A., & Poullet, Y. (2009). The right to informational self-determination and the value of self-development: reassessing the importance of privacy for democracy. In S. Gutwirth et al. (Eds.), *Reinventing data protection?* (pp. 45–76). Dordrecht, The Netherlands: Springer. doi:10.1007/978-1-4020-9498-9_2

Solove, D. (2008). *Understanding privacy*. Boston: Harvard University Press.

Tsiftsoglou, A., & Flogaitis, S. (2011). *Transposing the data retention directive in Greece: Lessons from Karlsruhe*. Academic Press.

Tzanou, M. (2011). Data protection in EU law: An analysis of the EU legal framework and the ECJ jurisprudence. In C. Akrivopoulou & A. Psygkas (Eds.), *Personal data privacy and protection in a surveillance era: Technologies and practices* (pp. 273–297). Hershey, PA: IGI Global. doi:10.4018/978-1-60960-083-9.ch016

Tzanou, M. (2013). Data protection as a fundamental right next to privacy? 'Reconstructing' a not so new right. *International Data Privacy Law*, 3(2), 88–99. doi:10.1093/idpl/ipt004

Tzanou, M. (2013). Is data protection the same as privacy? An analysis of telecommunications' metadata retention measures. *Journal of Internet Law*, 17(3), 20–33.

Warren, S. D., & Brandeis, L. D. (1890). Right to privacy. *Harvard Law Review*, 4(5), 193–220. doi:10.2307/1321160

Westin, A. (1970). *Privacy and freedom*. New York: Atheneum.

KEY TERMS AND DEFINITIONS

Commission Proposals for a New EU Data Protection Legal Framework: Major reform of the current EU data protection legal framework proposed by the Commission in 2012 and currently under negotiation. The proposal includes a Regulation aimed to replace the Data Protection Directive, and a Directive aimed to replace the Data Protection Framework Decision.

Data Controller: The natural or legal person, which alone or jointly with others determines the purposes and means of the processing of personal data.

Data Protection: A set of rules that aim to protect the rights, freedoms and interests of individuals when information related to them is being processed.

Data Retention Directive: The Directive adopted in the aftermath of the Madrid and London terrorist attacks requiring the retention of telecommunications metadata by service providers in order to fight 'serious crime'. The Directive was invalidated by the Court of Justice of the EU on April 8th, 2014.

Lisbon Treaty: The latest Treaty that amends the constitutional framework of the European Union. The Lisbon Treaty entered into force on December 1st, 2009.

Personal Data: Information relating to an identified or identifiable natural person.

Processing: Any operation performed upon personal data, such as, collection, recording, storage, use, disclosure, dissemination, erasure and destruction.

APPENDIX: TABLE OF CASES

European Court of Justice and Court of First Instance

- Joined Cases C-465/00, C-138/01 & C-139/01, *Österreichischer Rundfunk*, Judgment of 20 May 2003, Full Court, [2003] ECR I-4989.
- Case C-101/01 *Bodil Lindqvist* [2003] ECR I-12971.
- Joined Cases C-317/04 and C-318/04, *European Parliament v. Council and Commission (PNR)*, Judgment of the Grand Chamber of 30 May 2006, [2006] ECR I-4721.
- Case T- 194/04 *Bavarian Lager Co. Ltd v Commission*, judgment of 8 November 2007.
- Case C-275/06 *Productores de Música de España (Promusicae) v Telefónica de España SAU*, judgment of 29 January 2008.
- Case C-524/06 *Huber v Bundesrepublik Deutschland*, judgment of 16 December 2008.
- Case C-73/07 *Satakunnan Markkinapörssi and Satamedia*, judgment of 16 December 2008.
- Case C-301/06 *Ireland v. European Parliament and Council*, Judgment of the Grand Chamber of 10 February 2009.
- Case C-553/07 *Rijkeboer*, judgment of 7 May 2009.
- Case C-518/07 *Commission v Germany*, judgment of 9 March 2010.
- Case C- 28/08P *Bavarian Lager II,* judgment of 29 June 2010.
- Joined Cases C-92/09 and C-93/09 *Volker und Markus Schecke GbR*, *Hartmut Eifert v Land Hessen*, Judgment of the Court (Grand Chamber) of 9 November 2010.
- Case C-70/10 *Scarlet Extended*, judgment of 24 November 2011.
- Case C-288/12 *Commission v Hungary*, judgment of 8 April 2014.
- Joined Cases C-293/12 and C-594/12 *Digital Rights Ireland and Seitlinger and others,* judgment of 8 April 2014.
- C-131/12 *Google Spain v. Agencia Española de Protección de Datos (AEPD) and Mario Costeja González*, judgment of 13 May 2014.

German Constitutional Court

- 1 BvR 256/08 of 2 March 2010.

Romanian Constitutional Court

- Decision No. 1258 of 8 October 2009.

Czech Constitutional Court

- 2011/03/22 Pl. ÚS 24/10.

Chapter 3

File–Sharing of Copyrighted Works, P2P, and the Cloud:
Reconciling Copyright and Privacy Rights

Pedro Pina
Polytechnic Institute of Coimbra, Portugal

ABSTRACT

In cyberspace, copyright enforcement and privacy rights have become two clashing realities. In fact, with the arrival of digital technology, especially the Internet, right holders, facing massive online infringements to their reproduction or distribution exclusive rights, mainly by file-sharers on Peer-to-Peer (P2P) systems or Cloud storage systems clients, started developing more and more intrusive new enforcement strategies in electronic communications as a means to identify the infringers and the committed infractions. The goal of the chapter is to study how the boundaries between what is public or private become fainter, whether the use of tracking software is consistent with personal data protection legislation, and whether it is possible to reconcile these two human rights, proposing a reflection on a possible extension of the use of levies in order to compensate right holders for private copies originating from unlawful sources.

INTRODUCTION

The tension between copyright and privacy is a relatively recent phenomenon.

In fact, until the dawn of the 21st century, the mere idea of the existence of a conflict between copyright and privacy rights would cause some strangeness. The tension between these rights was indeed almost imperceptible, since the referred branches of law, despite the fact that both are recognized as human rights, related to the development of an individual's personality as an ethical entity in articles 12 and 27 § 2 of the Universal Declaration of Human Rights, have developed autonomously, in tangentially unrelated grounds, which allowed them to co-exist peacefully.

Traditionally, in the pre-digital world, the boundaries between copyright and privacy were perfectly drawn in the context of the enforcement of the patrimonial rights granted to a copyright holder. Although copyright cannot be reduced to a mere patrimonial right – since beyond the recognition of such kind of rights, law grants the creators moral rights over their intellectual aesthetic works,

DOI: 10.4018/978-1-4666-7381-6.ch003

such as the right to claim authorship of the work and to object to any distortion, mutilation or other modification of or other derogatory action in relation to the said work which would be prejudicial to his honor or reputation – both in the common law copyright system and in the droit d'auteur system that prevails in European legislations, where the copyrightable intellectual work is considered an extent of its creator's personality and, therefore, the legal copyright regime directly regards the development of his/her personality and subsequently promotes cultural diversity despite their different bases and principles, copyright has been drawn primarily as an instrument to grant the holder, amongst other rights, the exclusive economic right to use and exploit his/her original work. Not disregarding the referred mixed nature of copyright, the possible conflict with privacy rights could only be perceived in the field of patrimonial rights' enforcement. If, on the one side, rightholders had the exclusive right to exploit publicly their copyrighted work, on the other side, private and non-commercial uses of the copyrighted work were free and escaped their control, since they were integrated in the private sphere of its consumer.

However, with the advent of digital technology, especially the internet, this state of things has altered dramatically. Rightholders, facing massive on-line copyright infringements or others unauthorized uses of works, mainly by file-sharers on peer-to-peer (p2p) systems or, more recently, by users of cloud computing platforms, started developing more and more intrusive new enforcement strategies in electronic communications as a means to identify the infringers and the committed infractions, reaching personal electronic information of consumers of online copyrighted works.

As a consequence of recognizing the importance of creative contents to the digital economy, legislators around the world have been escorting the rightholders' efforts to strengthen copyright protection in the digital environment, by creating not only sectorial substantive legislation but also in the field of digital copyright enforcement.

Cyber world's peculiarities, such as its specific structure and architecture and the fact that the enforcement is no longer only related to the apprehension of tangible things physically supporting the protected works but with the control of information and data, have been revealing copyright's highly porous new external boundaries that have been forcing it to leave the ivory tower where it used to stand in the old analogical world and, therefore, to confront itself with other rights like freedom of expression, privacy or consumers' rights.

In the digital relationship established with privacy rights, copyright's boundaries are becoming dimly defined, since it has been becoming more and more difficult to trace the line between what is public and what is private in p2p systems or in the cloud. In fact, considering that all data flowing through the internet is basically computer code, it is not possible for rightholders' tracking software to distinguish which collected data is public or private, lawful or unlawful, without a subsequent human normative evaluation. This simple example demonstrates clearly how thin can be the line between the violation of the users' right to privacy and the lawful exercise of a private surveillance power granted by law to the intellectual property's owner or to a regulatory administrative agency.

The present chapter aims to examine how digital technology like p2p systems or cloud computing constantly allows new unauthorized uses of protected works, the tension that has been arising in the digital world between intrusive copyright surveillance and enforcement mechanisms and internet users' privacy, suggesting how these rights can be reconciled.

Background

Technology has always been an essential element for copyright regulation. In fact, traditionally, since copyright regards the protection of intellectual aesthetic creations or, in other words, immaterial goods, the exteriorization of such kind of object needs the mediation of a physical support which may transform and evolve according to the known technology. That is the basis for the well-known dichotomy between the corpus mysticum, i.e., the copyrighted creative expression, and the corpus mechanicum that reveals the former. For that reason, it can be considered that copyright, per se, is not a tangible right, but an intangible sui generis quasi-property right over intellectual creations that can be embodied in tangible objects such as books or records.

When the corpus mechanicum was truly corporeal, it was relatively easy for rightholders to control the usages of their works, considering that material objects are scarce by nature. However, digital technology has generated a sort of a Copernican revolution in the field of copyright as it allowed creative works' consumers to experience and to share works without a corporeal fixation, just by watching movies or listening to music via streaming on video or music portals on the internet or by downloading or uploading protected content.

Digital technology has, thus, favored an enormous, global and almost uncontrolled flow of intangible information, including copyrighted content, which could easily escape rightholders' control. Nonetheless, the core of copyright patrimonial protection remains the same today as in the pre-digital era since rightholders have the power to exclusively exploit all the non-private usages of their creations, excluding others from using it without proper authorization and, normally, remuneration. Unlike the holders of tangible property, copyright holders do not have rights on things, namely the things that embody intellectual such as cd's, dvd's or books. For a limited period of time, they have the right to impose abstention behaviours to others, i. e., the right to exclude others from the use or consumption of the work without proper authorization, except in the case of mere private uses of copyrighted works or public interest concerned exceptions or limitations, such as for academic or scientific research, amongst others. Intellectual property rights, including copyright, and tangible property were, therefore, never totally equivalent.

Digitization, however, has changed in quality and in quantity the possibilities of infringement and of other unauthorized uses: it is possible to make huge amounts of perfect copies of digitized works and to easily share and spread them globally throughout the internet, since no corporeal body is needed, unlike what happened in the analogical era.

In legal terms, digital technology, not disregarding its possible lawful uses, has thus facilitated several possible violations of patrimonial rights that copyright laws usually grant exclusively to copyright holders: the right to display the copyrighted work publicly, the right to perform works publicly, the right to publicly distribute copies of the copyrighted works or the right to reproduce the works in copies. As a consequence, technological progress has permitted the establishment of genuine parallel economies based on counterfeiting and some non-commercial uses, such as the exchange of digital files through p2p networks have grown to such an extent that they are competing with the normal exploitation of works and challenging established commercial models (Geiger, 2010, p. 4).

The impact of the internet in the copyright field was, in fact, huge and lead to an unbalanced clash between massive and globalized digital unauthorized uses of copyrighted content and the old fashioned, reactive and obsolete copyright enforcement legal instruments that were designed in an analogical and tangible context where it was relatively easy to find infringers and the physical supports of works illegally reproduced and distributed. Creative contents and information flowing on the internet not only wanted to be free but also seemed to be liberated from rightholders' control and from judicial reaction. For a long time, based on the technology of the medium, the geographical and globalized distribution of its users and the intangible nature of its content, digital libertarians thought that the cyber world provided an unavoidable shift from a legal regime to a technological regime where speech and the flow of information were liberated from public or private heteronomous constrictions (Boyle, 1997).

Truly, the plurilocalized distribution of the infringers and the immense quantity of online infractions revealed how unprepared the international copyright legal system was to enforce rights in the digital context. Public enforcement mechanisms based on national courts were slow, merely reactive and inefficient since they were localized (i.e., limited by territorial sovereignty) and analogic. Therefore, such circumstances left most of the infractions unpunished and did not prevent the patrimonial damages that rightholders had suffered.

As rightholders were not able to find an efficient reaction from the judiciary system, therefore facing an insufficient state protection, they started developing self-help systems based upon technological protection measures (TPM) such as, inter alia, steganography, encryption or electronic agents like web crawlers or spy-bots, that could be able to hinder online infringements and economic losses. Copyright law started to seem an inefficient tool to protect creators' interests. It is in this context marked by the tendency to diminish the importance of copyright in a digital environment in favour of a control-by-code based solution that Clark (1996) elegantly declares that "the answer to the machine is in the machine" (p. 139). According to this point of view, technology would be the most relevant instrument to lock-up access to creative expression and information in a digital environment and architectural design would become the preferred or, at least, a popular method of regulating the emerging global communication networks (Lessig, 2006). In fact, considering that the basic functions of TPM are:

1. Controlling access to copyright works (and possibly other information products);
2. Restricting unauthorised reproduction (and possibly other usage) of such works;
3. Identifying the works, the relevant right–holders (and possibly the conditions for authorised usage of the works); and (4) protecting the authenticity of the latter identification data (Bygrave, 2003, pp. 420-421), technology gives rightholders the means to fully control the usages of their works.

The referred approach wasn't sufficient per se as TPM could be circumvented by other technological devices or software and so, as a result, the information and communication technologies (ICT) industry started lobbying for the enactment of new laws whereby both copyright and technology protection measures were recognized. The goal was to technologically transform the copyright legal by internalizing and recognizing self-help digital systems.

Several international treaties and digital copyright national laws – from the Agreement on Trade Related Aspects of Intellectual Property Rights (TRIPS) or the World Intellectual Property Organization (WIPO) Copyright Treaty and the WIPO Performances and Phonograms Treaty, at the international level, to the Digital Millennium Copyright Act (DMCA), in the USA, or the Directive 2001/29/EC of the European Parliament and of the Council of 22 May 2001 on the harmonisation of certain aspects of copyright and related rights in the information society (InfoSoc Directive), in the European Union, followed by subsequent transpositions into member state laws –, adopted the legal-technological approach for protecting creative expression by recognizing that the use of TPM was a lawful means to a digital rights management system. Moreover, the referred new generation of copyright laws provided that circumvention acts and the creation or dissemination of circumvention devices were forbidden and punished as criminal offenses. In this context, it is proper to conclude with Werra (2001) that rightholders are entitled to

... three levels of cumulative protection: the first is the legal protection by copyright. The second level is the technical protection of works through measures protection techniques. The third level is the new legal protection against circumvention of TPM introduced by the WIPO Treaties (p. 77).

According to the current legal background, technology can be combined with contractual provisions included in end user license agreements consequently creating what can apparently be the perfect digital rights management system taking into consideration that licensors can contractually predict which users' behaviours are lawful or not and have the means to digitally control it. That is to say that in these specific cases, copyright may be partially overridden and substituted by the combination of technology and contract law. Since this kind of provisions had substantially more to with copyright enforcement than to the material regulation of creative expression, some authors distinguish it from primary substantive copyright and called it paracopyright (Jaszi, 1988) or *übercopyright* (Helberger & Hugenholtz, 2007).

However, despite their obvious theoretical advantages to rightholders, who are granted the right to create private systems of copyright monitoring, the online surveillance measures contained in digital rights management systems have the potential to undermine some fundamental rights of internet users, such as freedom of expression, in its broadest sense, including in its scope the right of access to knowledge and information, or the right to privacy – or, in its multifaceted dimension, the right to informational and communicational self determination. Considering the above mentioned features of TPM and digital rights management systems, their intrusive nature on users' privacy becomes evident. The capabilities of an ideal digital rights management system are detecting and preventing a wide range of operations – including opening, printing, exporting, sharing, copying, modifying, mixing or excerpting; maintaining records of lawful or unlawful

users' behaviors and sending this information to rightholders. The collectors may then manipulate the acquired data to generate predictive profiles of infringers or lawful consumers for use in future marketing activities, or for sale to other vendors (Cohen, 1997, pp. 186-187).

As indicated above, digital rights management systems apply, in the first place, to legitimate users or purchasers of copyrighted digital works whose habits of reading, listening to or accessing copyrighted works can be monitored by rightholders: in these cases, the latter players go beyond the limits of the users' private sphere since they are capable in some cases to monitor their private tastes and behaviours (Cohen, 1996). Given that "intellectual privacy resides partly in the ability to exert (a reasonable degree of) control over the physical and temporal circumstances of intellectual consumption within private spaces" (Cohen, 2003, p. 582) the described use of digital rights management systems may trump users' privacy rights.

Navigating the Internet and the World Wide Web leaves a digital track that can be used to reconstitute the actions of the users (without his/her knowledge or consent). Taking those technologic possibilities into account, several authors have pointed out that, on matters like electronic surveillance, the architecture of cyberspace closely resembles Bentham's Panopticon as re-imagined by Michel Foucault. The latter's reflections on the disciplinary society have been used as a major reference for the study of electronic control and surveillance in the digital environment. The Panopticon was an ideal type of a prison imagined by Jeremy Bentham. According to this English utilitarian philosopher, the panoptic structure should be based on a central watchtower encircled by a peripheral ring divided into cells facing the center. As the cells were backlit from the outside, all the prisoners could be seen by those standing in the watchtower. However, the guards in the center couldn't be seen because of the use of venetian blinds on the towers' windows. This way, in the ring, one is totally seen; at the same time, in the watchtower, one is never seen. By dissociating the see/being seen binomial, this scenario creates in the prisoners' minds the feeling of being permanently watched and controlled even when the guards are not actually standing in the tower. From the Bentham's proposal, Foucault conceptualized the disciplinary society based on the panopticism. According to him,

... disciplinary power [...] is exercised through its invisibility; at the same time it imposes on those whom it subjects a principle of compulsory visibility. In discipline, it is the subjects who have to be seen. Their visibility assures the hold of the power that is exercised over them. It is the fact of being constantly seen, of being able always to be seen, that maintains the disciplined individual in his subjection (Foucault, 1977, p. 187).

Although the scope of privacy rights cannot be reduced to the protection against intrusion by digital Panopticon watchers, the present chapter focuses on one of the most controversial issues in this field related to the use of intrusive software regarding copyright enforcement within p2p networks and in the cloud, two environments where users and file-sharers frequently share and swap copyrighted content, reproduce and synchronize it in several devices without rightholders' authorization.

The architecture of p2p systems promotes a distributed and decentralized network that enables a computer to find files directly on the hard drive of another network connected device without the need for central servers. As a result, each user can be a consumer and a supplier of files simultaneously. In such a decentralized network, the boundaries between what is public and what is private within a computer's memory grow blurrier since users allow their peers to access the hard disk of their computers. Therefore, the number of potential invasions by surveillors to the computer's memory and the number of unknown accesses to

personal data stored in the device is facilitated and may increase rapidly. As in the Panopticon, one user cannot or may not know when another one is accessing to the contents stored on his/her computer. The digital panopticism is thus a behaviors detection system mediated by the use of digital technology characterized by the fact that there might have been not just a hyper-vigilant – a role that, traditionally, fits the government and that, in Orwell's novel 1984, is personalized in the Big Brother –, but many Little Brothers, individuals or private entities, peers of the observed user, moved by the defense of their material interests.

In this context, given the extent of illegal file-sharing of copyrighted or patented works and the inefficient reaction of public enforcement mechanisms, the private enforcement technology-based strategy turned very attractive for rights' holders. However, what could be justified as a defensive mechanism, revealed itself an intrusive and, sometimes, disproportioned means. As Katyal (2004) states,

... the problem of piracy has led some private entities to respond even more forcefully than necessary, seeking to destroy not only the peer-to-peer networks that have sprouted across the Internet, but the very boundaries of privacy, anonymity, and autonomy in cyberspace.

If p2p's architecture revealed itself to be an outstanding mechanism of content distribution, its connatural openness also enhances an attractive panoptic structure of private surveillance and control by rightholders seeking for copyright infringers using unauthorized content. In such a context, it becomes relatively easy to collect file-sharers' data like their IP addresses, the files stored in their computer or the record of uploads and downloads. Since the judgment over the legality of the files' content is made afterwards, it is possible that data has been collected and analyzed for nothing, infringing p2p networks users' privacy rights.

Cloud computing, defined by the National Institute of Standards and Technology as "a model for enabling convenient, on-demand network access to a shared pool of configurable computing resources (e.g., networks, servers, storage, applications, and services) that can be rapidly provisioned and released with minimal management effort or service provider interaction" (Mell and Grance, 2009), has been getting more and more popular recently. A cloud storage infrastructure allows its users to access files remotely over a network. Although Cloud providers offer services that usually are divided into different categories, such as Infrastructure-as-a-Service (IaaS), Platform-as-a-Service (PaaS) and Software-as-a-Service (SaaS), this chapter will focus mainly on the latter, specifically on Cloud storage services where platforms like iCloud, Amazon Cloud Drive, SkyDrive or Dropbox can be included, as they enable users to store files containing texts, music, movies or photos on remote cloud servers and to share such files within a synchronized format.

Compared to p2p systems, Cloud storage can be similar as it is also meant to be a sharing platform, but has a different architecture. In fact, the Cloud operated a major shift in internet users' behaviors. According to Gervais and Hyndman (2012),

... pre-Cloud, the Internet was used to transport data and allow hundreds of millions of individual and corporate computers on which content was stored to exchange using their Internet identity (an IP address). Switching from this connection paradigm, in which the Internet was essentially a network connecting computers, to an amalgamation paradigm, where user computers and devices are merely tools used to access private and commercial content amalgamated on server farms operated by major intermediaries (p. 55).

Amongst others, Cloud Storage providers may offer services like providing digital personal lockers, synchronizing, sharing or matching.

In the first case, the provider offers a remote memory space allowing users to duplicate the contents of their digital library on all digital devices. Users start by uploading digital content – where it can be included copyright protected works – to the Cloud and, afterwards, they have the possibility to download the stored content to any other device. The referred acts may, in theory, collide with the reproduction right foreseen in Article 9 of the Berne Convention, since, as it was agreed in the WIPO Copyright Treaty:

The reproduction right, as set out in Article 9 of the Berne Convention, and the exceptions permitted thereunder, fully apply in the digital environment, in particular to the use of works in digital form. It is understood that the storage of a protected work in digital form in an electronic medium constitutes a reproduction within the meaning of Article 9 of the Berne Convention.

Since uploading a file containing a protected work legally acquired to a digital personal locker is equivalent to making a digital backup, it seems reasonable to considered such act as a fair use of the work, according to laws like the US Copyright Act, or that it must fall into the private copy exception, when this space of users' freedom is foreseen in national copyright legislations, normally accompanied by the obligation to pay a compensation. Problems may arise and we may be facing a copyright infringement when the identified exceptions aren't foreseen in a specific country, when the work that the user wants to upload is protected by TPM, since anti-circumvention is forbidden, or when that work came from an unlawful source.

Similar problems may arise in the case of synchronization services associated to sales, such as Google Play or Apple's AppStore. The user buys the copyrighted content and automatically stores it on the Cloud so that it can be accessed, by acts of downloading or streaming on multiple devices.

If the Cloud Storage provider offers the user the possibility of sharing files, it won't be considered no longer a simple host as it allows users to infringe the exclusive rightholders' right of distribution and of making the work available online.

When the user uploads files, matching services, like iTunes' Match, scan the user's computer to determine which files are there and, after finding a match in the provider's database, gives that user access to an equivalent provider's file containing the same work. In that process,

iTunes matches song titles with those in its database, but reportedly it can also determine whether each song on the user's computer was originally an iTunes download, ripped from a CD or acquired (presumably illegally) via peer-to-peer (p2p) networks.3 If and when this occurs, a list is generated on Apple's servers matching the user's iTunes account with a specific number of p2p acquired songs (Gervais and Hyndman, 2012, p. 55).

Cloud storage providers offering matching services have therefore a great amount of information on copyrighted works consumers' behaviors and on eventual infringements on copyright which may of great interest to rightholders.

PRIVACY AND THE RIGHT TO INFORMATIONAL SELF-DETERMINATION

The advent of digital ICT has promoted a profusion of digital transmission and communication of data that, given the electronic trail that it leaves, can easily be surveyed, collected and controlled. Since a substantial part of digital data regards personal matters, safeguards against the treatment and misuse of computerized personal data are becoming increasingly important (Canotilho & Moreira, 2007, pp. 550-551).

Recent European responses to the exposed problem are inspired by a Germany Federal Constitutional Court (BVerfGE, 1983) ruling according to which,

... in the context of modern data processing, the protection of the individual against unlimited collection, storage, use and disclosure of his/her personal data is encompassed by the general personal rights constitutional provisions. This basic right warrants in this respect the capacity of the individual to determine in principle the disclosure and use of his/her personal data [and consists in] the authority of the individual to decide himself, on the basis of the idea of self-determination, when and within what limits information about his private life should be communicated to others.

This perspective recognizes the right to privacy with a broader scope than the traditional United States law understanding of this right as "the right to be left alone" (Warren and Brandeis, 1890), imposing an obligation of no trespassing.

Following Ferrajoli's teachings on the distinction between rights and their guarantees (2001), we could note that, although a negative dimension is included in the scope of the right to communicational and informational self-determination, this right is conceptualized not only as a mere guarantee of the right to privacy, but as a true fundamental right with an independent meaning; this meaning consists in the recognition of the freedom to control the use of information (if it is personal), and in the protection against attacks arising from the use of such information" (Castro, 2005, pp. 65*ff*.).

Therefore, the right to communicational and informational self-determination reveals two autonomous but intrinsically linked facets. The first one has a defensive nature, similar to the guarantee for the secrecy of correspondence and of other means of private communication, and is built as a negative right that protects the holder against interference by the State or by individuals who are responsible for processing digital or analogical data or others. The second facet constitutes a positive right to dispose of your own personal information, a power of controlling it and determining what others can, at every moment, know about you (Castro, 2006, p. 16). That is to say, the holder does not only have the right to remain opaque to others but also the right to control the use of his/her personal data and establish the terms of its use by third parties.

The right to communicational and informational self-determination is a true fundamental right, related to the development of the personality of each individual, established in article 8 of the European Union Charter of Fundamental Rights:

1. "Everyone has the right to the protection of personal data concerning him or her.
2. Such data must be processed fairly for specified purposes and on the basis of the consent of the person concerned or some other legitimate basis laid down by law. Everyone has the right of access to data which has been collected concerning him or her, and the right to have it rectified.
3. Compliance with these rules shall be subject to control by an independent authority."

The Charter's legislator followed the tracks of the European Convention on Human Rights and the jurisprudence of the European Court of Human Rights, according to which "the State is not merely under the obligation to abstain from interfering with individuals' privacy, but also to provide individuals with the material conditions needed to allow them to effectively implement their right to private and family life" (Rouvroy/Poullet, 2007, p. 20).

At the European Union derivative law level, three directives directly regulate privacy matters:

1. Directive 95/46/EC of the European Parliament and of the Council of 24 October 1995 on the protection of individuals with regard to the processing of personal data and on the free movement of such data;
2. Directive 2002/58/EC of the European Parliament and of the Council of 12 July 2002 concerning the processing of personal data and the protection of privacy in the electronic communications sector (Directive on privacy and electronic communications); and
3. Directive 2000/31/EC of the European Parliament and of the Council of 8 June 2000 on certain legal aspects of information society services, in particular electronic commerce, in the Internal Market (Directive on electronic commerce).

Through the mentioned directives, the European legislator created a legal framework to regulate the activity of electronic data collecting and subsequent treatment guided by the following principles:

1. The principle of lawful collecting, meaning that collecting and processing of data constitute a restriction on the holder's informational self-determination and are only permitted within the parameters of the law and, particularly, with the holder's knowledge and consent;
2. The finality principle, according to which data collecting and the data processing can only be made with a clearly determined, specific and socially acceptable finality that has to be identifiable in the moment when the activity is being executed;
3. The principle of objective limitation, meaning that the use of the collected data must be restricted to the purposes that were communicated to the holder, and must respect the general principles of proportionality, necessity and adequacy;
4. The principle of temporal limitation, which implies that data shall not be kept by more than the time needed to achieve the finality that justified the activity;
5. The principle of data quality, meaning that the collected data must be correct and up-to-date;
6. The principle of free access to data, according to which the holder must be able to know the

existence of the collection and the storage of his/her personal data and, if he/she wants, to rectify, erase or block the information when incomplete or inaccurate; and

7. The security principle, under which the controller must implement appropriate technical and organizational measures to protect personal data against accidental or arbitrary unlawful destruction or accidental loss, alteration, unauthorized disclosure or access, in particular where the processing involves the transmission of data over a network. As it is regulated in the European Union, the right to communicational and informational self-determination gives an individual the power to control all the possible usages of his/her personal data.

In the United States of America, market regulation of privacy is prevalent. Therefore, despite the provisions of the Privacy Act of 1974, 5 U.S.C. § 552a, "with limited exceptions, the processing and transferring of data per se is not among those activities that either the state or federal governments monitor" (Garcia, 2005, p. 1238, n. 206). In fact, except for the government regulation of specific sectors like the protection of children online, all the procedures related to collecting, keeping or transferring consumer data are left to industry self-regulation. The Federal Trade Commission (FTC) has an important role in promoting fair privacy policies, but has only prosecution powers against firms that act inconsistently with their disclosed policy if existent.

Consequently, without public regulation imposing duties to data collectors, and in the absence of the collectors' disclosure of privacy policy, personal data holders may not have the information or the powers to control what personal information is collected, when or how it is collected, how it will be used, or if it will be disclosed or transferred to third parties, amongst other possible usages.

DIGITAL COPYRIGHT ENFORCEMENT SURVEILLANCE MECHANISMS

One of the major pieces of European legislation in the field of copyright enforcement is Directive 2004/48/EC of the European Parliament and the Council of 29 April 2004 on the enforcement of intellectual property rights ("Enforcement" Directive). This directive does not only apply to infringements committed on a commercial scale, although some provisions – Articles 6(2), 8(1) and 9(2) – are only applicable in such cases. But even the concept of "commercial scale" proposed by the Directive is vague: in Recital (14) it is stated that acts carried out on a commercial scale "are those carried out for direct or indirect economic or commercial advantage; this would normally exclude acts carried out by end-consumers acting in good faith." There is no definition of the concepts of economic advantage or good faith, which may bring several interpretation problems, especially because in recital (15) it is recognized that the Directive should not affect substantive law on intellectual property and, consequently, the exclusive rights to distribute the work or to make it available to the public, which leaves space to a maximalist interpretation of the concept of commercial scale.

In Article 6, paragraph 1, of the "Enforcement" Directive it is stated that:

Member States shall ensure that, on application by a party which has presented reasonably available evidence sufficient to support its claims, and has, in substantiating those claims, specified evidence which lies in the control of the opposing party, the competent judicial authorities may order that such evidence be presented by the opposing party, subject to the protection of confidential information. For the purposes of this paragraph, Member States may provide that a reasonable sample of a substantial number of copies of a work or any other protected object be considered by the competent judicial authorities to constitute reasonable evidence.

In face of this provision, it seems correct to conclude that the European legislator assumed that collecting IP is a lawful rightholder's behavior if functionally directed to subsequent copyright enforcement, since in the context of p2p networks it will be the adequate means to present "reasonable evidence." Such assumption could also be supported by Article 8, paragraph 3, of the Infosoc Directive, which provides that "[m]ember States shall ensure that rightholders are in a position to apply for an injunction against intermediaries whose services are used by a third party to infringe a copyright or related right." In fact, the European Union solution was influenced by the US notice and take down solution provided for in the DMCA, § 512,(c)(3), and (h)(1), which grants the rightholders the right to "request the clerk of any United States district court to issue a subpoena to a service provider for identification of an alleged infringer." Such request may be made by filing with the clerk one notification of claimed infringement that must be a written communication provided to the designated agent of a service provider that includes substantially, amongst other elements, the identification of the copyrighted work claimed to have been infringed, the identification of the material that is claimed to be infringing or to be the subject of infringing activity and that is to be removed or access to which is to be disabled, and information reasonably sufficient to permit the service provider to contact the complaining party, such as an address, telephone number, and, if available, an electronic mail address at which the complaining party may be contacted.

One of the most controversial provisions of the "Enforcement" Directive is article 8, paragraph 1, which creates, under the epigraph "Right to information," a broad sub pœna that permits intellectual property holders to easily obtain the names and addresses of alleged infringers. In fact, according to the identified provision,

Member States shall ensure that, in the context of proceedings concerning an infringement of an intellectual property right and in response to a justified and proportionate request of the claimant, the competent judicial authorities may order that information on the origin and distribution networks of the goods or services which infringe an intellectual property right be provided by the infringer and/or any other person who:

(a) was found in possession of the infringing goods on a commercial scale;

(b) was found to be using the infringing services on a commercial scale;

(c) was found to be providing on a commercial scale services used in infringing activities; or

(d) was indicated by the person referred to in point (a), (b) or (c) as being involved in the production, manufacture or distribution of the goods or the provision of the services".

This right to information is considered absolutely essential to ensure a high level of protection of intellectual property as it may be the only means to identify the infringer. Nevertheless, it is not absolute: paragraph 3 (e) of article 8, expressly stipulates that paragraph's 1 provision "shall apply without prejudice to other statutory provisions which […] govern the protection of confidentiality of information sources or the processing of personal data." In reality, European Union's concern over the protection of personal data is clearly manifested in recital 2 of the "Enforcement" Directive, where it is stated that, although the protection of intellectual property should allow the inventor or creator to derive a legitimate profit from his invention or creation and to allow the widest possible dissemination of works, ideas and new know-how, "[a]t the same time, it should not hamper freedom of expression, the free movement of information, or the protection of personal data."

One of the greatest obstacles that rightholders have been facing in this field is precisely the protection of personal data argument that is used by Internet Service Providers (ISPs), such as Cloud storage providers, for not disclosing their clients' identity. Given the contractual relationships established with the users, ISPs are the best positioned to give an identity to the IP address collected by the rightholder. Indeed,

ISPs have developed into a relatively new form of governance in cyberspace because they maintain a substantial amount of private, consumer information regarding users' online activities, and because they often control the transmission and distribution of requested information. For these reasons, many consider the ISP the principal repository for all identifying information regarding individual users and their Web activities. (Katyal, 2004, p. 311)

In order to escape personal data collecting and treatment laws, some groups of rightholders have been defending the idea that IP addresses are not personal data and, therefore, that ISPs may disclose their clients' identity even without a previous jurisdictional decision. The main argument relied on the fact that an IP address is per se insufficient to identify the individual behind it.

Although several cases related to this subject have been discussed throughout Europe, one in particular has become well known. In France, on May, 23, 2007, the *Conseil d'État* revoked a decision from the *Commission Nationale de l'Informatique et des Libertés* (CNIL), according to which this independent agency had refused to give an authorization to four collective management entities regarding the use of digital devices that could automatically detect copyright infringements and forward messages to the alleged online infringers. The CNIL understood that those devices constituted disproportional measures because they were not designed just to implement occasional actions strictly limited to the specific needs of

the fight against counterfeiting, but may lead to a massive collection of personal data and provide an exhaustive and continuous surveillance over the p2p networks (2005).

The *Conseil d'État* revoked that decision, announcing that the CNIL had erred in applying the law, namely on the proportionality issue, considering on the one hand, the quantitative dimension of copyright infringements on the Internet, and, on the other hand, that the survey related only to users who shared or provided copyrighted works up from a certain number. Later on, the *Cour d'appel* de Paris held that IP addresses should not be qualified as personal data and that they were not protected under the right to privacy or to informational self-determination. This understanding clearly diverges from the general understanding that IP addresses must be considered personal data. Such conclusion is, in my view, the right one and is consistent with the Opinion 4/2007 on the concept of personal data, from the Working Party set up under Article 29 of Directive 95/46/EC, whereby it considered IP addresses as data relating to an identifiable person. The Working Party stated:

Internet access providers and managers of local area networks can, using reasonable means, identify Internet users to whom they have attributed IP addresses as they normally systematically "log" in a file the date, time, duration and dynamic IP address given to the Internet user. The same can be said about Internet Service Providers that keep a logbook on the HTTP server. In these cases there is no doubt about the fact that one can talk about personal data in the sense of Article 2 a) of the Directive. Especially in those cases where the processing of IP addresses is carried out with the purpose of identifying the users of the computer (for instance, by Copyright holders in order to prosecute computer users for violation of intellectual property rights), the controller anticipates that the "means likely reasonably to be used" to identify the persons will be available e.g. through the courts appealed to (otherwise the collection of the information makes no sense), and therefore the information should be considered as personal data. (Article 29 data protection working party, 2007, p. 16)

In fact, considering that personal data is defined in Article 2 (a) of the Directive 95/46/EC as

… any information relating to an identified or identifiable natural person [and that] an identifiable person is one who can be identified, directly or indirectly, in particular by reference to an identification number or to one or more factors specific to his physical, physiological, mental, economic, cultural or social identity, it will be very difficult to sustain that a person cannot be identified through an IP address. More recently, other courts' decisions have declared that IPs are indeed personal data, based on the Article 29 data protection working party opinion; but there is still an undesirable lack of unanimity over this issue.

In the case C-275/06, the Court of Justice of the European Communities decided one of the most important cases related to the discussion on the balance between intellectual property enforcement and privacy. Promusicae, a Spanish collective management society, asked the ISP Telefonica de España to reveal personal data on their users in order to enable the latter to subsequently bring civil law charges against the detected copyright infringers. Since, under Spanish law, ISPs only have to reveal personal data to judiciary authorities in cases of criminal investigations and prosecutions, the Spanish court (*Juzgado de lo Mercantil n.° 5 de Madrid*) wanted to know from the Court of Justice if that material restriction was in conformity with European Union law. Advocate-General Juliane Kokott concluded that it is compatible with Community law for Member States to exclude the communication of personal traffic data for the purpose of bringing civil proceedings against copyright infringements.

Kokott noted that up to now the legislature has not considered that a more far-reaching protection of the holders of copyrights is necessary.

On the contrary, in adopting Directives 2000/31, 2001/29 and 2004/48, it provided for the unaltered continued applicability of data protection and saw no reason, when adopting the sector-specific Directives 2002/58 and 2006/24, to introduce restrictions of data protection in favour of the protection of intellectual property. Directive 2006/24 could, on the contrary, lead to a strengthening of data protection under Community law with regard to disputes concerning infringements of copyright. The question then arises, even in criminal investigations, as to the extent to which it is compatible with the fundamental right to data protection under Community law to grant aggrieved rightholders access to the results of the investigation if the latter are based on the evaluation of retained traffic data within the meaning of Directive 2006/24. Up to now, that question is not affected by Community law since the Data Protection Directives do not apply to the prosecution of criminal offences. (CJEC, 2007)

In its final decision, the Court decided that EU law does not require Member States to lay down an obligation to communicate personal data in order to ensure effective protection of copyright in the context of civil proceedings. This approach is extremely relevant, since it clearly indicates that a balance between copyright enforcement and personal data protection is needed and required by European Union Law, even though isolated readings of the legislation may suggest the pre-eminence of one over the other.

THE GRADUATED RESPONSE: AN ENFORCEMENT MECHANISM

Large controversy was raised in France recently over the implications of the *Creation and Internet* law for internet users' freedom of expression – a matter that shall not be treated in the present paper

– and privacy. This law, also known as HADOPI law, the acronym of *Haute Autorité pour la Diffusion des Œuvres et la Protection des Droits sur Internet* (High Authority for the Diffusion of Art Works and for the Protection of Rights on Internet), embraces new normative strategies regarding the enforcement of copyright in a digital environment, such as the graduated response mechanism.

More than a sanctionatory procedure based on the direct applicability of substantial copyright rules, the graduated response is a compelling mechanism that "intends primarily to reduce the scale of infringements through an (automated) educational notification mechanism for alleged online infringers" (Strowel, 2009, p. 78). It is based on a three-strike procedure that implies ISPs cooperation with rightholders and with the High Authority.

Once the individuals behind the IPs of alleged online infringers collected by rightholders or by the High Authority have been identified, with the cooperation of ISPs, the first step of the procedure is to send online warnings to the subscriber potentially committing copyright infringement, whereby he/she is advised about the illegality of his/her behavior and also about the possibility of legal online offer of creative content. If the infringement continues, six months after the first warning, a new one is sent. If, even so, the unlawful activity continues, in the last step of this procedure, a court may order the suspension of the broadband accounts of file-sharers of copyrighted material online.

This kind of solution has been spreading throughout the world and is being discussed with similar controversy in the United Kingdom, Australia, New Zealand, Germany or Spain. Furthermore, at the European Union legislative level, after the approval in November 2009 of the telecommunications package and the insertion of the new article 3a in the text of the Directive 2002/21/EC, it seems that the graduated response mechanism has found space in future member state legislation provided that a prior fair and impartial procedure is to be guaranteed. According to the referred provision, measures taken by Member States regarding end-users access' to, or use of, services and applications through electronic communications networks shall respect the fundamental rights and freedoms of natural persons, as guaranteed by the European Convention for the Protection of Human Rights and Fundamental Freedoms and general principles of Community law.

Accordingly, in the European Union, copyright infringements committed through electronic networks may lead to the application of enforcement measures against ISPs' clients. Nevertheless, measures, such as the ones provided in the graduated response mechanism, may only be taken with due respect for the principle of presumption of innocence and the right to privacy. In fact, pursuant to the new article 3a, "a prior, fair and impartial procedure shall be guaranteed, including the right to be heard of the person or persons concerned, subject to the need for appropriate conditions and procedural arrangements in duly substantiated cases of urgency in conformity with the European Convention for the Protection of Human Rights and Fundamental Freedoms," and "the right to effective and timely judicial review shall be guaranteed."

From a personal data protection point of view, solutions like the graduated response may be considered acceptable only if they respect the collecting and treatment principles discussed above and the general principles of proportionality, necessity and adequacy. For instance, a solution that imposes on ISPs the obligation of filtering data content without a court previous decision where, on an ad-hoc basis, all the factual and normative elements are available, should not be acceptable. Otherwise, all private communications, lawful or not, would be monitored by ISPs and government agencies: this would clearly violate the most basic foundations of a democratic society. Furthermore, the mere collection of IP addresses needs, at least in the European Union context, to be previously authorized, for instance, by the CNIL in France, or corresponding member state agencies. This would be an adequate way to ensure that a specific rightholder will objectively and proportionally collect IP addresses respecting the rights of the data owners providing them with a means to control the collector's actions. However, even if legal, solutions like the one established by the HADOPI Law aren't consistent with the dynamics of the digital economy and put in danger net neutrality. Moreover, the referred solution didn't have the results that the French legislator predicted, as music sales have continued to drop.

CONCLUSION: REVISITING AND EXTENDING LEVIES

Both copyright and privacy, especially the right to informational self-determination, have been dramatically affected by new digital technologies and by the enormous quantity of massive, plurilocalized, transnational and apparently anonymous infringements that these technologies facilitate in addition to their possible lawful uses.

If the first answers to the digital challenge resembled legal capitulation ("the answer to the machine is in the machine") and assumed the death of copyright and privacy laws in cyber world, defined as a space free from external regulation by national laws, soon such a technological determinism approach had to be abandoned. In fact, considering the potential harmfulness of online infringements, the equivalence between real and digital worlds had to be proclaimed, which led to the technological transformation of the legal regimes that had to rapidly adapt to the new contexts. Modern legislations recognize that both technology and law may concur to protect copyright and privacy: beyond substantive legal provisions regarding the scope of protection and the substantial powers granted to rightholders, it is also possible to use privacy enhancement technologies and copyright digital management systems.

However, in the field of digital copyright enforcement, intrusive technological measures created to identify online infringers were developed, putting in risk the privacy sphere of internet users, since their navigation and identification data can be collected and treated by a copyright holder. In this context, it is neither possible nor correct to offer an a priori hierarchy of copyright and the right to privacy. Both rights are recognized as human rights that are fundamental to the development of an individual's personality. For this reason, it is not up to the ordinary legislator to decide which right should prevail in abstract terms. Seeking for a harmonization or a practical concordance between two fundamental rights when in collision is a delicate task that cannot be strictly foreseen. A fundamental right may be restricted only when this restriction is proportionate, adequate and necessary to protect another right with similar value. Consequently, one cannot a priori emphasize copyright's protection and importance in disfavor of privacy concerns and vice-versa.

Digital copyright is facing an enormous challenge, since the number of online infractions is growing every day, causing significant economic losses to rightholders. The seeming opacity of the right to privacy should not allow unlawful behaviors to go unpunished. However, not every infringement may permit the disclosure of personal data. This can only be authorized if it is necessary to protect a value or a right with similar or greater value. This means that, first, the collection of IP addresses needs to be previously acknowledged by law or authorized by an independent agency; subsequently, only when copyright infringement constitutes simultaneously a criminal offense, privacy rights of the alleged infringer can be proportionately sacrificed.

It is, therefore, desirable that a harmonized legal framework regarding the criminalization of copyright infringements is settled; this is a difficult task to perform, considering how connected to national sovereignty such a matter is, even at the European Union level and despite the proposed Directive on this subject. Until then, litigation in courts will surely increase regarding the conflict between copyright enforcement and privacy rights and the casuistic definition of each one's scope; and legal uncertainty and insecurity will foment privacy self-regulation mechanisms, mainly through the use of privacy enhancing technology to protect users' personally identifiable information.

The tendency is to criminalize copyright infringement only when it occurs in a commercial scale, leaving private non-profit oriented uses out of its object. That means that, since privacy rights and copyright have the same dignity has human rights, it will be very difficult to justify intrusive solutions with the potential to cause harm in the privacy sphere of internet users. At the same time, it is undeniable that the unauthorized huge flow of creative information harms rightholders' interests.

One possible way to reconcile copyright and privacy rights in the cyber world is to extend the application of levies meant to compensate rightholders for legitimate exceptions to their exclusive rights by applying them also to mass unauthorized acts of reproduction, communication to the public and distribution.

Recently, in Case C-435/12 - ACI Adam and Others, where it was discussed if, when calculating the amount of the levy for private copy, should copies originating from unlawful sources be taken into account side by side with lawful copies, Advocate General Pedro Cruz Villalón concluded that a negative answer should be given, as, according to the three-step test foreseen in the Berne Convention and in Article 5(5) of the InfoSoc Directive, an exception to exclusive rights can only be accepted if it is not in conflict with the normal exploitation of the work and does not unreasonably prejudice the legitimate interests of rightholders. Such conclusion follows the optimistic understanding that was on the basis of the InfoSoc Directive according to which technology permitted rightholders to control every online use of their works, favoring online licensing schemes, and that DRM systems would turn levies obsolete. Reality has proven that despite some casuistic relevant

success cases (e. g. iTunes music store), if users can obtain copies for free in file-sharing systems, they will hardly migrate to licensed platforms where they will have to pay for the works.

On February 11, 2014, the European Parliament approved a not binding resolution based on a report made by Françoise Castex – where it was also proposed calling on the Commission to examine the possibility of legalizing works sharing for non-commercial purposes, which was rejected – calling on the Commission to assess the impact on the private copying system of the use of cloud computing technology for the private recording and storage of protected works, so as to determine whether these private copies of protected works should be taken into account by the private copying compensation mechanisms and, if so, how this should be done.

Extending levies to compensate rightholders for private copies originating from unlawful sources may trigger a shift from proprietary rules to liability rules, securing only rights to remuneration and not recognizing the right to exclude others from using copyrighted works without the rightholders' consent, in the field of digital copyright. Nevertheless, historically it has been a successful scheme aimed to recast the balance between copyright and technology and its implications on users' privacy. If the only way to implement licensed online schemes or to enforce digital copyright implies that consumers' behaviors have to be monitored, than a balanced solution must be achieved so that privacy rights aren't sacrificed when, after a necessary a posteriori analysis, one finds out that the surveilled behaviors weren't infringing copyright.

Although both may harm rightholders' interests, separating private copies from commercial scale piracy seems to be an imperative so that the Internet continues to be an infrastructure allowing free flows of information and that its users no longer have to be seen as potential copyright law infringers who must be preventively surveilled and controlled. Section title should be "Conclusion", not "Conclusions". Provide discussion of the overall coverage of the chapter and concluding remarks.

REFERENCES

Article 29 Data Protection Working Party. (2007). *Opinion 4/2007 on the concept of personal data.* Retrieved February 28, 2014, from http://www.droit-technologie.org/upload/actuality/doc/1063-1.pdf

Boyle, J. (1997). *Foucault in cyberspace: Surveillance, sovereignty, and hard-wired censors.* Retrieved February 28, 2014, from http://www.law.duke.edu/boylesite/foucault.htm

Bygrave, L. A. (2003). Digital rights management and privacy. In E. Becker, W. Buhse, D. Günnewig, & N. Rump (Eds.), *Digital rights management: Technological, economic, legal and political aspects* (pp. 418–446). New York: Springer. doi:10.1007/10941270_27

Canotilho, J. G., & Moreira, V. (2007). *Constituição da República Portuguesa Anotada.* Coimbra: Coimbra Editora.

Castro, C. S. (2005). O direito à autodeterminação informativa e os novos desafios gerados pelo direito à liberdade e à segurança no pós 11 de Setembro. In *Estudos em homenagem ao Conselheiro José Manuel Cardoso da Costa, II.* Coimbra: Coimbra Editora.

Castro, C. S. (2006). *Protecção de dados pessoais na Internet.* Coimbra, Portugal: Almedina.

Clark, C. (1996). The answer to the machine is in the machine. In P. Bernt Hugenholtz (Ed.), *The future of copyright in a digital environment.* The Hague, The Netherlands: Kluwer Law International.

CNIL. (2005, October 18). *Délibération no. 2005-235.* Retrieved March 27, 2010, from http://www.legifrance.gouv.fr/affichCnil.do?oldAction=rechExpCnilandid=CNILTEXT000017652059andfastReqId=137369379andfastPos=1

Cohen, J. (1996). A right to read anonymously: A closer look at 'copyright management' in cyberspace. *Connecticut Law Review, 28,* 981–1039.

Cohen, J. (1997). Some reflections on copyright management systems and laws designed to protect them. *Berkeley Technology Law Journal, 12,* 161–190.

Cohen, J. (2003). DRM and privacy. *Berkeley Technological Law Journal, 18,* 575-617. Retrieved February 28, 2014, from http://ssrn.com/abstract=372741

Court of Justice of the European Communities. (2007). *Opinion of advocate General Kokott* [CJEC Case C-275/06]. Author.

Ferrajoli, L. (2001). Fundamental rights. *International Journal for the Semiotics of Law, 14*(1), 1–33. doi:10.1023/A:1011290509568

Foucault, M. (1977). *Discipline and Punish: The Birth of the Prison* (A. Sheridan, Trans.). New York: Pantheon Books.

Garcia, F. J. (2005). Bodil Lindqvist: A Swedish churchgoer's violation of the European Union's Data Protection Directive should be a warning to U.S. legislators. *Fordham Intellectual Property, Media, and Entertainment Law Journal, 15,* 1204–1243.

Geiger, C. (2010). The future of copyright in Europe: Striking a fair balance between protection and access to information. *Intellectual Property Quarterly, 1,* 1–14.

Gervais, D. J., & Hyndman, D. J. (2012). Cloud control: Copyright, global memes and privacy. *Journal on Telecommunications & High Technology Law, 10,* 53–92. Retrieved from http://ssrn.com/abstract=372741

Helberger, N., & Hugenholtz, P. B. (2007). No place like home for making a copy: Private copying in European copyright law and consumer law. *Berkeley Technology Law Journal, 22*, 1061–1098.

Jaszi, P. (1998). *Intellectual property legislative update: Copyright, paracopyright, and pseudocopyright.* Paper presented at the Association of Research Libraries Conference: The Future Network: Transforming Learning and Scholarship, Eugene, OR. Retrieved February 28, 2014, from http://old.arl.org/resources/pubs/mmproceedings/132mmjaszi~print.shtml

Katyal, S. (2004). The new surveillance. *Case Western Reserve Law Review, 54*, 297–386.

Lessig, L. (2006). *Code 2.0.* New York: Basic Books.

Mell, Peter, & Grance. (2009). *The NIST definition of cloud computing.* National Institute of Standards and Technology, Information Technology Laboratory. Retrieved February 28, 2014, from http://www.nist.gov/itl/cloud/upload/cloud-def-v15.pdf

Rouvroy, A., & Poullet, Y. (2008). The right to informational self-determination and the value of self-development: Reassessing the importance of privacy for democracy. In *Reinventing Data Protection: Proceedings of the International Conference.* Berlin: Springer.

Strowel, A. (2009). Internet piracy as a wake-up call for copyright law makers – Is the ''graduated response'' a good reply? *World Intellectual Property Organization Journal, 1*, 75–86.

Warren, S., & Brandeis, L. (1890). The right to privacy. *Harvard Law Review, 4*(5), 193–220. doi:10.2307/1321160

Werra, J. (2001). Le régime juridique des mesures techniques de protection des oeuvres selon les Traités de l'OMPI, le Digital Millennium Copyright Act, les Directives Européennes et d'autres legislations (Japon, Australie). *Revue Internationale du Droit d'Auteur, 189*, 66–213.

KEY TERMS AND DEFINITIONS

Cloud Computing: A model for enabling convenient, on-demand network access to a shared pool of configurable computing resources (e.g., networks, servers, storage, applications, and services) that can be rapidly provisioned and released with minimal management effort or service provider interaction.

Copyright: The set of exclusive moral and economic rights granted to the author or creator of an original intellectual work, including the right to copy, distribute and adapt the work.

Digital Rights Management (DRM): A copyrighted work's management system based on digital technology that, amongst other powers, allows copyright holders to control access to works or to prevent unauthorized copies.

Enforcement: Ensuring obedience to the laws.

File-Sharing: The practice of sharing computer data or space on a network.

Informational Self-Determination: The capacity of the individual to determine the disclosure and the use of his/her personal data, to control and to determine what others can, at every moment, know about his/her respect.

Levy: To impose and collect a tariff or a tax.

Peer-to-Peer (P2P): A computer network designed so that computers can send information directly to one another without passing through a centralized server.

Chapter 4
Dataveillance in the Workplace:
Privacy Threat or Market Imperative?

Regina Connolly
Dublin City University, Ireland

ABSTRACT

The work environment is changing in response to market pressures, and the psychological contract that previously typified many employer and employee work relationships is coming under distinct threat as pervasive Internet-based technologies now enable management to monitor employees' email, computer interactions, and general work productivity. Although in some cases management may have legitimate reasons to monitor employees' actions, it is becoming increasingly evident that the use of these technologies has the potential to negatively impact employee productivity and morale, and in some cases employee health and wellbeing. This chapter outlines some of the emerging issues relating to workplace surveillance from the employees' perspective, as well as the motivation behind management's decision to employ technologies in order monitor their employees.

INTRODUCTION

The changing contours of global economics and shifting market pressures have resulted in a work environment that is now characterised by less job security, stagnant wages and where the nature of work has become more intense and ideosyncratic. Many employers feel that they must satisfy a market imperative that is constantly pushing for greater productivity, if their organisations are to remain competitive. Attempts to satisfy that imperative have resulted in a relentless drive for efficiency and a focus on rigorous performance quotas, which in turn have become key determinants of both employment and promotion.

Recent technological advancements have facilitated the achievement of those efficencies and in particular have enabled employers to gain more detailed insights into employee performance, including their own use of technology both during and after work hours. However, this has generated understandable privacy concerns for employees. The pervasive computing environment is characterised by the seamless integration of technologies into society, and it is this transparent nature which has fuelled much of these privacy concerns. For example employees are becoming increasingly aware of the ways in which management can employ such technologies to monitor their email and computer interactions in the workplace, measure

DOI: 10.4018/978-1-4666-7381-6.ch004

their performance and even monitor their social media activity. That workplace surveillance, or dataveillance, can negatively impact employee productivity and motivation as well as their trust in employers and consequent commitment to the organisation.

A SHIFTING CONTEXT

As profit driven organisations strive to manage their business in an efficient and productive manner, it is perhaps unrealistic to expect that such organisations would not avail of the obvious empowering benefits that communication monitoring technologies afford them. Furthermore it can be argued that they may in fact have legitimate reasons to monitor employee actions in the first place. However, an inevitable outcome of these changes is that employees' relationship with their employers is changing in line with the changing balance of power in the workplace.

For an employee, knowing that their performance is being monitored and that that information may against them as part of performance assessment or promotion evaluation exercises, changes their perspective of the parameters of the employment relationship. Employee-employer relationships are typically perceived as being a two-way exchange, with the focus squarely upon the perceptions of reciprocal promises and obligations of both parties (Guest, 2004). These perceived obligations form a psychological contract that has been described as an individual employees' "belief in mutual obligations between that person and another party such as an employer" (Rousseau and Tijoriwala, 1998: 679). In short, employees have implicit and sometimes unvoiced expectations regarding employee contributions, in terms of effort, loyalty and ability for organizational inducements such as pay, promotion and job security (Morrison and Robinson, 1997; Conway and Briner, 2002).

However, the monitoring of performance presents a threat to that previously accepted contract and indeed can be perceived as a breach of expectations by the employer, which in turn can lead to feelings of injustice or betrayal of employees (Morrison and Robinson, 1997). Employees' reactions to contract violation have been shown to effect their organizational commitment (Lemire and Rouillard, 2005), work satisfaction (Sutton and Griffin, 2003), job security (Kramer *et al.* 2005) and motivation (Lester *et al.* 2001), as well as increasing their stress levels (Gakovic and Tetrick, 2003). Trust and fairness are core aspects of any psychological contract (Guest 2004) and workplace surveillance presents a considerable threat to the previously perceived trustworthiness and fairness of employers who now have the potential to leverage performance information against employees.

Many questions surround the issue of workplace surveillance in particular relating to the ethical nature of management's ability to monitor employees computer interactions. The aim of this chapter therefore is to outline some of the major issues relating to workplace surveillance, identifying the emerging issues and subsequent privacy concerns from the employee's perspective, as well as the motivation behind managements' decision to employ monitoring technologies in the workplace. As such this chapter explores the ethical impact of monitoring in the computer-mediated work environment, addressing whether management's ability to monitor employee actions in workplace represents good business practice or constitutes an invasion of privacy.

PRIVACY AND SURVEILLANCE

It is a common belief that one of the greatest threats to personal privacy lies in the monitoring and surveillance capabilities of modern technology. Privacy is a complex construct that remains beset by conceptual and operational confusion. It is an ambiguous concept that for many is difficult to either define or understand. For example for every definition of privacy sourced from the literature, a counterexample can be easily produced (Introna, 1996). Understandably therefore, privacy is often defined and measured in terms of a specific study, event or situation and as a result the conceptual confusion that surrounds the construct as well as the ways in which best to manage it remains a hot discussion topic. In order to gain a full understanding of the privacy construct it is reasonable to suggest that one considers it from a multiplicity of viewpoints and as such privacy is often examined as a psychological state, a form of power, an inherent right or an aspect of freedom (Parker, 1974; Acquisti, 2002; Rust *et al.,* 2002)

One aspect of privacy of which for many is central to our understanding of the construct is the issue of control, specifically the individual's need to have control over their personal information. Control has been defined as "the power of directing command, the power of restraining" (Oxford, 1996: 291) and is consistently proposed in the literature as a key factor in relation to understanding individual privacy concerns. Personal control is important as it relates to the interest of individuals to control or significantly influence the handling of personal data (Clarke, 1988). Practitioner reports confirm the importance that individuals attribute to being able to control their personal information particularly in relation to the use of Internet-based systems. For example a 1999 Louis Harris poll indicated that 70% of online users felt uncomfortable disclosing personal information while a 2003 Harris poll of 1010 adults also found that 69% of those surveyed described their ability to control the collection of personal information as being 'exceptionally important'. Statistics like these indicate the increasing concern of individuals regarding the violation of their privacy and their desire to be able to control their personal information.

Interestingly, while individuals' sensitivity to control of private information is an issue of increasing concern, the truth regarding the extent of control over that personal information is often misunderstood, particularly amongst the Internet-using public. This is confirmed by a 2005 study by the Annenberg Public Policy Centre which discovered that 47% of the 1500 adults surveyed falsely believed they were able to control personal information distributed about them online simply because they had the right to view data collated by the on-line vendor, while a further 50% falsely believed they could control the depth of information contained on them by having the ability to edit information as and when they saw fit (Turow *et al.,* 2005). The value of such practitioner reports lies in the acknowledgement that individuals yearn to become empowered decision makers relating to the level of control they maintain over their sensitive information, thus providing a basis for future research from a rigour and relevance perspective.

This issue of control and privacy may not always be as clear cut as it at first seems however. In fact it can be argued that not every loss or gain or control necessarily constitutes a loss or gain of privacy (Parker, 1974). For example a user of an Internet-based technology who voluntarily provides personal information in the course of their interaction may not necessarily view this as a loss of control and consequently a loss of privacy. Even if the knowledge that each of their computer-based interactions leaves behind a detailed trail of information regarding who they are, their behaviour and habits and other potentially sensitive information about themselves – it may not necessarily constitute a lack of control or loss of privacy in their eyes. Once again it becomes apparent that the definition and scope of privacy is dependent upon the situation or event in question as well as attitudes and perceptions of those involved.

There is a general consensus that the advent of the information age has made the art of communication significantly easier. However, as previously noted, the influx and increased adoption of technology has also made it significantly easier for third parties to intercept and collate communications by others (Ghosh, 1998). In fact the adoption of the Internet for both business and recreational purposes simply fuels the privacy debate as the potential for individuals to gain unauthorised access to electronic networks poses as a significant threat (Laudon and Laudon, 2002). The increasing pervasiveness of technologies into our working lives has opened up a spectrum of unregulated behaviour whereby previously accepted distinctions regarding correct and immoral behaviour are no longer always clear (Turban, 2006). Researchers such as Safire (2002) note how extreme pervasive surveillance tends to result in a 'creepy feeling' among those being monitored despite the fact that they may have done nothing wrong to merit such scrutiny. In some cases individuals may be conscious that they are being monitored, they are just not sure of the extent and detail of that monitoring. Neither are they aware of how that collated information is being used by the monitoring body. As such it is clear that there are two distinct issues relating to surveillance – one relating to the actual act of monitoring or surveillance itself, the second relating to how the collated information can be used.

While it is clear that the exponential growth of Internet-based technologies has changed the scope and indeed the capabilities of such practices it is important to note that many of these monitoring techniques have a long established presence in the offline world also. One of the earliest known examples relates to an observation unit designed to house prison inmates by English philosopher Jeremy Bentham in the 18th century. The unit was designed to allow an observer to observe undetected so that prison inmates were seamlessly individualised, were made constantly visible, were always seen but could never see themselves (Foucault, 1977). In this way they were a constant source of information but subsequently unable to communicate in the existing relationship. The basic principals of this observation system played on the fundamental vulnerability of human nature, turning visibility into a trap and ensuring that a covert presence held the power.

Examples of modern day computer-mediated surveillance techniques rely heavily on these basic principles. Clarke (1988) coined the term dataveillance to describe the systematic monitoring of the actions or communications of individuals. Modern technologies provide the opportunity for constant observation and continuous data collection ensuring that surveillance is employed through an individual not over them. In fact, the monitoring of employees' computer-related interactions has previously been described as an 'electronic whip' used unfairly by management (Tavani, 2004). In this way employees are now facing an electronic form of panopticism whereby they can be observed by an electronic supervisor who never leaves the office (Wen *et al.*, 2007).

THE EMPLOYER PERSPECTIVE

The rapid growth of the Internet has been matched by an explosion in the use of email and Internet for business use in the workplace environment. In fact email is very much a fundamental part of the communication structure of many organisations today. While the speed and productivity benefits of email are immense from an organisational perspective, the placing of stringent controls by management on the use of email systems may also jeopardise an employee's privacy. For example a recent study carried out by AMA (2005) found that as many as 55% of US firms not only retain but review an employee's email messages, a figure which has risen 8% since 2001. Managements' ability to monitor employee actions also stretches to use of the Internet within the workplace. AMA (2005) further revealed that 76% of organisations monitor an employee's Internet usage, 65% of which are blocking access to particular websites highlighting Web surfing as a primary concern for many organisations. It is now estimated that as many as 80% of organisations monitor employee activities in the workplace – a figure which has doubled since 1997 (AMA, 2001; D'Urso, 2006).

Despite the fact that management are entitled to monitor employee behaviour primarily for 'business-related reasons' a recent study carried out by McParland and Connolly (2009) found that only 45% of employees surveyed knew their actions could be monitored by management while in the workplace. From this, only 22% believed that their actions were monitored on a regular – such as daily or weekly – basis. Interestingly however a significant number of respondents indicated a strong degree of privacy concerns in relation to managements' ability to monitor their email interactions in the workplace, despite the fact that many were unsure of whether or not such activities actually occurred. For example 35% were concerned that employers could log into and record their personal emails, 42% were concerned that they could access their emails without their knowledge and 45% were concerned with how management would or could use information obtained from their personal emails. Employees indicated a stronger level of concern regarding the monitoring of personal emails they receive (32%) as opposed to those they send themselves from their work email account (12%) confirming the notion that control is an important aspect in relation to privacy issues.

The concept and art of surveillance is based on the notion that one is 'under watch' or being observed in some way. However based on the fundamental principles of the 'Hawthorne Effect' it is reasonable to assume that if one is aware they are under observation they may alter their actions according. For example McParland and Connolly (2009) found that 84% of employees surveyed were careful about the type of information they would send in an email while in the

workplace with only 32% sending a personal email if they thought their employer could not see them. Furthermore 57% sent emails from their own personal (Yahoo, Gmail) account in order to prevent management from tracking their behaviour with only 54% of the overall sample accepting managements' right to monitor staff email interactions in the workplace.

While it is apparent that employees often alter or modify their behaviour in response to management monitoring activities, it is important to note that the use of such techniques may result in other more worrying outcomes. For example many workers experience high degrees of stress because their activities and interactions can be monitored by employers (Tavani, 2004). Once again based on the fundamental principles of panopticism the question can be raised as to whether it is the presence of the 'invisible supervisor' that generates or in part fuels this distress. Ironically however, it is the computer-based information worker whose work is dependent upon the use of computer systems that is often the one most subjected to this form of monitoring. In a study carried out by McParland and Connolly (2009) it was found that many individuals felt extremely uncomfortable being under watch by management expressing explicit concerns, questioning how the information collated is used and in some instances even translating it into a failing performance or lack of ability on their behalf. This obvious negative impact that such surveillance techniques have on employee morale is a serious issue and one which must be addressed. In fact the use of electronic surveillance in the workplace has been compared to that of a work environment tantamount to an 'electronic sweatshop' in some instances (Tavani, 2004).

Workplace surveillance clearly raises many ethical and social issues. However in order to adequately address many of these issues we must first consider the motivations behind managements decision to employ monitoring technologies in the first place.

SURVEILLANCE: MANAGEMENTS MOTIVATION

While many reports emphasis the risks faced by the employee, it is reasonable to assume that in some instances management may have legitimate reasons to monitor their employee's actions. For example profit driven organisations aim to manage their business in an efficient and productive manner and as such it may be unreasonable to expect that such companies would not avail of methods or employ technologies to ensure that their employees are completing the job they are being paid to do. Furthermore and perhaps more notably, organisations continually face the risk of adverse publicity resulting from offensive or explicit material circulating within the company and as such many employ monitoring technologies to protect themselves from costly litigation claims (Laudon and Laudon, 2001). The Internet has increased the possible threat of hostile work environment claims by providing access to inappropriate jokes or images that can be transmitted internally or externally at the click of a button (Lane, 2003). In fact, a study carried out in 2000 concluded that 70% of the traffic on pornographic Websites occurs during office hours, with ComScore networks reporting 37% of such visits actually taking place in the office environment (Alder *et al.,* 2006).

Moreover, the risks to organisations stretch also to the abuse of the email system, with virtually all the respondents in an AMA (2003) survey reporting some sort of disruption resulting from employee's email use. For example, 33% of the respondents experienced a computer virus, 34% reporting business interruptions and 38% of which had a computer system disabled for some time as the result of a bogus email. In a similar vein, Jackson *et al.,* (2001) conducted a study to investigate the cost management endure as a result of such email interruption. The study indicated that it took the average employee between 1 and 44 seconds to respond to a new email when the icon or pop up box appeared on their screen. 70% of these mails were reacted to within 6 seconds of them appearing and a further 15% were reacted to within a 2 minute time period. Overall the study found that it took on average 64 seconds for an employee to return to a productive state of work for every one new mail sent. Other practitioner reports also identify the potential cost of email usage with as many as 76% reporting a loss of business time due to email problems, 24% of which estimating a significant two day loss of company time (AMA, 2003). These statistics are not so surprising given the amount of time the average employee spends online. The survey further reported that the average employee spends 25% of his or her working day solely on their emails, with a further 90% admitting to sending and receiving personal mails during company time.

Whilst the need to improve productivity is a common rationale for employee monitoring, other motivations such as minimising theft and preventing workplace litigation can be considered equally justifiable in the eyes of management seeking to protect the interests of the organisation. The former motivation is particularly understandable as research shows that employees stole over 15 billion dollars in inventory from their employers in the year 2001 alone (Lane, 2003). In addition, the seamless integration of technology into the workplace has increased the threat of internal attacks with Lane (2003) noting the ease at which sensitive corporate data and trade secrets can be downloaded, transmitted, copied or posted onto a Web page by an aggrieved employee. Internal attacks typically target specific exploitable information, causing significant amounts of damage to an organisation (IBM, 2006). Management need to ensure that their employees use their working time productively and are therefore benefiting the organisation as a whole (Nord *et al.,* 2006). It is apparent however, that tensions will remain constant between both parties unless some form of harmony or balance between the interests of both the employer and employee is achieved.

In order to balance this conflict of interests however it is vital that clearly defined rules and disciplinary offences are implemented into the workplace (Craver, 2006). The need for structure becomes all the more apparent when one considers the differing views and tolerance levels certain managers may hold (Selmi, 2006). For example, if an employee is hired to work, then technically they should refrain from sending personal emails or shopping online during working hours. However, as a general rule, most management will overlook these misdemeanours as good practice or in order to boost worker morale. The situation becomes more serious however when the abuse of Internet privileges threatens to affect the company itself, be it through loss of profits or adverse publicity for the company. Furthermore, the problem increases as boundaries in the modern workplace begin to blur and confusion between formal and informal working conditions arise (Evans, 2007). For example by allowing an employee to take a company laptop into the privacy of their own home, management could be sending out a message that the computer can be used for personal use which may lead to the employee storing personal data on management's property. Legally, the employer would have claims over all of the data stored on the computer and could use it to discipline or even terminate an employee. In fact it is this apparent lack of natural limit in regards what is acceptable or indeed unacceptable relating to workplace privacy which makes the task of defining appropriate principles all the more difficult to comprehend (Godfrey, 2001).

AN ETHICAL PARADOX: ORGANISATIONAL JUSTICE, TRUST, AND RISK

The recent surge in the use of communication monitoring technologies within the computer-mediated work environment has further brought the issues of justice and fairness centre stage in the literature. In fact justice and fairness are often cited as key drivers in managing the ethical and privacy concerns of employees who are subjected to monitoring practices within the computer-mediated work environment (Stanton, 2000a and 2000b; Zweig and Webster, 2002). Organisational justice is an overarching term used to describe individuals' perceptions of what is fair and just within the workplace. For researchers such as Stanton (2000b) justice theories thus provide researchers with a solid framework to help predict the perceived fairness of specific organisational procedures, outcomes and actions.

Justice perceptions for the main are separated into three specific forms notably

1. Procedural justice,
2. Distributive justice, and
3. Interactional justice.

The first of these antecedents, procedural justice centres around an individuals' perception that the organisational decision-making process will produce fair and just outcomes (Barrett-Howard and Tyler, 1986; Stanton, 2000b and Hauenstein *et al.*, 2001). In this way, procedural justice act as a critical factor for understanding the relations between the supervisors' social power and the employees' subsequent reactions to it whereby they perceive positive outcomes in a more favourable light (Mossholder *et al.*, 1998). Distributive justice refers to the distribution of outcomes, measuring the extent to which employees feel recognised and therefore appropriately rewarded for their efforts within the workplace (Stanton, 2000b; Cohen-Charash and Spector, 2001 and Hauenstein *et al.*, 2001). In this way management are required to treat employees who are similar in respect to a certain outcome in the same manner, as opposed to basing decisions on arbitrary characteristics (Daft, 2000). According to Cohen-Charash and Spector (2001) if a distributive injustice is perceived, it will affect an employee's emotions, cognitions and their overall behaviour. The final facet of organisational justice, interactional justice stems from the interpersonal communications of the workplace, examining the quality of the interpersonal treatment employees experience at the hands of the company power- holders (Bies and Moag, 1986; Cohen-Charash and Spector, 2001). More specifically it examines the extent to which employees' believe they have been treated with dignity, sincerity and respect during the distribution of outcomes as well as the process undertaken to achieve them by company decision-makers (Stanton, 2000b; Helne, 2005). Consequently if an employee perceives interpersonal injustice they are more likely to act negatively towards their direct supervisor as opposed to the organisation or the injustice in question (Cohen-Charash and Spector, 2001).

Organisational justice theories have been linked to research on performance monitoring – specifically electronic performance monitoring [EPM] in the literature (Stanton & Barnes-Farrell, 1991; Stanton, 2000a; Stanton, 2000b). EPM differs from traditional (non-electronic) forms of monitoring in that it can be carried out on a continuous, large scale basis recording multiple dimensions of a single workers performance (Stanton, 2000a). The ubiquitous nature of these monitoring technologies contributes to the employees' ethical concerns relating to loss of personal privacy in the workplace.

Trust and risk perceptions also play an important role in the issue of workplace surveillance. For example studies on trust – in particular relating to trust in leaders - are becoming increasingly prominent in the literature. Mayer *et al.* (1995) for example developed a model which suggested that integrity, benevolence and ability were major factors which had the potential to affect an individual's perception of trustworthiness in a leader. Similarly a study carried out by Robinson and Rousseau (1994) found that as many as 55% of respondents reported a reduced level of trust in an employer as a result of management violating a psychological contract with them. The seamless integration of communication-monitoring technologies into the workplace can influence an employee's perception of the risks they face working in the computer-mediated environment. Therefore it is conceivable that an employees' attitude towards the technology will act as an important determinant in the implementation process of communication-monitoring technologies into the workplace.

Furthermore it is apparent that risk perceptions can affect how an individual makes specific decisions, subsequently influencing their behaviour. In fact studies show that when an employee is aware they are under surveillance, they modify their behaviour accordingly. For example, a recent study carried out by SHRM in 2005 found that as many as 75% of employees display a certain degree of caution in relation to what they write in emails due to possible monitoring by the organisation. Similarly the study showed that 47% are equally cautious in relation to telephone conversations while in the workplace environment. Studies show however that the degree of risk perceived by an individual can be reduced if trust exists in a particular situation (So and Sculli, 2002). In this way the significance of trust within studies on risk perception cannot be understated. In fact an individuals' need to trust often relates directly to the risks involved in a given situation and consequently the pervasive nature of communication-monitoring practices within the computer-mediated organisation hold risks that are unique to that context (Mayer *et al.*, 1995). In order for trust to be engendered however, employees must feel confident that the boundaries between what is acceptable and unacceptable in relation to information monitoring are clearly and openly stated. Those companies that are successful at building that trust and managing the uncertainty associated with communication monitoring practices will benefit from increased employee confidence.

It is becoming increasingly apparent that there is a significant disparity between management and employee perspectives on the issue of workplace surveillance. The uncertainty and lack of control related to the use of these communication monitoring technologies in the workplace reflects the significant asymmetry that exists in terms of what they mean to management versus the employee. While it is apparent that technology has created better, faster and cheaper ways for individuals to satisfy their own needs, the capability to leverage this technology is far higher for companies than for the employee. Because unequal forces, leading to asymmetric information availability, tilt the playing field significantly in favour of industry, such technologies do not create market benefit to all parties in an equitable manner (Prakhaber, 2000). As such one of the major tasks facing the computer-mediated organisation is that of identifying the factors to improve employees' attitudes and behavioural reactions towards surveillance in the workplace. There is a distinct need for clear measures to be implemented, that govern the effective and fair use of communication technologies in the workplace allowing management to monitor their staff in a reasonable and rational manner. Management should consider the ethical and social impacts that surveillance techniques may have within the workplace and employ specific policies which may both minimise the negative implications associated with the use of such technology as well as helping to improve employee receptiveness overall.

A CODE OF ETHICS FOR WORKPLACE SURVEILLANCE

Organisations looking for ways in which to balance this conflict of interest between management and employees are focusing towards the use of workplace policies, many of which are framed on established or predefined codes of ethics. For example Marx and Sherizen (1991) argue that employees should be made aware in advance of any monitoring practices conducted in the workplace before it actually occurs. In this way the individual can electively decide whether or not he or she wishes to work for that particular organisation. Furthermore the authors suggest that the employee should have the right to both view information collated on them and challenge inaccurate information before it can be used against them. This idea of 'transparency' in relation to surveillance methods is commonly supported by privacy advocates however it can be argued that it goes against fundamental principles of the act of surveillance. Similarly we can once again note the impact of the 'Hawthorne Effect' in that individuals will alter their behaviour if they believe they are being observed in some way. In this way management need to have clearly defined sanctions in place within the organisation informing employees of the depth and detail of monitoring practices in the company whilst deterring them from abusing workplace systems.

Other ethical strategies focus solely on how management use the information collated on employees in the workplace. Again we can note that the scope of surveillance is generally divided into two main components - one relating to the actual act of monitoring or surveillance itself, the second relating to how the collated information can be used. In some cases it is reasonable to assume that employees may not fear the act of surveillance but more so how the information could be used and whether or not employers will make subsequent judgements about them (Introna, 2001). For example, McParland and Connolly (2009) found that 33% of employees they surveyed were concerned that their employers would react negatively to their use of personal email in the workplace however 24% still thought it was reasonable to use work email to chat freely with their friends and colleagues. Once again the lines regarding what are acceptable or indeed unacceptable forms of behaviour begin to blur.

In order to alleviate much of this confusion other researchers such as Turban *et al.,* (2010) apply the basic ethical principles to information collected in an online environment. It is apparent however that these basic ethical principals can also be applied to the use of communication-monitoring technologies in the workplace environment thus providing a solid framework to guide management in their efforts to monitor employees in a fair and effective manner. The basic principals include the following;

1. **Notice or Awareness:** Employees should be made aware of the extent and detail of monitoring techniques, prior to the collection or use of personal information.

2. **Choice or Consent:** Employees should be made aware of how the collated information can be used and consent must be granted by the employee by signing a workplace policy or notification which outlines the companies monitoring practices.

3. **Access or Participation:** Employees should be able to access certain information on them and challenge the validity of the data.

4. **Integration or Security:** Employees should be assured that their personal information is kept secure within the organisation and cannot be used in a way which was not intended.

5. **Enforcement or Redress:** Employees must be made aware of organisational sanctions set in place such that a misuse of workplace systems will be detected and punished by management. Otherwise there is no deterrent or indeed enforceability to protect privacy issues.

Effective workplace policies need to protect the interests of all parties involved. A code needs to be developed that protects the interests of both the employee and the employer. Little progress can be made in this area however unless the current privacy legislation is addressed.

LEGAL PROTECTIONS: THE ROLE OF PRIVACY LEGISLATION

Privacy legislation differs considerably between Europe and the United States. While both Europe and the United States define privacy in a similar way, it is the fundamental objective of their information privacy laws that signifies the major difference between the two. For example in Europe privacy protection is considerably stronger than in the United States as it focuses on controlling and regulating managements' collection and use of employee data. While the European Directive is based on the Fair Information Doctrine of the United States it extends the level of control an individual can exercise over their own personal information (Laudon & Traver, 2010). In this way European law lends itself more to the protection of data – and therefore the individual – compared to the United States which focuses more on the use and collection of data. Any country that is a member state of the European Union [EU] must comply with the legislation that is passed by any one of its major institutions as well as any national laws or regulations set in place. Furthermore, under the Directive 95/46/EC and Article 29 WP55 all monitoring in the organisation must pass a number of specified criteria before being implemented into the workplace.

Under current EU legislation, the employer must prove that electronic observation is a necessary course of action for a specific purpose before engaging in it. In this way, management are encouraged to consider traditional and less intrusive measures of observation before resorting to electronic means (Directive 95/46/EC). For the purpose of Internet or indeed email surveillance, it is likely that some form of electronic monitoring would be enlisted, however in such instances the employer by law can only keep the data in question no longer than necessary for the specific monitoring action. In a similar vein, the second principal of finality denotes that any data collected, must be used for an explicit purpose and therefore cannot be processed or used for any other purpose than initially intended (Directive 95/46/EC).

Under EU law, management must also be clear and open regarding the surveillance practices of the organisation and are therefore obliged to provide employees with information regarding organisational monitoring policies. In this way employees are advised of improper procedures and disciplinary offences that justify the scope of invasive monitoring techniques (Directive 95/46/EC). Furthermore details of the surveillance measures undertaken are also provided so as the employee will know who is monitoring them, how they are being monitored as well as when these actions are taking place. This principal of transparency also provides individuals with access rights to personal data processed or collated by management, allowing them to request its rectification or deletion where appropriate (Directive 95/46/EC).

The fourth criterion, legitimacy is similar to that of necessity in so far as data can only be obtained for a justifiable purpose and must not contravene an employee's fundamental or inherent right to privacy. Under this element of the legislation however, data of a very sensitive nature can be deemed too personal to collect and collection therefore must be specifically authorised by a national law in extreme circumstances (Directive 95/46/EC). Organisations must also comply with the notion of proportionality, using the most non-intrusive or least excessive action in order to obtain the desired information. For example the monitoring of emails should if possible focus on the general information such as the time and transmission as opposed to the content if the situation permits. If however viewing of the email content is deemed necessary then the law presides that the privacy of those outside of the organisation should also be taken into account and that reasonable efforts be made to inform the outside world of any monitoring practices (Directive 95/46/EC).

Any data that is collated on an employee must only be retained for as long as is necessary under this European law and data that is no lon-

ger needed should then be deleted. Management should specify a particular retention period based on their business needs so as employees are constantly aware of the ongoing process (Directive 95/46/EC). Furthermore, provisions should be set in place to ensure that any data that is held by the employer will remain secure and safe from any form of intrusion or disturbance. The employer is also required to protect the technological medium from the threat of virus as a further means of protecting the personal data (Directive 95/46/EC).

It is apparent that the central concept of the European Directive relates to the processing and flow of information (Elgesem, 1999). As a result researchers such as Evans (2007) note how the existence of these European laws that favour the employee are consequently putting considerable pressure on the United States to adopt similar laws. In fact it has been previously suggested that the various proposals and directives – or at least the relevant aspects of them – should be combined into one robust comprehensive model (Tavani, 2004). While such a model combining the interests of both the organisation and the employee would appear to be a sensible solution however for Wang, Lee and Wang (1998) it poses 'one of the most challenging public policy issues of the information age'.

CONCLUSION

The primary objective of this chapter was to address the issue of electronic monitoring of employees in the computer-mediated work environment. The use of Internet-based technologies in the workplace presents businesses and employees with opportunities to engage in behaviours for which comprehensive understandings or rules have not yet been established. While it is apparent that management may have legitimate reasons to monitor employees' actions in the workplace, the privacy rights of the employee cannot be ignored. In this way it is paramount that some form of harmony or balance between the interests of the employer and the employee is achieved if the psychological contract is to remain intact.

This chapter explored the ethical impact of monitoring in the computer-mediated work environment, addressing whether employer ability to monitor employee actions in workplace represents good business practice or constitutes an invasion of privacy. Although there is increasing evidence that workplace surveillance is on the rise, the factors influencing management to electively employ monitoring technologies remains ambiguous. Furthermore the lines regarding what are correct and moral forms of behaviour continually blur thus limiting our overall understanding of the main issues involved as well as the ways in which to target them. As a result, our understanding of these issues, and the ways in which employee privacy concerns can be more effectively addressed, thus positively influencing productivity and morale, remains a matter of speculation and a fruitful avenue for future research.

REFERENCES

Acquisti, A. (2002). Protecting privacy with economic: Economic incentives for preventive technologies in ubiquitous computing environment. In *Proceedings of Workshop on Socially-Informed Design of Privacy-Enhancing Solutions in Ubiquitous Computing*. Ubicomp.

Alder, G. S., Noel, T. W., & Ambrose, M. L. (2006). Clarifying the effects of internet monitoring on job attitudes: The mediating role of employee trust. *Information & Management*, *43*(7), 894–903. doi:10.1016/j.im.2006.08.008

Barrett-Howard, E., & Tyler, T. R. (1986). Procedural justice as a criterion in allocation decisions. *Journal of Personality and Social Psychology*, *50*(2), 296–304. doi:10.1037/0022-3514.50.2.296 PMID:3746613

Bies, R. J., & Moag, J. F. (1986). Interactional justice: Communication criteria of fairness. *Research on Negotiations in Organisations*, *1*, 43–55.

Clarke, R. A. (1988). Information technology and dataveillance. *Communications of the ACM*, *31*(5), 498–512. doi:10.1145/42411.42413

Cohen-Charash, Y., & Spector, P. E. (2001). The role of justice in organizations: A meta-analysis. *Organizational Behavior and Human Decision Processes*, *86*(2), 278–321. doi:10.1006/obhd.2001.2958

Concise Oxford dictionary of current english. (1996). Oxford University Press.

Conway, N., & Briner, R. B. (2002). Full-time versus part-time employees: Understanding the links between work status, the psychological contract and attitudes. *Journal of Vocational Behavior*, *61*(2), 279–301. doi:10.1006/jvbe.2001.1857

Craver, C. B. (2006). Privacy issues affecting employers, employees and labour organizations. *Louisiana Law Review*, *66*, 1057–1078.

Cullinane, N., & Dundon, T. (2006). The psychological contract: A critical review. *International Journal of Management Reviews*, *8*(2), 113–129. doi:10.1111/j.1468-2370.2006.00123.x

D'Urso, S. C. (2006). Who's watching us at work? Toward a structural-perceptual model of electronic monitoring and surveillance in organisations. *Communication Theory*, *16*(3), 281–303. doi:10.1111/j.1468-2885.2006.00271.x

Daft, R. L. (2000). Management (5th ed.). The Dryden Press.

Directive 95/46/EC: Article 29 WP55. (2002). Retrieved November 14, 2014, from http://ec.europa.eu/justice_home/fsj/privacy/docs/wpdocs/2002/wpss_en.pdf

Elgesem, D. (1999). The structure of rights in directive 95/46/EC on the protection of individuals with regard to the processing of personal data and the free movement of such data. *Ethics and Information Technology, 1*(4), 283–293. doi:10.1023/A:1010076422893

Evans, L. (2007). Monitoring technology in the American workplace: Would adopting English privacy standards better balance employee privacy and productivity? *California Law Review, 95*, 1115–1149.

Foucault, M. (1977). *Discipline and punish: The birth of the prison*. Penguin Books.

Gakovic, A., & Tetrick, L. E. (2003). Psychological contract breach as a source of strain for employees. *Journal of Business and Psychology, 18*(2), 235–246. doi:10.1023/A:1027301232116

Ghosh, A. P. (1998). *E-commerce security – Weak links, best defences*. John Wiley and Sons, Inc.

Godfrey, B. (2001). *Electronic work monitoring: An ethical model*. Australian Computer Society.

Guest, D. (2004). The psychology of the employment relationship: An analysis based on the psychological contract. *Applied Psychology, 53*(4), 541–555. doi:10.1111/j.1464-0597.2004.00187.x

Harris Poll. (2003). *Harris interactive* [online]. Retrieved November 10, 2014, from http://www.harrisinteractive.com/harris_poll/index.asp?PID=365

Hauenstein, N. M. A., McGonigle, T., & Flinder, S. W. (2001). A meta-analysis of the relationship between procedural justice and distributive justice: Implications for justice research. *Employee Responsibilities and Rights Journal, 13*(1), 39–56. doi:10.1023/A:1014482124497

Helne, C. A. (2005). Predicting workplace deviance from the interaction between organizational justice and personality. *Journal of Managerial Issues, 17*(2), 247–263.

IBM. (2006). *Stopping insider attacks: How organizations can protect their sensitive information* [online]. Retrieved November 10, 2014, from http://www-935.ibm.com/services/us/imc/pdf/gsw00316-usen-00-insider-threats-wp.pdf

Introna, L. D. (1996). Privacy and the computer: Why we need privacy in the information society. *Ethicomp e-Journal, 1.*

Introna, L. D. (2001). Workplace surveillance, privacy and distributive justice. In Readings in CyberEthics. Sudbury, MA: Jones and Barlett Publishers.

Jackson, T., Dawson, R., & Wilson, D. (2001). *The cost of email interruption*. Loughborough University Institutional Repository: Item 2134/495 [online]. Retrieved November 10, 2014, from http://km.lboro.ac.uk/iii/pdf/JOSIT%202001.pdf

Kramer, M. L., Wayne, S. J., Liden, R. C., & Sparrowe, R. T. (2005). The role of job security in understanding the relationship between employee's perceptions of temporary workers and employee performance. *The Journal of Applied Psychology, 90*(2), 389–398. doi:10.1037/0021-9010.90.2.389 PMID:15769247

Lane, F. S. (2003). *The naked employee: How technology is compromising workplace privacy*. New York: AMACOM, American Management Association.

Laudon, K. C., & Laudon, J. P. (2001). *Essentials of management information systems: Organisation and technology in the networked enterprise* (4th ed.). Prentice Hall.

Laudon, K. C., & Laudon, J. P. (2002). *Management information systems: Managing the digital firm* (7th ed.). Prentice Hall International.

Laudon, K. C., & Traver, C. G. (2010). *E-commerce 2010 – Business, technology, society* (6th ed.). Boston: Pearson.

Lemire, L., & Rouillard, C. (2005). An empirical exploration of the psychological contract violation and individual behaviour. *Journal of Managerial Psychology, 20*(2), 150–163. doi:10.1108/02683940510579786

Lester, S. W., Claire, E., & Kickull, J. (2001). Psychological contracts in the 21st century: What employees values most and how well organizations are responding to these expectations. *Human Resource Planning, 24*, 10–21.

Louis Harris Poll. (1999). Available from http://www.natlconsumersleague.org/FNLSUM1.PDF

Marx, G., & Sherizen, S. (1991). Monitoring on the job: How to protect privacy as well as property. In Computers in the human context: Information technology, productivity, and people. Cambridge, MA: MIT Press.

Mayer, R. C., Davis, J. D., & Schoorman, F. D. (1995). An integrative model of organisational trust. *Academy of Management Review, 20*(3), 709–734.

McParland, C., & Connolly, R. (2009). *The role of dataveillance in the organsiation: Some emerging trends.* Paper presented at the Irish Academy of Management Conference, Galway, Ireland.

Morrison, E. W., & Robinson, S. (1997). When employees feel betrayed: A model of how psychological contract violation develops. *Academy of Management Review, 22*, 226–256.

Mossholder, K. W., Bennett, N., Kemery, E. R., & Wesolowski, M. A. (1998). Relationships between bases of power and work reactions: The mediational role of procedural justice. *Journal of Management, 24*(4), 533–552. doi:10.1016/S0149-2063(99)80072-5

Nord, G. D., McCubbins, T. F., & Horn Nord, J. (2006). Email monitoring in the workplace: Privacy, legislation, and surveillance software. *Communications of the ACM, 49*(8), 73–77.

Parker, R. B. (1974). A definition of privacy. *Rutgers Law Review, 27*(1), 275.

Prakhaber, P. R. (2000). Who owns the online consumer? *Journal of Consumer Marketing, 17*(2), 158–171. doi:10.1108/07363760010317213

Robinson, S. L., & Rousseau, D. M. (1994). Violating the psychological contract: Not the exception but the norm. *Journal of Organizational Behavior, 15*(3), 245–259. doi:10.1002/job.4030150306

Rousseau, D., & Tijoriwala, S. (1998). Assessing psychological contracts: Issues, alternatives and measures. *Journal of Organizational Behavior, 19*(S1), 679–696. doi:10.1002/(SICI)1099-1379(1998)19:1+<679::AID-JOB971>3.0.CO;2-N

Rust, R. T., Kannan, P. K., & Peng, N. (2002). The customer economics of internet privacy. *Journal of the Academy of Marketing Science, 30*(4), 455–464. doi:10.1177/009207002236917

Safire, W. (2002). The great unwatched. *New York Times.* Retrieved November 10, 2014, from http://query.nytimes.com/gst/fullpage.html?res=9A03E7DB1E3FF93BA25751C0A9649C8B63

Selmi, M. (2006). Privacy for the working class: Public work and private lives. *Louisiana Law Review, 66*, 1035–1056.

SHRM. (2005). *Workplace privacy – Poll findings: A study by the society for human resource management and careerjournal.com, January 2005.* Author.

So, M. W. C., & Sculli, D. (2002). The role of trust, quality, value and risk in conducting e-business. *Industrial Management & Data Systems, 102*(9), 503–512. doi:10.1108/02635570210450181

Stanton, J. M. (2000a). Reactions to employee performance monitoring: Framework, review, and research directions. *Human Performance, 13*(1), 85–113. doi:10.1207/S15327043HUP1301_4

Stanton, J. M. (2000b). Traditional and electronic monitoring from an organizational justice perspective. *Journal of Business and Psychology, 15*(1), 129–147. doi:10.1023/A:1007775020214

Stanton, J. M., & Barnes-Farrell, J. L. (1996). Effects of electronic performance-monitoring on personal control, satisfaction and performance. *The Journal of Applied Psychology, 81*(6), 738–745. doi:10.1037/0021-9010.81.6.738

AMA Survey. (2001). *Workplace monitoring and surveillance* [online]. Retrieved November 8, 2014, from http://www.amanet.org/research/pdfs/ems_short2001.pdf

AMA Survey. (2003). *Email rules, policies and practices survey* [online]. Retrieved November 10, 2014, from http://www.amanet.org/research/pdfs/email_policies_practices.pdf

AMA Survey. (2005). *Electronic monitoring and surveillance survey* [online]. Retrieved November 10, 2014, from http://www.amanet.org/research/pdfs/ems_summary05.pdf

Sutton, G., & Griffen, M. (2004). Integrating expectations, experiences and psychological contract violations: A longitudinal study of new professionals. *Journal of Occupational and Organizational Psychology, 77*(4), 493–514. doi:10.1348/0963179042596487

Tavani, H. T. (2004). *Ethics and technology: ethical issues in an age of information and communication technology* (International Edition). John Wiley and Sons.

Turban, E., King, D., Lee, J., Liang, T. P., & Turban, D. (2010). *Electronic commerce 2010: A managerial perspective* (6th ed.). Boston: Pearson.

Turban, E., Leidner, D., McClean, E., & Wetherbe, J. (2006). *Information technology for management – Transforming organisations in the digital economy* (5th ed.). John Wiley & Sons Inc.

Turow, J., Feldman, L., & Metlzer, K. (2005). *Open to exploitation: American shoppers online and offline*. A Report from the Annenberg Public Policy Centre of the University of Pennsylvania, June 2005.

Wang, H., Lee, M. K. O., & Wang, C. (1998). Consumer privacy concerns about internet marketing. *Communications of the ACM, 41*(3), 63–70. doi:10.1145/272287.272299

Wen, H. J., Schwieger, D., & Gershuny, P. (2007). Internet usage monitoring in the workplace: Its legal challenges and implementation strategies. *Information Systems Management, 24*(2), 185–196. doi:10.1080/10580530701221072

Zweig, D., & Webster, J. (2002). Where is the line between benign and invasive? An examination of psychological barriers to the acceptance of awareness monitoring system. *Journal of Organizational Behavior, 23*(5), 605–633. doi:10.1002/job.157

KEY TERMS AND DEFINITIONS

Distributive Justice: The perception of being adequately recognised and appropriately rewarded for efforts.

Informational Control: The right to have control over your personal information.

Interactional Justice: The perception that interactions with a third party such as an employer indicate sincerity and respect towards the employee.

Monitoring of Employees: Systematic observance of an employee over a period of time.

Pervasive Technologies: Widely adopted technologies.

Privacy: A state of being free from observance or disturbance.

Procedural Justice: The individuals' perception that the organisation's decision-making processes will be fair and just.

Psychological Contract: The relationship and expectations between an employer and employee regarding behaviour and treatment.

Workplace Surveillance: Close observation of someone or some action in the workplace.

Chapter 5

Social Engineering Techniques, Password Selection, and Health Care Legislation:
A Health Care Setting

B. Dawn Medlin
Appalachian State University, USA

Joseph A. Cazier
Appalachian State University, USA

ABSTRACT

Healthcare employees generally have access to view hospital patient's medical records. This access can be simply viewing their chart or reviewing information on a computer screen. With this type of accessibly, hospital employees have the opportunity to view diagnosis, personal medical histories, as well as demographic information such as age and gender. Social engineers can use methods such as familiarity with co-workers for instance to obtain this information from unsuspecting health care workers. In addition, weak password selection can provide opportunities for a wealth of information to be stolen. In this chapter, current security legislation that addresses the security of patient's health care records, social engineering tactics, and passwords are explored.

INTRODUCTION

There are many threats to the privacy of a patient's information, and one of the largest threats is social engineers or the act of social engineering. Social engineering is generally defined to include the use of trickery, personal relationships and trust to obtain information; more specifically, it is the art of deceiving people into giving confidential, private or privileged information or access to a hacker (Gragg, 2007).

Another threat to the privacy of security of patient's information can be the employees themselves. Internal employees actually can pose the largest threat to the security and privacy of information as they can exploit the trust of their

DOI: 10.4018/978-1-4666-7381-6.ch005

co-workers, and they generally are the individuals who have or have had authorized access to the health care organization's network. As well, they are generally familiar with the internal policies and procedures of the organization. Additionally, internal employees can exploit that knowledge to facilitate attacks and even collude with external attackers (http://www.cert.org/insider_threat/).

A patient's personal information, such as address, phone number, and social security number, are all items that may be included and accessible to some or all healthcare employees. PHR (Personal Health Care Records) are available to many who neither touch nor need access to patient's health care information. With the accessibility and sheer volume of patient's data and information patients may be even more vulnerable to security breaches. If the information is not easily accessible, hackers and social engineers have been very successful in founding ways to circumvent networked health data systems by simply asking for the information or by finding weaknesses within the system (Medin & Cazier, 2007).

Due to the number or increase to either losing or sharing information or the severity of these issues, HITECH or the Health Information Technology for Economic and Clinical Health Act of 2009 was enacted. Under Title XIII, HIPPA appears to remain the law that is most discussed in relation to privacy and security within the health care industry. One of the core aspects and a basic goal of the Health Insurance Portability and Accountability Act of 1996 (HIPAA) is to provide more electronic medical information. HIPAA addresses security and privacy measures, either directly or indirectly, in the standards related to management processes, user education and training, and access control (http://www.hhs.gov/news/facts/privacy.html). HIPAA regulations were enacted to protect the privacy and security of patients and their medical records; simply put, they make it illegal for unauthorized personnel to access or release information from someone's medical records.

Despite its legal requirements, however, HIPAA standards have been known to be difficult to implement and are not always followed. As required by HIPAA, healthcare institutions are required to provide security methods in order to protect patient's information. One such method is through the authentication of the individual requesting access. Healthcare employees are generally subjected to some type of authentication process. Although there are different ways of authenticating employees, most systems are based on the use of a physical token (something one has), secret knowledge (something one knows) or biometrics (something one is) (Burnett & Kleiman, 2006).

Due to increased regulations and the increased opportunities for exploitation that exist in today's digital world, it is even more important for healthcare providers to keep healthcare records and the information held within, safe and private. Governmental agencies have adopted initiatives that specifically address the issues and rights of healthcare patients. More specifically, the security and privacy of healthcare information is protected by the Health Insurance Portability and Accountability Act (HIPAA), requiring healthcare agencies to do everything possible to protect their information.

In addition to the various security measures discussed above, it is important for security managers and personnel to be familiar with the psychological weapons and motivations behind social engineering and its malicious use. Hasan, Prajapati and Vohara illustrate how social engineers will take advantage of human's innate tendency to trust and be helpful (Hasan et al, 2010). Many social engineers will play to the emotions of the victim by impersonating a staff member who has forgotten a password, thus imploring the victim to help someone in need (Hasan et al, 2010). According to Maan and Sharma there are multiple different types of social engineering (Maan et al, 2012).

These can include both human-based attacks as well as computer-based attacks. Human-based attacks typically play to the victim's sympathies through telephone communications, in which no face to face interaction is needed, and convincing the victim to allow them access because of a forgotten password (Hasan et al, 2012). Computer-based attacks are more technologically minded. An attacker can employ a phishing attack through falsified email messages that lure victims to a seemingly trustworthy site where they will be willing to input sensitive information as well as a pop-up window attack in which the social engineer will send pop-up windows resembling trusted services that require a username and password (Hasan et al, 2012).

BACKGROUND

With the availability of information comes the opportunity for more fraudulent activity such as social engineering attacks. According to Christopher Hadnagy in his book (2010), "social engineering is the art or better yet, science, of skillfully maneuvering human beings to take action in some aspect of their lives," (Hadnagy, 2010, p. 10). For many social engineers the process of obtaining meaningful information may lead to the insight of the organization's security policy, the countermeasures the organization has put in place and specifics relating to personnel and their level of security privilege.

If a social engineer is attempting to find out about one particular patient, they may target that person's medical health record. A patient's medical record may include gender, race, family history, sexual history including types of birth control, sexual activity and treatment, any history or diagnosis of substance abuse, and diagnosis of mental illness. Other medical information, such as HIV status, may also be included. The accessibility of this confidential information may open the door to various forms of discrimination. For instance,

chronic diseases such as HIV and AIDS may result in an increase in insurance rates or even denial of coverage, due to the extensive medical treatment usually needed by these patients. Individuals may even be ostracized or stigmatized because of their disease type. Patients expect the information contained in their records to remain secure and private, to be seen only by those individuals whose access is medically or administratively necessary.

Unfortunately, patient's medical records are being provided in public information and very easily accessed when a breach occurs. Table 1 represents some of the current security breaches that are occurring within the medical community.

As noted in Table 1, thousands of health care records and information is being made very public, and sometimes through simple carelessness or through the use of social engineering techniques or by asking simple questions. These examples also show that basic security policies are being ignored when dealing with non-technology related data points. Numbers of security breaches are growing as more and more medical records are going online and becoming accessible to both patients, health care providers and third party vendors.

Healthcare organizations as well as their employees must be made well aware of those factors related to password choice that may compromise medical records and information. Essentially, employees and the systems within healthcare organizations are the gatekeepers of accessibility.

Using a password as the only type of authentication into a system can offer to employees the ability to quickly enter into a system, but human practices such as using the same password on different systems and writing down a password may degrade the quality of password security (Pfleeger and Pfleeger, 2007). For healthcare organizations the password functions like the key to a lock, anyone who has it can get in to see the patient's information. Toward that end, there have been recommendations from governmental agencies to hospitals on how to construct a password. One of the first guidelines in creating good passwords

Table 1. List of recent hospital security breaches

Date	Organization	Event	Records Affected
2014	L.A. Care Health Plan	A processing error on the L.A. Care Health Plan payment website allowed some members to see the demographic information of other members (http://www.usatoday.com/story/tech/2014/02/27/california-data-breaches-hit-213-million-accounts/5868191/)	213 million accounts
2013	South Carolina Department of Health and Human Services Columbia South Carolina	Former Medicaid employee Christopher Lykes transferred to his personal Yahoo account 17 Excel spreadsheets. These spreadsheets contained social security numbers and other personal information. (http://healthitsecurity.com/2013/07/23/healthcare-data-breaches-reviewing-the-ramifications/).	230,000 patients
2012	Utah Department of Health Salt Lake City, Utah	The default network password was not changed on a network server creating a weak password policy. Protected information, including social security numbers, was exposed. (http://healthitsecurity.com/2013/07/23/healthcare-data-breaches-reviewing-the-ramifications).	780,000 patients
2012	Emory Health Care Atlanta, Georgia	Ten backup disks containing patient information, over 17 years, were lost from a storage facility. Two-thirds of the disks contained patient social-security numbers, names, and dates of surgery, diagnoses, medical procedures, and related doctors (http://healthitsecurity.com/2013/07/23/healthcare-data-breaches-reviewing-the-ramifications/)	315,000 patients

was published in 1985 by the Department of Defense and is still relevant today (http://www.alw.nih.gov/Security/FIRST/papers/password/dodpwman.txt). Their guidelines recommended the following:

1. Passwords must be memorized;
2. Passwords must be at least six characters long,
3. Passwords must be replaced periodically, and
4. Passwords must contain a mixture of letters (both upper- and lowercase), numbers, and punctuation characters.

Most networks administrators and security experts would concur with all of the above Department of Defense recommendations, however, that was in 1985 when the advice was given and when social engineering as well as other types of attacks were not as common as they are today.

According to CERT (the Computer Emergency Response Team), the advice to use upper and lower case alpha characters for Novell and/or VMS systems is useless since both of these systems are case insensitive.

Strong password guidelines must be a part of the educational system of health care employees as required by HIPPA. Strong passwords versus weak passwords should have at least eight characters. In addition, they will use the entire keyboard to create a string of characters. However, note that it is insufficient to merely exchange some words for letters; for example, software designed to hack programs will automatically check ampersands for "and" and the number 2 for "to."

Training and guidelines to health care employees is essential to remind employees of the importance of the security of medical records and information, but at the end of the day, these employees are simply human. Therefore, many of the deficiencies of password authentication systems arise from the limitations of human cognitive ability (Pond et al., 2000). If humans were not required to remember a password, a maximally secure password would be one with maximum length that could consist of a string of numbers, character, and symbols, and would make it very difficult for others to guess or remember. In fact, the requirements to remember long and complicated passwords are contrary to the way the human memory functions. First, the capacity of human memory in its capacity to remember a sequence of items is temporally limited, with a short-term capacity of around seven items plus or minus two (Kanaley, R., 2001). Second, when humans remember a sequence of items, those items cannot be drawn from an arbitrary and unfamiliar rang, but must be familiar 'chunks' such as words or familiar symbols. Third, the human memory thrives on redundancy.

In fact, studies have shown that individuals' short term memory will retain a password for approximately 30 seconds thereby requiring individuals to attempt to immediately memorize their passwords. It has also been shown that if an individual is interrupted before they fully memorize the password; it will fall out of their working memory and most likely be lost.

Also, if an individual is in a hurry when the system demands a new password, individuals must sacrifice either the concentration of the critical task at hand or the recollection of the new password. Related to this issue is having to create the content for this new quickly demanded password. The pressure to choose creative and secure passwords quickly generally results in individuals failing in their attempt to memorize this new password. For healthcare organizations this can result in reset rates at one per reset per every four to five users per month (Brostoff and Sasse, 2001).

In order to combat the issue of having to remember so many different passwords some users have resorted to the selecting familiar terms such as a pet or family name, their own name, their phone number, or other common terms that could be found in a dictionary. British psychologist Helen Petrie, Ph.D., a professor of human/computer interaction at City University in London analyzed the passwords of 1,200 British office workers who participated in a survey funded by CentralNic, an Internet domain-name company in 2001. She found that most individuals' passwords fell into one of four distinct password categories which were family, fan, fantasists, and cryptic.

The first category of "family," comprised nearly half of the respondents. These individuals selected their own name, the name of a child, partner or pet, birth date, or significant number such as a social security number. Further, Dr. Petrie found that individuals also choose passwords that symbolized people or events with emotional value or ties.

One third of the survey participants were identified as "fans," using the names of athletes, singers, movie stars, fictional characters, or sports teams. Dr. Petrie also found that these individuals wanted to align themselves with the lifestyle represented by or surrounded around a celebrity status. Two of the most popular names were Madonna and Homer Simpson.

Fantasists made up eleven percent of survey responses. Dr. Petrie found that their passwords were comprised of sexual terms or topics. Some examples included in this category were terms such as "sexy," "stud" and "goddess." The final ten percent of participants were identified as "cryptics." These users were seemingly the most security-conscious, but it should also be noted that they were also the smallest of all of the four identified categories. These individuals selected unintelligible passwords that included a random string of letters, numerals, and symbols such as Jxa+157.

Self-created computer passwords are generally personal, and they reflect the personalities of millions of people as they attempt to summarize their life through a few taps on the keyboard. As psychologists know, people and personalities are often very predictable in the aggregate, as may be their choices of passwords. Psychologists have found that humans can store only five to nine random bits of information in their short-term memory (Andrews, 2004), making it difficult to remember long and complicated passwords. Therefore, users have often chosen passwords with personal meanings that they can associate with something in their long-term memory.

Most social engineers rely on employees to unknowingly help them attack company networks and systems by simply answering a series of simple questions. Today, most healthcare agencies have intrusion detection/prevention systems such as firewalls that can be used to alert organizations in the event of a security breach, but these systems cannot prevent employees from inadvertently sharing information with others. Therefore, the question still remains, "how much information might an employee provide to a stranger or to a co-worker?"

Additionally, social engineers can obtain information from the employee by pretending to innocently ask questions about hobbies, family members and pets, or the employee's birth location, and can then assume the legitimate employee's identity. Next, they are able to gain access to all of the information that the employee is authorized to view. It is therefore imperative that employees be taught about the need for strong passwords and the tactics of social engineers.

It is important for security managers and personnel to be familiar with the psychological weapons and motivations behind social engineering and its malicious use. Hasan, Prajapati and Vohara illustrate how social engineers will take advantage of human's innate tendency to trust and be helpful (Hasan *et al*, 2010). Many social engineers will play to the emotions of the victim by impersonating a staff member who has forgotten a password, thus imploring the victim to help someone in need (Hasan *et al*, 2010). According to Maan and Sharma there are multiple different types of social engineering (Maan *et al*, 2012). These can include both human-based attacks as well as computer-based

attacks. Human-based attacks typically play to the victim's sympathies through telephone communications, in which no face to face interaction is needed, and convincing the victim to allow them access because of a forgotten password (Hasan *et al*, 2012). Computer-based attacks are more technologically minded. An attacker can employ a phishing attack through falsified email messages that lure victims to a seemingly trustworthy site where they will be willing to input sensitive information as well as a pop-up window attack in which the social engineer will send pop-up windows resembling trusted services that require a username and password (Hasan *et al*, 2012).

RESEARCH METHODOLOGY

Instrument

To simulate a real social engineering attack and to obtain a fair statistical representation of the security in relation to healthcare organizations, a survey was administered to employees of five hospitals. These hospitals consisted of varying sizes and were in different regions of the state. Hospital administration approval was obtained before administering the instrument, but the administration did not endorse the survey to respondents, nor did they ask them to participate.

Data was gathered to not only determine how many employees would disclose their passwords and other personal information such as their address, phone number and email, but also simulated the types of information individuals were willing to share with co-workers, colleagues, or friends of colleagues. The information that employees were willing to share, including their passwords and other personal information, would certainly make it easier to hack into a system instead of having to "guess" at the necessary authentication information.

Data Collection

The data set was comprised of 118 responses, with respondents working in small rural areas with approximately 5,000 people, to larger, more urban populations of 500,000. Fifty-three of the respondents filled out entry forms for a drawing, and thus provided the researchers with additional personal and identifiable information.

Analysis and Results

Interestingly, the findings noted in Table 2 indicate that most respondents were often required to use a password to access systems, but rarely changed their passwords or where required to change their passwords. The requirement of "not" being forced to change passwords by system policies or systems further allows for individuals to choose weak passwords. As further indicated, most of the respondents used the same password on multiple accounts. The practice of rarely changing passwords and/or using the same password for multiple accounts would assist social engineers, thus allowing them to easily attain access to one system and possibly more.

Analyzing the results related to employees' other password practices listed in Table 3 found that eighty-nine percent (89%) were allowed to choose their own passwords, with the average password being about seven characters in length. In addition, only sixteen percent (16%) of the employees included special characters, adding to the problem of less than secure passwords.

Most interesting, of the 118 respondents, seventy-three percent (73%) of the employees shared their passwords with a co-worker or the friend of a co-worker through this survey instrument. It should be noted that one of the largest threats is that of the internal employee and again, the confidentiality of the password. Internal employees can also act as social engineers to gain access to additional resources.

As seen in Table 4, half of the respondents created passwords consisting of family names, including their own name or nickname, the name of a child, or significant other. It is obvious that a very small percentage of employees are using most of the best practices recommended by governmental, educational, and private organizations.

Table 2. Survey question results

Variable Name	Question	Answers	N	Mean	Std. Dev.
Pass_Freq	How often do you use a password to access systems?	1 = Very Often 5 = Never	118	1.23	0.59
Pass_Change	How often do you change your passwords?	1 = Very Often 5 = Never	117	2.85	1.13
Reuse	Most people use the same password on multiple accounts. How often do you do this?	1 = Very Often 5 = Never	118	2.47	1.32
Choose_Pass	On average, do you choose your own password or have one assigned?	1 = Choose Own 0 = Assigned	117	0.89	0.32
Characters	How many characters are in your most commonly used password?	1 = 1-3, 2 = 4, 3 = 5, 4 = 6, 5 = 7, 6 = 8, 7 = 9, 8 = 10+	116	5.03	1.71
Numbers	Do your passwords contain any numbers?	1 = Yes, 0 = No	117	0.87	0.34
Special_Char	Do your passwords have any special characters in them (@, #, %, &, etc)	1 = Yes, 0 = No	118	0.16	0.37
Password	Please tell us your password	1 = Shared 0 = Did Not Share	118	0.73	0.45

Table 3. Password statistics

Variable Name	Question	Answers	N	Mean	Std. Dev.
Pass_Freq	How often do you use a password to access systems?	1 = Very Often 5 = Never	118	1.23	0.59
Pass_Change	How often do you change your passwords?	1 = Very Often 5 = Never	117	2.85	1.13
Reuse	Most people use the same password on multiple accounts. How often do you do this?	1 = Very Often 5 = Never	118	2.47	1.32
Choose_Pass	On average, do you choose your own password or have one assigned?	1 = Choose Own 0 = Assigned	117	0.89	0.32
Characters	How many characters are in your most commonly used password?	1 = 1-3, 2 = 4, 3 = 5, 4 = 6, 5 = 7, 6 = 8, 7 = 9, 8 = 10+	116	5.03	1.71
Numbers	Do your passwords contain any numbers?	1 = Yes, 0 = No	117	0.87	0.34
Special_Char	Do your passwords have any special characters in them (@, #, %, &, etc)	1 = Yes, 0 = No	118	0.16	0.37
Password	Please tell us your password	1 = Shared 0 = Did Not Share	118	0.73	0.45

Table 4. Password categories

Variable Name	Question	Answers	N	Mean	Std. Dev.
Family	Does your password fit into this category?	1 = Yes, 0 = No	118	0.50	0.50
Cryptic	Does your password fit into this category?	1 = Yes, 0 = No	118	0.05	0.22
Number	Does your password fit into this category?	1 = Yes, 0 = No	118	0.45	0.50
Fan	Does your password fit into this category?	1 = Yes, 0 = No	118	0.15	0.95
Faith	Does your password fit into this category?	1 = Yes, 0 = No	118	0.03	0.18
School	Does your password fit into this category?	1 = Yes, 0 = No	118	0.02	0.13
Fantasy	Does your password fit into this category?	1 = Yes, 0 = No	118	0.00	0.00
Place	Does your password fit into this category?	1 = Yes, 0 = No	118	0.14	0.34
Other	Does your password fit into this category?	1 = Yes, 0 = No	118	0.51	0.50

Table 5. Employees willing to share or not share passwords

	Shared Password			Did Not Share Password			Difference	
	N	Mean	Std. Dev.	N	Mean	Std. Dev.	Mean Dif.	Sig.
Pass_Freq	86	1.14	0.41	32	1.47	0.88	-0.33	0.01
Pass_Change	85	2.69	1.09	32	3.28	1.14	-0.59	0.01
Reuse	86	2.48	1.26	32	2.44	1.50	0.04	0.89
Pass_Train	84	0.51	0.50	31	0.61	0.50	0.10	0.34
Awar_Train	83	0.53	0.50	30	0.70	0.47	0.17	0.11
Current_Train	85	4.13	1.09	30	3.97	1.07	0.16	0.48
Choose_Pass	85	0.93	0.26	32	0.78	0.42	-0.15	0.02
Family	86	0.58	0.50	32	0.28	0.46	0.30	0.00
Cryptic	86	0.05	0.21	32	0.06	0.25	-0.02	0.73
Number	86	0.50	0.50	32	0.31	0.47	0.19	0.07
Fan	86	0.20	1.10	32	0.03	0.18	0.17	0.40
Faith	86	0.02	0.15	32	0.06	0.25	-0.04	0.30
School	86	0.01	0.11	32	0.03	0.18	-0.02	0.47
Fantasy	86	0.00	0.00	32	0.00	0.00	0.00	NA
Place	86	0.14	0.35	32	0.13	0.34	0.01	0.84
Other	86	0.55	0.50	32	0.41	0.50	0.14	0.18
Characters	86	5.26	1.62	30	4.37	1.81	0.89	0.01
Numbers	86	0.91	0.29	31	0.77	0.43	0.13	0.06
Special_Char	86	0.20	0.40	32	0.06	0.25	0.14	0.08

The category of "other," with forty-five percent (45%) of the respondents indicated that their passwords included a number. The choice to integrate a number is important, but just as important is the placement of that number and whether or not the number relates to meaningful and informative information such as a phone number or birth date.

Fifteen percent (15%) of the respondents self-reported the inclusion of "fan-based" words, which could include names of athletes, singers, movie stars, and fictional characters or sports teams. "Place" was the next highest category, with fourteen percent (14%), using another identifiable piece of information such as the city where the employee works or lives.

The smallest of all of the self-identified password categories was "fantasy," followed closely by the categories of school and faith. Five percent (5%) of the employees selected the "cryptic" category, suggesting that these employees are security-conscious since that category includes passwords that are unintelligible or include a random string of letters, numbers, and symbols. Unfortunately, as noted earlier, is it also the smallest of all of the eight self-reported categories.

A T-test was conducted to show see if there were significant differences between those that shared their password versus those that did not share their password in relation to the categories established by Petri and others. Those that used family as a part of their password were also more willing to share their password (see Table 5). A significant difference was found between those who shared their passwords in comparison to those who did not in relation to how often they changed their passwords.

Several findings were significant. Sixty-three percent of those who included family as a part of their passwords were willing to share it. Employees who included numbers in their passwords were willing to share their passwords at a rate of 50%; this seems counter intuitive, as one would assume that employees who have created stronger passwords by including numbers would be less likely to share their passwords. Employees who were more security conscious with the inclusion of a special character were not as willing to share it.

DISCUSSION

This study reveals several interesting findings. As noted earlier, most employees used the same passwords on multiple accounts, even though they frequently changed them. The actions of repeatedly using the same password are contrary to suggested recommendations by most security experts, because a hacker who can gain access to one account could more easily access other systems. Requiring individuals to maintain a new password for each system or application would obviously make systems more secure, but is in conflict with humans' short-term human memory capabilities. Employees may consider it necessary to include familiar names, places, and numbers in their passwords so that they can easily recall them.

Though most employees indicated that their employers offered password security training either very often or often, it appears that either the types of training very not very effective or that the employees did not take it very seriously. As noted in Table 4 and on the positive side of good password practices, those employees offered password training were significantly more likely to NOT use a dictionary word as their password and were more likely to have a password that was at least 6 characters in length. On the negative side, however, those same employees were just as willing to share their passwords even after

receiving the training as those that had not received training, suggesting that today's training is deficient in some way.

Other interesting findings emerged in relation to sharing or not sharing passwords. Employees who changed their password frequently were also more likely to share it. This action is contradictory in the fact that employees on one hand appear to be very security conscious while changing their password often and at the same time feeling secure enough to share it with others. Perhaps they were less concerned about sharing it because they thought it would be changed soon and so they perceived less risk.

In comparison, those individuals who were assigned passwords were less likely to share them, which may be a question of remembrance, where they don't share it because they don't remember it. Another possibility may be that if assigned a password, they considered it more sensitive and not to be shared. It may also be that those that are assigned passwords treat them with more respect due to the care the organization gives in giving it to them.

Also, those respondents who had longer passwords were more likely to share them, giving credence to the idea that, because most individuals do not retain information for more than 30 seconds, they would not remember a long password even if told to them by another. Whether or not this is the case, it is inconsistency that on one hand the employee has the awareness of good security practices to create a long password, but on the other hand offers it freely to others.

FUTURE TRENDS

The current standard of using a password where end-user's must remember and create a long string of characters, numbers, and symbols as a form of validating a user's identity may finally be replaced according to DARPA with a new program called Active Authentication (http://www.darpa.mil/Our_Work/I2O/Programs/Active_Authentication.aspx). This new program uses software-based biometrics and is moving away from hardware requirements. New aspects include features such as intrinsic behavioral or physical traits.

Smart cards may also be used as these operate with a chip that includes stored memory, and an operating system. A patient's entire clinical history is stored on the smart card which can only be accessed via reading devices in a physician's office, primary care center, hospital, or other medical institution. Through the use of this device, exposed paper records will not be a concern. An added benefit of smart cards is the ability for users to electronically forward patient information to other health care authorities and insurers. Specifically, Java-based card technology emerges as a leading platform because of its ability to support multiple health care applications securely, while incorporating biometrics for positive identification and authentication.

HIPAA calls for a tiered approach to data access in which staff members only have access to the information they require to perform their jobs. Biometrics makes possible such a tiered approach, while eliminating the security breaches that result from shared passwords or lost badges. Biometric applications are being used more often than ten years ago, due to decreasing cost, increasing accuracy, emerging technology, public acceptance, and stricter compliance regulations. Newer biometrics, for instance can capture a way a person walks or their gait can provide information about the individual.

CONCLUSION

As existing technological trends advance and new technology enters the marketplace, it is important to remember that both the employee and the patient must always be vigilant in protecting the information within the patient's record and on healthcare agency networks. Computerized systems and security methods cannot prevent individuals from talking or providing information to the shrewd, cunning and calculating social engineer.

The simulation that was carried out during this study demonstrated that many employees may currently be in violation of HIPAA and HITECH regulations due to their willingness to share their information and their practice of creating weak passwords, thus allowing for easy access into a system. Hospitals and other healthcare agencies must identify ways to educate employees regarding HIPAA and HITECH regulations to protect patients and prevent penalties for sharing or misusing information.

Within the area of health care systems, simply using the password method of authentication may be inefficient, and it is an absolutely essential element of a typical security model to address the types of authentication that may be most efficient. It is the process of confirming the identification of a user (or in some cases, a machine) that is trying to log on or access resources. There are a number of different authentication mechanisms, but all serve this same purpose, to stop intruders or those not authorized to have access. The question of what type of authentication may be different for each health care agency, but as seen through this study it is imperative that organizations address the important topics of passwords and techniques used by social engineers.

REFERENCES

Active Authentication. (n.d.). Retrieved March 12, 2014, from http://www.darpa.mil/Our_Work/I2O/Programs/Active_Authentication.aspx

Analytics, I. D. (2007). *Data breach harm analysis from ID analytics uncovers new patterns of misuse arising from breaches of identity data*. Retrieved November 12, 2009, from http://www.idanalytics.com/news_and_events/20071107.html

Andrews, L. W. (2004). *Passwords reveal your personality*. Retrieved March 13, 2007, from http://cms.psychologytoday.com/articles/pto-20020101-000006.html

Brostoff, S., & Sasse, M. A. (2001). *Safe and sound: A safety-critical approach to security*. Paper presented at the New Security Paradigms Workshop 2001, Cloudcroft, NM. doi:10.1145/508176.508178

Burnett, M., & Kleiman, D. (2006). *Perfect passwords, selection, protection, authentication*. Syngress.

CERT. (2009). *Insider threat research*. Retrieved December 1, 2009 from http://www.cert.org/insider_threat

Data Breaches. (n.d.). *A source of chronic pain*. Retrieved August 15, 2013 from http://www.experian.com/blogs/data-breach/2013/05/01/medical-data-breaches-a-source-of-chronic-pain

Department of Defense. (1985). *Password management guideline*. Retrieved September 3, 2004, from http://www.alw.nih.gov/Security/FIRST/papers/password/dodpwman.txt

Emory Health Care. (n.d.). Retrieved August 4, 2013 from http://healthitsecurity.com/2013/07/23/healthcare-data-breaches-reviewing-the-ramifications/

Experian: A World of Insight. (n.d.). *Data breach resolution*. Retrieved August 13, 2013 from http://www.experian.com/blogs/data-breach/2013/05/01/medical-data-breaches-a-source-of-chronic-pain%E2%80%8E

Gostin, L. O. (2000). *Public health law: Power, duty, restraint*. Berkeley, CA: University of California Press.

Gragg, D. (2007). *A multi-level defense against social engineering*. SANS. Retrieved July 1, 2009, from http://www.sans.org/reading_room/whitepapers/engineering/920.php

Hasan, M., Prajapati, N., & Vohara, S. (2010). Case study on social engineering techniques for persuasion. *GRAPH-HOC*, *2*(2), 17–23. doi:10.5121/jgraphoc.2010.2202

Intelegen, Inc. (2008). *Human memory*. Retrieved December 1, 2009, from http://brain.web-us.com/memory/human_memory.htm

Kanaley, R. (2001). Login error trouble keeping track of all your sign-ons? Here's a place to keep your electronic keys, but you better remember the password. *San Jose Mercury News*, p. 3G.

Kleyman, B. (2013). *Healthcare data breaches: Reviewing the ramifications*. Retrieved August 13, 2013, from http://healthitsecurity.com/2013/07/23/healthcare-data-breaches-reviewing-the-ramifications/

Laio, K. H., & Chueh, H. E. (2012). An evaluation model of information security management of medical staff. *International Journal of Innovation*, *8*(11), 7865–7873.

Mann, P. S., & Sharma, M. (2012). Social engineering: A partial technical attack. *International Journal of Computer Science Issues*, *9*(2), 557–559.

Medlin, B. D., & Cazier, J. A. (2007). An empirical investigation: Health care employee passwords and their crack times in relationship to HIPAA security standards. *International Journal of Healthcare Information Systems and Informatics*, *2*(3), 39–48. doi:10.4018/jhisi.2007070104

Mickle, M. (2012). *Top ten security breaches in 2012*. Retrieved July 21, 2013, from http://www.healthcarefinancenews.com/news/top-10-data-security-breaches-2012

Nixon Peabody. (2009). *Health law alert*. Retrieved November 15, 2009, from http://www.nixonpeabody.com/publications_detail3.asp?ID=2621

Paquette, A., Painter, F., & Jackson, J. L. (2011). Management and risk assessment of wireless medical devices in the hospital. *Biomedical Instrumentation & Technology*, *45*(3), 243–248. doi:10.2345/0899-8205-45.3.243 PMID:21639775

Pfleeger, C. P., & Pfleeger, S. L. (2007). *Security in computing* (4th ed.). Prentice Hall.

Pond, R., Podd, J., Bunnell, J., & Henderson, R. (2000). Word association computer passwords: The effect of formulation techniques on recall and guessing rates. *Computers & Security*, *19*(7), 645–656. doi:10.1016/S0167-4048(00)07023-1

Simpson, R. L. (2002). Chicago. *Nursing Management*, *33*(12), 46–48. doi:10.1097/00006247-200212000-00017 PMID:12488639

South Carolina Department of Health and Human Services. (n.d.). Retrieved August 5, 2013, from http://healthitsecurity.com/2013/07/23/health-care-data-breaches-reviewing-the-ramifications/

Stanford Hospital. (n.d.). Retrieved August 3, 2013, from http://www.nytimes.com/2011/09/09/us/09breach.html?pagewanted=all&_r=0

Thompson, S. T. (2006). Helping the hacker? Library information, security, and social engineering. *Information Technology and Libraries*, *25*(4), 222–226.

Thornburgh, T. (2004). Social engineering: The dark art. In *Proceedings of the 1st Annual Conference on Information Security Curriculum Development*. Kennesaw State University.

Ur, B., Kelley, P. G., Komanduri, S., Lee, J., Maass, M., & Mazurek, M. L. … Shay, L.F. (n.d.). *How does your password measure up? The effect of strength meters on password creation*. Carnegie Mellon University. Retrieved March 2, 2014, from https://www.ece.cmu.edu/~lbauer/papers/2012/usenix2012-meters.pdf

US Department of Health and Human Services. (2009). *Protecting the privacy of patients' health information*. Retrieved November 12, 2009, from http://www.hhs.gov/news/facts/privacy.html

Utah Department of Health. (n.d.). Retrieved August 2, 2013, from http://healthitsecurity.com/2013/07/23/healthcare-data-breaches-reviewing-the-ramifications/

Utimaco. (2009). *Health IT data breaches: No harm, no foul*. Retrieved November 12, 2009, from http://compliance.utimaco.com/na/tag/hitech-act

Welcome to AWPHD: Keeping Quality Care Local. (2013). Retrieved August 20, 2013, from http://www.awphd.org/presentations/.../Model%20Password%20Policy.doc

Werner, S., & Hoover, C. (2012). *Cognitive approaches to password memorability – The possible role of story-based passwords*. Retrieved March 2, 2014, from http://pro.sagepub.com/content/56/1/1243

KEY TERMS AND DEFINITIONS

Biometrics: A marker of someone's identity based on tangible and observable physical characteristics.

Computer-Based Attack: An attack on a system using and targeting primarily technologies directly.

Hacker: Someone with the skill and ability to modify a part of a system to use it in ways not originally intended, such as gaining unauthorized access and information.

HIPPA: The Health Insurance Portability and Accountability Act; a Federal law regulating health information privacy.

HITECH: The Health Information Technology for Economic and Clinical Health Act is another Federal law regulating health information sharing, security, and privacy.

Human-Based Attack: An attack on a system using and targeting primarily humans as a way to get to through the technology to the information they desire.

Password: A secret word known only to the individual and computer systems created proven a person's identity and grant them access to a system.

Social Engineering: The art and science of manipulating people and processes to get what an attacker wants.

APPENDIX: CONDENSED SURVEY

Gender: [ ] Male [ ] Female Place of Birth: _____

  Favorite TV Show: _____ Favorite Movie: _____

  Favorite Sport and Team: _____

  Favorite Singer/Band: _____ Favorite Song: _____

  Favorite Type of Pet: _____ Pet Name(s): _____

  Do you have kids: [ ] Yes [ ] No

  Please list the first names of the one (or two) most important person (or people) in your life:

_____

  To help with our research study, please tell us a little about your organizations security

  How often do you use a password to access systems?

  [1] Very Often [2] Often [3] Occasionally [4] Not Often [5] Never

  How often do you change your passwords?

  [1] Very Often [2] Often [3] Occasionally [4] Not Often [5] Never

  Most people use the same password on multiple accounts. How often do you do this?

  [1] Very Often [2] Often [3] Occasionally [4] Not Often [5] Never

  Does your employer offer password security training? [1] Yes [0] No

  Does your employer offer any other security awareness training? [1] Yes [0] No

  When was the last time you participated in either a password or another security awareness training program?

  [1] Last week [2] Last month [3] Last 6 months [4] Last Year [5] Never

  On average, do you choose your own password or have one assigned?

  [1] Choose Own [0] Assigned

  Most passwords fall into the following categories, please mark if yours fits in any of these (select all that apply) Family, Fan, Fantasy, Cryptic, Faith, Place, Numbers, School, Other

  How many characters are in your most commonly used password?

  [1] 1-3 [2] 4 [3] 5 [4] 6 [5] 7 [6] 8 [7] 9 [8] 10+

  Do your passwords contain any numbers? [1] Yes [0] No

  Do your passwords have any special characters in them (@, #, %, &, etc) [1] Yes [0] No

  In order to facilitate creation of solid data, we would appreciate if you would provide one of your passwords. This information will be held in the strictest of confidence, and will be used only to generate a number that describes the characteristics of your password and then destroyed.

  My Home/Work/Both password is: _____

  Comments:

Section 2
Identity Protection

Chapter 6
Play That Funky Password!
Recent Advances in Authentication with Music

Marcia Gibson
University of Bedfordshire, UK

Marc Conrad
University of Bedfordshire, UK

Karen Renaud
University of Glasgow, UK

Carsten Maple
University of Warwick, UK

ABSTRACT

Over the last few years, there has been emerging interest in authenticating users through the medium of music. Historically, developers of alternate modality systems have focused on image- and haptic-based techniques, instinctively shying away from music. This might be due to the inherently temporal nature of the listening task and the belief that this would be impractical and frustrating for users. In this chapter, the authors discuss and present new research in this field that, to the contrary, indicates that the "enjoyability factor" means users may be more willing to spend additional time authenticating with music than they would with other techniques. Although undeniably not the optimal solution in time-critical contexts, for many other pursuits music-based authentication could feasibly replace passwords, easing the number of secure strings the average user is expected to remember. Music may also offer a better solution for those suffering memory or cognitive impairments. This chapter incorporates discussion on recent advances in the field of authentication research within the context of a changing threat landscape. A prototype musical password system is presented and a summary of results from online user testing and a lab-based controlled experiment are presented which further reinforce the importance of accounting for "enjoyability" in the assessment of recognition-based authentication schemes.

1. INTRODUCTION

The most widely employed method of establishing an individual's eligibility to access an online file, site or service is to test their knowledge of a secret key: the familiar alphanumeric password. The level of security passwords offer against brute-force and dictionary attacks theoretically depends upon the degree of informational entropy (Shannon, 1948) they contain. However, it is widely acknowledged that passwords constructed of random letters, digits, and special characters are difficult to recall

DOI: 10.4018/978-1-4666-7381-6.ch006

(Yan, Blackwell, Anderson, and Grant, 2004). For this reason, naïvely selected passwords are often derived from meaningful objects (Brostoff and Sasse, 2000), or will contain predictable patterns. These passwords offer reduced entropy, although they assist in imprinting (Paivio, 1983) the password to memory.

Organizations often impose password construction policies. This seems a fitting strategy given that the rationale for password use is usually to protect assets. However, these policies usually revert a password to its prior arbitrary and unmemorable format. When faced with onerous password policies, users cope by writing passwords down or sharing one password over numerous accounts; therefore a policy intended to enhance security will often weaken it in practice (Inglesant and Sasse, 2010).

These issues become exacerbated on the web. This may emerge from the absence of security cultures which could be fostered in other settings (Johnson and Goetz, 2007), large numbers of sites requiring registration for trivial purposes (Renaud and De Angeli, 2009), user's perceptions of the economic costs involved in adhering to policy as greater than the costs of not following it (Herley, 2009), difficulties in visualizing online threats (Gaw and Felten, 2006) and because many websites are accessed infrequently; whereas the neural pathways through which memories are accessed deteriorate without frequent use (Sapolsky, 2005).

Another emerging issue is that web content is increasingly accessed via smartphones and tablets. Researchers at the Georgia Institute of Technology estimate that by the end of 2014 there will be more mobile devices on the planet than people (GTISC, 2013). Even though many of our online activities require authentication, using a password on these devices can be difficult or inconvenient due to their typically small screens and soft keyboards. Add to this the seemingly upward trend in frequency and scale of online password database breaches (and subsequent leaks) in recent years, and it is

clear there is a very real problem where passwords are concerned. On the other hand, most if not all of these mobile devices have *audio* capabilities.

The aim of this chapter is to incorporate discussion on recent advances in the field of sound-based authentication research within the context of the changing threat landscape. We will detail one approach: the musical password, which aims to address the weaknesses of the alphanumeric scheme while remaining suitable for inclusion in online environments. A prototype system, "Musipass" will be presented and a summary of results from user testing online, and in a lab-based controlled environment, will be presented. Later in the chapter, implementation issues will be explored and opportunities for future research identified.

2. BACKGROUND

There are two reasons that we forget; either the information no longer exists ("trace-dependent forgetting"); or it exists, but cannot be retrieved ("cue-dependent forgetting") (Tulving, 1974). Trace-dependent forgetting happens when an item is not imprinted strongly enough, if the item has not been successfully consolidated or has become corrupted by other memory items ("interference"). Cue-dependent forgetting occurs when a retrieval trigger ("cue") is not associated with the item.

It is difficult to generate a cue for a random password and cues cannot usually be provided to the user during authentication, as it cannot be ascertained whether the user is a friend or a foe. When John in accounts creates the password "Fluffy" based on his pet's name or writes passwords down, what he is really trying to do is provide himself with a cue as insurance against forgetting. So, what happens when John has three pets, Fluffy, Lois and Ruff? In this case interference may be experienced, where John is able to recall numerous passwords, but not the precise one to access the system in question. When an individual reuses a password over numerous accounts he or she is effectually limiting the effort required to generate and memorize the password, as well as reducing the possibility interference will occur.

Passwords must be recalled precisely and entered correctly without feedback (i.e. they are obfuscated to prevent observation). This makes passwords more difficult to enter, especially for users with cognitive, physical or other impairments who often experience usability issues on the web more severely than others (Petrie and Keir, 2007). These problems are exacerbated when a user is entering the password via a smartphone or tablet. This is due to the relative smaller size of keys incorporated and because soft keyboards lack the tactile feedback which normally assists users in distinguishing keys during entry (Clarkson et al., 2005; Lee and Zhai, 2009). In normal text entry tasks, to overcome these difficulties, such devices often make use of predictive dictionary matching to correct spelling and auto-complete words. However, it is not advisable to ease the password entry task using these techniques. The secret nature of passwords requires they should not appear in such dictionaries as this would lead to the dictionary itself becoming a new target for compromise (Jakobsson and Akavipat, 2012).

For these reasons, on many devices, users can opt to receive feedback when entering passwords. Here, password letters are displayed during entry. This may be a suitable solution for recovering from errors in environments where the user can be sure their interaction is not being observed, but still does not make passwords any faster or less error-prone to input.

There are also a wide range of cognitive factors that can impact an individual's ability to remember and input passwords: Dyslexic users often spell words unpredictably, dyspraxic users experience difficulties sequencing, users may have developmental or language difficulties (Schmidt, Kölbl, Wagner, and Strassmeier, 2004), elderly users often have difficulties retaining newly learned information (Small, Stern, Tang, and Mayeux,

1999) and some have poor reading skills (Schmidt, et al., 2004) or are unfamiliar with the designated alphabet script (Mendori, Kubouchi, Okada and Shimizu, 2002).

Mnemonic passwords have been proposed as one possible solution. These are constructed by transforming an obscure but easily remembered phrase, replacing some letters with numbers or symbols to increase entropy. Yan et al. (2004) found these superior in terms of memorability and security, to weak passwords. A standard password cracking dictionary was used in the experiment and it has been noted that in reality an attacker may opt to use a specialized mnemonic dictionary, bringing the practical applicability of the findings into question. Kuo, Romanosky and Cranor, (2006) found many of the phrases were well-known, suggesting that the construction of a mnemonic dictionary might be trivial.

The ease of use mnemonic passwords offer is unclear. Forget et al. (2007) found that six of sixteen subjects misunderstood how to create one. Participants in Yan et al.'s study may have understood what was required to use the mnemonic technique; however this may not always be the case in a real-world setting. Mnemonic passwords do not solve the problem of interference, as multiple mnemonics must be memorized. They also do not increase accessibility, because they still must be entered correctly while obfuscated.

Another group who disproportionately suffer the negative effects of passwords are novice users. Novices are less successful at using passwords safely than average or expert users, deviating from recommended secure password practices (such as, not re-using passwords over unrelated accounts and writing them down), more frequently than other groups (Hoonakker et al., 2009). However, novices also report increased fear of privacy violation and fraud as a result of their use of online services compared to more experienced users (Featherman and Pavlou, 2003). It seems unlikely therefore that this group simply do not take the security of their passwords seriously.

Instead it is more likely they misunderstand the password composition and management rules or are already stretched with the overall learning process involved in early web use, finding the additional password related procedures enough to overload them altogether.

3. ALTERNATIVE APPROACHES

There are other approaches that aim to resolve the issues outlined above. In the main, these include:

- **Hardware-Based Solutions:** This category includes biometrics and tokens. However the outlay cost (Florencio and Herley, 2007) and lack of installation and operating knowledge (Coventry, De Angeli and Johnson, 2003) can be prohibitive, especially in online environments. Some biometric scanners have difficulties capturing due to environmental factors such as humidity or when the user is unwell or injured. An example of the latter being people who work with their hands having thin ridges or none at all on their fingertips trying to use fingerprint readers to authenticate.
- **Visual Passwords:** Where the usual alphanumeric alphabet is replaced with images. Depending upon implementation, while forming a password the user will:
  - Select images from a larger challenge set ("Recognition-based").
  - Select coordinates within an image ("Location-based").
  - Draw a picture or create a path of actions in a visual environment ("Path-based").

The idea is based on the "Picture superiority effect" (Paivio and Csapo, 1973) which describes our tendency to be able to remember images more accurately than semantic or syntactic memories, although alphabets must be chosen carefully to avoid predictable passwords being selected (Davis, Monrose, and Reiter, 2004; Thorpe and van Oorschot, 2007). They can be prone to observation (Wiedenbeck, Waters, Sobrado, and Birget, 2006) and reliance on the visual channel alone impacts accessibility.

4. MUSICAL PASSWORDS

Sound could potentially form the basis for a very large password alphabet. People enjoy listening to music (Renflow and Gosling 2003) and perhaps uniquely of the proposed modalities it has a physio-emotional effect upon many; who report feeling intense chills when an especially pleasurable composition is heard (Nusbaum and Silvia, 2010). We are naturally predisposed to process music and this is triggered during everyday exposures (Bigand and Poulin-Charronnat, 2006).

Scherer and Zentner (2001) point out music often accompanies emotionally charged events, such as weddings and funerals. If this is correct, musical pieces could act as very efficacious memory cues. Secondly, music is processed at a lower level of the brain than other semantic memories, increasing resistance to interference (LeDoux, 1992). Observability may be less problematic than in visual schemes because earphones can be used to shield sounds from being overheard, at least by the casual observer.

4.1 Related Work

Liddell, Renaud and De Angeli (2003) asked users to listen to music and then choose an associated picture to authenticate. In reality, users concentrated on the pictures alone, considering the listening phase to be too time-consuming. Liddell et al. used students as participants, most of whom were young with few memory difficulties. On the contrary, older users are plagued by memory problems and more willing to accept some inconvenience in return for increased memorability. Renaud and Ramsay (2007) found that older users were not concerned about the time-consuming nature of a visual scheme they tested, their memory difficulties made the memorability of the mechanism far more important than how long it took to authenticate.

Wobbrock (2009) discussed a system called "TapSongs" which was designed for use in systems where there is no keyboard or screen. A single button is used to tap a rhythm in time with a tune as it is listened to. Each tune consists of 6-8 notes played on a piano and is an opening line from a well-known composition. Examples include: "Isty-bitsy spider", "Old Macdonald" and "London Bridge". TapSongs utilized earphones to guard against observation attacks. A small sample ($n = 10$) of participants were asked to set up and authenticate twenty-five times in a row using TapSongs. An 83% log in success rate was observed. In addition, vulnerability of TapSongs to observation attacks was tested. Subjects were asked to aurally and visually eavesdrop from 3 feet away while the experimenters tapped along to one of 15 tunes. The attackers did not know the name of the tunes the experimenter was tapping along to, so they could not "play" them along in their heads whilst listening to the tapping. More importantly, they could not hear the tunes playing from the earphones. This made the task of memorising the rhythm very difficult. No other security analysis of the technique has been carried out.

Biddle et al. (2011) created "ObPwd". In this scheme, users selected a digital object or objects from their storage device (e.g. documents, email messages, images, music or videos). A hash value was computed from the chosen file(s) and translated into a password string which was then passed to web-based log in forms. The system was trialed by 32 participants and showed to provide excellent memorability. Ninety percent of participants were able to authenticate using the system within three attempts and over ninety percent were able to authenticate on their first

attempt after a period of 7-10 days. Not all of the objects selected were based on music and there was no breakdown in the analysis to cover the memorability of password objects of different types. It is also unclear whether users listened to the music tracks during the enrolment and authentication process, or if they instead simply selected by clicking the file name without listening. One very interesting finding was that although the task of finding the appropriate password objects was time-consuming, it was not perceived as onerous by participants – to the contrary they enjoyed it.

Kumar (2012) used a simulated on-screen piano and used this to create password "compositions". The scheme is said to be somewhat resistant to shoulder surfing as the observer can hear a tune as it is entered but many of the notes are input using multiple keys concurrently, which it is reasoned may make it more difficult for observers to note which keys are pressed. To guard against mouse-tracking spyware, the window position is changed between uses. A security analysis is conducted, wherein the system is found to be more resistant to brute force and dictionary attacks due to the large size of the password space offered. A proof-of-concept version with a reduced number of keys (8 white and 5 black) was tested by 32 participants. However all experimental analysis focused on functional aspects of the software – no results about performance or usability of the scheme are available to date.

4.2 Designing Musipass

We set about designing a prototype, "Musipass" to see whether we could leverage the attributes of music to create a secure and memorable authentication scheme.

Interaction Style

When enrolling, we decided users would listen to a number of clips, and select a subset consisting of their favorites to form a password.

Using favorites was opted for as it was felt it might be enjoyable and easy to understand without overburdening novice users with complicated construction rules. At authentication they would be presented with "their" password clips, along with a set of distractors and asked to identify those contained in their password to authenticate.

Each musical clip is represented as an icon, with playback triggered when an icon is moused over (sighted individuals) or tabbed into focus (non-sighted individuals). To select a password clip, the user presses "Enter" or clicks the icon.

Password Length and Number of Distractors

Musical passwords are a new technology, we did not know prior to our investigation how users would react to them. We decided to ask users to select a short sequence of four clips from a relatively small set of 32 distractors, with all clips played back to the user separately. This should minimise frustration resulting from a too time-consuming authentication.

Number of Attempts

In our prototype, once a user had entered an incorrect password sequence, they would be offered the option to retry or quit to a questionnaire. For experimental purposes, we did not limit the number of retries.

Password Letter Repetition

Allowing repetition enhances security in traditional passwords as it increases the overall password space. In Musipass, allowing repetition increases the risk users will opt to reduce the effort required by memorizing only one or two secret clips. This would be predictable and negatively impact security, therefore repetition is not supported.

Sequential or Non-Sequential Password

If multiple password letters (clips) are selected in sequence from a single group of distractors, the user must recognize the clips *and* free-recall the order in which they were selected. This adds an additional level of complexity and may cause difficulties for some users. We removed the burden by breaking the alphabet the user selects from into small subgroups, with one password symbol per group and presenting these in sequence.

Alphabet Design

- **Push or Pull:** People are often open about their musical preferences and some are fairly predictable (Hirsch, 2007; Jackson, 2005). It is infeasible to allow users to upload their own sound clips: we will use a fixed set of clips and ask users to choose from these.
- **Musical Style:** We used familiar melodies - so called "old-familiar" tunes. Smith (1932) argues that we gain pleasure from familiar things, and this lies behind our inertia for change. Lazarsfeld and Field (1946) found that 76% liked to listen to music and, of those, 16% favored familiar music. Lower percentages preferred other music types. People are likely to have been exposed to well-known tunes, aiding autobiographical cue creation (Rentflow and Gosling, 2003).
- **Duration:** Bella, Peretz and Aronoff (2003) found familiarity for a melody could be experienced after 3 to 6 notes and recognition after a further 2 notes were heard. We used musical excerpts which are short enough in duration to minimize authentication time while remaining lengthy enough to enable recognition.
- **Rhythm:** Wells, Burnett and Moriarty (1989) found that rhythmic music enhances memorability. Mélen and Deliége

(1995) found that recognition was better for rhythmic transformations of musical pieces. We exploited this, offering clips with easily-recognized rhythms.

- **Vocal or Instrumental:** We used clips containing lyrics and melody. Vocal music is more memorable than instrumental music (Sewell and Sarel, 1986). The words and tune are processed independently (Besson,Faïta, Bonnel and Requin, 2002) but there are strong connections between the areas of the brain processing them (Peretz, Radeau, and Arguin, 2004). Crowder and Serafine (1986) showed that the lyrics and melody of a song could cue one another, especially when the music is familiar.

- **Hooks:** Monaco and Riordan (1980) define a hook as: "a musical or lyrical phrase that stands out and is easily remembered" (p178). A hook is a series of notes that endures in memory. We chose approximately five second vocal hooks originating from songs predominantly from the 1920s-1970s. Examples are, "I got it bad" by Ella Fitzgerald and "I can't control myself" by The Troggs.

Underlying Architecture

Research into improving the security of recognition-based authentication (Gibson, Conrad and Maple, 2010), considers the number of alphabet letters available for use in visual and sound-based schemes as being virtually infinite, only bounded by the processing capabilities of the system on which the alphabet is generated. Although some letters will be indistinguishable, the virtual infinity of the alphabet means a suitably abundant number of distinguishable letters should still be available. Examples of virtually infinite alphabets are the set of unique images indexed in Google or all top selling singles in a given country and time frame.

To mitigate the risk posed by the limited number of letters that can be presented before the effort required in searching becomes problematic and to overcome practical issues of storage and transmission, this model proposes the alphabet be distributed over the systems requiring it and that a unique child set of these (also unique) per-system subsets be presented to each user during authentication. Research into the security of conventional passwords finds that reducing password popularity is key to securing internet-scale systems (Schechter, Herley and Mitzenmacher, 2010), this sits well with the infinite alphabet password (IAP) model, where the uniqueness of each user's alphabet ultimately forces the selection of unique passwords.

When every password is unique, any leaked password becomes less useful to attackers. It cannot be used to access other accounts where the user may have reused the password, because password reuse is not possible. Neither would they be useful in the creation of cracking dictionaries, because no one but the original user would be able to select the same password.

In practically implementable IAP systems, of course not every password can be truly unique. However by forcing increased uniqueness (i.e. by minimizing the probability that two randomly chosen passwords are perceived the same), the damage from these attacks can be very much limited. Furthermore, a system like IAP lends itself easily to being used within a federated identity scheme. This would make it possible to know which distinct information systems have used a shared alphabet and therefore security professionals in the process of dealing with the aftermath of password leaks can know which other systems are at risk of unauthorized access, and which are not.

Instead of having to advise every user to change every password, only holders of "at-risk" accounts would be advised accordingly. This would not only reduce significantly the labor involved in the reparation task but also the interference suffered by large numbers of users after having to learn numerous new passwords after *en-masse* resets. More formally, in IAP:

The set of letters that can be combined to formulate passwords, $A = \{a1, a2, ...\} \cong N$ is modelled to be infinite. For illustrative purposes, we assume a user wants to authenticate to a server, S via a client node over a network, with the password itself stored as a database entry on a server. As a consequence of the infinity of A, we let different servers carry different alphabets such that Σ denotes a system of servers with $S \in \Sigma$ and $As \subseteq A$ denotes an alphabet for use in authentication onto $S \in \Sigma$ then $A_S \cap A_T = \varnothing$ for any $T \in \Sigma$ with $S \neq T$. Since $N \times N \cong N$, this is possible if $\Sigma \cong N$ is modelled as an infinite set of servers.

The enrolment process is accompanied by the user supplying to the system a unique identifier, u. Formats for u can be biometric data, hardware token, PIN or a username. u is then stored via a one-way hash function as a record on $S \in \Sigma$. The server S on receipt of the user id u generates randomly a finite subset $A_{S,u} \subseteq A_S$ which becomes that user's password alphabet. This is sent to the client device for presentation, where the user selects from $A_{S,u}$ a predefined number of elements to form a password. This password is transmitted to S, where it is also associated with u, concluding the enrolment process.

At authentication to S, the user presents their unique identifier u the server returns the finite set of letters namely $A_{S,u}$ which is presented to the user. At this point, no explicit confirmation is given as to whether the supplied identifier u was correct. If an incorrect identifier $v \neq u$ is entered, an alternate set $A_{S,v} \cap A_{S,u} = \varnothing$ is presented. When the identifier u is correct, $A_{S,u}$ is presented to the user over a number of stages (or screens) $A_{S,u}(1), A_{S,u}(2), ...$ with $\bigcup_i A_{S,u}(i) = A_{S,u}$. In the stage m, the user is presented with the set $A_{S,u}(m)$ and subsequently selects a predefined number of password elements before being presented with set $A_{S,u}(m+1)$. It should also be noted that the order of letters is randomized at each presentation (i.e. their *placement*).

To ensure that symbols do not appear in more than one presentation set $A_{S,u}(i)$, thus removing the requirement that the user memorizes sequences as well as the identity of their password members, it can optionally be required that the password sequence is injective, by specifying that $A_{S,u}(i) \cap A_{S,u}(j) = \varnothing$ for any $i \neq j$. In a conventional alphabet, this would reduce security, because the average search time for a brute force attack would be reduced. However as the alphabet itself is modelled as infinite, so too is the resulting theoretical search space.

An added benefit of the IAP model is that error feedback and recovery can be provided to the authentic user without inadvertently providing the same for an attacker. Here we assume (for example) that the user selects two password letters from each presented set of letters. The user's password $(a_{l(1)}, ..., a_{l(n)})$ with n even and $a_{l(2m-1)}, a_{l(2m)} \in A_{S,u}(m)$ for $1 \leq m \leq n/2$. When the password letter selection (b,c) from m is correct i.e. $(b,c) = [a_{l(2m-1)}, a_{l(2m)}]$ the user is presented with set $A_{S,u}(m+1)$ unless $2m = n$ in which case access is granted. When the selection is incorrect however, the user is exposed to a different unrelated set also randomized in placement $B_{S,u}(m,b,c) \subseteq A$ with all sets $A_{S,u}(m)$ and $B_{S,u}(m,b,c)$ being disjunct to prevent the possibility of an intersection attack. On presentation of $B_{S,u}(m,b,c)$ the authentic user may notice that the presented set is unfamiliar and different from the expected set $A_{S,u}(m)$ and opt to restart the authentication attempt from the beginning. The user who does not recognize the disjunctive nature of $A_{S,u}(m)$ may be identified as a potential intruder and is implicitly excluded from the system due to the inability to select the password elements which are not included in the decoy set $B_{S,u}(m,b,c)$.

We decided to design our prototype system so that it appears to be identical to the IAP scheme for the end user, although we only used one server and to gather information on the popularity of musical passwords selected, we opted for a small A_S set of 201 sounds and selected at random 36 of these to populate each user's individual $A_{S,u}$ set. Hence we weakened the condition that $A_{S,u}$ is completely disjunct for any two users. Therefore, in Musipass (assuming the attacker knows the username), an online brute force attack would achieve a positive result on average in 6561/2 attempts and in an offline attack, 1,583,960,400/2 attempts. The latter is roughly equivalent to a 5 character randomly selected traditional password over an alphabet of 62 letters (i.e. a-z, A-Z and 0-9).

In a "real-world" implementation we assume a lock-out mechanism would be used after a number of failed attempts to mitigate the online threat and that A_s would be larger than the 201 clips we used, strengthening against the offline threat. For example, if we used 2,000 clips on the server, the average offline attack would yield a result in around $1.595 \times 10^{13}/2$ attempts, equivalently closer to a 7 or 8 character randomly selected conventional password, yet there is no reduction is usability as the user is never exposed to this alphabet in its entirety. Even with a lock-out mechanism, there is a risk of low and slow attacks. Here options

for mitigation include intrusion monitoring techniques or adoption of longer password sequences (a possibility we plan to address in future). Finally, by generating individualized user alphabets, the authentication in effect becomes two-way. Not only does the user authenticate himself to the server, but the server authenticates itself to the user due to the absence of his personal alphabet on a masquerading server. IAP is therefore particularly useful for deployment in systems where users are at high risk of phishing and spoofing attacks.

5. LARGE SCALE ONLINE TESTING OF MUSIPASS

Musipass was implemented in Flash and embedded in a PHP web page, this allowed rapid development. A database was used to collect data about interactions and user's reactions were collected via questionnaires. Participants were invited to visit the site and test Musipass. Links to the experiment were provided via email, Facebook, to personal contacts and via groups and mailing

Figure 1. Musipass setup and training screens

lists specifically selected for their international participation, or interests in music, accessibility or security.

Visitors were provided with a description of the experiment and where they opted to participate, were asked to:

1. Provide an email address (as username and means for communication).
2. Create a traditional password that had not been used previously and that they felt would be secure.
3. Re-enter the password.
4. Authenticate using the new password.

Once the user had authenticated (or gave up their attempt), the Musipass interface was loaded. We then asked participants to:

5. Select a song clip from a choice of nine over each of four screens.
6. Enter a short description for each chosen clip (to strengthen the memory trace – akin to asking users to re-type their password).
7. Authenticate with the new musical password.
8. Fill out a questionnaire to express their opinion.

A week later, emails were sent inviting them to return and attempt a second authentication with their traditional and Musipass passwords. Any user returning before the end of the seven days was prohibited from accessing the test. Participants were then given the opportunity to complete a final post-evaluation questionnaire.

6. RESULTS FROM ONLINE EXPERIMENT

The experiment ran for 52 days. 133 people carried out the initial enrollment and authentication, "phase one", 94 returned to carry out a second authentication, "phase two".

6.1 Demographics

- **Age:** During both phases the majority of users were aged between 26 and 35 (39.8% overall during phase one and 39.3% in phase two). Participation of older users was minimal, with only 2.2% (three users) in the 56-65 age group and 1.5% (two users) in the over 65 category at phase one. During phase two, two users returned to participate from each of the 56-65 and over 65 groups.

- **Country:** We looked up the location of page requests based upon IP addresses, most came from the US (60%) and the UK (19%). A further 14% originated in Europe, including Germany, France, Ireland, Austria, Sweden, Norway, Italy and Spain. Just over 1% of requests were from Australia. Countries making up less than 1% each of page requests were Canada, Jordan, the Russian Federation, Mexico and Japan. A further 1% of requests could not be resolved. This suggests our results are mainly relevant to Western audiences. Particularly as those from outside this area may not have had exposure to the clips we deemed as being "old-familiar".

- **Impairments:** Almost all phase one respondents had full hearing, with exceptions being one with mild hearing loss, and one whose hearing is corrected to normal with an aid. One of the two returned for phase two. Four phase one participants (3%) had suffered a 20% loss of vision, all others had normal or corrected to normal vision. All four returned to participate in phase two. Four participants had a disability, one a color vision deficiency, one dyslexia, and one attention deficit hyperactivity disorder. One participant opted not to disclose the nature of their disability. Three of the four returned for phase two.

- **Musical Experience:** Musical experience might affect performance. We asked participants to categorize their experience as, "None", "Listen Frequently", "Play instrument", "Professional Musician" or "Other". Nineteen gave their experience as "Other", but on closer inspection could be mapped to one of the four categories. For example, one participant described their experience as "married to a pianist and composer" and was reclassified as, "Listen frequently". Another said: "degree in e-music; musical performer since age 5 - some pro; improvisor" and was re-categorized as "Professional musician". In phase one, the number of participants with no experience was 18 (13.5%), those who listen frequently was 49 (36.8%), those playing an instrument was 44 (33%) finally, 22 (16.5%) of the sample were professional musicians. In phase two, these were, "None" 11 (11.7%), "Listen frequently" 33 (35.1%), Play instrument (35.1%), Professional musician (18%).

- **Connection Speed:** Connections typically ranged between 300 and 10,000 Kbps. The lowest recorded download speed was 198 Kbps, this user was able to authenticate successfully in both phases. Our results however, might not be relevant for those with slower connections.

6.2 Memorability of Passwords and Reactions to Musipass during Phase One

We coded the result from each Musipass authentication attempt as:

- **Successful:** The participant successfully logged in.
- **Failed:** The participant had failed to recognize and recover from instances of decoy

clip set presentation, and who on reaching the final log in screen subsequently selected a non-password element, and

- **Quit:** The participant realized decoy clips were offered, but when given the choice of re-attempting or quitting to the questionnaire, opted to quit.

Traditional passwords were more memorable than musical passwords after initial enrollment (Table 1). However the difference was statistically insignificant (Fisher's $p > 0.05$).

Table 1. Phase one results (p = 0.4982)

	Successful	Failed	Quit	% Success Rate
Traditional	133	0	N/A	100
Musipass	131	0	2	98.4

6.2.1 Phase One Questionnaire

We asked how long it took to recognize the password clips, offering four options: "Almost immediately", "After 2-3 seconds", "Only after a full clip" or, "I needed to listen more than once". Most participants (74.4%), recognized their clips almost immediately, whilst 19.5% recognized their clips after 2-3 seconds. The remaining 6% said that they had to listen in full, or needed to listen more than once.

When asked to rate how much they liked Musipass on a scale of 1 (disliked very much) to 5, (liked very much), the mode average response was four - most users liked the system.

We asked how easy it was to remember their clips on a scale of 1 (very difficult) to 5 (very easy). The mode average response was five, "very easy". We asked users how satisfied they were after Musipass setup and training was complete with the amount of time it took to carry out the log in on a scale from 1 (Very dissatisfied) to 5 (Very satisfied). The mode response was two, overall participants were unsatisfied with the time taken. When asked how easy it was to go through the process of choosing their clips on a scale from 1 (Very difficult) to 5 (Very easy) the mode response was four, suggesting most users found this easy to do. Participants rated how time consuming it was to choose password clips from 1 (Not time consuming) to 5 (Very time consuming). The mode average response was four, users felt it took too long to enroll. We asked how much mental effort was involved in choosing the sounds on a scale of 1 (Very little effort) to 5 (A great deal of effort), the average response was two. When asked if they thought someone who knew them well would be able to guess the clips they chose, on a scale of 1 (Yes) to 5 (No). The mode average response was two, indicating most people thought their musical passwords could be guessed.

6.3 Clip Popularity

Dictionary attacks utilize non-standard frequencies in the distribution of passwords over the available space. For this attack to be successful, non-standard frequencies must exist in the passwords selected (i.e. there are common passwords). The strength of a musical password against this attack is a result of relative clip popularity. If a small group of clips are more popular, it is likely they would be included in passwords more often, increasing the likelihood that common passwords will be created. We tested clip popularity based upon each clip's number of appearances during enrollment and the number of times it was selected as part of a password. The hypotheses tested are as follows:

- **Alternative Hypothesis:** $H_A \equiv$ Sound is popular.
- **True Null Hypothesis:** $H_T \equiv$ Sound is unpopular.

- **Effective Null Hypothesis:** $H_0 \equiv$ Sound is not popular or unpopular.

We then applied the following in statistical hypothesis testing with 0.05 the threshold for acceptance:

H_0: $\mu_{popularity} = \mu_{binomial}$.
H_T: $\mu_{popularity} \leq \mu_{binomial}$.

Overall, 62% of the alphabet was found neither popular or unpopular. 15% were popular and 21% unpopular. In practice traditional passwords tend to utilize a smaller subset of the space they theoretically provide, although this alphabet is available to all users, all the time. When we scale our figures over the 36 sounds a single user would be exposed to during enrollment in Musipass, we expect, on average to see around five popular sounds included. To form the sounds into a password, at least one must appear per selection screen, the chance of this is 27% (104,976 of 376,992 permutations). This seems why, after comparing passwords created in Musipass we observe that none were identical. We also note that had IAP been implemented fully, it would (regardless of clip popularity) not be possible to create an off-the-shelf dictionary, as each alphabet is individual to each user.

6.4 Memorability and Reactions during Phase Two

Participants found it easier to remember musical passwords than traditional passwords during the second phase, with a 91% success rate in Musipass compared to 62% for traditional passwords (Table 2). Many participants returned after a period of disuse that was longer than seven days (mode=7, mean=9) with one user successfully authenticating with Musipass after 36 days away from the system.

Table 2. Phase two results (p = 0.4982)

	Successful	Failed	Quit	% Success Rate
Traditional	58	36	N/A	62
Musipass	86	5	3	91

Full details of success rates grouped by number of days passing between the phases are given in Figure 2.

A high success rate (88-100%) was achieved up until the eleventh day, after which time the dataset became sparse and we began to observe less of a marked difference between the two methods.

6.4.1 Effect of Demographic Variables

The number of days passing between the initial enrollment and authentication during phase two was identified as a confounding variable. This was removed by isolating results gathered from participants returning on the seventh day. We reordered this data by age and musical experience (Figures 3 and 4). Here, we did not find a positive correlation between age and ability to authenticate with either password type up to the 46-55 age group (we were unable to carry out the analysis for older users, as the sample for this group was too small). This led us to conclude that at least up to the age of 55, age did not affect success rate.

Professional musicians and non-musicians tested similarly for traditional password authentication success rates, but there was a higher success rate in Musipass from professional musicians then there was from the non-musical group. However, only four non-musical participants returned on the seventh day and without more data we still could not be sure about the existence of a relationship between level of musical experience and the ability to log in with Musipass.

Figure 2. Success rates by days passing

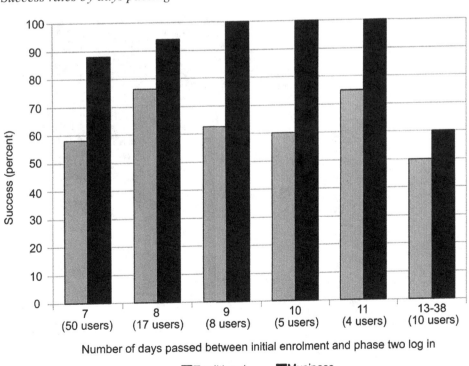

Figure 3. Traditional password success rate by musical experience and age

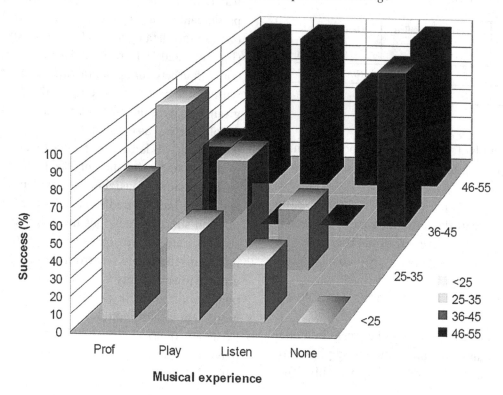

Figure 4. Musipass success rate by experience and age

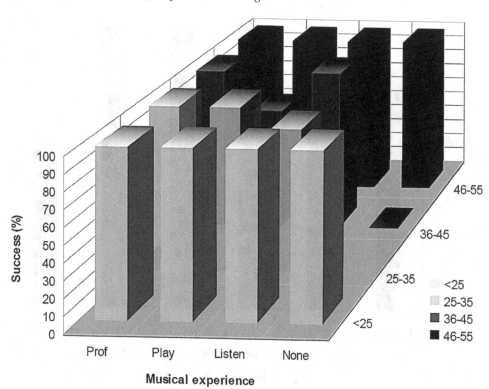

Data from participants in the "Listen frequently", "Play instrument" and "Professional musician" categories was more abundant. We observed a positive correlation for traditional password memorability within data from these groups – the more experienced people were, the better they remembered their password strings. Since ability to recall text strings is not usually associated with musical ability, we conclude that musical experience most likely affects memory in general, possibly due to the way musicians are trained to recall complicated patterns whilst performing; strengthening memory as a whole.

6.4.2 Phase Two Questionnaire

The overall response from phase two participants was very positive. When asked how much mental effort was involved logging in with Musipass on a scale of 1 (very little mental effort) to 5, (too much mental effort). The mode response was '1: very little mental effort.' Likewise, most participants found recognizing their clips very easy, rating this as 1, on a scale from 1 (very easy) to 5 (very difficult).

Below we include some typical comments regarding memorability:

I thought it worked very well and found it very easy, without cheating! Though I did recognize some of the other songs in each group I knew instinctively that they were not the right ones. When I came across my choice I immediately knew it and moved on without listening to the others. Million times more easy to recall using the songs, I couldn't remember my text password having a random word.

... i'm also amazed on how easy it was to identify the selected clips (believe it was by emotional connections but also by negative relationships with the other clips; btw i still can't remember my textual password!)

After trying unsuccessfully to log in with my alphanumeric password, the usefulness of Musipass became clear. I wouldn't want to have to use it for things I log in to often, such as online banking or email, but for lesser used passwords, this would be a better option than guessing, trying to retrieve it from a note or document, or waiting to have it emailed to me...

Although most users were able to authenticate successfully with Musipass, a few expressed concerns about interference:

... well, I couldn't remember my text password either, so it's a wash!:) it was particularly confusing when there were two or more songs on the same screen that i'm fond of or familiar with; it was hard to find a reason to choose one over the other during password selection, and hard to remember which I'd picked when I returned.

If several other sites were using Musipass and, potentially, using similar songs I'm not sure it will work.

I recognized "the songs I liked" and I would need to be persuaded that I could successfully disambiguate different selections of songs. I hope you'll pursue it.

We asked users how long it took them to recognize their clips: "Almost immediately", "After 2-3 seconds", "Only after I had listened to the full clip" or, "I had to listen to the options more than once". The figures had not changed much from the phase one responses, with 50% able to recognize their clips almost immediately and 40.4% recognizing them after 2-3 seconds. The remaining 9.5% listened in full or multiple times. One participant made an interesting point, again related to interference:

I was pleasantly surprised by the immediacy of my recognition of the music clips. Perhaps this is because my mind is less clogged with musical passwords than with text-based passwords?

We asked how frustrated participants felt during authentication on a scale of 1 (Not frustrated at all) to 5, (Very frustrated), the average response was 1 (Not frustrated at all). When asked how they felt about the time involved in logging in to Musipass on a scale from 1 (It was very quick) to 5 (It took too much time), the average response was four. Even though participants enjoyed using the system, they did not think the time required was practical. Typical feedback was:

I remebered the music login easily, though had forgotten the text one. Probably if i had to log in more often than the one week gap I prob would have remembered it. Also if I was trying to log in for something specific that I really needed to know then the time required for loggin in may get annoying. However in the scenario given, ie leasurly login with no urgency, it was pretty much the most fun login I've ever done:D.

I think it was really fun, but I am not sure how I would like it if I had to play so many clips just to login to my email, or something like that, which I want to do quickly.

Finally, we asked participants how much they liked Musipass overall on a scale of 1 (Disliked very much) to 5, (Liked very much), the average response was four, most users liked the system. A few participants expressed concerns about observation and password strength (we didn't want to complicate instructions, so did not explain that alphabets would differ between users, extending the range of possibilities, or that the placement of icons was shuffled). We feel it is important to consider these viewpoints, as perception of functionality is often indicative of technology acceptance. Typical comments were:

… even though it sometimes takes me several attempts to remember which of 5 passwords I have used for a site, this still felt longer, and i was also conscious that if it wen't wrong I was potentially going to have to do it again which would definately be longer. I also am always using my computer in public space and would not want to long into anything confidential in an audible way that others could overhear"

… it's an interesting concept but I'm not sure how it would work in practice while making the paranoid nerd types like myself feel secure in our password selections. (nothing like random strings to make you sleep better at night!)

Doesn't seem very secure, and takes a while to log in. Reusing an easy-to-remember text password would be faster.

7. TESTING TASK TIME

Reporting task times from our online study would have been misleading. It cannot be guaranteed that participants did not stop during the experiment to do other things (at least one told us they *did* do this). Although the authentication was time consuming, the question remained as to exactly how long it took. We decided to repeat the experiment in the lab to gather data on this. The lab-based trial was identical to the web-based trial described in the previous section. However, this time participants returned exactly seven days after the date of initial enrolment. Measures were also taken to ensure participants were fully focused on the test so that information about task time could be recorded accurately.

7.1 Sampling

Participation was sought from members of staff in the University of Bedfordshire and students in the Department of Computer Science and Technology. This convenience sample, is nevertheless relevant as they would have spent at least some time in a western cultural environment and should all have similar levels of computing experience (in this case, intermediate to expert).

7.2 Equipment

The equipment and where applicable, software settings used were identical in all experiments. A mid-range laptop with Microsoft Windows operating system was used. Other than antivirus and firewall applications, no additional software ran during the time of the experiment. The browser used to access the test was Mozilla Firefox, with the Musipass test page being the only browser tab open. The experiment required that the user wear over the ear style headphones during their interactions. This would inherently filter out some ambient noise, however the specific model used are not "noise cancelling" - some sounds from the surrounding environment would be perceived by participants. The participants were given the option to use a mouse, should they prefer it to the laptop's built-in trackpad.

The Internet connection speed used during the experiment was 100Mb/s. Although no metric was found in the operating system for volume measurement, the volume was set to the third notch up in the volume control panel with all other settings at default. This level was selected after listening to the sounds through the headphones to find a level deemed comfortable. It should be noted that the Musipass interface itself includes a volume control for any user who might want to change the volume according to their preference.

Participants were asked to attend a small yet busy working office in which the experiment was to be conducted. The idea of carrying out the experiment in an office was to simulate a typical operating environment, where external sounds may be audible during the setup and authentication process. The office itself contained five staff members (including the researcher), and occasionally one or two students would come in at a time with queries and to request technical support.

7.3 Participant Demographics

A total of thirty-six users agreed to participate in the experiment, with twenty-seven returning for the second phase a week later.

7.3.1 Age

In the first week, 28 per cent of participants were under 25, 42 per cent were aged 25-35. 16 per cent were aged 36-45 and 14 percent were aged 46-55. No older users participated. During the second week, these figures were 26 per cent under 25, 44 percent 25-35, 15 per cent 36-45 and 15 per cent 46-55. A cumulative frequency analysis was carried out to compare the ages of participants between this and the web-based experiment. It was found that these roughly corresponded, with the average age group in both trials being 26-35 years.

7.3.2 Vision and Hearing

All participants had full hearing. During week one all but one participant had normal vision, or had it corrected to normal with glasses. The one exception was mildly visually impaired, with 20 per cent vision loss. Unfortunately, this user did not return to participate during week two.

7.3.3 Other Disabilities

As with the online version of the experiment, participants were asked whether they had any other disabilities that might affect their ability to use the systems. One user said they had a painful back problem and two said they have Dyslexia. All three returned to participate in week two.

7.3.4 Musical Experience

Participants were asked about their level of Musical experience. 10 participants (28 per cent) said that they had no musical experience, 18 (50 per cent) said they listen frequently and 8 participants (22 percent) said that they play a musical instrument. No participant classified their experience as "Professional musician". These figures include two participants who rated their experience as "Other", but on inspection of descriptions were able to be included in the existing categories. Specifically, one participant who gave their experience as "Listen to music frequently and sing" was reclassified as "Listen frequently", another said they "Listen to music sometimes" and was reclassified as "None". A cumulative frequency analysis was carried out on this data, and the data gathered via the web-based experiment, here it was found that there was a large difference in Musical experience between participants of the two, with participants of the web-based study being more musically experienced in general.

8. LAB BASED TASK TIME RESULTS

8.1 Week One Set Up

Musipass was substantially more time consuming to set up than the traditional password, taking over 6 minutes on average compared to 27 seconds for traditional passwords. It should be noted that all time measures contained in this chapter do not exclude the Musipass interface or music clip download times. This is because the Musipass program was cached in the browser prior to the experiments taking place and the (non-cached) 36 clips (approximately 24 Mb in total) each user would have downloaded during both phases of the experiment would have taken < 1 second given the 100Mb/s Internet connection speed. In the following figures, outliers (measures more than 1.5 times above or below the interquartile range) are denoted with the "•" symbol.

As the Musipass setup time was so lengthy, it was decided to break it down during the analysis, to see where the time was being spent. Length of time participants spent reading the instruction screens, time spent selecting the music clips and time spent listening to the clips and writing descriptions in training were all analysed (Figures

Figure 5. Traditional password setup time

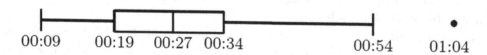

Figure 6. Musipass password setup time

Figure 7. Time spent on instruction screens in Musipass

Figure 8. Time spent selecting password clips in Musipass

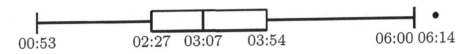

Figure 9. Time spent training in Musipass

7, 8, and 9). Overall, participants spent around 1 minute reading the instruction screens. It can be expected that if users were more familiar with musical passwords, they would not need to read instructions in detail to use the system. Most time was spent selecting the clips, with users on average spending 3 minutes and 7 seconds to complete. This was not surprising - to listen to 36 clips in full, each averaging approximately 5 seconds in duration, would result in a total of three minutes listening time. It is expected that users who were quicker had either listened to the beginning of some tracks only, or selected a clip they liked and moved on without listening to the remaining alternatives.

Finally, the second largest proportion of time spent was in training. This took on average 2 minutes and 6 seconds to complete, with nearly all participants listening to their chosen clips and entering descriptions within 3 minutes and 6 seconds. However there were a few outliers who took longer, including one who took 13 minutes and 58 seconds to finish the task. This participant did not write anything in the questionnaire that would explain why training had taken such a long time. The log data gathered during this participant's training session was inspected, to get some insight into what they did and what they wrote. They had listened to each of the song clips only once, so the length of time spent cannot be explained by the duration of the clips. The descriptions entered were a little on the lengthier side in relation to some others, but not excessively so. The descriptions given and time to complete each one are presented in Table 3. The longest time of the four clips was spent by this user making notes about the last.

The description is quite emotive and it is possible they may have taken some extra time to remember the artist, Michael Jackson who had passed away.

8.2 Week One Log In

Musipass was more time consuming to authenticate with than the traditional password, as is shown in Figures 10 and 11. Users spent on average 17 seconds to log in with their traditional password, compared with 1 minute and 5 seconds for Musipass passwords.

8.3 Week Two Log In

As expected, authentication using the traditional password was much faster, on average taking 16 seconds, compared with 1 minute and 52 seconds overall in Musipass. Of the time spent authenticating to Musipass, an average of 10 seconds was spent reading the instructions, these were less involved than those given in the first week, due to there being no clip selection or training procedure to explain.

Users spent on average 1 minute and 39 seconds on the Musipass log in process itself. Even though those who were able to authenticate successfully with their traditional passwords did so quickly, there was a clear distinction in terms of time spent attempting to authenticate from the seven participants (26 percent) who could not.

This group (which incidentally included both with Dyslexia), spent between 48 seconds and 3 minutes 48 seconds making incorrect guesses before exhausting the ten guess limit, or giving up and moving on. However, all of the seven were able to log in successfully with Musipass, spending (without instruction reading) between 1 minute and 16 seconds and 1 minute 48 seconds to authenticate. Overall this group spent less time authenticating to Musipass successfully than they did unsuccessfully attempting authentication with the traditional passwords (Table 4).

8.4 Questionnaire

8.4.1 Expended Effort

After using the systems following the one week break, participants were asked again, "How much effort was involved in logging in with your musical password?" on a scale of '1: Very little effort' to '5: A great deal of effort.' The average response received was 1.89 (median 2, mode 1). Most users felt it took a fair amount or very little effort to do. This response was almost identical to that received in the previous week (average 1.92) - there was no evidence indicating Musipass log in was perceived as less demanding with a second use. However, the mode value given in both weeks was 5, so for many participants there would be no option available to express any relative improvement.

Table 3. Log data from training session that took 13:58 secs to complete

Clip Number	Time Taken (mm:ss)	Description "[Sic]"
1	02:48	This music reminds me of sister, she loves Frank Sinatia and had most of his Albums at home.
2	03:41	I love little susie, but i cannot remember the name of the band. it is nice to dance to, and listen to when with friends.
3	03:00	When the night has come is a romatic music and my ex-husband i use to has played this record many a time and dance to it.
4	04:29	Mike Jacson has passed away, so this is to say, Mikel i will always love you. I grew up with him and he has entertained up for many, many years. We miss you.

Figure 10. Time taken to authenticate with traditional password

Figure 11. Time taken to authenticate with Musipass password

Figure 12. Time taken to authenticate with traditional password in week two

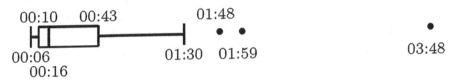

Figure 13. Time taken to authenticate with a Musipass password in week two

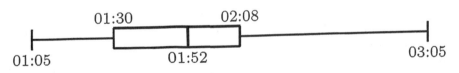

Figure 14. Task time breakdown – time spent reading instructions in Musipass

Figure 15. Task time breakdown – time spent logging in with Musipass

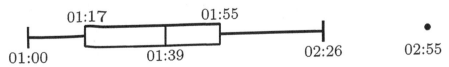

Table 4. Comparison of time spent by users unsuccessfully attempting to authenticate with their traditional password, compared with time they spent authenticating successfully to Musipass

Participant	Traditional Password Time	Musical Password Time	Difference
1	0:48s	1:35s	+ 0:47s
2	0:48s	1:52s	+1:04s
3	1:18s	1:21s	+0:03s
4	1:30s	1:43s	+0:13s
5	1:48s	1:28s	-0:20s
6	1:59s	1:16s	-0:43s
7	3:48s	1:58s	-1:50s
Totals	11:59s	11:13s	-0:46s

Participants were also asked "How much effort was involved in logging in with your text password?". Here the average response was 2.22 (median 2, mode 1) - this was a surprise. Straight after set up participants had responded to this question with an average 1.47 (median 1, mode 1). This means that after 1 week of disuse, participants felt that:

1. The traditional password was more demanding in terms of effort than in the previous week, and
2. The amount of effort required to authenticate with the traditional password was more than it was authenticating with Musipass.

8.4.2 Expended Time

When asked "How time consuming was it to log in with your text password?" on a scale of '1: Not time consuming' to '5: Very time consuming.' The average response was 2 (median 2, mode 1). Most people thought it took a fair amount or very little time to do. Again this value had changed since the first week, where participants had responded with 1.53 (median 1, mode 1).

When asked "How time consuming was it to log in with your musical password?" on a scale of '1: Not time consuming' to '5: Very time

consuming.' The average response received was 2.26 (median 2, mode 3) most participants felt this took a while, in particular longer than when compared to the traditional password. Again, this value was almost identical to the response to the same question given in the previous week (this was 2.31). However, what is very interesting is that although in actuality the musical password log in took almost four times as long as the traditional password during week one and six times as long in week two, users did not seem to perceive the time difference in this way. If they had, based on the values they gave in response to the question regarding text passwords, one would have expected the responses to the same question about Musipass to be closer on the scale to 4 or 5. Considering on the 5-point scale, 3 is usually considered to be "neutral", participants did not seem to show any strong dislike for the time aspect of the task.

The questionnaire also included a section for additional comments. During week one, some participants commented on the time aspect, saying:

Choosing the songs is time-consuming but also fun.

I could have set up my musical password and logged in much quicker but I was enjoying listening to the songs.

These were interesting points. It had not occurred to us previously that the enjoyability of Musipass might unfairly bias measures of task times in comparison with the less entertaining traditional password scheme. It was decided to check whether this affect was more widespread. Did many users really take longer than needed to listen to clips during enrolment and authentication with Musipass? Or was this participant simply an outlier? If more widespread, might the effect be observable in other alternative media systems such as those using images to authenticate users? The following additional question was added to the week two questionnaire to probe further with regard to this point.

- *Please select the option that you most agree with. LAST WEEK:*
  - *I only spent as long as I needed to listening to the songs,*
  - *I spent a longer time than I needed to listening to the songs because I enjoyed them,*
  - *I spent a longer time than I needed to listening to the songs for a different reason (please specify).*

16 participants (59.2 percent) said they only spent as long as needed. However 9 participants (33.3 percent) said they had spent longer because they enjoyed listening and two participants (7.4 percent) said they had taken longer for other reasons. Specifically one said,

I wanted to be sure I was choosing my favourite.

and the other,

I am not familiar with those songs, So I need time to recognise them.

Participants were also asked,

- *Please select the option that you most agree with. THIS WEEK:*
  - *I only spent as long as I needed to listening to the songs,*
  - *I spent a longer time than I needed to listening to the songs because I enjoyed them.*
  - *I spent a longer time than I needed to listening to the songs for a different reason (please specify).*

This time, 21 participants (77.7 percent) said they only spent as long as needed and 6 (22.2 percent) said they had spent longer because they enjoyed listening. No participants said they had taken longer for other reasons.

Although there was a chance participant's recall when trying to remember back to the previous week would be more error-prone, it was felt inclusion of the question regarding week one was still worthwhile. This is because, it could have turned out this "enjoyability" factor might not last into a second authentication attempt due to the novelty of the system wearing off, and if this is the case, asking only about the second week would shed no light on the matter. Whereas there was a chance some participants might still be able to accurately recall spending longer than needed during the first week. Answers received did seem to indicate this happened to some extent, and the "enjoyability effect" was not fully diminished by week two, with the number of participants spending longer decreasing by around 11 percent by the second week's login (33 percent in the first week, compared with 22 percent in the second week).

It may be that the enjoyability effect would wear off completely with frequent use and so this is a ripe area for future research. Even so, it seems sensible to assume that when comparatively measuring task times in other musical password schemes, and quite possibly some visual schemes, any "enjoyable" properties of the alphabets should be taken into consideration in order to avoid incorrect conclusions being drawn.

9. DISCUSSION

Musipass is highly memorable. We carried out a large scale online experiment, where users authenticated successfully after a full week away from the system. They appeared to like the system, enjoying the experience of choosing the sound clips and returning to attempt to remember them a week later. They found Musipass easy to use and were not at all frustrated during enrollment or authentication.

Participants had concerns about the guessability of choices. Our analysis suggests that the prevalence of easy to guess passwords (particularly if IAP is implemented) is lower than in traditional passwords, which are all too often easy to guess. However the question remains whether this is also the case when the attacker is a friend or a family member, or who is able to research preferences perhaps via social networking websites. Guessability may be worsened if we allow users to upload their own choices into the system, this could also lead to copyright problems. If our user's perceptions are correct and passwords in Musipass *are* easy to guess, this does not necessarily make Musipass superfluous in the world of authentication. Many systems ask users to authenticate themselves more for convenience than to achieve any measure of protection. In these systems, where authentication is required to deliver a measure of customization or support attribution, or when users are at high risk of phishing or spoofing attacks we could feasibly make use of a system like Musipass.

Techniques for hardening Musipass against guessing might include issuing the clips rather than allowing freedom of choice. This option may however, impact negatively on memorability. Another option is to populate the system with many musical genres and to vary these between users. It is then less likely that choices will be predictable. We could also personalize alphabets further, for example populating one with songs by Elvis Presley for an Elvis Presley fan. Here, guessability would be reduced and enjoyment enhanced - although interference might occur due to the similarity of the tracks. On the other hand a user who listens to them regularly, knowing them well and having built strong biographical associations might experience *enhanced* distinguishability and memorability.

Even though people complain about traditional passwords, the fact is they are very convenient (Morris and Thompson, 1979). Although participants in the online experiment indicated liking Musipass some of their comments show that they were exasperated due to its time-consuming nature. If users anticipate having to authenticate with a time-consuming mechanism a number of times a day, one can readily anticipate their dismay. One question that remained was how long did use of Musipass take. We repeated the experiment in a controlled lab-based environment to find out. Here we found that Musipass took from 4 to 6 times longer to authenticate with than a traditional password, however even though participants perceived this to take longer, they did not perceive the time required to be excessive. Participants also reported feeling that after one week away from both systems, Musipass required less effort to authenticate with than their traditional passwords. A number of participants reported spending longer using the system than they functionally had to. due to their enjoyment of the scheme and listening to the songs.

A task time breakdown analysis was carried out, wherein it was found a large proportion of time spent when using Musipass was in training and reading instructions. The inherent memorability of music may mean that training is unnecessary and this is an area for future work. Indeed the large password space that can be supported by schemes like Musipass and the high level of memorability it offers, may result in it being less necessary for users to change their passwords (and in turn unlikely they will undergo the training portion of the interaction frequently).

In its current form, perhaps the future of Musipass lies within the context of low risk systems, which are used infrequently, by users who are more concerned about forgetting than convenience. As Musipass provides long-term memorability, it may also prove useful as a recovery mechanism once a conventional password is forgotten. Here Musipass might be offered as an alternative to security questions, which are prone to interference and tend to be based on personal (hence researchable) information or attributes.

10. CONCLUSION

We reported on the development and trials of a scheme called "Musipass". Musipass used musical clips as an alphabet and utilized the IAP model as its architecture. IAP allows many of the criticisms commonly aimed at recognition-based authentication, in particular with regard to vulnerability to brute force and dictionary attacks to be mitigated. Sound-based passwords can be designed to rely on recognition or cued-recall for authentication and music especially, is pleasant to experience for a large proportion of users and is highly memorable. Musipass offers some of the memorability of image-based schemes to which it is well suited as counterpart; catering to the needs of users unable to gain access via the visual channel. When used with earphones, musical passwords are less prone to eavesdropping than image-based or conventional passwords. Attacks using specialized hardware, such as directional microphones cannot be categorically ruled out and further research is required into the possibility and success rates of these. It should be noted that the additional equipment required would make this attack more difficult to achieve than simply glancing over while an alphanumeric password is entered.

We tested Musipass and traditional passwords for memorability after a period of disuse. Overall, Musipass offered better performance, with 48% more successful authentication attempts than with traditional naively selected passwords. Participants returned for the second phase of the experiment from seven to thirty-eight days from the date of initial set up. We found that when we isolated data from participants returning on the seventh day, there was no identifiable correlation between age and password memorability. We did identify a correlation between musical experience and ability to authenticate using a traditional password; suggesting music performance strengthens the memory as a whole. The overall reaction to Musipass was positive, with the majority of participants liking it and finding it easy to use. Like other recognition-based schemes, a drawback for some users is the amount of time required during the process, however many users reported spending longer interacting with the system as they enjoyed using it.

11. FUTURE WORK

We hope to encourage further research into the efficacy and feasibility of alternate modality authentication systems. In addition to questions already raised, areas for future investigation include, whether users might persevere with previously unfamiliar tunes long enough for them to become familiar.

If this turns out to be the case, the possibilities for alphabet inclusion are increased. We might for example, use creative-commons music. Ours was a research prototype and in US and UK copyright law would be treated as "fair use" (UK Copyright Service, n.d.; US Copyright Office, n.d.). In a non-research system, even if non-profit making, this may not be the case and the clips will need to be paid for. If we are to remain faithful to our originally intended purpose, ensuring inclusivity for groups who find conventional approaches difficult, it seems unfair to ask them to pay for the service, or to view advertisements only to be given the same opportunity to authenticate that others take for granted. Perhaps record companies could submit password clips, in return for showcasing the work of artists. As people have a preference for the familiar, this could positively affect sales.

Another question is how many musical passwords people can remember. Research suggests that music memories are less prone to interference than other types, though it seems advisable to test this in the context of authentication. If multiple musical passwords are difficult to remember, implementation as single-sign-on may provide a viable alternative. The majority of participants said they didn't have to listen to all clips presented, selecting "theirs" as soon as they heard them and moving on. This serves as anecdotal evidence that people do not find the distractors becoming as familiar to them as their password clips. Both our studies involved a lengthy delay between enrollment and authentication. Trials involving regular use, perhaps on a daily basis, might be better placed to confirm this as fact.

Finally, our design should be considered as one possible implementation for a sound-based password. The choices made for the alphabet and password selection procedure were based on research into enhancing memorability and security. The literature on the subject is vast, and it may prove useful to populate sound-based systems and interaction therewith differently, enhancing efficacy.

REFERENCES

Bella, S. D., Peretz, I., & Aronoff, N. (2003). Time course of melody recognition: A gating paradigm study. *Perception & Psychophysics*, 65(7), 1019–1028. doi:10.3758/BF03194831 PMID:14674630

Besson, M., Faïta, F., Bonnel, A.-M., & Requin, J. (2002). Singing in the brain: Independence of music and tunes. *Psychological Science*, 9(6), 494–498. doi:10.1111/1467-9280.00091

Biddle, R., Mannan, M., van Oorschot, P. C., & Whalen, T. (2011). User study, analysis, and usable security of passwords based on digital objects. *IEEE Transactions on Information Forensics and Security*, 6(3), 970–979.

Bigand, E., & Poulin-Charronnat, B. (2006). Are we "experienced listeners"? A review of the musical capacities that do not depend on formal musical training. *Cognition*, 100(1), 100–130. doi:10.1016/j.cognition.2005.11.007 PMID:16412412

Brostoff, S., & Sasse, M. A. (2000). Are passfaces more usable than passwords? a field trial investigation. In S. McDonald, (Ed.), *People and computers XIV - Usability or else! Proceedings of HCI 2000* (pp. 405-424). Springer. doi:10.1007/978-1-4471-0515-2_27

Clarkson, E., Clawson, J., Lyons, K., & Starner, T. (2005). An empirical study of typing rates on mini-QWERTY keyboards. In *CHI'05 extended abstracts on Human factors in computing systems* (pp. 1288-1291). ACM. doi:10.1145/1056808.1056898

Coventry, L., De Angeli, A., & Johnson, G. (2003). Usability and biometric verification at the ATM interface. In *Proceedings of the SIGCHI Conference on Human Factors in Computing Systems* (pp. 153-160). ACM Press. doi:10.1145/642611.642639

Crowder, R. G., Serafine, M. L., & Repp, B. (1986). Physical interaction and association by contiguity in memory for the words and melodies of songs. *Memory & Cognition*, 18(5), 469–476. doi:10.3758/BF03198480 PMID:2233260

Davis, D., Monrose, F., & Reiter, M. K. (2004). On user choice in graphical password schemes. In *Proceedings of the 13th Conference on USENIX Security Symposium* (p. 11). Berkeley, CA: USENIX Association.

Featherman, M. S., & Pavlou, P. A. (2003). Predicting e-services adoption: A perceived risk facets perspective. *International Journal of Human-Computer Studies*, 59(4), 451–474. doi:10.1016/S1071-5819(03)00111-3

Florencio, D., & Herley, C. (2007). A large-scale study of web password habits. In *Proceedings of the 16th International Conference on World Wide Web* (pp. 657-666). ACM. doi:10.1145/1242572.1242661

Forget, A., Chiasson, S., & Biddle, R. (2007). Helping users create better passwords: Is this the right approach? In *Proceedings of the Third Symposium on Usable Privacy and Security* (pp. 151-152). ACM. doi:10.1145/1280680.1280703

Gaw, S., & Felten, E. W. (2006). Password management strategies for online accounts. In *Proceedings of the Second Symposium on Usable Privacy and Security* (pp. 44-55). ACM. doi:10.1145/1143120.1143127

Gibson, M., Conrad, M., & Maple, C. (2010). Infinite alphabet passwords: A unified model for a class of authentication systems. In S. K. Katsikas & P. Samarati (Eds.), SECRYPT (pp. 94–99). SciTePress.

Gibson, M., Renaud, K., Conrad, M., & Maple, C. (2009). Musipass: Authenticating me softly with "my" song. In *NSPW'09: New security paradigms workshop* (pp. 85–100). New York, NY: ACM. doi:10.1145/1719030.1719043

Gibson, M., Renaud, K., Conrad, M., & Maple, C. (2012). Music is the key: Using our enduring memory for songs to help users log on. In M. Gupta, J. Walp, & R. Sharman (Eds.), *Strategic and practical approaches for information security governance: Technologies and applied solutions*. IGI Global. doi:10.4018/978-1-4666-0197-0.ch008

GTISC. (2013). *Emerging cyber threats report 2014*. The Georgia Tech Information Security Center and Georgia Tech Research Institute. Retrieved from http://www.gtsecuritysummit.com/2014Report.pdf

Herley, C. (2009). So long and no thanks for the externalities: The rational rejection of security advice by users. In *NSPW'09: New security paradigms workshop* (pp. 133–144). New York, NY: ACM. doi:10.1145/1719030.1719050

Hirsch, L. E. (2007). Weaponizing classical music: Crime prevention and symbolic power in the age of repetition. *Journal of Popular Music Studies*, 19(4), 342–358. doi:10.1111/j.1533-1598.2007.00132.x

Hoonakker, P., Bornoe, N., & Carayon, P. (2009). Password authentication from a human factors perspective: Results of a survey among end-users. In *Proceedings of the Human Factors and Ergonomics Society Annual Meeting* (Vol. 53, No. 6, pp. 459-463). SAGE Publications. doi:10.1177/154193120905300605

Inglesant, P. G., & Sasse, M. A. (2010). The true cost of unusable password policies: password use in the wild. In *Proceedings of the 28th International Conference on Human Factors in Computing Systems (CHI '10)* (pp. 383-392). ACM. doi:10.1145/1753326.1753384

Jackson, M. (2005, January 10). Music to deter yobs by. *BBC News Magazine*. Retrieved December 12, 2010 from http://news.bbc.co.uk/1/hi/magazine/4154711.stm

Jakobsson, M., & Akavipat, R. (2012). Rethinking passwords to adapt to constrained keyboards. In *Proc. IEEE MoST*. IEEE.

Johnson, M. E., & Goetz, E. (2007). Embedding information security into the organization. *IEEE Security and Privacy*, 5(May/June), 16–24. doi:10.1109/MSP.2007.59

Kuo, C., Romanosky, S., & Cranor, L. F. (2006). Human selection of mnemonic phrase-based passwords. In *Proceedings of the Second Symposium on Usable Privacy and Security* (pp. 67–78). ACM. doi:10.1145/1143120.1143129

Lazarsfeld, P., & Field, H. (1946). *The people look at radio*. Chapel Hill, NC: University of North Carolina Press.

LeDoux, J. E. (1992). Emotion as memory: Anatomical systems underlying indelible neural traces. In S. Christianson (Ed.), *Handbook of emotion and memory: Theory and research* (pp. 269–288). Hillsdale, NJ: Erlbaum.

Lee, S., & Zhai, S. (2009). The performance of touch screen soft buttons. In *Proceedings of the SIGCHI Conference on Human Factors in Computing Systems* (pp. 309-318). ACM. doi:10.1145/1518701.1518750

Liddell, J., Renaud, K. V., & De Angeli, A. (2003). *Authenticating users using a combination of sound and images*. Paper presented at British Computer Society, Bath, UK.

Mélen, M., & Deliége, I. (1995). Extraction of cues or underlying harmonic structure: Which guides recognition of familiar melodies? *The European Journal of Cognitive Psychology*, 7(1), 81–106. doi:10.1080/09541449508520159

Mendori, T., Kubouchi, M., Okada, M., & Shimizu, A. (2002). Password input interface for primary school children. In *Proceedings of the International Conference on Computers in Education (ICCE02)*. Auckland, New Zealand: IEEE Computer Society. doi:10.1109/CIE.2002.1186069

Monaco, B., & Riordan, J. (1987). *The platinum rainbow... How to make it big in the music business*. Sherman Oaks, CA: Omnibus Books.

Morris, R., & Thomson, K. (1979). Password security: A case history. *Communications of the ACM*, 22(11), 594–597. doi:10.1145/359168.359172

Nusbaum, E. C., & Silvia, P. J. (2010). Shivers and timbres: Personality and the experience of chills from music. *Social Psychological & Personality Science*, (October), 2010.

Paivio, A. (1983). The empirical case for dual coding. In J. Yuille (Ed.), *Imagery, memory and cognition: Essays in honour of Allan Paivio* (pp. 307–322). Hillsdale, NJ: Erlbaum.

Paivio, A., & Csapo, K. (1973). Picture superiority in free recall: Imagery or dual coding? *Cognitive Psychology*, 5(2), 176–206. doi:10.1016/0010-0285(73)90032-7

Peretz, I., Radeau, M., & Arguin, M. (2004). Two-way interactions between music and language: Evidence from priming recognition of tune and lyrics in familiar songs. *Memory & Cognition*, 32(1), 142–152. doi:10.3758/BF03195827 PMID:15078051

Petrie, H., & Kheir, O. (2007). The relationship between accessibility and usability of websites. In *Proceedings of the SIGCHI Conference on Human Factors in Computing Systems* (pp. 397-406). ACM. doi:10.1145/1240624.1240688

Renaud, K., & De Angeli, A. (2009). Visual passwords: Cure-all or snake-oil? *Communications of the ACM, 52*(12), 135–140. doi:10.1145/1610252.1610287

Renaud, K., & Ramsay, J. (2007). Now what was that password again? A more flexible way of identifying and authenticating our seniors. *Behaviour & Information Technology, 26*(4), 309–322. doi:10.1080/01449290601173770

Rentfrow, P. J., & Gosling, S. D. (2003). The do re mi's of everyday life: The structure and personality correlates of music preferences. *Journal of Personality and Social Psychology, 84*(6), 1236–1256. doi:10.1037/0022-3514.84.6.1236 PMID:12793587

Sapolsky, R. (2005). Stressed out memories. *Scientific American Mind, 14*(5), 28.

Schechter, S., Herley, C., & Mitzenmacher, M. (2010). Popularity is everything: A new approach to protecting passwords from statistical guessing attacks. In *Proceedings of the 5th USENIX Workshop on Hot Topics in Security*. USENIX Association.

Scherer, K. R., & Zentner, M. R. (2001). Emotional effects of music: Production rules. In Music and emotion: Theory and research (pp. 361–392). Oxford, UK: Oxford University Press.

Schmidt, A., Kölbl, T., Wagner, S., & Strassmeier, W. (2004). Enabling access to computers for people with poor reading skills. In *Proceedings of 8th ERCIM Workshop on User Interfaces for All* (LNCS), (Vol. 3196, pp. 96–115). Vienna, Austria: Springer. doi:10.1007/978-3-540-30111-0_8

Sewall, M. A., & Sarel, D. (1986). Characteristics of radio commercials and their recall effectiveness. *Journal of Marketing, 50*(1), 52–60. doi:10.2307/1251278

Shannon, C. (1948). A mathematical theory of communication. *The Bell System Technical Journal, 27*, 379-423.

Small, A., Stern, Y., Tang, M., & Mayeux, R. (1999). Selective decline in memory function among healthy elderly. *Neurology, 52*(7), 1392–1396. doi:10.1212/WNL.52.7.1392 PMID:10227623

Smith, A. B. (1932). The pleasures of recognition. *Music & Letters, 13*(1), 80–84. doi:10.1093/ml/XIII.1.80

Spafford, E. (1992). Observing reusable password choices. In *Proceedings of 3rd USENIX Security Symposium* (pp. 299-312). Berkeley, CA: USENIX Association.

Thorpe, J., & van Oorschot, P. C. (2007). Human-seeded attacks and exploiting hot-spots in graphical passwords. In *Proceedings of the 16th Conference on USENIX Security Symposium*. Berkeley, CA: USENIX Association.

Tulving, E. (1974). Cue-dependent forgetting. *American Scientist, 62*, 74–82.

UK Copyright Service. (n.d.). *Factsheet P-01: UK copyright law*. Retrieved December 12, 2010 from http://www.copyrightservice.co.uk/copyright/p01_uk_copyright_law

US Copyright Office. (n.d.). *Fair use*. Retrieved December 12, 2010 from http://www.copyright.gov/fls/fl102.html

Wells, W. D., Burnett, J., & Moriarty, S. (1989). *Advertising: Principles and practice*. Prentice Hall.

Wiedenbeck, S., Waters, J., Sobrado, L., & Birget, J.-C. (2006). Design and evaluation of a shoulder-surfing resistant graphical password scheme. In *Proceedings of the Working Conference on Advanced Visual Interfaces* (pp. 177-184). ACM. doi:10.1145/1133265.1133303

Wobbrock, J. O. (2009, October). Tapsongs: Tapping rhythm-based passwords on a single binary sensor. In *Proceedings of the 22nd Annual ACM Symposium on User Interface Software and Technology* (pp. 93-96). ACM. doi:10.1145/1622176.1622194

Yan, J., Blackwell, A., Anderson, R., & Grant, A. (2004). Password memorability and security: Empirical results. *IEEE Security and Privacy*, *2*(5), 25–31. doi:10.1109/MSP.2004.81

ADDITIONAL READING

Adams, A., & Sasse, M. A. (1999). Users are not the enemy. *Communications of the ACM*, *42*(12), 40–46. doi:10.1145/322796.322806

Barton, B. F., & Barton, M. S. (1984). User-friendly password methods for computer-mediated information systems. *Computers & Security*, *3*(3), 186–195. doi:10.1016/0167-4048(84)90040-3

Blood, A. J., & Zatorre, R. J. (2001). Intensely pleasurable responses to music correlate with activity in brain regions implicated in reward and emotion. *Proceedings of the National Academy of Sciences of the United States of America*, *98*(11), 818–823. PMID:11573015

Conrad, M., French, T., & Gibson, M. (2006). A pragmatic and musically pleasing production system for sonic events. *In IV'06: Proceedings of Tenth International Conference on Information Visualization*, (pp 630–635). IEEE Computer Society. doi:10.1109/IV.2006.10

Dhamija, R., & Perrig, A. (2000). Déjà vu: A user study using images for authentication. In *Proceedings of USENIX Security Symposium*, (pp 45–58), Denver, Colorado, USA. USENIX Association.

Dunphy, P., Heiner, A. P., & Asokan, N. (2010). A closer look at recognition-based graphical passwords on mobile devices. In *SOUPS'10:Proceedings of the Sixth Symposium on Usable Privacy and Security*. (Article 3). ACM: New York, NY, USA. doi:10.1145/1837110.1837114

Eschrich, S., Munte, T. F., & Altenmüller, E. O. (2008). Unforgettable film music: The role of emotion in episodic long-term memory for music. *BMC Neuroscience*, *9*(1), 48. doi:10.1186/1471-2202-9-48 PMID:18505596

Franklin, K. M., & Roberts, J. C. (2004). A path based model for sonification. In *IV'04: Proceedings of Eighth International Conference on Information Visualization*, (pp. 865–870). IEEE Computer Society.

Gallace, A., & Spence, C. (2008). The cognitive and neural correlates of "tactile consciousness": A multisensory perspective. *Consciousness and Cognition*, *17*(1), 370–407. doi:10.1016/j.concog.2007.01.005 PMID:17398116

Gibson, M., Conrad, M., Maple, C., & Renaud, K. (2010). Accessible and Secure? Design Constraints on Image and Sound Based Passwords, In *i-Society'10: Proceedings of International Conference on Information Society*. IEEE Computer Society.

Herley, C., Oorschot, P. C., & Patrick, A. S. (2009). Passwords: If We're So Smart, Why Are We Still Using Them? In Dingledine, R. Golle, P. (Eds.) Financial Cryptography and Data Security. Lecture Notes In Computer Science, Vol. 5628. pp.230-237. Springer-Verlag, Berlin, Heidelberg

Kaufman, E., Lord, M., Reese, T., & Volkman, J. (1949). The discrimination of visual number. *The American Journal of Psychology, 62*(4), 498–525. doi:10.2307/1418556 PMID:15392567

Kuber, R., & Yu, W. (2006). Authentication using tactile feedback. Paper presented at *British Computer Society, HCI Engage 2006, Interactive experiences*. London, UK.

Kuber, R., & Yu, W. (2010). Feasibility study of tactile-based authentication. *International Journal of Human-Computer Studies, 68*(3), 158–181. doi:10.1016/j.ijhcs.2009.11.001

Moncur, M., & Leplâtre, G. (2007). Pictures at the ATM: exploring the usability of multiple graphical passwords. In *CHI'07: Proceedings of the SIGCHI conference on Human factors in computing systems* (pp. 887-894). ACM, New York, NY, USA. doi:10.1145/1240624.1240758

Nanayakkara, S., Taylor, E., Wyse, L., & Ong, S. H. (2009). An enhanced musical experience for the deaf: design and evaluation of a music display and a haptic chair. In *CHI'09: Proceedings of the 27th international conference on Human factors in computing systems*. ACM, New York, NY, USA. doi:10.1145/1518701.1518756

Open, I. D. Foundation (n.d.). *About the Open ID foundation*. Retrieved December 12, 2010 from http://openid.net/foundation/

Renaud, K. (2009). Web authentication using Mikon images. In *CONGRESS'09: World conference on privacy, security, trust and the management of e-business*, (pp. 79-88). IEEE Computer Society. doi:10.1109/CONGRESS.2009.10

Shay, R., Komanduri, S., Kelley, P. G., Leon, P. G., Mazurek, M. L., Bauer, L., et al. (2010). Encountering stronger password requirements: user attitudes and behaviors. In *SOUPS'10: Proceedings of the Sixth Symposium on Usable Privacy and Security*. (Article 2). ACM, New York, NY, USA. doi:10.1145/1837110.1837113

Shibata, D. (2001) Brains of deaf people "hear" music. *International Arts-Medicine Association Newsletter,* 16,4.Retrieved December 12, 2010 from http://www.iamaonline.org/Dec01_IAMA_NL.PDF

United States Access Board. (2000). *Electronic and Information Technology Accessibility Standards (Section 508)*. Retrieved December 12, 2010 from http://www.access-board.gov/sec508/standards.htm

Web Accessibility Initiative. (2006). *Policies Relating to Web Accessibility*. Retrieved December 12, 2010 from http://www.w3.org/WAI/Policy/

Yan, J. J. (2001). A note on proactive password checking. In *NSPW'01: Proceedings of the 2001 workshop on New security paradigms*, (pp. 127-135). ACM, New York, NY, USA. doi:10.1145/508171.508194

KEY TERMS AND DEFINITIONS

Brute Force Attack: Attacker sequentially works through all possible passwords until a valid one is obtained. Can be "offline" where attacker obtains a file containing hashed passwords, subsequently encodes possibilities and compares to file or, "online" where guesses are made directly at interface. Will find all passwords given sufficient time and space.

Dictionary Attack: Attacker uses a dictionary of common passwords and uses these in an attempt to gain access. Can also be implemented on or off-line. Saves time compared to brute force, though not guaranteed to find every password.

Entropy: In this context, the randomness or lack of predictability of a password's distribution throughout the available space.

Low and Slow Attack: Similar to a brute force attack, although attacker distributes guesses over a number of accounts to avoid detection.

Musical Password: A password which utilizes music as the alphabet.

Password Alphabet: The set of letters that can be included to form passwords.

Password Space: The number of unique passwords that can be created from an alphabet.

Single-Sign-On (SSO): A system which allows access to numerous accounts once authenticated to a single session – reduces the number of passwords requiring memorization.

Chapter 7
Privacy, Security, and Identity Theft Protection:
Advances and Trends

Guillermo A. Francia III
Jacksonville State University, USA

Frances Shannon Hutchinson
ITEL Laboratories, USA

Xavier Paris Francia
Jacksonville State University, USA

ABSTRACT

The proliferation of the Internet has intensified the privacy protection and identity theft crises. A December 2013 report by the U.S. Department of Justice indicates that 16.6 million persons were victims of identity theft with direct and indirect losses amounting to almost $24.7 billion in 2012 (Harrell & Langton, 2013). These startling and apparently persistent statistics have prompted the United States and other foreign governments to initiate strategic plans and to enact several regulations in order to curb the crisis. This chapter surveys recently enacted national and international laws pertaining to identity theft and privacy issues. Further, it discusses the interplay between privacy and security, the various incentives and deterrence for privacy protection, and the prospects for the simulation of the social and behavioral aspects of privacy using the agent-based modeling.

INTRODUCTION

As an extension of an earlier work (Francia & Hutchinson, 2012) on regulations and compliance pertaining to identity theft prevention, detection, and response policies, we describe recently enacted national and international laws pertaining to identity theft. We also expound on the relationship between privacy and security, the various incentives and deterrence for privacy protection, and possible research extensions that include the social and behavioral study on privacy protection through agent-based modeling and simulation.

DOI: 10.4018/978-1-4666-7381-6.ch007

Figure 1. Types of identity theft

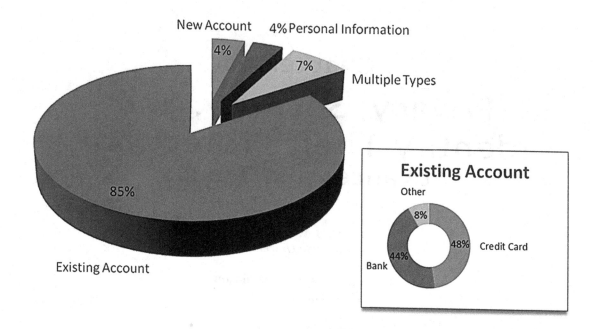

BACKGROUND

Identity theft is a threat that has confounded society since the biblical times. The ubiquity of the Internet and the convenience of electronic transactions have exacerbated the threat and made it even much easier to execute. A most recent report by the Department of Justice indicates staggering losses amounting to almost $25 billion incurred due to almost 17 million cases of identity theft losses (Harrell & Langton, 2013). Snapshots of several alarming statistics, which are gathered from the same source and are pertinent to identity theft, are shown in Figure 1 and Table 1. Figure 1 depicts the allocation of ID thefts by type. The inner chart further breaks the existing account slice into three categories: credit card, bank account, and other account.

Table 1 shows the actions taken by individuals to reduce their risk of identity theft. Note the alarming percentage of people using an ID theft protection service.

Table 1. Actions taken to reduce the risk of ID theft

Action Taken	Percentage
Checked credit report	37.9
Changed passwords on financial accounts	28.6
Purchased identity theft insurance/credit monitoring service	5.3
Shredded/destroyed documents with personal information	67.4
Checked bank or credit statements	74.8
Used identity theft security program on computer	16.6
Purchased identity theft protection	3.5

(Harrell & Langton, 2013).

These alarming statistics and their perceived persistent nature should motivate everyone, most importantly private and public institutions, to adhere and remain in compliance with policies and regulations that promote privacy and security protections. We begin with the definition of important concepts pertaining to regulatory compliance and identity theft.

REGULATORY LAWS AND COMPLIANCE

ID Theft protection is a subject of a variety of additional security-focused legislation. For example, health care providers and their affiliates are subject to the Health Insurance Portability and Accountability Act of 1996 (HIPAA), which specifically protects the rights and information of patients and health care plan participants (Salomon, Cassat, & Thibeau, 2003). Educators must contend with the Family Education Rights and Privacy Act, or FERPA, which strives to protect the information of students (Salomon et al., 2003). In fact, some educational institutions may find themselves covered by both FERPA and HIPAA if that institution is affiliated with a health care provider.

An update to an earlier work (Francia & Hutchinson, 2012) which describes several laws and regulations that pertain to information security and identity theft prevention or response is presented in the following.

HITECH Act

The Health Information Technology for Economic and Clinical Health (HITECH) Act is part of the American Recovery and Reinvestment Act (ARRA) of 2009 (U.S. Government Printing Office Public Law 111-5, 2009). Among its many purposes is the promotion of health information technology which ensures that the patient's health information is secure and protected. The security provisions closely related to the protection of health information includes:

- Notification of affected patients in cases of security breaches;
- Restrictions on the sale and marketing of health information;
- The provision of patient access to electronic health information;
- Accounting of disclosures of health information to patients; and
- Additional HIPAA regulations covering business partners such as vendors and exchanges.

COPPA

The Children's Online Privacy Protection Act (COPPA), which was enacted in 1998 and became effective in April, 2000, applies to the online collection of personal information of children under the age of 13. It includes provisions to protect the children's privacy rights, to restrict marketing to those children, and to seek verifiable consent from the parent or guardian (Legal Information Institute, 2014). The authority to issue regulations and enforce COPPA is with the Federal Trade Commission (FTC). In December 2012, the FTC issued revisions to the rules which include four new categories to the definition of personal information: geolocation information; photo, videos or audio files; user names; and persistent identifiers that can be used to identify a user over time and across multiple websites. Enforcement actions of the FTC include a deterrent civil penalty of up to $16,000 per violation (Bureau of Consumer Protection, 2014).

U.S.-EU Safe Harbor Framework

The U.S. Safe Harbor Framework is a process with which U.S. companies can transfer personal data from the European Union (EU) to the United States. This process is consistent with the requirements of the EU Data Protection Directive (Bureau of Consumer Protection, 2014B). It would take a U.S. company's self-certification of compliance with the seven principles and other requirements by the Commerce Department to be able to join the U.S.-EU Safe Harbor. The seven principles are:

- **Notice:** Organizations must notify an individual about the purpose of privacy-related data collection.
- **Choice:** Organizations must provide an individual the option to choose whether personal data collection can or cannot be continued and/or disclosed to a third party.
- **Onward Transfer:** Organizations must apply the notice and choice principles when disclosing to a third party.
- **Access:** Individuals must be provided access to their own personal data and must be able to correct, amend, or delete any of that information.
- **Security:** Organizations must provide adequate protection of personal data.
- **Data Integrity:** Organization must ensure that the personal information remain accurate, complete, and current for its intended purpose.
- **Enforcement:** To ensure compliance, effective means of enforcement of these rules must be in place.

Other International Privacy Laws

During the last decade other countries have vigorously pursued and enacted legislation on privacy rights protection. Among these countries are Malta (*Personal Data and Protection of Privacy Regulation (SL 399.25)*), Romania (*Processing of Personal Data and the Protection of Privacy in the Electronic Communications Sector; Law no. 506 (2004)*), and Singapore (*Banking Act, the Statistics Act, the Official Secrets Act, and the Statutory Bodies and Government Companies (Protection of Secrecy) Act*). (Francia and Ciganek, 2010).

Recently enacted laws related to privacy rights protection include Australia's *Personally Controlled Electronic Health Records Act 2012* (*ALRC, 2014*), Mexico's *Protection of Personal Data Held by Private Parties Law 2010* (IAPP, 2014), and Belgium's *Royal Decree on Data Retention 2013* (Data Guidance, 2014).

PRIVACY AND SECURITY

The Difference between Privacy and Security

The words "privacy" and "security" can invoke similar imagery, such as a picture of a closed door or thoughts of one's home; however, the two are separate concepts that must both be taken into account whenever someone's information or safety is at risk. Privacy may be defined as "the quality or state of being apart from company or observation", "freedom from unauthorized intrusion", or simply "the state of being alone" (Merriam-Webster, Incorporated, 2014).

One of the key issues when attempting to protect privacy or security is a difference in expectations. United States law on the subject remains ambiguous, stating that citizens have a "reasonable" expectation of privacy and should be protected from "unreasonable" searches and seizures, but what is and is not reasonable is ill-defined and must often be revisited with the emergence of new technologies (Verrecchia & Weiss, 2013). The now-famous case of *Olmstead v. United States* first brought this issue to light as the country struggled to determine how private a telephone conversation really is, and who would be allowed to listen in (and to what extent, and under what circumstances) without penalty. This same issue has been revisited recently in light of even more advanced technology that allows for the collection of massive amounts of data, which has been used by the National Security Agency (NSA) to amass a bulk collection of citizens' phone record metadata in the name of preventing potential terrorist attacks and other threats (Savage, 2013). In the Olmstead case, it was ruled that citizens had a right to an expectation of privacy when speaking on the telephone; in a later case (*Smith v. Maryland*), the ruling stated that while the content of a phone conversation was expected to be private, records of the call itself (such as the parties involved, the time of the call, and its length) were considered to be public information kept by the phone companies and could be used in police investigations (Verrecchia & Weiss, 2013). The more recent question seems to be, given the newfound ease with which such large amounts of metadata can be collected and analyzed to infer additional information, can the collection of such data on this scale still be considered a "reasonable" breach of the average citizen's privacy? While firm action has not been taken one way or the other as of this writing, the ruling of at least one District Court judge Richard J. Leon indicates that such behavior is unconstitutional, opposing the fifteen Foreign Intelligence Surveillance Court judges who have previously examined this issue (Savage, 2013).

Privacy vs. Security

Several recent political debates have chosen to frame issues in this context: would you rather be private or secure? While this "either-or" mentality has always had some presence in courtrooms due to concerns over unconstitutional searches and seizures in the name of preventing future crimes, it has become far more prevalent following the United States' long anti-terrorism campaign and its attempts to justify ever more invasive security measures. This approach of gathering data on everyone in an attempt to locate a few potential criminals is called a dragnet approach (Noble, 2013).

Some security experts argue that the privacy versus security standpoint is in itself a "false choice" and that traditional security measures have always been designed to reinforce security without compromising privacy, such as door locks, fences, and firewalls (Sullivan, 2013). One oft-quoted

argument of those willing to give up their privacy is "nothing to hide", which is used to insinuate that anyone who wants to protect their privacy must have something to hide and is therefore to be treated with suspicion. The fallacy of this argument lies in the fact that everyone does, in fact, have something to hide – personal information in the wrong hands can be used to directly harm an individual financially, emotionally, or even physically, and it is not always apparent who will abuse that information until they have already done so.

The legal decisions currently being made about massive data collection and dragnet techniques are important because they will play a part in defining what personal data can be collected by government entities, corporations, and individuals and how that data may be handled by those who collect it.

INCENTIVES AND DETERRENCE FOR PRIVACY PROTECTION

Incentives for Individuals

The primary incentive for an individual to protect his or her private information is a strong one; aside from the general feeling of security that accompanies control over one's personal information, maintaining privacy greatly reduces the risk of identity theft, which can have lasting fiscal and social repercussions for the victim. While everyone can benefit from basic security measures like using strong passwords or shredding sensitive documents, particular circumstances or statistics can further incentivize individuals to invest in their privacy and the privacy of those around them.

Another area of privacy protection that is easily overlooked is the protection of one's personal information from friends, family, neighbors, and coworkers. Sadly, not all cases of identity theft are the work of major data breaches or faceless hackers in far-away locations. In a 2007 FTC report, sixteen percent of surveyed identity theft victims reported that they knew the perpetrator personally with an alarming six percent reporting a family member (Federal Trade Commission, 2007). Keeping sensitive documents out of sight, not lending credit and debit cards for others to use, and keeping passwords or lock combinations private are all simple precautions that can help to reduce the temptation of someone close to home in committing identity theft.

In spite of all preventative measures, the truth is that no amount of precaution, monitoring, or paid services can guarantee identity theft protection. Major data breaches are becoming more commonplace, and sensitive data has become cheap. According to a set of statistics reported by Robert Siciliano, a compromised U.S. bank account with a balance of $70,000 - $150,000 can be purchased online for as little as $300, while as little as $8 will buy a stolen U.S. credit card (CVV number included) and a mere $40 will purchase a stolen U.S. identity (Siciliano, 2014). Persons and businesses whose information has not yet been compromised cannot feel entirely safe, either; $25 to $100 will buy a dedicated criminal to extract substantial information on a given person or business through means such as Trojan infiltration or social engineering (Siciliano, 2014).

Incentives for Corporations

Various organizations gather immense amounts of personal data about their customers, ranging from consumer shopping habits to names, credit card numbers, passwords, email addresses, and other information. Some of this information is required in order to conduct business. Medical facilities must keep their patients' medical histories on hand for the purpose of informed diagnosis and treatment. All of this personal data could be abused should the company suffer from a data breach.

Particular attention has been paid to large corporation data breaches of late as they appear to be growing in both frequency and scale. The potential for a data breach to occur should give any corporation reason to invest in the security of its collected information since the compromised data can result in millions of dollars' worth in damage control. Target in particular has suffered staggering losses from its 2013 holiday data breach, including $61 million expenses in 2013 alone as well as more than 80 as of yet unresolved lawsuits against the company (Lobosco, 2014). In an infographic posted by security researchers, the financial costs of another major data breach – Sony in 2011 – are listed as $171 million as of the time the research was conducted with an estimated potential for up to $24 billion total in damages before the lingering effects of the data breach would subside (Veracode, 2014). Both breaches could have been prevented, or at least mitigated, by stronger security precautions such as more careful system monitoring or code checks.

Major credit card companies also suffer from each data breach because they may be responsible for partially or fully absorbing the cost of an identity theft, depending on how much protection the company offers its card holders and whether the thief is ever proven or apprehended. For this reason, several U.S. credit companies are pressuring other corporations to adopt the Europay, Mastercard and Visa (EMV) technology currently used in Europe (Harris, Perlroth, & Popper, 2014). This technology embeds small chips into credit and debit cards which produce a new code for each transaction, making them much more difficult to counterfeit than a card which only uses traditional CVV information and protecting users from having their card information easily stolen by point-of-sale attacks at a cash register. The United States has been slow to adopt this technology even though this country accounts for roughly 47% of all credit card fraud (though, interestingly, only 27% of all credit transactions) (Harris, Perlroth, & Popper, 2014).

Deterrence for Individuals

Despite the enormous damages that can be incurred from having one's personal information used in a malicious way, there is a great deal of deterrence in the modern world against keeping such information private. The mere existence of social media sites such as Facebook and Twitter encourage users to share large amounts of personal information such as likes and dislikes, phone numbers, marital status, current location, schools and universities attended, and anything else that a person might be convinced to share with friends online. For users, sharing this information may allow them to locate long-lost contacts or connect with people who claim to share similar interests. The value of this data for the social media sites is that it can be collected and used to provide marketers with targeted advertisements for users of the site to generate more revenue by tailoring ads to those whom are most likely to follow through and make purchases from them. However, widely available personal data can also be used maliciously in social engineering, fraud, or harassment.

Social media aside, many individuals may be convinced to part with a little bit of privacy here and there in order to receive some other benefit; for instance, whenever a consumer signs up for a loyalty card at a local retail outlet, the outlet is likely to collect data about that user such as an identifying name, phone number, or email address as well as more particular data about how often the user shops at that location and what items he or she tends to purchase (Privacy and Data Security: Protecting Consumers in the Modern World, 2011). In return for this personal information, the consumer may receive a discount on goods purchased, though perhaps without knowledge of the precise quantity of information that has just been traded or what will be done with it.

A less obvious but far more common means of deterrence against privacy can be found in the average terms of service or privacy policy itself.

In 2008, it was estimated that it would take the average American over 200 hours every year to read the privacy policies of every site they were likely to use – and that is assuming that the reader is able to understand the policy the first time it is read, if at all (Misener, 2014). It is likely that this number has increased over the years as more companies use the Internet to provide additional services and reach new audiences. Additionally, companies are not always required to notify their users when the terms of service or privacy policies change, and can reserve the right to alter them at any time and any number of times within a given year (Misener, 2014). It should come as no surprise, then, that the average user "accepts" these terms and policies without having the slightest idea about what he or she is agreeing to.

Deterrence for Corporations

Just as the potential loss of profit and trust can incentivize large companies or organizations to protect the personal data they collect, so too can the potential for greater profit deter them from sharing this data.

Marketing is a common driving force behind data sharing. A 2003 study highlighted some of the benefits for marketers when choosing targeted advertising as a medium; in particular, fewer wasted dollars are spent advertising to users who were unlikely to ever follow through with a purchase and greater spending occurs in the advertising industry overall since targeted ads tend to generate more revenue than other, more traditional mediums (Iyer, Soberman, & Villas-Boas, 2003). By knowing the age, location, and personal preferences of many individuals, advertising companies can further refine their marketing strategies by choosing whether to target specific advertisements and offers toward those who are mostly likely to buy the product or toward consumers who are thought to have weak branding preferences and therefore may be swayed to try a product for the first time or to leave competing brands (Iyer, Soberman, & Villas-Boas, 2003).

Facebook in particular is known for collecting large amounts of data on its users over time and then offering to target advertisements based on that data. It has been a successful business strategy, generating over $2.34 billion in advertisement revenue alone as of the end of quarter on December 31, 2013 (Goel, 2014).

Aside from its use in generating advertising revenue and allowing retailers to adjust their stock and marketing campaigns to suit the interests of the consumers who are most likely to spend money, there is pure profit to be made by simply selling collected information. Entities that deal primarily in the buying and selling of personal information are called data brokers, and the information they trade could include anything from one's religious views and political affiliations to user names, income, medical history, web browsing history, known contacts and psychiatric profile (Kroft, 2014). This information may appear useful not only to those in the marketing or sales industries, but also to researchers or even prospective employers conducting a background check.

FURTHER RESEARCH DIRECTIONS

In theory, personal data protection appears simple; just perform the risk assessment, create the policy and procedures, then audit and revise as necessary. Unfortunately, it is often much more complex in practice.

Privacy laws can significantly differ across physical and cultural boundaries. Although humans are bound by core ethical standards, societal and business laws may be greatly influenced by culture. The need for an in-depth study of privacy laws that transcends physical and cultural boundaries provides a challenging extension to this research project.

The weakest link in the enforcement of privacy protection policies is always the people involved. Some individuals are especially prone to social engineering no matter how many information security awareness training they have undergone. Discovering the actual thoughts and actions of those that handle confidential information can be a tricky process, and changing a person's nature, beliefs or daily habits can prove nearly impossible. Thus, a study on the social behavior towards privacy protection and trust is a logical extension to this research.

In economics, utility functions have been used to describe and explain the behavior of consumers (users) within a system of constraint. Traditional, normative economic theory posits that human behavior is rational whereas behavioral economists have come to the conclusion that human behavior is best described as irrational. By incorporating psychological factors and processes into utility functions, behavioral economists have been able to describe human behavior with much more accuracy, and this increased precision has led to improvements in altering human behavior for the benefit of society (Kahneman & Tversky, 2000). Although this research has substantial implications for decision making involving privacy, there has been little attempt to evaluate the predictions of prospect theory as it relates to risky decisions in cyberspace, particularly in privacy protection. Thus, another natural extension to this work is the design and implementation of an agent-based model that can be used to simulate cyber risks and decision making processes in light of privacy protection.

CONCLUSION

Our discussions on the recently enacted national and international laws pertaining to privacy protection and identity theft prevention reveal a common thread: a continuous enhancement of the existing laws and regulations. It is easy to recognize that this phenomenon is brought about by technological advancements that are rapidly obliterating several restrictions to information access. As such, there is a constant need to improve various incentives and deterrence for privacy protection. Further, as we become more intimately bound by technology, a solid comprehension and understanding of our social and behavioral attitude on privacy and risky decisions in cyber space must be fully developed.

REFERENCES

Australian Law Reform Commission (ALRC). (2014). *Health information privacy.* Retrieved May 1, 2014 from http://www.alrc.gov.au/publications/3-overview-current-law/health-information-privacy#_ftnref20

Bureau of Consumer Protection. (2014). *Complying with COPPA: Frequently asked questions.* Retrieved April 30, 2013 from http://www.business.ftc.gov/documents/0493-Complying-with-COPPA-Frequently-Asked-Questions

Bureau of Consumer Protection. (2014B). *Federal trade commission enforcement of the U.S.- EU and U.S.-Swiss safe harbor frameworks.* Retrieved April 30, 2013 from http://www.business.ftc.gov/documents/0494-federal-trade-commission-enforcement-us-eu-and-us-swiss-safe-harbor-frameworks

Federal Trade Commission. (2007, November 27). *FTC releases survey of identity theft in the U.S. study shows 8.3 million victims in 2005.* Retrieved March 12, 2014, from Federal Trade Commission: http://www.ftc.gov/news-events/press-releases/2007/11/ftc-releases-survey-identity-theft-usstudy-shows-83-million

Federal Trade Commission. (2010, March 9). *LifeLock will pay $12 million to settle charges by the FTC and 35 states that identify theft prevention and data security claims were false.* Retrieved March 7, 2014, from Federal Trade Commission: http://www.ftc.gov/news-events/press-releases/2010/03/lifelock-will-pay-12-million-settle-charges-ftc-35-states

Federal Trade Commission. (2012, July). *How to keep your personal information secure.* Retrieved March 12, 2014, from Federal Trade Commission: http://www.consumer.ftc.gov/articles/0272-how-keep-your-personal-information-secure

Francia, G. A., & Ciganek, A. (2010). Global information security regulations, case studies and cultural issues. In M. E. Whitman & H. J. Mattord (Eds.), Readings and cases in the management of information security, volume II: Legal and ethical issues in information security management. Course Technology.

Francia, G. A., & Hutchinson, F. (2012). Regulatory and policy compliance with regard to identity theft prevention, detection, and response. In T.-S. Chou (Ed.), *Information assurance and security technologies for risk assessment and threat management: Advances* (pp. 292–322). IGI Global Pub. doi:10.4018/978-1-61350-507-6.ch012

Goel, V. (2014, January 29). *Big profit at Facebook as it tilts to mobile.* Retrieved March 15, 2014, from The New York Times Company: http://www.nytimes.com/2014/01/30/technology/rise-in-mobile-ads-pushes-up-revenue- and-profit-at-facebook.html

Guidance, D. (2014). *Belgium: Decree fully transposes data retention directive.* Retrieved May 1, 2014 from http://www.dataguidance.com/dataguidance_privacy_this_week.asp?id=2128

Harrell, E., & Langton, L. (2013). *Victims of identity theft, 2012.* U.S. Department of Justice, Bureau of Justice Statistics, December, 2013, NCJ 243779. Retrieved April 30, 2014, from http://www.bjs.gov/content/pub/pdf/vit12.pdf

Harris, E. A., Perlroth, N., & Popper, N. (2014, January 24). *Neiman Marcus data breach worse than first said.* Retrieved March 15, 2014, from The New York Times Company: http://www.nytimes.com/2014/01/24/business/neiman-marcus-breach-affected-1-1- million-cards.html?_r=1

Identity Theft Assistance Center. (2013). Retrieved March 7, 2014, from http://www.identitytheftassistance.org/pageview.php?cateid=47#childIDfraudReport

International Association of Privacy Professionals (IAPP). (2014). *Mexico federal data protection act*. Retrieved May 01, 2014 from https://www.privacyassociation.org/media/pdf/knowledge_center/Mexico_Federal_Data_ Protection_Act_July2010.pdf

Iyer, G., Soberman, D., & Villas-Boas, J. M. (2003, May). *The targeting of advertising*. Retrieved March 15, 2014, from http://groups.haas.berkeley.edu/marketing/PAPERS/VILLAS/tgtadv1_apr03.pdf

Kahneman, D., & Tversky, A. (2000). *Choices, values, and frames*. Cambridge University Press.

Kroft, S. (2014, March 9). *The data brokers: Selling your personal information*. Retrieved March 15, 2014, from http://www.cbsnews.com/news/the-data-brokers- selling-your-personal-information/

Legal Information Institute (LII). (2014). *TOPN: Children's online privacy protection act of 1998*. Retrieved April 30, 2014, from http://www.law.cornell.edu/topn/childrens_online_privacy_protection_act_of_1998

Lobosco, K. (2014, March 14). *Target details risks from giant data breach*. Retrieved March 15, 2014, from Cable News Network: http://money.cnn.com/2014/03/14/news/companies/target-breach/

Merriam-Webster, Incorporated. (2014). Retrieved February 28, 2014, from Merriam- Webster.com: www.merriam-webster.com

Misener, D. (2014, January 21). *Google's Nest deal highlights privacy-policy issues: Dan Misener*. Retrieved March 15, 2014, from http://www.cbc.ca/news/technology/google-s-nest-deal-highlights-privacy-policy-issues-dan-misener-1.2504839

Noble, J. (2013, September 11). *U.S. debates security vs privacy 12 years after 9/11*. Retrieved March 10, 2014, from USA Today: http://www.usatoday.com/story/news/nation/2013/09/10/us-debates-security-vs-privacy- 12-years-after-911/2796399/

Russer, M. (2010, June). *Maximize profits through hyper-targeted Facebook ads*. Retrieved March 15, 2014, from http://realtormag.realtor.org/technology/mr-internet/article/2010/06/maximize-profits-through-hyper-targeted-facebook-ads

Salomon, K. D., Cassat, P. C., & Thibeau, B. E. (2003, March 20). *IT security for higher education: A legal perspective*. Retrieved September 22, 2010, from http://net.educause.edu/ir/library/pdf/CSD2746.pdf

Savage, C. (2013, December 16). Judge questions legality of N.S.A. phone records. *The New York Times*. Retrieved March 2, 2014, from http://www.nytimes.com/2013/12/17/us/politics/federal-judge-rules-against-nsa-phone-data-program.html?pagewanted=1&_r=2

Siciliano, R. (2014, January 27). *Stolen identities are cheap on the darknet*. Retrieved March 10, 2014, from http://bestidtheftcompanys.com/2014/stolen-identities-are-cheap-on-the-darknet

Sullivan, B. (2013, July 6). *Privacy vs. security: 'False choice' poisons debate on NSA leaks*. Retrieved March 7, 2014, from http://www.nbcnews.com/business/consumer/privacy-vs-security-false-choice-poisons-debate-nsa-leaks-f6C10536226

Talbot, D. (2013, September 16). *Encrypted heartbeats keep hackers from medical implants*. Retrieved March 12, 2014, from MIT Technology Review: http://www.technologyreview.com/news/519266/encrypted-heartbeats-keep-hackers- from-medical-implants/

U.S. Government Printing Office Public Law 111-5. (2009). *American Recovery and reinvestment act of 2009*. Retrieved April 24, 2014 from http://www.gpo.gov/fdsys/pkg/PLAW-111publ5/pdf/PLAW-111publ5.pdf

Veracode. (2014). *Sony PSN breach infographic.* Retrieved March 15, 2014, from http://www.veracode.com/sony-psn-breach-infographic

Verrecchia, P., & Weiss, D. M. (2013). *Privacy vs. security.* Retrieved March 2, 2014, from York College of Pennsylvania: http://www.ycp.edu/offices-and- services/advancement/communications/york-college-magazine/fall-2013/privacy-vs.- security/

ADDITIONAL READING

Birrell, E., & Schneider, F. (2013, September-October). B. "Federated Identity Management Systems: A Privacy-Based Characterization. *IEEE Security and Privacy, 11*(5), 36–48.

De Cristofaro, E. (2014, March-April). Genomic Privacy and the Rise of a New Research Community. *IEEE Security and Privacy, 12*(2), 80–83.

Ellyatt, H. (2013, December 9). *How business can shed light on the 'dark net'*. Retrieved March 7, 2014, from CNBC.com: http://www.cnbc.com/id/101234129

Greene, S. S. (2006). *Security Policies and Procedures: Principles and Practices.* Upper Saddle River: Pearson Education, Inc.

Kahneman, D., & Tversky, A. (1979). Prospect theory: An analysis of decision under risk. *Econometrica, 47*, 263–291.

Singla, A., & Krause, A. (n.d.). *Truthful Incentives for Privacy Tradeoff: Mechanisms for Data Gathering in Community Sensing.* Retrieved March 10, 2014, from http://www.ics.uci.edu/~qliu1/MLcrowd_ICML_workshop/Papers/ActivePaper3.pdf

Tormo, G., Marmol, F., Girao, J., & Perez, G. (2013, November-December). Identity Management--In Privacy We Trust: Bridging the Trust Gap in eHealth Environments. *IEEE Security and Privacy, 11*(6), 34–41.

KEY TERMS AND DEFINITIONS

Compliance: The act of being in conformity with official regulations.

Identity Theft: The fraudulent use of another person's personal information.

Personally Identifiable Information: Any personal information by which an individual may be identified (SSN, bank account number, username/password combination, etc.).

Policy Compliance: A goal set by an organization in its attempt to encourage and achieve compliance by its members/employees with regard to the organization's policies.

Privacy: The state of being free of infringement.

Regulatory Compliance: A goal set by an organization in its attempt to comply with all laws or regulations relevant to that organization.

Security: The state being of being safe from danger.

Chapter 8
Identity Management Systems:
Models, Standards, and COTS Offerings

Reema Bhatt
State University of New York – Buffalo, USA

Manish Gupta
State University of New York – Buffalo, USA

Raj Sharman
State University of New York – Buffalo, USA

ABSTRACT

Identity management is the administration of an individual's access rights and privileges in the form of authentication and authorization within or across systems and organizations. An Identity Management system (IdM) helps manage an individual's credentials through the establishment, maintenance, and eventual destruction of their digital identity. Numerous products, applications, and platforms exist to address the privacy requirements of individuals and organizations. This chapter highlights the importance of IdM systems in the highly vulnerable security scenario that we live in. It defines and elaborates on the attributes and requirements of an effective identity management system. The chapter helps in establishing an understanding of frameworks that IdM systems follow while helping the reader contrast between different IdM architecture models. The latter part of this chapter elaborates on some of today's most popular IdM solutions.

1. INTRODUCTION

We live in an age where information systems dominate our world. For everything, from paying bills to ordering food or from buying apparel to managing bank accounts; we make use of the vulnerable and susceptible medium-the internet. Organizations-whether commercial or governmental, rely heavily on their intranet and internal information systems for efficient operations, management and day to day functioning. When making services available via computer networks, there is often a need to know who the users of the system are and what information they are authorized to view or access (Jøsang & Pope). Almost all websites and web services require users to present their identities

DOI: 10.4018/978-1-4666-7381-6.ch008

in order to be authenticated and granted access. Users are identified by their digital identities that comprise of usernames passwords, date of birth, search history, purchasing behavior, passphrases etc. This calls for user privacy management and related issues. Researchers argue that information exchanged online is susceptible to numerous threats which arise from two main factors. Firstly, users have no control over who views their information for e.g. a user knows that their passwords are stored in a database but they have no control over people who access the database. Secondary to this threat is the fact that the user's information is stored indefinitely which means that the identity thief can lie in the future as well (Alkhalifah & D'Ambra, 2012). According to a recent Forrester Research (Kark, 2010) identity and access management was identified as a top security issue for 2011 that needed to be considered as a critical component of corporate security strategies (Cser, 2008).

Two parts of identity management are identified by:

1. Providing users with credentials that can uniquely identify them; and
2. Using these credentials to authenticate users and grant them access and privileges based on these credentials (Jøsang & Pope). The dominance of digital identities, however, also raises concerns about protecting user privacy. Privacy is one of the most challenging issues related to identity management. Privacy related requirements impose several restrictions on identity management systems and therefore are extremely critical (Glasser & Vajihollahi). Users seldom have control over their own digital identity. Information that they provide as a part of mandatory disclosure is stored indefinitely in systems and databases that the users themselves have no control over. This has made it possible for hackers and criminals to rob people off money and information from the comfort

of their own homes. Identity theft is thus increasingly becoming one of the prominent cyber-crimes; hackers that can manage to steal an individual's digital identity get access to confidential information such as credit card numbers, bank passwords, SSN etc. Identity management systems, IdM, were therefore created to address these security concerns.

The contributions of this chapter are manifold. First it provides an overview of different architectures and applications of IdM systems. It provides an insightful discourse on the components and attributes of IdM systems so as to be able to decide what kind of systems will best fit the reader's organizational needs and requirements. It will serve as an excellent primer for IT and security professionals in understanding what options are available to them, which can immensely help them in decision making. It also presents a rich discussion of the background of IdM systems and the challenges that today's organizations can face in management of IdM systems. The last section presents some of the most popular and effective commercial off the shelf IdM systems that are available for purchase. This section will benefit organizations that do not wish to build customized IdM solutions but instead purchase one from commercial software vendors; which is not only the most widely used but also considered to be the most cost effective approach. Discussions and presentations in this chapter can act as an aid for security managers and professionals in understanding the current identity management solutions and technologies while facilitating their decision making and risk management. The goal of this chapter is to provide a broad view of IdM systems and help professionals make decisions that would benefit their company.

The organization of this chapter is as follows. Section 2 throws light on why IdM systems should be used, how they help a business and how they work. Section 3 highlights the key components of identity management systems while section 4 outlines the most common architectures of IdM systems. Section 5 details the attributes of a good IdM system. Section 6 describes some commercial software solutions available off the shelf from the market. Section 7 describes some challenges that can be anticipated while implementing IdM systems. Section 8 describes the applications of identity management. Sections 9 describes some industry standards used for identity management while section 10 outlines some of the risks associated with IdM implementation.

2. BACKGROUND

An identity management system is a framework of processes including the technology that facilitates management of digital identities in systems and organizations. The technology initiates, records and manages a user's identity and administers access rights and privileges based on the user's identity. IdM systems are a tool for IT managers to control access and protect critical systems and information from unauthorized use. Numerous technologies such as password management, monitoring software, digital certificates etc. fall under this category. After going through years of evolution and enhancements, today these technologies are available as software suits that provide sophisticated capabilities such as federated identity management, credential administration and management.

2.1 Functional Attributes of Identity Management Systems

IdM systems typically consist of the following functional attributes (Balasubramaniam, A.Lewis, Morris, Simanta, & B.Smith, 2009):

- **Identity Provisioning:** Provisioning is the process of creating and maintaining a user's identity. An example of this would be creating a user account on your bank's web portal.

- **Storage Management and Retrieval of ID Information:** User created digital identities are stored in databases and repositories, and consulted when a user seeks access to information assets.

- **Authentication and Authorization:** Often implemented using ID repositories, databases and directory services; these attributes identify, authorize and authenticate users seeking access to systems by verifying their credentials against their established identities.

- **Single Sign-On:** This allows users the flexibility to use the same identity and credentials across various systems, making them user friendy. This can be implemented using technologies such as Security Assertion Markup Language (SAML).

- **Auditing and Reporting:** An auditing system that periodically stores all activities taking place across the organization.

2.2 Identity Management Terminology

Identity management has two principal components – management of identity and management by identity. Management of identity is the process of issuing and using digital identities and credentials (such as usernames and passwords). Management by identity combines the proven identity of the user with their authorization, in order to grant access to resources (Wood, 2005). Listed below are some commonly used terms in the identity management domain:

- **Provisioning:** As mentioned earlier, the process of creating user identities, defining their access privileges and saving them in the ID repository.

- **De-Provisioning:** The process of deleting a user's identity from the repository and revoking all access rights.

- **Federated Identity Management:** Also known as single sign-on, federated identity management is a mechanism that allows users to share the same credentials across multiple systems among trusted partners.
- **Identity Synchronization:** The process of keeping all identity repositories consistent.
- **Identity Lifecycle Management:** This is the set of all processes such as provisioning, de-provisioning, synchronizing etc. for maintaining digital identities.

2.3 Why Should One Invest in Identity Management?

In order for organizations to enhance business productivity by protecting their digital assets and information, IdM needs to be an integral part of their systems for numerous reasons.

- **Security:** Managing the humongous information systems and interconnected computer systems, especially for large enterprises, becomes a little less complex and cost effective by making ID management a centralized process.
- **Controlled Access:** Considering the increase in commercial use of hand held devices such as cell phones, PDAs, laptops; ID management helps an organization keep track of the devices that are connected to its network—a must to ensure security.
- **Government:** Laws and government regulations such as Sarbanes-Oxley, Gramm-Leach-Bliley, HIPAA etc. require organizations to ensure confidentiality of client and employee information.
- **Competitive Advantage:** Implementing IdM is a best practice; it can give an organization a competitive edge over rivals. It provides a way for providing better customer service, by providing them access to your information systems, without having to compromise on security.
- **Cost Savings:** A study has revealed that most of the help desk calls received are for password resets, thus making automated password reset one of the biggest cost saving techniques for organizations. IdM systems automate password resetting and various other time intensive tasks.

3. COMPONENTS OF IDM SYSTEMS

According to Mark Berman and Joel Cooper, an identity management infrastructure is a collection of technology, business processes, and underlying network systems that determines access and authorization parameters (Tracy, 2008). This definition highlights the following basic components of IdM systems:

- A repository that defines and stores the digital identities of all users,
- A set of tools that can be used for adding, modifying or deleting that user data,
- A system for enforcing security policies and access control mechanisms, and
- An auditing system that records all the activities that take place on the system.

These components can be architected by an IdM system based on the requirements of enterprise such as security and privacy concerns, sensitivity of data that is protected, number of users, ease of use and so on. To aid such technical specifications, there are several approaches that have been suggested.

4. ARCHITECTURE

A general design is usually followed while designing and developing IdM systems. First and foremost, the system must have a source of information that verifies which users should and should not exist, as well as what their access permissions should be. If every random user can create a user account on an organization's intranet; the purpose of using identity management is lost. This is usually controlled through the use of an enterprise resource planner (ERP) such as SAP. The basic functions of the IdM server are to assign resources, remove resources, and disable resources. The IdM server creates user accounts and allocates resources based upon the information provided by the ERP system. With IdM in place a user may log in to an e-mail system and as a result of the credentials being checked, may also be granted access to their active directory without having to do anything else (Tracy, 2008). However, this is just a general architecture, there is lots of room for variation. IdM systems can be broadly classified into three main models i.e. isolated, centralized and federated identity systems (Miyata, Koga, Madsen, & Adachi, 2006):

4.1 Isolated Model

This identity model is one where the service provider also acts as the identity provider, and both identity and user operations are provided by the same server (Cao & Yang, 2010) . The service provider manages both the name space and authentication for all of its users, making it the identity provider as well. Unique users create their own identifiers and set their own authentication passwords within the system. The biggest advantages of this model are its simplicity and the fact that personal information being exposed solely to the service provider.

However, a disadvantage of this model is that it used solely for access to one system, and thus a user must create their own identifier and authentication criteria for every service provider they encounter. It is not uncommon for users to forget the details to service providers they use infrequently, preventing the services from being used to their full potential (Jøsang et al., 2007). Resultantly, user account and password management have long been major expenses for organizations (Gupta and Sharman, 2008a).

Figure 1. Silo model

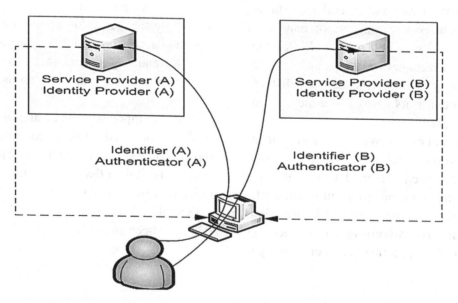

4.2 Common Identity Domain Model

In the Common Identity Domain Model, there is only one common identity provider that encompasses multiple service providers. In this method a user could use the same identity information over multiple services. A common authentication token in this model is to use a public-key certificate. Such a solution would be good for an organization that is able to assign a single, non-changing identifier to a user. Advantage of this model is that it is simple to manage for both the service provider and user. Only one set of identifiers and authentication information is needed by users, and thus it is easier to maintain.

On the other side, this can also turn into a disadvantage. It is difficult to manage a set of unique name spaces and identifiers for a huge number of users that are considered to be both stable and without privacy implications. For e.g., users are likely to have numerous e-mail addresses and as a result e-mail would not be a good identifier.

4.3 Centralized Single Sign-on Identity Model

This model allows for the use of a centralized identity provider that manages the name space, authentication tokens, and authentication of users. In sequence, a user sends their identifier and authentication information to the identity provider, the provider then sends a security assertion to the service provider(s); the service provider then grants the requested access. This model fits well into closed networks where multiple service providers are managed by a single organization. In such closed networks it is assumed that the identity and service providers are governed by the same authority with the same policies in place, making implementation a simpler process. A disadvantage of this model could be that it is considered to be unsuitable for environments where the service providers are not governed by a common authority. It is

Figure 2. Common identity domain model

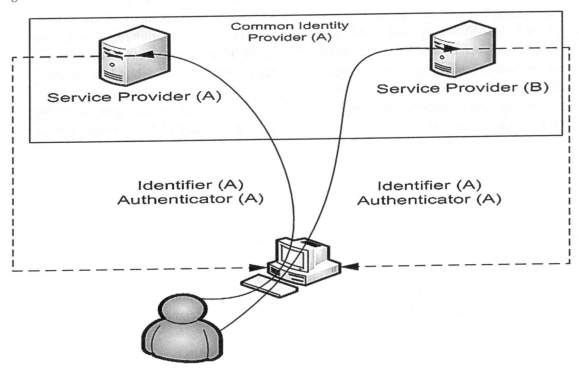

Figure 3. Centralized single sign-on model

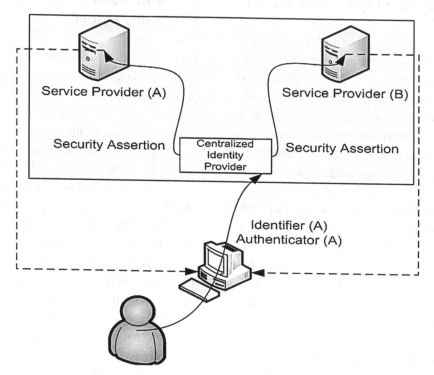

not that the model itself does not allow for easy implementation, but that it is unlikely that different service providers would accept an outside identity provider to manage and authenticate identities on their behalf. It would violate certain privacy protection principles regarding exposure of personal information (Jøsang et al., 2007). Recent research has proposed some improvements to commonly adopted SSO architectures (Cahill et al., 2011; Chadwick et al., 2011; Sun et al., 2010; Takeda et al., 2006).

However, in spite of the disadvantages; increased security and compliance, improved user productivity and convenience and real cost savings are few motivations that drive SSO implementation (Impravata, n.d, 2009). At the same time, there has been good amount of research done in the SSO domain to recommend improvements and to address some of the

identified concerns. For example, Mustafic et al. (2011) and Suoranta et al. (2012) proposed solution to single point of failure issue by suggesting improving strength of authentication. Alsaleh and Adams (2006) also suggest privacy enhancements, while Linden and Vapula (2005) propose improvements around usability. According to a Gartner report Single Sign-On system can save up to $300 per user per year which can account to huge amounts (Connolly, 2000). Single Sign-On (SSO) systems provide users the convenience of accessing multiple applications and systems while having to provide credentials only once (Gupta and Sharman, 2010). Most of the cross-enterprise SSO implementations are done using standards such as SAML or OAuth (Cantor and Kemp, 2005; Hirsch et al., 2005; Hardt, 2012), which also used by many commercially available products.

4.4 Centralized Model with Browser Support

It essentially takes the centralized single sign on method that Microsoft attempted to implement through the Passport service, but with multiple identity providers would be involved. The idea is that a user may want to use different identities for different situations. In such a system, a user has multiple 'InfoCards' stored on a computer contained in a 'CardSpace,' which do not contain any sensitive information. Each of these InfoCards points to a centralized identity provider where the sensitive information is stored. In this method a security assertion is first sent from an identity provider to the CardSpace module, and further forwarded to the service provider. The advantage of this model is that it improves upon centralized single sign on where service providers are not governed by a common authority. By allowing for support of multiple identity providers and centralized domains, the problem of leaving personal information in the hands of one giant identity provider is no longer a problem.

When it comes to disadvantages it can be said that they are amplified over the previous centralized model. The same problem exists with a third party identity provider holding personal information, albeit it is multiple providers instead of just one. This model also brings back a problem seen in the silo model. A user will be responsible for remembering multiple sets of identifier and authentication information due to the likeliness that they will be interacting with multiple identity providers for the different services they are using. Finally, if someone with ill intentions finds a way to exploit the CardSpace system, they could use the InfoCards and pointers that they have to identity providers to utilize a person's identity without having to actually steal it (Jøsang et al., 2007).

4.5 Federated Single Sign-on Identity Model

This model builds on single sign-on, with the idea that groups of service providers enter into a mutual security and authentication agreement. This agreement enables service providers to recognize user identities from other service providers (Rochet and Tirole, 2003). Like in the silo model, each identity provider is also its own service provider. The difference, however, is that the providers are linked. As an example, when logging in Provider A, a user will be identified as Identifier A. Provider A can send a security assertion to Provider B verifying the authenticity of the user that has Identifier A. The user will then be authenticated in the other providers system with its own unique Identifier B. The biggest advantage to this model is that it allows for single sign-on in environments where multiple entities are involved. It can also be retrofitted to an existing silo model, allowing for service providers to keep existing name space and authentication systems without the worry of conflict.

Federated identity management has its own drawbacks such as high investment costs, trust issues between partners, data synchronization and consistency and interoperability (Jensen, 2012). The main disadvantage here is that it relies heavily on trust between multiple organizations. Service providers must be able to trust security assertions from each other and have confidence that another providers will not try to exploit this in any way. This demands enterprises to enable convenient and secure business interactions with internal and external stakeholders, and create relationships to trust the electronic identities to access critical information resources. Federated identity management (FIM) is a system that enables individuals to use the same credentials or identification data to obtain access to the networks of multiple enterprises to conduct business transactions. FIM has demonstrated huge potential in providing reliable and scalable solutions to problems in systems security and access management. SAML (Security Assertion Markup

Figure 4. Centralized model with browser support

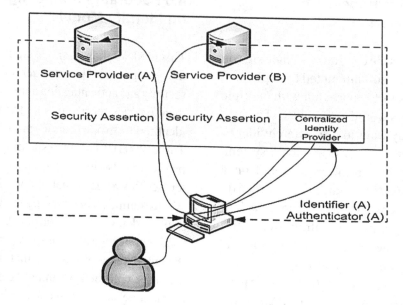

Language) is the dominant web services standard   for FIM (Gupta and Sharman, 2008b).

Figure 5. Federated single sign-on model

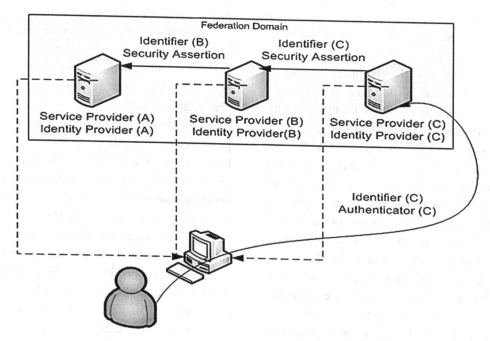

5. ATTRIBUTES OF A GOOD IDM SYSTEM

Listed below are some attributes to look out for, when selecting an identity management system (Alotaibi & Wald, 2012):

- **Multifactor Authentication:** Use of multiple authentication mechanisms for e.g. a combination of passwords and biometrics strengthens security of the system. However, this also depends on the criticality of the resource being protected.

- **Compliance with Standards:** Complying with international IdM standards facilitates an organization to implement hassle free updates, extensions and integration with other systems; if the need may arise in future.

- **Effectiveness and Efficiency:** The system should ensure that users are able to perform their tasks effectively with minimum time delay and should require users to perform minimum number of steps for authentication.

- **Usability and Memorability:** The system should implement uncomplicated account setup, recovery management and access management procedures that do not require lengthy interactions from the user's end. It should provide users with clear and concise instructions and error messages, where required. Functions and operations must be set in a logical order that are not very difficult for users to memorize.

- **Consistency:** Consistent procedures and operations across the system make it easy for users to grasp and comprehend information.

- **Security:** The most important attribute of an IdM system, strong and reliable authentication and authorization mechanisms that enforce access control. For e.g. a system that uses nonce based authentication

makes replay attacks almost impossible, as opposed to one that uses timestamp based authentication. A nonce is a random value that is generated every time encryption is done, and therefore has a new random value every time a user attempts authentication. This leads to a stronger notion of not only privacy but also authenticity (Rogaway, 2004).

6. MOST POPULAR SOFTWARE SOLUTIONS

In this section, we discuss some of the most popular IdM solutions available in the market today. These discussions are based completely off of information found on the websites of said solutions. The software systems are listed by company name in a random fashion order without any bias through the order.

1. **NetIQ Identity Manager 4:** NetIQ Identity Manager 4 was awarded the Readers Trust Award for "Best Identity Management Solution" at the 2014 SC Awards ceremony on February 25, 2014. It is a comprehensive identity management suite that provides an intelligent identity framework to leverage new as well as existing IT assets by reducing costs and ensuring compliance across various environments. NetIQ Identity Manager includes integration modules for several commonly used systems such as MS Active Directory, LDAP, eDirec-tory, Lotus Notes etc. in order to cater to the diver user base, Identity Management solution is available in two different editions—the standard as well as advanced version. Their motto is to provide "simple, secure access for the right people at the right time." (NetIQ, 2014)

2. **CyberArk Application Identity Manager:** This is one of the numerous software solution offered by CyberArk in the domains of

threat protection, security, secured access etc. It helps businesses protect the valuable information that lies in their internal information systems by implementing secure and robust authentication mechanisms. It eliminates all hard coded passwords from scripts, application code and configuration files thus making them inaccessible to developers and support staff. It aims to deliver high availability, redundancy and business continuity through secured caching capabilities. The Identity Manager provides accountability through maintaining logs of each transaction, password synchronization and encryption, and simple integration with third party applications (CyberArk, 2014).

3. **Enterprise Random Password Manager by Lieberman Software:** The Enterprise Random Password Generator (ERPG) is a privileged identity management product that can discover, track, secure and audit privileged accounts across an enterprise. Some of the features ERPG provides are super-user login accounts for that are used for configuration settings and other administrative tasks, service accounts that require privileged login ID and password, and application to application passwords that are used to connect databases, middleware and more. ERPM also has a feature called as True Discovery™ that on addition of new hardware or software, continuously discovers and secures new privileged identities. With the help of real time visualization ERPM provides dashboards that help organizations identify security and productivity issues (Lieberman Software, 2014).

4. **Identity and Access Management Suite by Evidian:** Awarded the best IAM Solution by SC Magazine in 2013, the Identity and access management system by Evidian helps organizations deploy a step by step a coherent access policy. It helps organizations unify digital identities from multiple sources such as HR, payroll etc. It automates the implementation of the access policy by creating roles directly at the IT system and constantly monitors its application. It implements a clean and simple system that facilitates quick and thorough audits. Evidian I&A Manager can efficiently integrate with existing systems to accommodate existing users without having to replace them. Its interoperability with other user access services, multilingual support and scalability make it a comprehensive solution (Evidian, 2014).

5. **CloudMinder™ Identity Management by CA Technologies:** A robust cloud-based service, the CloudMiner IAM solution helps organizations realize the benefits of cloud computing while at the same time miminizing security risks. Some of the features of CA CloudMiner are advanced authentication via multifactor credentials and device identification with SaaS model, federated single sign-on to cloud as well as on premise applications, automated user provisioning and de-provisioning along with synchronization with LDAP/Active directory. Some of the benefits that CloudMiner aims to provide organizations with are; reduction in deployment time, minimal operational and administration costs, better user productivity and reduced costs (CA Technologies, 2014).

6. **Centrify Server Suite by Centrify:** The Centrify Server Suite aims to protect mission critical servers from identity related risks and threats by leveraging existing Active Directory infrastructures to centrally manage authentication, access control, policy enforcement and compliance. They have a patented 'Zone' technology that provides unique access control. The Centrify Server Suite 2014 provides full activity audit trails and videos that can trace back every activity to individuals. The latest version supports over 450 platforms including various ver-

sions of Windows, Linux and Unix operating systems. By combining privilege management, Active Directory bridging and user activity monitoring in one comprehensive solution, Centrify provides organizations with a unique solution (Centrify, 2014).

7. **Universal Key Manager by SSH Communications Security:** The Universal SSH Key Manager (UKM) is a multiplatform, scalable solution that reduces the risks of unauthorized access from internal as well as external entities. It claims to implement identity management using a non-disruptive approach that allows enterprises to gain control of SSH infrastructure without having to replace any existing systems. This approach is based on three principles: discover trust relationships and policy violations, remediate invalid keys and incorrect policy compliance and manage by eliminating manual processes, enforcing compliance and maintaining proper audit trails. This highly scalable solution guarantees high availability, simpler compliance, stronger security while leveraging existing IAM infrastructures (SSH Communications Security, 2014).

8. **OneLogin, Identity Management in the Cloud:** OneLogin is one of the fastest IdM systems available for use with the cloud infrastructure that simplifies identity management among various users and across various devices and applications. It provides on demand solutions and services such as single sign-on, user provisioning, directory integration by connecting users Active Directory or LDAP servers with OneLogin, real time cloud search, strong authentication using PKI certificates, mobile access, password vaulting and reporting and analytics. OneLogin makes use of multiple data centers, redundant DNS app and database servers to guarantee a 99.99% system uptime. It is simple to use- has a clean interface and

fast setup process. One of the best features of OneLogin is that they offer clients numerous subscription plans to choose from (OneLogin, 2014).

9. **HID Global's 4TRESS Authentication Appliance for Enterprises:** The 4TRESS authentication appliance is an identity assurance solution for enterprises that provides strong authentication for all employees seeking access various applications such as cloud, VPN, workstations etc. it makes uses of multiple authentication technologies such as OTP tokens, smart cards, temporary activation codes, LDAP passwords, PKI, third party tokens among others to strengthen security at client systems. 4TRESS has a robust and resilient architecture that can accommodate from a 100 to a million users. It is compliant with OATH industry standards, thus preventing vendor lock-in; and provides easy integration with existing systems. 4TRESS aims to improve organizational productivity by allowing employees to connect to internal information systems through a variety of devices and at the same time decreasing risks by implementing robust, multifactor authentication that inhibits breaches (4TRESS, 2014).

10. **Access Sentinel by ViewDS Identity Solutions:** ViewDS is a developer of innovative Identity and access management software products that are deployed in a variety of industries. The ViewDS suite comprises of three products; ViewDS Directory Server-an XML enabled search server that offers search capability, Access Sentinel-an authorization server and Identity Bridge- a synchronization and integration tool. Access Sentinel Authorization Policy Server for Attribute Based Access Control built on ViewDS solutions, thus enabling storage of roles, policies and identity information on a single repository. It is an XACML (Extensible Access Control Markup Language) V3 standard

based solution that manages authorization for clients making their systems faster and safer to use. It provides added security and flexibility via attribute based access control (ABAC) and role-based access control (RBAC). Access Sentinel is a scalable, secure and efficient solution with a unique architecture that provides indexed search on any attribute (ViewDS Solutions, 2014).

11. **Access: One by Pirean Software:** Access: One is a leading, award winning access management platform that provides authentication, federated identity management and single sign n functionality. One of the striking features of this software is that it gives the organization full flexibility over interactions that users have in its digital presence. It provides services such as: Webtop- a central, cross platform launchpad that allows secure access from multiple devices, Access Store-enable users to manage access to numerous applications; and QRyptoLogin- a multifactor authentication mechanism that allows users to scan QR codes based on one time passwords. Access: One provides support for Automated User Management, LDAP Integration, Contextual Step-Up authentication, integration with Google and other applications, audit reporting, identity intelligence among various other services (Access: One, 2014).

12. **Shibboleth® by Internet2®:** Shibboleth, one of the world's most popularly deployed federated identity solutions, is a standards based open source software that allows single sign-on across and within organizational boundaries. It implements the OASIS Security Assertion Markup Language (SAML) to provide an attribute exchange framework. It provides extended privacy by allowing users to control attributes released to applications. Developed as an open source software, Shibboleth is released under the Apache License (Shibboleth, 2014).

13. **TridentHE by Aegis Identity Software:** Aegis Identity offers identity management solutions for the educational market. The TridentHE Identity Manager from Aegis is the education market's first open standards identity management solution specifically built for higher education. It provides features like provisioning-managing user roles and resources, password management-password synchronization, maintaining password policy, reconciliation and fine grained audit policies. Based on open standards such as SPML, SCIM, Eclipse among others, its SOA facilitates integration between systems. It aims to reduce the total cost of ownership by implementing a system that is simple, easy to install and maintain (Aegis Identity, 2014).

14. **ForeFront Identity Manager 2010 R2 by Microsoft:** Microsoft's ForeFront Identity Manager aims to reduce complexity of identity management by offering self-service identity management for e.g. by automation of remediation like password reset, automated lifecycle and role management, and a strong framework for corporate security policies and audit. The four feature areas provided by this solution are policy management, credential management, user management, and group management. It uses a SharePoint based console for policy enforcement and authoring. ForeFront supports heterogeneous identity synchronization and cross platform support. Easy extensibility and easy to use interface makes it a user friendly portal where users can manage their own identities (Microsoft, 2014).

15. **Oracle Identity Management:** Oracle Identity Management facilitates organizations to manage the user identity lifecycle within or beyond organizational boundaries via identity governance, access management, and directory services. Oracle has numerous different identity management suites

which can be licensed separately or bundled together. These are Oracle Identity Manager, Oracle Identity Analytics, Oracle Access manager, Oracle Web Services Manager, Oracle Identity Federation, Security Token Service, Oracle Enterprise Single Sign-On, Oracle Entitlements Server, Oracle Adaptive Access manager, Oracle Directory Services, and Oracle Platform Security Services. Separately they do such things as manage privileges, deal with regulatory compliance, implement single-sign on, protection of web services access and dealing with security token issuance, validation, and exchange amongst other things. (Oracle-IDM, 2014).

16. **Tivoli® Identity Manager by IBM®:** IBM Tivoli is a policy based Identity Manager that provides a secure, automated user man agement system that helps legacy and e-business systems. Some of the striking features of Tivoli are a role based administration model, web administrative interface and automated submission and approval of user requests. Highlights of this system include centralized web administration to reduce complexity, scalability, user identity lifecycle management support, and easy updates via the application management toolkit (Tivoli, 2014).

17. **PingFederate® by Ping Identity:** PingFederate is a lightweight identity management system that provides federated access management over the client's existing architecture or over the cloud. It uses token based security for authenticating users. Using adaptive federation, it encourages user customization of access scenarios. One of the striking features of PingFederate is that it can be deployed in any environment in less than a day. Some of the features of PingFederate include secured mobile access, integration with social media and automated user provisioning.

7. EVALUATION FACTORS FOR COMPARING VARIOUS SOLUTIONS

With the innumerable options for off the shelf software solutions available in the market, how does one decide which solution will maximize profits for their implementation effort? How do we compare various IdM solutions so as to pick the best one for our organization's needs? Given below are some evaluation criteria that help professionals distinguish between features of various commercial IdM solutions and make a decision on the best suited product for their business needs as well as technological environment.

- **Effort Required for Integrating with Current Applications, User Base, and Business Processes:** The solution that seamlessly integrates with the technological and organizational infrastructure should be the best bet, since it minimizes effort as well as cost.

- **Simplified Account Provisioning:** Comparing user account management functions i.e. creating, deleting, updating user profiles can help provide a good estimate of the effectiveness of the chosen system. These functions should be automated and available via a remotely accessible interface, so as to limit dependency on administrators for non-critical tasks. Critical tasks such as revoking access rights, recognizing illegitimate accounts, terminating users should be executed with minimum time delay. Select the system that can be altered to suit your specific business requirements, such as specific formats for auto generated user IDs.

- **Role Based Access:** In the best solution, different kinds of users should be able to access different, specific sets of information depending on their role/account type.

- **Compatibility with Servers:** Since every IdM needs to interface with various databases and application servers, evaluate solutions based on their compatibility with the leading names in the industry.

- **Speed of Access:** Does the solution create its own identity repository on implantation? Or can it integrate with the existing repository? Does it use indexing or any other such fast retrieval methods for? Organizations generate a humongous amount of user traffic on a daily basis and undoubtedly, the best solution is one that best manages the ever increasing user traffic with negligible down time.

- **Flexibility and Long Term Support:** In order to ensure easy maintenance, support and future enhancements, it is very important for the selected solution to adhere to industry standards. Using tools and technologies that are on the verge of extinction is not just monetarily but also technologically a bad decision; no matter how simple, cost effective or advantageous they may seem.

- **Scalability:** How many users and applications can the system support? Does it allow to extend these numbers in the future? How time/effort consuming would this be? Non scalable systems are usually a bad choice.

- **Accountability:** A good solution is one that supports full accountability by maintaining exhaustive object, user and application level audit trails. Flexibility in generating audit reports such as predefined v/s on demand reports, access control, compatibility with other reporting tools are desirable features.

- **Performance Tracking:** Does the system allow tracking details on system performance metrics such as user provisioning time, response time, number of users online, disabled accounts, locked-out accounts etc.? This makes evaluating performance of the IdM system a simple and comprehensible task. Availability of visu-

alization of these metrics via a graphical user interface is a huge advantage.

- **Strength of Security:** Needless to say, this is the most important factor while evaluating different IdM systems. The best solution will be one that enforces multifactor authentication, strong passwords and identities, simple yet secure password recovery, secure communication over networks etc. among others.

- **Synchronization:** Although identity synchronization is a choice of the organization, a solution that supports federated identity management and single is almost always desirable over one that supports a silo model so as to ease the process of future enhancements and extensions.

- **Usability:** Even the most secure, most profitable and easily deployable systems can be unsuccessful if the end users fail to use it with ease. Over complicated account setup, extremely stringent password rules, lengthy authentication process are features that you should avoid in a solution.

Although trying to find a single software that matches all these factors will be like looking for a droplet in the rain, the best way to go is prioritize on a set of factors necessary for your business and use them for evaluating options.

8. CHALLENGES

Implementing an identity management system for an organization requires thorough knowledge of not only the organization's internal information systems but also its functional/non-functional requirements; along with a good understanding of what solutions are available and which best fits the organization's specifications. Although it may seem to be a straight forward task, implementation of identity management is faced with numerous challenges. The most common ones are explained below.

- **User Access Control via Definition of Roles:** Companies are increasingly moving towards allowing external users to access their internal information systems. In order to provide access rights to internal users such as employees and contractors as well as to external users such as customers, vendors etc.; companies need to be able to distinguish between these users and accordingly provide access rights. This gives rise to the challenge of defining various user roles and assigning specific privileges to those roles. For e.g. a user may be able to view their utility bill on the web portal using their own credentials, but only an authenticated employee can make amendments to the bill.

- **User Administration/Account Setup:** Each kind of user requires their own account setup process. In order to enforce strict security, only legitimate members of the organization should be able to create user accounts with the system. When a user initiates account setup, the system should be able to recognize whether the user is authorized to hold an account. A generic example of this is when customers need to verify their email address and phone numbers in order to complete the account setup process. Employees can be identified by their employee ID's, names, date of birth or a combination of these factors.

- **User Provisioning/Account Maintenance:** Account maintenance can cost a company millions of dollars, if the optimal account setup processes are not in place. Managing the hundreds of users and maintaining their accounts can become a nightmare if accounts are incorrectly setup or worse if user roles are incorrectly defined. When a system has a large number of users, even a small task like resetting password becomes resource and time intensive. A study says that 45% of calls to IT help desks are from users who face issues in account setup, password resetting etc (Lee, 2003). The key here is to automate as many processes as possible.

- **Configuration for Account/Access Termination:** In the absence of accurate documentation that details all the rights and privileges that a user has been granted, account termination can be tricky. The identity management system should be configured for a simple and easy account termination process. Delay in revoking access rights of terminated users can prove to be a major security hazard.

- **Integrated Identity:** There are numerous applications and resources in organizations that users seek to access. Employees require credentials to access payroll, network systems, databases, email etc. Enforcing different credentials for use with every system complicates it not only for the user but also is an unnecessary overhead for the system. This calls for integrated or federated identity that allows users to use the same identity (credentials) across various systems.

- **Ensuring Regulatory Compliance:** Compliance to regulations and government laws that state what user information can be stored, storage restrictions; performing periodic audits and maintaining audit trails. This can be challenging when different national and state laws, organizational regulations and work domain specifications exist.

- **User Privacy:** Identity management systems store sensitive user information such as date of birth, passwords etc. This information is protected by user privacy laws. Adherence to these laws and strict compliance is of utmost importance.

- **User Acceptance:** Often the most neglected attribute, user acceptance often determines the success or failure of an implementation. A system that is too compli-cated for users has a high chance of failure. A simplified end user interface, quick and concise processes, procedures and access to resources, integrated identities, appro-priate error messages and quick recovery management are some usability attributes that make a good system.

- **Performance:** In order to obtain ROI on implementing identity management, the system should be quick in activation and deactivation of user accounts; require min-imal manual intervention; be flexible i.e. changing and updating user profiles and roles should be simple; robust i.e. should be able to handle increasing volume of us-ers efficiently, and consistent i.e. user iden-tities and information about users should be maintained consistent across the differ-ent data stores (Hitachi ID Systems Inc, 2014).

9. APPLICATIONS

We make use of computer networks and the inter-net for almost every activity from our lives- from maintaining a balanced diet and keeping count of calories to maintaining bank accounts and keeping track of our finances. This exhibits the omnipresence of user accounts and thus identity management. Identity management is used in various areas that include but are not limited to an individual's personal documents, work connectiv-ity, and attachment to social media networks etc.

9.1 Consumer

Consumer IdM systems aim to enable smooth in-teractions between the customers and user services by eliminating the need for users to maintain vari-ous identities and credentials and allowing them to use the same credentials across multiple systems. Various consumer domains that can benefit from

identity management are Ecommerce, healthcare, education, banking, finance, cloud storage among others. In this area there is typically a trusted third party who acts as the identity service provider and also as a point of authentication to the consumer to access their services. We can see this at play in various systems. Numerous websites allow new users to register with their existing Facebook, Twitter or Google credentials. Microsoft also now allows users to access their Windows 8 account, MS Office, Skype, and other services through a single account. An example of where this is cur-rently in wide use is with Microsoft's Windows Live platform. Windows Live is a freely available service which allows a user to integrate their e-mail, Windows Live Messenger, online storage, Xbox gaming experience, and other Microsoft provided services. When a user logs in to one of these services and continues on to use another of the services included in Windows Live, they are automatically logged in and are able to continue on without any further proof of identification. When registering to create a Windows Live ID, it is marketed as something that "gets you in to all Windows Live services," and that is exactly what it does (MS Live, 2010)

9.2 Commercial

In the commercial workspace, the administration of user accounts has, and will most likely continue to be a task that that consumes a large amount of an IT department's time and resources. In most organizations that have the ability and means to do so, IdM solutions have been implemented which allow for easier modification of user roles across the entire organization as opposed to an individual basis. This does not eliminate the administration of individual users on a case by case basis, but does greatly simplify the task of performing updates to groups of user accounts.

An important aspect of commercial based IdM which utilizes the technology to its fullest is when inter-organization shared space is involved. When two organizations collaborate, it brings about a situation where both security and quick access are required; and both organizations are likely to need access to certain parts of the others system. Having an appropriate IdM solution in place, allows for the needs of both organizations to be met without much overhead. When collaboration ends, the organizations are also able to easily cut access ties with little to no hassle.

9.3 Government

In the government realm there is a never-ending list of forms of identities issued with the most common ones including a driver's license, passport, and social security number. The management of identities within this realm is considered to be fragmented as citizens are identified by different government institutions through different credentials.

Implementation of IdM in the government sector involves exposing government services on the Internet and integrating mechanisms that allow for the proper identification of citizens. In government usage, citizens would essentially have IdM forced upon them whereas in consumer uses it is by choice; in commercial uses it is as a result of employment. The government must weigh social and legislative aspects of implementation across an nation. Privacy and freedom that the government would both need to guarantee to the public, and follow through with law establishing all aspects of the system (Casassa et al., 2002).

9.4 Mobile

The Pew Internet Project's research related to mobile technology revealed that 90% of American adults own a cell phone out of which 58% own smartphones (Pewinternet.org). It also revealed that more than making phone calls, people use their smart phones to connect to social media, share pictures, share their location, access the

internet, pay bills, send/receive email, share/store work related documents, coordinate meetings etc. Not only are people shifting from desktop computers to laptops, tablets and netbooks for everyday chores, but the usage of smartphones is at an all-time high.

With every operating system on a phone comes a different type of IdM that will connect the user to different services. A few of the more popular operating systems are Microsoft's Windows Mobile, Apple's iPhone OS, and Google's Android. As an example, on phones running the Android operating system, the screen a user encounters upon first boot of the phone asks for their Google Mail login information. Once a user does this, their phone syncs with their Google account and pulls mail, contacts, calendar events, and anything else they may use through Google. When the user updates or changes anything either through their phone or personal computer, the other is instantly updated.

10. STANDARDS RELATED TO IDM SYSTEMS

In order to establish definitive and widely accepted definitions of identity management methods, processes and terminology, various groups are working towards developing and establishing standards and frameworks that promote best practices in identity management solutions, and enable simple integration between different disparate systems. Some of the most widely used standards are discussed below:

- **INCITS/CS1:** Established in 2005, the InterNational Committee for Information Technology Standards- Cyber Security 1 includes standardization in the area of identity management in the form of an identity management framework, role based access control, single-sign on, privacy framework, role-based access control, anonymity and credentials among others. It also includes the areas of entity-authentication, non-repudiation and key management (INCITIS, 2014) .

- **ISO/IEC JTC 1/SC 27:** The ISO/IEC JTC 1/SC 27 is a sub-committee of the ISO/IEC JTC 1 of the International Standards Organization (ISO). This group works towards general methods, standards and techniques for protecting information and privacy. Some of the published standards under this area are ISO/IEC 9798-3:1998/Cor 2:2012, ISO/IEC 9798-1:2010 and ISO/IEC 9798-2:2008 for entity authentication, ISO/IEC 13888-3:2009, ISO/IEC 13888-2:2010 for non-repudiation. It also has published a framework for identity management ISO/IEC 24760-1:2011- that defines identity management terminology and core concepts (ISO, 2014).
- **SAML by OASIS:** The Security Assertion Markup Language by the Security Services Technical Committee of OASIS is an XML based framework for exchanging security information. There are four main components of SAML. Packets of information known as assertions-, protocols, mappings from SAML messages to standard message protocols called as bindings and profiles that define the usage of SAML specific to the applications (Cantor et al., 2005; Hirsch et al., 2005). The latest version of SAML i.e. V2.0 is used in a number of applications such as single sign-on, attribute based authentication and securing web services (OASIS, 2014).
- **WS Security by OASIS:** Web Service Security, WSS is a set of security policy assertions for use with the WS Policy framework. It defines use of token types and defines cryptographic algorithms, transport level security among other parameters, in an attempt to promote interoperability and

compatibility among different web service participants. WS Security mainly describes three components: signing SOAP messages to ascertain integrity, encryption of SOAP messages to guarantee integrity maintain security tokens to confirm message sender's identity (OASIS, 2014).

- **XACML by OASIS:** Extensible Access Control Markup Language, XACML, is a standard for representing and evaluating access control policies. XACML is primarily an Attribute Based Access Control (ABAC) system, however, Role Based Access Control (RBAC) can also be implemented in XACML. Applications of XACML include defining access control policies for web servers and services, gateways, firewalls, applications etc. (OASIS, 2014).
- **XCBF by OASIS:** The OASIS XML Common Biometric Format that provides a standard way to describe biometric information such as DNA, fingerprint, iris scan etc. The standard can widely help in various applications in areas of law enforcement, government, and corporate privacy (OASIS, 2014).

11. RISK ASSESSMENT

The primary goal of implementing identity management is to ensure that access to an organization's private and confidential information is granted only after execution of appropriate security processes and controls. It is a convoluted process with a simple goal- to protect organizational assets from unauthorized access. Although successful implementation reduces the security risks in an organization by a huge factor, it also brings business, usability and other risks that should be managed and mitigated. The implementation of identity and access management systems entails risks and challenges. A successful implementation will require changes to the processes and security operations, which introduces business risks (Aldhizer et al., 2008; Reymann, 2008). At the same time, they also introduce new risks in the technical and operational environments of any company while helping mitigate security risks through strong access management enforcement (Rai,et al., 2007; Engelbert, 2009; Links, 2008). Some of these are presented next.

- **Identity Chaos:** In the absence of federated identity or single sign-on systems, decentralized management of identities can result in a situation known as identity or password chaos where individuals seek access to numerous systems and have different credentials or each of these systems. To add to the confusion, different systems have different rules and constraints, expiration dates etc. on passwords. This leads to two things, increased support and maintenance costs because users will frequently forget their passwords and reduced learnability, and usability.

- **Extremely Stringent Constraints Can Reduce Productivity:** Stringent password rules such as use of alphanumeric characters, frequent update policy, lengthy passwords, account lock out after failed attempts etc.; that aim to strengthen security; can result in reduced user productivity when they fail to remember their complex passwords and frequently need to reset their password.

- **Insider Threat:** When the IdM system carries a huge amount of personal data from users, employee negligence as well as employees with malicious intent pose a great threat to data confidentiality. The people who are in control of the IdM system often have root access and all privileges to access all systems. Such people should be closely monitored, there should be thorough accountability and auditability in order to ensure non repudiation.

- **Securing Data Centers:** The databases, data stores and data centers where user's private information is store should also be highly protected via information security as well as physical security measures. Communication networks that are used for exchanging messages containing user identity attributes are common entry points for hackers and identity thieves. Securing these channels is of utmost importance to maintain user privacy

- **Business Risk:** One of the greatest risks, while implementing IdM systems is that of gaining a return on investment, ROI. The implemented security policies should not only help the organization move towards its goals and objectives, but the implementation project also should be able to fetch appropriate returns. Assessment to identify the level of security appropriate for the organization can help in minimizing business risk.

Numerous risk metrics for identity management systems facilitate reporting, interpreting audit logs and quantifying the risks related to and effectiveness of the IdM system. Some of these metrics are listed below:

- **Identity Count:** The number of user profiles that the identity repository holds.
- **Authentication Claims Count:** The number of successful and unsuccessful attempts made by users for authentication/authorization purposes.
- **Provisioning/De-Provisioning Efficiency:** The amount of time/resources expended in account setup and termination processes.
- **Password Strength:** The amount of time required to crack passwords.
- **Audit System Usage:** The percentage of successful/failed authentication or authorization activities logged, change tracking.

- **Compliance Scores:** A measure of how closely the system matches industry best practices and regulations.
- **Security Systems Coverage:** A measure of how well the organization is protected from the most common threats. In other words, the percentage of potential threats covered by antivirus, firewalls, antispyware systems, etc.

12. CONCLUSION

Identity Management covers the spectrum of tools and processes that are used to represent and administer digital identities and manage access for those identities (Allan et al., 2008). Usually people use different digital identities in different contexts depending on association of different information with each identity (Gupta and Sharman, 2008c). The three main business drivers for identity management solutions are security efficiency (lower costs and improved service), security effectiveness (including regulatory compliance) and business agility and performance (including workforce effectiveness and customer convenience) (Allan et al., 2008). Identity Management is a means to reduce such risks, representing a vital part of a company's security and auditing infrastructure (Buell and Sandhu, 2003). The secure and efficient administration of numerous personal attributes that make up digital identities is one of the key requirements in open and closed networks. Especially in respect to confidentiality and integrity, the users themselves, rather than popular external threads like viruses, phishing, or pharming attacks represent the main risk (Stanton et al, 2005). As a result of incorrect account management and inadequately enforced security policies users accumulate a number of excessive rights within the organizations' IT systems over time, violating the principle of the least privilege (Ferraiolo et al., 2003). Moreover, people have a hectic life and cannot spend their time administering their digital

identities (El Maliki and Seigneur, 2007). Identity Management in open networks like the Internet has received tremendous attention throughout the last years with researchers. Although considered important, Identity Management in closed networks, however, has not gained comparable significance within the research community.

Identity management has shown to enhance employee efficiency and also bolster security posture while containing costs (Penn, 2002). Enterprises, including commercial corporations and government agencies, are increasingly relying on identities of customers and citizens to provide services and consummate transactions over Internet (Mont et al., 2000). While recent laws and legislations (S.761, 2006)(1999/93/EC, 1999) aim at speeding up the process of adoption of digital identities by recognizing the legal validity of digital signatures both on electronic documents and electronic transactions, Internet identity thefts, and related frauds (Arnold, 2000; Coates et al., 2000) are fast growing crimes that take advantage of poor security and privacy practices and the underestimation of the involved risks. The maintenance of security of IdM systems has become challenging due to the diversity of today's specifications concerning, for example, privacy, system integrity and distribution on the Web (Gaedke, Meinecke, & Nussbaumer, 2005).

IdM software and solutions are used in practically all digital interactions where a person must identify themselves whether people realize it or not. The current status of IdM is one where users have learned to jump from one method to the other in their everyday lives with little thought of the inefficiencies that still exist, purely because each advancement in this area is still one step in the direction of becoming more efficient. A user that at one point was required to have twenty sets of identifier and authentication information will certainly be happy with being able to lower it to ten; no complaints will be made about wanting to have only one. In the scheme of things IdM is fairly matured, at least in the product offerings and architectures given the current state of technologies. At the same time, with new threats emerging all the time, there are enough growth opportunities in this field for further improvement and innovation.

Through taking a quick outside look at all of the aforementioned companies, it can be said that many provide similar services. However, it would be impossible to recommend any of these software solutions because just like every lock has a different key; every organization has different needs that an IdM system fulfills. And how well a solution fits into the organizational structure is determined by the organizational goals and requirements. A risk assessment against company's IDM requirements is very vital in ensuring right selection of tools for best risk management. There are many security risk management methods and tools available that can be leveraged for this purpose (Matulevicius et al., 2008) and they do offer flexibility in terms of analyzing certain aspects such as processes or issues in more details (Smojver, 2011; Taubenberger, 2011). Even more growing in importance in last few years is the emphasis on data privacy concerns which should be included in these assessments (Lund et al., 2011).

REFERENCES

1999/93/EC – Directive. (1999). *1999/93/EC of the European Parliament and of the Council of 13, December 1999 on a Community Framework for Electronic Signature – 1999*. Author.

Access: One. (2014). Retrieved online on 4/12/2014 from http://pirean.com/access-one/

Aegis Identity Software. (2014). Retrieved online on 4/12/2014 from http://aegisidentity.com/identity-software/products/tridenthe/

Aldhizer, G. III, Juras, P., & Martin, D. (2008). Using automated identity and access management controls. *The CPA Journal, 78*(9), 66–71.

Alkhalifah, A., & D'Ambra, J. (2012). The role of identity management systems in enhancing protection of user privacy, cyber security, cyber warfare and digital forensic. In *Proceedings of 2012 International Conference*. SyberSec.

Allan, A., Perkins, E., Carpenter, P., & Wagner, R. (2008). What is identity 2.0? Key issues for identity and access management, 2008. *Gartner Research Report*, ID Number: G00157012.

Alotaibi, S. J., & Mike, W. (2012). Security, user experience, acceptability attributes for the integration of physical and virtual identity access management systems. In *Proceedings of International Conference on Information Society (i-Society 2012)*. Academic Press.

Alsaleh, M., & Adams, C. (2006). Enhancing consumer privacy in the liberty alliance identity federation and web servies frameworks. In *Proceedings of the 6th International conference on Privacy Enhancing Technologies (PET'06)*. Springer-Verlag. doi:10.1007/11957454_4

Arnold, T. (2000). *Internet identity theft: A tragedy for victims* (White Paper). SIIA.

Balasubramaniam, S., Lewis, G. A., Morris, E., Simanta, S., & Smith, D. B. (2009). Identity management and its impact on federation in a system-of-systems context. In *Proceedings of 3rd Annual IEEE International Systems Conference*. IEEE.

Buell, A. D., & Sandhu, R. (2003). Identity management. *IEEE Internet Computing, 7*(6), 26–28. doi:10.1109/MIC.2003.1250580

Cahill, C. P., Martin, J., Phegade, V., Rajan, A., & Pagano, M. W. (2011). Client-based authentication technology: User-centric authentication using secure containers. In *Proceedings of the 7th ACM Workshop on Digital Identity Management*. Chicago: ACM. doi:10.1145/2046642.2046659

Cantor, S., & Kemp, J. (2005). *Liberty ID-FF protocols and schema specification.* Technical Report for Liberty Alliance Project, version: 1.2- errata-v3.0; 2004-2005.

Cao, Y., & Yang, L. (2010). A survey of identity management technology. In *Proceedings of 2010 IEEE International Conference on Information Theory and Information Security (ICITIS).* IEEE.

CA Technologies. (2014). Retrieved online on 4/12/2014 from http://www.ca.com/us/products/detail/ca-cloudminder-identity-management/details.aspx

Casassa, M., Bramhall, P., Gittler, M., Pato, J., & Rees, O. (2002). Identity management: A key e-business enabler. Paper presented at SSGR2002s, L'Aquila, Italy.

Centrify Corporation. (n.d.). Retrieved from http://www.centrify.com/blogs/tomkemp/privilege_management_made_easy.asp

Chadwick, D. W., Inman, G. L., Siu, K. W., & Ferdous, M. S. (2011). Leveraging social networks to gain access to organizational resources. In *Proceedings of the 7th ACM Workshop on Digital Identity Management.* ACM. doi:10.1145/2046642.2046653

Chappell, D. (2006, April). *Introducing Windows CardSpace.* Retrieved from http://msdn.microsoft.com/en-us/library/Aa480189

Coates, D., Adams, J., Dattilo, G., & Turner, M. (2000). *Identity theft and the Internet.* Colorado University.

Connolly, P. (2000, September 29). *Single signon dangles prospect of lower help desk costs.* Retrieved march 21, 2009, from infoworld: http://www.infoworld.com/articles/es/xml/00/10/02/001002esnsso.html

Cser, A., & Penn, J. (2008). *Identity management market forecast: 2007 to 2014.* Forrester Research Report. Retrieved on 4/18/2014 from http://www.securelyyoursllc.com/files/Identity%20Management%20Market%20Forecast%202007%20To%202014.pdf

CyberArk Software Inc. (2014). Retrieved online on 4/12/2014 from http://www.cyberark.com/product-etail/application-identity-manager-features

El Maliki, T., & Seigneur, J.-M. (2007). A survey of user-centric identity management technol ogies. In *Proceedings of Emerging Security Information, Systems, and Technologies, 2007.* Academic Press.

Engelbert, P. (2009). *5 keys to a successful identity and access management implementation.* A CA white paper. Retrieved on 4/18/2014 from http://www.ca.com/files/whitepapers/iam_services_implementation_whitepaper.pdf

Evidian. (2014). Retrieved online on 4/12/2014 from Retrieved from http://www.evidian.com/pdf/fl-iamanager-en.pdf

Ferraiolo, D. F., Kuhn, R. D., & Chandramouli, R. (2003). Role-based access control. Artech House Computer Security Series.

Gaedke, M., Meinecke, J., & Nussbaumer, M. (2005). A modeling approach to federated identity and access management. In *Proceedings of International World Wide Web Conference.* Academic Press. doi:10.1145/1062745.1062916

Glasser, U., & Mona, V. (2008). Identity management architecture. In *Proceedings of IEEE International Conference on Intelligence and Security Informatics.* IEEE.

Gupta, M., & Sharman, R. (2008a). Security-efficient identity management using service provisioning (markup language). In Handbook of research on information security and assurance (pp. 83-90). Hershey, PA: IGI Global.

Gupta, M., & Sharman, R. (2008b, December). Dimensions of identity federation: A case study in financial services. *Journal of Information Assurance and Security*, 3(4), 244–256.

Gupta, M., & Sharman, R. (2008c). Emerging frameworks in user-focused identity management. In Handbook of research on enterprise systems (pp 362-377). Hershey, PA: IGI Global.

Gupta, M., & Sharman, R. (2010). Activity governance for managing risks in role design for SSO systems. *Journal of Information Assurance and Security, 5*(6).

Hardt, D. (2012). *The OAuth 2.0 authorization framework*. RFC 6749, IETF; October 2012.

HID Global's 4TRESS Authentication Appliance. (n.d.). Retrieved from http://www.hidglobal.com/sites/hidglobal.com/files/resource_files/identity-assurance-4tress-authentication-appliance-ds-en.pdf

Hirsch, F., Philpott, R., & Maler, E. (2005). *Security and privacy considerations for the OASIS security assertion markup language (SAML) v2.0*. Technical report, OASIS; March 2005.

Hitachi ID Systems Inc. (2014). Retrieved online on 4/12/2014 from User Provisioning Best Practices.

Imprivata. (n.d.). *Benefits of single sign on*. Retrieved March 22, 2009, from Imprivata: http://www.imprivata.com/contentmgr/showdetails.php ?id=1170

INCITS. (2014). Retrieved online on 4/12/2014 from https://standards.incits.org/a/public/group/cs1

ISO. (n.d.). Retrieved from http://www.iso.org/iso/iso_catalogue/catalogue_tc/catalogue_tc_browse.htm?commid=45306

Jensen, J. (2012). Federated identity management challenges. In *Proceedings of 2012 Seventh International Conference on Availability, Reliability and Security (ARES)*. Academic Press. doi:10.1109/ARES.2012.68

Jøsang, A., Al Zomai, M., & Suriadi, S. (2007). Usability and privacy in identity management architectures. In *Proceedings of the Australasian Information Security Workshop 2007*. Ballarat, Australia: Academic Press.

Jøsang, A., & Pope, S. (n.d.). User centric identity management. *CRC for Enterprise Distributed Systems Technology* (DSTC Pty Ltd). The University of Queensland.

Kark, K. (2010). *Twelve recommendations for your 2011 security strategy*. Forrester Research Report. Retrieved on 4/18/2014 from http://www.forrester.com/Twelve+Recommendations+For+Your+2011+Security+Strategy/fulltext/-/E-RES57684

Lee, S. (2003). An introduction to identity management systems. *SANS Institute InfoSec Reading Room*. Retrieved online on 4/12/2014 http://sans.org/reading_room/whitepapers/authentication/introduction-identity-management_852

Lieberman Software. (2014). Retrieved online on 4/12/2014 from http://www.liebsoft.com/Enterprise_Random_Password_Manager/

Linden, M., & Vilpola, I. (2005). An empirical study on the usability of logout in a single sign-on system. In *Proceedings of the 1st International Conference in Information Security Practice and Experience* (LNCS), (vol. 3439, pp. 243-254). Springer-Verlag. doi:10.1007/978-3-540-31979-5_21

Links, C. H. (2008). *IAM success tips: Identity and access management success strategies*. CreateSpace Independent Publishing Platform.

Lund, M. S., Solhaug, B., & Stølen, K. (2011). *Model-driven risk analysis: The CORAS approach.* Springer.

Matulevicius, R., Mayer, N., Mouratidis, H., Dubois, E., Heymans, P., & Genon, N. (2008). Adapting secure tropos for security risk management in the early phases of information systems development. In *Proceedings of CAiSE* (pp. 541–555). CAiSE. doi:10.1007/978-3-540-69534-9_40

Microsoft. (2014). Retrieved online on 4/12/2014 from file:///C:/Users/Reema/Dropbox/Sem%202/ IDM%20Chapter/FIM_datasheet_MSForeFront. pdf

Miyata, T., Koga, Y., Madsen, P., & Adachi, S. (2006, January). A survey on identity management protocols and standards. *IEICE Transactions on Information and Systems, E89-D*(1), 112–123. doi:10.1093/ietisy/e89-d.1.112

Mont, M. C., Bramhall, P., Gittler, M., Pato, J., & Rees, O. (2000). *Identity management: A key e-business enabler.* Retrieved from hpl.hp.com

MS-Live. (2010). *Home - Windows Live.* Retrieved online from http://home.live.com

Mustafic, T., Messerman, A., Camtepe, S. A., Schmidt, A. D., & Albayrak, S. (2011). Behavioral biometrics for persistent single sign-on. In *Proceedings of the 7th ACM Workshop on Digital Identity Management.* ACM. doi:10.1145/2046642.2046658

NetIQ Identity Management. (2014). Retrieved online on 4/12/2014 from https://www.netiq. com/solutions/identity-access- management/

OASIS. (2014a). Retrieved online on 4/12/2014 from http://docs.oasis-open.org/ws-sx/ws-securitypolicy/v1.3/errata01/os/ws-securitypolicy-1.3-errata01-os-complete.pdf

OASIS. (2014b). Retrieved online on 4/12/2014 from http://docs.oasis-open.org/xacml/3.0/ xacml-3.0-core-spec-os-en.pdf

OASIS. (2014c). Retrieved online on 4/12/2014 from https://www.oasis-open.org/committees/ tc_home.php?wg_abbrev=security

OASIS. (2014d). Retrieved online on 4/12/2014 from https://www.oasis-open.org/committees/ xcbf/ipr.php

OneLogin. (2014). Retrieved online on 4/12/2014 from http://www.onelogin.com/ product/

Oracle-IDM. (n.d.). Retrieved from http://www. oracle.com/technetwork/middleware/id-mgmt/ overview/index.html?ssSourceSiteId=opn

Penn, J. (2002). *IT trends 2002: Directories and directory-enabled applications.* GIGA Report.

Rai, S., Bresz, F., Renshaw, T., Rozek, J., & White, T. (2007). *Global Technology Audit Guide: Identity and Access Management.* The Institute of Internal Auditors.

Reymann, P. (2008). *Aligning people, processes, and technology for effective risk management.* Retrieved on 4/18/2014 from: http://www.theiia. org/intAuditor/itaudit/archives/2008/january/ aligning-people-processes-andtechnology-for-effective-risk-management

Rochet, J—C., & Tirole, J. (2003). Platform competition in two–sided markets. *Journal of the European Economic Association, 1*(4), 990–1029.

Rogaway, P. (2004). *Nonce-based symmetric encryption.* International Association for Cryptologic Research. Retrieved from: http://www. pewinternet.org/fact-sheets/mobile- technology-fact-sheet/

Shibboleth. (2014). Retrieved online on 4/12/2014 from https://shibboleth.net/about/

Smojver, S. (2011). Selection of information security risk management method using analytic hierarchy process (ahp). In *Proceedings of Central European Conference on Information and Intelligent Systems*. Academic Press.

SSH Communications Security. (2014). Retrieved on 04/17/2014 from http://www.ssh.com/resources/datasheets/3-universal-ssh-key-manager

Stanton, J. M., Stam, K. R., Mastrangelo, P., & Jolton, J. (2005). Analysis of end user security behaviors. *Computers & Security*, *24*(2), 124–133. doi:10.1016/j.cose.2004.07.001

Sun, S.-T., Boshmaf, Y., Hawkey, K., & Beznosov, K. (2010). A billion keys, but few locks: The crisis of web single sign-on. In Proceedings of the 2010 Workshop on New Security Paradigms. Academic Press. doi:10.1145/1900546.1900556

Suoranta, S., Tontti, A., Ruuskanen, J., & Aura, T. (2013). Logout in single sign on systems. In Policies and research in identity management: Third IFIP WG 11.6 working conference. London: Springer.

Takeda, Y., Kondo, S., Kitayama, Y., Torato, M., & Motegi, T. (2006). Avoidance of performance bottlenecks caused by HTTP redirect in identity management protocols. In *Proceedings of the Second ACM Workshop on Digital Identity Management*. ACM. doi:10.1145/1179529.1179535

Taubenberger, S., Jürjens, J., Yu, Y., & Nuseibeh, B. (2011). Problem analysis of traditional IT-security risk assessment methods – An experience report from the insurance and auditing domain. In *Proceedings of SEC* (pp. 259–270). SEC.

IBM Tivoli. (n.d.). Retrieved on 2/2/2011 from http://www.rv-nrw.de/content/koop/tim/identity-mgr_43.pdf

Tracy, K. (2008). Identity management systems. *IEEE Potentials*, (November/December), 2008.

ViewDS Identity Solutions. (2014). Retrieved online on 4/12/2014 from http://www.viewds.com/images/pdf/AccessSentinel.pdf

Wood, P. (2005, September). Implementing identity management security - An ethical hacker's view. *Network Security*, *2005*(9), 12–15. doi:10.1016/S1353-4858(05)70282-8

KEY TERMS AND DEFINITIONS

Authentication: Verifying user's assertion of its identification through credentials.

Authorization: Verifying user's privileges to a system.

Identity Management Architecture: Design of identity system for managing credentials and entitlements for users of covered system(s).

Identity Management System: A system for managing user identities.

Multiple Factor Authentication: An authentication system that is based on more than one factor of authentication such as something user knows (knowledge), something that user possesses (possession) and something user is (behavioral or physical trait).

Password Management: Managing users' passwords for purpose of authenticating users.

Role Management: Managing users' entitlements and rights to application(s).

Single Sign On: Use of single set of credentials to provide access to multiple applications and systems.

Chapter 9
How Private Is Your Financial Data?
Survey of Authentication Methods in Web and Mobile Banking

Vidya Mulukutla
State University of New York – Buffalo, USA

Manish Gupta
State University of New York – Buffalo, USA

H. R. Rao
State University of New York – Buffalo, USA

ABSTRACT

The ease and convenience of Internet Banking or e-banking has made it the most preferred way for customers as well as the banking industry alike. The fact that e-banking enables remote accessibility of a customer's account translates to round-the-clock service from the bank and has made this mode of operation a success in every sense. The starting and most important point for which would be the authentication to customer's financial data. This chapter sheds light on the different authentication mechanisms that could be followed as per the situational demands taking into consideration the various threat environments and possible vulnerabilities in the system. The advantages and disadvantages arising out of different authentication mechanisms are presented with the possible attack scenarios enumerated. An overview of the personal computer environ and the mobile environ are discussed. The chapter will be invaluable for managers and professionals in understanding the current authentication landscape.

DOI: 10.4018/978-1-4666-7381-6.ch009

INTRODUCTION

The online banking is a service provided by many banks to their customers to access their account from anywhere with a computer and Internet connection with them (Online Banking, 2010). The users prefer this service as they can save time by accessing their bank transaction through the Internet from home or any place. The factors that drive accelerated growth of banking on the Internet are as listed below (Hutchinson & Warren, 2003):

- Increase the demand of customers.
- With more and more players in the market, there is increasing competition to stand out and satisfy customer needs.
- In order to cut down on costs and maintain high levels of efficiency.
- Relaxation of regulations in the financial services market world-wide.

With increase in fraud and identity theft, the banking sector is constantly on its toes and is struggling a lot with the authentication issues. The authentication of the user is of utmost importance as fraud should be avoided on this service and bank should also ensure that only authorized person accesses the account. Though the banks have taken keen interest in developing secure authentication mechanisms for the users, the fraud is still growing and the improvement in the authentication processes are much needed. At present banks follow different methods to secure their service.

Authentication is a process of verifying that the right person is provided access when requested (Authentication, 2007). Using the authentication we can ensure that the right person is provided with exact identity such as driving license, passport etc to show that he/she is the authorized person to hold those identity cards. There are different types of authentication methods available to authorize a person. The person once verified using those methods are permitted to access the particular resource where the authentication is required. The access control is a term where the authorized person is provided with authorization to access particular factor in the web resources which can be granted or declined as per the service provider (control, 2010).

The authentication can be provided through many methods and authentication is an essential factor in banking sectors to provide complete security to the online banking service. Banks are investing more in providing security to their online banking services. However, with the lack of robust authentication mechanisms for users who access their accounts from multiple number of devices, be it personal computers or shared computers or mobile devices and from any corner of the world, all efforts to make the network secure can turn out futile. For a really long time, passwords were the most common and a de-facto standard for authentication. With recent changes in the stakes and increasing value of underlying information, users are required to remember longer and more complex passwords while also requiring them to change them frequently. This has led to more insecurity and inconvenience (see for example, Bunnell et al., 1997; Furnell et al, 2000; Pond et al, 2000, Bishop & Klein, 1995); and alternative and more secure methods of authentication have made their way in the mainstream. There are different types of authentication methods and each had their unique qualities in providing authentication. There many different issues that are faced by the banking sectors in the online banking and are described in detail in this paper.

AUTHENTICATION: BACKGROUND

Authentication is a process where one has to prove his identity. A user can be authenticated to the server by means of providing identity in the form of username and authenticating by means of a password. Further mechanisms can be added to strengthen security. Reliable customer authentication is imperative for financial institutions engaging in electronic banking (Gupta et al,, 2004). In today's online financial services environment, authentication is the bedrock of information security. Simple password authentication is the prevailing paradigm, but its weaknesses are all too evident in today's context (Gupta et al, 2008). The authorization is a term which is provided to identify whether the identified person is authorized to enjoy the service. This is verified based on the records that are maintained in the database and it should match the identification provided by the person. Authorization is like the boarding pass that is used to board airplanes. The access control is another term relevant in this context, which refers to varying level of access to different users depending on their ability to prove their identity, by means of controls enforced by the system. The service provider has the full rights to grant or denied the access level to the user. In general, means controlling the full access of the user (control, 2010). There are many different methods are used to provide a secure authentication.

Need for Authentication

The delivery of the services through the publicly accessible infrastructure (i.e Internet) has increased to a great level. The transactions in the e-commerce are done using the Internet as medium and the provider cannot see the user as he/she may be from anywhere in the world. So the service providers should ensure that only the right person is accessing the right account. To identify that, the authentication of the users is essential to perform the transactions through Internet as it's an open network and anyone can access it. (Liang & Wang, 2005). Authentication is provided by the concept of cryptography using the encryption and decryption technique. The basic authentication can be provided by the user's password. The authentication can be created only when the user submits any authentication code like passwords when requested (Liang & Wang, 2005).

The corporate world has now started to use the web technology to improve their operations and they use the Internet as the medium. The corporations have also started to share confidential information to their users through the Internet. Some organizations are even operating their servers from one place to another using the remote accessing technique and which needs a high secure authentication so that the data can be transferred within the certain authenticated groups. Most of the organizations use the intranet and hence they need to secure their web server and only the authorized persons can access the server and authentication method provides a good security (Byron, 2003). "In an April 2002 report, the FBI/Computer Security Institute (CSI) noted that ninety percent of respondents (primarily large corporations and government agencies) detected computer security breaches within the last twelve months. As in previous years, the most serious financial losses occurred through theft of proprietary information and financial fraud. (Byron, 2003)".

With increasing amount of sensitive information being shared over the internet and advancements in technologies, there are more ways in which intruders are finding way to penetrate into systems leading to fraudulent activity. To overcome this issue the authentication process is created and using this process the right person alone is allowed to access the right resources. A secret code (passwords, PINS etc) are provided to the users and so they can access only using those access codes and so that the organization can have only the authorized persons accessing their intranet and this reduces the fraud to a higher extent (Byron, 2003).

Types of Authentication

The authentication is provided differently by different web servers and all servers have their own authentication methodology and properties for authentication. The authentication in general can be classified into eight types and are as follows,

1. Basic authentication,
2. Client certificates and Server certificates,
3. Digest authentication,
4. Integrated authentication,
5. Customized authentication with HTTP module,
6. Pass through authentication,
7. Windows integrated authentication, and
8. URL authentication.

Basic Authentication

The basic authentication type means where the user name and passwords are requested and when entered data are sent in a format with the full document as normal text and only the user name and password are encoded. The passwords are encoded and this provides the basic authentication to the user's data. It's the user's responsibility to remember the password and also its properties like case sensitive etc. The user will enter the data to the application when requested by the servers and the entered data are stored in the server. Later when the user access the application, the data that are requested by the server and when the user enters the data are being matched by the saved data and finally the user is allowed to access the application only if the data matches the stored data in the server. This is the method followed in the basic authentication technique (Magalhaes, 2001). While passwords, still, are the most authentication mechanism, extensive research has shown that passwords have their own inherent security issues (Morris & Thompson, 1979). And when complex passwords provide some respite in that regard, they pose a bigger usability concern (Adams & Sasse, 1999; Gaw & Felten; 2006)), so different mechanisms for authentication needs to be investigated and implemented (Herley & Oorschot, 2012).

Client Certificates and Server Certificates

- **Client Certificates:** The authentication in this type is performed such that the server requests the client to provide the client certificate before the client request to connect to the service provider. After the client sends the certificate the server checks with the earlier stored details about the client and matches it. If the details provided matched, then it request the service provider the details about the client and it provides the certificates that are supplies earlier from the service provider to the client. After the client accepts that certificate and ensures that he is getting the response from the correct service provider and not a fraud, he/she provides the details and then after matching with those details it allows the client to connect the service provider (Magalhaes, 2001).

- **Server Certificates:** The service providers have to register their server certificates with the ISA servers when they obtain the server. The client when trying to connect to the service provider will be provided with the certificate that will be used for verifying the client. The client accepts the certificate means the ISA server will link the client and the service provider. Thus authentication is made and both the client and server can ensure that they are working with the authorized persons (Magalhaes, 2001).

Digest Authentication

This is advanced version of the basic authentication where the user's data is sent in the encrypted form using the hashing methodology whereas in the basic methodology the data is transferred unencrypted. In the digest authentication it provides more security as the encryption and also hash (message digest) makes the data more secure so that intruders cannot decipher the text that are transferred in the Internet. The hash strings added will easily locate the place, computer's details, username and domain. More security is available than to the basic authentication methodology (Magalhaes, 2001).

Integrated Authentication

This is another type where we are able to get more security as the exchange of the username and passwords among the service provider and the client is not done and so the intruders can't trace any details. This scenario is very similar to federation identity management where Identity and access management systems are used by online service providers (SP) to authenticate and authorize users to services based on access policies (Gupta & Sharman, 2008). The verification in this authentication type is provided in such a way that use of the inbuilt challenge/response authentication protocol. The IE 5.5 (and above) that comes with Microsoft Windows operating system has the inbuilt authentication protocol which verifies the certificate and provides a reliable authentication to transaction (Magalhaes, 2001).

Customized Authentication with HTTP Module

The authentication is provided faster than the web method in this type. The ASP.NET will create series of events and all the events perform their operation till the verification is made and this will be complete in a quick manner than that of the web method. The data can be edited even after the request is on progress and this helps the users more easier and convenient way to get accessed (Liu, 2004).

Pass through Authentication

This type of authentication occurs when the ISA server passes the clients information to the server and this is provided for both the incoming and outgoing web requests. The following are the steps involved in pass-through authentication:

1. The request to the server from the client is made through the web server.

2. The web server request for the authentication code and type the server supports.
3. The client provides the required authentication code and it will be directed by the web servers to the appropriate service providers.
4. The response from the service providers will be taken into account and then the client is made to communicate with the service providers directly.

Windows Integrated Authentication

This is another type which is similar to basic authentication but also an advanced version of it. In this type the authentication is provided based on the hashing algorithm. This type is used in most organizations where the intranet is used and they want to control the access. This authentication helps in providing good access control inside the organization (Liu, 2004).

URL Authentication

This is another type of authentication such that it based on the verification done using the ASP.NET. Here when the client provides the authentication code the server checks for the occurrence of the username in the database. It will scroll top-down the database till it obtain the username in the database and then it checks for authentication code and then provide access to the client (Liu, 2004).

Methods of Authentication

The authentication can be provided by means of three different methods based on the authentication technique and the human nature and are as follows:

- **What You Have:** The physical cards that the user has and use it to prove his identity. This includes the tokens, smart cards, pass cards, etc.
- **What You Know:** These are known to the user only. This can be obtained only by

forcing the user and only if the user wishes can be provided. This includes passwords, PIN, pass phrases, etc.

- **What You Are:** This can be obtained only from the user's physical appearance and characteristics. This term differs from all the individuals. This includes all Biometrics, DNA, etc (Kay, 2005).

Authentication Techniques

The authentication which is provided to obtain more security for accessing certain services through Internet had follows various methods of authentication technique. Each authentication technique had its own unique properties and each provide authentication in different forms. Using a combination of these have also been researched and shown to have mixed results (Wimberly & Liebrock, 2011; Gormon, 2003) There are many different techniques in the authentication and some techniques are as follows:

- Usernames and passwords,
- PIN,
- Identifiable picture,
- One-time password,
- Swipe card,
- Token,
- Biometric,
- Keyboard rhythm, and
- OTP Scratch card.

Usernames and Passwords

The usernames and passwords authentication technique is the first and old technique where the user will be provided with unique username and a secret phrase known as the passwords. These data's are stored in the database and are verified all times when the user enters the information. The password can be numeric, alphabetic, symbols etc based on the service provider's terms and condi-

tions. This is the basic, common technique but a weak technique to provide authentication. The user provides the username and then the existence of the username in database is to be verified and if available the password is requested from the user. The user then enters the secret phrase and then after checking with the database it allows the user to access and hence the authentication is provided (Thigpen, 2005). A recent research (Vance, 2010) shows that about 5000 passwords constitute around 20% of all passwords. At the same time complex password requirements such as long passwords using special characters and numbers, frequent forced changes present usability issues and challenges (Enleman et al., 2013; Karole et al., 2011; Weiss and Deluca, 2008; Kamnduri et al., 2011; Zezschwitz, 2013) which take direct toll on productivity and satisfaction, something financial companies want to avoid at any cost. This paves way for multiple factor authentication mechanisms, but that is also fraught with issues. Some of the recent studies have shown that multiple factor authentication are difficult and cumbersome to use for users, while being complex and expensive for companies (Bauer et al., 2007; Bonneau et al., 2012; Braz and Robert, 2006; Gunson et al, 2011; Sabzevar & A. Stavrou, 2008; Strouble et al., 2009).

PIN (Personal Identification Number)

The PIN is another technique which is similar to that of passwords but contains only numeric terms and it should be kept in secret. The PIN is a four digit number and it's used mostly in the Automated Teller Machine (ATM) to identify the personal identification. If the user enters the wrong PIN a certain number of times, his/her account gets locked automatically. The number of combinations for guessing the PIN number are high so it is not easy to guess and so a safer method and its used as the authentication method in ATMs at present (Thigpen, 2005).

Identifiable Picture

This is another technique of authentication which is provided by means of using the picture. This system is used as a subsidiary term for entering passwords and personal identification numbers. The user is provided with a picture when he registers his account and so that the user can easily remember the picture. When the user needs to access the account many pictures are provided as choice and the user has to select the appropriate picture and after that access will be granted only if the correct picture is identified (Thigpen, 2005). This technique has matured a lot in today's technological environment (see for example: Renaud, 2009; Komanduri and Hutchings, 2008; Wiedenbeck et al., 2005; Chiasson et al., 2008).

One-Time Password

This is the advanced form of the passwords that overcome the vulnerable that are in the basic authentication techniques. The user enters the password once and they are associated with many hashing techniques and the data are then exchanged with the server and will be stored. So when user tries to connect multiple times the hash technique helps to identify the password and so it will be more secure and the user can avoid changing the passwords many times (Thigpen, 2005).

Swipe Card

The swipe card's data is stored in an encrypted form and has magnetic strip that is used to read the data. The best example for the swipe cards are credit and debit cards. The user can swipe this card and transactions are made based on the information provided in the magnetic strips. The possibility of fraud is more in this card as the card can be theft and duplication of the magnetic strip can be made this result in misuse of the card (Thigpen, 2005).

Token

The token is the device that is provided to the user and the user will physically submit the device which provides authentication. The tokens can be classified into three types:

- **USB Token:** The device can be connected to the system directly and the software is not needed. The device requests for a password upon connecting to the machine which gives it a double authentication (Authentication Techniques, 2006).
- **Smart Card:** This is another device, which is of similar form factor as of a credit card and contains small microprocessor. The user inserts the card into the appropriate reader and the inbuilt identity provides the basic information about the user and after checking the details the user provides a password to authenticate (Authentication Techniques, 2006).
- **Password Generating Token:** This is a token where the token itself generates a new password after every use of the old password. The token generates the OTP (One Time Password) or the unique pass code each time and ensures that the password is not used consequently. The generated password is provided by the token and the user will enter his existing username and password and then enters the newly generated OTP. This provides a higher degree of strength to the authentication process. This technique is more secure than other token (Authentication Techniques, 2006).

Biometric

Another attractive method of authorization or identification is using the biometrics, which has been suggested to have shown increased security (Normalini and Ramayah, 2012). "Biometrics are automated methods of identifying a person or verifying the identity of a person based on a physiological or behavioral characteristic (Podio & Dunn, 2001)". A biometric typically refers to a feature or characteristic measured from a biological body. Biometric authentication systems use these features to distinguish users and for establishing an identity. Some of the most common biometrics used include fingerprints, retina, iris, voice, face, hand, etc (Jain et al., 1998; Jain et al, 2006). Bioemteric technology is already playing an increasingly important role on banking environments for authentication (Venkatraman & Delpachitra, 2008)

The biometrics will be compared between the enrolled data and the currently captured data. The identification mode of this technique will search for the captured data with the central database and finally the exact data of the user that has been enrolled earlier will be matched and provided using the "One-to-Many Matching" technique. The verification mode is that when the user provides the data the captured data is identified using the "One-to-One technique" matching. There are many different forms of biometric test forms available like fingerprint recognition, face recognition, voice recognition, retinal scan, signatures, Iris feature etc.

- **Fingerprint Recognition:** This is an interesting method of authentication where the user's finger print is recognized. Each and every individual had their unique finger print and this technique had followed earlier by the law and order of the government. At present they are stored using the finger print reader machines and stored electronically and used when ever needed. Each finger had different form of prints and even the difference can be found among twins and so the individual can be identified easily. This is a good replacing technique than entering the passwords (Podio & Dunn, 2001).

- **Face Recognition:** In this technique the facial image of the user is identified and accordingly the identification is obtained. The user's face has been recognized using some inexpensive cameras where the image of the face in the visible spectrum is captured. It can be done using the IR (Infrared) of facial heat image. Even though the user changed his appearance the user's hair properties and facial expressions will never change and this provides the proper identification of the user (Podio & Dunn, 2001).

- **Voice Recognition:** This is another technique to authenticate such that the user's voice is used as the identification code for verification. The user had to register the voice to the service providers while the authentication is initially made and when ever needed the user has to speak (ex: the user can say his/her name) and the voice will be matched with the voice in the database. The requirement for this system to execute is need of the system and voice recognizing software. The software calculates the user's vocal track and the characteristics that are present in the user's voice and finally it will be matched when the user used them finally. The main drawback of this process is that if the user affected with any throat related problem, the system cannot able to recognize the voice and the access cannot be provided until the reset in done.

- **Iris Recognition:** This feature provides identification using the featured iris of the eyes which is a colored portion that covers the pupil in the eyes. Each and every individual had their unique difference in their iris and this is recognized by the system and can able to identify the exact match for that iris. Both the verification and identification is done easily using this method and the increase in this type of technique is increasing at recent trends. Nowadays many users are using contact lens and eyeglasses and at present the teat of the iris can be done even with that. This system also provides good identification of the users.

- **Hand and Finger Geometry:** This is an old method for more than about twenty years and in this method the user's hand characteristics are analyzed. The characteristic includes the length, width, surface, thickness etc. The distance among the fingers are calculated and used to later identification. This system is tough to handle and need more space when compared to other biometrics technique and so the usage of this technique is reducing (Podio & Dunn, 2001).

Digital Signature

This is a process where the user's signature is used to identify the person. The user can enroll the signature digitally and the pressure, angle and modes used to create that signature is calculated and stored. So when the user need to authenticate using the signature the characters of the signature is analyzed with the enrolled one and matched and finally the access will be provided if it matched with the existed signature.

Keyboard Rhythm

This technique is followed in some workplaces where the user's usage of the keyboard is calculated and accordingly the authentication is provided to the user. The pressure the user uses the keyboard, the time needed to strike between the keys used by the user is calculated and accordingly the authentication is provided. This is also a different technique that is used in some workplace to reduce unauthorized access of the system (Thigpen, 2005).

OTP Scratch Card

The scratch card is a low expensive card that contains the numbers arranged in rows and column format like grids. The number of the grids in the card is recognized. The user when use this card will enter the username and password first time and then will enter the randomly generated passwords that are created by the scratch card with the numbers in it. This is easy for the user to carry as he can place it in wallets and the drawback of this method is that the physical misuse and theft of the product (Authentication Techniques, 2006).

ROLE OF AUTHENTICATION IN ONLINE BANKING

Nowadays the usage of the Internet banking has increased a lot and the possibility of fraud also increased. Since many users started to use the online banking and also the intruders increased in order to hack the users details and to steal the money from others account without their knowledge. Because of this problem many users stopped using these services from the banks. It's bank's responsibility to provide users the account security and so banks prefer to authenticate the user so that they can ensure that only the right person is using the appropriate account. Attacking the banks server had started to occur often and the banks are pushed to authenticate their users (CEPIS, 2007).

Some banks provide authentication based on the 'Two Factor Authentication' which has two basic authentication factors. The security is more essential factor in banks and they depend only on the two factor authentication and are as follows,

- What the user knows (PIN, Password, Pass phrases),
- What the user has (Smart cards, Tokens, etc).

Most of the banks use only the username and password or pass phrase as their authentication factor over the Internet. The users are requested to provide the PIN/Passwords/Passphrase when they try to access the online banking. These are used as the basic authentication term in online banking. If the security provided to be more means then the bank will provide with extra hardware security devices like tokens along with the password provided to the users. The authentication factor provided are implemented in the following ways and are as follows:

- One-time password approach,
- Certificate based approach,
- Time based password approach.

Certificate Based Approach

In this approach a certificate is provided along with the password to the user. The certificates are software token that is installed inside a USB or any Smart card device and it should be provided by the user. The bank server will execute the card along with the passwords provided and will be used for the authentication purpose.

One-Time Password Approach

This is another method where the passwords are provided to the user by the server and can be used only once for a transaction and after single use, it expires. The user will have to request new password for next attempt to login. The passwords that are created temporarily are termed as TAN's (Transaction Authorization Numbers). There are three types of TAN's and are iTAN (TAN's distributed in lists), eTAN (TAN's created using special hardware devices) and mTAN (Tan created through mobile phones). The operation of the TAN's are represented in Figure 1. The iTAN process is also described in the figure which is done using the lists for each TAN request. The same approach is followed in the eTAN and mTAN where the SMS messages and other media devices are used as the medium of transaction; and these are successfully deployed at many Ausrian and German banks (Wiesmaier et al, 2004).

Time-Based Password Approach

This is another method which is more secure than the one-time password approach. The operation is similar to that of one-time password approach

Figure 1. Authentication – TAN approach (CEPIS, 2007).

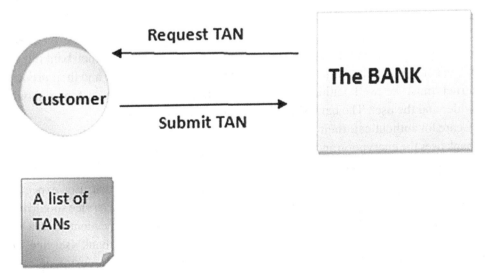

but there will be certain time limit provided to it such that after the password is generated it will be there only for certain time after that it will expire. This is created with a design that the hackers cannot have sufficient time to calculate the codes and so it will be more secure (CEPIS, 2007).

INTERNET BANKING: ISSUES

In recent trends, the use of the Internet in the organization had increased to higher extend and many organizations follow Internet as their major business medium. Similarly the banking sector also introduces the Internet banking to their customers as an easier method to perform their transactions. Since a greater portion of population now uses Internet, the amount of information on Internet has exploded, securing which has become a major issue in the Internet banking (OCC, 1999). Some of the issues in the Internet banking are as follows,

- Authentication,
- Trust,
- Non-repudiation,
- Privacy, and
- Availability.

Authentication

Another issue in the Internet banking is the Authentication. The banking operations performed through Internet must be well authenticated with the provider and the user. The bank should provide more care for authenticate their users. In general, the bank uses the encryption and decryption technique to transfer the authentication code where the public key and private key are used for the authentication. Later on the passwords used as codes are transferred and now they are using biometric identification codes are used as latest form of authentication codes.

Trust

This is another issue in Internet banking. Since the transactions are made through the Internet, authentication service provider for Internet i.e, Certificate Authority is essential and it's a trust oriented part that the bank relies on the third party for their security. The certificate authorities provide the "Digital Signatures" which helps in providing good security with good mix of the preventive, detective and corrective controls to provide authentications.

Non-Repudiation

The participation by both the sender and receiver in transferring their authentication codes are undeniable proof and this is one of the issues in the Internet banking. While banks, which technically have dedicated Internet connections, are at risk of being perpetrated by unauthorized personnel, electronic banking system users face greater risks due to the remote accessibility and therefore, more exposure of sensitive information. Therefore, it becomes a cardinal rule for banks to ensure non-repudiability by means of attestation by a third party, who holds the identity certificates, the identities of the sender and receiver. (Fatima, 2011)

Privacy

This is consumer issue in the Internet banking. Consumers in the Internet banking should be provided more security and their privacy in more essential such that the customer should rely on their security services.

Availability

This is a major part that user expects from the service providers. The service should be provided all times and no inconvenient should be faced by the customers from the bank's service. The service should be provided to the customers twenty hours a day and seven days a week. The customer should be comfortable with all sort of service provided by the Internet banking service providers.

Authentication Issues in Online Banking

Due to the volume of sensitive information handled by banks, it is always under pressure to uphold the privacy of its customers from perpetrators. As is commonly quoted, 'Human is the weakest link', which is what makes user authentication one of the most important vulnerable areas to be taken care of by banks. There are various ways in which web applications could be subjected to attack. Below listed provide a broad categorization of the same:

- Online Channel Breaking Attacks.
- Offline Credential Stealing Attack.
- Software based Attacks.
- Phishing.
- Data Breaches.

Online Channel Breaking Attacks

This is a system where the intruders attack web application of banks. The intruders will never aim to obtain the user's credential instead they try to hijack the information that was transferred between the user and the bank, which is seen in the cookie information. The intruders will watch the transactions and also will intercept the messages from the client and the server and will record the authentication codes used by the user. The intruders will make use of those cookies and may access that account as an authenticated user. This is one way of attacking the authentication of the online banking. Most of the intruders are using this methodology to attack the bank servers (Weigold, 2006). Two examples of online attacks that can render Public Key Infrastructure (PKI) inefficient are Cross-site Scripting Attack and Cross-Site request forgery.

Offline Credential Stealing Attacks

This is another type of attack that is faced by the banking sector. This attack is performed when the system is placed in offline mode. The system is hacked by means of miscellaneous software that contains viruses and Trojan horses. This viruses and Trojan horses will get rooted into the system and will be used to store the confidential data is processed by the system and is then provided to the attackers. The hackers install software through un-trusted sites and downloads from the Internet. (Weigold, 2006).

Software Based Attacks

Usually, banks use software based protection for their servers. Banks use software protection rather than the hardware-based protection because former is cheaper (Yang, 1997). There are many drawbacks in this system and are as follows,

1. The encryption algorithm used to encrypt the data in these software based protection system can be attacked by the attackers.
2. Direct approach of trying the combination of the possible occurrence of the PIN can be calculated by the attackers.
3. Hacking the bank's server and accessing all the confidential data.
4. Hacking client's personal computers through miscellaneous programs.

Phishing

This is a process where the fake websites like bank's website, financial institution website or government websites are created to and fraud users into revealing confidential data such as passwords and access codes; and then to access their accounts to indulge in fraud. There are many organizations that are affected by phishing websites created by the attackers. Many e-commerce organizations are still trying to reduce the effect of these phishing websites attacks. "There are several different types of phishing attacks including misleading e-mails, man-in-the-middle, URL obfuscation, page content overriding, malware phishing, key loggers and screen grabbers, session hijackers, web Trojans, IP address manipulation, and system reconfiguration attacks (Williamson, 2006)". While organizations try to track and bring down these fake websites creation, the perpetrators continuously invent new ways to phish. In year 2005 alone, the number of phishing sites almost quadrupled (Williamson, 2006).

A recent survey (APWG, 2013) shows that about 77% of all phishing attacks in the first half of 2013 targeted the financial sector. One of the most common technical countermeasures for protection against phishing that has been adopted by many financial services firms is use of Extended Validation Secure Socket Layer (EV SSL). EV SSL is used for server-client mutual authentication and for also encryption of data in transmission. It also facilitates verification of certificate on the servers by furnishing more information such as company location, corporate name and a registration number for the server website (CA, 2012). However, it has also been shown that this method is also vulnerable to phishing (Marlinspike, 2009). Another method is to show customer-selected image at the time of any online interaction with the company, usually at the time of login. Bank of America's SiteKey is an example of such technique(BOA, 2014). According to a survey by Anti Phishing Working Group(APWG-1, 2012; APWG-2, 2012), the average lifetime of phishing sites has gone down from 46 hours in 2011 to 26 hours in 2012, while their number had climbed from 50,298 to 89,748. Another recent solution against phishing is based on black lists maintained and published by leading browser companies such as Google Chrome's Safe Browsing, Microsoft Internet Explorer's Phishing Filter and the Phishing Protection by Mozilla Firefox (Mozilla, 2014; Google, 2014)

Data Breaches

This is another type of attack that is used to obtain users confidential information. The Internet is used as the medium and the users are provided with names of famous organizations to provide different offers and terms. There are billions of records of personal and private information stored and processed by universities, healthcare institutions, businesses, government agencies and other entities for providing services and products. The personal information stored include social security numbers, credit card numbers, data of birth, driver license number, addresses and much more. Risks from unintended disclosure of personal information include privacy risks and risks from potential identity theft frauds. The damages done from these risks alone already cost billions of dollars in detection and remediation (Hasan & Yurcik, 2006). There are several organizations, for-profit and non-profit that has been actively engaged in maintaining the incidents of security breaches. There also have lot of organizations that suffered a breach and have disclosed it to mass media (Attrition.org, 2009; Tehan, 2005). Privacy Rights ClearingHouse (PRC, 2009) estimates that around 100 million records containing sensitive personal information have been compromised over last few years. The users are lured into entering Credit Card details, Social Security Number, Date of Birth etc that is stolen by the attackers. The users tend to provide the information as the links seem to be coming from banks, high level financial organizations, big organizations etc. After the trap is successful, the stolen information is used to launch fraudulent activities (Williamson, 2006).

FRAUD PREVENTION STRATEGIES

The fraud in the Internet banking has become common and prevention has become more essential and banks have to take precautionary steps to perform the process without fraud (BITS, 2003). ACFE defines fraud as "the use of one's occupation for personal enrichment through the deliberate misuse or application of the employing organization's resources or assets". Companies and individuals lose billions of dollars every year to various types of fraud (Levi & Burrows, 2008; Chan et al., 1999; Chen et. al., 2006; McAlearney, 2008). The proceedings from these frauds helps fund organized crime, international trafficking, and even cross-border terrorist financing (McAlearney, 2008). There are three different stages where strategies are followed to prevent the fraud and some are provided below:

- Application process,
- Application Authentication,
- After application approval.

Application Process

- **Limit Timeframes:** This process is implemented when the application is filled up by the customers and it is provided with time limit so that it will be closed before the provided time and application should be finished by the user within the provided time.
- **Provide a Secure Channel:** This is provided to the user immediately so that the user can verify provided details and also check for any intruders or intercept of the data.
- **Create an Audit Trail:** This feature will automatically record the user's IP address and time for the further references.

Application Authentication

- **Use a Real Time Process:** This is created to verify whether the provided details by the user are accurate. It also verifies the details provided by the user during applying through online and the user should register to the concern authority before applying.

- **Ask "In Wallet" Question:** The wallet questions are the one of the confidential question where the user can provide like social security number, driving license number and date of birth etc where the intruders can hack these wallets but don't know whether they are applying for a new application or an existing application.
- **Use "Out-of Wallet" Questions:** This is automatically generated questions asked to the user about the exact value of the monthly chargers to be paid. So that the intruders can be avoided if wrong details are provided.
- **Use of "Out-of Credit" Questions:** These are about the personal questions about the user apart from the credit of the account. This also secures the server from the intruders.
- **Provide Standard Field Variation:** This is to ensure that whether the user is using the application correctly.
- **Verify Application Data:** The user details are verified with the central database and the information provided is correct and to ensure the user also that he/ she enters only the correct information.

After Application Approval

- **Wait for Funding Prior to Opening an Account:** The waiting time is provided by the financial institutions for the user to enter the PIN numbers in ATM centers so that perpetrators would not be able to identify the code within the provided time.
- **Require That a Signed Application on File:** The user's signature is verified with the signature recorded in the database and so that unauthorized users cannot misuse the user's checks or any other transactions.

- **Require Customer Authentication to be Completed in the Branch or through Customer Call Centers:** The information about the user is to be recorded earlier in the particular branch where the user operates the accounts. If not the information should be registered either through the customer call centers.

- **Implementing Manual Fraud Screening on Initial Deposits:** The image that is captured when the check is dropped and the machine also captures the image of the person who deposits the initial amount and it can be helpful to avoid unauthorized access to the account.

SYSTEMS AND SOLUTIONS TO ATTACKS IN ONLINE BANKING

The online banking should be provided with high security so that the attacks in the authentication of the Internet banking can be stopped and the server can be secured (Yang, 1997). The solutions are provided by means of the two terms namely,

- Software based security system, and
- Hardware based security system.

Software Based Security System

In this system the authentication is based on the software programs. Encryption is the main method used to encrypt the code. Encryption is a technique where the data is jumbled and can be retrieved using some shared secret. This process needs both the public key and private key. In one method only one key is used by both the client and server where both for encryption and decryption the key is used (symmetric encryption). The second method is that using a private key and public key (asymmetric encryption). The public key should be made available to both the client and the server. The

data can be transferred using the public key in the public domain but retrieved by means of the private key. This method is more secure than that of first encryption method. The encryption methodology can be classified in to four classifications such as Digital signatures, Secure Electronic Transactions, Pretty good privacy and Kerberos (Yang, 1997).

- **Digital Signatures:** A digital signature is used to identify the sender by the receiver using the signature placed along with the messages. The private key is used to encrypt and the public key to decrypt. The user's signature is used as the private key in this case. Only the user can create the signature and it is difficult to copy the signature.

- **Secure Electronic Transactions (SET):** This is another method based on the software to create a secure card which can be used to do the payments in Internet. These cards are provided with the world wide accessible terms such as Visa Master Card, IBM, Microsoft, Netscape communication corp, Verisign. The online bank transaction can be done securely using the SET technology. RSA public key encryption technique is used in this method. The digital signature is created using a unique public and private key. A digital signature is provided with the data and it encrypted using some hashing techniques. The encrypted data will be sent along with the user's private key which helps to provide users identity to the bank so that the receiver can get the details of the sender. The receiver uses the hashing algorithm to generate the messages and should match the old one.

- **Pretty Good Privacy (PGP):** This is another method where its functions are based on the combination of the public key algorithm and private key algorithm. No transmitted channel medium is required for this technique. The received public key can be decrypted with the user's private key and so the identity of the sender can be verified. This method also provides more security for the data transfer.

- **Kerberos:** This is a private key encryption technique. It creates an encrypted data packet called ticket and it will be transferred through Internet. The tickets are used to identify the user and the tickets can be transferred only between Kerberos servers. The private keys are shared between the two systems.

Hardware Based System

It is another more secure form of exchanging data over Internet and comprises physical devices which are expensive and difficult to handle. There are many hardware based systems and most common is the Smart card and MeChip (Yang, 1997).

- **Smart Card:** This card is mechanically designed with the programs and chips are inbuilt and it can store data related to the user's personal identification terms. The user can use this card when needed to retrieve the information. The virus can affect this card but this will be used mostly in outdoors and the Internet usage cannot be made in this card.
- **MeChip:** This is a device that is connected using the USB port of a personal computer. The information that needed to be sent in a secure manner is added to the device, which transfers the data and checks the status of the transmission.

Comparison of Authentication Techniques

In this section, we present a comparison of different authentication methods that are most commonly used. Table 1 presents a summary of the comparison based on handling (support and maintenance from user standpoint), cost (to the company) and security of the solution. As we can see, tokens and OTP scratch pads are the most difficult methods for support and for handling (more from a convenience standpoint). Biometrics has the most costs in terms of implementing a solution and on-going maintenance. However, there are several methods that score "High" on security or on authentication strength including biometrics, which has the highest score.

AUTHENTICATION IN MOBILE BANKING

Mobile phones, today, provide many more luxuries that they did not provide a few years ago. From the basic functionality of making and receiving calls to sending emails to making transactions, mobile devices have made lives, both personal and professional, more convenient and much easier. The constantly evolving mobile environment calls for more functionality where mobile phones are increasingly becoming reflections of the personal computers implying more storage and processing capabilities. Mobile phones are thus, a miniature portable version of personal computers (Ben-Asher et al., 2011). As mobile phones increasingly become an indispensable commodity, enriching user experience is key which is achieved by means of creating rich mobile applications which in turn need to be supported by developing powerful mobile operating systems that have capabilities of running the applications in the most efficient manner. While

Table 1. Comparison of authentication techniques

S. No.	Technique	Handling	Cost	Security
1	Username & Passwords	Easy	Nil	Average
2	PIN	Easy	Nil	Average
3	Identifiable picture	Easy	Nil	Moderate
4	One-Time Password	Moderate	Nil	Moderate
5	Swipe Card	Easy	Low	Average
6	Tokens	Hard	Medium	High
7	Biometric	Easy	High	Very High
8	Keyboard Rhythm	Moderate	Medium	Moderate
9	OTP Scratch Card	Hard	Medium	Moderate
10	Digital Signatures	Easy	Medium	High
11	Secure Electronic Transactions (SET)	Easy	Medium	High
12	Pretty Good Privacy (PGP)	Moderate	Medium	High
13	Kerberos	Easy	Medium	High
14	Smart Cards	Easy	Low	Moderate
15	MeChip	Moderate	Medium	Moderate

these platforms may draw a parlance from existing desktop operating systems, they introduce a gamut of security mechanisms relevant to the mobile landscape. (Singh, 2012)

As much as mobile phones may derive functionality from traditional personal computers, they offer a different perspective in terms of usage. While personal computers are used over a long continuous stretch of time, mobile phones are accessed intermittently for more number of times and shorter periods whenever there is the need, for example, an email notification. This introduces an additional security mechanism to authenticate the device multiple number of times as compared to a personal computer. Being the handy devices that they are, the idea of security in a mobile phone overwhelms users as it is perceived to hinder convenience and ease of usability. A recent study notes that, more than 30% of mobile phone users do not use a PIN on their phones. On the contrary, there is increasingly a large amount of high value data being stored on mobile devices; with mobile payment and money

transfer applications as well as enterprise data becoming available on mobile devices (Riva, et. al., 2012). In this context it is pertinent that the banking industry acquaints itself with the security aspect of the mobile environment in order to avoid ramifications that could be detrimental to stakeholders. In the digital world where impersonation is the gravest form of security breach, non-repudiation, which means the identity of the sending and receiving party is attested by an authorized third party, is a prudent step towards keeping intruders and illegal activities at bay (Fatima, 2011).

Methods of Authentication in Mobile Banking

There are a few common and very widely used methods of authentication in mobile banking environment including (but not limited to):

1. Basic Password Authentication System,
2. Implicit Password Authentication System,

3. Multi-factor Authentication System,
4. Progressive Authentication System, and
5. Client Server Authentication System.

Basic Password Authentication System

The basic password authentication system is the traditional means of authentication, where the user is required to register a username and password which is used for every instance of authenticating to the system. In order to make the application resistant to brute force attacks and simple dictionary attacks, character restrictions and specifications are set on the password. For instance, the application may accept passwords only if they satisfy the criteria of – 8 characters in length, alphanumeric and at least one special character. The user's session is timed such that it expires/logs the user out when the application is idle for some time. The session idle time after which the user is force logged out can be set according to the severity of the application. Additional layer of protection could be added by the system by means of remembering the device from which the user generally logs in and send out an email or SMS for any unusual activity.

- **Benefits:**
  - If the system implements strong password policy, the application is secure from brute force attacks or simple dictionary attacks.
  - It is the easiest to implement among authentication methods.
- **Drawbacks:**
  - Unless there is strong server security, the database that stores all passwords could be compromised.
  - Due to the difficulty in remembering or keying in the password, most users save the password in the device, which can make it a vulnerability in the case of a stolen device or borrowed device.

By providing just a single layer of security, the system could be vulnerable to several other threats which are attempted to be overcome by some of the methods discussed next.

Implicit Password Authentication System

Know Your User

The user logs in with the basic username and password. Subsequently, the server picks a couple of questions (the number of questions depends on the level of service requested) out of the 10-20 questions selected by the user out of 100-200 standard questions in the bank's database during the registration process. For example, the user may choose the following questions:

- The name if the city you were born?
- The name of the breed of your pet animal?
- Date of birth?

The server creates and henceforth associates every question to images where the answers can implicitly be implied from the corresponding images. Every question chosen by the user, triggers a randomly selected image from the authentication space which is presented to the user as a challenge. The user is expected to navigate his/her way through the image to get the answer that is embedded in the image. For instance, the server may present the user with a geographical map. The user should correlate to Question 1. If Los Angeles is the city the user was born, he needs to click on North America. It will then zoom into North America where the user can choose Los Angeles. Every other time the user wants to authenticate to the server, a different question may be presented or if the same question repeats, a different scenario is presented. Hence, an outsider cannot make sense of the authentication scheme, as it is a fuzzy system. Also, session keys could be generated from the correct clickable area in the image in order to ensure there are no static keys that can give leeway to intruders. (Almuairfi, Veeraraghavan, & Chilamkurti, 2011)

- **Benefits:**
  - This authentication method helps secure the application from shoulder surfing and screen dump/screen capture attacks.
  - Due to the implicit nature of the authentication, only a legitimate user can make sense of the challenge posed by the server and therefore decode it to gain access to perform an authorized transaction through the application.
- **Drawbacks:**
  - A drawback of implementing this method of authentication could be that the system could ask a very easy question at the time of registration – an alphanumeric question – and ask the user to key in the answer through a graphical keyboard (Almuairfi et al., 2011)

Audio and Haptic Cues

While the audio modality has been considerably explored, authentication by means of haptic cues is a less trodden path and may gain more momentum given its implicit nature and thus the security it has to offer. Based on tactile feedback technology, haptic cues take advantage of the sense of touch by decoding the pressure or force, vibrations or any mechanical association of the user to the device, which is unique to the user.

There is a PIN lock system and the PIN is derived from a set of tactile or audio cues. The PIN is, therefore, a sequence of the audio and haptic cues. Accordingly, the size of the cues and length of the PIN can be changed. (Bianchi, et. al, 2011)

- **Benefits:**
  - The system employs cues, which cannot be interpreted or seen due to the fact that they are observation resistant and more importantly unique to every user.
  - Protects from shoulder surfing.

Multifactor Authentication Systems

Traditional M-Banking Process

In the basic traditional M-Banking process, the client side presents a request. Subsequently, the server side transfers the message containing the On-Time-Password (OTP) to the client side. An authentic user who is in possession of the device will receive the OTP and therefore, key in the correct OTP to the server side. In order to avoid hacking or spoofing, the OTP should be verified from the webpage of the server side for non-repudiation (so that the OTP is actually sent from the authentic server side), after which, the client side will register/input the OTP on the webpage of the server side. The server side then checks for validity of the OTP. The transaction is accepted or rejected depending on the validity of the OTP. (Tsai, Chen, & Zhuang, 2012)

- **Benefits:**
  - Unless the right device is possessed, the OTP cannot be accessed and hence unauthorized transactions cannot be made.
  - Also, the OTP is valid for a limited time and therefore cannot be reused making it immune to replay attacks.
- **Drawbacks:**
  - A stolen device can help gain unauthorized access into the system.
  - Also, man-in-the-middle attacks could be successfully done if the OTP is not strongly encrypted.

Authentication Using OTP and Biometric

This authentication is similar to the traditional two-factor authentication discussed above up until the point where the OTP is sent to the server side. An extra layer of defense is added in this case - if the OTP sent is valid, the server sends one more request to client for biometric information. If the information sent is correct, the user can perform the transaction. This model can be modified and implemented towards progressive authentication, which is discussed later in the chapter. (Tsai et al., 2012)

Authentication Using TIC

TIC Authentication: TIC authentication is the technique used to verify both the user and the ongoing transaction. A TIC code is used to certify that the right person has initiated the current transaction and that it is a legitimate user who is trying to access his/her account. TIC codes are:

- Issued by the Bank or Financial institution to its customers.
- An 8 bit or 16 bit Pseudo randomly generated code which is assigned to the customers.
- May be a complicated digit sequence or combination of numeric and alpha numeric characters.

So, Multifactor Authentication can be used to verify the user and the transaction by using the following steps:

1. **Web-Based Basic Authentication:** First, a basic traditional authentication – username/password based protocol – is required to gain initial access into the system by proving one's identity to the web server.
2. **TIC Authentication:** Once authentication to the web server is successful using the basic username/password, a TIC code is demanded from the user. The TIC code is decrypted at user end and the user then inserts the one time TIC code that helps in uniquely identifying his/her transaction and thereby proving his/her identity to the web Authentication server.
3. **SMS Confirmation:** An extra layer of defense is added by means of an SMS confirmation in order to confirm one's financial transaction. The web Authentication server sends an SMS to the web user for confirmation of the transaction made. The strength of security of the system also depends on the security of the messages sent by SMS and WAP, which are encrypted. The transaction can be confirmed by the user by means of replying to the SMS with a 'YES' or a 'NO'. This helps in further ensuring the authenticity of transactions made every single time.

Mobile phones cannot handle the highly computation intensive nature of Public Key Infrastructure. Therefore, PKI can be used to encrypt the symmetric key while the entire data that can simply be encrypted using the symmetric key.

- **Benefits:**
    ○ The two-way authentication protocol addresses several of the shortcomings of the Secure Electronic Transmission. Data is always in an encrypted form making the information that is vital to a user highly secure and available to the merchant in an encrypted form.
- **Stolen Device:** In the case of a stolen device, despite the intruder having the user's password he cannot surpass the extra layers of authentication, as the TIC code is also encrypted whose key is known only to the valid user.
- **Man-in-the-Middle Attack:** The fact that there is no unencrypted data sent over untrusted network at any stage during the

authentication process protects and secures the system from man-in-the-middle attacks. Additionally, the benefit of having OTPs which expire in a timely fashion making them available for only one single transaction (Tiwari et al., 2011).

Bio-Cryptography: Combination of Biometrics and Cryptography

Biometrics and cryptography could be used in combination in a way that they could complement each other and derive the best of both worlds. The fingerprint biometric is used to generate a cryptographic key, by means of employing it to work with the Elliptical Curve Cryptography (ECC) public key cryptography. The key retrieval process is thus protected by means of fingerprint verification. A successful fingerprint authentication results in generation of correct keys.

The basic idea is to transfer the locally matched fuzzy vault index to the central server for biometric authentication using the PKI which offloads the computation demand to the central server. The keys generated are dynamic as they change for every biometric authentication while the minutia details are never exposed externally, Vulnerability risk is further notched down as the establishment of symmetric session keys does not need a conventional key exchange process.

RSA is the most widely accepted standard in the industry. However, owing to the computational demands posed, ECC which offers the same security strength as RSA but with smaller key sizes, is employed in the mobile environment, where small memories and lower computational capacities are expected.

Recent significant research outcome on bio-cryptographic includes bio hashing, cancelable template, fuzzy extractor and fuzzy vault.

- **Benefits:** Secures application from:
  - **Trojan Horse Attack:** Even in the worst case scenario where the attacker compromises the private key of the

PKI which has been stored in the mobile device, it does not help break the system as the attacker has to surpass the biometric authentication at the central server in the first place. Also, the cryptographic key being generated from the biometric information which is unique to every user makes it unpredictable. Furthermore, it is not stored at either mobile client side or server side.

  - **Brute Force Attack:** No static key stored in hardware - Both genuine minutiae and chaff points can be used to generate the session key.
  - **Biometric Template Attack:** Increasing the total number of minutiae from the usually collected 10-20 or increasing the difficulty for attackers to capture the minutiae information are two possible solutions.
  - The other attacks from which this method can secure the system are Transmission channel attack – ECC algorithm provides security that RSA algorithm provides; Replay attack – adoption of timestamps; Man-in-the-middle attack – use of Public Key Infrastructure (PKI) and truly random session keys generated from biometrics (Xi et al., 2011).

Progressive Authentication Methods

Graded Security

Graded security is a means of granting graduated access to a user. Graded security can be seen from two different perspectives: One way of which is user-based access control where access is granted on the basis of role held by the user often described in a hierarchical manner – guest-user to super- user. Second, graded security can be seen as a content- based system. In this case, access is provisioned on the basis of content alone. The user is required to authenticate to the system every single time he/she is to be provided with content requested with no overlap to other content thus making each content accessible independently only. (Ben-Asher et al., 2011)

Implicit Password Authentication

This method of authentication has been described earlier in the chapter, which could be used to provide graded security. The user would be granted with the initial level of access when he authenticates to the system with username and password which could be sent as plain text. As per the level of access required, the system might choose relevant questions that have been registered by the user during the time of registration process.

Progressive Authentication by Means of Sensors

Mobile systems can progressively authenticate (and de-authenticate) users by constantly collecting cues about the user, such that at any point in time the user is authenticated with a certain level of confidence. Several authentication signals are used. Sensors such as the voice recognition or haptic cues can be used to establish knowledge about the user and henceforth pose authentication challenges to gain access to critical information. In order to extend the validity of the user and avoid cases wherein, an illegitimate user is exploiting a session that has been idle for hours. This method can make the best use of the technological advancements in the mobile environment. With mobile phones being increasingly networked, proximity and motion sensors can be used to detect whether the phone is next to another device of the same user where he is currently authenticated and active.

- **Benefits:**
  - This approach makes the authentication overhead lower and proportional to the value of the content being accessed.

- **Drawbacks:**
  - There is inherent noise in sensing data as well as energy and performance constraints. If sensor streams are the only source used for detection, the system is likely to suffer a high number of false rejections (inability to recognize the owner) or cases of unauthorized accesses.
  - Moreover, it is a challenging task to process the sensor data and run the inference stack on a mobile device. Continuously recording data from the sensors can drain the battery of the mobile phone at faster rate (Riva et al., 2012).

Client-Server Authentication

In order to cryptographically protect the communication channel between the client and server, e-commerce applications employ a secure sockets layer/ transport layer security protocol. The server side authenticates itself to the client using a public key certificate and so should the client. One disadvantage of this pre-shared key based approach is that every server needs to generate and securely distribute a key-bearing token to every user, which is likely to be a significant burden in practice. Another disadvantage is its poor scalability. Therefore, Transport Layer Security-Session Aware user authentication (TLS-SA) using a GAA (General Authentication Architecture) bootstrapped key is a viable approach. The scheme employs a GAA-enabled user device with a display and an input capability (e.g. a 3G mobile phone) and a GAA-aware server, and binds the user authentication process to the TLS session without modifying the operation of TLS. A GAA bootstrapped session key is used in the computation of the user authentication code, there is no need to generate and securely distribute a key-bearing token to every user (Chen et. al., 2011). The main benefit is that it secures application from Man-in-the-middle attacks.

CONCLUSION

The security of the bank operations is essential, more so when the intensity and frequency of attacks is higher than ever. So, the need of authentication in a secure manner is more essential than ever. There are many different authentication techniques available and each has its own unique properties in providing authentication. The online and mobile banking which is now used worldwide has more useful functions than ever, but the growth in fraud and identity theft shows failure in securing the information. Authentication has emerged to be the one of the most vital pieces of strengthening security and ensuring privacy of financial date. The chapter presented several authentication methods and the solutions to some potential types of attacks, for both web banking and mobile banking We discussed our survey of different authentication issues, some of the most important factors in selecting an authentication mechanism. The discussions and conclusions in the chapter can be used by managers and security professionals in understanding different approaches to authentication and will aid them during the decision making process.

REFERENCES

Adams, A., & Sasse, M. (1999). Users are not the enemy. *Communications of the ACM, 42*(12), 41–46. doi:10.1145/322796.322806

Almuairfi, S., Veeraraghavan, P., & Chilamkurti, N. (2011). *IPAS: Implicit password authentication system.* Paper presented at the Advanced Information Networking and Applications (WAINA), New York, NY.

APWG. (2012a) Anti-phishing working group. *Global Phishing Survey.* Retrieved 1st August, 2012 from http://docs.apwg.org/reports/APWG_GlobalPhishingSurvey_1H2012.pdf

APWG. (2012b). Anti-phishing working group. *Global Phishing Survey.* Retrieved 1st August, 2012 from http://docs.apwg.org/reports/APWG_GlobalPhishingSurvey_2H2012.pdf

APWG. (2013). Anti-phishing working group. *Global Phishing Survey.* Retrieved 1st August, 2012 from http://docs.apwg.org/reports/APWG_GlobalPhishingSurvey_1H2013.pdf

Attrition.org. (2009). Retrieved from 3rd March, 2013 from Attrition.org http://attrition.org/security/dataloss.html

Authentication. (2007, June 4). Retrieved 3rd April, 2010 from www.searchsecurity.techtarget.com

Authentication Techniques. (2006, January 10). Retrieved 3rd April, 2010 from www.sheshunoff.com: http://www.sheshunoff.com/ideanet/index.php?itemid=204&catid=4

Bauer, L., Cranor, L. F., Reiter, M. K., & Vaniea, K. (2007). Lessons learned from the deployment of a smartphone-based access-control system. In *Proceedings of the 3rd Symposium on Usable Privacy and Security* (pp. 64-75). ACM.

Ben-Asher, N., Kirschnick, N., Sieger, H., Meyer, J., Ben-Oved, A., & Möller, S. (2011). On the need for different security methods on mobile phones. In *Proceedings of the 13th International Conference on Human Computer Interaction with Mobile Devices and Services.* Academic Press.

Bianchi, A., Oakley, I., Kostakos, V., & Kwon, D. S. (2011). The phone lock: Audio and haptic shoulder-surfing resistant PIN entry methods for mobile devices. In *Proceedings of the Fifth International Conference on Tangible, Embedded, and Embodied Interaction* (pp. 197-200). Madeira, Portugal: Academic Press. doi:10.1145/1935701.1935740

Bishop, M., & Klein, D. V. (1995). Improving system security via proactive password checking. *Computers & Security, 14*(3), 233–249. doi:10.1016/0167-4048(95)00003-Q

BITS. (2003, April). *Fraud prevention strategies for internet banking.* Retrieved 3rd April, 2010 from http://www.bits.org/downloads/Publications%20Page /mointernetwp.pdf

BOA. (2014). *Bank of America SiteKey.* Retrieved 6th June 2013 from https://www.bankofamerica. com/privacy/online-mobile-banking-privacy/ SiteKey.go

Bonneau, J., Herley, C., van Oorschot, P. C., & Stajano, F. (2012). The quest to replace passwords: A framework for comparative evaluation of web authentication schemes. In *Proceedings of IEEE Symposium on Security and Privacy* (pp. 553 – 567). IEEE. doi:10.1109/SP.2012.44

Braz, C., & Robert, J.-M. (2006). Security and usability: the case of the user authentication methods. In *Proceedings of the 18th International Conference of the Association Francophone d'Interaction Homme-Machine* (pp. 199 – 203). ACM. doi:10.1145/1132736.1132768

Bunnell, J., Podd, J., Henderson, R., Napier, R., & Kennedy-Moffat, J. (1997). Cognitive, associative, and conventional passwords: Recall and guessing rates. *Computers & Security, 16*(7), 645–657. doi:10.1016/S0167-4048(97)00008-4

Byron, B. (2003, August 1). *The need for authentication & authorization.* Retrieved on 3rd April, 2010 from http://www.redbooks.ibm.com/ abstracts/tips0266.html?Open

CA. (2012). *Guidelines for the issuance and management of extended validation certificates.* Retrieved from www.cabforum.org

CEPIS. (2007, October 27). *Authentication approach for online banking.* Retrieved 3rd April, 2010 from http://www.cepis.org/files/ cepis/20090901104203_Authentication%20approaches%20for%20.pdf

Chan, P. K., Fan, W., Prodromidis, A. L., & Stolfo, S. J. (1999). Distributed data mining in credit card fraud detection, data mining. *IEEE Intelligent Systems & their Applications, 14*(6), 67–74.

Chen, C., Mitchell, C. J., & Tang, S. (2011). SSL/ TLS session-aware user authentication using a GAA bootstrapped key information security theory and practice. In *Security and privacy of mobile devices in wireless communication* (pp. 54–68). Springer.

Chen, R. C., Chen, T. S., & Lin, C. C. (2006). A new binary support vector system for increasing detection rate of credit card fraud. *International Journal of Pattern Recognition, 20*(2), 227–239. doi:10.1142/S0218001406004624

Chiasson, S., van Oorschot, P. C., & Biddle, R. (2008). Lecture notes in computer science: Vol. 4734: Graphical password authentication using cued click points. Springer.

Control, A. (2010). *Authentication, authorization and access control.* Retrieved 3rd April, 2010 from http://eregie.premier-ministre.gouv.fr/manual/ howto/auth.html

Egelman, S., Sotirakopoulos, A., Muslukhov, I., Beznosov, Z., & Herley, C. (2013). Does my password go up to eleven? The impact of password meters on password selection. In *Proceedings of the SIGCHI Conference on Human Factors in Computing Systems* (pp. 2379-2388). ACM. doi:10.1145/2470654.2481329

Fatima, A. (2011). E-banking security issues--Is there a solution in biometrics? *Journal of Internet Banking & Commerce, 16*(2), 1–9.

Furnell, S. M., Dowland, P. S., Illingworth, H. M., & Reynolds, P. L. (2000). Authentication and supervision: A survey of user attitudes. *Computers & Security, 19*(6), 529–539. doi:10.1016/S0167-4048(00)06027-2

Gaw, S., & Felten, E. W. (2006). Password management strategies for online accounts. In *Proceedings of the 2nd Symposium on Usable Privacy and Security* (pp. 44–55). Academic Press. doi:10.1145/1143120.1143127

Google. (2014). *Google safe browsing*. Retrieved from http:///www.google.com/chrome/intl/ko/more/security.html

Gunson, N., Marshall, D., Morton, H., & Jack, M. (2011). User perceptions of security and usability of single-factor and two-factor authentication in automated telephone banking. *Computers & Security*, *30*(4), 208–220. doi:10.1016/j.cose.2010.12.001

Gupta, M., Lee, J., & Rao, H. R. (2008). Implications of FFIEC guidance on authentication in electronic banking. In Handbook of research on information security and assurance. Hershey, PA: IGI Global.

Gupta, M., Rao, H. R., & Upadhyaya, S. (2004, July-September). Electronic banking and information assurance issues: Survey and synthesis. *Journal of Organizational and End User Computing*, *16*(3), 1–21. doi:10.4018/joeuc.2004070101

Gupta, M., & Sharman, R. (2008, December). Dimensions of identity federation: A case study in financial services. *Journal of Information Assurance and Security*, *3*(4), 244–256.

Hasan, R., & Yurcik, W. (2006). A statistical analysis of disclosed storage security breaches. In *Proceedings of 2nd International Workshop on Storage Security and Survivability* (StorageSS '06). Academic Press. doi:10.1145/1179559.1179561

Herley, C., & Oorschot, P. C. V. (2012). A research agenda acknowledging the persistence of passwords. *IEEE Security and Privacy*, *10*(1), 28–36. doi:10.1109/MSP.2011.150

Hutchinson, D., & Warren, M. (2003). Security for internet banking: A framework. *Logistics, Information, &. Management*, *16*(1), 64–73.

Jain, A., Bolle, R., & Pankanti, S. (Eds.). (1998). Biometrics: Personal identification in networked society. Dordrecht, The Netherlands: Kluwer.

Jain, A. K., Ross, A., & Pankanti, S. (2006). Biometrics: A tool for information security. *IEEE Transactions of Information Forensics and Security*, *1*(2), 125–143. doi:10.1109/TIFS.2006.873653

Karole, A., Saxena, N., & Christin, N. (2010). A comparative usability evaluation of traditional password managers. In *Proceedings of the 13th International Conference on Information Security and Cryptology* (pp. 233-251). Springer-Verlag.

Kay, R. (2005, April 4). *Biometric authentication*. Retrieved 3rd April 2010 from http://www.computerworld.com/s/article/100772/Biometric_Authentication?taxonomyId=17&pageNumber=1

Komanduri, S., & Hutchings, D. (2008). Order and entropy in picture passwords. In *Proceedings of Graphics Interface*. Academic Press.

Komanduri, S., Shay, R., Kelley, P. G., Mazurek, M. L., Bauer, L., & Christin, N. et al. (2011). Of passwords and people: Measuring the effect of password-composition policies. In *Proceedings of ACM CHI Conference on Human Factors in Computing Systems* (pp. 2595 – 2604). ACM.

Levi, M., & Burrows, M. (2008). Measuring the impact of fraud in the UK: A conceptual and empirical journey. *The British Journal of Criminology*, *48*(3), 293–318. doi:10.1093/bjc/azn001

Liang, W., & Wang, W. (2005). *A quatitative study of authentication & QoS in wirless IP network*. Retrieved 8th April, 2010 from http://www.ece.ncsu.edu/netwis/papers/05LW-INFOCOM

Liu, S. (2004, February). *Authentication in ASP. NET web servers.* Retrieved from 3rd March 2010 from http://progtutorials.tripod.com/Authen.htm

Magalhaes, R. M. (2001, November 19). *Understanding ISA's different types of authentication.* Retrieved 3rd April 2010 from www.isaserver.org/tutorials/Understanding_ISAs_different_Authentication_types.html

Marlinspike, M. (2009). *New tricks for defeating SSL in practice, Blackhat.* Retrieved 21st April, 2011 from https://www.blackhat.com/presentations/bh-dc-09/Marlinspike/BlackHat-DC-09-Marlinspike-Defeating-SSL.pdf

McAlearney, S. (2008, August 7). TJX data breach: Ignore cost lessons and weep. *CIO Magazine.*

Morris, R., & Thompson, K. (1979). Password security: A case history. *Communications of the ACM, 22*(11), 594–597. doi:10.1145/359168.359172

Mozilla. (2014). *Phishing protection: Design documentation, Mozila Wiki.* Retrieved from https://wiki.mozilla.org/Phishing_Protection:_Design_Documentation

Normalini, M. K., & Ramayah, T. (2012). Biometrics technologies implementation in internet banking reduce security issues? In *Proceedings of International Congress on Interdisciplinary Business and Social Sciences 2012* (ICIBSoS 2012) (vol. 65, pp. 364–369). Academic Press. doi:10.1016/j.sbspro.2012.11.135

O'Gorman, L. (2003, December). Comparing passwords, tokens, and biometrics for user authentication. *Proceedings of the IEEE, 91*(12), 2019–2040. doi:10.1109/JPROC.2003.819605

OCC. (1999, October). *Internet banking.* Retrieved 3rd April, 2010 from http://www.occ.treas.gov/handbook/intbank.pdf

Online Banking. (2010). Retrieved 3rd April, 2010, from http://www.investorglossary.com/online-banking.htm

Podio, F. L., & Dunn, J. S. (2001). *Biometric authentication technology.* Retrieved 3rd April, 2010, from http://www.itl.nist.gov/div893/biometrics/Biometricsfromthemovies.pdf

Pond, R., Podd, J., Bunnell, J., & Henderson, R. (2000). Word association computer passwords: The effect of formulation techniques on recall and guessing rates. *Computers & Security, 19*(7), 645–656. doi:10.1016/S0167-4048(00)07023-1

PRC. (2009). *A chronology of data breaches reported since the choicepoint incident (list).* Privacy Rights Clearinghouse. Retrieved January 24th 2010 from http://www.privacyrights.org/ar/ChronDataBreaches.htm

Renaud, K. (2009, February). On user involvement in production of images used in visual authentication. *Journal of Visual Languages and Computing, 20*(1), 1–15. doi:10.1016/j.jvlc.2008.04.001

Riva, O., Qin, C., Strauss, K., & Lymberopoulos, D. (2012). Progressive authentication: Deciding when to authenticate on mobile phones. In *Proceedings of the 21st USENIX Security Symposium.* USENIX.

Sabzevar, A. P., & Stavrou, A. (2008). Universal multi-factor authentication using graphical passwords. In *Proceedings of IEEE International Conference on Signal Image Technology and Internet Based Systems.* IEEE. doi:10.1109/SITIS.2008.92

Singh, K. (2012). Can mobile learn from the web. In *Proceedings of IEEE Computer Society Security and Privacy Workshops, WPSP '12.* IEEE.

Strouble, D., Schechtman, G., & Alsop, A. S. (2009). Productivity and usability effects of using a two-factor security system. In *Proceedings of the Southern Association for Information Systems Conference* (pp. 195-201). Academic Press.

Tehan, R. (2005, December 16). *Personal data security breaches: Context and incident summaries.* Congressional Research Service Report for Congress.

Thigpen, S. (2005, July 17). *Banking authentication methods.* Retrieved 3rd April, 2010 from http://www.infosecwriters.com/text_resources/ pdf/ Authentication_Methods_For_Banking. pdf

Tiwari, A., Sanyal, S., Abraham, A., Knapskog, S. J., & Sanyal, S. (2011). A multi-factor security protocol for wireless payment-secure web authentication using mobile devices. In *Proceedings of IADIS International Conference on Applied Computing.* IADIS.

Tsai, C., Chen, C., & Zhuang, D. (2012). Trusted m-banking verification scheme based on a combination of OTP and biometrics. *Journal of Convergence, 3*(3), 23–30.

Vance, A. (2010). If your password is 123456, just make it hackme. *New York Times.* Retrieved 15th March, 2010 from http://www.nytimes. com/2010/01/21/technology/21password.html

Venkatraman, S., & Delpachitra, I. (2008). Biometrics in banking security: A case study. *Information Management & Computer Security, 16*(4), 415–430. doi:10.1108/09685220810908813

Weigold, T. K. (2006, March/April). *Secure internet banking and authentication.* Retrieved 3rd April 2010 from http://www.zurich.ibm. com/pdf/csc/SecureInternetBanking Authentication.pdf

Weiss, R., & De Luca, A. (2008). Passshapes: Utilizing stroke based authentication to increase password memorability. In *Proceedings of the 5th Nordic Conference on Human-Computer Interaction.* Academic Press. doi:10.1145/1463160.1463202

Wiedenbeck, S., Waters, J., Birget, J., Brodskiy, A., & Memon, N. (2005, July). PassPoints: Design and longitudinal evaluation of a graphical password system. *International Journal of Human-Computer Studies, 63*(1-2), 102–127. doi:10.1016/j.ijhcs.2005.04.010

Wiesmaier, A., Fischer, M., Karatsiolis, E. G., & Lippert, M. (2004). *Proceedings of the 2005 International Conference on Security and Management.* Retrieved from arxiv.org/pdf/ cs.CR/0410025

Williamson, G. D. (2006). Enhanced authentication in online banking. *Journal of Economic Crime Management, 42*(2).

Wimberly, H., & Liebrock, L. M. (2011). Using fingerprint authentication to reduce system security: An empirical study. In *Proceedings of IEEE Symposium on Security and Privacy* (pp. 32–46). IEEE. doi:10.1109/SP.2011.35

Xi, K., Ahmad, T., Han, F., & Hu, J. (2011). A fingerprint based bio-cryptographic security protocol designed for client/server authentication in mobile computing environment. *Security and Communication Networks, 4*(5), 487–499. doi:10.1002/sec.225

Yang, Y.-J. (1997). *The security of electronic banking.* Retrieved 3rd April, 2010, from http:// csrc.nist.gov/nissc/1997/proceedings/041.pdf

Zezschwitz, E., De Luca, A., & Hussmann, H. (2013). Survival of the shortest: A retrospective analysis of influencing factors on password composition. In *Proceedings of Human-Computer Interaction.* Academic Press.

KEY TERMS AND DEFINITIONS

Authentication Factor: One of three possible factors – something the user knows (knowledge), something user possesses (possession) and something user is (behavioral).

Authentication: Verifying user's assertion of its identification through credentials.

Authorization: Verifying user's privileges to a system.

Identity Federation: Asserting user's identification information to a trusting partner for purpose of user's identification and authorization.

Identity Management Architecture: Design of identity system for managing credentials and entitlements for users of covered systems.

Identity Management System: A system for managing user identities and related privileges.

Multiple Factor Authentication: An authentication system that is based on more than one factor or authentication.

Password Management: Managing users' passwords for purpose of authentication.

Role Management: Managing user's roles for purpose of authorization and entitlements.

Single Sign On: Use of a single set of credentials to provide access to multiple systems and applications.

Section 3
Trust and Security

Chapter 10
Security and Privacy Requirements Engineering

Nancy R. Mead
Carnegie Mellon University, USA

Saeed Abu-Nimeh
Damballa Inc., USA

ABSTRACT

Security requirements engineering identifies security risks in software in the early stages of the development cycle. In this chapter, the authors present the SQUARE security requirements method. They integrate privacy requirements into SQUARE to identify privacy risks in addition to security risks. They then present a privacy elicitation technique and subsequently combine security risk assessment techniques with privacy risk assessment techniques. The authors discuss prototype tools that have been developed to support SQUARE for security and privacy as well as recent workshops that have focused on additional results in the security and privacy requirements area. Finally, the authors suggest future research and case studies needed to further contribute to early lifecycle activities that will address security and privacy-related issues.

INTRODUCTION

Several initiatives have tried to standardize the processes of the software lifecycle, yet ISO/IEC 12207:2008 is considered the standard of software lifecycle processes (ISO/IEC 12207, 2008) by most. This standard divides software lifecycle processes into five high-level phases:

1. Acquisition,
2. Supply,
3. Development,
4. Operation, and
5. Maintenance.

The acquisition phase concentrates on initiating the project. The supply phase concentrates on developing a project management plan. In the development phase, the software product is designed, created, and tested. In the operation phase, users start utilizing the product. Finally, in the maintenance phase, the product is maintained to stay operational.

DOI: 10.4018/978-1-4666-7381-6.ch010

Software requirements are discussed and addressed at an early stage in the software development phase. Requirements engineering concentrates on the real-world goals for, functions of, and constraints on software systems. In addition, it covers the relationship of these factors to precise specifications of software behavior and to their evolution over time and across software families (Zave, 1997).

Requirements elicitation in software development concentrates on functional and nonfunctional requirements. Functional or end-user requirements are the tasks that the system under development is expected to perform. Nonfunctional requirements are the qualities that the system must adhere to. Functional requirements are not as difficult to tackle, as it is easier to test their implementation in the system under development. Security and privacy requirements are considered nonfunctional requirements, although in many instances they do have functionality (Abu-Nimeh, Miyazaki, & Mead, 2009).

The Security Quality Requirements Engineering (SQUARE) method is used to identify software security issues in the early stages of the development lifecycle. In the following sections, we present the SQUARE method in detail and discuss the integration of privacy requirements into SQUARE.

It is essential to identify the security and privacy issues in a software risk assessment. Conducting a risk assessment is a step in a risk management process that involves the identification, assessment, and prioritization of risks related to a situation. A risk assessment determines, in a quantitative or qualitative way, the value of these risks. A security risk assessment identifies the threats to systems, while a privacy risk assessment identifies data sensitivities in systems. The SQUARE method relies on security risk assessment techniques to assess the levels of security risk in systems. However, these security risk assessment techniques are not adequate to address privacy risks. Therefore, we combine the security risk assessment techniques in the SQUARE method with privacy risk assessment techniques.

Background

While the Security Quality Requirements Engineering (SQUARE) method (Mead, Hough, & Stehney, 2005) aims to identify software security risks in the early stages of the software development process, privacy requirements engineering (Chiasera, Casati, Daniel, & Velegrakis, 2008) serves to identify privacy risks early in the design process. Some research studies (Pfleeger & Pfleeger, 2009) indicate that privacy requirements engineering is a less mature discipline than security engineering and that underlying engineering principles give little attention to privacy requirements. However, more recently, privacy requirements engineering has evolved through work at a number of workshops, notably the RELAW workshops at the IEEE International Requirements Engineering Conference (RE).

Some (Adams & Sasse, 2001) claim that most privacy disclosures happen due to defects in design and are not the result of an intentional attack. Nevertheless, security is necessary but not sufficient to ensure privacy.

Although security and privacy risks overlap, relying merely on protecting the security of users does not imply the protection of their privacy. For instance, health records can be secured from various types of intrusions; however, the security of such assets does not guarantee that the privacy of patients is secure. The security of such records does not protect against improper authorized access or disclosure of records.

The SQUARE method generates categorized and prioritized security requirements following its nine steps (Mead et al., 2005):

1. Technical definitions are agreed upon by the requirements engineering team and project stakeholders.
2. Assets, business, and security goals are identified.
3. In order to facilitate full understanding of the studied system, artifacts and documentation are created.

4. A security risk assessment is applied to determine the likelihood and impact of possible threats to the system.
5. The best method for eliciting security requirements is determined by the requirements engineering team and the stakeholders.
6. Security requirements are elicited.
7. Security requirements are categorized.
8. Security requirements are prioritized.
9. The security requirements are inspected to ensure consistency and accuracy.

In the next section, we present modified steps to address privacy issues in software and to perform a privacy risk assessment.

SQUARE FOR PRIVACY

The following nine steps modify the SQUARE method to adapt the whole process for privacy requirements engineering (Bijwe & Mead, 2010):

1. **Agreeing on Definitions:** The engineering team and the stakeholders create a comprehensive list of terms that will aid effective communication and reduce ambiguity. A list of terms that are applicable to privacy is provided. This list can include terms such as, access, anonymity, authentication, pseudonymity, etc. Then, suggested definitions for the proposed terms with their sources are provided to help the stakeholders understand the basic scope of each term and select one of its definitions.
2. **Identifying Assets and Privacy Goals:** In this step, a discussion is initiated among the stakeholders regarding their assets and overall privacy goals for the project. Privacy goals include:
   a. Ensure that personal data is collected with the user's permission,
   b. Ensure that the data collected for a specific purpose is not used for other purposes without appropriate authorization, and
   c. Ensure that the user is aware of the purpose for which personal data is collected.
3. **Collecting Artifacts:** Artifacts that are relevant to privacy include system architecture diagrams, use-case scenarios and diagrams, misuse-case scenarios and diagrams, attack trees, and user-role hierarchies. System architecture diagrams provide an overview of the system as it exists and shows how data flows among the different components. Privacy use cases will mostly be related to how the system handles user data and how the system components interact with each other. Misuse cases identify the vulnerabilities of the system and the risks that the system is prone to. Misuse cases can be used to make the system more resistant to such attacks. Attack trees model threats to the system by focusing on the attackers and the ways they may attack the system. User-role hierarchies can determine the access control requirements based on user roles.
4. **Conducting the Risk Assessment:** The security risk assessment techniques in SQUARE are combined with privacy risk assessment techniques to address privacy risks. (The section "Combining Security and Privacy Risk Assessment Techniques" covers the process in detail.)
5. **Selecting an Elicitation Technique:** The privacy requirements elicitation technique (PRET) can be used in this step to select a suitable elicitation technique for privacy. (The section "Privacy Requirements Elicitation Technique" covers PRET in detail.)

6. **Eliciting Privacy Requirements:** To elicit privacy requirements, PRET can be used in this step as well.

7. **Categorizing Requirements:** Privacy requirements can have legal implications; therefore, a categorization that suits privacy requirements is needed. (Massey, Otto, & Anton, 2009) use three categories to prioritize legal requirements:
   a. Nonlegal requirements,
   b. Legal requirements needing further refinement, and
   c. Implementation-ready legal requirements.

8. **Prioritizing Requirements:** The list of requirements provided by the risk assessment (step 4) and categorization (step 7) are prioritized in this step. (Karlsson, 1996) proposed the pairwise comparison method to prioritize requirements. The method is based on the analytical hierarchy process (AHP) and derives the relative importance of one requirement over another. Given a set of n requirements, the method requires $n * (n - 1)/2$ comparisons. Using the values given for each comparison, mathematical formulas can be used to derive the prioritization for the n requirements. (Massey, Otto, & Anton, 2009) proposed a method to prioritize requirements using two steps. In the first step of finding legal implications, we use the required legal text as input. The main goal of this step is to map the requirements to the subsections in the legal text with the help of legal-domain experts. The second step is calculating a prioritization score for every requirement. This step uses the mapping from the first step to calculate a prioritization score based on a predefined formula.

9. **Inspecting Requirements:** Inspections remove defects and clarify ambiguities in the requirements. A number of methods exist that are used to carry out inspections, ranging from ad-hoc inspections to the use of checklists, and even Fagan reviews and scenario-based inspections. Research has shown that scenario-based inspection methods provide a better defect-detection rate than checklist or ad-hoc inspections (Porter, Votta, & Basili, 1995).

The outcome of this nine-step process is a final privacy requirements document that has been agreed upon and verified by all stakeholders and the requirements engineering team. In the next section, we discuss modifications to steps 4, 5, and 6 in further detail.

Combining Security and Privacy Risk Assessment Techniques

Security and privacy risk assessment techniques overlap, yet they address different problems. Generally, security risk assessments protect systems' resources, including software, storage, networks, and users. However, privacy risk assessments concentrate on data protection, which includes the application of various policies and procedures to collect and protect data (Abu-Nimeh & Mead, 2010).

The goals of a security risk assessment include the implementation of authentication and authorization systems, whereas the goals of a privacy risk assessment relate to privacy policies and procedures. The following are the different procedures used in privacy impact assessments and security risk assessments (Mitrano, Kirby, & Maltz, 2005):

Security Risk Assessment

- Threat identification;
- Vulnerability identification;
- Control analysis;
- Likelihood determination;
- Impact analysis;
- Risk determination.

Privacy Impact Assessment

- Data description;
- Data sources;
- Data collection process, data accuracy, data completeness, and data currentness;
- Data comprehensiveness and documentation;
- Data access description, access procedures, access controls, and access responsibilities;
- Access levels and restrictions;
- Authorized access misuse;
- Shared data restrictions and controls;
- Data relevancy and necessity;
- Possibility of data derivation and aggregation;
- Protection and control of consolidated data;
- Data retrieval;
- Equitable treatment of users;
- Data retention and disposal;
- User monitoring and protection against unauthorized monitoring.

The SQUARE method relies on two risk assessment techniques in step 4:

1. The Risk Management Guide for Information Technology Systems (NIST SP 800-30) (Stonebuner, Goguen, & Feringa, 2002).
2. Yacov Haimes's Risk Filtering, Ranking, and Management Framework (RFRM) (Haimes, 2004).

The RFRM approach contains eight phases, some of which were found to be out of scope. Only two relevant phases of RFRM are included in the SQUARE method: phase III, bi-criteria filtering and ranking, and phase IV, multi-criteria filtering and ranking.

The NIST model for risk assessment is broken into nine steps, each with an output that serves as the input to the next step. The SQUARE method excludes steps 1, 8, and 9 in the NIST model, as they are irrelevant or redundant for our purposes. Therefore, the steps from the NIST model included in the SQUARE method are threat identification, vulnerability identification, control analysis, likelihood determination, impact analysis, and risk determination.

Clearly, the risk assessment in the SQUARE method corresponds to the system under analysis. Most importantly, the risk assessment should categorize the likelihood and impact of the major threats to the system (Mead, Hough, & Stehney, 2005).

Microsoft's Threat Modeling method is another widely used method that can be used to identify risks (Ingalsbe, Kunimatsu, Baeten, & Mead, 2008). Threat modeling is based on the STRIDE method for risk identification. STRIDE is an acronym for Spoofing of user identity, Tampering, Repudiation, Information disclosure (privacy breach or data leak), Denial of Service (DoS), and Elevation of privilege. Threat modeling presentation material, videos, and tools are available for download from the Microsoft website. Threat Modeling workshops are also available from Microsoft.

Several laws and regulations provide a set of guidelines that can be used to assess privacy risks. For example, the Health Insurance Portability and Accountability Act (HIPAA) addresses privacy concerns of health information systems by enforcing data exchange standards.

In addition, Privacy Impact Assessment (PIA) (Flaherty, 2000) is a comprehensive process for determining the privacy, confidentiality, and security risks associated with the collection, use, and disclosure of personal information.

In the following sections, we discuss the combination of PIA and HIPAA with security risk assessment techniques that are used in the SQUARE method. In the next section, we discuss a classification of PIA and HIPAA following the methodology in (Campbell & Stamp, 2004), after which we explain the addition of privacy impact and risk assessment techniques to the current SQUARE method.

Privacy Impact Assessment

According to (Statistics Canada, 2008), the PIA process is used to determine the privacy, confidentiality, and security risks associated with the collection, use, and disclosure of personal information. It also defines how to mitigate and eliminate the identified risks. Any new program or service delivery initiative should consider the PIA process and should communicate to the public about the privacy and confidentiality of their information.

According to US-CERT (United States Computer Emergency Readiness Team, 2008), the following should be addressed when conducting a PIA on systems:

1. **Characterization of the Information:** What information is collected and maintained in the system.
2. **Uses of the Information:** Use of information and tools to analyze data.
3. **Information Retention:** How long information is retained.
4. **Internal Sharing and Disclosure:** Which internal organizations share the information.
5. **External Sharing and Disclosure:** Which external organizations share the information.
6. **Notice of Collection of Information:** Notifying individuals prior to collection of information.
7. **Individual Access, Redress, and Correction:** How individuals can access their information.
8. **Technical Access and Security:** Who can access the information or the system.
9. **Technology:** What development process was used to develop the system.

Previous research (Heckle & Holden, 2006) proved that PIA works well in combination with other risk assessment techniques. PIA helped to identify the data sensitivities of vote verification systems, while other risk assessments were used to identify the full spectrum of threats to these systems. In the next section, we discuss the integration of HIPAA as a privacy risk assessment technique.

HIPAA Privacy Risk Assessment

HIPAA (Health Insurance Portability and Accountability Act) addresses privacy concerns of health information systems by enforcing data exchange standards. The act also provides a guideline for analyzing risks. The overall objective of a HIPAA risk analysis is to document the potential risks and vulnerabilities of confidentiality, integrity, or availability of electronically protected health information (ePHI). In addition, this risk analysis determines the appropriate safeguards needed to bring the degree of risk to an acceptable and manageable level. Risks found by this analysis fall into three categories: access, storage, and transmission.

The entities of interest in a HIPAA risk analysis are called Covered Entities (CEs). These entities must comply with the HIPAA Security Rule. CEs can be health plans (e.g., HMOs, group health plans), health care clearinghouses (e.g., billing and repricing companies), and health care providers (e.g., doctors, dentists, hospitals) who transmit ePHI.

There are seven steps in an HIPAA risk assessment:

1. Inventory and classify assets.
2. Document likely threats to each asset.
3. Conduct a vulnerability assessment.
4. Evaluate current safeguards (administrative, physical, or technical).
5. Document risks.
6. Recommend appropriate safeguards.
7. Create a report of results.

Table 1. Classification matrix

Level		Approach		
		Temporal	Functional	Comparative
Abstract	Expert	Engagement (1)	Sequence (4)	Principles (7)
Mid-level	Collaborative	Exercise (2)	Assistant (5)	Best Practice (8)
Concrete	Owner	Compliance Testing (3)	Matrix (6)	Audit (9)

Table 2. Approach level

Level	Abstract	Mid-Level	Concrete
	High Level (3)	Mid-Level (2)	Low Level (1)
Expertise	Requires expert knowledge	Requires both expert and owner knowledge	Requires user knowledge
Description	How an expert performs an assessment	How both (an expert and an owner) perform an assessment	How a system owner performs an assessment
Application	Broad	Middle	Narrow
Driver	Expert	Collaborative (both expert and owner)	Owner

CLASSIFICATION OF RISK ASSESSMENT TECHNIQUES

To make sure that both the existing security and proposed privacy risk assessment techniques follow the same methodology and require the same expertise, we apply the classification scheme presented in (Campbell & Stamp, 2004). The proposed privacy risk assessment techniques must conform to the methodology used by the risk assessment techniques in the SQUARE method, except that they address privacy rather than security. In (Campbell & Stamp, 2004), the authors propose a classification scheme for risk assessment methods based on the level of detail of the assessment method and the approach used in that assessment method. They summarize the strengths and weaknesses of assessment methods in a nine-cell matrix as shown in Table 1.

This matrix helps the user understand what to expect from an assessment method, what the relationship is among different assessment methods, and what the best way is to use an assessment method. This classification scheme does not help to determine which methods are appropriate for addressing security risks and which are appropriate for addressing privacy risks, yet it does help us analyze the methods suitable for privacy and those suitable for security relative to their detail and the assessment approach they follow.

As shown in Table 2, an assessment method can belong to one of three levels: abstract, midlevel, and concrete. An abstract method requires an expert to drive the method. A concrete method requires someone who knows the details of the system to drive the method——that is, the owner of the system. A mid-level method requires collaborative effort between an expert and the owner of the system to drive the method.

Table 3 shows the three different approaches that can be taken in risk assessment methods. An assessment method can use one of three approaches:

Table 3. Approach classification

	Temporal	**Functional**	**Comparative**
Procedure	It stresses a system and actual tests are applied in real time	It is a blend of the other two approaches. It performs a threat analysis, which focuses on how a system functions without testing	It is a comparison against an explicit standard. The system model and the threat lists are only implicitly present in a generic form
Outcome	The performance of the system as a consequence of the application of those tests	Threat analysis	Comparing the system with an explicit standard
Advantages	Testing the system clears misconceptions	Considers specific threats, vulnerabilities, assets, and countermeasures	Simple and focused
Disadvantages	Impractical to test the system, so a model of the system is tested. Similarly, cannot perform all attacks on the system and a subset of attacks is performed.	No testing involved	No testing or examination of function and no explicit system model is involved.

1. A temporal approach stress-tests a system in real-time.
2. A functional approach performs threat analysis on the system without testing.
3. A comparative approach compares the system against an explicit standard.

The nine numbered cells in Table 1 (i.e., engagement (1) through audit (9)) show what needs to be done by the driver of the method. These activities are summarized as follows:

1. **Engagement:** Experts try to compromise a system without the owner's help.
2. **Exercise:** The owner collaborates with experts to compromise a system.
3. **Compliance Testing:** The owner performs an activity similar to door rattling of the system.
4. **Sequence:** The user answers a series of questions or completes a flow chart.
5. **Assistance:** An assistant, or similar, records and tracks system details.
6. **Matrix:** The user looks up a table.
7. **Principles:** The user applies principles to the system and keeps a list of comparative types.
8. **Best Practice:** The owner keeps a more specific list than the principle's list.

9. **Audit:** The owner keeps a list based on an explicit standard, but this list more specific than the best practices list.

Refer to (Campbell & Stamp, 2004) for further details on these methods.

Classification of Security Risk Assessment Methods in SQUARE

As we mentioned earlier, the SQUARE method relies on two risk assessment techniques in step 4: NIST SP 800-30 and RFRM.

(Campbell & Stamp, 2004) lists NIST SP 800-30 as an assistant method. This risk assessment approach is performed by an expert and is a functional approach (see Table 3). However, (Campbell & Stamp, 2004) do not list RFRM as a risk assessment method. NIST and RFRM both deal with hardware failure or destruction; however, they rank importance differently and their outputs concentrate on different aspects. In NIST, the output concentrates on what the attacker can do once inside the system (e.g., destroy data, disclose information). In RFRM, the output concentrates on the attacker's ability to break the frontline of a defense system (Mead et al., 2005). Due to the similarity of the NIST model and RFRM, we consider RFRM an assistant method as well.

Classification of Privacy Risk Assessment Methods

PIA and HIPAA are driven by experts, which means they require someone other than the owner of the system to perform the risk assessment. Further, these methods perform threat analysis on a system without testing it. These methods actually consist of a series of questions that are answered by the users of the system as shown in the previous subsections.

Both methods require the same level of expertise (i.e., expert) used in NIST SP 80030 and RFRM. Both methods also follow the same methodology (i.e., functional) used in NIST SP 800-30 and RFRM. Consequently, PIA and HIPAA are regarded as assistant methods.

The following goals were met by integrating the PIA and HIPAA risk assessment methods:

1. Introduce risk assessment techniques that address privacy in addition to security.
2. Follow the same assessment methodology.
3. Require the same level of expertise used by the security risk assessment techniques in SQUARE.

Based on this discussion, our goal is met. We introduced risk assessment techniques that address privacy rather than security, follow the same assessment methodology, and require the same level of expertise used by the security risk assessment techniques in the SQUARE method (Abu-Nimeh & Mead, 2009).

Privacy Requirements Elicitation Technique

The privacy requirements elicitation technique (PRET) (Miyazaki, Mead, & Zhan, 2008) is based on the SQUARE method. This technique helps software engineers and stakeholders elicit privacy requirements using a computer-aided approach. PRET uses a questionnaire to elicit information that the requirements engineers and stakeholders

complete. The tool contains a database of privacy requirements that is searched to use the input from the questionnaire and provide results.

Figure 1 depicts the integration of the PRET technique into the SQUARE method. The first four steps in the SQUARE method remain the same. In the fifth step, when elicitation techniques are chosen, PRET can be selected to elicit privacy requirements. This step is where the PRET process starts, the questionnaire is answered, and the privacy requirements are elicited. Finally, the privacy requirements are verified and fed back to the SQUARE method.

In the SQUARE method, the privacy requirements are categorized, prioritized, and inspected in the seventh, eighth, and ninth steps respectively. Recently, privacy and security requirements engineering were integrated more fully in the P-SQUARE tool, which supports security, privacy, or both (CERT Division, 2014).

Next, we describe questionnaire design, discuss the various sources used to identify privacy requirements, and illustrate the process involved in requirements elicitation.

Questionnaire Design

Privacy Seal Programs (Markert, 2002) and the OECD Privacy Statement Generator[1] are used to prepare the stakeholder questionnaire. The OECD generator is a tool that provides users with useful input in the development of a privacy policy and statement. Using the generator and other privacy seal policies, such as TRUSTe and PrivacyMark, 10 questions are developed to include in the questionnaire as shown in Table 4.

Identification of Privacy Requirements

Privacy requirements are collected from multiple sources, which are generally various publicly available privacy laws and principles. In addition, we apply misuse cases to identify privacy requirements. We outline each of these approaches in the following sections.

Figure 1. Integration of PRET into SQUARE
©2014 Carnegie Mellon University. Used with permission.

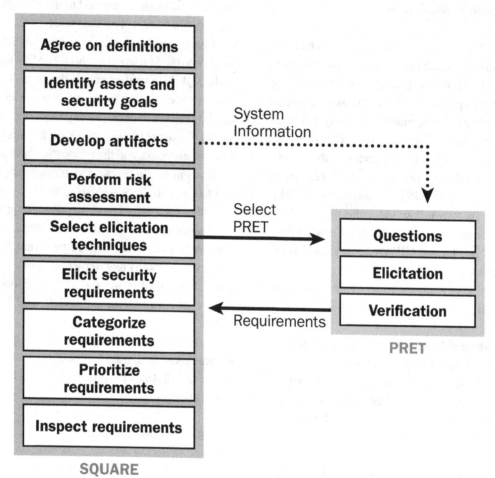

Privacy Laws and Principles

To identify privacy requirements, six privacy principles and laws are studied, from which a subset of privacy requirements are selected. The following are the laws and principles studied:

1. OECD Guidelines on the Protection of Privacy.
2. The European Commission's Directive on Data Protection.
3. Japan's Personal Information Protection Act.
4. Privacy laws in the US:
   a. Privacy Protection Act.
   b. Video Privacy Protection Act.
   c. CA–SB–1386 (California).
   d. Family Educational Rights and Privacy Act.
   e. Health Insurance Portability and Accountability Act.
   f. Children's Online Privacy Protection Act.
5. Common Criteria.
6. W3C Web Services Architecture Requirements.

Table 4. Questions included in the questionnaire

Question	Response
11. Does the service provider process personal information?	Yes / No
12. In which country or area is the service provided?	USA / EU / Canada / Japan / Other

13. What type of service provider?
    13.1. If industrial, does the service provider belong to any of these fields?
    13.2. If governmental, does the service provider belong to any of these fields?
    13.3. Is the purpose of the service related to journalism, literary work, academic studies, religious activities, or political activities?
	Industrial / Governmental / Academic / Other
	Medicine / Communication / Education
	Military branch / Non-military branch / Research body
	Yes / No

14. What kind of personal information does the service provider process?	Point of contact / Social identification / Personal identity data / Demographic information / Age, education / Health information / Financial information / Personal information of children / Other sensitive personal data
15. How does the service provider obtain personal information?	Provided by users / Provided by third parties / Collected automatically from users / Collected automatically from third parties
16. Where does the service provider store personal information?	Client side / Server side / Third-party client side / Third-party server side
17. How long does the service provider store personal information?	Does not store / One transaction / Certain period of time / Forever
18. Does the service provider use personal information for another purpose?	Yes / No
19. Does the service provider share personal information with others?	Yes / No
20. What privacy protection level does the service provider set?	High / Mid / Low

Table 5. Answers to the auto insurance service questionnaire

Question	Answer
1	Yes
2	USA
3	Industrial
3.1	–
3.2	–
3.3	No
4	Point, Social, Demographic, Age
5	Provided by users, Provided by third parties
6	Server side
7	Forever
8	No
9	No
10	Mid

Misuse Cases

Misuse cases are used to elicit requirements. The idea behind using these cases is to document and decide how software should act proactively to prevent malicious activities. Misuse cases are derived from the use case technique, which is a modular way to describe a way in which a complex system is employed by its users (Armour & Miller, 2000).

With slight modifications, use cases can be used to aid in the identification of security requirements. Misuse cases specify behavior that is not wanted in the proposed system. Many security breaches can be described in a stepwise fashion that resembles ordinary use cases. Misuse cases can also be associated with a use case, indicated with a "threaten" relationship; that is, the misuse case represents a threat to normal use (Sindre & Opdahl, 2000). This whole process has proven to be useful in mitigating future attacks.

Table 6. Auto insurance service PRET results

Privacy Requirements	Derivation	Explanation	Priority Level
The service architecture shall describe privacy policy statements and enable a user to access them.	W3C–AR020.1, 20.3	Personal data usage (Q1, Q2)	Mid
Before collecting personal data, the data controller shall specify the purpose.	OECD–PP–P9	Personal data usage (Q1)	Mid
The service provider shall limit the collection of personal data and obtain such data by lawful and fair means.	OECD–PP–P7	Personal data collection (Q6)	Mid
The system network communications must be protected from unauthorized information gathering and/or eavesdropping.	Misuse–case–1	Personal data collection (Q6)	Mid
The system should have functional audit logs and usage reports without disclosing identity information.	Misuse–case–2	Personal data collection (Q6)	Mid
The system shall have strong authentication measures in place at all system gateways and entrance points.	Misuse–case–3	Personal data storage (Q7)	Mid
Personal data should be protected by reasonable security safeguards against risks such as loss, unauthorized access, destruction, use, modification, or disclosure of data.	OECD–PP–P11	Personal data storage (Q7)	Mid
Personal data shall be accurate, complete, and kept up-to-date, if possible.	OECD–PP–P8	Personal data storage (Q7)	Mid
The system shall provide a mechanism by which users can verify their data.	OECD–PP–P13	Personal data storage (Q7)	Mid
The system shall provide a data backup mechanism.	Misuse–case–4	Personal data storage (Q7)	Mid
The system shall have a verification process to check whether there is a disclosure agreement between the third party and the person.	Misuse–case–5	Personal data collection from the third party (Q5)	Mid
The service provider shall report to all the customers if the privacy information is breached.	CA–SB–1386	Breach report in JP, USA (Q1,Q2, Q3)	High

Decision Process

A decision tree of requirements is built to traverse multiple combinations of question paths. The introduction of subsequent questions is based on the answers to the current question. While the user goes through different nodes in the decision tree, a different set of questions is introduced. Several constraints are checked to ensure that privacy requirements dedicated to certain areas, (e.g., in the US, in the EU), are met. In addition, each one of the requirements is assigned a priority based on its source. For instance, requirements derived from laws have a higher priority than requirements derived from principles and misuse cases.

Table 7. Answers to the health care ring questionnaire

Question	Answer
1	Yes
2	Japan
3	Industrial
3.1	Medicine
3.2	–
3.3	No
4	Point, Demographic, Health, Age,
5	Provided by users
6	Server side
7	Certain period of time
8	No
9	Yes
10	High

Table 8. Health care ring results

Privacy Requirements	Derivation	Explanation	Priority Level
The service provider shall describe privacy policy statements and enable a user to access them.	W3C–AR020.1, 20.3	Personal data usage (Q1, Q2)	Mid
Before collecting personal data, the service provider shall specify the purpose.	OECD–PP–P9	Personal data usage (Q1)	Mid
The service provider shall obtain prior consent of the person, except for following cases: (1) Handling of personal information is based on laws. (2) Handling of personal information is based on the necessity for the protection of the life, body, or property of an individual. (3) Handling of personal information is based on the necessity for improving public hygiene or promoting the growth of children. (4) Handling of personal information is based on the necessity for cooperating with a state institution, a local public body, or an individual or entity entrusted by one in executing the operations prescribed by laws.	PIPA–Article–16	Personal data usage in JP (Q1, Q2, Q3)	High
The service provider shall handle personal information within the scope of its purpose of use.	PIPA–Article–16	Personal data usage in JP (Q1, Q2, Q3)	High
The service provider shall limit the collection of personal data and obtain such data by lawful and fair means.	OECD–PP–P7	Personal data collection (Q6)	Mid
The system network communications must be protected from unauthorized information gathering and/or eavesdropping.	Misuse–case–1	Personal data collection (Q6)	Mid
The system should have functional audit logs and usage reports without disclosing identity information.	Misuse–case–2	Personal data collection (Q6)	Mid
The system shall have strong authentication measures in place at all system gateways and entrance points.	Misuse–case–3	Personal data storage (Q7)	Mid
Personal data shall be accurate, complete, and kept up-to-date, if possible.	OECD– PP–P8	Personal data storage (Q7)	Mid
The system shall provide a mechanism by which users can verify their data.	OECD–PP–P13	Personal data storage (Q7)	Mid
The system shall provide a data backup mechanism.	Misuse–case–4	Personal data storage (Q7)	Mid
The service provider must take necessary and proper measures for the prevention of leakage, loss, or damage, and for other control of security of personal data.	PIPA–Article–20	Personal data storage in JP (Q2, Q7)	High
The service provider shall disclose personal data only with the consent of data subject to or by the authority of law.	OECD–PP–P10	Personal data sharing (Q9)	Mid
The service provider shall enable delegation and propagation of privacy policy to third parties.	W3C–AR020.5	Personal data sharing (Q9)	Mid
The service provider shall gain consensus from users about what data they are sharing.	PIPA–Article–23	Personal data sharing in JP (Q2, Q3, Q9)	High
The service provider shall report to all the customers if the privacy of information is breached.	CA–SB–1386	Breach report in JP, USA (Q1,Q2, Q3)	High
The system should provide anonymity. Anonymity means other users or subjects are unable to determine the identity of a user bound to a subject or operation.	CC–FPR–ANO	Privacy enhancing technology usage (Q10)	Low

continued on following page

Table 8. Continued

Privacy Requirements	Derivation	Explanation	Priority Level
The system should provide pseudonymity. Pseudonymity means a set of users and/or subjects are unable to determine the identity of a user bound to a subject or operation, but that this user is still accountable for his or her actions.	CC–FPR–PSE	Privacy enhancing technology usage (Q10)	Low
The system should provide unlinkability. Unlinkability means users and/or subjects are unable to determine whether the same user caused certain specific operations.	CC–FPR–UNL	Privacy enhancing technology usage (Q10)	Low
The system should provide unobservability. Unobservability means users and/or subjects cannot determine whether an operation is being performed.	CC–FPR–UNO	Privacy enhancing technology usage (Q10)	Low

EVALUATION CASE STUDIES

We initially evaluated our model using two pseudo-software development projects: an auto insurance service and a health care ring. In Table 5, we show the answers to the questionnaire for the auto insurance service. Then, we show the corresponding privacy requirements elicited by PRET in Table 6. The health care ring's answers to the questionnaire are shown in Table 7 and the elicited privacy requirements are shown in Table 8. When the P-SQUARE tool was developed, we were able to conduct additional case studies using the tool to validate the ability of SQUARE supplemented with PRET to address security requirements, privacy requirements, and both.

CONCLUSION AND FUTURE RESEARCH DIRECTIONS

In this chapter, we discussed SQUARE, a security requirements engineering approach designed to be used to address software security issues in early stages of the development lifecycle. We also discussed the integration of privacy requirements into the SQUARE method.

First, we introduced PRET, a technique designed to elicit privacy requirements in software. PRET relies on SQUARE in some steps, but introduces extra steps to be applicable to privacy issues. We evaluated PRET using the pseudo-software projects of an auto insurance service and a health care ring.

We showed that the security risk assessment methods used in SQUARE cannot be used as an alternative to privacy risk assessment methods. We presented the addition of privacy risk and impact assessment methods (HIPAA and PIA) to SQUARE.

To make sure that both the existing security and the privacy risk assessment techniques follow the same methodology and require the same expertise, we applied a classification scheme of risk assessment methods. Then, we combined the existing security risk assessment methods in SQUARE, namely NIST SP 800-30 and RFRM, with PIA and HIPAA. More recent risk assessment research may result in additional improvements in this area, but our extensions to SQUARE took us further down the path of privacy requirements engineering.

We described the privacy requirements engineering tool called SQUARE for Privacy (P-SQUARE), including all nine steps of SQUARE. Thus, SQUARE targets both privacy and security risks in software. We also developed a prototype tool to address SQUARE for Acquisition (A-SQUARE).

In the future, we plan to show how malware analysis can contribute to early lifecycle activities such as security requirements engineering (Mead & Morales 2014), and revise the SQUARE method accordingly.

REFERENCES

Abu-Nimeh, S., & Mead, N. R. (2009). Privacy risk assessment in privacy requirements engineering. In *Proceedings of Requirements Engineering and Law (RELAW) 2009 Second International Workshop* (pp. 17-18). Hoboken, NJ: IEEE.

Abu-Nimeh, S., & Mead, N. R. (2010). *Combining privacy and security risk assessment in security quality requirements engineering*. Paper presented at the 2010 Association for the Advancement of Artificial Intelligence (AAAI) Spring Symposium Series, Intelligent Information Privacy Management, Palo Alto, CA.

Abu-Nimeh, S., Miyazaki, S., & Mead, N. R. (2009). Integrating privacy requirements into security requirements engineering. In *Proceedings of the Twenty-First International Conference on Software Engineering and Knowledge Engineering* (pp. 542–547). Skokie: Knowledge Systems Institute Graduate School.

Adams, A., & Sasse, M. A. (2001). Privacy in multimedia communications: Protecting users, not just data. In *People and computers XV-Interaction without frontiers* (pp. 49–64). London: Springer. doi:10.1007/978-1-4471-0353-0_4

Armour, F., & Miller, G. (2000). *Advanced use case modeling: Software systems*. Boston, MA: Addison-Wesley Professional.

Bijwe, A., & Mead, N. R. (2010). *Adapting the SQUARE process for privacy requirements engineering* (CMU/SEI-2010-TN-022). Retrieved July 8, 2014, from the Software Engineering Institute, Carnegie Mellon University website: http://resources. sei.cmu.edu/library/asset-view.cfm?AssetID=9357

Campbell, P. L., & Stamp, J. E. (2004). *A classification scheme for risk assessment methods* (SAND2004-4233). Retrieved July 8, 2014, from the Sandia National Laboratories website: http://prod.sandia.gov/techlib/access-control. cgi/2004/044233.pdf

CERT Division of the Carnegie Mellon University Software Engineering Institute. (2011). *SQUARE for privacy (P-SQUARE)* [tool]. Retrieved July 8, 2014, from http://www.cert.org/cybersecurity-engineering/products-services/p-square-tool.cfm

Chiasera, A., Casati, F., Daniel, F., & Velegrakis, Y. (2008). Engineering privacy requirements in business intelligence applications. In *Secure data management* (pp. 219–228). Berlin: Springer-Verlag. doi:10.1007/978-3-540-85259-9_15

Flaherty, D. H. (2000). Privacy impact assessments: An essential tool for data protection. *Privacy Law & Policy Reporter*, *7*(5), 85–90.

Haimes, Y. Y. (2004). *Risk modeling, assessment, and management* (Vol. 40). Hoboken, NJ: John Wiley & Sons. doi:10.1002/0471723908

Heckle, R. R., & Holden, S. H. (2006). Analytical tools for privacy risks: Assessing efficacy on vote verification technologies. In *Symposium on Usable Privacy and Security*. Pittsburgh, PA: Carnegie Mellon University. Retrieved July 8, 2014, from the Carnegie Mellon University website: http://cups.cs.cmu. edu/soups/2006/posters/heckle-poster_abstract.pdf

Ingalsbe, J. A., Kunimatsu, L., Baeten, T., & Mead, N. R. (2008). Threat modeling: Diving into the deep end. *IEEE Software*, *25*(1), 28–34. doi:10.1109/MS.2008.25

Karlsson, J. (1996). Software requirements prioritizing. *Requirements Engineering*, *1996*, 110–116.

Markert, B. K. (2002). *Comparison of three online privacy seal programs*. Bethesda, MD: SANS Institute. Retrieved July 8, 2014, from http://www.sans. org/reading-room/whitepapers/privacy/comparison-online-privacy-seal-programs-685

Massey, A. K., Otto, P. N., & Anton, A. I. (2009). Prioritizing legal requirements. In *Proceedings of Requirements Engineering and Law (RELAW) 2009 Second International Workshop* (pp. 27–32). Hoboken, NJ: IEEE.

Mead, N. R., Hough, E., & Stehney, T. (2005). *Security quality requirements engineering* (CMU/SEI-2005-TR-009). Retrieved July 8, 2014, from the Software Engineering Institute, Carnegie Mellon University website: http://resources.sei.cmu.edu/library/asset-view.cfm?AssetID=7657

Mead, N. R., & Morales, J. A. (2014). *Using malware analysis to improve security requirements on future systems*. Paper presented at the Evolving Security and Privacy Requirements Engineering (ESPRE) Workshop, International Requirements Engineering Conference (RE) 2014, Karlskrona, Sweden. doi:10.1109/ESPRE.2014.6890526

Mitrano, T., Kirby, D. R., & Maltz, L. (2005). *What does privacy have to do with it?* Paper presented at the Security Professionals Conference, St. Louis, MO.

Miyazaki, S., Mead, N., & Zhan, J. (2008). Computer-aided privacy requirements elicitation technique. In *Proceedings of Asia-Pacific Services Computing Conference* (pp. 367-372). Hoboken, NJ: IEEE.

OECD & Microsoft Corporation. (2000). *OECD privacy statement generator*. Retrieved April 25, 2009, from http://www2.oecd.org/pwv3/

Pfleeger, S. L., & Pfleeger, C. P. (2009). Harmonizing privacy with security principles and practices. *IBM Journal of Research and Development, 53*(2), 273–289. doi:10.1147/JRD.2009.5429048

Porter, A., Votta, L., & Basili, V. (1995). Comparing detection methods for software requirements inspections: A replicated experiment. *IEEE Transactions on Software Engineering, 21*(6), 563–575. doi:10.1109/32.391380

Sindre, G., & Opdahl, A. L. (2000). Eliciting security requirements by misuse cases. In *Proceedings of the 37th International Conference on Technology of Object-Oriented Languages* (pp. 120-131). Los Alamitos, CA: IEEE Computer Society.

Statistics Canada. (2008). *Privacy impact assessment*. Retrieved July 8, 2014, from http://www.statcan.gc.ca/about-apercu/pia-efrvp/gloss-eng.htm

Stoneburner, G., Goguen, A., & Feringa, A. (2002). *Risk management guide for information technology systems* (NIST Special Publication 800-30). Retrieved July 8, 2014, from http://csrc.nist.gov/publications/nistpubs/800-30/sp800-30.pdf

United States Computer Emergency Readiness Team. (2008). *Privacy impact assessment for EINSTEIN 2*. United States Department of Homeland Security. Retrieved July 8, 2014, from https://www.dhs.gov/xlibrary/assets/privacy/privacy_pia_einstein2.pdf

Zave, P. (1997). Classification of research efforts in requirements engineering. *ACM Computing Surveys, 29*(4), 315–321. doi:10.1145/267580.267581

ADDITIONAL READING

ISO. IEC 12207 (2008). *Systems and software engineering -- Software life cycle processes* (ISO/IEC 12207:2008). Retrieved July 8, 2014, from http://www.iso.org/iso/home/store/catalogue_tc/catalogue_detail.htm?csnumber=43447

KEY TERMS AND DEFINITIONS

HIPAA (Health Insurance Portability and Accountability Act): A U.S. law that addresses privacy concerns of health information systems by enforcing data exchange standards and providing a guideline for analyzing risks.

Privacy Impact Assessment (PIA): An assessment used to determine the privacy, confidentiality, and security risks associated with the collection, use, and disclosure of personal information as well as how to mitigate and eliminate the identified risks.

Privacy Risk Assessment: A risk assessment that is specific to privacy concerns and has goals that relate to privacy policies and procedures.

Requirements Engineering: A field that includes requirements identification, requirements analysis, requirements specification, requirements verification and validation, and requirements management.

Risk Assessment: A step in a risk management process that involves the identification, assessment, and prioritization of risks related to a situation; thereby determining, in a quantitative or qualitative way, the value of the risks.

Security Quality Requirements Engineering (SQUARE) Method: A method that generates categorized and prioritized security requirements following a nine-step process.

Security Requirements Engineering: A field that identifies security risks and mitigation strategies in the early stages of the system development cycle.

Security Risk Assessment: A risk assessment that is specific to security concerns and has goals that include the implementation of authentication and authorization systems.

Threat Modeling: A process used to identify and document security risks (threats) to a system.

ENDNOTE

[1] OECD & Microsoft Corporation (2000). OECD Privacy Statement Generator. Retrieved April 25, 2009, from http://www2.oecd.org/pwv3/ (The OECD Privacy Statement Generator was retired in 2010 and no public site for the tool is currently available.)

Chapter 11
An Information Security Model for Implementing the New ISO 27001

Margareth Stoll
Independent Researcher, Italy

ABSTRACT

The importance of data privacy, information availability, and integrity is increasingly recognized. Sharpened legal requirements and increasing data leakages have further promoted data privacy. In order to implement the different requirements in an effective, efficient, and sustainable way, the authors integrate different governance frameworks to their holistic information security and data privacy model. More than 1.5 million organizations worldwide are implementing a standard-based management system. In order to promote the integration of different standards, the International Standard Organization (ISO) released a common structure. ISO/IEC 27001 for information security management was changed accordingly in October 2013. The holistic model fulfills all requirements of the new version. Its implementation in several organizations and the study's results are described. In that way data privacy and security are part of all strategic, tactical, and operational business processes, promote corporate governance and living security, as well as the fulfillment of all standard requirements.

INTRODUCTION

Due to globalization and increasing competition, information and supporting technology have become key asset and differentiators for modern organizations. Organizations and their information and information systems are faced with security threats from a wide range of sources, including computer-assisted fraud, espionage, sabotage, vandalism, fire or flood. 92% of large enterprises had a security incident in the last year with an average cost of 280.000-690.000 £ for the worst incident (PricewaterhouseCoopers, 2010). Threat agents have increased in the last years sophistication of their attacks and their tools (ENISA, 2013). The security incident have increased 25% over the previous year, while the average financial cost of incidents are up 18% (PricewaterhouseCoopers, 2013). Mobile and cloud computing, off-shoring, social networks and the increasingly intercon-

DOI: 10.4018/978-1-4666-7381-6.ch011

nected, flexible and virtualized business complexity and dependencies are still great challenges for data privacy and information security.

In the last years, the legal and regulatory requirements in this area have been sharpened. Most modern corporate governance guidelines, and always more laws, make the board and specifically the CEO responsible for the well-being of the organization. Data breaches and lack of security compliance may result in loss of confidence of customers, partners and shareholders, as well as severe civil and criminal penalties for board members (Saint-Germain, 2005; Clinch, 2009). More and more organizations are reducing their business risks by seeking assurance that their supplier and partners are properly protecting information assets and ensuring business continuity (Saint-Germain, 2005). In this respect the availability of all essential assets, confidentiality, data privacy, data integrity and legal and regulatory compliance are central for organizations' success (Bélanger & Crossler, 2011; Da Veiga & Eloff, 2007; Solms & Solms, 2009; Sowa, Tsinas & Gabriel, 2009). This poses great challenges for small and medium sized organizations. They need a very efficient and functional approach, which can be smoothly integrated in their daily business.

More than 1.5 million organizations worldwide are implementing a standard based management system based on international standards (e.g. quality ISO 9001, or environment ISO 14001, IT service management ISO 22000 and others) (ISO, 2013a). In order to promote an efficient integration of different standards, the International Standard Organization [ISO] released a common structure for all management systems' standards, the Annex SL of the ISO/IEC Directives (ISO, 2013d). In accordance to this new structure, ISO published in October 2013 the new version of the ISO/IEC 27001 (ISO, 2013b) and ISO/IEC 27002:2013 (ISO, 2013c) information security management standards. More than 19.500 organizations worldwide have just implemented an information security management system in accordance to

the old version of ISO/IEC 27001 (ISO, 2013a). In order to maintain their certificate they have to adjust their system to the new requirements. The international standard provides requirements for establishing, implementing, maintaining and continually improving an information security management system to meet the specific security and business needs/objectives of the organization. It is important that the information security management system is part of and integrated with the organization's processes and overall management structure and that information security is considered in the design of processes, information systems, and controls (ISO, 2013b; 2013c).

Despite the huge amount of research on privacy and information security (see Bélanger &Crossler; 2011; Pavlou, 2011; Smith, Dinev & Xu, 2011), the calls for more interdisciplinary information security research (Dhillon & Backhouse, 2000; Dinev, 2014; Pavlou, 2011; Warkentin &Willison 2009) and for studies at the group and organizational level (Bélanger &Crossler; 2011; Pavlou, 2011;), the current understanding of information security and data privacy (Dinev, Xu, Smith, & Hart; 2013) is largely fragmented. We found no integrated information security and data privacy framework. Several international best practices for information security management have been developed to provide guidance and ensure comprehensiveness. Some of the most commonly used include Control Objectives for Information and related Technology (COBIT), Information Technology Infrastructure Library (ITIL) and national guidelines, such as NIST SP 800 series in the US or IT Security Guidelines from the Federal Office for Information Security in Germany.

To meet optimally all data privacy and information security requirements we have developed an efficient, effective and sustainable information security and data privacy model. This model integrates the different information security governance frameworks with different best-practice methods (COBIT, ITIL) (IT Governance Institute, 2007; Office of Government Commerce [OGC], 2007). The holistic approach integrates data privacy and information security into all strategic, tactical and operational business processes and promotes thereby living data privacy and information security as part of corporate governance. In addition it fulfills the requirements of the new ISO/IEC 27001:2013 and provides guidance for the implementation or the revision of an implemented system.

The next subsection analyzes some information security governance frameworks and best-practice methods in order to construct our holistic information security governance model (subsection 3). We explain the main requirements of the new ISO/IEC 27001:2013 and discuss the fulfillment of the standard' requirements by our model. After the implementation of the model is presented (subsection 4) and we report and discuss our case studies experiences (subsection 5). At the end we give an outlook with proposals for further research directions (subsection 6) and our conclusions (subsection 7).

RESEARCH FRAMEWORK

Information Security Governance Oriented Frameworks

To achieve effectiveness and sustainability in today's complex, interconnected world, information security must be addressed at the highest levels of the organization. It must be an integral part of corporate governance (Solms & Solms, 2009; Da Veiga & Eloff, 2007; Sowa, Tsinas & Gabriel, 2009; IT Governance Institute, 2007; OGC, 2007; ISO, 2013b, 2013c).

The board and executive management should (Organization for Economic Co-operation and Development [OECD], 2004; IT Governance Institute, 2006):

- Provide and review the strategic direction, major plans of action, risk policy, and the annual budgets and business plans;
- Set performance objectives;
- Monitor implementation and corporate performance; and
- Oversee major capital expenditures, acquisitions and divestitures.

The corporate information security policy is part of or aligned with the corporate policy. It provides direction for short and long-term business security requirements to deliver enhanced business value to all stakeholders. Business and relevant legal and regulatory requirements must be taken into account. The board indicates how important the protection of the assets is to the organization (Solms & Solms, 2009). They decide the criteria for accepting risks and the acceptable levels of risk in the context of the organization's overall business risks (ISO, 2013b). From these strategic directives a set of relevant policies, standards and procedures are deduced for the middle management (tactical layer). These are the inputs for the operational procedures and guidelines (Solms & Solms, 2009; Sowa, Tsinas & Gabriel, 2009; Da Veiga & Eloff, 2007; IT Governance Institute, 2007; OGC, 2007).

All documents produced during the top down 'direct' part must be formulated in such a way that the compliance to the specific document can be measured (Solms & Solms, 2009). To conclude the direct-execute-control cycle measurement data are extracted on the operational level. They are compiled and integrated to perform measurement and monitoring against the requirements on the tactical level. For the board and executive management strategic level reports are produced. They reflect the actual risk situation, as well as compliance and conformance to relevant directives (Solms & Solms, 2009; Sowa, Tsinas & Gabriel, 2009; Da Veiga & Eloff, 2007; IT Governance Institute, 2007). By linking transparently operational, tacti-

Figure 1. The holistic information security and data privacy model

cal and strategic information to security objectives and to business objectives the board and executive management is supported to find and define cost benefit balanced investment strategies (Sowa, Tsinas & Gabriel, 2009), programs, projects and resource decisions.

HOLISTIC INFORMATION SECURITY GOVERNANCE MODEL

In consolidation of the different frameworks discussed above, best-practice methods (COBIT, ITIL) and based on our practical experiences we developed a holistic information security and data privacy model (Figure 1):

- The corporate vision and policy are established by regarding the requirements of all stakeholders, as well as legal and regulatory requirements. Objectives and strategies are deduced from corporate vision

and policy. Relevant information security aspects are integrated (see top of Figure 1).

- A risk assessment is conducted to establish a risk treatment plan to reduce security risks to an acceptable level of risk. For the identified remaining risks a business continuity plan is developed, implemented, maintained, tested and updated regularly (see the graphic under the top of Figure 1).

- Business process objectives are deduced from the corporate objectives by regarding the specific business, contractual, legal and regulatory requirements for each single process. In accordance to these, we analyze and optimize all business processes in a strategically aligned way (see middle of Figure 1: the main business processes start from the first contact with the customer and end with the delivery of the product/service and the customers' satisfaction). In that way stakeholder requirements together with information security are improved. Information security measures and controls, identified in the risk assessment and business continuity planning, are suitably integrated into the operational processes. Thus, they are implemented, maintained, tested and updated regularly to ensure effectiveness. The process description establishes for all process steps the associated responsible and accountable function and relevant information security requirements. Clear and traceable information security roles and responsibilities are assigned.

- The resource management (see bottom of Figure 1) specifies necessary resources, technologies and infrastructures to obtain and continually improve adequate information security. Competence objectives are deduced for all functions from the process models in alignment to corporate objectives. Appropriate trainings and awareness for all collaborators and involved partners are promoted. Their effectiveness is evaluated.

- The effectiveness, performance, compliance and adequacy of the established holistic information security system are continually measured, analyzed and reported using suitable methods for monitoring and measurement. Based on the actual risk situation, compliance and the achievement of established objectives necessary measures to maintain and improve corporate governance are elaborated and implemented proactively. In that way the whole system is continually improved accordingly to corporate governance objectives and strategies (see the measurement, analysis and improvement circle around Figure 1).

Main Requirements of the New ISO/IEC 27001:2013

In accordance to the new common structure for all management systems' standards - the Annex SL of the ISO/IEC Directives (ISO, 2013d) –the new ISO/IEC 27001:2013 (ISO, 2013b) and ISO/IEC 27002:2013 (ISO, 2013c) for information security management require following main principles:

- The information security policy and objectives of the organization must be established and communicated to fulfill the requirements of all interested parties (stakeholders).

- A risk assessment must be conducted to establish a risk treatment plan in order to reduce risks to acceptable levels of risk. For the identified remaining risks a business continuity plan must be developed, implemented, maintained, tested and updated regularly.

- All necessary information security risk assessments, treatments and controls must be integrated within all organization's processes in order to meet the organizations' security objectives.

- The needed resources must be determined and provided. The established management system must be documented, structured and communicated systematically. All collaborators must be competent to perform their tasks and be aware of the relevance and importance of their information security activities. Each collaborator must contribute to the achievement of the established information security objectives.

- The effectiveness and adequacy of the information security management system must be continually improved by monitoring, measuring, analyzing, auditing, evaluating and applying corrective and preventive actions in the sense of a PDCA cycle (plan, do, check / study, act).

Table 1. The holistic model and the requirements of the new ISO/IEC 2700x

Requirements of ISO/IEC 27001:2013 and ISO/IEC 27002:2013	The Holistic Information Security and Data Privacy Model
Information security policy and objectives (context of the organization and leadership)	We go a step further and integrate the security policy and objectives within the corporate policy and objectives.
Risk Assessment (Planning)	It is fully fulfilled.
Business Processes and operation	We require stronger than the standard to integrate information security suitably into the operational processes. We integrate, for example, the security objectives within business process objectives.
Support (=resource management)	In addition to the information security standard we deduce competence objectives for all functions. In that way we fulfill the requirements of the ISO 9001 standard for quality management.
Performance evaluation and improvement	It is fully fulfilled.

IMPLEMENTATION

In this section we describe in detail the implementation of our holistic information security and data privacy model with applied methods and examples. We focus overall on governance elements (direction, process integration, controlling) and describe the methods, process and applied tools to implement the new version of the ISO/IEC 2700x family, information security frameworks and best-practice methods.

To implement our holistic information security and data privacy model we execute following steps:

1. We elaborate the policy, deduce objectives and elaborate adequate strategies (see Policy and Objectives).

2. The risk assessment, risk treatment, and business continuity planning are conducted intermeshed with the process analysis and process improvement (see corresponding subsections). Firstly we deduce business process objectives from corporate objectives. In the next step we analyze the processes, define relevant assets and deduce for these information security objectives from process objectives. Based on this we conduct the risk assessment and elaborate risk treatments and business continuity plans. At the end we optimize the business processes in ac-

cordance to established process objectives and integrate suitable identified information security measures, risk treatments and business continuity activities into all processes.

3. From the optimized business processes we deduce the organizational structure with function profiles and competence objectives and assign roles and responsibilities (see Resource Management). To fulfill established objectives we determine and provide necessary human, financial and technical resources accordingly to optimized resource processes (part of business processes, see step 2).

4. The whole system documentation must be documented, reviewed, approved, communicated, trained and implemented (see System Documentation). It is composed by directives, policies, standards, procedures, guidelines, controls, legal and regulatory interpretations, templates, checklists and other relevant documents (further regulations), as well as policy, objectives, strategies, process models, risk assessment, business continuity plans, the organizational structure, function profiles, role and responsibility assignment matrix and others. Its adequacy and effectiveness is periodically evaluated and optimized.

5. The whole information security and data privacy system must be measured, analyzed, adjusted to changing requirements and continually improved to promote sustainable information security (see Continually Measurement, Analysis and Improvement). In that way it may be also necessary to restart from an earlier step, for example to change the policy. After that we must perform all successive steps again.

Policy and Objectives

We elaborate the corporate policy. Based on Quality Function Deployment (Akao, 1990) we:

1. Identify and prioritize all relevant stakeholders,
2. Determine the requirements of all stakeholders, the relevant legal and regulatory requirements for all locations and markets, all contractual and statutory obligations and the characteristics of the business and market and
3. Define the capabilities, assets and technology, and the physical environment of the organization.
4. From the focus of the single stakeholders, weighted by their priority, we prioritize all requirements and obligations. Thereby we take into account the characteristics of the business and markets and the organizational strengths and weakness.
5. We establish the corporate policy accordingly to the prioritized requirements.

Information security aspects are integrated within the holistic corporate policy. In that way the quality and information security policy, as well as scope and boundaries of the holistic management system are defined.

From the corporate policy we deduce corporate objectives together with information security objectives, such as availability, confidentiality and

integrity. To each objective we assign long-term, medium-term and annual goals with appropriate metrics, targets and measurement methods to monitor their achievement and to evaluate compliance. To fulfill the established information security objectives we elaborate adequate information security strategies. Thus the entire organization is focused to accomplish the stakeholder's requirements inclusive information security, as well as legal, regulatory and standard compliance and conformance. Information security becomes an integral part of corporate governance.

Risk Assessment

A risk assessment is conducted for establishing a risk treatment plan to reduce risks on acceptable levels of risk in collaboration with all collaborators and partners concerned.

We deduce business process objectives from corporate objectives and analyze the processes (see Process Analysis and Process Improvement). Thereby we determine relevant assets and deduce from process objectives their required information security objectives, e.g., confidentiality, integrity and availability. This is elaborated with the executive management and approved by the board. In that way the risk assessment is aligned with strategic objectives and corporate governance. Further a good understanding of the board and executives for potential security impacts and necessary changes, projects and investments is promoted.

Regarding the corporate risk management, the enterprise context and all relevant legal, regulatory, contractual and business requirements we identify threats to those assets. The likelihood of the threats occurrence and the impacts that losses of security requirements may have on the assets are estimated by regarding currently implemented controls. For the higher risks adequate risk treatment plans (controls) are elaborated. To each control or group of controls appropriate control objectives and measurement methods are formulated in such a way that the compliance can be controlled. The board decides the criteria for accepting risks and whether the remaining levels of risk are acceptable in the context of the organization's overall business risks or further risk treatments must be developed and implemented.

The ISO/IEC 27002 and ISO/IEC 27005, national guidelines, such as NIST SP 800 series in the US or IT Security Guidelines from the Federal Office for Information Security in Germany provide helpful information for the threat analysis and risk assessment.

The risk treatment plan is integrated into the operational processes (see Process Analysis and Process Improvement). In that way the risk treatments and the existing standard based management system are integrated.

For the identified remaining risks a business continuity plan is developed and integrated into the operational processes. Thus it is implemented, maintained, tested and updated regularly to ensure that it is effective to maintain or restore operations and ensure availability at the required level and in the required time scale following interruption to, or failure of, critical business processes.

Business Processes and Operation

Standard based management systems require the analysis and improvement of all business processes to achieve established corporate objectives and to regard all requirements of the relevant standard and relevant business, legal and regulatory obligations.

We deduce in accordance to the requirements of ISO 9001, COBIT and ITIL for all business processes process objectives from corporate objectives by taking into account business, contractual, legal and regulatory requirements for each single process. In that way the process objectives are aligned with strategic corporate security objectives. To propagate corporate objectives to business process objectives Quality Function Deployment (Akao, 1990) and balanced scorecard (Kaplan, 1996) provide helpful approaches.

In the next step we analyze all business processes bottom up by interviewing the collaborators involved. Beginning from the management process, we examine all production or service processes, as well as all supporting processes, resources processes and improvement processes. In that way we study also the development of new products or services.

For process modeling we use a simple structured flow-charts (see Figure 2) with three or four columns (4th for annotations, conditions, and terms), limited to one page. In that way the processes are sufficiently deeply structured. For time critical descriptions we use also Gantt charts.

The process models (see Figure 2) establish for all activities:

- Involved functions,
- Relevant laws, regulations and obligations,
- Procedures and directives, which must be regarded,

Figure 2. Process modeling method

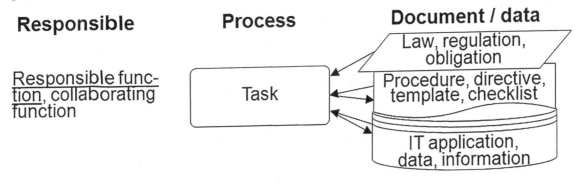

- Applied templates, documents, checklists, forms, IT applications, processed and exchanged data, and information.

These process models define for all documents and data the accountable, responsible and involved functions over the whole document lifecycle (creation, review, approval, signature, release, distribution, retrieval, modification, archive and disposal). External information sources or receivers are also documented. Thus the whole document and data logistic is described. The European and most national data protection laws require for example that the data subject has the right to receive among others the information about the recipients and data processors of his data. By integrating information security with data privacy and standard based management systems this legal requirement can be deduced efficiently from established process models.

In accordance to relevant legal and regulative security requirements we establish for each document and data class the data protection class and required protection methods for the whole data lifecycle. Examples for such information security policies are:

- Necessary and licit access rights,
- Segregation of duties,
- Data encryption,
- Signature policies with signature rights and signature procedures,
- Archiving methods and duration for current, intermediate and historical archives,
- Destruction or disposal procedures and methods.

After all business processes are harmonized and optimized together with the concerned collaborators by taking into account deduced information security objectives, as well as quality, efficiency, effectiveness and all other corporate, business, legal and regulatory requirements. In accordance to the corporate objectives we consider and integrate all relevant aspects (e.g., environment, human resource development, resource management, information management, communication management, controlling, knowledge management or others). Entire documents and data are examined for necessity and lawfulness. The general manager of a public organization, for example, appreciated overall the performance improvement by eliminating all indispensable data.

By optimizing the processes the identified controls (risk countermeasures) and business continuity tasks and tests are integrated, implemented and maintained by appropriate IT systems and workflows, if possible. Many organizations for example implement the user registration and de-registration as a sub-process, which is initiated by the human resource management application. In that way all information security aspects, which are identified in the risk assessment, are regarded and best integrated. Based on our case studies experiences it is essential to integrate all information security tasks into the daily work of the collaborators in a suitable and efficient way (see Case Studies Results and Experiences).

Other information security controls and tasks, which cannot be supported by IT in business processes are integrated in existing directives, code of conducts, process models, policies, standards, procedures, guidelines, controls, legal and regulatory interpretations, or others (further regulations). For each control an appropriate compliance clause specifying in which way compliance will be evaluated is defined. By the process analysis we recognize these process steps, in which experiences and interpretations of laws or regulations (lessons learned) are developed. These should be documented for later use. Thus data collection and information processing are planned and implemented systematically and structured in accordance to relevant legal and regulative requirements.

To harmonize processes and data over the whole organization we define firstly the main services or products with their corresponding processes and analyze these with the involved departments. Afterwards we harmonize and integrate common process segments, law interpretations, regulations, checklists and forms. Thus we establish a reduced number of common main processes (ca. one until five) with harmonized documents, regulations and law interpretations. Templates are developed for all necessary documents and forms (e.g., contract forms for standardized products or services). They are examined only once by specialized experts and jurisprudents. Afterwards every collaborator can fill them easily with the personal data of the customer and the required product/ service. The specialized knowledge of experts is integrated also into all checklists. In that way implicit knowledge is externalized. Knowledge and information management is also improved (Davenport, 2005; Stoll, 2007a).

Resource Management (Support)

Standard based management systems require that the organization determines and provides necessary resources to obtain established objectives and to continually improve the effectiveness. Thus collaborators with adequate competences and optimal technologies, infrastructures, tools and instruments are promoted. This supports also information security:

- We deduce the organizational structure with function profiles from the assigned roles to each function at the single process steps. The function profiles consist at least of objectives, main tasks, responsibilities and required competences. Regarding the different roles of each collaborator we assign him functional objectives, responsibilities, main tasks and required competences. In that way a suitable human resource development is planned and implemented ac-

cordingly to defined, optimized processes (human resource development is a part of business processes, see step 2). The effectiveness is evaluated. The competences of all collaborators with assigned information security responsibilities are also promoted systematically, structured and sustainable. All collaborators are aware of the relevance and importance of their activities and contribute to the achievement of the established objectives.

- An optimal infrastructure and appropriate maintenance and facility management processes promote overall physical and environmental security and the availability and reliability of supporting utilities, such as power, telecommunication or air condition supply.

- Adequate technology and IT system management are essential for communications, network, operations and application security. The strong strategic alignment of all necessary information security changes, projects and investments promotes the understanding for potential security impacts of the board and executives and an appropriate funding.

System Documentation

After the establishment the whole system documentation (see Implementation step 4) must be reviewed, approved and communicated. Every collaborator must be trained on the relevant regulations for him. The collaborators and particularly the managers must implement continually the established processes and regulations. The documentation must be always actual. Laws, regulations and standards require a traceable communication and adequate training for the collaborators concerned.

Commonly the system documentation is now distributed electronically through web-based intranets, document management platforms or as pdf. New collaborators are trained on the whole documentation at their start. After periodical trainings communicate changes and promote awareness. In that way the collaborators get often too much information at once and forget it until they need it.

To provide need-oriented, operations integrated learning we elaborate the regulations regarding media-pedagogical, motivation-psychological and didactical principles (Rosenberg, 2001; Reinmann-Rothmeier, 2002). According to these principles and the analyzed expectations of the collaborators, the way for accessing the single modules should be as short as possible, clear structured and practice oriented. The documentation should be written:

- Clearly understandable and compact,
- Simply and motivating worded,
- Adjusted to the skills of the readers,
- Using expressive terms applied in the organization,
- Corresponding with organizational objectives and values,
- Offering concrete instructions and templates,
- Including a lot of examples of everyday practice, and
- An extensive index.

We divide the system documentation in small modules and structure these in accordance to our holistic information security and data privacy model. Further we offer different start assistances depending on the competences and needs of the users (e.g., for new collaborators, department oriented, management oriented, topics referred, based on the standard and others). In that way the documentation is comprehensive in the whole and compact for the single collaborator (see Figure 3).

Changes and improvements are commonly isolated from the documentation and cannot be discussed in a context-sensitive way. The documentation is primarily used to fulfill legal, regulative and standard requirements and changed only prior to external audits. Thus the documentation frequently is not corresponding to lived processes. Changes or improvements are quite frequently developed as hidden systems. In some organizations of our case studies we stored the system documentation on an organizational learning and knowledge system (Stoll, 2008). This system offers context sensitive, collaborative discussions and improvements. It promotes the actuality, practice-orientation, comprehensiveness, usability and efficiency of the documentation, as well as operations integrated, need-oriented learning, employee involvement and collaborative information security improvement (Stoll, 2008).

Figure 3. The didactical preparation of the system documentation

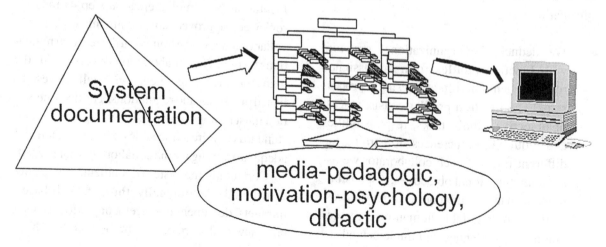

Performance Evaluation and Improvement

An increasingly faster changing environment (market, customer, technology, law or regulations) requires continual adaption of objectives, processes, risk assessment, regulations, technology and collaborators. It is a widely accepted principle that an activity cannot be managed and overall not improved continually if it cannot be measured. Thus the effectiveness and performance of the information security management system and the actual risk and compliance situation has to be ongoing evaluated and improved. Effectively implemented security measurements demonstrate the value of information security to top management, face informed decision making, demonstrate compliance, improve security confidence and enable stakeholders to continually improve information security. This is a critical success factor for sustainable information security (ISO, 2013c).

From established corporate objectives we deduced business process objectives and control objectives according to regulatory, legal and contractual requirements (see Process Analysis and Process Improvement). Due to our integrated approach we elaborate in that way also information security objectives. Appropriate measurement methods are defined to control the achievement of planned results and the effectiveness of the selected controls, as well as to improve information security and data privacy. In accordance to NIST SP 800-55 (National Institute of Standards and Technology [NIST], 2008) and ISO/IEC 27004 (ISO, 2009) the relevant stakeholders are involved in each step of information security measures development to ensure commitment and promote a sense of ownership for information security compliance and performance.

We extract measurement data at the operational level and analyze them. These data are aggregated and integrated with audit, review, assessment and test results, the feedback from different stakeholders (e.g., customers, collaborators, suppliers, partners), as well as environment observations (e.g., changed business conditions, legal and/or regulative requirements, surveys and technical reports). They are reported to all relevant stakeholders of the tactical and strategic level (Stoll & Breu, in press).

Based on our holistic information security approach we integrate information security evaluation with corporate controlling. Thus information security measurement and compliance information are part of the corporate business cockpit and corporate management. Based on the achievement of established objectives, and the actual risk and compliance situation necessary measures to maintain and improve information security and data privacy are elaborated and implemented proactively and on time. The directives are assisted in identifying and evaluating noncompliant and ineffective security processes and controls, as well as in prioritizing and deciding actions for improving or changing strategies, processes and/or controls.

Information security management requires a systemic and holistic approach. For example, if a new customer or law requires stronger confidentiality for certain data, a risk assessment over the whole data lifecycle (from receipt to disposal) must be conducted. The adequacy of the implemented regulations and the applied technical and physical security protection for all treatments and locations must be checked and eventually improved. The affected parts of the system documentation must be appropriately changed, approved, trained, implemented and evaluated in accordance to defined processes. In compliance to legal, regulatory and business requirements tracks of all changes and their communication must be maintained traceably.

At the operational level information security metrics support the identification of previously undetected or unknown information security issues, the identification of attempted security breaches and incidents, and the detection of security events. If planned results are not achieved or security issues or breaches occur, appropriate corrective and eventually preventive actions are taken accordingly to defined optimized processes (see Process Analysis and Process Improvement).

Organizational knowledge is changed and so new individual and organizational learning becomes possible (Takeuchi & Nonaka, 2004; Senge, 2003). Thus the knowledge and learning spiral, as well as the information security life-cycle are constantly pushed again (Takeuchi & Nonaka, 2004). Information security and data privacy is sustainable maintained and improved.

CASE STUDIES: RESULTS AND EXPERIENCES

This holistic information security and data privacy model was implemented over several years within diverse process oriented standard based management systems in different small and medium sized organizations of distinct sectors and countries. The following case studies results were collected by established process and system measurement methods and interviewing managers and collaborators:

- **Applicability and Evaluation:** The participants of the case studies passed over the years all external compliance audits. They received and maintained the international recognized ISO/IEC 27001 certificate and other management system certificates. In addition the organizations passed on the new version of the standard without problems.
- **Understandable:** This model reduces complexity and is based on the new common structure for all management systems' standards - the Annex SL of the ISO/IEC Directives (ISO, 2013d). More than 1.5 million organizations worldwide are implementing such standard based management systems (ISO, 2013a). By the next revision of each standard, it must be written in accordance to the new structure. For organizations with an implemented quality management system, the risk assessment is

for example a new part. Thus, the quality management system can benefit from the risk assessment experiences of information security management. Other management systems, such as environmental or hygienic or health and safety, have also just implemented risk assessment, but from a different technical perspective. In our case studies, for example, in a technical organization and in technical departments the collaborators regard information security aspects more helpfully for their daily work than others. In that way the existing standard based management system benefits from information security management. The collaborators consider in addition the integration of different management standards more than an extension and enriching.

- **Adaptable to Specific Requirements:** This model provides a generic and systemic approach, which can be best adapted to the specific requirements of each organization. For example, the same business process of an organization requires in different departments in accordance to legal requirements and the type of treated data classes (personal in one and high sensitive health data in the other) on one hand a very high confidentiality and on the other hand low or medium confidentiality. These different requirements are integrated into one single management system (including requirement analysis, risk assessment, measurement, analysis and improvement and all other elements).
- **Easy to Use:** This model was simple to use for all organizations involved. The lead time to implement information security and data privacy varies in our case studies from three months to two years. It is depending on the complexity and diversity of an organization, their information security requirements, the degree of organization, the management commitment and overall the time invested by the collaborators involved.

- **Efficiency and Cost Reduction:** By integrating information security with other standard based management systems synergies are used, such as an integrated policy, the establishment and communication of objectives, the management process, system thinking, the systematic process oriented approach, the training and improvement processes, and others. In that way the effort and costs for the introduction could be reduced in our case studies about 10-20%. The advantages are still higher during the implementation, where only the audit is extended, and the security and data privacy specific risk assessment and business continuity planning must be maintained.

- **Effectiveness:** The tight integration of information security objectives with corporate objectives, the strategic alignment of all information security projects and measures, the employee involvement and continual information security controlling promote the fulfillment of established objectives. The studied organizations achieve their planned objectives in average more than 92%.

- **Sustainability:** The first organization of the case studies obtained the certificate in 2003 and maintained it over all the years. Different chief information security officers state a tight alignment of information security with corporate objectives and strategies, a suitable integration with all business processes, and the continual measurement, analysis and improvement as great challenges, but crucial success factor for effective and ongoing information security.

- **Compliance:** Legal, regulatory, standard and business information security requirements are analyzed, implemented and maintained by defined controlling and improvement processes. In that way

legal, regulatory and standard compliance and conformance are sustainable implemented. This is specially appreciated by board members and CEOs. During the period of the case studies different legal requirements, for example, were changed. They could be integrated easily and efficiently in the established security system. Based on our holistic and preventive approach most of the requirements were already implemented. The requirements of the new version of ISO/IEC 27001 were also just mainly implemented. The structured and systematic approach was appreciated by the chief information security officer as helpful tool for an efficient risk assessment, the establishment of new or change of existing regulations or processes and their communication and implementation.

Success Factors and Discussion

Here we present and discuss some case studies experiences, challenges and success factors of our case studies.

Integrating data privacy and information security into standard based management systems requires a business-focused and suitable management system for the specific requirements of the organization. This certainly cannot be achieved by using a purchased generic manual, which does not correspond with lived processes and is not aligned with corporate objectives and strategies. The standard based management system must be evidently committed by the board and directives and implemented ongoing and effectively. If information security is integrated with a management system, which is only an alibi to certificate, information security and data privacy cannot be supported. It may be much better to start from zero. In that way the new information security system offers a new chance to relaunch the management system. As ISO/IEC 27001 was one of the first published standards accordingly the new structure of annex SL, it promotes also the recertification of other standards.

It seems obviously that information security and data privacy must be business-focused and suitable for the specific organization. Many organizations want to implement information security with the minimalist possible effort. They require, for example generic risk assessments and information security regulations. If an organization uses such tools not only as framework or guidelines, they implement some common information security aspects, but never holistic information security and data privacy. Information security governance per definition must be part of corporate governance to sustain and extend organization's strategies and objectives for sustainable organizations' success (IT Governance Institute, 2006).

In discussion with the information security manager, they face great challenge to deduce transparently measureable information security objectives from corporate objectives to all business processes and organizational units. Information security for long time was seen fundamentally as an only technical job and integral part of the information technology department. A lot of technical information security objectives, such as system availability, network security or secure authentication with appropriate controls and metrics were developed and implemented. Information security problems persisted and increased. Information security is complex and requires a collaborative and holistic approach by regarding all business processes and organizational units. Thus, we go a step further than ISO/IEC 27001 and integrate information security measurement and evaluation within process controlling. For one organization, for example, the confidential treatment of all internal information and customer related information is essential. We assigned to each document and group of data the data protection class accordingly to legal requirements. How helpful would be only data encryption, if on the other side, for example, the collaborators speak very open about this data

outside the organization. Practice-oriented regulations for the data treatment over the whole data lifecycle and continual security awareness by all collaborators were most important.

Based on our case studies experiences it is crucial to implement and improve information security in accordance to business and legal requirements in all business processes over the whole value network to archive sustainable information security. We invested a lot of effort in each organization to link information security requirements for each business process with corporate objectives and legal and regulatory requirements.

Information security metrics and measurement were also a great challenge for all organizations and can be still improved. The new ISO/IEC 27001:2013 requires now also enhanced information security measurement and evaluation. Information security controlling is in most of these organizations integrated with corporate controlling. In that way information security is a topic of each board meeting and management review. It was much easier to implement information security controlling for IT service provider than for other organizations, where overall data privacy and legal compliance are main information security objectives. These require more human related controls than technical controls. They are difficult to measure and must be overall audited and assessed.

Based on the case study the best way to implement sustainable information security was to integrate identified controls suitable and optimal IT supported into the everyday practice of all collaborators. To harmonize and balance the single process requirements to each other was a challenge. These discussions were excellent trainings to improve information security awareness by all collaborators involved.

Clear assigned roles and responsibilities promoted also security and privacy awareness. In that way all collaborators feel information security and privacy as part of their work and not as an add-on and take ownership for information security. We received, for example, in all organizations of the case studies suggestions for potential security breaches and improvement proposal from the collaborators. It was evident that security and privacy awareness are directly influenced by the way how actively executives take ownership for information security: they practice established directives itself, they incorporate security by all their decisions and actions and they enable and control collaborators in following these principles.

To integrate information security ongoing into the everyday business practice it is further essential to check all programs, projects and events for potential security and compliance risks and requirements. Information security and data privacy must be an integral part of program/project management, product/system development, incident management and change management. We have implemented this aspect in all organizations with a first approach. The great influence for the most organizations was recognized over a longer period and will be further improved. The new standard supports these experiences and requires a stronger integration than the old version.

The collaborators appreciate an effectively accessible, reader friendly, clear understandably and practice-oriented documentation. An efficient and effective search function and a clear structured management system are most important for them. The invested effort to prepare the documentation regarding didactical principals was fully honoured by the collaborators. They accessed the documentation more frequently in these organizations, which regarded more didactical principals than in others.

To maintain ongoing information security and data privacy we must improve our system dynamically and flexibly to all internal and external changes. The new version of the standard enhanced the requirements for performance evaluation and improvement. The information security life-cycle must be pushed constantly. This requires continual organizational and technical development, which can be supported by organizational and technical tools so far as this is admitted by corporate culture. In an organiza-

tion with an open, confident based, participative corporate learning culture the security awareness was much more appreciated by the same external auditors than in other organizations with a more hierarchical culture.

OUTLOOK

Based on our case studies experiences in several organizations with different management systems we can clearly state that a key success factor for information security and data privacy is the tightly integration with other standard based management systems, such as ISO 9001 for quality management. In that way information security and data privacy is introduced and improved in an effective, efficient and sustainable way, provided that the standard based management system is suitable for the organization and implemented at an adequate maturity level. Due to the decision of the international standard organization to harmonize the standards for management systems, we provide as first the empirical evidence for the potential of this new approach.

Due to the stronger management focus of the new ISO/IEC 27001 we presented our approach by underlining strategic and controlling aspects. Further publications and research will integrate in this model technical and architecture oriented security models, as well as socio-organizational and cultural approaches.

Based on our case studies results and the new or improved requirements of ISO/IEC 27001 we suggest most different future research streams with great practice relevance by the main success factors and challenges, such as:

- **Information Security Controlling:** Objective deployment, metrics and stakeholder oriented reporting, as well as the integration of information security controlling, reporting and escalation with corporate controlling, performance and information management are ongoing main research streams. The strategic and corporate management dimension of information security research should be still promoted.

- **Holistic, Integrated Information Security:** The integration of information security into all business processes over the whole value network and specially the integration with program/project management, product/system development, incident management and change management offer a wide range of research questions. An adequate assessment and treatment of information security risks, for example must be tightly integrated with project or change management or product/system development.

- **Sustainable Information Security:** An important future research avenue is ongoing information security. It requires an interdisciplinary approach of most different disciplines, such as corporate management, information technology, engineering, information and knowledge management, organizational development, communication science, service management, facility management, civil protection, sociology, psychology, and others.

CONCLUSION

We presented a holistic information security and data privacy model to meet information security and data privacy requirements, as well as legal, regulatory and standard compliance and conformance requirements. It integrates different information security governance frameworks and fulfills all requirements of the new ISO/IEC 27001: 2013. It provides firstly a model for implementing the new requirements and gives empirically evidence of the challenges and success factors for implementing the new version of the standard for information security management. In addition it guides the integration of information security and data privacy within other standard based management systems, such as ISO 9001 for quality management.

A main success factor for this holistic information security and data privacy model approach is a suitable integration of information security into all strategic, tactical and operational business processes:

- Information security objectives are deduced coherently from corporate objectives for all business processes, assets and organizational functions,
- An adequate and strategically aligned risk assessment is conducted,
- All business processes are optimized for information security and the established risk treatments and business continuity plans are integrated with the daily work of all collaborators,
- The effectiveness, compliance and adequacy of the implementation are continually measured, analyzed and improved.

In that way information security and data privacy is fully integrated with corporate governance.

Based on our practical experiences over several years in distinct small and medium sized organizations this holistic information security and data privacy model can be introduced in standard based management systems efficiently and smoothly. It supports sustainable information security and data privacy effectively.

The confidence of customers, partners and shareholders, the availability of essential assets and data integrity, as well as legal and regulatory compliance are promoted. The price is the development, implementation and maintenance of this model.

Due to the importance of information and information systems for modern organizations as key differentiator and the sharpened data privacy requirements, information security must be recognized as valuable contribution to strategies and organizations' success. It must become integral part of all strategic, tactical and operational business processes and activities. This requires a practice-oriented, holistic, interdisciplinary approach for information security and information security research. Further research must be done in the direction of information security controlling, holistic integrated information security and sustainable, living information security.

REFERENCES

Akao, Y. (1990). *Quality function deployment, integrating customer requirements into product design*. Cambridge, MA: Productivity Press.

Bélanger, F., & Crossler, R. E. (2011). Privacy in the digital age: A review of information privacy research in information systems. *Management Information Systems Quarterly, 35*(4), 1017–A36.

Clinch, J. (2009). *ITIL V3 and Information security*. Retrieved November 03, 2010 from www.best-management-practice.com/gempdf/ ITILV3_and_Information_Security_White_Paper_May09.pdf

Da Veiga, A., & Eloff, J. H. P. (2007). An information security governance framework. *Information Systems Management, 24*(4), 361–372. doi:10.1080/10580530701586136

Davenport, T. H. (2005). *Thinking for a living, how to get better performance and results from knowledge workers*. Boston, MA: Harvard Business School Press.

Dhillon, G., & Backhouse, J. (2000). Technical opinion: Information system security management in the new millennium. *Communication of the European ACM, 43*(7), 125–128. doi:10.1145/341852.341877

Dinev, T. (2014). Why would we care about privacy? *European Journal of Information Systems, 23*(2), 97–102. doi:10.1057/ejis.2014.1

Dinev, T., Xu, H., Smith, J. H., & Hart, P. (2013). Information privacy and correlates: An empirical attempt to bridge and distinguish privacy-related concepts. *European Journal of Information Systems, 22*(3), 295–316. doi:10.1057/ejis.2012.23

European Union Agency for Network and Information Security (ENISA). (2013). *Threat landscape 2013, Overview of current and emerging cyber-threats*. Retrieved December 24, 2013 from http://www.enisa.europa.eu/activities/risk-management/evolving-threat-environment/enisa-threat-landscape-2013-overview-of-current-and-emerging-cyber-threats

Great Britain Office of Government Commerce (OGC). (2007). *Service design (SD): ITIL*. London: The Stationery Office.

International Standard Organization (ISO). (2008). *ISO 9001:2008, quality management systems – Requirements*. Geneva, Switzerland: ISO.

International Standard Organization (ISO). (2009). *ISO/IEC 27004:2009, information technology, security techniques, information security management measurement*. Geneva, Switzerland: ISO.

International Standard Organization (ISO). (2013a). *ISO survey of certifications 2012*. Retrieved March 15, 2014 from http://www.iso.org/iso/home/standards/certification/iso-survey.html

International Standard Organization (ISO). (2013b). *ISO/IEC 27001:2013, information technology, security techniques, information security management systems requirements.* Geneva, Switzerland: ISO.

International Standard Organization (ISO). (2013c). *ISO/IEC 27002:2013, information technology, security techniques, code of practice for information security management.* Geneva, Switzerland: ISO.

International Standard Organization (ISO). (2013d). *ISO/IEC directives, part 1, consolidated ISO supplement, procedures specific to ISO.* Geneva, Switzerland: ISO.

IT Governance Institute. (2006). *Information security governance: Guidance for boards of directors and executive management.* IT Governance Institute.

IT Governance Institute. (2007). *COBIT® 4.1: Framework, control objectives, management guidelines, maturity models.* Rolling Meadows, IL: IT Governance Institute.

Kaplan, R. S., & Norton, D. P. (1996). *The balanced scorecard: Translating strategy into action* (reprinted ed.). Boston, MA: Harvard Business School Press.

National Institute of Standards and Technology (NIST). (2008). *Performance measurement guide for information security, NIST special publication 800-55 revision 1.* Retrieved January 28, 2010 from http://csrc.nist.gov/publications/nistpubs/800-55-Rev1/SP800-55-rev1.pdf

Organization for Economic Co-operation and Development (OECD). (2004). *Principles of corporate governance.* Retrieved November 03, 2010 from http://www.oecd.org/dataoecd/32/18/31557724.pdf

Pavlou, P. A. (2011). State of the information privacy literature: Where are we now and where should we go? *Management Information Systems Quarterly, 35*(4), 977–988.

PricewaterhouseCoopers LLP. (2010). *Information security breaches survey 2010, technical report.* Retrieved July 13, 2010 from http://www.pwc.co.uk/pdf/isbs_survey_2010_technical_report.pdf

PricewaterhouseCoopers LLP. (2013). *Defending yesterday, key findings from the global state of information security survey 2014.* Retrieved December 25, 2013 from http://www.pwc.com/gx/en/consulting-services/information-security-survey/download.jhtml

Reinmann-Rothmeier, G. (2002). Mediendidaktik und wissensmanagement. *MedienPädagogik, 2*(2), 1-27. Retrieved August 18, 2006 from www.medienpaed.com/02-2/reinmann1.pdf

Rosenberg, M. J. (2001). *E-learning: Strategies for delivering knowledge in the digital age.* New York, NY: McGraw-Hill.

Saint-Germain, R. (2005). Information security management best practice based on ISO/IEC 17799. *Information Management Journal, 39*(4), 60–66.

Senge, P. (2003). Taking personal change seriously: The impact of organizational learning on management practice. *The Academy of Management Executive, 17*(2), 47–50. doi:10.5465/AME.2003.10025191

Smith, H. J., Dinev, T., & Xu, H. (2011). Information privacy research: An interdisciplinary review. *Management Information Systems Quarterly, 35*(4), 980–A27.

Sowa, S., Tsinas, L., & Gabriel, R. (2009). BORinformation security - Business ORiented management of information security. In M. E. Johnson (Ed.), *Managing information risk and the economics of security* (pp. 81–97). New York, NY: Springer; doi:10.1007/978-0-387-09762-6_4

Stoll, M. (2007). Managementsysteme und prozessorientiertes wissensmanagement. In N. Gronau (Ed.), *Proc. 4th Conference on Professional Knowledge Management – Experiences and Visions* (vol. 1, pp. 433-434). Berlin: Gito Verlag.

Stoll, M. (2008). E-learning promotes information security. In M. Iskander (Ed.), *Innovative techniques in instruction technology, e-learning, e-assessment, and education.* Dordrecht, The Netherlands: Springer; doi:10.1007/978-1-4020-8739-4_54

Stoll, M., & Breu, R. (2013). Information security measurement roles and responsibilities. In T. Sobh & K. Elleithy (Eds.), *Emerging trends in computing, informatics, systems sciences, and engineering* (pp. 11–23). Springer. doi:10.1007/978-1-4614-3558-7_2

Takeuchi, H., & Nonaka, I. (2004). *Hitotsubashi on knowledge management.* Singapore: John Wiley & Sons.

von Solms, S. H., & Solms, R. v. (2009). *Information security governance.* New York, NY: Springer. doi:10.1007/978-0-387-79984-1

Warkentin, M., & Willison, R. (2009). Behavioral and policy issues in information systems security: The insider threat. *European Journal of Information Systems, 18*(2), 101–105. doi:10.1057/ejis.2009.12

ADDITIONAL READING

Anderson, C. L., & Agarwal, R. (2010). Practicing safe computing: A multimethod empirical examination of home computer user security behavioral intentions. *Management Information Systems Quarterly, 34*(3), 613–A15.

Argyris, C., & Schön, D. A. (1978; 1996). *Organizational learning.* Reading, Mass u.a.: Addison-Wesley Pub. Co.

Arnason, S. T. (2007). *How to achieve 27001 certification: An example of applied compliance management.* Abingdon: Taylor & Francis Group.

Bernard, R. (2007). Information lifecycle security risk assessment: A tool for closing security gaps. *Computers & Security, 26*(1), 26–30. doi:10.1016/j.cose.2006.12.005

Bleicher, K. (2004). *Das Konzept Integriertes Management: Visionen, Missionen, Programme.* Frankfurt: Campus-Verlag.

Brotby, K. (2009). *Information security governance: A practical development and implementation approach.* Chichester: John Wiley & Sons, Limited. doi:10.1002/9780470476017

Bulgurcu, B., Cavusoglu, H., & Benbasat, I. (2010). Information security policy compliance: An empirical study of rationality-based beliefs and information security awareness. *Management Information Systems Quarterly, 34*(3), 523–A7.

Deming, W. E. (1986). *Out of the crisis: Quality, productivity and competitive position.* Cambridge: Cambridge Univ. Press.

Dhillon, G., & Backhouse, J. (2001). Current directions in IS security research: Towards socio-organizational perspectives. *Information Systems Journal, 11*(2), 127–153. doi:10.1046/j.1365-2575.2001.00099.x

Dhillon, G., & Torkzadeh, G. (2006). Value-focused assessment of information system security in organizations. *Information Systems Journal, 16*(3), 293–314. doi:10.1111/j.1365-2575.2006.00219.x

Ezingeard, J., & Bowen-Schrire, M. (2007). Triggers of change in information security management practices. *Journal of General Management, 32*(4), 53–72.

Federal Office for Information Security [BSI]. (2007). *IT Security Guidelines*. Retrieved January 28, 2010 from www.bsi.bund.de/cae/servlet/contentblob/475854/publicationFile/28012/guidelines_pdf.pdf

Federal Office for Information Security [BSI]. (2008). *BSI Standard 100-1 Information Security Management Systems (ISMS)*. Retrieved January 28, 2010 from https://www.bsi.bund.de/SharedDocs/Downloads/EN/BSI/Publications/BSIStandards/standard_100-1_e_pdf.pdf?__blob=publicationFile

Federal Office for Information Security [BSI]. (2009). *BSI-Standard 100-4: Business Continuity Management*. Retrieved January 28, 2010 from https://www.bsi.bund.de/SharedDocs/Downloads/EN/BSI/Publications/BSIStandards/standard_100-4_e_pdf.pdf?__blob=publicationFile

Gordon, L. A., Loeb, M. P., & Sohail, T. (2010). Market value of voluntary disclosures concerning information security. *Management Information Systems Quarterly, 34*(3), 567–A2.

Hayden, L. (2010). *IT security metrics: A practical framework for measuring security & protecting data. New York u.a.* McGraw Hill.

Humphreys, E. (2007). *Implementing the ISO/IEC 27001 information security management standard*. Boston: Artech House.

Imai, M. (1986). *Kaizen: The key to japan's competitive success*. New York, NY: Random House.

International Standard Organization [ISO]. (2008). *ISO/IEC 21827, Information technology, Security techniques, Systems Security Engineering, Capability Maturity Model® (SSE-CMM®)*. Geneva, Switzerland: ISO.

International Standard Organization [ISO]. (2008). *ISO/IEC 27005:2008 Information technology, Security techniques, Information security risk management*. Geneva, Switzerland: ISO.

International Standard Organization [ISO]. (2010). *ISO/IEC 27003:2010, Information technology, Security techniques, Information security management system implementation guidance*. Geneva, Switzerland: ISO.

Jaquith, A. (2008). Security metrics: Replacing fear, uncertainty, and doubt (4 print ed.). Upper Saddle River, NJ u.a.: Addison-Wesley.

Johnston, A. C., & Warkentin, M. (2010). Fear appeals and information security behaviors: An empirical study. *Management Information Systems Quarterly, 34*(3), 549–A4.

Juran, J. M. (1951). *Quality-control handbook*. New York: McGraw-Hill.

Kankanhalli, A., Teo, H., Tan, B. C. Y., & Wei, K. (2003). An integrative study of information systems security effectiveness. *International Journal of Information Management, 23*(2), 139–154. doi:10.1016/S0268-4012(02)00105-6

Savola, R. (2007). Towards a security metrics taxonomy for the information and communication technology industry. Paper presented at the *International Conference on Software Engineering Advances, 2007. ICSEA 2007*. 60-66. http://doi.ieeecomputersociety.org/10.1109/ICSEA.2007.79

Siponen, M., & Vance, A. (2010). Neutralization: New insights into the problem of employee information systems security policy violations. *Management Information Systems Quarterly, 34*(3), 487–A12.

Siponen, M. T. (2001). An analysis of the recent IS security development approaches: descriptive and prescriptive implications. In G. Dhillon (Ed.), *Information security management: Global challenges in the new millennium.* Hershey, PA: IGI Global. doi:10.4018/978-1-878289-78-0.ch008

Smith, S., Winchester, D., Bunker, D., & Jamieson, R. (2010). Circuits of power: A study of mandated compliance to an information systems security de jure standard in a government organization. *Management Information Systems Quarterly, 34*(3), 463–486.

Spears, J. L., & Barki, H. (2010). User participation in information systems security risk management. *Management Information Systems Quarterly, 34*(3), 503–A5.

Stewart, J. M., Tittel, E., & Chapple, M. (2008). *CISSP: Certified information systems security professional study guide. Serious skills.* Indianapolis, IN: Wiley Pub.

Stoll, M., Felderer, M., & Breu, R. (2013). Information Management for Collaborative Information Security. *Proceedings of the 2010 IEEE international conference systems, computing sciences and software engineering (SCSS2010).*

Tiemeyer, E., & Bachmann, W. (2009). Handbuch IT-management: Konzepte, Methoden, Lösungen und Arbeitshilfen für die Praxis (3, ed.). Munich, Germany: Hanser.

Trcek, D. (2003). An integral framework for information systems security management. *Computers & Security, 22*(4), 337–360. doi:10.1016/S0167-4048(03)00413-9

Weill, P., & Ross, J. W. (2004). *IT governance: How top performers manage IT decision rights for superior results.* Boston, Mass.: Harvard Business School Press.

Wood, C. (2003). *Information Security Roles & Responsibilities Made Easy.* Houston: Information Shield.

KEY TERMS AND DEFINITIONS

Business Process: A business process is a set of interrelated or interacting activities which transforms inputs into outputs to meet defined objectives by respecting constraints and requiring resources.

Information Security Governance: Information security governance is an integral part of corporate governance. It provides the strategic direction for information security, ensures that objectives are achieved, and ascertains that risks are managed appropriately and responsibly. In that way information security sustains and extends organizations strategies, objectives and controlling for sustainable organizations' success.

Information Security Management System: An information security management system is part of the overall management system (see Management System). It is based on a business risk approach, to establish, implement, operate, monitor, review, maintain and improve information security accordingly to stakeholder, business, standard, legal and regulatory requirements.

Information Security: Information security is the preservation of confidentiality, integrity and availability of information. In accordance to corporate objectives and strategies, as well as stakeholder's, legal, regulatory, business and standard requirements other properties, such as authenticity, accountability, non-repudiation and reliability can also be involved.

Management System: A management system identifies, understands and manages interrelated or interacting processes and activities to establish the organizations' objectives accordingly to stakeholders', legal, regulatory and standard requirements and to achieve those objectives sustainable. It consists of a corporate policy, objectives, planning activities, responsibilities, organizational structure, policies, practices, procedures, processes and resources. Due to external and internal changes it must be continually adjusted and improved.

Policy: The policy provides the overall intention, direction, principles and values of an organization in accordance to stakeholders', legal, regulatory and standard requirements and the characteristics of the business, the organization, its location, assets and resources. It is a framework for setting objectives and measuring their achievement.

Quality Management System: A quality management system is a management system (see "Management system") to direct and control an organization to fulfill stakeholder requirements. It includes the establishment of the quality policy and objectives, as well as quality planning, quality control, quality assurance and quality improvement.

Risk Assessment: A risk assessment is a systematic use of information to identify sources of risk, to estimate the risk and to compare the estimated risk against given risk criteria to determine the significance of the risk.

Chapter 12
Health IT:
A Framework for Managing Privacy Impact Assessment of Personally Identifiable Data

Cyril Onwubiko
Research Series Limited, UK

ABSTRACT

Health IT is the use of Information Technology (IT) in healthcare to improve patients' experience, enable quality care, efficiency, speed, and security of the collection, exchange, sharing, and storage of sensitive personal information. But Health IT faces a number of notable challenges ranging from privacy risks to trust and confidence in the use of EHRs. In this chapter, a framework for conducting Privacy Impact Assessment (PIA) of Health IT projects is discussed. Privacy impact assessment is a process through which privacy risks are assessed. The chapter includes recommendations for mitigating identified risks and ensuring compliance to policy and processes for handling and processing of highly sensitive and Personally Identifiable Information (PII).

INTRODUCTION

In 2009 the US government signed the passage of the Health Information Technology for Economic and Clinical Health Act (HITECH Act, 2009), a federal initiative that seeks to improve American health care delivery and patient care through an unprecedented investment in Health Information Technology (Health IT). Simply, Health IT is the use of IT in healthcare to improve patients' experience, enable quality care, efficiency, speed and security of personal information collection, exchange, sharing and storage. So Health IT encourages and incentivizes the use of electronic health records (EHRs) instead of paper medical records to maintain people's health information, the secure use and sharing of health information, and the use of IT to improve the quality and efficiency of care.

The goals of Health IT were pretty clear – to convince all physicians and hospitals to adopt EHRs, incentivize care service providers to adopt EHRs and to use them in ways that improves patients experience, quality and efficiency of care. But five years down the line, have these goals been realised? What have improved, and what haven't? What are perceived major drawbacks, and what could be done to improve?

DOI: 10.4018/978-1-4666-7381-6.ch012

The use of IT in Health to improve patients experience, improve quality of care, reduce delays in treatment, and improve healthcare standards as a whole is a welcome development and should be encouraged. Lessons learnt from other countries that currently use EHR information systems attest to impressive results, improvements in patient care experience, overall healthcare efficiency as seen with lower levels of drug error rates in Europe. For example, Denmark has the lowest rate of inappropriate medication in eight European countries (Denmark, the Netherlands, the UK, Iceland, Norway, Finland, Italy and the Czech Republic) – a 5.8 percent rate, compared to 19.8 percent in these countries on average (Lesk, 2013). Meanwhile, the US is still struggling to reduce errors. According to the 2000 National Research Council report (Grady, 2010) estimated that approximately 100,000 deaths resulted from medical errors each year; this figure has not improved over a decade later (Lesk, 2013).

Unfortunately, IT in Health comes with some challenges, especially, when use of IT in health is going to fundamentally and radically change existing healthcare practices such as use of EHRs for patient information record management, culture change in terms of electronic use, sharing and transmission of patients' information. As with any change, both patients and practitioners are going to react to this change one way or another. Similarly, the implementation and operation of Health IT in accordance to the HITECH Act are going to be challenging, too. These challenges are going to be multifaceted, including but not limited to technical, policy, interoperability, interface, privacy, security and data formatting and presentation issues. This thought is not radical, as the Office of the National Coordinator for Health Information Technology (ONC) itself had envisaged this, leading to the initiation of the Strategic Health IT Advanced Research Projects (SHARP), a program researching into, and addressing some of the perceived challenges in four specific areas – security and health information

technology, patient-centered cognitive support, health care application and network design and secondary use of EHR information (Office of the National Coordinator for Health Information Technology, 2010).

According to the HITECH Act, Health IT includes hardware, software, integrated technologies or related licenses, intellectual property, upgrades, or packaged solutions sold as services that are designed for or support the use by health care entities or patients for the electronic creation, maintenance, access, or exchange of health information (HITECH Act, 2009). The adoption, building or 'migration' to EHR is going to be expensive, resource intensive, demanding and certainly challenging. Electronic health record as technology service is in itself complex, let alone policy, security, privacy and governance wrapper that are in them equally convoluted. For instance, Healthcare Trusts and Hospitals in the UK use a number of different electronic care record systems, such as EPR (Electronic Patients Record), PAS (Patient Administration System), CRS (Care Records System) etc. Compatibility between two EHR systems becomes an issue. Data format and data presentation from one system to another differs. How the same data is viewed or presented in one system is different to the other, nothing is seamless or straightforward between any two electronic health record systems. The same data is presented in different views making interpretation and understanding of health information a major concern.

The exchange, sharing and transmission of health information could span across enterprise boundaries, such as hospitals, care providers and could use technologies that traverse geographic boundaries, for example, cloud computing. This is likely to raise privacy concerns and could impact public trust and confidence, especially when it relates to personally identifiable information or personally identifiable data (PID), and when the sharing or exchange is not patient-consented. The use of networks, technologies and software that are inherently privacy-invasive, such as location-based technologies, smart cards, radio frequency identification (RFID) tags, and biometrics for health IT or for EHR systems can be a major concern.

Research surveys and polls consistently show that patients are enthusiastic about the adoption of EHRs but are equally concerned about the privacy of their digital health information. Nearly one in eight patients has withheld information from a healthcare provider due to privacy concerns (Agaku, Adisa, Ayo-Yusuf & Connolly, 2014). Failure to address these concerns could have real consequences for people's health (McGraw, 2013). Similar concerns resonate from privacy campaigners who believe patients should have a say in how their health information are shared, and who they are shared with. For example, currently in the UK, the National Health Service (NHS) initiated a Care.data project which supposed to compile a giant database of medical records showing how individuals have been cared for across the general practice (GP) and hospital sectors. According to the British Broadcasting Corporation (BBC), Care. data is believed will be shared with researchers for research purposes (BBC, 2014), and that records will be pseudo-anonymized, which means the identifiable data has been taken out. Instead, it will just contain the patient's age, gender and area they live in. Although there is provision for people to opt-out of the scheme should they wish to. The norm should have been for the initiative to have everyone opted-out so that people can willingly opt-in should they choose to. Such canny approach does not seat well with the public, and hence erodes public trust and confidence, and could raise serious questions around the actual intents behind the NHS database programme. Is the intention really for research purposes or shared for underground citizens' surveillance? Again, with the recent episodes and revelations regarding mass citizen surveillance programmes in the US and cooperation by the UK, this is bound to raise eyebrows. No wonder it has been

meant with stiff opposition and reluctance by the public. As at February 19, 2014, the NHS England Care.data project has been put on hold. The hesitation comes after polls suggested that less than half the population had heard of the scheme, concerns about the security of the data, the process for gaining consent, and data being available to commercial organisations.

To encourage public trust and confidence in Health IT, privacy risk assessment of all Heath IT components starting from HER systems and including data sharing and exchange policies and practices. This is in order that privacy risks relating to Health IT can be identified and mitigated appropriately.

Privacy impact assessment is used to assess privacy risks that may be associated with a project and to ensure that privacy legislations are not breached, and sensitive personally identifiable data are not compromised too. Privacy risk assessment is an assessment of risks associated with - failing to comply with state or federal privacy legislation - protecting personal information data of individuals, and satisfying privacy requirements of information systems, that may need to be redesigned or retro-fitted at considerable expense (Educause, 2010). This means that privacy risk assessment should be carried out on all projects, especially Health IT projects to ensure that:

1. They comply with privacy legislations or regulations;
2. They provide adequate safeguards to manage, handle, share, store or transport sensitive personal data or personally identifiable information (PII); and
3. Finally, they comply with Health IT-specific information systems' privacy requirements.

Managing privacy risks can be challenging, not because of the numerous issues of concern, but also because each project is unique and utilizes fundamentally different technologies and mechanisms to deliver its own service. While the steps involved in carrying out privacy impact assessment are the same for any project, but each assessment of privacy for any project is different. A 'project' in this chapter refers to a system, programme, initiative or scheme. A project may involve a collection of systems that are used to deliver service for a specific purpose. For example, a census programme is a project whose aim is to count the number of lawful citizens, by checking and verifying their name, age, address and social or religious inclination, of a particular nation. This project may require the use of information communications technology (ICT) systems, people, electronic, and manual processes. An 'in-service (existing) project' is a programme of work that is already been delivered and in operational use. A new project is a programme of work that is in the initiation stage of the project lifecycle.

There are a good number of sources that provide guidelines for conducting PIAs such as (UK Information Commissioner's Office, 2009; Educause, 2010; Radack, 2010; Gruteser & Grunwald, 2004; Peirce, 2009; Abu-Nimeh & Mead, 2001; Privacy by Design, 2014). Unfortunately, organizations still face difficulty assessing privacy risks associated to new and existing projects. Some of the most common challenges faced by organizations include:

1. Appropriate assessment of privacy invasive technologies;
2. Justification for project;
3. Difficulty finding privacy experts within own organization;
4. Lack of appropriate guideline for tailored privacy risks assessment, and how to determine the level of privacy assessments required for a particular project;
5. Appropriate gathering and handling of personal information data and compliance to privacy regulations and legislations.

In this chapter, improvement to our contribution on managing privacy impact assessment of personally identifiable information (Onwubiko, 2011) is presented; offering guidance on how to assess privacy risks of both new and in-service projects. Further, lessons learned from managing privacy risks for new and existing projects, especially relating to Health IT, resulting from collection, aggregation, sharing, handling and transportation of sensitive personal information are discussed.

PRIVACY IMPACT ASSESSMENT

Privacy impact assessment is an assessment of privacy related risks comprising of four distinct assessments:

1. Assessment of the project's characteristics or features such as technologies or mechanisms deployed or intended of use. This assessment is to check if the technologies or mechanisms would be privacy invasive.

2. Assessment of the project's compliance with privacy regulations, state, federal, national, bilateral or multilateral privacy legislations. This relates to compliance with privacy regulations and legislations, especially those that operate where the project is located or situated. For example, the Data Protection Act 1998 in the UK or the 'the Privacy Act' in the US, or other privacy related pieces of legislations in other parts of the world, such as Canada, Australia and Germany.

3. Assessment of personal information data being processed, or to be processed by the project. For example, is personal information data collected identifiable or not; are they sensitive personal data; are they 'obsolete' personal identifiable data, etc.

4. Finally, it is an assessment of the collection, sharing, distribution, storage and transportation of personal information data, and

Table 1. Personal identifiers

S/N	Personal Identifiers	S/N	Personal Identifiers
1	Names (firstname, surname or lastname)	12	Biometric identifiers such as fingerprints, voice prints etc
2	Addresses (home, business or both)	13	Bank, Financial or Credit card details
3	Post code or Zip code	14	Mother's maiden name
4	Email address	15	Tax, Benefit or Pension records or Record numbers
5	Telephone numbers (Fax numbers)	16	Employment records
6	Driving license number	17	School attendance or records
7	Date of birth	18	Vehicle identifiers and serial numbers including license plate numbers
8	Social insurance number / National insurance number	19	Web universal resource locators (URLs)
9	Medical record numbers / Health records	20	Internet protocol (IP) address numbers
10	DNA data	21	Full face photographic images and any comparable images
11	Any other materials relating to social services including child protection and housing	22	Any other unique identifying number, characteristic, or code.

Personal identifiers (shown in Table 1) comprise of both personal information that are in the public domain and sensitive personal data that when released is likely to cause harm or distress to the individual. These identifiers are derived from a couple of standards – HIPAA (HIPAA (2006) and HMG IA Standard No. 6 (HMG IA Standard No. 6, 2009).

whether the processing of personal information is in line with privacy legislations. It is important to mention that PIA is not only applied to a project, but also applied to a workstream, programme, task, policy, procedure, platform or ICT System.

According to NIST's ITL Security Bulletin 2010 (Radack, 2010), PII or PID is any information about an individual that is maintained by an agency, including information that can be used to distinguish or trace an individual's identity, such as name, social security number, date and place of birth, mother's maiden name, or biometric records; and any other information that is linked or linkable to an individual, such as medical, educational, financial, and employment information (based on General Accountability Office and Office of Management and Budget definitions). A list of PII is as shown in Table 1.

It is pertinent to mention that compliance with privacy legislation is dependent on where the project that is being assessed is located. For example, a project in the UK would have to comply with the UK privacy legislations and the wider European Union privacy legislations, and may comply with other privacy legislations of other countries if the organisation wishes to do so.

There are also bilateral and multilateral privacy legislations, such as the Safe Harbor Act (Directive 95/46/EC, 1995), which regulates the processing of personal data within the European Union in addition to Directive 2002/58/EC that protects privacy of electronic communications (Directive 2002/58/EC, 2002). Directive 95/46/EC is also available not only to EU member state (nations), but also, available to other countries outside the EU, which the United States (US) signed up to. Organization operating within bilateral or multilateral privacy legislation should comply with those pieces of privacy legislations. This means

Figure 1. PISA framework – privacy impact suitability assessment framework (Onwubiko, 2011).

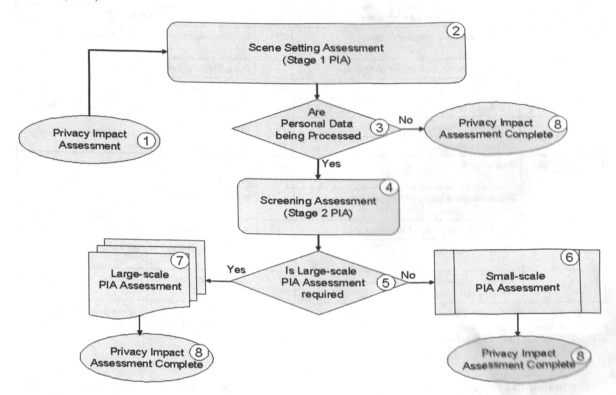

that a privacy impact assessment of a project operating in bilateral or multilateral privacy legislation must be equally assessed within the confinements of those bilateral or multilateral privacy agreements, and other specific privacy legislation of its own country. For example, privacy legislation compliance for a privacy impact assessment of a project in the UK would involve assessment of the project's compliance to both UK-specific privacy legislations and EU related privacy legislations.

Privacy impact assessment may seem onerous at times due to the numerous steps involved when carrying out PIA. Depending on the nature of the project, extensive privacy impact assessment maybe required. Some general purpose and useful guidelines exist such as handbook on PIA assessment (UK Information Commissioner's Office, 2009).

Our contribution in this chapter is rather unique and focused on providing a practical approach to conducting privacy impact assessment that is general-purpose and doctrinaire. The usefulness of our contribution can be seen in both the guidelines provided with respect to our Privacy Impact Suitability Assessment (PISA) Framework (see Figure 1) and Privacy Screening Framework (see Table 4).

In the private sector, for example, privacy impact assessments of projects are not as mandated as it is in the public or government sector. While, PIA may be conducted for certain projects based on best endeavours in the private sector, it is mandatory for all government and public sector projects as an essential risk management activity. For example, the Department of Homeland Security, National Cyber Security Division of the United States conducted privacy impact assessment of its

EINSTEIN 2 Program in 2008 to examine its privacy implications with collecting, analyzing and sharing of Computer Security Information across the Federal Civilian Government (US-CERT, 2008). According to the United States Computer Emergency Readiness Team (US-CERT), the Department of Homeland Security (DHS) must provide this publicly available PIA prior to initiating a new collection of information that uses information technology to collect, maintain or disseminate information that is in an identifiable form or collects identifiable information through the use of information technology as mandated by the US, E-Government Act of 2002. Similarly, in the UK, the Information Commissioners Office (ICO), Cabinet Office has recommended privacy impact assessment for all projects, new and existing, whose functionality may require the collection, sharing or use of personal information. This was driven from the UK Data Handling Review of 2008 (Cabinet Office, 2008).

PRIVACY IMPACT SUITABILITY ASSESSMENT (PISA) FRAMEWORK

The privacy impact suitability assessment framework is our proposed framework for assessing a project's suitability for PIA assessment (see Figure 1).

The PISA framework is an eight (8) step privacy assessment model, which aims to evaluate if a project is required to undergo PIA or not; and to determine the level of PIA required, where applicable. The first step (indicated by the small circle on each object) is the start of the PIA assessment. The second step is the scene setting assessment (a.k.a. stage 1 PIA). At this stage, the project is initially assessed as to whether personal information data will be processed by the project. For existing projects, the scene setting assessment will check if information being processed by the project involves personal information data. The third step is when a decision is reached whether

the project should or should not undergo a stage 2 PIA assessment. If the outcome shows that personal information data is not being or will not be processed, then PIA is completed (step 8) and that concludes privacy impact assessment for that project. If otherwise, then the fourth step begins. The fourth step is the stage 2 PIA.

The second stage PIA (Stage 2 PIA) starts with the screening exercise when privacy risks of the project are assessed in much more detail than stage 1. This involves assessing the project's characteristics, such as technologies or mechanisms that will be deployed in the project, for example, checking if such technologies are privacy invasive. It also assesses the type of personal data that will be collected, and to ensure the people providing these data are aware and willing. In addition, it assesses if there is good justification for the project. The fifth step is when a decision is reached as to whether small-scale PIA or large-scale PIA is pertinent for the project. The sixth step involves carrying out large-scale or small-scale PIA, and finally, the seventh step completes the assessment. Since every project should be assessed of privacy risk, we thought the framework is a foundational contribution, which assist privacy experts and organization conduct, in a practical way, a privacy assessment of their projects.

Scene Setting Assessment (Stage 1 PIA)

The scene setting assessment (SSA) is the first stage PIA of a project. It is aimed to ascertain if the project will process personal information data, or already processes personal information data. This is applicable to existing project (see Figure 1). To conduct a scene setting PIA assessment of a project, we have designed ten (10) fundamental scene setting questions to help with the assessment in order to deduce the suitability or appropriateness of privacy impact assessment of the project, as shown in Table 2.

Table 2. Privacy scene setting assessment

PD	Project Details	Response
PD1	Project Name:	
PD2	Country of Project Location:	
PD3	Project Reference:	
PD4	Project Registration Type:	
PD5	Project Owner:	
PD6	Assessor Name:	
PD7	Assessor Email Address:	
PD8	Assessor Expertise:	
PD9	Assessment Date:	
SSA	**Scene Setting Assessment**	**Response**
SSA1	Would the project consume, process, transport or store personal information data?	
SSA2	What personal information data would the project process?	
SSA3	Why is personal information collected by the project?	
SSA4	What is the intended use of personal information data being collected by the project?	
SSA5	How would personal information data be processed, this includes sharing, transporting, exchanging, storing and disposing of personal information?	
SSA6	Is the organisation that owns the project an authorised Data Controller?	
SSA7	Is the organisation that owns the project an authorised Data Processor?	
SSA8	With whom will personal information be shared, or/and exchanged?	
SSA9	How are service consumers consent obtained?	
SSA10	How will service consumers informed of the justification for the project?	
SSA11	How will personal information data at rest secured?	
SSA12	How will personal information data secured on transit?	
SSA13	Select applicable legislation for the project	
SSA14	What privacy regulations apply or are required for the project?	

Based on the outcome of this assessment (answers to questions on Table 2), a decision should be made, either to proceed, or stop further privacy impact assessment. If it is believed that the project will be used to process personal information data, then further PIA assessments are recommended, otherwise this concludes PIA assessment of the project. Suppose the outcome of the scene setting assessment turns out that the project is handling personal information data. This implies that a second stage PIA (screening assessment), which is a much more thorough assessment than the scene setting assessment, will be required. It is pertinent to mention that, the first stage PIA is mandatory for all projects.

Screening Assessment (Stage 2 PIA)

The second stage PIA is referred to as the screening assessment, during which project stakeholders are interviewed to determine the level of personal data the project intends to process, or has been processing, this is applicable to existing projects (see Figure 1).

The aim of the screening assessment is to determine whether a small-scale or large-scale PIA is deemed necessary for the project. A small-scale privacy impact assessment is an abridged privacy risks assessment of a project. It is recommended when a small percentage of the project characteristics underline some privacy concerns. For example, if one or two features of the project characteristics imply privacy concern, then it is justifiable to recommend a small-scale PIA assessment. If more than three aspects of the project characteristics underline privacy concerns, then a large-scale PIA is justifiable. Having said that, there are cases when a small-scale PIA is recommended even a number of a project features seems to underline privacy concerns.

For example, if it is perceived that personal data being processed are either none sensitive or the processing is infrequent. None sensitive personal data refers to personal data of a living individual that can only identify an individual when linked or combined with other personal data of that individual. For example, an email server project that collects only two sets of personal data during user registration such as name and email address of the user would justify a small-scale PIA, even though it aggregate significant volumes of personal information data. A large-scale PIA assessment is an extensive, thorough, and detailed privacy risks assessment. A large-scale PIA assessment is recommended when a good percentage of the project characteristics evaluated during a screening exercise underlines serious privacy concerns. For example, a data consolidation project of a health service that links data controllers or sources warrants large-scale privacy risks assessment. Both small-scale and large-scale privacy impact assessments require project stakeholders to be interviewed in order to determine the areas of the project that involve processing of personal information data, and the level of analysis or manipulation (source linkages) of personal data that are intended.

There is no empirical method of deciding which projects should undergo large-scale or small-scale privacy impact assessment. One approach that has been recommended to determining the level of assessment required for a project is the use of screening questions (Information Commissioner's Office 2009) developed by the ICO. The ICO's proposed screening process is extremely helpful; unfortunately, the screening process does not guarantee that the same project when assessed by two separate organisations would lead to the same level of PIA recommendations. For this reason, proposed the Privacy Screening Framework (see Table 4), in addition, we designed a general purpose legal and privacy assessment questions (see Table 3) to assist organizations assess legal and privacy compliance of projects during PIA assessments.

Table 3 consists of twelve (12) questions comprising legal, regulatory and legislative assessment of personal data handling, processing and sharing. The idea behind the provision of the legal and privacy compliance check is to ensure that PIA assessments are consistently evaluated by each organization by following the same prescriptive guideline. As seen in the table, there are ten (10) UK-specific directives that are also listed. The reason behind this is to include country-specific directive, so that dependent on where the project is located, assessment of country-specific directives are also assessed. In our future work, we hope to include country-specific privacy directives in the model.

After carrying out legal and privacy compliance checks of a project, the next activity in the PIA assessment is the privacy screening assessment.

PRIVACY SCREENING FRAMEWORK (PSF)

The privacy screening framework is our proposed framework that provides the required prescriptive guidance for carrying out large-scale PIA assessments. The PSF framework is flexible, adaptable and self-directing. It is flexible because the PIA assessor can choose to add or remove any non-applicable sections of the framework without influencing the end result of the assessment.

Table 3. Legal and privacy compliance check

PD	Project Details	Response
PD1	Project Name:	
PD2	Country of Project Location:	
PD3	Project Reference:	
PD4	Project Registration Type:	
PD5	Project Owner:	
PD6	Assessor Name:	
PD7	Assessor Email Address:	
PD8	Assessor Expertise:	
PD9	Assessment Date:	
GPC	**General Privacy Clauses**	**Response**
GPC1	Is the project compliant with all relevant regulation/directives	
GPC2	Are the business processes to be used (or been used) for the project compliant with all relevant regulation/directives	
GPC3	Are there legal compliance that this project must satisfy?	
GPC4	Are there standards and law that this project must comply?	
GPC5	Are there privacy related compliances stemming from a code of connection or code of interconnection contract?	
GPC6	Are there privacy related compliance arising from corporate/statutory privacy policy?	
GPC7	Are there specific privacy requirements or compliance arising from service consumers that must be satisfied?	
GPC8	Are there privacy related mandates from the Public that this project must satisfy?	
GPC9	Is the project, the processes of the project or the personal data collected compliant with Public Health requirements?	
GPC10	Is this project compliant with the Health Insurance Portability and Accountability Act (HIPAA)	
GPC11	Will personal data be shared or transport outside the Country of Origin?	
GPC12	Will personal data be shared or transport outside the Province of Origin but consumed within the Country of Origin?	
UK	**Country Specific Directives**	**Response**
UK1	Is the project compliant with the Data Protection Act 1998?	
UK2	Is the project, the personal data that it handles, and its business activities compliant with the Data Protection Principles (1-8)?	
UK3	Freedom of Information Act, 2000	
UK4	Is the project compliant with the Privacy and Electronic Communications Regulations 2003?	
UK5	Is the project compliant with the Freedom of Information Act 2000?	
UK6	Is the project compliant with the Privacy Act 1974?	
UK7	Is the project compliant with the EU Directive 2002/58 EC on Processing of Personal Data and the Protection of Privacy in the Electronic Communications Sector?	
UK8	Is the project compliant with the EU Directive 95/46 EC on the processing of personal data and on the free movement of such data	
UK9	Freedom of Information and Protection of Privacy Act (FIPPA)	
UK10	Is the project compliant with the Human Rights Act 1998?	

Table 4. Privacy Screening Framework (PSF)

High Level Privacy Impact Assessment		
1	Project Details	Response
PD1	Project Name:	
PD2	Project Reference:	
PD3	Country of Project Location:	
PD4	Project Registration Type:	
PD5	Project Owner:	
PD6	Assessor Name:	
PD7	Assessor Email Address:	
PD8	Assessor Expertise:	
PD9	Assessment Date:	
2	Technology Privacy Risk Assessment	
2a	Privacy-Invasive Technologies	Response
2a1	Please select technologies being deployed or in use by the project.	
2a2	Does the project use RFID or plan to deploy RFID (Radio frequency identification)?	
2a3	What is RFID used for? For example, tracking users, tracking people etc.	
2a4	Does the project use biometric technology (biometrics) or plan to deploy biometrics?	
2a5	What is biometrics used for in the project? For example, authentication, authorisation, tracking, gatekeeper etc.	
2a6	Are all technologies applied to the project well-understood by the organisation?	
2a7	Are all technologies applied to the project well-understood by the service consumers?	
2a8	Does the project use locator monitoring technologies or plan to deploy locator monitoring technologies, such as GIS, GPRS etc.?	
2a9	Which locator monitoring technology is in use or planned for use?	
2a10	What locator monitoring technologies used for in the project? For example, tracking users, tracking equipment, tracking both users and their actions	
2a11	Are there demonstrable concerns that the technologies used in the project may impact privacy	
2a12	Does the project use visual surveillance for its operation?	
2a13	Which visual surveillance tools are in use?	
2a14	What are the visual surveillance tools used for? For example, monitor people, monitor intruders, monitor both users and intruders, track object movement and interactions	
2a15	Are the privacy impacts (from the project) well-understood by the organisation, and by the service consumers	
2a16	Are there measures applied to avoid or mitigate negative privacy impacts, or at least reduce them to satisfactory levels of those whose privacy is affected	
2a17	What measure/controls are in place to address privacy concerns?	
2b	Event and Information Monitoring Technologies	Response
2b1	Does the project involve the use of event and information monitoring technologies such as SEIM, SEM and SIM such that user traffic, user actions and user locations can be monitored	
2b2	Are SIEMS used to track user activities and interactions	
2b3	Are cookies being monitored and used in various ways users are not aware of, and their consent not sort?	
2b4	Are service consumers' activities logged?	

continued on following page

Table 4. Continued

	High Level Privacy Impact Assessment	
2b5	For what purpose are service consumers' activities logged?	
2b6	How long are logs retained?	
2b7	Are the organisation and service consumers aware that their traffic are being monitored	
2b8	Is the use of the SEIM/SEM/SIM due to regulatory compliance?	
2b9	What regulatory compliance does the use of SIEM/SEM/SIM fulfil?	
2b10	If service consumer data are collected, are they subject to reprocessing that could lead to the identification of individuals	
2c	Data Capturing and Screening Technologies	Response
2c1	Does the project involve the use of data capturing, admission and screening technologies such as Biometrics, RFID, Blood sampling toolkit, Lab equipment, X-ray and digital imagery, data monitors (wireshark) such that user identifiable attributes, characteristics and features are monitored, captured or/and stored	
2c2	Which data capturing, admission, screening or registration technologies are in use?	
2c3	Are blood sampling toolkits used or will be used for the project?	
2c4	Are X-ray and digital imagery equipment in use?	
2c5	Is a medical monitor, such as heart monitors, pacemaker, or LCD implantation toolkits in use?	
2c6	Which traffic and data monitoring devices are in use?	
2c7	Which user registration equipment are in use?	
2c8	Is the use of the data capturing and screening tools due to regulatory compliance, if yes, please specify	
2c9	Which regulatory compliance mandates or recommends the use of data capturing and screening device?	
2c10	Are the organisation and service consumers aware that user traffic are monitored?	
2d	Cloud-Based Technologies	Response
2d1	Does the project use or intend to use Cloud-based services?	
2d2	What type of Cloud is used or will be used?	
2d3	Which Cloud delivery model is in use or may be used?	
2d4	Who is the Cloud Provider?	
2d5	Is the Cloud Provider Local, Provincial or International?	
2d6	What controls are offered to assets in the Cloud by Provider?	
2d7	Is the Cloud Provider an authorised Data Processor?	
2d8	Is the Cloud Provider an authorised Data Controller?	
2d9	Is the Cloud Provider compliant to DPA, Privacy Act or EU Directives 95/46 EC or EU Directive 2002/58 EC?	
2d10	Is the Cloud Provider's Data Centres local, overseas or both?	
3	Project Privacy Risk Justification	
3a	Privacy Notices	Response
3a1	Is there an appropriate privacy notice outlining the legitimate reasons/intention for processing of personal information?	
3a2	What does the privacy notice include?	
3a3	Are service consumers aware or informed as to why their personal data are being collected?	

continued on following page

Table 4. Continued

High Level Privacy Impact Assessment		
3a4	Is there a process in place to ensure privacy notice is provided prior to data collection to all intended service consumers?	
3a5	Is personal data/information collected through a 3rd-party for the project. That is, is data collection process outsourced via a 3rd-party?	
3a6	Is privacy notice communicated to service consumers about the use of 3rd-party data collector/processors?	
3a7	Is the 3rd-party collecting the data local, offshore, near offshore	
3a8	Where is the 3rd-party organisation located?	
3a9	Is the 3rd-party organisation a registered and authorised data collector or data processor?	
3a10	How is privacy notice communicated to service consumers?	
3a11	If user consent is required, how does the project seek to obtain this?	
3a12	Is personal data collected being used for the purposes outlined in the original privacy notice?	
3b	Justification for Data Handling	Response
3b1	Is there justification to why personal data are collected or processed?	
3b2	What justification exists for the collection and further processing of each type of personal information?	
3b3	Are service consumers aware or informed as to why their personal data are being collected?	
3b4	How did service consumers get to know about the benefits of the project for them or society?	
3b5	Is the project a government project, such as a national census project	
3b6	Do service consumers understand the benefits of the project to them or society?	
3c	Justification for New Data Acquisition	Response
3c1	Is the acquisition of new personal data required?	
3c2	Why is new data required?	
3c3	Will the new pieces of data collected be combined with existing data	
3c4	What new set of data or identify are or will be acquired?	
3c5	Do service consumers understand the benefits of the extra data supplied in the overall assessment of the project	
4	Identity Privacy Risk Assessment	
4a	Intrusive or Onerous Use of New or Substantially Changed Identity Authentication Requirements	Response
4a1	Will the enrolment or registration process require new identifiers to existing ones?	
4a2	Will the registration or enrolment process of the service requires three or more personal identifiable information such as (Name, Address, NI, DoB, SIN, email, Mother's Maiden name etc.)	
4a3	Will the authentication process of the service requires the use of new identifiers?	
4a4	Please, select the identifiers used?	
4a5	Will the project cache or store personal identifiable information of the service consumer during registration	
4a6	Does the enrolment or registration process require two or more processes (for example, collection of basic personal details and onerous PII details)	
4b	Use of a New Identifier for Multiple Purposes	Response

continued on following page

Table 4. Continued

	High Level Privacy Impact Assessment	
4b1	Will the project require a new ID (such as, username, DoB, eye colour, address, NI etc.) and would this new ID be combined with existing IDs	
4b2	Will the new ID be combined with existing IDs?	
4b3	Will an ID be used for multiple purposes such as used for registration, authentication and identification or service improvement contact	
4b4	How many identifiers are used in total for registration or authentication of service consumers?	
4c	Additional Use of an Existing Identifier	Response
4c1	Will the project make use of a combination of existing IDs (example, username, DoB, year, address etc.) in its processing or analysis	
4c2	How many identifiers are required?	
4c3	How many identifiers are combined?	
4c4	Please, select the identifiers used?	
4c5	Please, select identifiers that are combined?	
5	Data Privacy Risk Assessment	
5a	Sensitive and Personally Identifiable Data (PID/PII)	Response
5a1	Will sensitive or personally identifiable data be collected and further processed?	
5a2	Please, select sensitive or personally identifiable data that would be collected and processed by the project	
5a3	What are the reasons for collection and further processing of sensitive personal information?	
5a4	Will data collected for other purposes used in this project?	
5a5	Will the project use or combine personal data collected for other uses with those collected during service registration/enrolment?	
5a6	Will the project involve significant change in data linkages / data sources	
5b	Linkage of Personal Data with Data in Other Collections, or Significant Change in Data Linkages	Response
5b1	How many data linkages or data sources (transfer, consolidation or storage) of personal data are in use	
5b2	Will data collected for other purposes be used in this project	
5b3	Will the project use or combine personal data collected for other uses with those collected during service registration/enrolment or privacy notice?	
5b4	Will the project involve significant change in data linkages / data sources	
5b5	Will the project involve significant change in data linkages / data sources	
5c	Handling of a Significant Amount of New Data about Each Person, or Significant change in Existing Data-Holdings	Response
5c1	What is the estimated number of users who may use this system?	
5c2	What set or combination of user data are required during user registration/enrolment?	
5c3	Will the project result in the handling of a significant amount of new data about people such as Name, address, DoB, NI, Mother's maiden name etc.	
5c4	Will the project result in the handling of a significant change in existing data-holdings	
5c5	Will the Project Combine Both New and Existing Personal Data	
5d	Handling of New Data about a Significant Number of People, or a Significant Change in the Population Coverage	Response

continued on following page

Table 4. Continued

	High Level Privacy Impact Assessment	
5d1	Will the project result in the handling of new data about a significant number of service consumers	
5d2	What is the number of service consumers required to use the service?	
5d3	Will the project result in a significant change in the population coverage	
5d4	What population coverage is anticipated	
6	Data Handling, Processing, Protection & Mobility Privacy Risk Assessment	
6a	Compliance	Response
6a1	Is the project or organisation a registered Data Controller?	
6a2	Is the project or organisation a registered Data Processor?	
6a3	Is the project, programme or organisation register as data controller or data custodians in accordance with prevailing laws/directives?	
6a4	Does the project or the organisation have a privacy policy?	
6a5	Does the project have privacy policy statement?	
6a6	Does the project have a privacy notice statement for services offered by the project?	
6a7	Does the project or organisation have a data protection policy?	
6a8	Will the project have a privacy impact assessment policy or procedure?	
6b	Data Collection Policies or Practices	Response
6a1	Does the project involve new data collection policies that may be unclear or intrusive to service consumers	
6a2	Does the project require the modification of existing data collection policies that may be unclear or intrusive to service consumers	
6a3	Does the project involve new data collection practices or procedures that nay be unclear or intrusive to service consumers	
6a4	Does the project require the modification of existing data collection processes or procedures that may be unclear or intrusive to service consumers	
6a5	Are there mandatory learning and training courses for service providers and developers that are tailored for data protection and privacy controls and guidelines	
6c	Data Quality Assurance Processes or Standards	Response
6c1	Does the project have a data quality process or procedure?	
6c2	Are users aware of the quality assurance procedures of the project?	
6c3	Will the project use a new data quality processes or procedures that may be fundamentally different from existing data quality procedures?	
6c4	Will service consumers or users be notified of the new, or changes in data quality procedure?	
6c5	When was the data quality procedure changed?	
6c6	When will the new data quality procedure be implemented /deployed?	
6d	Data Security Arrangements, Practices, and Processes	Response
6d1	Does the project have a data security process or procedure?	
6d2	Are service consumers/users aware of the security assurance procedure of the project?	
6d3	Will the project use a new data security processes or procedures that may be fundamentally different from existing data quality procedures?	

continued on following page

Table 4. Continued

	High Level Privacy Impact Assessment	
6d4	What data security controls are in place for the project?	
6d5	Does the project use changed data security arrangement processes or procedures that may be unclear or intrusive to service consumers?	
6d6	When was the data security procedure changed?	
6d7	When will the new data security procedure be implemented /deployed?	
6e	Data Access or Disclosure Arrangements, Processes, and Practices	Response
6e1	Does the project or organisation have a data access and disclosure policy or process?	
6e2	Is there a subject access request policy?	
6e3	Does the project comply or will comply with subject access request?	
6e4	Does the project use existing data access or disclosure process that may be unclear or intrusive to service consumers?	
6e5	How often is existing data access or disclosure process reviewed?	
6e6	Does the project use new data access or disclosure process that may be unclear or intrusive to service consumers?	
6e7	When was the new data access or disclosure process deployed or signed-off?	
6e8	Are service consumers aware of, and agreed to, the new data access or disclosure process?	
6f	Data Retention Arrangements, Practices, and Processes	Response
6f1	Does the project or organisation have a data retention policy?	
6f2	When was the data retention process or policy signed-off?	
6f3	Does the data retention periods stipulated in the policy compliant with data protection principles?	
6f4	Is the existing data retention policy unclear or noncompliant with the Data Protection Principles?	
6f5	Is there an aspiration to change the existing data retention policy or process?	
6f6	Why would the existing data retention policy/process been changed?	
6f7	When will the new data retention process/policy be signed-off?	
6f8	Who signs off the data retention policy?	
6g	Disclosure for Publicly Available Information	Response
6g1	Does the project have a publicly accessible portal	
6g2	What sort of information would the portal hold about service consumers?	Name
6g3	Does the portal correlate or collate a set of personal information data, such as name, address, and user activities?	
6g4	Will the project make publicly available piece of personal information data readily accessible. For example, use of public Internet website that organize and aggregate personal information data, such as data mining?	
6g5	Who will have access to publicly available personal data from the portal?	
6h	Data Sharing	Response
6h1	Does the project share personal data with another organisation, institution or 3rd parties?	
6h2	Is personal data shared for commercial gain? For example marketing?	
6h3	Are service consumers aware of, and agreed to, the sharing of data with another entity?	

continued on following page

Table 4. Continued

	High Level Privacy Impact Assessment	
6h4	How is the data shared?	
6i	Data Mobility	Response
6i1	Does the project plan to send personal data to jurisdictions outside the EEA (EU, Iceland, Norway, and Liechtenstein)?	
6i2	Has the jurisdiction that the project is transferring the information to been assessed as "Adequate"	
6i3	Is personal data transferred to America to a company that signs up the Safe Harbor act?	
6i4	Which jurisdiction or country is data sent to?	
6i5	Is the project using any Cloud delivery mechanism or cloud type to transfer personal data?	
6i6	Which mechanisms are used to share or move personal data around?	
6j	Hosting	Response
6j1	Is the project outsourced to a provider outside of the organisation?	
6j2	Is any component of the project hosted overseas, offshore or near offshore?	
6j3	Is the outsourcee or 3rd-party organisation a Cloud Provider?	
6j4	Which jurisdiction or country is the outsourcee located?	
6j5	Is the project using any Cloud delivery mechanism or cloud type?	
6j6	Which Cloud delivery type is used?	
7	Data Archive Privacy Risk Assessment	
7a	Data Archival Policies, Practices, and Processes	Response
7a1	Does the project have a data archive policy or process?	
7a2	How long is personal data being archived	
7a3	Are data archived online or offline	
7a4	Will archived data be used for other purposes except for its original intentions	
7a5	What additional purposes would archived data serve?	
8	Assessing Privacy Risk resulting from Decommissioning	
8a	Secure Sanitisation	Response
8a1	Does the project or organisation have a decommissioning and secure disposal policy?	
8a2	Has any system components of the project been decommissioned, re-used or destroyed?	
8a3	Which system components of the project have ben decommissioned either for re-use, upgrade or destruction?	
8a4	Are systems sanitized before re-use?	
8a6	For systems re-use, have personal data stored on the system being securely destroyed such that their re-construction is impossible?	
8a5	How are the systems/components sanitised?	
8a7	How are paper-based assets containing personal data destroyed?	
9	Privacy Risks Business Impact Assessment	
9a	Vulnerability	Response
9a1	Are the public aware of the project?	
9a2	Is the project under any competition?	
9a3	Are the system components of the project located in vulnerable sites? For example, offshore premises, near offshore locations	
9a4	Will the project (portal) be accessible from vulnerable environment?	
10	Others	
	Please provide any comments you think may assist with the privacy risk assessment of the project or platform being evaluated.	

PSF is adaptable and self-directing because the PIA assessor is required to carry out the assessment, and can modify any sections of the framework that is deemed not applicable to the project's locality or operating environment (see Table 4). For example, when conducting a PIA assessment of a project in the UK, it may not be relevant to evaluate the project based on US-specific privacy legislations except where bilateral mandates are applicable. Similarly, privacy risk assessment of US-based projects should be evaluated against US-specific privacy legislations and applicable industry regulations, plus bilateral or multilateral privacy understandings, where applicable. Thus, it is equally the case with privacy risk assessment of project hosted in other EU countries such as Belgium, Germany or France.

The privacy screening framework is composed of eight (8) sections containing over 185 assessment questions. Each section contains over three subsections, and each subsection contains questions which are crafted to assessing in details the various aspects of the project privacy clauses, practices and policies, such as the data exchange policy, information sharing practices and data handling and storage requirements and principles.

Section 1 is about the project details, comprising project name, reference, organization, asset owner and name of PIA assessor. Section 2 is technology assessment, which focuses primarily on privacy risk assessment of three main areas – privacy-invasive technologies, event and information monitoring technologies, and data capturing and screening technologies. Section 3 is project justification assessment. It is aimed to ensure that the purpose and justification of the project are made known to the public or the users of the system. It has two subcategories – justification for data handling and justification for new data acquisition. Section 4 is identity assessment, which focuses on privacy risks associated to the use, combination and linkage of personal identifiers, such as username, date of birth, national insurance number etc. (see Table 1).

Section 5 is data assessment. This assesses the quantity and significance of personal data being processed (used, stored or transported). Section 6 is data handling assessment, which focuses on privacy risks associated with data collection policies, procedures and quality assurance. Section 7 is awareness assessment. It deals with privacy risks associated with the security of the information system processing personal information data for the project; in addition, it deals with secure disposal and destruction of the information system holding personal information data, when no longer in use. Finally, section 8 is miscellaneous, which affords the risk assessor the opportunity to profile other pertinent privacy risks particular to systems utilized for the project. For example, privacy concerns with legacy systems, bespoke design and customized solutions etc.

Privacy Impact Assessment of an In-Service Project

A project is said to be in-service when it is already being used to deliver a type of service or another. In every aspect, it means the project has gone live. There are five phases to any project lifecycle: initiation phase, development phase, test phase, in-service phase, and decommission phase. Privacy impact assessment of an in-service project is the retrospective privacy risk assessment of a project that is already being used to deliver a service. This means that risk assessment of the project was previously completed only on the basis of business and security requirements, without prior assessment of privacy risks associated with the project.

Privacy impact assessment of an existing project is the retrospective assessment of privacy risks associated to that project. First, privacy assessment suitability of the project should be established as shown in Figure 1. Second, privacy risks relating to technologies or mechanisms deployed in the project, data collection and handling procedures applied (see Privacy Screening Framework - Table 4), and compliance to privacy legislations and regulations (see Table 3) should be evaluated. Finally, specific project privacy requirements should be addressed.

Assessing privacy risks of an existing (in-service) project can be challenging, while the outcome is often astonishing and expensive, because of the following:

1. Asset owners and senior information risk owners do not have a clue how damaging results from such assessments may turn up.
2. Outcome could imply privacy violation or breach.
3. Outcome could show that certain technologies are privacy intrusive or that the data collection and handling procedures contravene privacy regulations or legislations. This may lead to such technologies being decommissioned from the project, consequently resulting to significant financial losses to the organization.
4. Outcome could be costly because the result may mean that certain assets in the project may have to be decommissioned, withdrawn or destroyed. It could also result in significant financial penalties such as fines due to breach of privacy. For example, in August 2010, the UK Government's Financial Services Authority (FSA) fined Zurich Insurance record data loss fine of £2.3M due to a breach on privacy (Shane, 2010). There are a number of cases of huge financial penalties being hit on organisations due to privacy breaches, and such breaches are now starting to be publicly disclosed as Government takes new stances to ensure organisations take privacy seriously.

To conduct privacy impact assessment of an existing project we recommend a quick assessment using our privacy impact assessment questionnaire (see Table 2). This assessment is meant to show if PIA is indeed relevant to the project or not. Based on the outcome of this assessment, further privacy assessments of the project will be decided. It is pertinent to mention that privacy impact assessment of in-service projects follow the same methodology as new projects (see Figure 1). This means that, first, privacy suitability assessment of the project (Stage 1 PIA). Second, based on the outcome of the Stage 1 PIA assessment, Stage 2 PIA will commence; otherwise the assessment is concluded. Following the second stage PIA, two sets of assessment is envisaged, either a small-scale or a large scale PIA assessment.

It is pertinent to re-iterate that the outcome of privacy impact assessment of an existing project can be insightful and expensive. We recommended organisations to consider conducting PIA as early as possible in the project lifecycle to minimize the consequences associated with in-service PIA. For example, PIA of an existing project could reveal that an organisation is in breach of privacy because of the use of technologies that are intrusive in the processing of personal information data. In another case, it may reveal that an organization does not comply with certain privacy regulations or legislations. Either case, the impact it will have on the organization is huge. For instance, it could lead to significant financial penalties, withdrawn accreditation, or/ and subsequent termination of the project. In a normal circumstance, breach of privacy attracts a fine and requires fresh risk assessment of the project, which costs both time and money. In an extreme case, it will lead to significant financial penalty (as a result of breach of customer service agreement and resultant fine from the government), affects the organisation brand (negative media publicity), and especially in situations where disclosure of security or privacy breaches are required due to regional or provincial legislation. Finally, it may lead to termination of the project.

Privacy Impact Assessment of a New Project

With new projects it is recommended that privacy requirements are assessed from the outset and consideration to these requirements are made prior to implementation. This does not mean that privacy impact assessment of new projects is a panacea to all privacy concerns. As shown in Table 5, the difficulty to carrying out privacy impact assessment of new projects are that at the early stages of a project, very little is known of the various components of the project. For example, the entire design of the project may not have been fully developed. Stakeholders may not fully understand all the requirements of the project and detailed functional features of all

the technological mechanisms to be deployed in the project may not have been known. Hence, privacy assessment of all the various components of the project, at this stage, is not feasible.

New projects afford an organization the opportunity to consider privacy requirements from the outset. As set out by local, national and international privacy agencies, privacy impact assessment is one way of ensuring that privacy concerns are addressed from the start of project initiation to the entire lifecycle risk management of the project. The fact that a project is new does not make privacy impact assessment of that project any easier compared to PIA assessment of an in-service project. As shown in Figure 1, the same framework is utilized to assess both new and existing projects.

Table 5. A comparison of privacy impact assessment of existing and new projects

Specific Issues to New and Existing Projects		
S/N	New Project	Existing Project
1	At the early stages of the project initiation phase, functional requirements of the different components of the project may not be known and well understood, hence privacy impact assessment of the project at this stage may be inconclusive.	Functional requirements are known, but the realisation that the project maybe combining multiple personal information identifiers may not have been considered.
2	Often, all the technologies, or mechanisms to be used in the project may not be properly identified, hence privacy assessment relating to technology or mechanism, or even the design cannot be properly evaluated.	Because the project is already in-service, even when privacy risks are identified, addressing all the identified risks may impact service, hence business needs often override privacy requirements.
3	Ownership of risk may become an issue, especially when information security roles and responsibilities have not been defined and agreed on.	Ownership of risk is also an issue with existing projects, especially when prior privacy risks have not been conducted.
4	Expertise in conducting privacy impact assessment for new projects within a single organisation (for example, small to medium-size organisation) is a challenge.	Expertise in conducting privacy impact assessment is also a challenge for existing projects, because: • Skills to do so may not exist within one organisation, and, • Expertise to assess existing projects, and manage relationships and interfaces that exist with in-service project can be onerous.
5	The scope or extent to which personal information to be collected will be processed (shared, stored, combined, exchanged) may not be known and well understood.	Where privacy impact assessment may reveal a high likelihood of privacy violation, business needs may override privacy requirements, especially if addressing privacy issues may result to service impacting consequences or significant financial expense.
6	The extent to which different personal information identifiers may be combined, processed or analysed may not be fully determined.	There may be a bias to suppress privacy risk in relation to business needs since privacy impact assessment was carried out retrospectively.
7	The justification of the project to service consumers (users of the systems, public or citizen) may not have been discussed or communicated to the public or wider service consumers.	The justification for existing projects are known, but the use of additional personal identifiers may have not been justified for existing projects, and when there is a scope change to existing project, this is not often communicated to the service consumers.

A major concern observed with most privacy impact assessments is that organisations do not often have the right mix of privacy skilled experts to carry out privacy impact assessments. Often, people with limited privacy expertise from varying but related disciplines such as information assurance, information security or information technology are asked to carryout privacy impact assessments. Our recommendation for organisations is to enlist the service of privacy experts to assist with PIA exercise, especially when large-scale PIA is recommended. A lesson learned from carrying out privacy impact assessments is that interpretation of privacy requirements does so often differ among stakeholders.

Table 5 provides some comparisons between PIA of new and existing projects. It is evident that there are issues that are common to both new and existing projects, such as compliance to privacy legislations and regulations. Nevertheless, there are issues that fall under one category but not the other. For example, privacy impact assessment of existing projects may require retrofitting of privacy, or risk acceptance of privacy non-compliant practices; whereas, for new projects, privacy considerations are recommended from the outset, hence retrofitting of privacy requirements are not applicable.

Risk Relating to Aggregation of Personal Identifiable Data

Personally identifiable information (PII) requires special handling/processing procedures in accordance to the Data Protection Act (DPA) Principles 1-8, the Privacy Act and other national and international privacy legislations. This is because the impact of privacy breaches to an individual, which could vary from prolonged personal distress to significant personal financial losses. Unfortunately, privacy breach of a project collecting PII data of citizens will impact a larger population of individuals, resulting to prolong distress to a population of individuals. The cumulative and interdependent risks resulting from the collection of significant number of aligned sensitive personal information data require proportionate risk mitigation procedures, and additional controls may seem plausible to address risk resulting from aggregation of these PII data. When carrying privacy impact assessment of a project, it is worth taking into consideration (at stage 2 of the PIA assessment) whether personal data from numerous data collectors or sources will be aggregated. That is when a significant number of personally identifiable information is collected or combined proportionate privacy-assurance controls should be required. For example, additional storage, processing and handling requirements may be needed.

Personally identifiable information requires special handling, sharing, storage and retention procedures. While these procedures are essential to protecting PIIs, additional handling and sharing procedures may be required if a significant amount of personal data is required. Further, if these information would be handled in new ways or ways that involved new linkages of personal data, additional controls should be used to address risks resulting from this new practice.

SOLUTIONS AND RECOMMENDATIONS

In this chapter guidance to conducting privacy impact assessment of both new and in-service projects are provided. Fundamentally, the Privacy Impact Suitability Assessment (PISA) framework is provided to enable organisations successfully carry out privacy impact assessment, knowing that every project should be assessed for privacy risks. The PISA framework is useful and straightforward to use and apply to any project with respect to privacy risks assessments.

To ensure PIA assessments are consistent and straightforward, we proposed the Privacy Screening Framework, which assists privacy assessors to assess projects prescriptively against all the seven categories of privacy risks. The PSF framework is flexible, adaptive and self-directing; which means that the person undertaking the assessment (assessor) can choose to adapt the framework to suit the needs of a particular project. The framework can be utilized and applied by any person. The framework is straightforward and derived based on lessons learned in carrying out PIA assessments for a number of organisations on a number of projects. Further to the frameworks provided, we provided the legal and privacy compliance check (see Table 3) to ensure consistency when assessing privacy regulations and directives compliance.

With the understanding that the earlier privacy assessment is planned in the project initiation programme the better the organization will be in addressing privacy requirements, issues or concerns. We recommend that privacy impact assessment should become an essential part of the risk management process of every project. We hope that this will help organisations plan PIA from the outset of the project, knowing that retrofitting of privacy assessment can be costly as we have seen with PIA assessment of in-service projects.

When planning privacy impact assessment, considerations should be made of risks resulting due to the sheer volume of personally identifiable information the project would process. And when data from different sources will be used, the impact of aggregation of these data should be considered. This should serve as an indicator as to when additional privacy controls may be required due to aggregation effect. Finally, we recommend that privacy impact assessment should be carried out by privacy experts within an organization, and where people with the right skills cannot be found, the services of external privacy agencies should be enlisted. There is new privacy legislation in the UK that empowers the UK Information Commissioner's Office to exact financial penalty to any organization in breach of privacy. This will, and has ushered a reawakening of privacy consciousness in organizations, especially, governmental organizations and agencies.

FUTURE RESEARCH DIRECTIONS

We plan to automate the PIA frameworks proposed in this chapter into a toolkit that will assist organizations when carrying out privacy risk assessments. The proposed toolkit will be available for download, or used from www.research-series.com. The provision of automated toolkits to assist with conducting PIA can be helpful, but the challenge will be on the coverage of relevant privacy legislations. This is because local or provincial privacy legislations are different among countries; hence, it will be challenging to cover all applicable privacy legislations in the toolkit.

CONCLUSION

In this chapter, we discussed the overriding benefits of Health IT, especially adoption of the electronic health records, providing very useful insights to Europe where EHRs are fully operational and functional. To assist with Health IT adoption in the US, especially encouraging public trust and confidence in EHR, we proposed a privacy impact assessment framework for managing privacy risks associated to the exchange, sharing and transmission of personally identifiable information. The privacy assessment framework aids to identifying and remedying privacy risks in Health IT. It provides assessments questions that can be tailored to any Health IT project in order to fully understand associated privacy risks and remediation plan.

The different issues relating to privacy impact assessment of new and in-service projects are demonstrated and discussed. It was found that in-service projects were challenging to be privacy assessed, and the outcome of privacy impact assessment to an in-service project could be insightful and expensive; and consequently could result to significant financial losses to the organization when found in breach of privacy. Privacy impact assessment frameworks were proposed, discussed and utilized to demonstrate their usefulness when conducting PIA assessments. Each aspect of the privacy framework was described such as the privacy impact suitability framework, legal and privacy compliance check and privacy screening framework. Finally, issues surrounding aggregation of personally identifiable information were discussed with the view to highlighting associated risks while recommending essential privacy controls to addressing these risks.

REFERENCES

Abu-Nimeh, S., & Mead, N. R. (2009). Privacy risk assessment in privacy requirements engineering. *2nd International Workshop on Requirements Engineering and Law*, *11*, 7-15.

HI TECH Act. (2010). *Health information technology for economic and clinical health act: Subtitle A, SEC 3000, definitions, 2009*. Retrieved from http://www.healthit.gov/sites/default/files/hitech_act_excerpt_from_arra_with_index.pdf

Agaku, I. T., Adisa, A. O., Ayo-Yusuf, O. A., & Connolly, G. N. (2014). Concern about security and privacy, and perceived control over collection and use of health information are related to withholding of health information from health care providers. *US National Library of Medicine, National Institutes of Health*. Retrieved from http://www.ncbi.nlm.nih.gov/pubmed/23975624/

British Broadcasting Corporation. (2014). *Care.data: How did it go so wrong?* Retrieved February 21, 2014 from http://www.bbc.co.uk/news/health-26259101

Cabinet Office. (2008). *The data handling procedure in government: Final report, June 2008*. Retrieved from http://www.cesg.gov.uk/products_services/iatp/documents/data_handling_review.pdf

NHS Database. (2014). *NHS bosses accused of 'climate of fear' over care data*. Retrieved from http://www.telegraph.co.uk/journalists/laura-donnelly/10628950/NHS-bosses-accused-of-climate-of-fear-over-care.data.html

Directive H. T. M. L. 2002/58/EC. (2002). *Protection of privacy to electronic communications*. Retrieved from http://eur-lex.europa.eu/LexUriServ/LexUriServ.do?uri=CELEX:32002L0058:EN:HTML

Directive 95/46/EC 1995. (n.d.). Directive 95/46/EC of the European Parliament and of the Council of 24 October 1995 on the protection of individuals with regard to the processing of personal data and on the free movement of such data. Retrieved from http://eur-lex.europa.eu/LexUriServ/LexUriServ.do?uri=CELEX:31995L0046:en

Educause. (2010). *Privacy risks assessment*. Retrieved from http://www.educause.edu/node/645/tid/30444?time=1281348515

Grady, D. (2010). *Study finds no progress in safety at hospitals*. Retrieved from http://www.nytimes.com/2010/11/25/health/research/25patient.html?_r=0

Gruteser, M., & Grunwald, D. (2004). A methodological assessment of location privacy risks in wireless hotspot networks in security in pervasive computing. *Lecture Notes in Computer Science*, (2802), 113–142.

HIPAA. (2006). *Saint Louis University institutional review board: HIPPA TIP sheet*. Retrieved from www.slu.edu/Documents/provost/irb/hipaa_tip_sheet.doc

HMG IA Standard No. 6. (2009). *Protecting personal data and managing information risk.* Cabinet Office, CESG National Technical Authority for Information Assurance, Issue 1.2.

Information Commissioner's Office. (2009). *Privacy impact assessment: Handbook version 2.0. appendix 1 – PIA screening process.* Retrieved from http://www.ico.gov.uk/upload/documents/pia_handbook_html_v2/html/3-app1.html

Lesk, M. (2013). Electronic medical records: Confidential, care and epidemiology. *IEEE Security & Privacy, Building Dependability, Reliability and Trust, 6*(11).

McGraw, D. (2013). Privacy and security as enabler, not barrier, to responsible health data uses. *IEEE Security & Privacy, Building Dependability, Reliability, and Trust, 6*(11).

Office of the National Coordinator for Health Information Technology. (2010). *Strategic health IT advanced research projects (SHARP).* Retrieved from http://www.healthit.gov/policy-researchers-implementers/strategic-health-it-advanced-research-projects-sharp

Onwubiko, C. (2011). Challenges to managing privacy impact assessment of personal identifiable data. In Information assurance and security technologies for risk assessment and threat management: Advances. Hershey, PA: IGI Global.

Peirce, T. (2009). RFID privacy & security. *IEEE International Conference on Communications, ICC, 24*, 11-15

Privacy by Design. (2014). *We must strongly protect privacy in electronic health records.* Retrieved from http://www.privacybydesign.ca/index.php/must-strongly-protect-privacy-electronic-health-records/

Radack, S. (2010). Guide to protecting personally identifiable information (PII). *NIST ITL Security Bulletin.* Retrieved from http://csrc.nist.gov/publications/nistbul/april-2010_guide-protecting-pii.pdf

Shane, D. (2010). *Zurich insurance hit with record data loss fine.* Retrieved from http://www.information-age.com/channels/security-and-continuity/news/1277718/zurich-insurance-hit-with-record-data-loss-fine.thtml

US-CERT. (2008). *Privacy impact assessment EINSTEIN program.* Department of Homeland Security, National Cyber Security Division, United States. Retrieved from http://www.dhs.gov/xlibrary/assets/privacy/privacy_pia_einstein2.pdf

KEY TERMS AND DEFINITIONS

Data Protection Act (DPA): This is a piece of legislation that governs how personal information of living individuals is processed. Processing of personal information means, how personal information are obtained, shared, recorded or stored (held). This piece of legislation was enacted in 1998 in the United Kingdom (UK).

Personal Data: Personal data is data that relates to a living person who can be identified by those data, or from those data plus other information which is in the possession of, or is likely to come into the possession of, the data controller. For example, first name, last name or/and date of birth of a living person.

Personal Identifiable Data (PID): These are sensitive and personal data that can be used to identify an individual. Personal identifiable data is the same as Personally Identifiable Information (PII), while the former is associated to Europe; the latter is associated with America. Examples of PII include a combination of one or more personal identifiers such as full face photographic images and any comparable images plus name, or date of birth plus address and health records. A full list of personal identifiers is shown in Table 1.

Sensitive Personal Data: These are identifiable personal data whose release would put those persons at significant risk of harm or distress, unless otherwise disclosed by the persons. For example, a person's medical records, bank details, social insurance number (national insurance) or tax records, etc.

Chapter 13
Do We Need Security Management Systems for Data Privacy?

Wolfgang Boehmer
Technische Universität Darmstadt, Germany

ABSTRACT

The importance of personal data and managing them is increasing worldwide. However first, one must be able to distinguish between data, information, and knowledge, before one turns to protecting them. Furthermore, it must be considered that, in open systems, security is a relative term and can be characterized only with the term risk. This suggests that security is not a state in open and dynamic systems but can only be maintained on a pre-defined level (conservation status) with a security management system. Data privacy therefore requires security management systems to ensure sustainable protection at a previously defined level. Pure guidelines and policies are just not sufficient for the protection of data in open systems, as is typical in companies.

INTRODUCTION: THINKING IN SYSTEMS

This contribution can be classified thematically to the field of Security Engineering. This assignment is based on both computer science and engineering alike. For this assignment, Ross Anderson provided an apt definition in his eponymous book.

Security Engineering is about building systems to remain dependable in the face of malice, error, or mischance. As a discipline, it focuses on the tools, processes, and method needed to design, implement, and test complete systems, and to adapt existing systems as their environment evolves (Anderson, 2008).

From the view of R. Anderson (2008), four interacting components are addressed, which are illustrated in Figure 1. Firstly, a policy is postulated that describes what can be achieved. On the other hand, so-called mechanisms are required in response to this that is necessary to enforce the policy. This could, for example, be cryptographic protocols, access configuration and access arrangements, tamper-resistant hardware, etc.

DOI: 10.4018/978-1-4666-7381-6.ch013

Figure 1. Security engineering framework based on policies (Anderson, 2006).

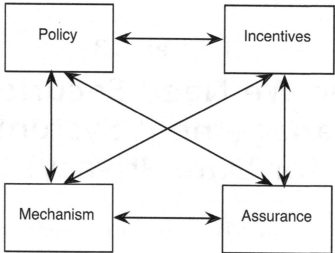

The third component is the assurance in these mechanisms, according to Anderson (2008), or the security, which is provided, by these mechanisms and the last component is addressed by the incentives. He considers the incentives from two perspectives. Firstly, from the perspective of the persons who want to protect themselves and secondly the group of people who try to circumvent these mechanisms in an unauthorized manner.

It is an interactive system, as illustrated by the cross-references (arrows) between the components.

A significant disadvantage of policies becomes apparent if they alone are used to secure the value chain of a company. This disadvantage is that the policies do not provide feedback about their effects. Especially in an open system such as a company, this lack of response has proved to be a disadvantage.

To assess the overall security of a company, it is invaluable to obtain feedback on security status, for only then can an adequate response be generated if necessary. As a suitable method for complete protection of a company, standardized management systems based on systems theory have become the established practice. Based on

the desire for complete security, for example in terms of the value chain, a universal framework for a risk-oriented management system can be outlined.

The framework is illustrated in Figure 2 based on the concept of systems theory. It is dominated by adjustments in response to perturbations (deviations) and shows policies and procedures as the dependent variables of the control loop. A disturbance will, in most cases, affect the value chain of the company. This point of view is aligned with overall enterprise security rather than with individual components.

Security is seen to be one facet of Quality of Service (QoS) and to include classical security goals such as confidentiality, availability, and integrity. All components of the framework are in constant interaction with each other. The aim of the management system as implemented is to adjust for deviations proactively; this is a typical case for an Information Security Management System (ISMS). However, if the risk decision for a specific deviation is to act reactively after the occurrence of the deviation, this is a typical task for a Business Continuity Management System (BCMS) argued Boehmer (2009b).

Figure 2. Security engineering system framework (Boehmer, 2011).

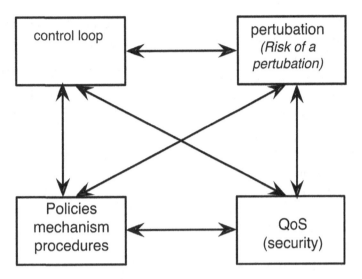

The previously addressed question of the distinction between the definition of policies and management systems with regard to their application leads to the discussion and definition of open, closed, and isolated systems. Originally, this systems concept was defined in thermodynamics, but it has now been transferred to information technologies and to companies. By analogy, the various types of systems can be described as follows:

- An example of an isolated system could be a single computer that is not networked and that does not communicate with its environment, e.g., with a user. Typical examples are embedded systems, which are implemented as autonomous systems.
- A computer connected with a network could represent a closed system. Important for a closed system is the exchange of data and information with its environment.
- An open system can be exemplified by a company, which exchanges matter (people, computers, materials) with its environment and is also linked with this environment. Companies are often described in the liter-

ature as open systems because they do not act independently, but are in many ways integrated into their environment and are therefore exposed to pressures and conditions that from the system viewpoint must be regarded as no modifiable (Leimer, 1990, p. 22). Moreover, Capra (1996) argued that organizations could be described as open systems from the point of view of systems theory.

The recognition that policies are well suited to secure isolated and closed systems has become prevalent over the last decade. However, in the case of open systems, such as companies, policies are not the ideal method. It has been shown that open systems such as companies can be better protected by a risk-based management system with a control loop than by policies. Control loops can be well described using discrete-event systems theory (DES), and many of the characteristics of control loops can be transferred directly to management systems. Control loops are widely used in engineering technology for purely technical systems. For socio-technical systems such as a value chain, the features and knowledge of control loops have been used only rarely.

In the following section, the relationship between management systems and systems theory is explained in more detail.

The definition of Matt Bishop (2004) goes beyond the concept of a system, which Matt Bishop has used for his definition of a policy. Bishops system limit refers to a computer. An expanded view of policies was created in 1995 by (Lindup, 1995). A policy for Matt Bishop is an axiomatic description. A policy is initially static in nature to encourage allowed states and discourage not-allowed states in a system, process, or object (Bishop, 2004). In his book, in section 4.1, Bishop describes a security policy as follows:

Security policy divides a system in authorized, or secure states $sZ = \{z_1, z_2\}$ and non-authorized or un-secure states $uZ = \{z_3, z_4\}$. A secure system is a system that starts to run in a secure state and is never able to change into an un-secure state.

Figure 3 sketches the different states of a system. A system is considered a computer, which is seen as a state machine. z denotes the single possible states $z_1, ..., z_n \in Z$ and $\partial = z_n \xrightarrow{\sigma_n} z_{n+1}$ denotes the transitions between the states. The exchange between two states e.g. z_1, z_2 is marked with black arrows labeled transitions σ_1, σ_2 as a secure transition. Correspondingly, transitions labeled with gray arrows show the uncertain transitions σ_3, σ_4.

On the basis of the possible changes of states of a system, different systems can be classified.

If all secure states are described by sZ, a security mechanism $N_{Ma} = \{m_1^{Ma}, ..., m_{Ma}^{Ma}\}$ can be defined as a set of appropriate measures. These N_{Ma} limit the system on the set of secure states sZ. With $sZ \subseteq Z$ and $|N_{Ma}|$ describes the cardinality of the subset of $Z' \subseteq Z$. With these elements one can define a secure, a precise and a vague system:

- **Secure System (sS):** The system can reach only the states of z_n, which satisfy the condition $Z' \subseteq sZ$. The measures $|N_{Ma}|$ ensure that a subset of possible states, $Z' \subseteq sZ$, of all possible states Z are secure.

- **Precise System (pS):** The system can reach only the states of z_n, which satisfy the condition $Z' \subseteq sZ$. Actually, the definitions above should be declared as a precise and a secure system, because only those states z_n will be reached for which the requirement is that the subset $z_n \in Z'$ coincide exactly with the set of secure states $z_n \in sZ$.

- **Vague System (vS):** The system can reach only the states of z_n, which satisfy the condition $z_n \in Z'$ and $z_n \notin sZ$. With the definition vS, a vague and possibly also an insecure system is described for the

Figure 3. Secure and unsecure states (Bishop, 2004).

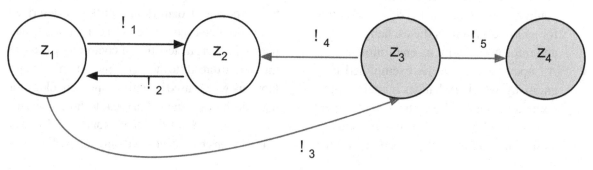

states reached Z_n, because the states Z_n are not in the subset of the secure states sZ, but in the subset Z'. The subset Z' is associated with the $\left| N_{Ma} \right|$. This expresses that the measures, or part of the measures, are not sufficient to limit the states sZ to the states Z. Consequently, there may be a shortage.

While a system is postulated with the three definitions sS, pS, vS, the system, however, is not specified. Likewise, no statement is made on the time period the system has, does not have, or hopes to achieve these properties. Furthermore, no statement was made regarding by what methods the measures $\left| N_{Ma} \right|$ should be identified. We will come back later to this point in the discussion of the measures and methods for achieving a secure state.

Furthermore, it was stated earlier that the system is a computer. However, other IT objects could also be subsumed in a system. To specify the term of the system in more detail, we will make a classification of possible systems below.

In the context of this work, the notion of a system - similar to that of Anderson (2008) is expanded and borrowed more from the field of physics (thermodynamics). In thermodynamics, three different systems (definition of iS, cS and oS) are defined:

- **Isolated Systems** (iS): Neither exchanging of asset nor flow of information. A system that exchanges neither matter (assets) nor energy (information) with its environment.
- **Closed Systems** (cS): No exchanging of assets but flow of information. A system that does not exchange assets but exchanges information with its environment.
- **Open System** (oS): Exchanging of assets and flow of information. A system that does exchange assets and information with its environment.

- **Behavior Systems** (bS): Flow of information between subjects. A system behavior is influenced by the interaction of subjects that exchange information.

The term asset is taken from ISO 27001:2005. In the context of this contribution, asset is treated as a made-up word, which include roles and resources.

The affinity with the computer science systems iS, cS, bS is established via the second law of thermodynamics (entropy) according to Shannon (1948), in which an energy exchange can be interpreted as an information exchange.

But the system bS according to the definition of a behavior system cannot be derived from thermodynamics. The inclusion of behavioral systems in information security is a relatively new branch and is dominated by the game theory. We will investigate the behavioral systems using, as an example, the route of infection of the virus "Stuxnet".

Under a closed (isolated) system (iS) in the sense of definition of a isolated system, a computer could be understood which is not cross-linked and does not communicate with its environment, e.g. with a user or another computer (e.g. router, firewall, etc.). On the other hand, a closed system (cS) according to the Definition above could be represented by a networked computer, which shares data and information over the network with its environment (communication partners).

A company can be understood as an open system (oS) according to the definition above, because it exchanges matter (people, computers, equipment) with its environment and is also linked its environment. Regarding companies open systems is widespread in the literature. Companies or Organizations in general are open systems, because they do not act independently, but are in many ways integrated into the environment and thereby exposed to constraints and conditions that are normally regarded as unchangeable by the system itself (Leimer, 1990, p. 22). Organizations are described as open systems in systems theory, such as Capra (1984, 1997) wrote in the mid-eighties. A system is a whole, consisting of sub-systems and can be distinguished from other systems. It draws the environmental inputs that are transformed into outputs. These act on other sub-systems and the environmental system and thus contribute to the objective of the overall system. Furthermore, F. Capra states, the organizational systems exhibit features as they appear in scientific systems. The realization that a company is a system is discussed in economics much later by Wilms (2003, p. 6).

In terms of computer science, the concept of matter can also be considered an asset (resource, role). Based on this idea, the terms IT security (security of information technology) and information security (security of data and information) are distinguishable.

For closed systems (cS) according to the definition above, as previously outlined by the IT objects. This means that in the context of IT security, there are therefore sufficient definitions to protect the IT infrastructure of a company and to put it into a secure state (sS). With this view of closed systems, securing a computer can be done through measures. If the development of regulations and standards for IT security are considered against this background, it becomes clear that these were purely driven by (technical) measures in the years 1990 - 2005. Mention should be made, for example, of RFC 2196 (IETF, 1997) and its predecessor RFC 1244 (IETF, 1991), as well as the regulations ITSEC (1991) or the British Standard BS7799-1 (1995). In Germany, this development was forced by the IT Baseline Protection Manual controls. It is essentially about security policies and security mechanisms that are mainly established on IT assets.

In this decade, it was first attempted to incorporate this policy-based perspective in the whole infrastructure of the company. But a purely policy-based security infrastructure is without economic

efficiency. Furthermore it is an open system and not a closed system. The limits of this development became more obvious at the end of the 90s more by many companies, the consequence being that the IT departments were converted for economic reasons into independent legal bodies. As an example, In Germany, one can name DREGIS (Dresdner Bank IT service), AGIS (Allianz Group IT Services), BIS (BASF IT Services), etc. These spin-offs triggered rethinking. A novel development of so-called management systems started and still continues today. Management systems seem to be better suited for safeguarding enterprises, according to present knowledge, as pure policy-based rules. However, to date, these management systems defy formal description.

Although thinking in systems is described extensively in the literature, these ideas are hardly used in companies. Representative of this is the popular book by Donella H. Meadows (1993). She wrote the following about systems:

A system isn't just any old collection of elements of thinks. A system is an interconnected set of elements that is coherently organized in a way that achieves something. A system must consist three kinds of thinks: elements, interconnections, and function or purpose... the word function is generally used for nonhuman systems, the word purpose is used a human one, but the distinction is not absolute, since so many systems have both human and nonhuman elements (Meadows, 1993).

Turning to corporate security, it is clear that the systems theory is not the basis of safeguarding of enterprise architectures. It can be stated that currently security concepts are used for safeguarding corporate and industrial systems and the system theory plays little to no role in this.

Furthermore, it can be shown that good security concepts cannot be reduced to only a list of measures; the security measures listed in the concepts are always a result of an underlying method.

A plethora of articles about the development of security concepts can be found in the literature. The control objectives pursued within security concepts are also discussed variously and differently in the literature. A number of control objectives stemming from different perspectives can be found. However, the security concept rooted in standards e.g. ISO 27001 stem from three main objectives (availability, confidentiality, integrity). In addition to these three core objectives, however, other goals, such as authenticity, anonymity, privacy, etc. are also often addressed. The three main objectives are described below:

- **Availability:** It is an agreement regarding the availability of a file, information, services or property for a certain percentage per year. That means the expression 97% availability with respect to 365 days means that if 10 days of outage are recorded, the percentages for a service are fulfilled.
- **Confidentiality:** Is not expressed as a percentage, but it as a binary variable. The confidentiality is either given or not. Intermediate values cannot exist. Main mechanisms for protecting confidentiality in information systems are cryptography and access controls.
- **Integrity:** Is to be understood, like confidentiality, as a binary variable. The integrity either exists or not. Intermediate values cannot exist. Integrity is concerned with the trustworthiness, origin, completeness, and correctness of information, as well as the prevention of improper or unauthorized modification of information.

The three above-mentioned control objectives cannot be run in a prosaic way for use in the modeling of a security concept. Therefore, the control objectives and their behavior will also be investigated.

The three control objectives behave in a communication relationship as random variables in a probability space. With proper security concepts those control objectives can be protected from risk of breach.

Now if the confidentiality [Conf] and integrity [Int] are seen as discrete sets of random variables in a probability space, it is possible to describe these two security objectives as the sets of given indicator functions.

Due to the binary property of the two subsets [Int], [Conf] with [Int], $\subseteq X$ and [Conf] $\subseteq X$, for every x on [0,1], which $x \subseteq X$ for is 1 when $x \subseteq$ [Int] or $x \subseteq$ [Conf], otherwise $x = 0$ It is

$$X \rightarrow \left[0,1\right], x \mapsto \begin{cases} 1, if(x) \in Int \\ 0, if(x) \notin Int \end{cases}$$

Also [Int] can be used for the random variable [Conf], if we used [Conf] instead [Int], then we can derive

$$X \rightarrow \left[0,1\right], x \mapsto \begin{cases} 1, if(x) \in Conf \\ 0, if(x) \notin Conf \end{cases}$$

Thus, the binary properties of the two discrete random variables are formally described. In this contribution we write $\mathbf{1}_{Int}$ for the discrete indicator function, integrity, and $\mathbf{1}_{conf}$ to use the discrete indicator function confidentiality.

It is different with the availability (Av), which can be formally described as a Complete Partial Order, *CPO*. With a *CPO* we can easily find intermediate values in the interval [0,1] in R$^+$ which are the subject of a binary relation. A binary relation over the set (Av) availability of all elements is a partial order, if a,b $\in$(Av) and a $\leq$ b holds. We use the following notation in this paper

$$(Av \leq) \mapsto \left[a \leq b\right] \text{ or short (Av).}$$

The control objectives are linearly independent of each other. Linear independence is expressed through a vector space over a body and an index set. In this context, the control objectives are considered vectors on a time axis (365 days). Thus, the value of the vectors by the equations [Int], [Conf] and (Av) and the direction is defined by the time axis t ∈ T with T = 365 days. Often, the period T, or one year, is understood as the planning horizon. This makes it possible to formulate the following definition.

Linear independence of the protection goals] The protection goals of confidentiality (1_{conf}), integrity (1_{Int}) and availability (Av) behave as vectors on a time axis (t) and are linearly independent.

Finally a security concept [SecCon] is the illustration of the measures (N_{Ma}) and integrity (1_{Int}), confidentiality (1_{conf}), and (Av) and the map to the Information Security Management System (ISMS)

$$SecCon|NMa|: = ISMS\ ((Av),\ (1_{Int}),\ (1_{conf})) \mapsto \Psi$$

for a system $(oS, cS, iS, bS) \mapsto \Psi$.

However, the security concepts are not only the power of the measures $|N_{Ma}|$ for reducing the risk of a possible breach of the three security objectives for a system, but it is necessary that the measures $|N_{Ma}|$ were developed using a methodology like an ISMS. The ISMS must be able to map the different risk types according to the underlying (open, closed, isolated) systems. So, the identified measures $|N_{Ma}|$ included in a security concept based on a ISMS (see the definition later on). With reference to equation SecCon|N$_{Ma}$|, it's possible to define the following statement for the three main protection goals for a common security concept:

- **Common Security Concept:** A security concept includes measures $|N_{Ma}|$ to ensure the security objectives of confidentiality,

availability and integrity for a system (oS, cS, iS, bS) aligned to a predefined level.

With the aid of the different defined and addressed systems, a differentiation between IT security and information security can be formulated.

- **IT Security:** Is characterized by the attempt to adhere to the control objectives of confidentiality, integrity and availability with respect to a predefined level for one or more closed system (IT object) or IT assets.

Here, the term IT object refers to communication objects from, for example, computers, active and passive network elements as well as firewall systems and web servers, to name but a few. If the term policies is applied in the classic definition by Matt Bishop on a closed system, as applied to a computer, it quickly becomes clear that this is a conductive definition of policies for closed systems.

For the present contribution, the application of IT security, which is closely linked with the development and application of security policies, is therefore not the focus. It is about the security of information flows in open systems, such as in companies. We call this enterprise security.

While IT security provides a set of methods and procedures that are established, a similar approach has not yet been explored in the field of information security. IT Security is focused on the IT assets and information security is focused on the information flows within an organization. However, information flow models relevant to the information flows within a company have not yet been developed, even though there are the traditional methods of Bell and LaPadula, describing a state-based machine as a theoretical model. This model is intended to get access to confidential information. Furthermore the integrity-oriented models of BiBa and Clark & Wilson (1987) also exist; however, information flows are not yet modeled for a whole company. Currently based in the company's approach the theory is to disturb and treat this disturbance with so-called management systems.

Often in this context the term Enterprise Security or Enterprise Security Management (ESM) is used to describe the safeguarding of a whole company. Similarly, the term Enterprise Architecture is used for enterprise-wide communication structures. In the application of open systems, it is therefore appropriate to speak about information security. The concept of information security is broader and includes IT security. Thus, the information security is defined as follows:

- **Information Security:** Is characterized by the attempt to adhere to the control objectives of confidentiality, integrity and availability with respect to a predefined level for an open system on an enterprise level. Furthermore, the information and the flow of information are independent from any media (object).

The development of management systems with a focus on IT security and information security began in the late 90s and continues today. This is partly because the concepts of the IT security and information security have not yet been differentiated and on the other hand, the term of the management system has not been specified using formal methods. This is reflected by the fact that information security management systems are used incorrectly for IT security. It can be shown in many examples in the economy, but also observed in the doctrine, that this misapplication is still widespread. But the opposite can be also observed when a management system for IT security is used for information security. The IT Baseline Protection Manual (ITGSHB) is one example. ITGSHB is called IT Baseline

Protection Manual since the 2006-year version. The IT Baseline Protection Manual includes a catalog of hazards and measures related mainly to IT assets.

Figure 4 is the result of trying to qualitatively illustrate the relationship between IT Security and Information Security and Privacy in the context of an open system such as a Company. The shaded area represents the company and receives information, data and assets from the environment as input. After processing in the value chain, the input leaves the Company also as information, data and assets.

It is important to note that the information, data and asset flows go beyond the borders of the Company. Furthermore, it is seen that the information security surrounds IT security. Privacy issues are also illustrated; these go beyond the IT security, but not beyond the information security.

In this contribution the basic assumption is:

- **Enterprise Security Management (ESM):** In open systems alone are not sufficient as either static or dynamic policies to maintain a given level of security for a certain (long) period. In open systems, it is more conducive to act contrary to a control system and risk-oriented management system to effectively and efficiently achieve a planned level of security.
- **Information Security Management System (ISMS):** An ISMS is characterized by set points in open systems for confidentiality, availability, integrity to eliminate disturbances or disruption risks on a value chain (controlled system) in an effective and / or efficient way. It is a feedback- and risk-based control system that works stably and robustly to meet the pre-defined level of security in a range of tolerance.

Figure 4. IT security vs. information security in an open system

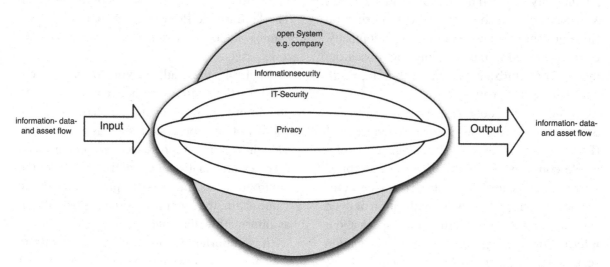

Definition for an ISMS is a modification of Equation SecCon|NMa|, because in a process-oriented management of a company two other control objectives have to be taken also into account.

First is the process quality Pq, which behaves as a partial order. This can be formulated analogous to the availability according to equation (Pq) as follows:

$$(Pq \leq) \mapsto \left[a \leq b\right] \text{ or short } (Pq \leq)$$

Six Sigma can be viewed as one of the methods for the optimization of the process quality, Pq Six Sigma is a statistical quality method and is based on a standardized normal distribution. Meanwhile, Six Sigma is used not only in production but also in software development. Six Sigma is a systematic approach to improving processes (business processes, emergency processes, software development processes), using analytical and statistical methods. Like the presented thesis, this perturbation theory and system theory is used for the improvement of security management systems based also on mathematical methods. It is assumed in both methods (Six Sigma and Management systems) that each business process can be described as a mathematical function.

Thus, for example, these methods go beyond the maturity model (CMMI) of Carnegie Mellon University. Second, it is the process cycle time, Pt, which is important for the value chain of a company. The process cycle time can again be seen as a partial order. This can be defined analogous to the process quality (Pq $\leq$) according to equation (Pt $\leq$) as follows:

$$(Pt \leq) \mapsto \left[a \leq b\right] \text{ or short } (Pt \leq)$$

The process cycle times (Pt) are closely linked to the overall business success. If the process time is too slow or even stops, business continuity methods are required. Here, the business continuity methods are part of a Business Continuity Plan (BCP) to a Business Continuity Management System (BCMS), such as BS 25999. If process cycle time stops, the MTPD (maximum tolerable period of disruption) starts to run.

Using equation [SConE] one can formulate a company-wide (enterprise) security concept with the measures |NMa| for an arbitrary system $(oS, cS, iS, bS) \mapsto \Psi$, taking into account the definitions SecCon, Pq, Pt according to equation

SecConE|NMa|: = ISMS ((Av), (1Int), (1conf),
(Pq $\leq$), (Pt $\leq$)) $\mapsto \Psi$.

Using equation [SConE] we can describe the following definition of an Enterprise Security Concept:

A company-wide security concept [SConE] includes measures to ensure the control objectives of confidentiality, availability, integrity, process-quality and process cycle time for a system Ψ to a predefined level.

We will show later that risk indicators can be defined with the variables specified in the company-wide security concept [SConE] with the partially ordered set ($Av \leq$, Pq $\leq$), (Pt $\leq$)).

Furthermore in this contribution, the basic theory and the definition of ISMS are discussed, both from the theoretical as well as its application-specific view and differentiated from the properties and applications of policies.

In the contribution a secure system [sS] and definition for ISMS, a security level (pre-defined level) is addressed. However, the detailed specification is still an open issue. The desire to develop a metric or a security measure for information security or IT security is covered in the literature by several publications, e.g. to name a few by Jaquith (2007) and Conway (1972). However, so far no satisfactory definition of a metric has established itself in IT/Information security. This could be due to the mandatory requirement of a measure of the IT/Information security.

MEASURING SECURITY INDIRECTLY BY THE RISK

The complementary relationship between security and risk for a system Ψ is reflected in an IT/Inf. security concept. This complementary relationship is that the lower the security (Sec), the higher the risk (Risk) of a violation of the three control objectives for a system $(oS, cS, iS, bS) \mapsto \Psi$; therefore risk and security are negatively correlated. Figure 5 illustrated this relationship qualitatively.

To describe this negative correlation in a formal way, risk and security simplified are normalized by the interval [0,1]. For the interval [0,1] the limits 0 and 1 must be set. In the case where the safeguarding of a company reaches the value of 1, this is equivalent to saying that a company cannot act irreversibly, or the company is in the state of a bankruptcy.

$$Sec = (1 - Risk)[R^-] \mapsto \Psi$$

Two extreme (theoretical) situations for IT/Inf.-Security (Sec) can be carved out using definition [Security]. For the case in equation IT/Inf.- security, Sec = 0 would be given, if all risks could occur and no security concept exists for the prevention of the risks

$$Sec = \begin{cases} 0, if(Risk) = 1 \\ > 0 \leq 1, otherwise \end{cases}$$

The opposite theoretical case could occur, if the assumption was that all possible risks would be treated preventively, so that they may not strike. Then, the case would be that the IT/Inf.- security would be equal to 100%, that is Sec = 1 in the following equation

$$Risk = \begin{cases} 0, if(Sec) = 1 \\ > 0 \leq 1, otherwise \end{cases}$$

These two considerations (equation $Sec, Risk$) and Figure 4 consider two extreme theoretical situations that will probably rarely arise in practice. So the option (otherwise) primarily remains from equations Sec and $Risk$, which we will discuss in more detail in this chapter.

Figure 5. Security versus risk

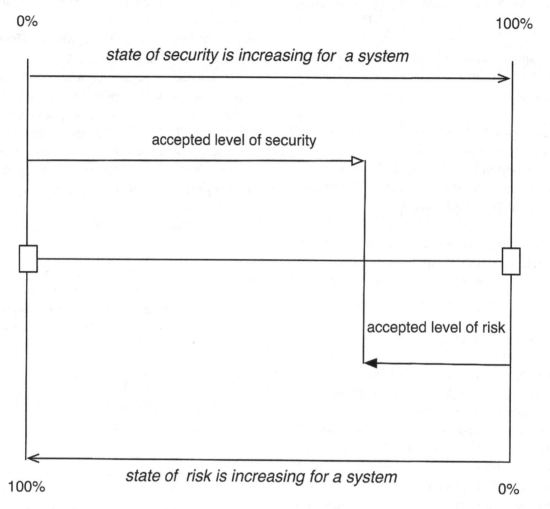

The risk in the sense of operational risk[1] is obtained as the probability (Pr) of an event (E) on the impact on a system, e.g. on an open system (oS) as a value chain with a negative outcome (Loss, L) in monetary units (€), in R⁻ see [Giacometti et al. 2008]. This relationship can be expressed as follows:

$$Risk = (\mathrm{Pr}_E \times L)[R^-] \mapsto \Psi .$$

This definition was developed in line with the article by Courtney (1977). In his article R. Courtney defined the fundamental relationship between risk, probability and impact (cost) as a cross product for a one year time period. However, the relationship is defined independent of any system – unlike the equation for the risk [Risk]. In the equation [Risk] the risk acts on a set of systems $(oS, cS, iS, bS) \mapsto \Psi$. Baskerville (1993) drew an extensive discussion of methods and procedures in the field of information security in his literary work. The relationship between risk processes and systems is illustrated in Figure 4. The relationship shown there will be explored in more detail in this chapter.

With our definition of security (see [Sec]) and risk (see [RISK]) the thoughts of R. Courtney and R. Baskerville are expanded upon. The risk [Risk] is regarded as a random variable in a probability space. A random variable $X : \Omega \to R$ is a measurable function on a probability space, if it satisfies the triple $\Omega, A(\Omega), P$. Where P called the power set and $A(\Omega)$ is a σ-algebra. In other words, this means that if a random variable X obeys the conditions of a σ-algebra, a measurement of the random variable X is possible. Above, it was explained that the control objectives behave as random variables. When the non-empty set G of measurable random variables obey a σ-algebra and can be assigned to a probability measure P, we can define a risk metric ρ for Ω as a set of results.

$$\rho : G \rightarrow R^-$$

Thus, the random variables in G on the probability space $\Omega, A(\Omega), P$ describe the potential harm in the field of IT/Inf.- Security for a given time interval $t \in T$.

The set A is a σ-algebra, which can be viewed as a subset in a probability space, leads directly to the measure theory, which has set itself the task of generalizing the elementary geometrical concepts such as path length, surface area and volume, to allow this complex to assign a measure quantities. The quantities to be measured are summarized in set systems, which are different when finished strong against set operations.

The power set P is the most comprehensive set of all measure systems and contains any subset A over the ground set Ω. On the other hand, the σ-algebra[2] is the most important class of sets of measure theory, which is closely associated with the power set. Using the σ-algebra, it is possible to define measurable quantities. A measurable set of random variables in probability space leads to a risk metric. The risk metric for a random variable $\rho(X)$ requires four characteristics to be satisfied to meet two random variables (X, Y). A risk metric provides information about the quantification of risk exposure.

A frequently used metric of risk is described by the variance of a random variable in probability space. Because the variance represents the average of the squared deviations from the average of a random variable X (Artzner et al., 2001). The universal risk measure, the variance, which is also known as Value at Risk (VaR) and its coherent version (C-VaR), can be used both for market and financial risks, as well as for operational risks, because it is possible to control a company by the risk and determine the risks on the same risk metric.

In this contribution, the risk is used as a metric for the provision of IT/Inf.- security as described in definition [Sec]. In the article by Saydjari (2006), the question of whether the risk is an appropriate metric for the provision of IT/Inf.- security is pursued. In his paper, he discussed the number of attacks as a metric, compliance criteria, intrusion detection based measurements, as well as fault-based incidents. Finally, there six general conclusions he drew for a good metric, which should be mentioned here.

1. The right things must be measured (to eventually be able to make a decision).
2. There must be a quantifiable metric (It can be expressed in monetary units as profit or loss, generally (R).
3. An accurate measurement must be possible.
4. There must be a validation against a basic assumption (ground truth).
5. There must be a cost/benefit-driven implementation.
6. An independent review must be possible.
7. It must be possible to repeat the results.

The requirements above of number 1 to 4 relate directly to the metric and the number 5 to 8, according to Saydjari (2006), are desirable properties. It should be noted at this point that the risk measure, as defined in equation [risk], satisfies all these requirements and also the desirable properties of number 5 to 8.

If one still considers that the risk in Basel II is used as a metric, and this has received a correspondingly wide acceptance in the financial services sector, it is concluded that only the risk is to be used as an accepted practice.

If the definition of risk [risk] is used in the definition of the security [Sec], then the following equation can be derived.

$$Sec = (1 - (\Pr_E \times L)[R^-] \mapsto \Psi$$

With the equation above, it can be expressed that the IT/Inf.- security is negatively correlated and spanned in the two-dimensional space by the cross product of probability and damage, and the values of security and risk moves (see Figure 5) within the interval [0,1]. Thus, security can be measured indirectly by measuring the risk.

A quantification of a random variable $X \in G$ (see equation [rho]) is performed formally by assigning a value x for a range of values W using a certain event E. For the random variable X the image of a discrete probability space then applies to the discrete result set $\Omega = \{\omega_1, \omega_2, ...,\}$ such that $X : \Omega \to \mathrm{Re}$ with Re = real number. For discrete random variables for the discrete value range that is interpreted in the context of operational risk as a monetary loss (L)

$$Lx = Wx := X(\Omega) = \{x \in \mathrm{Re} \mid \exists \omega \in \Omega\} \text{ with } X(\omega) = x$$

In the field of operational risks, the probability ($\Pr$) with the random variable (X) which may accept certain values (Wx) and losses (Lx) is of interest. For any event (E) with $1 \leq i \leq n$ and $x_i \in \mathrm{N}$:

$$E_i := \{\omega \in \Omega \mid X(\Omega) = x_i\} = \Pr[\{\omega \in \Omega \mid X(\omega) = x_i\}]$$

Since, in this context, only numerical random variables are considered, each random variable can be assigned to two real functions. We assign any real number (x) the probability that the random variable takes that value or a maximum of such a great value. Then the function [fx] with

$$f_x : \mathrm{Re} \to [0,1], x \mapsto \Pr[X = x]$$

is called a discrete (exogenous) density (function) of X. Furthermore, a distribution function [Fx] is defined with

$$Fx : \mathrm{Re} \to [0,1], x \mapsto \Pr[X \leq x]$$
$$\sum_{x \in L_x : x' \leq x} \Pr[X = x']$$

The value (Wx) can have both positive and negative values, depending on which is discussed in the context, the density or the distribution of values.

The equations [fx] and [Fx] are based on an existing exogenous set of data. In the field of finance and the insurance industry this is often given, but often not in the IT/Inf.- security fields. This fact is already recognized in Basel II, the ambitious approach (AMA) (see Figure 6). Against this background, the scenario technique has been established as an adequate tool.

THE INFLUENCE OF BASEL II ON IT/INF. SECURITY

A general, colloquial definition of the term risk (see definition [risk]) is written in the minimum requirements for risk management (German abbreviation is MaRisk) according to the BaFin.

Risk is understood as the possibility of not reaching an explicitly formulated or implicitly defined objective. All risks identified by the management

Figure 6. Different causes for operational risk according to BASEL II

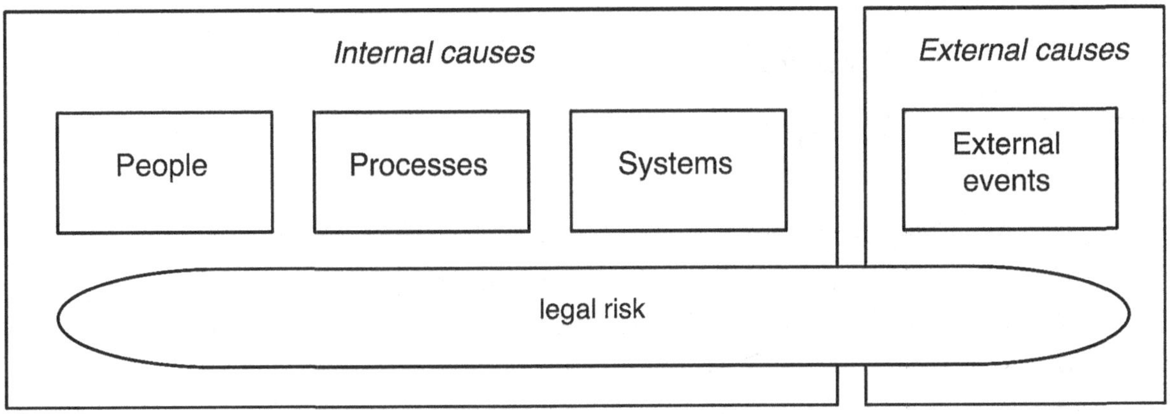

that present a lasting negative impact on the economic, financial position or results of the company may have to be considered as much as possible.

These statements above are made in accordance with BASEL II. We will discuss BASEL II and the so-called operational risks (see Figure 5) later in more detail.

A generally accepted definition of risk areas has been made with Basel II. It assigns all the risk areas that are not unique to the market and financial risks to operational risks.

... the risk of loss resulting from inadequate or failed internal processes, people and systems from external events, including legal risk but not strategic and reputational risk.

The Figure 6 sketches the definition of the operational risk in accordance with the Committees of Basel.

If the legal risk is excluded for the time being, processes, systems and people (actors) in the systems or processes remain so for the operational risks, the internal causes. Thus, makes sense to carry out a business process analysis, at least for the critical business processes.

However, the trend most recently observed in the banks, is that the banks want meet not only the purely regulatory requirements under Basel II in the area of operational risk, but they are increasingly involving commercial aspects. The trend of increasing use of the Advanced Measurement Approach (AMA) under Basel II is easily visible compared to the previous use of the Basic Indicator Approach (BIA) or the even simpler standardized approach (STA).

A similar trend can also be observed in the industry, in which the management systems for corporate safeguarding that involve a risk assessment are preferred. The increasing number has for example, seen this significant trend each year since 2005 of about 1000 certificates[3] against ISO/IEC 27001:2005 in 2011 a new version was created by the. More than 20000 certificates have been registered as of 2014 worldwide a number that had increased by more than 10% since the year before. The realization that risk management is not an end in itself, but represents a key instrument to assist management in achieving corporate goals has been establishing itself more and more. This is particularly true for operational risk.

In the general definition of the risk according to eq. [risk], both state risk (event risk) and risk behavior (behavioral risk) are subsumed. They differ in the influence exerted by a person on the result. If a person (role) influences the risk, we are referring to behavioral risks. In the absence of human influence we are referring to state risks that are analyzed using stochastic risk theory. The stochastic risks put forward an exogenous density function,

Figure 7. Sketch of the ambitious measurement approach

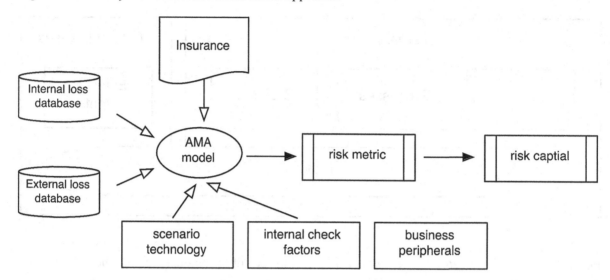

argued Alchian et al. (1983) in his paper. For the purposes of ISO/IEC 27001 and the requirements defined therein, an *Information Security Management System* must consider both types of risk in the management system.

Consequently the standard ISO 27001:2005 addressed the operational risks in the sense of Basel II. The standard defines the objectives clearly For the purpose of ISO27001 in its Section 1.1:

Citation ISO/IEC 27001:2005, Section 1.1: This International Standard specifies the requirements for establishing, implementing, operating, monitoring, reviewing, maintaining and improving a documented ISMS within the context of the organization's overall business risks.

From the above citation, it is clear that from the perspective of Basel II, operational risks (OpRisk) are inherently connected with the business and are not purposely pursued, unlike e.g. market risks and financial risks. Sufficient capital must be provided to combat these inherent operational risks by the requirement of the Basel Committees (Basel II).

The Figure 7 sketches, in a block diagram, the elements belonging to the ambitious measurement approach. In the environment of the banks the value

at risk (VaR) and an improved variant the conditional Value at Risk (CVaR) are generally used.

The ISO/IEC 27001 provides the necessary reference to the business goals. For the control of a company merely a pure analysis of risks (ISO 27005) is not very helpful. Therein lies the connection between ISO/IEC 27001 and ISO/IEC 27005. A concrete indication of how to deal with the consideration of business processes related to ISO/IEC 27001 is described in ISO/IEC 27003.

To secure the business processes of a company, the security concept, see eq. [SecCon] on page respectively [SConE], with the protection of the confidentiality, integrity and availability of various means of safeguarding practices (policies and management systems) is used for isolated, closed and open systems.

The causes or events (see equation [Ei]) which can lead to a state of risk, typically in the range of frequent low-scale up to the rare-scale, events with severe consequences can be transcribed. Preferably, the rare events are put through a continuity plan (business continuity plan BCP). The extremely rare risks are often analyzed using extreme value theory (EVT) according to the Fisher-Tippet-Gnedenko theorem. The frequent events, however, can be countered by means of

ISMS according to ISO/IEC 27001. For the purely behavioral risks, the mathematical game theory of the potential behavior of the actors offers lessons to learn, which in turn can then be incorporated into a security concept.

In the context of this contribution, market and financial risks are neglected, so that we analyze only the operational risks. Returning to Figure 5 it is thus clear that the state of security (see definition [Sec]) and risk (see definition [risk]) must determined by the company itself. In other words, on an enterprise level, security management is the equivalent of risk management. The risk treatment is enforced with a control system (closed loop), which is converted to a subsystem level or at an object level through appropriate policies, mechanisms and procedures.

This section can finally be summarized as follows. Companies are open systems, which in turn consist of systems and subsystems. For safeguarding a company, Enterprise Security Management Systems (ESM) is necessary to consider individual risks related to the value chain, systems and people. To control the risks, the company is required to quantify and possibly aggregated them on a risk measure when different business units should be considered from a management level.

THEMATIC DISCUSSION

From the perspective of the overall safeguarding of a company and protection of data privacy the two types, the static and the dynamic policies, have the same disadvantage: they do not provide feedback on its effect. Thus superior control ability is lacking in the corporate management.

It can be observed that in order to safeguard a company, management systems will use in accordance with e.g. ISO 27001, BS25999 and ISO/IEC 20000, which follow the Deming cycle (Plan-Do-Check-Act). The increasing number of global certifications demonstrates the importance of these management systems. The ISO 27001 standard provides requirements for an Information Security Management System (ISMS) and the BS 25999 Business Continuity Management System (BCMS) and the ISO 20000 describe an IT Service Management (ITSM). These management systems are described by the Deming cycle (PDCA cycle); they depict a continuous improvement cycle. However, to date, there is no formal description of these management systems.

The aforementioned security management systems to the ISO 27001, BS25999 and ISO 20000 can be described as best practice procedures. Best practice methods often play an important role at the beginning of a new technological development. They are a temporary solution to the mathematical method, when the overall trend is seen in retrospect. A similar development can be, from the perspective of the author, observed for information security management systems. The time has come to change from the pure best practice to procedures that supported on mathematical methods.

A first step towards to a formal description of management systems was discussed in the paper by Boehmer (2010). He shows how the theory of discrete-event control circuits for technical systems and socio-technical systems, such as the above management systems can be transferred. It has been shown how the transition from a dynamic policy to a feedback policy can be understood. In addition, feedback policies can be interpreted as management systems, because it can show, with the method of bi-simulation between the Deming cycle and a control loop, if they are expressed as standard machines. At first glance, the above Management systems have similarities, but also differences with the technical control circuits of discrete event systems theory (DES).

Policies with feedback have, in general, been under-appreciated in computer science research. In contrast, control system engineering research regularly implements control loops with built-in feedback capabilities to monitor technical systems, and these loops can be modeled by the framework of discrete event systems (DES) theory. In systems theory, the concept of the signal and the system is fundamental. This thesis focuses mainly on discrete signals (disturbances) and discrete systems. In the simplest case, it is a system known as an input / output control circuit (IO-automaton, as is shown in Figure 7, upon which a discrete disturbance acts.

The control loops are composed of four elements connected sequentially to form a loop: the control system, the sensor, the controller, and the actuator. In general, control system engineering is a discipline that mathematically models diverse systems in nature by analyzing their dynamic behavior. Control theory is applied to create a controller mechanism that shifts the system behavior in a desired manner. Control loops have gained far-reaching significance because they are not purely technical models; the control loops define general organizing principles that incorporate concepts of self-regulation observed in biology, sociology/psychology, and general systems theory. An extensive body of literature discusses control loops, and the reader is referred, e.g., to Miller, R. M. (1988). Loops follow the basic principle of 'measurement - comparison - control.' In order to meet this control task, the current value of the control variable the actual value must be measured and compared with the nominal value. When deviations occur appropriate adjustments must be made. In the realm of control system engineering, the task of control loops can be defined as follows:

Control Circuits

Control circuits maintain processes time-dependent parameters within a predetermined range of values, particularly in response to disturbances.

In Figure 8, an I/O automaton with its two elements is shown. The dashed lines illustrate the scope of the discrete correction device (K_s) and the discrete transfer function (G_s). The general set point function ($G_v s$) is interpreted as an output signal. The solid lines with arrows outline the cycle, which starts as soon as the deviation (d_k) acts on the controlled system. Between set point and the alleged deviation, several activities are carried out in order to achieve a trouble-free operation of the controlled system. The control objectives of IT/Inf.-security (confidentiality, availability, integrity) are used as a reference value (v_k).

The reference value (v_k) determines in Figure 8 the level of security for the mentioned security concept control objectives of a company. The reference value must be provided from outside or from the companies themselves. Deviation (d_k) and set-point (v_k) are sketched as lines with open arrowheads in Figure 8. These two exogenous events that act on the system cause the activities in the system. Accordingly, w_k is the deviation

Figure 8. Regular control loop as an I/O automaton

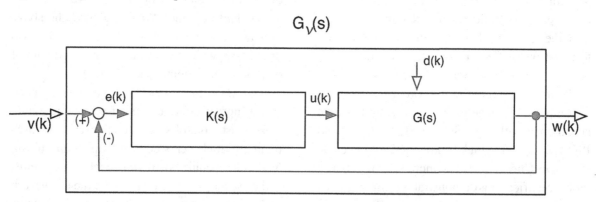

measured by the sensor and thus, the actual value of e_k is the difference between set-point and actual value. The signal that goes from the controller to the actuator, with u_k and the correcting signal or control value by the actuator on the controlled system, is characterized with u_k.

For purely technical systems, the timing (t) of an I/O automaton is important, which can be described with a first order differential equation. In the context of this contribution only the discrete behavior is of interest, which is usually expressed by an algebraic equation. The discrete case is indicated by the discrete variable k in the signal and the index (s).

This I/O automaton – also known as a single input / single output (SISO) system – can be viewed as a deterministic finite automaton. This simple control loop can be expanded to four elements.

The decisive factor in a control loop is the controller. With the help of the controller the disturbance (d_k) is regulated out of the controlled system in the course of time (t).

Within an Information Security Management System (ISMS) the measures for the risk prevention counteract the disturbance. The function of the PID controller is essentially in the verification phase (check phase) and phase correction (act phase). In the Figure 9, damped harmonic oscillation (step response) occurs to some extent in a management system on the one hand due to the different types of risk prevention (prevention, reduction, transfer, accept, eliminate) that can be designated the effectiveness of the elimination of disturbance and, on the other hand with the cost of risk prevention (efficiency of the elimination of an disturbance).

Depending on how well the effectiveness of the measure harmonizes with the cost of the action, the step response emerges, as shown in Figure 9. Later on we will address the effectiveness and economic efficiency of a security management system in more detail, by discussing a target function. Through the orthogonal behavior of the effectiveness and economic efficiency the target conflict arises, which can only be solved heuristically.

MANAGEMENT SYSTEMS AND THE DEMING CYCLE

From the perspective of the overall security of an enterprise, the two types of policy, static and dynamic, have the same disadvantage in that they do not provide any feedback about their effect. This makes higher-level control by corporate management impossible, but such control is essential to enterprise security. Furthermore, economic issues play a wide-ranging role in company security.

Boehmer (2010) has shown that the theory of control loops for technical systems can also be applied to socio-technical systems such as the information security management systems mentioned earlier. The above-mentioned three best-practice management systems (ISMS, BCMS, and ITSM), which are based on the Deming cycle, involve a four-phase cycle, Plan-Do-Check-Act (PDCA). The PDCA cycle is based on the imperfection of socio-technical systems and the consequent need for feedback argued Deming (1986).

Historically (since 1939), management systems, or rather the PDCA cycle, for quality assurance and statistical evaluation, were discussed for the first time by Shewhart (reprint 1980 (1939) and Shewhart, 1986). The idea was popularized by Deming (1986), from whom the cycle gets its name. The necessity of information security for management systems has been identified by Elo J., H., P. & Elo M. (2003), and an implementation has been presented by Salehl et al. (2007). The close relationship between information security and business processes has been discussed by Solms B. & Solms R. (2005).

Figure 9. Using PID control loop parameters

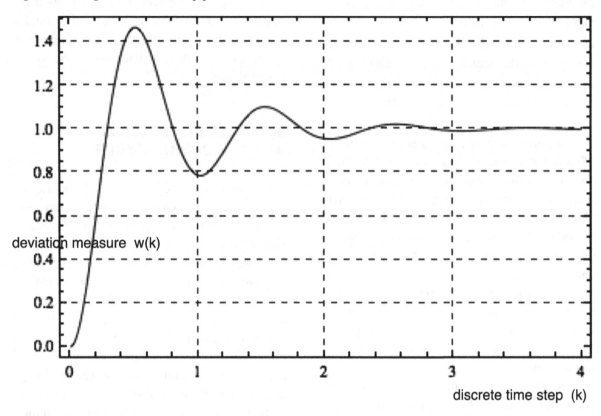

If the four phases are interpreted as states, the PDCA cycle can be shown to generate a standard automaton. Figure sketches the Deming cycle as a state transition diagram. The four phases are presented as states $Z = \{z_1, z_2, z_3, z_4\}$, and the state transitions are presented as events $\Sigma = \{\sigma_1, \sigma_2, \sigma_3, \sigma_4\}$. σ_0 indicates the initial event in Figure . The final state Z_F is provided for the standard state automaton, but may not exist as a single state because the system undergoes a continuous improvement process that is represented as a cycle (loop).

To compare the Deming cycle with a control loop, it is necessary to describe both methods as standard automatons. Then the behavior of two standard automatons can be compared by the bisimulation technique. The Deming cycle D can be expressed as a quintuple:

$$D = \{Z, \Sigma, \delta, z_0, Z_F\}. \tag{1}$$

The transitions δ allow the system to change state, for example $z_n \xrightarrow{\sigma_n} z_{n+1}$, with the successor state determined by the transition function $z' = \delta(z, \sigma)$. Then the Deming cycle can be described by a standard automaton D as presented in Equation 1.

A further improvement can be achieved if $Z_F = 1' \neq 1$, so that $z_1 \neq z'_1$ in the Deming cycle. This improvement criterion, applied over n cycles, yields a final stable state. As discussed by Boehmer (2009a), this condition produces a balance in the system that can be interpreted as an equilibrium state, or in other words, one in which the state of the system no longer changes. The Deming cycle is then balanced. For this case $Z_F = 1$. The Check (check for improvements) and Act (perform improvements) functions are responsible for attaining the equilibrium state. In an ideal case, the system reaches equilibrium after a certain period of time.

Figure 11 sketches the Deming cycle as a state transition diagram. By analogy to the quintuple representing the Deming cycle, a control loop can also be described by a standard automaton $\hat{A}$:

$$\hat{A} = \left\{ \hat{Z}, \hat{\Sigma}, \hat{\delta}, \hat{z}_0, \hat{Z}_F \right\}. \tag{2}$$

The elements needed to understand the quintuple representing the standard automaton $\hat{A}$ are analogous to the states and events of the quintuple of the Deming cycle (see Equation 1). The states can be described as $\hat{Z} = \left\{ \hat{z}_1, \hat{z}_2, \hat{z}_3, \hat{z}_4 \right\}$ and the events as $\hat{\Sigma} = \left\{ \hat{\sigma}_1, \hat{\sigma}_2, \hat{\sigma}_3, \hat{\sigma}_4 \right\}$. The transition function is given by $\hat{\delta}$ and indicates a transition from one state to another, for example $\hat{z}_n \xrightarrow{\hat{\sigma}_n} \hat{z}_{n+1}$.

The two machines can be compared based on the similarity and equivalence of their response behavior. Here, similarity is determined only by the input and output values of the automaton. This type of similarity is called interface equivalence. This topic will not be discussed further here in order to pay more attention to the bisimulation. According to Milner's axiom, two states are considered equal if they cannot be distinguished by (a combination of) observations (Milner, 2006). A bisimulation between two objects is therefore a transition system that reproduces an observed behavior that is identical for two objects. If a relation exists between the states of a Deming quintuple D and a standard automaton $\hat{A}$ then the bisimulation $S_{\hat{A}D}$ applies, such that

$$S_{\hat{A}D} \subset \hat{A} \times D, \tag{3}$$

where Z_D and $\hat{Z}_{\hat{A}}$ indicate the state sets of the two automata D and $\hat{A}$. Equation 3 shows the

Figure 10. PDCA cycle as a standard automaton according to Deming

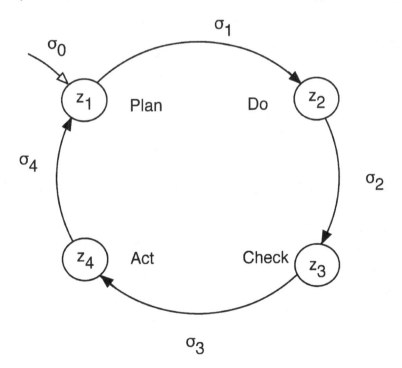

Figure 11. Control loop for an ISMS as defined by ISO 27001

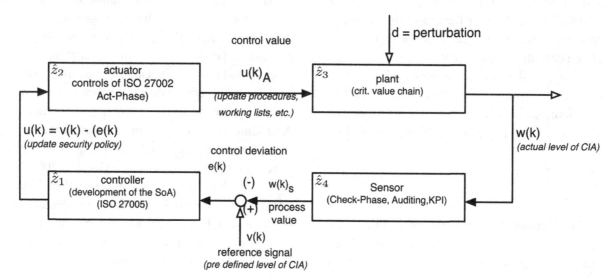

relation between the automata $\hat{A}$ and D. The simulation relation $S_{\hat{A}D}$ maps the states of the automaton $D\big|z_1$ and $\hat{A}\big|z_1$ in the sense that the second element of the pair, e.g., $(z_1, \hat{z}_1) \in S$, is simulated by the first, and therefore $z_1 \sim \hat{z}_1$ applies. The number of states may be different in the two machines, but this does not present a contradiction within the relation S. If $D\big|z_k$ and $\hat{A}\big|z_k$ are equivalent for all input sequences k, they are called k-equivalent. In the Deming cycle, $k = 4$ (see Figure 3). The k-equivalent states are also l-equivalent for all $l \leq k$. Nonequivalent states are called 'distinguishable.' All states that are distinguishable by input sequences of length k are k-distinct.

The preceding paragraph has shown that a Deming cycle may be expressed as a quintuple (see Equation 1) and that this behavior may be compared with any other automaton, such as $\hat{A}$ (see Equation 2) using the bisimulation function S (see Equation 3). The following paragraph describes the conversion of the control loops of a management system (ISMS) into a standard automaton $\hat{A}_{ISMS}$ and subsequently the equivalence of this automaton to the Deming standard automaton D.

Policies with feedback have, in general, been underappreciated in computer science research. In contrast, control systems engineering regularly implements control loops with built-in feedback capabilities to monitor technical systems, and these loops can be modeled in the framework of discrete-event systems (DES) theory. In general, control systems engineering is a discipline that mathematically models diverse systems in nature by analyzing their dynamic behavior. Control theory is used to create a controller mechanism that can shift the system behavior in a desired manner. Control loops have gained far-reaching significance because they are not purely technical models; they define general organizing principles that incorporate various concepts of self-regulation observed in biology, sociology, psychology, and general systems theory. An extensive body of literature discusses control loops; the reader is referred, for example, to (Miller, 1989). In the realm of control systems engineering, the task of a control loop can be defined as follows:

Def. 1: A control loop maintains the time-dependent parameters of a process within a predetermined range of values, particularly in response to disturbances.

The management systems defined in the ISO 27001, BS 25999, and ISO 20000 standards can be interpreted as socio-technical systems. Socio-technical systems differ from purely technical systems in that a subject is part of these systems. This chapter focuses only on these socio-technical management systems and in particular on their discrete-time behavior. A socio-technical system must have a controller, sensor, and actuator that must be customized for each company because the value chain differs from one company to another.

In essence, an ISMS follows a PDCA cycle, as shown in Figure 11. However, if the elements of an ISMS are transformed into the elements of a control loop, the control loop shown in Figure 11 is obtained. This representation illustrates the four elements of a Deming-cycle management system and the four elements of a control loop. Figure 11 illustrates a reference signal (setpoint) $v(k)$ within a loop that maintains the requirements for confidentiality, integrity, and availability (CIA) at predefined levels. The current security level $w(k)$ is generated by the disturbance (d) acting on the plant (the controlled system). The sensor(s) measure the current security level, denoted by $w(k)_S$. The controller is then adjusted by means of the reference signal $v(k)$ to restore the previously defined security level. As a corrective action, the signal $u(k) = v(k) - e(k)$ is created. This signal reflects the updating of the current security policy. The controller, sensor, and actuator specify, measure, and implement procedures and working instructions in the plant. The quantity $u(k)_A$ represents this signal, which acts on the plant to eliminate the perturbation (d).

The equivalence between the standard Deming cycle automaton D and the standard closed-loop automaton $\hat{A}_{ISMS}$, as expressed by Equation 4, will now be investigated. During conversion of the control loop into a standard automaton $\hat{A}_{ISMS}$, four states were defined: $\hat{z}_1$ = controller, $\hat{z}_2$ = actuator, $\hat{z}_3$ = plant (controlled system), and $\hat{z}_4$ = sensor (see Figure 11). The four states

of $\hat{A}_{ISMS}$ can be compared with those of the standard Deming cycle automaton using Equation 4:

$$
\begin{aligned}
(z_1, \hat{z}_1) &= \in S = z_1 \sim \hat{z}_1 \\
(z_2, \hat{z}_2) &= \in S = z_2 \sim \hat{z}_2 \\
(z_3, \hat{z}_4) &= \in S = z_3 \sim \hat{z}_4 \\
(z_4, \hat{z}_2) &= \in S = z_4 \sim \hat{z}_2
\end{aligned}
\tag{4}
$$

Clearly, Equation 4 can be interpreted from the perspective of the standard automaton D as follows:

State 1: Plan $\rightarrow$ risk analysis according to ISO 27005, statement of applicability $\rightarrow$ Controller.

State 2: Do $\rightarrow$ implement measurements (e.g., according to ISO 27002) $\rightarrow$ Actuator.

State 4: Check $\rightarrow$ Check phase $\rightarrow$ Sensor.

State 2: Act $\rightarrow$ Action phase, corrective action $\rightarrow$ Actuator.

It is evident from Equation 4 and the states in the above list that a bisimulation does not exist for all k states of the Deming cycle ($k = 4$). For instance, no bisimulation exists for state $\hat{z}_3$. This indicates that the plant cannot be directly represented by the Deming cycle. The plant is defined only implicitly by the scope of the standard. The scope of an ISMS, as defined by ISO 27001, describes the value chain of a company, which is the plant (the controlled system). In contrast with control system engineering, here the controlled system (the plant) is part of the standard automaton. Consequently, an l-equivalence exists only because the state $\hat{z}_{k=3}$ is distinguishable. From the viewpoint of Discrete Event System theory, these four phases comprise a control loop, as shown in Figure 11.

This section has discussed the elements of a control loop and of management systems and has shown their equivalence to a standard automaton with a feedback function. It has also been shown that the bisimulation (see Equation 4) between the standard automatons of the PDCA cycle using the elements of a standard loop can be expressed by the standard ISO 27001 automaton. Boehmer (2010b) has performed further investigations of management systems defined by the BS 25999 and ISO 20000 standards. The question also arises of whether management systems can occur only in isolation in a company, or whether multiple management systems can exist in parallel. This question has been investigated by Boehmer (2010b). From these investigations, it is clear that the three management systems can frequently be found coupled together in companies. It can be shown that ISO 20000 management systems are closely linked with ISO 27001 management systems, but only a loose link can be established between an ISO 27001 (ISMS) management system and a BS 25999 (BCMS) management system.

Modeling of the Plant

The previous section showed that the controlled system in the Deming-cycle automaton could not be represented by a control loop. In a control loop, the controlled system and the disturbances acting on the controlled system play a decisive role. This section will therefore consider some aspects of quantitative modeling and discuss the controlled system.

A control system or the value chain of a company can be modeled qualitatively or quantitatively. Methods for the qualitative modeling of business processes (the value chain) include the Pi-Calculus, developed by Milner (1992), which formed the basis for the Business Process Management Notation (BPMN) and has become widespread in many areas of industry. Examples of tools based on this notation include ARIS-Designer, developed by A.W. Scheer of the University of Saarland (Scheer, 2001) and ADONIS from the University of Vienna (Kühn et. al., 1996). These studies describe BPMN implementations of busi-

ness processes using a qualitative representation. This qualitative approach is of great importance if the descriptions of business processes, definitions of interfaces, and assigned roles and resources need to be modeled. Use of a qualitative method can make business processes more transparent and improve the generation of working instructions.

A Business Continuity Experiment

On the other hand, if quantification of business processes is desired, formal methods and their implementation in tools are more appropriate. The interest in quantification may arise, for example, when determining the level of functionality needed to achieve compliance with the security criteria of a Business Continuity Plan (BCP). So far, in practice, only elaborate field experiments have been carried out. Boehmer et al. (2009c) published theoretical estimates based on the MCRL2 tool and related to formal methods. Especially in the case of a BCP, such an analysis is considered rare and has been previously verified only by a field study. The quantitative assessment of a BCP is of vital importance for a company because a BCP, in the event of a disaster, takes over responsibility for the objectives of the controlled system for a period of time. The need to establish a Business Continuity Management System (BCMS) incorporating several BCPs in case of catastrophic events in a company has been, since the Oxford study by Knight and Pretty (1996), assumed as a matter of course.

In a study by Boehmer et al. (2009c), it has been shown that formal methods can be used with process algebra, modal logic, and mu-calculus to examine BCP-based emergency processes for their performance (throughput) and their compliance with security requirements (the four-eyes principle). For these analyses, the MCRL2 tool from the *TU/e* toolkit was used. The field study involved a business process (value chain) — that is, a controlled system — and an existing emergency process (BCP), with MCRL2 used to test their performance and their level of compliance with security policies.

In this investigation, the whole state space was analyzed. From this test, non-intuitive results were obtained and are presented here. It was recognized that with the required capabilities of the previously defined emergency process (BCP), the viability of the system was not sufficient. A modification of the emergency process (BCP) was then performed, which showed that the required capabilities (throughput) and level of compliance with security policy (the four-eyes principle) could be achieved (Boehmer et al., 2009c). Use of a quantification method can make business processes more transparent and improve the generation of working instructions.

PREVENTIVE ADJUSTMENT OF RISKS WITH MANAGEMENT SYSTEMS

In terms of operational risks (OpRisk), the question is to define the potential loss (damage) that may arise in business operations and how it can be corrected proactively. In contrast to the market or the credit sector, no industry standard has emerged for identifying, quantifying, and managing operational risk, as noted by Boos and Schulte-Mattler (2001). An important consideration for operational risk analysis of the interaction between threats and vulnerabilities on an asset in a business process is that this analysis can retroactively affect the business process. The terms 'asset,' 'threat,' and 'vulnerability' in this chapter are as defined in the ISO 27000 standard, sections 2.3, 2.45, and 2.46.

Unlike stock exchanges, which function under operational risks—according to Basel II, internal causes are considered in the foreground—the analysis of the possible exploitation of vulnerabilities must consider all appropriate threats. Furthermore, reliability theory plays a major role in the case of technical components.

Although the approaches used in the market and financial sector are very different from those used in the field of operational risk, a desire exists, argues Leipold and Vanini (2003), to obtain a single uniform measure to assess risk in the areas of market, finance, and operations. The risk measure can be expressed as a non-empty set G of measurable random variables associated with a σ-algebra A and a probability P:

$$\rho : G \to \mathbb{R}_{(5)}.$$

The random variable $X(\omega)$ (see Figure) describes for the actual finite probability space (Ω, A, P) the potential harm over the time interval ($t \in T$). The measure of risk interprets as necessary capital (risk capital) the amount that is necessary to drive to zero the possible loss incurred to forestall risk. The risk measure can be expected to have a number of properties (translation invariance, subadditivity, positive homogeneity, and monotonicity), as required in the pioneering work of Artzner et al. (2001) for a coherent risk measure. The corresponding measure space is determined by (Ω, A, ρ).

In the area of market and financial risks, the Value at Risk (VaR) measure is favored, or even more so, its coherent version, the Conditional Value at Risk. This measure describes the value at risk as the risk of the expected loss for a given confidence level (confidence interval α), which in a specific time interval ($t \in T$) will not be exceeded. The CVaR describes the expected loss in the case that the VaR is exceeded. It can also be interpreted as the average worst-case loss if α (the confidence level of the VaR) is exceeded.

The operational value at risk (OpVaR) has been discussed in the literature, but there is a wide gap between theory and practice. In practice, a simple ordinal scale is still predominantly used, as proposed in the Basel Accord (2001). Also according to the Basel Accord, a textual description of risks by dividing them into classes relating to expected probability (P-robability) and severity of impact (I-mpact) is commonly used. Such methods are known as semi-quantitative methods. Through the use of two ordinal values, the risk values are entered as cell values in a P × I risk matrix, from which the risk level can then be read. If this *ad hoc* approach is used for all the risks in a value chain, a dot pattern is created in the P × I risk matrix. This risk matrix is often used to define three risk levels: low, medium, and high.

The semi-quantitative method for deriving risk level very quickly encounters its limits when several semi-quantitatively described risks need to be aggregated. The question has been raised whether the overall risks in a value chain need to be compared to the yield of the value chain. To study quantitative risk assessment in a value chain in which a management system was used for preventive mitigation of risks, a field study was performed from 2007 to 2010 in an energy company in Germany. In the following section, this field study and its findings will be presented.

FIELD STUDIES (2007–2010) AT 26 POWER STATIONS AND 3 SURFACE MINING OPERATIONS

In a three-year field study, a leading energy company in Germany implemented an ISMS as defined by ISO 27001 at 29 locations with SCADA systems (Boehmer, 2011). Previously, the SCADA systems had been secured on the basis of security policies, but it had been increasingly recognized in recent years that the security policies were ineffective. Based on further analysis, it became clear that this company constituted an open system, and therefore an information security management system (ISMS) was implemented in accordance with ISO 27001.

The value-added processes were first extensively (qualitative) described (using ARIS-Designer) to provide as much detail as possible to the experts on the ground and to obtain a reliable description of the risk scenarios (possible undesirable changes of state of a process). It became apparent during the field study that it was easier for experts to think within a scenario and then assign different outcomes for this

scenario (best case, most likely case, worst case, as shown in Figure 12) than to determine a single value of a probability density function. Similar experience with three-point estimation in the field of project management has been reported, for example in (Palmer, 1996).

The Beta-PERT distribution or the underlying three-point estimate (best case, most likely case, worst case) is ideal for the determination of expert opinion and is often used for assessment of project risks. However, the Beta-PERT distribution has until now not been mentioned in the literature for assessment of operational risks. It is clear, however, that if the quality of the input data is inferior, then the processed data (output data) in a distribution cannot be better; in short, garbage in, garbage out.

In this respect, the field study (the investigation of 29 power plants) placed particular emphasis on the input values for the risk scenario analysis. A risk scenario is understood to be a stochastic event described as follows:

Def. 2: A risk scenario is understood to be a model of a possible (stochastic) event (incident), contained in a set of events Ω that could happen in the future, and caused by violation of the protection objectives (confidentiality, availability, integrity) by the interaction of one or more threats representing a vulnerability.

Generally, a scenario is a possible, conceivable (stochastic) event, as expressed formally in Equation 6. It assigns a particular value to a random variable. In this context, a stochastic event can be seen as a risk event (Rsz). It will be estimated by a three-point risk estimate which assigns different loss probabilities (Pr) to a risk event (best case (bc), most likely case (mc), worst case (wc), as shown in Figure 12.

Equation 6 (Box 1) defines a risk scenario (Rsz) with $\varsigma = \{bc, mc, wc\}$ as the possible outcomes of this random variable $X(\omega)$ interpreted as a risk event.

Figure 12. Risk scenario with three different outcomes

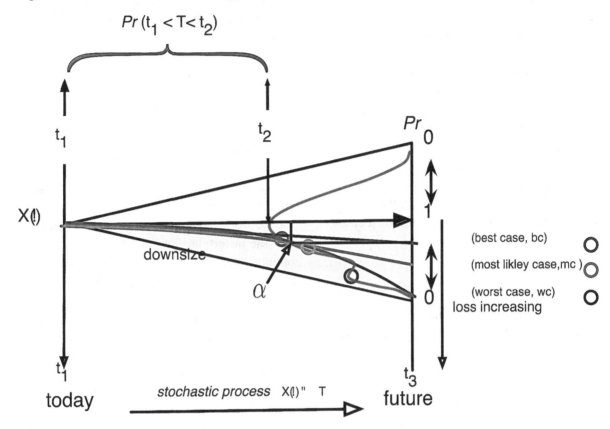

$$X(\omega) = Rsz_\varsigma := \begin{cases} if\varsigma = bc \mid \left(x_{bc} \ll x_{mc}\right) \wedge \Pr\left[X(\omega) = x_{bc}\right] \to best\ case \\ if\varsigma = mc \mid \left(x_{mc} > x_{bc}\right) \wedge \Pr\left[X(\omega) = x_{mc}\right] \to most\ likely\ case\ (6) \\ if\varsigma = wc \mid \left(x_{wc} \gg x_{bc} \wedge x_{mc}\right) \wedge \Pr\left[X(\omega) = x_{wc}\right] \to worst\ case \end{cases}$$

The possible types of outcomes (Rszç) of risk events were estimated in workshops by local experts. An illustration of the stochastic process described by Equation 6 can be found in Figure. Furthermore, a distribution (the red line) of the three points representing the estimates was defined; this line shows the distribution of possible losses to absorb. In this case, the certain event (Pr = 1) is no longer a random event.

In terms of operational risks, only the grey shaded area of interest is normally referred to as a downside risk measure with $X(\omega) = \{0, -\infty\}$. Assuming a time interval (t1, t3) in the probability space (Pr), the expected loss (VaR) can be determined for a confidence interval (α) by means of Equation 7, which provides a lower bound:

$$VaR_\alpha := \min\left\{x \mid \left(\Pr\left[X \leq x\right] > \alpha\right)\right\}, \qquad (7)$$

As mentioned previously, the VaR is not a coherent risk measure, as demonstrated by Artzner [2001], because the VaR is based on a normal distribution. Figure illustrates the distribution function, which was determined by the three-point risk estimation procedure. The drawback of the VaR is clearly illustrated by the reddish-brown line, which illustrates the confidence interval α. It can be clearly seen in Figure that the worst-case scenario is not covered by the approximation of a purely normal distribution. Therefore, to assess single risks, the conditional VaR (CVaR) was used. The CVaR is the average loss of the worst cases:

$$CVaR := \left\{ x \mid \left(\Pr\left[X \leq x \right] < \alpha \right) \right\}, \tag{8}$$

In this context, only certain losses of interest are considered, those that are based on the intersection of assets, threats, and vulnerabilities with critical business processes.

As mentioned previously, special attention has been paid to the estimation of input variables using the three-point estimate (best case, most likely case, worst case). In addition, in the favorable consideration of the expert scenarios, an interval estimate was preferred instead of a point estimate, because probability theory is characterized by point estimation, which has so far been prevalent in risk analysis. However, it is often difficult in practice to estimate exactly the probability of an impact (best case, most likely case, worst case), as has been shown in practice in the field studies at the 29 locations. It was much easier for the surveyed experts to indicate a probability range (from - to), which is essentially a tolerance range.

Consequently, as a precise estimate, the information from expert opinion was incomplete, being only an indication of the lower (Lo) and upper limits (Up) between which a possible event can occur in a distribution function (see Figure). Therefore, each event (scenario $\varsigma = \{bc, mc, wc\}$) was mapped into a closed interval [0,1] as a probability component. According to Weichselberger

[2001], the interval probability (IP) for the closed interval $Z_0[0,1]$ can be defined with an σ-algebra A as follows:

$$IP = A \rightarrow Z_0\left[0,1\right]$$
$$\varsigma \mapsto IP(\varsigma)\left[L_o(\varsigma), U_p(\varsigma)\right], \tag{9}$$

Equation 9 describes the uncertainty (error tolerance) of the expert opinions $\varsigma \mapsto IP(\varsigma)$ to the precise scenario estimates (ς) for the best case, most likely case, and worst case. Especially for the worst-case scenarios, it has been shown that the uncertainty in the estimate (the expert opinion) increases with increasing extent of damage and decreasing probability of occurrence. At this point, the limit of measurability is achieved. However, rare but high-impact risk events are of great importance in determining the value.

The three-year field study was carried out in various power plants, surface mines, gas-fired plants, coal-fired power plants, and hydroelectric plants. The goal of all power-plant processes is to produce energy (electricity) and thus to realize added value.

Energy is produced by burning fuel and operating a turbine. In addition, there are waste materials that must be disposed of. Figure 13 shows a section of the core processes, which operate in all power plants in a similar manner. To operate the main process plant (KP-0), the following key processes must occur sequentially: provide assistance and supplies (P-1), produce steam and electricity (P-2), and dispose of waste (P-3).

As an example, considering a detailed view only of the core process (P-2), it essentially consists of the parallel processes of process engineering (P-2V), control (P-2L), PDV (P-2P), and electrical (P-2E controlled). In other words, the operation of P-2 depends on the operation of subprocesses P-2V, P-2L, P-2P, and P-2E. If one of the subprocesses is not working properly, then the core process P-2 will be disrupted, and the power plant may even shut down.

Figure 13. Core processes of a power plant

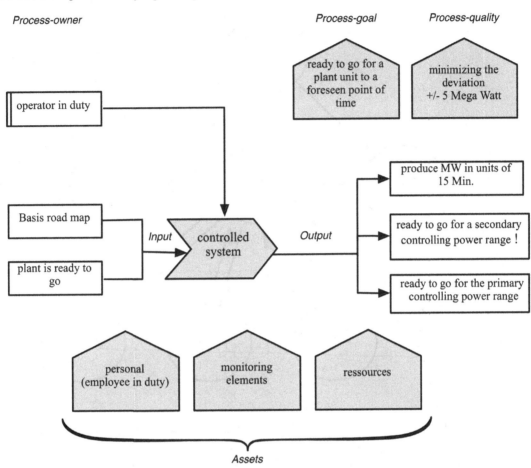

On the detailed subprocess level, considering here P-2P (as shown in Figure 14), it is possible for the experts to estimate risk scenarios (best case, most likely case, worst case) and their potential effects (see Figure 12) for the process of steam and power generation. In a minority of cases, the impact can be understood by comparing the performance to the basic schedule and identifying episodes of non-fulfillment of the basic plan. The term 'damage' means in this example that no energy is output from the power plant for an accounting unit of 15 minutes, thus creating a loss for the power plant owner. The core processes (P-1, P-2, P-3) must run sequentially, but in the case of P-2 only, if P-2P is operating (works). Figure 14 illustrates the process elements.

In the scenarios examined, conditions that could occur with a nonzero probability (control operations) do not follow a regular pattern. For frequent (k) repetitions of the state sequence (or control), it has been shown that the state described by Equation 10 is a very common condition (trend). Here, the common condition of the random variable $X(\omega)$ is determined as:

$$\Pr\left[X(\omega) = x_a\right] \approx 1. \tag{10}$$

This means that the deviation x_a in energy production, to a tolerance of $+/-$ 5 MW, is higher than in the initial schedule, and therefore no loss occurred in the discrete time step (k). The

Figure 14. Process element P-2P modeled with ARIS

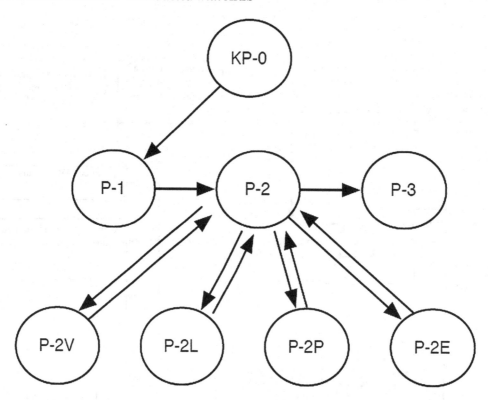

other scenarios are described by Equation 6 and illustrated in Figure. The results of the risk scenarios are shown in Figure 12. The risk scenarios have been evaluated using the extended three-point estimate, represented by the blue lines or indicated by the color-coded stripes. The two arrows indicate the reduction of the loss by the implementation of the two management systems with repeated risk analysis. Boehmer (2011) has pointed out in his paper that Figure 16 provides a compressed representation (aggregation of single risks by means of a convolution of the density distribution) across all sites and all SCADA processes.

As a result, it can be stated that the greater the uncertainty in the approximation, the greater will be the loss and the less often it will occur (Figure 15). The lower (beige) dashed line represents the potential loss distribution after implementation of the two management systems (ISMS and BCMS).

Therefore, the beige line also describes the remaining risks that are accepted by the locations. Boehmer [2009] showed that an ISMS designed to respond proactively to risks and a reactive BCMS which activates emergency processes are aligned. Decision theory has resolved the issues of which management system should be implemented for which risk scenarios and which context should be preferred to provide protection that is effective, economically efficient, or both. The following paragraph discusses further this conflict in management systems.

The reductions in expected loss which were achieved by the implementation of management systems (ISMS, BCMS) are remarkable. Although both management systems contribute to a reduction in possible losses (see the vertical arrows in Figure 15), the remaining loss expectation for rare but serious damage incidents is higher than for small but frequent losses. This is a non-intuitive result and shows the importance of developing a Business Con-

Figure 15. Reduction of the expected loss distribution by security management systems

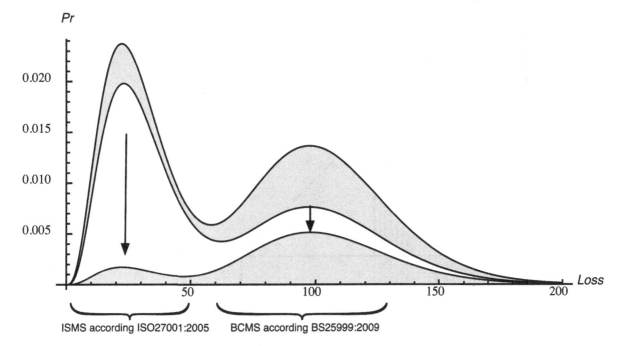

ISMS according ISO27001:2005   BCMS according BS25999:2009

tinuity Management System and associated Business Continuity Plan (BCP). Quantifying various aspects of a Business Continuity Plan was discussed in the previous section (see the BCP experiment). Finally, it should be noted that prior assessment and reduction of operational risk, which could lead to a significant reduction in the required risk capital through the use of management systems, has not yet been discussed in the literature.

The following section will address the different objectives of economic efficiency and effectiveness of protection for the controlled system in a socio-technical loop and how to handle them in an information security management system.

TARGET FUNCTIONS AND MANAGEMENT SYSTEMS

This section addresses the measurement of management systems. From the literature, two methods are known to be suitable in principle for the measurement of management processes. The

first is the maturity model, developed at Carnegie Mellon University. This concept, known by the acronym CMMI, is today used not only for its original purpose of measuring software development processes, but also now for measuring the maturity of information security management systems such as an ISMS. The second method is the indicator or metrics method, also known as the Key Performance Indicator (KPI) method.

Both methods have their strengths and weaknesses, but a company needs to be able to evaluate the effectiveness and efficiency of its management system, which is impossible with the maturity model. Therefore, the indicator method and the derivation of an objective function for an information security management system will now be discussed.

In purely economically oriented management systems, the company is essentially set up to pursue profit objectives only argued Chamberlin (1965). This purely economically oriented management system is not suitable as a model for an information security management system.

Figure 16. Defining the governing objective function for a management system

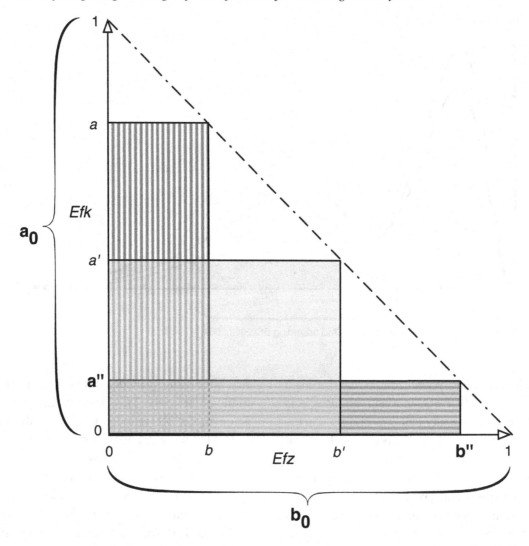

A number of previous studies by Boehmer (2008, 2009b, 2009c) have clarified the role of the effectiveness and efficiency of a management system. However, no target function can be derived from these considerations. Therefore, a target function must be derived from the characteristics of effectiveness and economic efficiency to define a requirement for management systems of second order.

The opposing system characteristics of effectiveness and efficiency can be formulated as an optimization problem, in which the levels of

effectiveness and economic efficiency are normalized to 1 and vary over an interval [0,1] to define the hypotenuse and leg of a right triangle.

Figure 16 illustrates this situation. The effectiveness values, (Efk = a, a', a'' | Efk $\in$ R), and the efficiency values, (Efz = b, b', b'' | Efz $\in$ R), in the interval [0,1] transform this optimization problem into a graphic optimization problem. To illustrate this principle, Figure 16 shows four rectangles. The first rectangle is delimited by the values (a, b) and is marked by vertical hatching. The second rectangle is delimited by the values (a', b') and is transparent. The third rectangle is delimited by the values (a'', b''). The optimization problem is solved by maximizing the area spanned by the rectangle embedded in the triangle (see Figure 16). The sides of the rectangle are denoted by a_0 and b_0. Given Efz = b'' and Efk = a'' and letting f represent the area of the rectangle, the target function can then be defined as the product of the lengths of each side:

$$f(a'', b'') = a'' \times b'',\qquad(11)$$

Maximizing the area of the rectangle delimited by a'' and b'' (see Figure 16) yields the following triangle relationship if b'' is given:

$$\frac{a_0}{b_0} = \frac{a''}{b_0 - b''} \rightarrow a'' = \frac{a_0}{b_0} \times (b_0 - b''),\qquad(12)$$

Maximizing the area by substituting the right side of Equation 12 into Equation 11 yields:

$$f(b'') = \frac{a_0}{b_0} \times b''(b_0 - b''),\qquad(13)$$

The question then arises of determining the point at which the function f has a global maximum. Because f is differentiable as a polynomial function, it follows that:

$$f(b'') = \frac{a_0}{b_0} \times (b_0 - 2b'').\qquad(14)$$

Any solution to this equation is also a root of the function f (b''). A solution that also gives f (b'') = 0 and b'' = 0 is a useful solution. However, the best solution is given by Efk = a' and Efz = b'. This discussion concludes with a summary of the importance of the target function for operation of the control loop (see Figure 11) in the management systems discussed previously, which were designed in accordance with the ISO 27001 standard.

From the equation for a linear control loop in an ISMS as proposed by Boehmer (2010a), it can be shown that a perturbation can be compensated for in different ways, depending on how the controller and actuator are defined. From the manner in which the actions of the controller and actuator are adjusted, management systems can be divided into two classes, as discussed Boehmer (2010a).

Def. 3: A first-order management system describes the compensation behavior after a disturbance in a socio-technical system.

Def. 4: A second-order management system meets the conditions of a first-order management system and also satisfies other requirements. Compensation after the disruption is also described by economic criteria. The controller operates under an overall objective function that affects the effectiveness and the economic efficiency of each compensation action.

The management system defined according to ISO 27001 satisfied the requirements of a control loop, but the standard addresses only the effectiveness of the management system (see ISO 27001, page 6, section 4.2.3.c). However, economic efficiency is not explicitly required, so the system meets the requirements for a second-order management system. Boehmer (2010a) has stated that in the ISO 27001 standard for the Check and Act phases, as well as for the Statement of Applicability (SoA), the target function must be supplemented to address effectiveness and economic efficiency. The reason is that, for management systems that influence the value chain through controller actions, it would be absurd if the risk compensation procedure did not take account of economic conditions.

SOLUTIONS AND RECOMMENDATIONS

In this chapter, it has been shown formally by equations and experimentally by a field study that information security management systems are preferable to security policies as a way to achieve enterprise security. The reason for this is the ability of management systems to compensate for disturbances in open systems. Policies are ideal, however, if the objective is to protect closed and isolated systems.

For the practical application of management systems, this means that whether a system is to be considered as an open, closed, or even an isolated system must be determined in advance. Only then can the next steps be addressed by the appropriate type of security method. If the decision is to implement a management system[4] to protect the information in a company, attention must be paid, not only to the ISO/IEC 27001 standard, but also to the ISO/IEC 27003 standard (Implementation Guide) as well as ISO/IEC 27004 (Measurement of the Management System) and ISO/IEC 27005 (information security risk management). The management system is implemented in the Check phase and continuously improved in the Act phase. However, this iterative continuous improvement process results in a state of balance or equilibrium state if the effectiveness and economic efficiency of the measures taken are carefully balanced to achieve risk prevention. This is an approach to obtaining an optimal operating condition for a company.

FUTURE RESEARCH DIRECTIONS

In spite of recent advances in management systems research, a number of interesting questions remain open, such as whether decision-making about risks is a matter for decision theory falls into the realm of game theory.

In this discussion, decision-making about risks will be addressed using decision theory. There is assumed to be a single agent, facing five alternatives with two different goals, and acting in a given environmental situation. The five alternatives for dealing with risks can be identified as reducing, avoiding, transferring, accepting, and elimination. The two objectives can be characterized as effective safeguarding versus protection of economic efficiency. However, certain cases could also be described as involving a technical expert to achieve optimal safeguarding and the owner of the plant (budget owner) who would prefer protection of economic efficiency. With this interpretation, the case would fall into the realm of game theory, which could identify other solutions. These aspects are currently the objects of a follow-up project involving the same field study analyzed in this chapter.

CONCLUSION

The properties of static and dynamic policies are often explored in computer science. There are a number of situations in which policies play a significant role, and consideration of the theoretical treatment of these policies is useful. In this chapter, it has been shown that the implementation of current policies is not necessarily adequate for meeting the requirements of today's enterprises. In particular, the field of information security often requires feedback on the effectiveness of a set of policies. A lack of feedback creates difficulties for both the classical static policies and the newer dynamic policies. This chapter has shown that dynamic policies can be expressed using system theory with feedback control loops. It has been demonstrated that control loops in the system theory of technical systems can be used to describe the behavior of socio-technical systems. These are known as management systems, and their behavior is equivalent to the behavior of technical control loops. As examples for analysis, one standard and one management system (ISO 27001) and the behaviors of a PDCA cycle and a loop were studied. It was demonstrated that this standard could be described using system theory for the control loops. In addition, an objective classification scheme for management systems was developed. Management systems that address a dysfunction using only one controller are defined as first-order management systems. Second-order management systems use a higher-level target function as the controller.

In contrast to purely economic management systems, where the target function can be defined by a single variable (revenue), the target function of a management system for enterprise security is determined by two variables that are subject to a tradeoff. The solution to this conflict leads to an optimization problem, which can only be solved iteratively. A practical implementation was derived for one example.

REFERENCES

Alchian, A., & Allen, W. R. (1983). *Exchange and production, competition, coordination & control* (3rd ed.; p. 184). Belmont, CA: Wadsworth Publishing Co.

Anderson, R. (2006). *Security engineering: A guide to building dependable distributed systems* (2nd ed.). Cambridge, UK: Wiley.

Artzner, P., Delbaen, F., Eber, J. M., & Heath, D. (2001). Coherent measures of risk. *Mathematical Finance, 9*(3), 203–228. doi:10.1111/1467-9965.00068

Basel Committee. (2001). *Operational risk.* Supporting Document to the New Basel Capital Accord on Banking Supervision (May 31).

Baskerville, R. (1993). Information systems security design methods: Implications for information systems development. *ACM Computing Surveys, 25*(4), 375–414. doi:10.1145/162124.162127

Boehmer, W. (2008). Appraisal of the effectiveness and efficiency of an information security management system based on ISO 27001. In *Proceedings, Second International Conference on Emerging Security Information, Systems and Technologies (SECUWARE 2008).* IEEE Computer Society. doi:10.1109/SECURWARE.2008.7

Boehmer, W. (2009a). Cost-benefit trade-off analysis of an ISMS based on ISO 27001. In *Proceedings of ARES Conference: The International Dependability Conference.* IEEE Computer Society.

Boehmer, W. (2009b). Survivability and business continuity management system according to BS 25999. In *Proceedings, Third International Conference on Emerging Security Information, Systems and Technologies (SECUWARE '09).* IEEE Computer Society. doi:10.1109/SECURWARE.2009.29

Boehmer, W. (2009c). Performance, survivability and cost aspects of business continuity processes according to BS25999. *International Journal on Advances in Security, 2*(4). Retrieved from http://www.iariajournals.org/security/

Boehmer, W. (2010a). Toward an objective function for an information security management system. In *Proceedings, Third IEEE International Symposium on Trust, Security and Privacy for Emerging Applications (TSP-2010).* IEEE Computer Society.

Boehmer, W. (2010b). Analysis of strongly and weakly coupled management systems in information security. In *Proceedings, Fourth International Conference on Emerging Security Information, Systems, and Technologies (SECURWARE 2010).* IEEE Computer Society. doi:10.1109/SECURWARE.2010.26

Boehmer, W. (2014). (in preparation). Application and formal description of discrete and event driven feedback systems in the IT/Inf. *Security.*

Boos, K. H., & Schulte-Mattler, H. (2001). Basel II: Methoden zur quantifizierung operationeller risiken. *Die Bank, 8,* 549–553.

Capra, F. (1984). *The turning point: Science, society, and the rising culture.* Bantam.

Capra, F. (1996). *The web of life: A new scientific understanding of living systems* (1st ed.). Anchor Books/Doubleday.

Chamberlin, E. (1965). The theory of monopolistic competition: A re-orientation of the theory of value (8th ed.). Harvard University Press.

Clark, D. D., & Wilson, D. R. (1987). A comparison of commercial and military computer security policies. In *Proceedings of the 1987 IEEE Symposium on Research in Security and Privacy (SP'87).* Oakland, CA: IEEE Press.

Conway, W., Maxwell, W. L., & Morgan, H. L. (1972). On the implementation of security measures in information systems. *Communications of the ACM, 15*(4), 211–220. doi:10.1145/361284.361287

Courtney, R. (1977). Security risk analysis in electronic data processing. In *Proceedings of the NatLonal Computer Conference 46.* AFIPS.

Deming, W. E. (1986). *Out of the crisis.* Cambridge, MA: MIT Press.

Elo, J. H. P., & Elo, M. (2003). Information security management: a new paradigm. In *Proceedings, 2003 Annual Research Conference of the South African Institute of Computer Scientists and Information Technologists on Enablement through Technology (SAICSIT '03).* South African Institute for Computer Scientists and Information Technologists.

Giacometti, R., Rachev, S., Chernobai, A., & Bertocchi, M. (2008). Aggregation issues in operational risk. *Journal of Operational Risk, 3*(3).

Jaquith, A. (2007). *Security metrics, replacing fear, unceartainty, and doubt.* Addison Wesley.

Knight, R., & Pretty, D. (1996). *The impact of catastrophes on shareholder value.* Oxford, UK: Templeton College, Oxford University.

Kühn, H., Karagiannis, D., & Junginger, S. (1996) *Metamodellierung in dem BPMS-Analysewerkzeug ADONIS, Konferenz Informatik '96.* Uni Klagenfurt.

Leimer, H. W. (1990). *Vernetztes denken im bank-management.* Gabler Verlag. doi:10.1007/978-3-322-91058-5

Leippold, M., & Vanini, P. (2003). *The quantification of operational risk.* Available at SSRN: http://ssrn.com/abstract=481742 or doi:10.2139/ssrn.481742

Lindup, K. R. (1995). A new model for information security policies. *Computers & Security, 14*(8), 691–695. doi:10.1016/0167-4048(96)81709-3

Meadows, D. H. (2008). Thinking in systems: A primer. Chelsea Green Publishing Company.

Miller, R. M. (1988). Market automation: Self-regulation in a distributed environment. *ACM SIGGROUP Bulletin, 9*(2–3), 299–308. doi:10.1145/966861.45443

Palmer, A. R. (1996). Waltzing with asymmetry. *Bioscience, 46*(7), 518–532. doi:10.2307/1312930

Pucella, R., & Weissman, V. (2004). Foundations of software science and computation structures. *Lecture Notes in Computer Science, 2987,* 453–467.

Salehl, M. S., Alrabiah, A., & Bakry, S. H. (2007). Using ISO 17799: 2005 information security management: A stope view with six sigma approach. *International Journal of Network Management, 7*(1), 85–97. doi:10.1002/nem.616

Saydjari, O. S. (2006). Is risk a good security metric? in *Proceedings of the 2nd ACM Workshop on Quality of Protection, QoP '06* (pp. 59–60). ACM. doi:10.1145/1179494.1179508

Scheer, A.-W. (2001) *ARIS-modellierungs-methoden, metamodelle, anwendungen.* Springer.

Shannon, C. (1948). A mathematical theory of communication. *Bell System Technical Journal*, 379-423, 623-656.

Shewhart, W. A. (1939, reprint 1986). Statistical method from the viewpoint of quality control. Dover Publications.

Shewhart, W. A. (1980). *Economic control of quality of manufactured product*. American Society for Quality Control.

Solms, B., & Solms, R. (2005). From information security to ... business security? *Computers & Security*, *24*(4), 271–273. doi:10.1016/j.cose.2005.04.004

van der Meyden, R. (1996). The dynamic logic of permission. *J. Log. Comput.*, *6*(3), 465–479. doi:10.1093/logcom/6.3.465

Wilms, F. (2003). Systemorientierte unternehmensfhrung von KMUs. In *Management von KMU und grndungsunternehmen* (pp. 3–26). Deutscher Universtätsverlag Wiesbaden.

KEY TERMS AND DEFINITIONS

Control Systems: Linear control loops, as well as socio-technical control loops both follow the general requirements and specifications of control systems. In open systems, it is more conducive to act contrary to a control system and risk-oriented management system to effectively and efficiently achieve a planned level of security.

Management Systems: Management systems follow the classical idea of the disturbance and system theory, which is an integral part of the engineering sciences. Disturbances, or better, a risk of a disturbance in terms of IT/Inf. security refers to any possible interference of the value chain of a company and the goal is to compensate for this possible disturbance through a preventive action.

Policies: A policy is an axiomatic description, according to Bishop's view, of how a secure state can be achieved from an unsecured state.

Systems Theory: Control circuits for technical systems in the context of systems theory. The concept of the signal, which can be time-continuous or non-time-continuous, and the concept of the system are fundamental in system theory. A signal is a rough representation of a piece of information.

Target Function: We derive a target function to define the requirements for a second-order management system based on the properties of effectiveness and efficiency.

Tradeoff: In this article, the effectiveness and the efficiency are proposed as substitute-sizes. It is defined a suitable, measurable KPI for every size. But the effectiveness and the economic efficiency are contradicting and constitute a trade-off. This trade-off can be interpreted as a knapsack problem. However, as a solution of this combinatorial optimization problem we propose a special branch and bounding algorithm.

ENDNOTES

[1] For the market and financial risks cannot only negative outputs (loss) can be, but it can also be a profit. It means that the risk (R) is in (R^+).

[2] The Greek letter σ – denotes a countable set, but the set can also be infinitely countable.

[3] See http://www.iso27001security.com/html/27001.html, last access October 2014.

[4] Cfg. http://www.iso27001security.com/index.html, last accessed October 2014.

Chapter 14
Trust and Trust Building of Virtual Communities in the Networked Age

Qing Zou
McGill University, Canada

Eun G. Park
McGill University, Canada

ABSTRACT

This is the networked age, when people participate in various virtual communities through a platform or network of communities. Members of the communities communicate in faster and more simultaneous interactions in invisible ways. Since the importance of trust in virtual communities has been widely recognized, trust as a complex, multi-faceted, and context-dependent concept has been examined by many researchers in several disciplines. In this chapter, the authors aim to examine the definitions and characteristics of trust in the context of virtual communities and discuss terms relevant to the concept and types of trust. Relevant issues on trust and trust building in virtual communities are discussed, and future research directions are suggested for further study.

INTRODUCTION

With the widespread use of internet, smart phones and social computing in recent years, people are becoming more engaged by participating in various virtual communities in everyday life. Virtual communities have their own unique characteristics such as anonymity and a lack of physical presence. Virtual communities make it possible for people who share similar values, interests, experiences, and knowledge and have similar beliefs and personal views to come together from various backgrounds and motivations. People can interact with other members of a virtual community anywhere at any time through any device. People can also be involved in multiple virtual communities and communicate with members of other virtual communities simultaneously. In doing so, trust and trust building between participants has become more significant than ever in order to maintain communication in virtual communities. In particular, virtual communities provide a platform or network

DOI: 10.4018/978-1-4666-7381-6.ch014

for members to communicate through faster and simultaneous interactions in a variety of ways. As the importance of the concept of trust in virtual communities has been widely accepted, it remains a complex, multifaceted and context-dependent concept (Kelton, Fleischmann, & Wallace, 2008; Stabb, Bhargava, Lilien, Rosenthal, Winslett, & Sloman, 2004).

In this chapter, first we examine the terms community and virtual community and describe their characteristics. Then, we examine the definitions and characteristics of the term trust in the new contexts of virtual communities and review relevant issues related to the concept of trust. Different types of trust and trust building are also investigated. Major research issues, challenges, and further research directions revolving around the term trust are discussed. In examining the concept of trust, this chapter focuses on the social aspects rather than the technical side of the term.

BACKGROUND

Community

There have been several different definitions of the term community, which reflects the fact that there may be difficulty and confusion with regards to defining the term (Bhattacharyya, 2004). Since a community seemingly refers to geographic proximity and the characteristics of defining community are similar to those of group (Christenson, Frendley, & Robinson, 1994), the term community is used interchangeably with the term group. Brandon and Hollingshead (2007) define the term group as "an entity comprised of people having interdependent goals, who are acquainted, interact with one another and have a sense of belonging associated with their membership" (p.106). Wilson and Ryder (1996) also agree that groups become communities, "when they interact with each other and stay together long enough to form a set of habits and conventions,

and when they come to depend upon each other for accomplishment of certain ends" (p. 801).

Turning to the term community, it is defined as "a constructed arena where multiple people with shared interests interact with each other" (Dehnart, 1999, A standard definition of community, para. 5). In comparing these definitions, we see that three components are shared: people, interaction, and a sense of belonging. In other words, community is composed of people who join as members, they socially interact, and their members have a set of shared denominators as their social identification or a sense of belonging to the community (Christenson et al., 1994). This third component is considered important since people need to have a sense of belonging by occupying a mutual and collective interest or intention to form a community. In line with this notion, the following definitions emphasize a sense of sharing, by saying that community is "any social configuration that possesses shared identity and norms" (Bahattacharyya, 2004, p. 12), or "a social organization of people who share knowledge, value and goals" (Jonassen, Peck, & Wilson, 1999, p. 118). To see whether the characteristics of the term community may apply to another term, virtual community, we now examine how differently or similarly people act in the virtual community.

Virtual Community

With the development of the Internet - also called virtual space, online space or cyberspace - people began to interact with each other through the medium. Rheingold (1993) defines the term virtual community as "social aggregations that emerge from the Net which is loosely interconnected computer networks, when sufficient people carry on those public discussions... to form webs of personal relationships in cyberspace" (p. 5). More specifically, Ridings, Gefen, and Arinze (2002) state that "virtual communities can be defined as groups of people with common interests and practices that communicate regularly and for some duration in an organized way over the Internet through a common… mechanism" (p. 273). In comparison with virtual communities, traditional communities tend to depend on a typical sense of location and relationships among their members and are generally bound to regional and physical proximity. Unlike traditional communities, virtual communities can work across and beyond space, time and physical organizational boundaries (Lipnack & Stamps, 1997; Mowshowitz, 1997). That is why virtual communities are considered a natural extension of traditional communities through a new medium in an online or virtual context (Ostwald, 1997).

Virtual communities have the same three components as the term community: people as members, social interaction, and a sense of belonging. Whittacher, Issaces, and O'Day (1997, p. 29) describe that:

1. "[M]embers of virtual communities have a shared goal, interest, need, or activity that provides the primary reason for belonging to community";
2. "[M]embers engage in repeated, active participation and often, intense interactions, strong emotional ties and shared activities occurring between participants";
3. "[M]embers also have access to share resources and there are policies for determining access to those resources"; and
4. "[R]eciprocity of information, support and services between members is considered significant". They also emphasize that there is a shared context of social conventions, language, and protocols (Whittacher et al., 1997).

Furthermore, social interactions are confined in a boundary within a virtual community. Members of a virtual community accept and follow rules (such as rules of admission, exclusion, and behavior). Hercheui (2011) emphasizes that a virtual community has boundaries and three characteristics of "common interests, rules, and voluntary membership" (p.5).

Regarding the specific differences of virtual communities from traditional communities, Dehnart (1999) describes the following noticeable changes: "media is becoming an arbiter, not just a creator, of community; communities can be entirely dependent upon technology for their survival; the identities of community members is [sic] becoming more ambiguous; communication is becoming less direct, requiring more proactive interaction among members of a community; and passive or anonymous participation is becoming standard" (Changing notions of community, para. 1). Among the three components mentioned above, Owston (1998) emphasizes that a virtual community is most of all "a group of people who regularly interact online and share common goals, ideals, or values" (p. 60). If a traditional community is a meeting place, virtual communities, rather than being places, exist as social networks (Wellman & Gulia, 1999). Ward (1999) supports this point by asserting "the spirit of community or communion that is found among networks of people is far more important than having a sense of place" (p. 98). People not only interact but also "learn from each other's work, and provide knowledge and information resources to the group related to certain agreed-upon topics of shared interest" (Hunter, 2002, p. 96). Therefore, social interactions in virtual communities are based on common interests and can also be considered as processes of transforming technology to meet people's needs. In addition, since members easily enter and leave a virtual community by following the rules of the community and their commitment to shared ideas and values could be ephemeral in virtual communities, the anonymity of members might impose different senses of identity in virtual communities.

As new digital technologies and communication tools emerge, communication methods change by reducing barriers of time and space that may hinder communication. Traditional face-to-face communication occurs only with people interacting simultaneously at the same location.

Unlike traditional forms of communication, with computer-mediated communication tools and new network technologies, people can use a lot of digital tools, such as video conferencing, a messenger program or an Internet phone, (e.g. Skype, Hangouts, etc.), and various applications over smartphones. These communication tools allow users to communicate anytime, anywhere, through any device simultaneously and ubiquitously. All of these technologies have a profound impact on the way people interact with each other and think of a community. New technologies make the creation of new or disguised identities possible. In particular, recent years have seen the proliferation of social networking and computing tools, such as Bulletin Board Systems (BBS), Internet Relay Chat (IRC), email listservs, Instant Messaging (IM), Really Simple Syndication (RSS) feeds, blogs, wikis, Facebook, Second Life, YouTube, Instgram, Twitter, etc. and accordingly members' social interactions also have become large and varied. As a result, new types of communication also emerge in virtual communities. Members' interactions are dichotomized into either synchronous or asynchronous types. Synchronous interactions can be found in IM, IRC, and Second Life, in which people communicate with each other in a more real-time sense. Asynchronous interactions and communications take place over a period of time in BBS, email listservs, blogs and social network web sites. For instance, while two individuals comment on a post in a blog, over time or (often) almost at the same time, they may become aware of other replies. Although those replies do not need real-time attention, this function is made possible by underlying systems. To take another example, in Facebook, most interactions are asynchronous, such as updating statuses and writing in responses to other members' posts. More and more systems support both types of interactions, which allow people to choose how they will interact with other members.

To consider social interaction in depth, researchers have made efforts in conceptualizing how people interact within virtual communities. In particular, some models and theories have been proposed for member relations in virtual communities. Short, Williams, and Christie (1976) propose a social presence theory. The theory defines social presence as the "degree of salience of the other person in the interaction and the consequent salience of the interpersonal relationships" (p. 65). They define social presence as a quality of the medium itself and hypothesize that "communications media vary in their degree of [s]ocial [p]resence, and that these variations are important in determining the way individuals interact" (Short et al., 1976, p. 65). More specifically, Swinth and Blascovich (2002) state "social presence can be thought of as whether or not there are social cues that signify the presence of others within some interactional context" (p. 319). In another model, Reduced Social Cues (Hiltz & Turoff, 1978; Kiesle, 1986; Sproull & Kiesler, 1991) are introduced where nonverbal, visual, status and position cues are largely missing in an online context. Personal identities are becoming ambiguous, and communication occurs in a social vacuum. They explain that cues indicate a person's social identity in virtual communities (Nass & Brave, 2005; Sproull & Kiesler, 1991; Tajfel & Turner, 1986). While some cues are in many ways missing, other cues might exist and may possibly be easier to change as well (Sproull & Kiesler, 1991). For example, online avatars have become very popular in some virtual communities. They represent some cues made by community members. However, it is also important to know that an avatar can be created, modified, and erased in a moment. In the reduced social cues approach, de-individuation means a state in which people lose their individuality, because group members do not feel they stand out as individuals and individuals act as if they are submerged in the group (Festinger, Pepitone, & Newcomb, 1952). This kind of impersonal view has been challenged by many studies on member relationships in virtual communities. The medium or underlying technology that supports a virtual community cannot predict its members' behavior. In spite of lacking nonverbal and social cues, personal relationships can still be further developed and fostered within virtual communities (Lea & Spears, 1991; Spears & Lea, 1992). Social capital theory is also used in virtual communities research that researchers found connections between social capital and virtual communities (Nip, 2004; Haythornthwaite, 2005; Chiu, Hsu, & Wang, 2006; Zhao et al. 2012) and there are other factors affect in forming the social capital within virtual communities, such as trust.

Regarding social interaction in virtual communities, the formation of social interaction and member communication is becoming more dependent upon the social context of virtual communities and the way to utilize the medium with members' needs (Jarvenpaa, Shaw, & Staples, 2004; Spears, Lea, Corneliessen, Postmes, & Ter Haar, 2003). Both the medium and members of virtual communities have an impact in shaping the complexity and quality of member relationships in the communities. The motivation and barriers to the formation of social interactions in virtual communities may vary. While familiarity among members of a community may increase precipitation (Ardichilli et al., 2003), a sense of belonging may be the most important factor in participation (Zhao et al., 2012). Ethical boundaries in virtual communities are critical, which affects members' participation and experience within the communities (Vanacker & Heider, 2012).

However, virtual communities are not created in a vacuum and they depend on technologies and the resources supporting the technologies. In other words, virtual communities cannot exist without connections with offline communities and technologies. The connections may pose restrictions or influence the communities in many ways. De Souza et al. (2004) relate the groupware software tools, such as Yahoo! Groups, SmartGroups

and MSN Groups, influence these communities through the rules and norms embedded in the tools. Institutions may have various types of connections to virtual communities, for example, providing financial support to hardware and software for virtual communities. Matzat (2004) shows that offline relations may influence the governance structure of the virtual communities. Hercheui (2011) reveals the existence of parallel governance structures in the studied virtual communities.

Then why do people join virtual communities? People gather and use virtual communities for different purposes and reasons. Some people want to share the common sense of community, others are just looking for various types of information, and the others may be in a virtual community for several more reasons. Rheingold (1993) states that virtual communities have two main functions for members, although there may be more: one is to act as a meeting or gathering place and the other is to act as a tool for members' use. The most frequently reported reason is to find information. Virtual communities bring together people with the same interests from all over the world. By searching or browsing a certain topic, people might get a breadth and depth of information from many virtual communities. This goes beyond a simple factual exchange, as search engines are powerful enough to find factual information. Knowledge exchange and information sharing are among the main reasons people use virtual communities (Constant, Sproull, & Kiesler, 1996; Ridings & Gefen, 2004; Wasko & Faraj, 2000). People also join virtual communities for recreational purposes, such as to play games. For example, Chess lovers play chess, share their experience, and improve skills with many unknown players from virtual communities. It is quite easy for game lovers to find numerous game sites in virtual communities (e.g. Computer, Xbox, PlayStation, Wii, etc.). Members socialize and make new friends easily within those virtual communities. Social support is another reason people join a virtual community (Sproull & Faraj, 1997). People with similar issues regarding health concerns or real estate problems join together in virtual communities to share their personal stories and past experiences. For instance, Radin (2006) studies an online breast cancer community sponsored by a nonprofit organization in Canada that consisted of members from New Zealand, Hong Kong, and Europe. Therefore, through their different purposes, virtual communities can be categorized into four communities:

1. Transaction communities,
2. Interest communities,
3. Relationship communities, and
4. Fantasy communities (Armstrong & Hagel, 1996).

Lu, Zhao, & Wang (2008) add one more type: mixed communities. Transaction communities "mainly focus on the transaction needs and from which people could get trading information"; In interest communities, "people share interest or expertise on a specific topic [and] gather together to communicate with each other"; Relationship communities refer to a space where "people with similar experience could come together and form meaningful interpersonal relationships"; And fantasy communities "usually refer to online games and in which people could come together get fantastic experience" (Lu et al., 2008, p. 1).

In summary, the unique characteristics of virtual communities mean that they are irrelevant of physical location, system-, technology- and medium-dependent, and social context-dependent. Members are relatively invisible or anonymous and they amass lower logistical and social costs (Sproull & Faraj, 1997). Knowledge exchange and information sharing seem to be closely related to virtual communities (Constant et al. 1996; Wasko & Faraj 2000). In comparison with traditional communities, the characteristics of virtual communities may bring some issues and challenges to the communities themselves. Considering social interaction and the sustainable membership of a community, we see there is a clear relationship between the issues of trust and virtual communities.

TRUST

Definitions and Characteristics

Since the concept of trust is complex, researchers have tried to define the term from interdisciplinary points of view, including sociology, philosophy, psychology, economics, political science, and others. Researchers tend to present several perspectives on trust because of the complexity and confusion revolving around trust. The three views of trust are identified by Brenkert (1998): attitudinal, predictability, and voluntarist. Among these, an attitudinal definition is given by Mayer, Davis, and Schoorman (1995) and agreed upon by the majority. They state, "trust is the willingness of a party to be vulnerable to the actions of another party based on the expectation that the other will perform a particular action important to the trustor, irrespective of the ability to monitor or control that other party" (p. 712). The predictability view of trust "stresses the importance of expectations about the behavioral predictability of the other party" (Connolly, 2008, p. 260). The voluntarist view of trust is that individuals voluntarily make themselves vulnerable and believe in another party's goodwill and harmlessness (Connolly, 2008).

In addition, trust has various aspects, such as an attitude, an attribution, an expectation, a feeling or belief, an intension, and a trait (Hoffman, Lee, Woods, Shadbolt, Miler, & Bradshaw, 2009), Accordingly, research on trust looks at trust with the following four aspects: 1) trust as an individual attribute; 2) trust as a behavior; 3) trust as a situational feature; and 4) trust as an institutional arrangement (Sitkin & Roth, 1993). Interestingly considering that the aspects of trust intertwine with each other, Govier (1997) points out that trust is fundamentally "an attitude, based on beliefs and feelings and implying expectations and dispositions" (p. 4). From this statement, trust is an attitude and likely to involve beliefs, feelings, and expectations. When people trust, they tend to expect kind and benevolent behaviors and actions toward themselves. Specifically, Govier (1997, p. 6) describes the detailed features of the attitude of trust:

1. Expectations of benign, not harmful, behavior based on beliefs about the trusted person's motivation and competence;
2. An attribution or assumption of general integrity on the part of the other, a sense that the trusted person is a good person;
3. A willingness to rely or depend on the trusted person, an acceptance of risk and vulnerability, and
4. A general disposition to interpret the trusted person's actions favorably.

Similarly, Gefen (2000) states that trust demonstrates the confidence in the trustees' benevolence, ability, integrity, and predictability in uncertain circumstances. Seen through these features, trust exists implicitly in many parts of our daily lives and social world (Govier, 1997).

Although people often are unaware of the trust processes, as Baier (1986) describes, "[m]ost of us notice a given form of trust most easily after its sudden demise or severe injury. We inhabit a climate of trust as we inhabit an atmosphere and notice it as we notice air, only when it becomes scarce or polluted" (p. 234). In addition, trust is based on the trustor's relevant experience and knowledge of others, and thus it is not just a game of chance (Jøsang, 1996). The willingness to rely or depend on the trusted person and to assume risk and vulnerability is vital to trust. Similar to the definition of trust given above by Mayer et al. (1995), trust is defined as "a psychological state comprising the intention to accept vulnerability based upon positive expectations of the intentions or behaviors of another" (Rousseau, Sitkin, Burt & Camerer, 1998, p. 395) in order to emphasize the two key elements – the willingness to accept vulnerability and the expectations of favorable treatment by another party. Chopra and Wallace (2003)

stress three elements: "a trustee to whom the trust is directed, confidence that the trust will be upheld, and a willingness to act on that confidence" (p. 2) and define that "trust is the willingness to rely on a specific other, based on confidence that one's trust will lead to lead to positive outcomes" (p. 3).

Trust is also context dependent. Grabner-Kräuter, Kaluscha, & Fladnitzer (2006) stress that context characteristics is one of three perspectives (context characteristics, trustor properties, and characteristics of the trusted object) in defining trust. Relationships and interactions between trustor and context, between trustee and context, among trustor, trustee, and context are acknowledged and addressed in many definitions of trust. Across disciplines there is agreement that people trust others in the context of their specific roles. Govier (1997) supports this fact by saying that "trust is not a binary choice between all and nothing. We may trust or distrust to various degrees… trust and distrust are often relativized to specific roles or contexts" (p. 5). Govier (1997) also points out that "trust on the whole does not mean trust in every context" (p. 5), since trust is not likely to be extended to other areas or specialties. For instance, we trust our physician with health-related matters. We trust our mechanics to fix our cars, but not our teachers on this matter.

Interestingly, regarding this aspect, people tend to trust based not on complete but incomplete knowledge, experience, and capabilities (Govier, 1997), only because people may not be able to get a complete picture of everything. Nevertheless, as Luhmann (1979) notes, people tend to judge, trust and assume that the outcomes will be beneficial. In this way, people assume that trust can broaden our possibilities and reduce the complexity of communication and social interactions. Since people have information about every aspect of life, even incomplete, and people tend to generalize from their experience, the outcome of any interaction still remains predictable. However, people do not trust blindly. Rather they know something about the people or situation they trust.

Therefore, trust is highly subject to a degree of belief about agents, not as an object property of an agent (McKnight & Chervany, 1996). The degree of such belief ranges from total trust to total distrust. For instance, there might be a situation in which an agent does not have an opinion of other agents' trustworthiness or is ignorant of others' trustworthiness. However, an agent will still make a trusting action, based on anticipation of a subjective judgment regarding the other agent (Abdul-Rahman & Hailes, 2000).

Trust is also created inductively, as Govier (1997, p. 8) remarks:

The attitude of trust presupposes inductively grounded beliefs and confident expectations that go further than strict induction world warrant. So it presupposes something we well know: we are creatures who reason inductively, and we have a tendency to extend our confidence beyond the evidence.

Since people trust inductively, based on their beliefs, Govier (1997) goes on to point out that:

… the attitude of trust presupposes inductively grounded beliefs and confident expectations…. We build more trust on the trust we have…. Trust is possible because we are inductive creatures who extend induction to provide ourselves with confident expectations about the future. Many of these expectations are about other people (p. 8).

The trust of other people is possible because people inductively extend their beliefs and responses to others, based upon their sense of themselves, position in the world and their values. This fact implies that trust is dynamic and value-added as additional experiences and evidence may increase or decrease the degree of trust in others later on (Abdul-Rahman & Hailes, 2000).

Trust as a complex concept is likely to be composed of many attributes. Grandison and Sloman (2000) identify the attributes of trust as the following: reliability, dependability, honesty, truthfulness, security, competence, and timeliness (p. 3). As some researchers agree, they also point out that these attributes are dependent on the environment, where trust resides with people (Grandison & Sloman, 2000, p. 3). Mayer et al.'s study includes three factors of perceived trustworthiness as ability, benevolence, and integrity (1995). Trust is also closely related to two conditions: risk and dependence (Rousseau, et al., 1998). Chopra and Wallace (2003) categorize a range of perspectives into the following areas: nature of trust, elements of trust, preconditions (dependence and risk), dimensions, trustworthiness (what attributes are desired of a potential recipient of trust), influences (what factors influence trust), and processes (how does trust build and evolve). More importantly, McEvily and Tortoriello (2011) review a number of trust related studies and existing trust measurement tools and state that trust can be measured.

Among all of these attributes, we only focus on antecedent, risk, and dependence that are crucial to trust building processes and examine them in a more detailed manner. Antecedents are conditions that lead to trust and support trust building. In different contexts, researchers have identified context-dependent and more common antecedents. Mayer et al. (1995) summarize that trust antecedents appearing in literature generally fall into three major categories: ability, benevolence, and integrity. In virtual communities, most of all, information technology factors are greatly considered as antecedents to trust.

Risk has also been studied in many disciplines. Risk and uncertainty exist in every aspect of our lives because our ability to gather and handle information is limited. Economist Knight (1921) makes his famous distinction between risk (randomness with knowable probabilities) and uncertainty (randomness with unknowable probabilities). More specifically, risk refers to "situations in which the outcome of an event is unknown, but the decision-maker knows the range of possible outcomes and the probabilities of each" (Klein,

2009, p. 326). Kahneman and Tversky (1979) propose Prospect Theory to explain the framing effects that human is likely to be risk aversion for gains and risk proness for losses by incorporating psychological mechanisms. Although the importance of risk in understanding trust has long been recognized (Luhmann, 1988), there is no consensus on risk and its relationship with trust. Importantly, researchers agree that complete certainty will not lead to trust and trust does not need to be involved in such circumstances. Mayer, et al. (1995) argue that trust would lead to risk taking and perceived risk moderates the relationship between trust and risk taking. Risk occurs when we do not have complete information about the situation we are in; if we take certain actions, the outcome may be unpredictable in such a way that the outcome is harmful to us. As a result, risk may lead to trust and trust building. Mayer, et al. (1995) address that "it is unclear whether risk is an antecedent to trust, is trust, or is an outcome of trust" (p. 711). We should note that not all risk taking or the presence of risk is related to trust. Although the relationship between risk and trust is complex, risk is necessary for the formation of trust (Chen & Dhillon, 2003). Pavlou (2003) finds that risk is not a causal predictor of trust and an antecedent to trust; on the other hand, trust is an antecedent of perceived risk.

Dependence refers to one party relying on others to achieve a desired result. Dependence can be categorized into shallow dependence, shallow inter-dependence, deep dependence, and deep inter-dependence (Sheppard, & Sherman, 1998). Shallow dependence "occur[s] when one's outcomes are contingent upon the action of another" (p. 424). In shallow inter-dependence, both parties must effectively coordinate behavior in order to achieve desired goals (p. 424). In deep dependence, "a trustee's behavior is often outside the trustor purview" (p. 425). Deep inter-dependence is characterized by shared values and norms. Sheppard and Sherman (1998) remark that "trust is the acceptance of the risks associated

with the type and depth of the inter-dependence inherent in a given relationship" (p. 425). The distinction between confidence and trust depends on perception and attribution and our ability to distinguish between dangers and risks (Luhmann, 1988). In a situation of confidence, people do not consider alternatives, while in a situation of trust, people choose one action over others in spite of the possibility of being disappointed by that action (Luhmann, 1988). Trust and confidence can lead to disappointment. In the case of confidence, people will "react to disappointment by external attribution" (Luhmann, 1988, p. 97). In the case of trust, people will "have to consider an internal attribution and eventually regret trusting choice" (Luhmann, 1988, p. 98).

We see that trust is considered a dynamic and social phenomenon. Trust evolves all the time. The characteristics of trust can be summarized as the following: 1) it exists as a subjective degree of trust; 2) it is established in a certain context; 3) it involves expectations of future outcomes; 4) it is not necessarily transitive (Abdul-Rahaman & Hailes, 2000); 5) trust might be based on prior experiences, and 6) trust might not be always beneficial. Viewed from different perspectives, there might be more characteristics of trust in different contexts.

Types of Trust

Unlike traditional communities, virtual communities may not have face-to-face contact and their visual cues are different. To understand trust better, some researchers have tried to identify the types of trust in virtual communities.

Lewis (1999) classifies trust into two types: deep trust and swift trust. Deep trust refers to not just an acknowledgement between two agents but trusting interpersonal relationships built on mutual appreciation. Swift trust, also called scatter trust (Govier, 1997) or thin trust (Putnam, 2000), refers to "a more generalized decision to give most people the benefit of the doubt" (Radin, 2006, p. 593).

Some researchers identify trust as consisting of three dimensions in an intertwined mode: ability, benevolence, and integrity (Mayer et al., 1995; Gefen & Straub, 2004). Ability refers to skills or competencies that allow an individual to be perceived as competent in a certain area, such as a mutual interest or hobby, in virtual communities. Benevolence means that others care about and treat the trustor well. Integrity is the expectation that the trustee will act in accordance with social norms or principles that the trustor accepts.

In order to produce an acceptable typology, McKnight and Chervany (2001) analyze numerous definitions of trust from various fields, including psychology, social psychology, sociology, economics, political science, management, and communications. They identify two kinds of trust: construct type and referent type. The construct type of trust refers to "what type of construct trust is" (p. 7025), while the referent type of trust "refers to the object of trust" (p. 7025). McKnight and Chervany (1996) categorize trust into three different types:

1. Interpersonal trust,
2. System trust or impersonal trust, and
3. Dispositional trust.

Interpersonal trust refers to direct trust between two or more people (or groups) in a specific context. System trust or impersonal trust refers to trust that is not founded upon any personal attributes or states but rather upon the perceived properties of a system or institution. Luhmann (1988) states "[a] system – economic, legal, or political – requires trust as an input condition. Without trust it cannot stimulate supportive activities in situations of uncertainty or risk" (p. 103). In the modern world, our societies build not only on interpersonal trust but also on system trust. Take the monetary system as an example: we may not trust what other people say about the value of money, but we do trust the banking system, which ensures the value of money. Another example would be the legal system. We do not trust other people but trust the legal system to ensure the justice of our society. In comparison with interpersonal trust, system trust "is incomparably easier to acquire than personal trust.... [B]ut, [o]n the other hand, it is incomparably more difficult to control" (Luhmann, 1979, p. 50). System trust implies that people depend on the system. In other words, people trust the information processed by others as the elements of the system and within the system only. System trust is closely related to impersonal structure. McKnight, Cumming, and Chervany (1998) suggest that two types of impersonal trust can be differentiated as: structural assurances and situational normality" (p. 478). Structural assurances include safeguards such as regulations, guarantees, or contracts (Shapiro, 1987; Zucker, 1986). Situational normality may include one's own role and others' roles in the situation (Baier, 1986). System trust is based on the perception that things appear normal (Baier, 1986) or in "proper order" (Lewis & Weigert, 1985, p. 974).

Dispositional trust is based on the personality attributes of the trusting party (McKnight & Chervany, 1996). Dispositional trust is a pervasive attitude toward others that exhibits a basic trust or general inclination to display faith in humanity (McKnight & Chervany, 1996). Dispositional trust is sometimes called "basic trust that... describes the general trusting attitude of the trustor" (Abdul-Rahman & Hailes, 2000, p. 3). It can be considered independent of any context. Therefore, there is no consensus in relation to dispositional versus situational trust. While dispositional trust is assuming that other people are always trustworthy, irrespective of whether people are good or bad, "one will obtain better outcomes by trusting them- hence, one should trust them" (McKnight & Chervany, 1996, p. 38). In virtual communities, people tend to depend on technology and media more than in traditional communities and the identity of members is very difficult to obtain and trust because of members' easy appearance and disguise.

Similarly, in classifying trust some researchers suggest that trust may be broadly categorized into three layers: dispositional, learnt, and situational trust (Dibben, Morris, & Lean, 2000; Giffin, 1967; Worchel, 1979). Dispositional trust refers to "the personal trait or disposition of an individual to be trusting or not" (Dibben, et al., 2000, p. 56). Dispositional trust here may be slightly different from that discussed above. Learnt trust is an individual's general tendency to trust. Situational trust is dependent on situational cues such as context or information available (Worchel, 1979).

Regarding trust building, some researchers categorize trust differently. Sarker, Valacich, & Sarker (2003) identify personality-based (that develops because of a person's trusting nature), institutional-based (that is a function of an individual's belief in institutional norms/procedures), and cognitive-based trust (which develops from social cues and impressions that an individual receives from the other). In another categorization, Lewicki and Bunker (1996) extend that trust is developed in transitional stages into three types of trust: calculus-based trust, identification-based trust, and knowledge-based trust. Calculus-based trust refers to trust that exists between individuals in the early stage of a relationship. This form of trust is grounded "not only in the fear of punishment for violating the trust but also in the rewards to be derived from preserving it" (Lewicki & Wiethoff, 2000, p. 88). Knowledge-based trust exists between two parties based on the predictability of the other party. Identification-based trust exists where the parties understand, appreciate and share one another's needs. In addition, Lucero and Wallerstein (2013) show that trust development can evolve in stages by the order of calculus-based, knowledge-based, and identification-based trust.

To assess interpersonal trust, McAllister (1995) divides interpersonal trust into affect-based trust and cognition-based trust. In his study, cognition-based trust is defined as choosing "whom we will trust in which respects and under what circumstances, and we base the choice on what we take

to be 'good reasons,' constituting evidence of trustworthiness" (Lewis & Wiegert, 1985, p. 970). Affect-based trust consists of the emotional bonds between individuals (Lewis & Wiegert, 1985). Some researchers stress affective (e.g., caring, emotional connection) elements along with the cognitive elements of trust (Kanawattanachai & Yoo, 2007). Emotional states have an effect on trust. Emotions may change the ability, benevolence, and integrity of the trusting individual in some way cognitively (Dunn & Scheweitzer, 2005). Trusting actions appear to be sudden and dramatic (Murnighan, Malhotra, & Weber, 2004). In the meantime, emotional attachments may cause a trusting individual to take a sudden risk and have irrational trust (Rawlins, 2009; Weber, Malhotra, and Murnighan, 2005). As we have seen in the several different types of trust from multiple perspectives, it is apparent that many factors are involved in identifying, grouping and assessing trust and we need to take a holistic approach in understanding trust and trust building.

Trust Building in Virtual Communities

When trust is considered in the particular setting of virtual communities, many researchers question whether the findings of trust and trust building in traditional communities can be applied to virtual communities, since there are differences in trust building in the two communities (Castelfranchi & Tan, 2001; Herring, 2002; Kollock, 1999).

Returning to the three types of trust (i.e. interpersonal trust, system trust, and dispositional trust), building trust in virtual communities mostly involves interpersonal trust (McKnight & Chervany, 1996; McKnight & Chervany, 2001; Ridings et al., 2002). Trust is built through social interactions among individual members and/or between members and the entire community. Most importantly, we need to pay attention to the fact that achieving trust in virtual communities is strongly dependent upon the technological medium of the Internet or built-in web systems and tools. In addition, as emerging social networking sites make social interaction over the Internet much easier than before, virtual communities start to leverage social networking technology. With the advancement of security technology, security measures may protect communities from attacks and unwarranted access. When no risk is involved, trust becomes redundant so that over-emphasizing security may lead to a climate of distrust (Kramer, 1999). Therefore, trust in virtual communities depends highly on system trust or impersonal trust, as social interaction activities are possible only though the capabilities of the technological medium and supporting systems. In line with this notion, the trust of members is likened to trusting a technological medium (including a remote agent, medium, and the technology in general) rather than members themselves, particularly when the true identity of members is not necessarily revealed to others (Burauska & Asldama, 2008).

The approach to the consideration of trust building as a process has been elaborated through theoretical models. Zucker (1986) proposes three different modes of trust production. They are characteristic-based, process-based, and institutional-based trust building mechanisms. Characteristic-based trust is produced based on personal characteristics such as ethnic background, religion, age, sex, etc. The major mechanism for the production of this type of trust is through a sense of shared commonality with other parties. Process-based trust is produced based on social exchanges between individuals and organizations. The exchanges may be obtained directly from previous successful experiences in building trust and indirectly from established reputation, brands, etc. Institutional-based trust is produced through a third party and is tied to broad societal institutions on intermediary mechanisms (Zucker, 1986).

When comparing types of trust, among deep trust and swift trust, swift trust seems more important at the early stage of building trust. Research suggests that reputation, self-efficacy, system

quality, and structural assurance are stable factors to foster initial trust in mobile banking (Zhou, 2011; Zhou, 2012). For long-term trust, cognition-based trust is followed by affect-based trust (McAllister, 1995). Among the three stages of trust building (i.e. calculus-based, knowledge-based and identification-base), the calculus-based distrust holds high negative expectations in impersonally interacting compared to others. The identification-based distrust has more negative emotional attachment than others and holds high confidence in negative expectations regarding others (Lewicki & Bunker, 1996; Lewicki & Wiethoff, 2000). In addition, the violation of trust is likely to be an emotional event for the trustor (Lewicki & Bunker, 1996; Morrison & Robinson, 1997). When parties are unable to conform to expectations, trust is violated. However, not every violation may change the trust between trustors and trustees. Frequent or severe violations of trust are likely to change the trusting relationship. Lewicki and Wiethoff (2000) discuss that violations of calculus-based trust are likely to encourage calculus-based distrust. Violations of identification-based trust have a greater effect on the parties' emotional well-being. Violations of identification-based trust are likely to end the relationship itself, if they are not properly addressed. To repair such a violation, parties must first communicate in an attempt to identify and understand the breach, and then explicitly recommit themselves to their trusting relationship (Lewicki & Wiethoff, 2000; Tomlinson & Mayer, 2009). Nooteboom criticizes (2002) that it is unlikely that knowledge-based trust will secede from the calculus-based trust because knowledge is required when forming calculus-based trust.

Empirically, some researchers propose several frameworks: a conceptual framework of trust where antecedents link to outcomes (Shankar, Urban, & Sultan, 2002; Lu, Zhao, & Wang, 2009) and trust antecedents with cognitive, affective, interpersonal, and social factors (Kramer, 1999). Among them, Gefen, Karahanna and Straub (2003) identify five categories of constructing trust antecedents:

1. **Knowledge-Based Trust:** Focuses on trust building through ongoing interactions;
2. **Institution-Based Trust:** Refers to relying upon an impersonal structure or third party to build trust (this corresponds to impersonal trust or system trust);
3. **Calculative-Based Trust:** Deals with rational assessments of ongoing relationships;
4. **Cognition-Based Trust:** Refers to trust building through impressions rather than repeated personal interactions over a longer period of time; and lastly
5. **Personality-Based Trust:** Refers to individual personalities that influence trust building.

The above categories and antecedents facilitate overall trust building and may influence the initial decision to trust.

In addition, the differences between offline and online interactions may influence the formation of trust. In virtual communities, interactions occur through a technological medium, which may potentially eliminate or reduce some important factors for trust building. Some antecedent conditions are compromised in virtual communities. Lack of authority to govern interactions, anonymity, and ease of joining, leaving, or lurking impose on trust building. Although lacking social and other traditional cues facilitate trust building, interactions within virtual communities are filled with other cues that might be interpreted as indices of trust (de Laat, 2005). For example, account name, email address, avatar, login time, and login frequency might be valuable cues to the information about individual members. In communicating with each other, most interactions are text-based, since people use language and write letters to convey meaning. Different people might have their own patterns, such as using specific words, spelling, or abbreviations. Different styles and forms of writing may reveal who the individuals are and give us a sense of how they interact with others.

As various factors contribute to trust building, the concept of trust is directly or indirectly related to several relevant terms as well, including authority, identity, authenticity, shared values, commitment, reputation, etc. "Trust involves beliefs about the intentions of the authority" (Tyler & Lind, 1992, p. 142) and authorities are "the subset of people or information perceived to be credible" (Rieh & Danielson, 2007, p.313). People come to trust because they believe that the authority can be trusted to try to behave fairly (Tyler & Lind, 1992). Authority is influenced by one's thoughts and institutional affiliation and at the same time, influences on people's actions (Wilson, 1983). Doyle (2012) investigates trust antecedents, trustworthiness signals, and inaccurate messaging related to trust building in wine blogs and suggests that authoritative knowledge drives ratings of the credibility of a blogger and leads to trust of its claims.

Lynch (2001) considers identity as related to trust and anonymity and pseudonymity as closely related to identity and trust building in virtual communities. Although account name, email address, and other cues including writing style and content may be sources for identity, those cues have limited reliability. They might be changed and not be persistent. It is becoming increasingly popular for members to have links to their personal web sites and weblogs in signature files (Donath, 1998). Some members may reveal their MSN or Facebook account to others during interactions. This may result in linking to more permanent online identities or even real identities. The authenticity of the identity is directly related to the authenticity of the cues associated with the identity. It is impractical to verify all the information on identity for members in virtual communities. On the other hand, authenticity of identity is tied to the authoritative identity for authorizing sources. In other words, authenticity is associated with a third-party authority. However, because identity alone cannot lead to trust, communications and interactions among members of virtual communities often lead to a sense of belonging and shared values, which often evoke social trust (Porter, 2004; Siegrist, Cvetkovich, & Gutscher, 2001). Commitment is also seen as a mandatory factor in maintaining trust (Hunt & Morgan, 1994). Reputation and a trusted third party have a strong influence on a member's initiative to participate in interactions and trust building (Kollock, 1999; Jarvenpaa, Tractinsky, & Vitale, 2000). Social networks make electronic word of mouth communication extremely easy among consumers through sharing knowledge concerning products and services (Jeong & Jang, 2011), which can lead to trust or distrust and influence on decision making (di Pietro & Pantano, 2013).

To better understand the relationships between trust and other concepts, a credibility assessment model may be applied to virtual communities (Hilligoss & Rieh, 2008). The proposed model consists of three levels of credibility judgments: construct, heuristics, and interaction. "The construct level pertains to how a person constructs, conceptualizes, or defines credibility.... The heuristics level involves general rules of thumb used to make judgments of credibility.... The interaction level refers to credibility judgments based on specific source or content cues" (Hilligoss & Rieh, 2008, p. 1473). This model shows that the three levels are interlinked and credibility is relative to the social context in information seeking and credibility judgments (Hilligoss & Rieh, 2008, p. 1482).

In summary, as virtual communities are distinctive from traditional communities in many ways, building trust in virtual communities also may differ. With the development of technology in recent years, new virtual communities are emerging and changing all the time in given contexts. Newly created web and smart phone tools and technological systems become substantial in building trust as those tools support communication and innovatively create member interaction. As seen in this section, many studies show that there are several types of trust and trust building. Importantly, as trust building is considered as a process through

social interaction in virtual communities, several factors in building trust are involved. Trust building is clearly critical in virtual communities and is still being discussed.

ISSUES AND DISCUSSION

As trust and trust building in virtual communities have heterogeneous and multifaceted aspects, literature about the two terms brings notable and valuable issues to research communities. Although many issues have been studied, more comprehensive studies are needed to further explore these topics theoretically and/or empirically in depth. Key research issues that we discuss in this section can be grouped into the following six issues:

1. Examining the nature and role of trust in perspectives consisting of trustor, trustee, and context;
2. Investigating kinds of factors that affect virtual communities in the given context;
3. Examining concepts such as distrust, antitrust, trust repair, and especially, the negative side of trust;
4. Investigating trust from a multi-dimensional perspective;
5. Exploring the identity of members and other personal traits that may affect trust building in a virtual community; and
6. Trust and distrust and their relationship in new types of virtual communities (e.g. social network sites, mobile based virtual communities).

Most of all, considering that trust and trust building are highly dependent on situational contexts (Granovetter, 1985), research on examining the specific context is one of the major issues in a certain type of virtual community. As e-commerce-related virtual communities in recent years are growing at an exponential rate, e-commerce-related virtual communities become "a new form of e-business medium" (Wu & Tsang, 2008, p. 115). Various communities (i.e. eBay, Amazon, PayPal, etc.) provide a valuable key to understanding electronic commerce and digital economy (Ridings et al., 2002). Since members benefit by acquiring electronic resources, the power to search for information is significant in expediting e-trading efficiently, speedily, and at greatly reduced transaction costs. In particular, as mobile based virtual communities are growing dramatically, trust and trust building are also important to them and their social interaction can be applied to mobile communities in the same manner (Yan et al., 2013). Lu, Zhao, and Wang (2008) point out that important factors to forming this kind of virtual community include familiarity, structural assurances, and perceived similarity to others in building trust between members' capabilities. In addition, research about trust and trust building associated with social media may leverage a social media framework with functional building blocks, such as identity, conversations, sharing, presence, relationships, reputation, and groups (Kietzmann et al., 2011).

Trust building in virtual communities is a complex process and it is affected by several factors. One issue in this matter is examining explicit and implicit factors in the given context of the communities. As trust and trust building in one type of virtual community may be different in another type, it is agreed that antecedent conditions of trust in one type of virtual community may be different from other kinds. As types of trust vary, different types of social interaction also have an impact on trust formation. Different types of available information may not cultivate trust in the same way. Types of information sought and exchanged in social interaction may be scrutinized in different types of communities. For example, to understand radical virtual communities (i.e. terrorist communities), some factors may have been taken for granted that should have had more attention (i.e. ethnicity, race, culture, etc.). Since virtual communities reflect the real world, trust and trust building need to be put into a wide context. Yan (2009) finds out that children and adolescents have limited knowledge and resources to develop their understanding on the complexity and potential harm of the Internet. Unsurprisingly, we could spot private information on social networking sites, such as Facebook, blogs, Twitter, etc. That information may lead to potential harm. According to Wolak, Finkelhor, & Mitchell (2004), trust is developed between sex predators and victims through communications on the Internet and may eventually lead to face-to-face meetings and sexual activities.

Contexts, cultures and personal traits are all important factors. Trust may have different influences, depending on gender, culture, and social network sites. According to Hofstede (1980), gender is an important dimension of culture. Buchan, Croson, and Solnick (2008) study trust and gender through behavior and beliefs in the investment game. They find that the relationship between expected return and trusting behavior is stronger among men than women. Connolly and Bannister (2007) compare antecedents of consumer trust in online shopping in Ireland and the United States and find that culture does play a role in relation to trust. Other researchers also confirm that trust may affect people in different cultures differently (Kim, 2008; Turel, Yuan, & Connelly, 2008). Stepanikova, et al. (2006) find through a study of patients that racial/ethnic/language-based differences are reflected in a patient's trust in a physician based on their perception of a physician's behaviors. Factors such as the average age of members in virtual communities and information technology artifacts used in virtual communities may affect trust as well. Mangum (2011) finds that African Americans interacting with others in social networks produce political trust - a special trust depends on interpersonal trust.

To understand trust better, distrust has been a focus of trust research and has become one of the most significant issues. Regarding distrust, there are two perspectives. Some researchers argue that distrust and trust are two distinct concepts, not two ends of one continuum (Lewicki, McAllister, & Bies, 1998; McKnight & Chervany, 2006), while others take the opposite view that trust and distrust are the opposite ends of the same continuum (Schoorman, Mayer, & Davis, 2007). Importantly, there is a dimension between trust and distrust, in which people neither trust nor distrust. Hardin (2002) suggests there are asymmetries between trust and distrust because they have "asymmetric grounds both motivational and epistemological" and they have "substantially asymmetric implications for behavior and for society" (p. 90). Distrust usually arises when a breach of trust happens and a trust building process may lead to either trust or distrust. Distrust seems to be related to strong, negative emotions. The importance of distrust has been recognized not only in e-commerce but also in other areas. For example, in e-commerce, vendors or online shops, whether they are legitimate or illegitimate, try to diminish distrust and foster trust. In virtual learning communities, distrust may have negative effects and discourage people from learning. Like trust, distrust may be related to gains or losses depending on different circumstances. McEvily, Radzevick, and Weber (2012) propose measuring trust based on measuring distrust (i.e. individuals' willingness to incur costs to mitigate vulnerability to others). Additionally, trust is not always positive and beneficial. In some senses, cyber bullying is a breach of trust and may lead to distrust. Mishna, Saini & Solomon (2009) suggest that cyber bullying occurs within the context of students' social groups and relationships. They have categorized cyber bulling into three types: posting, coercing and "backstabbing" and masquerading. Surprisingly, they have found that many students cyber bully their friends. When cyber bullying happens, students are unlikely to disclose it to parents. The reasons may be very complex when students decide to take risks to trust or distrust. Whether trust and distrust can coexist may be clear in critical situations. For example, Ho & Chau (2013) examine location accuracy and precision

of a location personalization mobile service and suggest that trust and distrust can coexist since they found that the service increases individuals' integrity and perceived location accuracy directly increases distrust. To reveal the relation of distrust and trust and the antecedents of distrust, further studies on this issue need to be conducted.

As mentioned in the previous section, trust has been recognized as a multidimensional and multi-faceted construct. Mitchell & Zigurs (2009) list more than twenty theories in literature of trust in virtual teams, such as social identity theory, social impact theory, media richness theory, etc. Putnam (1993) states "trust is an essential component of social capital" (p. 170). In other words, in social capital theory, trust is treated as a variable (Khodyakov, 2007). Some researchers recognize trust as an essential factor for collaborative behavior (Gambetta, 1988). Others suggest that trust is a conscious or rational choice (Hardin, 1992; Williamson, 1993). Lewis & Weigert (1985) define trust as the "undertaking of a risk in the course of action on the confident expectation that all persons involved in the action will act competently and dutifully" (p. 971).

Another perspective on obtaining trust is seeing it as a process. Trust building could be considered as stages of development since trust is built gradually as people interact with each other. Trust building is a continuous process and requires positive refinements (Ofuonye, Beatty, Reay, Dick, & Miller, 2008). Trust could be conceptualized as a psychological state in terms of an individual's disposition and interrelated internal cognitive and affective processes (Kramer, 1999) so that it may operate as a moderator after examining recent trust studies in organizational settings (Dirks & Ferrin, 2001). They further suggest that trust has an important impact on attitudinal and behavioral outcomes as well as on management. To some extent, virtual communities are loosely connected organizations. Some findings such as those on organizational settings may be applied directly to virtual communities. In general, various aspects in looking at trust from social, cognitive, affective and contextual perspectives need to be taken into account in order to develop a comprehensive theory on trust and trust building, since definitions and theories built upon one discipline alone may reveal a partial picture of trust and trust building. Studying multiple factors from multi-disciplines is an interesting area for further research and will add a new dimension to the existing theories and models.

Lastly, the identity of community members is significant. As web tools and technology are highly significant in virtual communities, it may be tricky and complicated to recognize community members' real identities through anonymous identification or online aliases. Therefore, confirming identities and gaining authority members are ongoing and noteworthy research issues. People might be at greater risk, if they reveal the web addresses of their personal web sites, wikis, blogs, or Facebook accounts, because it may be possible to determine their real identities through gathered information from those sources in a limited setting. In some virtual communities, online identity and off-line identity might be tangled or mixed together so that building trust through identities can be very complex. Different types of visual cues are emerging in virtual communities. This kind of visual cue is different from face-to-face environments and an important source of identification. Song and Kim (2006) investigate the effect of subjective norms, social comparison, and social identity on intention to use an avatar service in virtual communities. New virtual communities, like ones on Second Life, have even brought largely text-based social interactions to 3D level. One emerging class of online social network depends on users' sharing their location with others (including friends, members of communities, and anonymous). Location sharing creates new and distinct interactions that may encourage others to join in the activity (Coughlan, Linden, & Adams, 2012) and imposes risk to individuals who share their locations on the web. In addition, on social

network sites the interaction of trust and distrust is a critical factor. Russo (2012) suggests that both trust in the technology artifact and trust in other network users positively influence willingness to participate in location-based social interactions, while the usability of the technology artifact and structural assurances are the two most import antecedent conditions that lead to trust. He also notices that women have a much stronger willingness to participate in a community than men do. Examining trust and trust building needs to be revisited in these social network sites among virtual communities.

In summary, we agree that in a virtual environment, trust is based on beliefs in the trustworthiness of a trustee, which is composed of three distinct dimensions (that are mostly agreed upon): integrity, ability, and benevolence (McKnight & Chervany, 2002). It is important to examine the factors, dimensions, and major issues in a virtual community when reconsidering the construct of trust in the virtual context. Questions such as whether each dimension and factor is equally important and whether other factors or new dimensions exist can lead to a deeper understanding of trust.

FUTURE RESEARCH DIRECTIONS

Numerous aspects and issues need to be further examined, including the six key issues discussed above. In this section, we highlight some additional future research avenues, although this list is not limited.

First, we suggest that the focus should be on further investigation of the characteristics and factors of trust in virtual communities. Previous studies reveal that there are different types of virtual communities and different factors of trust building that affect virtual communities. With the development of network technology with various tools, it is quick and simple to stay connected with other people. For example, smart phones or other mobile devices are very popular and allow people to be in and out of virtual communities in a much easier and faster way. A person's real identity may be unknown but his or her current location may be tracked by the use of location personalization technology. Furthermore, social media introduces substantial and pervasive changes to communication between members of virtual communities and non-virtual communities. All of these factors may have an impact on the operation of virtual communities. Regarding this aspect, we ask some research questions that need to be investigated further: How do virtual communities get created? What activities and dynamics are actually going on in virtual communities? What factors cause virtual communities to merge, collapse and disappear? How do new technologies interact with the activities of virtual communities? and finally, what methods are appropriate for conducting this research to answer these questions? Given the multi-faceted phenomenon of virtual communities, it seems necessary to take a holistic approach with multi-faceted and multi-dimensional components. As virtual communities are social hubs, studies on the information searching and sharing behaviors of members and interaction between members and their relations may also shed light on more elusive issues such as group norms, community attachment, commitment, trust, and trust development.

Second, time is an inevitable factor among many of the factors in trust and trust building in virtual communities. One study of particular interest finds that although old or experienced members have gradually developed trust in the community over time, the importance of trust decreases with experience (Gefen, Karahanna, & Straub, 2003). Or new members of a virtual community may behave differently from old members. Some longitudinal studies in limited laboratory settings demonstrate that trust changes over time (Serino, Furner, & Smatt, 2005). Regarding this matter, more studies need to explore the relationship of time and other factors in trust building in real settings. The result of these studies may also be applied to both virtual and non-virtual communities.

Third, swift trust is formed in virtual communities with members who may only have limited information about the communities and other members. Some studies suggest swift trust is based on stereotypical impressions from categorical information and communication behaviors such as members' characteristic patterns of communication behavior (Jarvenpaa & Leidner, 1998). Regarding the swift trust issue, some questions arise: Is swift trust dependent on the type of virtual communities? What factors may affect long-term trust to be built from swift trust? Is there a relationship between swift trust and technology in building trust?

Fourth, as the use of mobile phone devices and services spreads, mobile-based virtual communities have quickly emerged as a new form of virtual communities and provide various mash-up and upgraded services for members. Trust and trust building in these communities are considered essential. Further research should be conducted to explore the unique and distinctive characteristics and social interaction within and across members in the communities.

Lastly, it is necessary to pay more attention to the violation of trust and trust repair. After trust has been violated or damaged, people in communities repair violated trust in order to re-build it. Understanding the trust-repairing processes will add valuable insight to research on the field. Regarding this matter, some research questions arise, such as: How is trust violated? How is trust repaired and rebuilt? What factors have an impact on the trust reparation process? What conditions or strategies are effective in repairing violated trust?

We would like to emphasize that the studies on trust and trust building need to be conducted not only with empirical data but also in theory. We expect that longitudinal studies on trust in virtual communities will produce important outcomes for the field and continue to draw the attention of researchers in the future.

CONCLUSION

Trust exists in every aspect of our society, in both traditional and virtual communities. We assume that as more new digital tools and technologies are developed, the more various virtual communities will emerge and trust and trust building might be more complicated. Trust as a multi-dimensional concept has been examined regarding its definition, nature, characteristics, types and factors in different approaches. It is not surprising to see that there are various models of trust and trust building. As virtual communities are built for many purposes, the importance of understanding trust and trust building has theoretical and practical implications on many aspects of our communities and all of society. In the near future, we hope there will be more technical solutions for trust management and that some concerns of trust may be solved. Nevertheless, as long as social aspects of virtual communities remain a similarly important issue, accordingly, trust building will continue to be a focus of research in virtual communities.

REFERENCES

Ardichivili, A., Page, V., & Wentling, T. (2003). Motivation and barriers to participation in virtual knowledge-sharing communities of practice. *Journal of Knowledge Management*, 7(1), 64–77. doi:10.1108/13673270310463626

Armstrong, A., &, J. (1996). The real value of on-line communities. *Harvard Business Review*, 74(3), 134–141.

Baier, A. (1986). Trust and antitrust. *Ethics*, 96(2), 231–260. doi:10.1086/292745

Bhattacharyya, J. (2004). Theorizing community development. *Journal of the Community Development Society*, 34(2), 5–34. doi:10.1080/15575330409490110

Brandon, D. P., & Hollingshead, A. B. (2007). Characterizing online groups. In A. N. Joinson, K. Y. A. McKenna, T. Postmes, & U. D. Reips (Eds.), *The Oxford handbook of Internet psychology* (pp. 105–119). Oxford, UK: Oxford University Press.

Brenkert, G. (1998). Trust, business and business ethics: An introduction. *Business Ethics Quarterly*, 8(2), 195–203. doi:10.5840/beq19988219

Buchan, N. R., Croson, R., & Solnick, S. J. (2008). Trust and gender: An examination of behavior, biases, and beliefs in the investment game. *Journal of Economic Behavior & Organization*, 68(3-4), 466–476. doi:10.1016/j.jebo.2007.10.006

Burauskas, G., & Aldama, J. I. (2008). *Trust in virtual community*. (Unpublished master thesis). Lund University, Lund, Sweden.

Castelfranchi, C., & Tan, Y. H. (2001). *Trust and deception in virtual societies*. Dordrecht, The Netherlands: Kluwer Academic Publishers. doi:10.1007/978-94-017-3614-5

Chen, S. C., & Dhillon, G. S. (2003). Interpreting dimensions of consumer in e-commerce. *Information Technology Management*, 4(2-3), 303–318. doi:10.1023/A:1022962631249

Chiu, C., Hsu, M., & Wang, E. (2006). Understanding knowledge sharing in virtual communities: An integration of social capital and social cognitive theories. *Decision Support Systems*, 42(3), 1872–1888. doi:10.1016/j.dss.2006.04.001

Chopra, K., & Wallace, W. A. (2003). Trust in electronic environments. In *Proceedings of the 36th Annual Hawaii international Conference on System Sciences*. IEEE Computer Society. doi:10.1109/HICSS.2003.1174902

Christenson, J., Fendley, K., & Robinson, J. (1994). Community development. In J. Christenson & J. Robinson (Eds.), *Community development in perspective* (pp. 3–25). Ames, IA: Iowa State University.

Connolly, R. (2008). Trust and the virtual environment: Research and methodological considerations. *International Journal of Networking and Virtual Organisation*, 5(3/4), 259–274. doi:10.1504/IJNVO.2008.018823

Connolly, R., & Bannister, F. (2007). Consumer trust in Internet shopping in Ireland: Towards the development of a more effective trust measurement instrument. *Journal of Information Technology*, 22(2), 102–118. doi:10.1057/palgrave.jit.2000071

Constant, D., Sproull, L., & Kiesler, S. (1996). The kindness of strangers: The usefulness of electronic weak ties for technical advice. *Organization Science*, 7(2), 119–135. doi:10.1287/orsc.7.2.119

Coughlan, T., van der Linden, J., & Adams, A. (2012). Local connections: Designing technologies for discovery and creativity within the community. *Interaction*, 19(1), 18–22.

De Laat, P. B. (2005). Trusting virtual trust. *Ethics and Information Technology*, 7(3), 167–180. doi:10.1007/s10676-006-0002-6

de Souza, C. S., Nicolaci-da-Costa, A. M., da Silva, E. J., & Prates, R. O. (2004). Compulsory institutionalisation: Investigating the paradox of computer-supported informal social processes. *Interacting with Computers*, 16(4), 635–656. doi:10.1016/j.intcom.2004.07.003

Dehnart, A. (1999). *Digital neighborhoods*. Retrieved January 12, 2010, from http://www.andydehnart.com/writing/articles/digital_neighborhoods

di Pietro, L., & Pantano, E. (2013). Social network influences on young tourists: An exploratory analysis of determinants of the purchasing intention. *Journal of Direct Data and Digital Marketing Practice*, 15(1), 4–19. doi:10.1057/dddmp.2013.33

Dibben, M. R., Morris, S. E., & Lean, M. E. J. (2000). Situational trust and co-operative partnerships between physicians and their patients: A theoretical explanation transferable from business practice. *QJM*, 93(1), 55–61. doi:10.1093/qjmed/93.1.55 PMID:10623783

Dirks, K. T., & Ferrin, D. L. (2001). The role of trust in organizational settings. *Organization Science*, 12(4), 450–467. doi:10.1287/orsc.12.4.450.10640

Donath, J. (1998). Identity and deception in the virtual community. In M. Smith & P. Kollock (Eds.), *Communities in cyberspace* (pp. 29–59). London: Rutledge.

Doyle, J. D. (2012). *Building it up and tearing it down: a three-study examination of trust, trust building, and the effects of erroneous messaging in the blogosphere*. (Doctoral dissertation). Retrieved from https://curve.carleton.ca/theses/31281

Dunn, J., & Schweitzer, M. (2005). Feeling and believing: The influence of emotion on trust. *Journal of Personality and Social Psychology*, 88(5), 736–748. doi:10.1037/0022-3514.88.5.736 PMID:15898872

Festinger, L., Pepitone, A., & Newcomb, T. (1952). Some consequences of deindividuation in a group. *Journal of Abnormal and Social Psychology*, 47(2, Suppl), 382–389. doi:10.1037/h0057906 PMID:14937978

Gambetta, D. (1988). Can we trust trust? In D. Gambetta (Ed.), *Trust: Making and breaking cooperative relationships* (pp. 213–237). New York: Basil Blackwell.

Gefen, D. (2000). E-commerce: The role of familiarity and trust. *Omega: The International Journal of Management Science*, 28(6), 725–737. doi:10.1016/S0305-0483(00)00021-9

Gefen, D., Karahanna, E., & Straub, D. W. (2003). Trust and TAM in online shopping. *Management Information Systems Quarterly*, *27*(1), 51–83.

Gefen, D., & Straub, D. W. (2004). Consumer trust in B2C e-commerce and the importance of social presence: Experiments in e-products and e-services. *Omega: The International Journal of Management Science*, *32*(6), 407–424. doi:10.1016/j.omega.2004.01.006

Giffin, K. (1967). The contribution of studies of source credibility to a theory of interpersonal trust in the communication process. *Psychological Bulletin*, *68*(2), 104–120. doi:10.1037/h0024833 PMID:6065581

Govier, T. (1997). *Social trust and human communities*. Montreal, Canada: McGill-Queen's University Press.

Grabner-Kräuter, S., Kaluscha, E. A., & Fladnitzer, M. (2006). Perspectives of online trust and similar constructs: A conceptual clarification. In *Proceedings of the 8th International Conference on Electronic Commerce: the New E-Commerce: Innovations for Conquering Current Barriers, Obstacles and Limitations to Conducting Successful Business on the Internet*. ACM. doi:10.1145/1151454.1151496

Grandison, T., & Sloman, M. (2000). A survey of trust in internet applications. *IEEE Communications Surveys and Tutorials*, *3*(4), 2–16. doi:10.1109/COMST.2000.5340804

Granovetter, M. S. (1985). Economic action and social structure: The problem of embeddedness. *American Journal of Sociology*, *91*(3), 481–510. doi:10.1086/228311

Hagel Abdul-Rahman, A., & Hailes, S. (2000). Support trust in virtual communities. In *Proceedings of the 33rd Hawaii International on System Science* (pp. 1769-1777). IEEE.

Hardin, R. (1992). The street-level epistemology of trust. *Analyse & Kritik*, *14*, 152–176.

Haythornthwaite, C. (2005). Social networks and internet connectivity effects. *Information Communication and Society*, *8*(2), 125–147. doi:10.1080/13691180500146185

Hercheui, M. D. (2011). A literature review of virtual communities. *Information Communication and Society*, *14*(1), 1–23. doi:10.1080/13691181003663593

Herring, S. C. (2002). Computer mediated communication on the internet. *Annual Review of Information Science & Technology*, *36*(1), 109–168. doi:10.1002/aris.1440360104

Hilligoss, B., & Rieh, S. Y. (2008). Developing a unifying framework of credibility assessment: Construct, heuristics, and interaction in context. *Information Processing & Management*, *44*(4), 1467–1484. doi:10.1016/j.ipm.2007.10.001

Hiltz, S. R., & Turoff, M. (1978). *The network nation: Human communication via computer*. Reading, MA: Addison-Wesley.

Ho, S. Y., & Chau, P. Y. K. (2013). The effects of location personalization on integrity trust and integrity distrust in mobile merchants. *International Journal of Electronic Commerce*, *17*(4), 39–71. doi:10.2753/JEC1086-4415170402

Hoffman, R. R., Lee, J. D., Woods, D. D., Shadbolt, N., Miler, J., & Bradshaw, J. M. (2009). The dynamics of trust in cyberdomain. *IEEE Intelligent Systems*, *24*(6), 5–11. doi:10.1109/MIS.2009.124

Hofstede, G. (1980). *Culture's consequences: International differences in work-related values*. Newbury Park, CA: Sage.

Hunt, S. D., & Morgan, R. M. (1994). Relationship marketing in the era of network competition. *Marketing Management*, *3*(1), 18–28.

Hunter, B. (2002). Learning in the virtual community depends upon changes in local communities. In K. A. Renninger & W. Shumar (Eds.), *Building virtual communities: Learning and change in cyberspace* (pp. 96–126). Cambridge, UK: Cambridge University Press. doi:10.1017/CBO9780511606373.009

Jarvenpaa, S. L., & Leidner, D. E. (1998). Communication and trust in global virtual teams. *Journal of Computer-Mediated Communication*, *3*(4). Retrieved from http://jcmc.indiana.edu/vol3/issue4/jarvenpaa.html

Jarvenpaa, S. L., Shaw, T. R., & Staples, D. S. (2004). Toward contextualized theories of trust: The role of trust in global virtual teams. *Information Systems Research*, *15*(3), 250–267. doi:10.1287/isre.1040.0028

Jarvenpaa, S. L., Tractinsky, N., & Vitale, M. (2000). Consumer trust in an internet store. *Information Technology Management*, *1*(1-2), 45–71. doi:10.1023/A:1019104520776

Jeong, E., & Jang, S. (2011). Restaurant experiences triggering positive electronic word of mouth (eWOM) motivations. *International Journal of Hospitality Management*, *30*(2), 356–366. doi:10.1016/j.ijhm.2010.08.005

Jonassen, D. H., Peck, K. L., & Wilson, B. G. (1999). *Learning with technology: A constructivist perspective*. Upper Saddle River, NJ: Merrill.

Jøsang, A. (1996). The right type of trust for distributed systems. In *Proceedings of the 1996 Workshop on New Security Paradigms*. Academic Press. doi:10.1145/304851.304877

Kahneman, D., & Tversky, A. (1979). Prospect theory: An analysis of decisions under risk. *Econometrica*, *47*(2), 313–327. doi:10.2307/1914185

Kanawattanachai, P., & Yoo, Y. (2007). The impact of knowledge coordination on virtual team performance over time. *Management Information Systems Quarterly*, *31*(4), 783–808.

Kelton, K., Fleischmann, K. R., & Wallace, W. A. (2008). Trust in digital information. *Journal of the American Society for Information Science and Technology*, *59*(3), 363–374. doi:10.1002/asi.20722

Khodyakov, D. (2007). Trust as a process: A three-dimensional approach. *Sociology*, *41*(1), 115–132. doi:10.1177/0038038507072285

Kiesler, S. (1986). Thinking ahead: The hidden messages in computer networks. *Harvard Business Review*, (January-February), 46–60.

Kietzmann, J. H., Hermkens, K., McCarthy, I. P., & Silvestre, B. S. (2011). Social media? Get serious! Understanding the functional building blocks of social media. *Business Horizons*, *54*(3), 241–251. doi:10.1016/j.bushor.2011.01.005

Kim, D. J. (2008). Self-perception-based versus transference-based trust determinants in computer-mediated transactions: A cross-cultural comparison study. *Journal of Management Information Systems*, *24*(4), 13–45. doi:10.2753/MIS0742-1222240401

Klein, P. G. (2009). Risk, uncertainty, and economic organization. In J. G. Hülsmann & S. Kinsella (Eds.), *Property, freedom, & society: Essays in honor of Hans-Hermann Hoppe* (pp. 325-338). Auburn, AL: Ludwig von Mises Institute. Retrieved on May 1st, 2010, from web site: http://mises.org/daily/3779

Knight, F. H. (1921). *Risk, uncertainty, and profit*. New York: Kelley and Millman, Inc.

Kollock, P. (1999). The production of trust in online markets. In E. J. Lawler, M. Macy, S. Thyne, & H. A. Walker (Eds.), *Advanced in group process* (vol. 16, pp. 99–123). Greenwich, CT: JAI Press.

Kramer, R. M. (1999). Trust and distrust in organizations: Emerging perspectives, enduring questions. *Annual Review of Psychology*, *50*(1), 569–598. doi:10.1146/annurev.psych.50.1.569 PMID:15012464

Lea, M., & Spears, R. (1991). Computer-mediated communication, de-individuation and group decision-making. *International Journal of Man-Machine Studies, 34*(2), 283–301. doi:10.1016/0020-7373(91)90045-9

Lewicki, R. J., & Bunker, B. B. (1996). Developing and maintaining trust in work relationships. In R. M. Kramer & T. R. Tyler (Eds.), *Trust in organization: Frontiers of theory and research* (pp. 114–139). Thousand Oaks, CA: Sage. doi:10.4135/9781452243610.n7

Lewicki, R. J., McAllister, D. J., & Bies, R. J. (1998). Trust and distrust: New relationships and realities. *Academy of Management Review, 23*(3), 438–458.

Lewicki, R. J., & Wiethoff, C. (2000). Trust, trust development, and trust repair. In M. Deutsch & P. T. Coleman (Eds.), *The handbook of conflict resolution: Theory and practice* (pp. 86–107). San Francisco, CA: Jossey-Bass.

Lewis, J. D. (1999). *Trusted partner: How companies build mutual trust and win together.* New York: Simon & Schuter.

Lewis, J. D., & Weigert, A. J. (1985). Trust as a social reality. *Social Forces, 63*(4), 967–985. doi:10.1093/sf/63.4.967

Lipnack, J., & Stamps, J. (1997). *Virtual teams.* New York: John Wiley and Sons, Inc.

Lu, Y., Zhao, L., & Wang, B. (2008). Exploring factors affecting trust and purchase behavior in virtual communities. In *Proceedings of IEEE Symposium on Advanced Management of Information for Globalized Enterprises.* IEEE. doi:10.1109/AMIGE.2008.ECP.11

Lu, Y., Zhao, L., & Wang, B. (2009). (in press). From virtual community members to C2C e-commerce buyers: Trust in virtual communities and its effect on consumers' purchase intention. *Electronic Commerce Research and Applications.* doi:10.1016/j.elerap.2009.07.003

Lucero, J., & Wallerstein, N. (2013). Trust in community–academic research partnerships: Increasing the consciousness of conflict and trust development. In J. Oetzel & S. Ting-Toomey (Eds.), *The SAGE handbook of conflict communication* (2nd ed.; pp. 537–563). Thousand Oaks, CA: SAGE Publications. doi:10.4135/9781452281988.n23

Luhmann, N. (1979). *Trust and power.* Toronto: John Wiley.

Luhmann, N. (1988). Familiarity, confidence, trust: Problems and alternatives. In D. Gamebetta (Ed.), *Trust: Marking and breaking cooperative relations* (pp. 94–107). New York: Basil Blackwell.

Lynch, C. (2001). When documents deceive: Trust and provenance as new factors for information retrieval in a tangled web. *Journal of the American Society for Information and Technology, 52*(1), 12–17. doi:10.1002/1532-2890(2000)52:1<12::AID-ASI1062>3.0.CO;2-V

Mangum, M. (2011). Explaining political trust among African Americans: Examining demographic, media, and social capital and social networks effects. *The Social Science Journal, 48*(4), 589–596. doi:10.1016/j.soscij.2011.03.002

Matzat, U. (2004). The social embeddedness of academic online groups in offline networks as a norm generating structure: An empirical test of the Coleman model on norm emergence. *Computational & Mathematical Organization Theory, 10*(3), 205–226. doi:10.1023/B:CMOT.0000045369.98848.71

Mayer, R. C., Davis, J. H., & Schoorman, F. D. (1995). An integrative model of organization trust. *Academy of Management Review, 20*(3), 709–734.

McAlister, D. J. (1995). Affect- and cognition-based trust as foundations for interpersonal cooperation in organizations. *Academy of Management Review, 38*(1), 24–59. doi:10.2307/256727

McEvily, B., Radzevick, J., & Weber, R. A. (2012). Whom do you trust and how much does it cost? An experiment on the measurment of trust. *Games and Economic Behavior*, *74*(1), 285–298. doi:10.1016/j.geb.2011.06.011

McEvily, B., & Tortoriello, M. (2011). Measuring trust in organisational research: Review and recommendations. *Journal of Trust Research*, *1*(1), 23–63. doi:10.1080/21515581.2011.552424

McKnight, D. H., & Chervany, N. L. (1996). *The meanings of trust* (Technical Report 94004). Carlson School of Management, University of Minnesota. Retrieved on February 1st, 2010, from http://misrc.umn.edu/wpaper/WorkingPapers/9604.pdf

McKnight, D. H., & Chervany, N. L. (2001). Conceptualizing trust: A typology and e-commerce customer relationships model. In *Proceedings of Hawaii International Conference on System Sciences*. IEEE Computer Society. doi:10.1109/HICSS.2001.927053

McKnight, D. H., & Chervany, N. L. (2002). What trust means in e-commerce customer relationships: An interdisciplinary conceptual typology. *International Journal of Electronic Commerce*, *6*(2), 35–59.

McKnight, D. H., & Chervany, N. L. (2006). Distrust and trust in B2C e-commerce: Do they differ? In *Proceedings of the Eighth International Conference on Electronic Commerce* (pp. 482-491). Fredericton, Canada: Association for Computing Machinery. doi:10.1145/1151454.1151527

McKnight, D. H., Cummings, L. L., & Chervany, N. L. (1998). Initial trust formation in new organizational relationships. *Academy of Management Review*, *23*(3), 473–490.

Mishna, F., Saini, M., & Solomon, S. (2009). Ongoing and online: Children and youth's perceptions of cyber bullying. *Children and Youth Services Review*, *31*(12), 1222–1228. doi:10.1016/j.childyouth.2009.05.004

Mitchell, A., & Zigurs, I. (2009). Trust in virtual teams: Solved or still a mystery? *The Data Base for Advances in Information Systems*, *40*(3), 61–83. doi:10.1145/1592401.1592407

Morrison, E. W., & Robinson, S. L. (1997). When employees feel betrayed: A model of how psychological contract violation develops. *Academy of Management Review*, *22*, 226–256.

Mowshowitz, A. (1997). Virtual organization - Introduction to the special section. *Communications of the ACM*, *40*(9), 30–37. doi:10.1145/260750.260759

Murnighan, J. K., Malhotra, D., & Weber, J. M. (2004). Paradoxes of trust: Empirical and theoretical departures from a traditional model. In R. M. Kramer & K. S. Cook (Eds.), *Trust and distrust in organizations: Emerging perspectives, enduring questions* (pp. 293–326). New York: Russell Sage Foundation.

Nass, C., & Brave, S. (2005). *Wired for speech*. Cambridge, MA: MIT Press.

Nip, J. Y. M. (2004). The relationship between online and offline communities: The case of the Queer Sisters. *Media Culture & Society*, *26*(3), 409–428. doi:10.1177/0163443704042262

Nooteboom, B. (2002). *Trust: Forms, foundations, functions, failures and figures*. Cheltenham, UK: Edward Elgar. doi:10.4337/9781781950883

Ofuonye, E., Beatty, P., Reay, I., Dick, S., & Miller, J. (2008). How do we build trust into ecommerce web sites? *IEEE Software*, *25*(5), 7–9. doi:10.1109/MS.2008.136

Ostwald, M. J. (1997). Virtual urban futures. In D. Holmes (Ed.), *Virtual politics: Identity & community in cyberspace* (pp. 125–144). London: Sage.

Owston, R. (1998). *Making the link: Teacher professional development on the internet*. Portsmouth, NH: Heinemann.

Pavlou, P. A. (2003). Consumer acceptance of electronic commerce: Integrating trust and risk with the technology acceptance model. *International Journal of Electronic Commerce, 7*(3), 69–103.

Porter, C. E. (2004). A typology of virtual communities: A multi-disciplinary foundation for future research. *Journal of Computer-Mediated Communication, 10*(1). Retrieved from http://jcmc.indiana.edu/vol10/issue1/porter.html

Putnam, R. (1993). *Making democracy work: Civic tradition in modern Italy.* Princeton, NJ: Princeton University Press.

Putnam, R. (2000). *Bowling alone: The collapse and revival of American community.* New York: Simon and Schuster. doi:10.1145/358916.361990

Radin, P. (2006). "To me, it's my life": Medical communication, trust, and activism in cyberspace. *Social Science & Medicine, 62*(3), 591–601. doi:10.1016/j.socscimed.2005.06.022 PMID:16039031

Rawlins, B. (2009). *Irrational trust.* Retrieved on May 1st, 2010, from http://www.instituteforpr.org/essential_knowledge/detail/irrational_trust_rawlins

Rheingold, H. (1993). *The virtual community: Homesteading on the electronic frontier.* Reading, MA: Addison-Wesley.

Ridings, C. M., & Gefen, D. (2004). Virtual community attraction: Why people hang out online. *Journal of Computer-Mediated Communication, 10*(1). Retrieved from http://jcmc.indiana.edu/vol10/issue1/ridings_gefen.html

Ridings, C. M., Gefen, D., & Arinze, B. (2002). Some antecedents and effects of trust in virtual communities. *The Journal of Strategic Information Systems, 11*(3-4), 271–295. doi:10.1016/S0963-8687(02)00021-5

Rieh, S. Y., & Danielson, D. R. (2007). Credibility: A multidisciplinary framework. *Annual Review of Information Science & Technology, 41*(1), 307–364. doi:10.1002/aris.2007.1440410114

Rousseau, D., Sitkin, S., Burt, R., & Camerer, C. (1998). Not so different after all: A cross-discipline view of trust. *Academy of Management Review, 23*(3), 393–404. doi:10.5465/AMR.1998.926617

Russo, P. (2012). *The antecedents, objects, and consequents of user trust in location-based social networks* (Doctroal dissertation). Available from ProQuest Dissertations and Theses database. (UMI No. 3518792).

Sarker, S., Valacich, J. S., & Sarker, S. (2003). Virtual team trust: Instrument development and validation. *Information Resources Management Journal, 16*(2), 35–55. doi:10.4018/irmj.2003040103

Schoorman, F. D., Mayer, R. C., & Davis, J. H. (2007). An integrative model of organizational trust: Past, present and future. *Academy of Management Review, 32*(2), 344–354. doi:10.5465/AMR.2007.24348410

Serino, C., Furner, C. P., & Smatt, C. M. (2005). Making it personal: How personalization affects trust over time. In *Proceedings of the Hawaii International Conference on System Sciences (ICIS)*. Waikoloa, HI: IEEE. doi:10.1109/HICSS.2005.398

Shankar, V., Urban, G. L., & Sultan, F. (2002). Online trust: A stakeholder perspective, concepts, implications, and future directions. *The Journal of Strategic Information Systems, 11*(3-4), 325–344. doi:10.1016/S0963-8687(02)00022-7

Shapiro, S. P. (1987). The social control of impersonal trust. *American Journal of Sociology, 93*(3), 623–658. doi:10.1086/228791

Sheppard, B. H., & Sherman, D. M. (1998). The grammars of trust: A model and general implications. *Academy of Management Review*, *23*(3), 422–437.

Short, J., Williams, E., & Christie, B. (1976). *The social psychology of telecommunications.* New York, NY: John Wiley.

Siegrist, M., Cvetkovich, G. T., & Gutscher, H. (2001). Shared values, social trust, and the perception of geographic cancer clusters. *Risk Analysis*, *21*(6), 1047–1054. doi:10.1111/0272-4332.216173 PMID:11824680

Sitkin, S. B., & Roth, N. L. (1993). Explaining the limited effectiveness of legalistic remedies for trust/distrust. *Organization Science*, *4*(3), 367–392. doi:10.1287/orsc.4.3.367

Song, J., & Kim, Y. J. (2006). Social influence process in the acceptance of a virtual community service. *Information Systems Frontiers*, *8*(3), 241–252. doi:10.1007/s10796-006-8782-0

Spears, R., & Lea, M. (1992). Social influence and the influence of the 'social' in computer mediated communication. In M. Lea (Ed.), *Contexts of computer-mediated communication* (pp. 30–65). Hemel Hempstead, UK: Harvester Wheatsheaf.

Spears, R., Lea, M., Corneliessen, R. A., Postemes, T., & Ter Harr, W. (2002). Computer-mediated communication as a channel for social resistance: The strategic side of SIDE. *Small Group Research*, *33*(5), 555–574. doi:10.1177/104649602237170

Sproull, L., & Faraj, S. (1997). Atheism, sex and databases: The net as a social technology. In S. Kiesler (Ed.), *Culture of the internet* (pp. 35–51). Mahwah, NJ: Lawrence Erlbaum Associates.

Sproull, L., & Kiesler, S. (1991). Computers, networks and work. *Scientific American*, (September), 84–91.

Stabb, S., Bhargava, B., Lilien, L., Rosenthal, A., Winslett, M., & Sloman, M. (2004). The pudding of trust. *IEEE Intelligent Systems*, *19*(5), 74–88. doi:10.1109/MIS.2004.52

Stepanikova, I., Mollborn, S., Cook, K. S., Thom, D. H., & Kramer, R. M. (2006). Patients' race, ethnicity, language, and trust in a physician. *Journal of Health and Social Behavior*, *47*(4), 390–405. doi:10.1177/002214650604700406 PMID:17240927

Swinth, K. R., & Blascovich, J. (2002). Perceiving and responding to others: Human-human and human-computer social interaction in collaborative virtual environments. In *Proceedings of the 5th Annual International Workshop on PRESENCE*. Porto, Portugal: Academic Press.

Tajfel, H., & Turner, J. C. (1986). *The social identity of intergroup relations.* Chicago: Nelson-Hall.

Tomlinson, E. C., & Mayer, R. C. (2009). The role of causal attribution dimensions in trust repair. *Academy of Management Review*, *34*(1), 85–104. doi:10.5465/AMR.2009.35713291

Turel, O., Yuan, Y., & Connelly, C. E. (2008). In justice we trust: Predicting user acceptance of e-customer services. *Journal of Management Information Systems*, *24*(4), 123–151. doi:10.2753/MIS0742-1222240405

Tyler, T. R., & Lind, E. A. (1992). A relational model of authority in group. *Advances in Experimental Social Psychology*, *25*, 115–192. doi:10.1016/S0065-2601(08)60283-X

Vanacker, B., & Heider, D. (2012). Ethical harm in virtual communities. *Convergence (London)*, *18*(1), 71–84. doi:10.1177/1354856511419916

Ward, K. J. (1999). The cyber-ethnographic and the emergence of the virtually new community. *Journal of Information Technology*, *14*(1), 95–105. doi:10.1080/026839699344773

Wasko, M. M., & Faraj, S. (2000). "It is what one does": Why people participate and help others in electronic communities of practice. *The Journal of Strategic Information Systems*, 9(2-3), 155–173. doi:10.1016/S0963-8687(00)00045-7

Weber, J. M., Malhotra, D., & Murnighan, J. K. (2005). Normal acts of irrational trust, motivated attributions, and the process of trust development. In B. M. Staw & R. M. Kramer (Eds.), *Research in organizational behavior* (pp. 75–102). Elsevier.

Wellman, B., & Gulia, M. (1999). Net surfers don't ride alone. In B. Wellman (Ed.), *Networks in the global village* (pp. 331–366). Boulder, CO: Westview Press.

Whittaker, S., Isaacs, E., & O'day, V. (1997). Widening the net: Workshop report on the theory and practice of physical and network communities. *SIGCHI Bulletin*, 18(1), 27–32. doi:10.1145/264853.264867

Williamson, O. E. (1993). Calculativeness, trust, and economic organization. *The Journal of Law & Economics*, 36(S1), 453–486. doi:10.1086/467284

Wilson, B., & Ryder, M. (1996). Dynamic learning communities: An alternative to designed instruction. In M. Simonson (Ed.), *Proceedings of selected research and development presentations* (pp. 800-809). Washington, DC: Association for Educational Communications and Technology. Retrieved on January 20, 2010, from http://carbon.ucdenver.edu/~mryder/dlc.html

Wilson, P. (1983). *Second-hand knowledge: An inquiry into cognitive authority*. Westport, CT: Greenwood Press.

Wolak, J., Finkelhor, D., & Mitchell, K. J. (2004). Internet-initiated sex crimes against minors: Implications for prevention based on findings from a national study. *The Journal of Adolescent Health*, 35(5), 424–433. doi:10.1016/j.jadohealth.2004.05.006 PMID:15488437

Worchel, P. (1979). Trust and distrust. In W. G. Austin & P. Worchel (Eds.), *Social psychology of intergroup relations* (pp. 174–187). Monterey, CA: Broks/Cole.

Wu, J. J., & Tsang, A. S. L. (2008). "Factors affecting members" trust belief and behaviour intention in virtual communities. *Behaviour & Information Technology*, 27(2), 115–125. doi:10.1080/01449290600961910

Yan, Z. (2009). Limited knowledge and limited resources: Children's and adolescents' understanding of the internet. *Journal of Applied Developmental Psychology*, 30(2), 103–115. doi:10.1016/j.appdev.2008.10.012

Yan, Z., Dong, Y., Niemi, V., & Yu, G. (2013). Exploring trust of mobile applications based on user behaviors: An empirical study. *Journal of Applied Social Psychology*, 43(3), 467–686. doi:10.1111/j.1559-1816.2013.01044.x

Zhao, L., Lu, Y., Wang, B., Chau, P., & Zhang, L. (2012). Cultivating the sense of belonging and motivating user participation in virtual communities: A social capital perspective. *International Journal of Information Management*, 32(6), 574–588. doi:10.1016/j.ijinfomgt.2012.02.006

Zhou, T. (2011). An empirical examination of intial trust in mobile banking. *Internet Research*, 21(5), 527–540. doi:10.1108/10662241111176353

Zhou, T. (2012). Understanding users' initial trust in mobile banking: An elaboration likelihood perspective. *Computers in Human Behavior*, 28(4), 1518–1525. doi:10.1016/j.chb.2012.03.021

Zucker, L. G. (1986). Production of trust: Institutional sources of economic structure. In B. M. Staw & L. L. Cummings (Eds.), *Research in organizational behavior* (pp. 53–111). Greenwich, CT: JAI Press.

ADDITIONAL READING

Ba, S. (2001). Establishing online trust through a community responsibility system. *Decision Support Systems, 31*(4), 323–336. doi:10.1016/S0167-9236(00)00144-5

Bachmann, R.: 2011, At the crossroads: future directions in trust research

Bachmann, R., & Zaheer, A. (Eds.). (2006). *Handbook of Trust Research*. Cheltenham, UK: Edward Elgar. doi:10.4337/9781847202819

Benbasat, I., Gefen, D., & Pavlou, P. A. (2010). Introduction to the Special Issue on Novel Perspectives on Trust in Information Systems. *Management Information Systems Quarterly, 34*(2), 367–371.

Dyer, J. H., & Chu, W. (2003). The role of trustworthiness in reducing transaction costs and improving performance: Empirical evidence from the United States, Japan, and Korea. *Organization Science, 14*(1), 57–68. doi:10.1287/orsc.14.1.57.12806

Frost-Arnold, K. (2014). Trustworthiness and truth: The epistemic pitfalls of internet accountability. *Episteme, 11*(1), 63–81. doi:10.1017/epi.2013.43

Gefen, D., Benbasat, I., & Pavlou, P. A. (2008). A Research Agenda for Trust in Online Environments. *Journal of Management Information Systems, 24*(4), 275–286. doi:10.2753/MIS0742-1222240411

Grabner-Kräuter, S., & Kaluscha, E. A. (2003). Empirical research in on-line trust: A review and critical assessment. *International Journal of Human-Computer Studies, 58*(6), 783–812. doi:10.1016/S1071-5819(03)00043-0

Kramer, R. M. (2006). *Organizational trust: a reader*. New York: Oxford University Press.

Kramer, R. M., & Cook, K. S. (Eds.). (2007). *Trust and Distrust in Organizations: Dilemmas and Approaches*. London: Sage.

Li, P. P. (2012). When trust matters the most: The imperatives for contextualising trust research. *Journal of Trust Research, 2*(2), 101–106. doi:10.1080/21515581.2012.708494

Marková, I., & Gillespie, A. (Eds.). (2007). *Trust and distrust: Socio-cultural perspectives*. Greenwich, CT: Information Age Publishing, Inc.

Pan, L.-Y., & Chiou, J.-S. (2011). How Much Can You Trust Online Information? Cues for Perceived Trustworthiness of Consumer-generated Online Information. *Journal of Interactive Marketing, 25*(2), 67–74. doi:10.1016/j.intmar.2011.01.002

Porter, C. E., & Donthu, N. (2008). Cultivating Trust and Harvesting Value in Virtual Communities. *Management Science, 54*(1), 113–128. doi:10.1287/mnsc.1070.0765

Vance, A., Elie-dit-cosaque, C., & Straub, D. W. (2008). Examining trust in information technology artifacts: The effects of system quality and culture. *Journal of Management Information Systems, 24*(4), 73–100. doi:10.2753/MIS0742-1222240403

Zahedi, F. M., & Song, J. (2008). Dynamics of trust revision: Using health infomediaries. *Journal of Management Information Systems, 24*(4), 225–248. doi:10.2753/MIS0742-1222240409

KEY TERMS AND DEFINITIONS

Antecedent: Conditions or factors to support trust building.

Identity: Representation or identification to be distinguished from the other party.

Online Community: A community that exists online, mainly on the Internet, where its members with similar interests, experience, or shared values take part in social interactions such as share information, knowledge, and experience with other members.

Social Networking: The use of web-based social media programs to interact with peoples for some purposes.

Trust Building: Trust formation or trust development during mutual communication and interaction of participants.

Trust: One party is willing to believe that the other party's behaviors should accord with the expectation or social norms of the party held.

Virtual Community: A community of members to share common purposes over the Internet and social media.

Chapter 15
The Security, Privacy, and Ethical Implications of Social Networking Sites

M. J. Warren
Deakin University, Australia

S. Leitch
RMIT, Australia

ABSTRACT

The chapter investigates the security and ethical issues relating to privacy and security. This chapter also examines the ethical issues of new forms of bullying that are being played out weekly in the media: cyber bulling, specifically on SNS such as Facebook. The traditional and direct forms of bullying are being replaced by consistent abuse via SNS due to the ease and accessibility of these new forms of communications.

BACKGROUND

The world has developed into a global community and the Internet is the thread that connects this global community. We have seen the Internet develop from the days of static web pages containing static information and static pictures (Web 1.0) to the current form of the Internet of today, Web 2.0. Today, Web 2.0 has moved away from utilising only static information and allows for the dynamic exchange of information through the use of video and audio. The important aspects of Web 2.0 is the social aspect of the technology development, which sees users generate new and ongoing content of pages via their interactions or commentary. We now see systems such as Facebook, Twitter being used by millions / billions of users across the global, this global usage results in developing ethical situations, this chapter explores two examples of social media and ethical situations.

DOI: 10.4018/978-1-4666-7381-6.ch015

INTRODUCTION

Information access, anytime, anywhere, any place, is one of the features of the twenty first century. Social Networking Sites (SNS's) are cyber spaces where people discuss ideas, share information, air their views and communicate to a global audience. SNS's such as Facebook, have become increasingly popular and are being used on a daily basis by millions of users across the globe. This vast usage can create fantastic opportunities but also brings with it a host of issues. One of these problems is the sharing of personal information with a wide audience and the associated security risks of doing so. The Internet has developed into a global social network and reflects many of the world wide social problems that society in general faces (Seendahera, 2009). This chapter examines a number of cases where physical, social and ethical situations have transferred into the technology mediated communication domains.

The chapter will investigate the security and ethical issues relating to privacy and security. This chapter will as well as examine the ethical issues of new forms of bullying that is being played out weekly in the media; that of cyber bulling, specifically on SNS such as Facebook. The traditional and direct forms of bullying are being replaced by consistent abuse via SNS due to the ease and accessibility of these new forms of communications.

SECURITY AND PRIVACY ISSUES OF SNS

Individuals often fail to understand the implications of making personal information public through SNS's such as Facebook. Research on various organisations by the Society of Corporate Compliance and Ethics and the Healthcare Compliance Association revealed that 24% of the organisations had disciplined their employees for inappropriate behaviour on SNS's and that

this behaviour had caused embarrassment for the organisation (Whitney, 2009). For example, pictures uploaded by a finance industry employee disclosed a colleague faking a sick day and the subsequent outcome was that the employee lost their job (McCarthy, 2008).

Research also has shown that SNS's are leaking individual's identity information to third parties including data aggregators, which track and aggregate user's viewing habits for targeted advertising purposes (Warren & Leitch, 2014). One implication for users is having tracking cookies associated with their user identity information taken from their SNS profile. This makes tracking user's movement across several websites much easier. Although user identities are not directly available to third parties who track users through IP (Internet Protocol) addresses, these IP addresses can be easily related to a particular user and therefore disclose their personal information obtained through the SNS's (Vijayan, 2009). The leakage of personal information means that the third parties not only obtain a collated collection of users' behavior but can also discover the viewing habits of specific individuals (Krishnamurthy & Wills, 2009).

Personal information may also be made available through secondary leakage targeting external applications (Krishnamurthy & Wills, 2009). Facebook uses a large number of third party applications as a part of its platform; these are provided for entertainment, education and social purposes. However, Facebook does not have any control over the third party application providers and websites supported through its platform. Publicly available information is made available to these third party applications and websites once a user begins to use them. Before approving third party applications or websites, Facebook requires the providers to agree to Facebook's terms of user information disclosure and takes technical measures to ensure that only authorised information is delivered to these third party vendors. Estimates in 2011, identified 100,000 third party applications that allowed information to be shared accidently between Facebook third party applications (BBC, 2011a).

SNS's enable malware to spread, which is due to malware's ability to access personal information. Increased use of SNS's such as Facebook and YouTube increase the chance of malware or peer phishing attacks that can potentially cause serious damage to organisational data security (Socialman, 2009). For example there were concerns regarding a data leak after a hacker broke into the 'Top Friends' application on Facebook' making users private information visible (Goldie, 2008). In 2012, a computer worm (Ramnit) stole 45,000 login credentials from Facebook users in the UK and France; this information could have been potentially used in a social engineering attack (BBC, 2012a).

Corporate organisations use SNS's for many different reasons. One use is to utilise their information to create strategic advantage by growing or gaining a competitive advantage. Another important use is that of a marketing tool in order to increase the organisation's business profile. Employees within the organisation generally create an organisational profile on Facebook as a way of informally communicating with customers, sharing information, promoting products, getting informal product feedback and building brand loyalties (New York Times, 2008). By building these organisational profiles, employees are able to communicate and interact with customers from all over the world, however this can result in data leakage and cause serious issues for the organisations as employees may accidently post information about the organisations latest products, for example, pictures of the latest iPhone.

Organisations may have concerns about Facebook and its usage; these concerns also relate to individuals that the organisation communicates with (employees, customers, etc.) and those individuals' right to privacy. Organisations can monitor current and potential employees through SNS's and some colleges and schools even keep track of their students' posts on SNS's. Police can use online information for investigative and tracking purposes (Jones et al, 2008), such as during the English riots of 2010. Facebook was used by the rioters to post information about their activities, and as a way to incite other individuals to join them in rioting. After the riots had ceased, police used the rioters posts as evidence to prosecute and imprison the individuals concerned (BBC, 2011b).

Facebook users can restrict certain information from being viewed from different cohorts, including friends. In 2009, Facebook altered its privacy settings, including the control over who sees individual messages (BBC, 2009). This meant that Facebook users could amend their access rights regarding information they posted so that specific individuals could, for example, view their postings but not their photos. In 2010, Facebook announced a new 'groups' feature that allowed users to specify circles of friends with whom they want to share data, in essence allowing users to categorise user friends and share information with only certain groups of friends (BBC, 2010). The ways in which information can be shared within Facebook is constantly changing, and one of the key issues is whether users are able to keep up with these changes and calibrate the settings so that their privacy is protected.

Another issue surrounding privacy and information safety in SNS's is the candidness of SNS's to communicate to users what information is private and what is public. This is clearly laid out in Facebook's policy documents, however, it is likely that very few of the 1.28 billion monthly users (Facebook, 2014) have taken adequate time to familiarize themselves with these documents and change their settings accordingly. Another privacy matter is trusting that those that have access to any personal information (such as those on a friend's list) will treat personal information, in the form of birth dates, status updates and photos in an ethical manner and not disseminate or use the information in an unethical fashion. This wholly relies on an individual and their own conscience, however it is prudent of users of such SNS's to take responsibility for their own actions rather than blaming a SNS. Taking responsibility would include making sure that they check their privacy settings; only making information available that they are comfortable with sharing; and only adding people to their "friend list" who are actually friends, or known to the user, in keeping with the original purpose of Facebook, rather than the more recent use of adding as many "friends" as possible.

There is also the worrying trend of whether Facebook friends actually exist in reality. An internal review of Facebook's customer base identified 83 million illegitimate accounts (BBC, 2012b). These fake pages ranged from companies settings up individual profile pages, so that these fake individuals can "like" the companies products or services to fake pages setup for pets that can "like" and interact with their owners.

ETHICAL ISSUES OF CYBER BULLYING AND ANTISOCIAL BEHAVIOUR

In recent years there has been extensive research conducted in the sphere of bullying via electronic means, often termed cyber bullying. Previously, work undertaken in this arena was mainly in workplaces that used technology mediated communication means for group work, team and skill building. This chapter will look at cyber bullying in adolescent cases and online antisocial behaviour.

What constitutes bullying as opposed to everyday conflicts that often occurs with children and teenagers, is that bullying is defined as "repeatedly and over time, to negative actions on the part of one or more other students who are or perceived to be stronger" (Olweus, 1993). Bullying also highlight the motivation, where there is a genuine intent to cause harm and that the abuse is consistently repeated over a period of time, rather than an on-off conflict or argument (Whitney & Smith, 1993; Olweus, 1999, Mishna, 2011).

The traditional view of bullying in the school yard, such as name calling and other verbal abuse, physical assault, or humiliation, has now expanded into cyber bullying. Cyber bullying can take many forms and can refer to the use of emails, mobile communication messaging, website postings, blogging, and the misuse of pictures as a way to spread rumours, humiliate, isolate, embarrass of frighten those being victimised (Smith et al, 2006; Willard 2005).

Those engaging in bullying who are pre-pubescent tend to engage in direct bullying behaviours, whilst those who are in their teenage years move more towards cyber bulling. Female bullies tend to use less direct strategies than their male counterparts (Wolke, 2010). Unlike traditional bullying, cyber bullying is not only perpetuated by individuals against another individual. It is becoming more prominent for groups to become the attacker, perhaps due to the anonymity of the Internet and the fact that this anonymity can lead to individuals forming a group with a pack mentality. This pack mentality has developed into the concept of flaming, Flaming is defined as displaying online hostility by insulting, swearing or using otherwise offensive language (Moor et al, 2010). A United Kingdom study in 2008 reported that up to 10% of students had been cyber bullied (Smith et al, 2008) whilst a Canadian study undertaken in 2009 reported a rate of 35% (Cassidy et al, 2009). A predominant conclusion in much research (Olweus, 1993, Wilton, 2011) is that rather than having school policies push to eradicate bullying, a better method for extinguishing bullying would be to "teach" young people in the home about the unacceptable nature of bullying behaviour. This raises an even more important aspect relating to cyber bullying in that in a technologically savvy world many parents are unaware of their children's actions and behaviours online, due to them not being aware about how the SNS and other technologies work which results in them not closely monitoring what is occurring. It is easy for a parent to chastise bullying behaviour between siblings or friends when it occurs in the home, but less easy to control and monitor such interactions and behaviours when they take place through technological means (Leitch & Warren, 2012) in an unmediated space.

Another element of antisocial behaviour is that of vigilantism. Whilst the perpetrators believe they are in the "right" and are defending others they are often engaging in the same behaviours as cyber bullies by defacing and attacking individual's SNS pages and engaging in patterns of harassment (Wehmhoener, 2010).

The chapter will explore a number of case studies and highlight the issues related to SNS's.

CASE STUDY 1: THE JESSI SLAUGHTER INCIDENT, A USA CASE

Based upon news reports (ABC 2010a, ABC 2010b, CBS, 2010 Farquhar, 2010). Jessi Slaughter was a pseudonym (real name Jessica Leonhardt) for an 11 year old girl (living in the USA) who rose to prominence in the media through dramatic events that unfolded through her use of SNS. The situation began with postings on a website called StickyDrama (which can be described as a blogging, rumour and gossip site contributed to by teenagers). The postings on this website accused Jessi of being involved with a member of a band, which she denied. She reacted to this by posting videos and content of herself and attacking the people she thought had defamed her. The situation escalated when individuals gained personal information including home phone numbers and Twitter account details about her and posted this information on various other sites. She was a victim of prank calls at home and she received numerous hate emails. In spite of this, Jessi continued to taunt the anonymous posters by blogging and commenting on the situation (Mathieu, 2011). In a final act, the young girl created a video which was subsequently posted on YouTube, in which she delivered a tearful and angry rant to those

perpetuating the acts, at one point her father is present in the video and delivers his own angry message to the anonymous posters. This video brought global attention to Jessi and the issue of cyber bullying and received over 785,000 views.

An important aspect of the case study was that personal information related to Jessi was posted on 4Chan. 4Chan is a simple image based bulletin board where anyone can post comments and share images and is governed by a site set of rules that do not allow "flaming" (4Chan, 2012). What happened was that Jessi story appeared on the message boards of 4Chan, with the threats against Jessi coming fast and furious (ABC, 2010a). This enflamed the situation even further. A sad aftermath of the situation was that people made fun of Jessi by making parody videos of her (including song remixe's and comedy sketches) and posted them on YouTube. The most popular of these videos received over 900,000 views on YouTube.

Jessi's story highlights a number of ethical issues which, depending on the perspective of the parties involved, will change the interpretation of the case. In regards to Jessi Slaughter, a major issue was the ability and desire of an 11 year old to post inappropriate material on SNS. Another concern was the sub optimal parental control and the lack of awareness regarding her online activities.

Another factor was the action of the 4Chan site which allowed for the systematic attack on an 11 year old (legally a child) by anonymous posters, enabling the use of SNS to escalate an issue rather than reporting the inappropriate material to legal authorities. Further, posts on 4Chan breached their own behaviour rules; they were unable to police themselves, and remove, or stop bullying posts.

These ethical issues highlight that SNS's have a social responsibility to have some control over the content and behaviour of those using their services. In recent years SNS have taken active steps to control bullying issues, however incidences have not decreased dramatically regarding the number of cyber bullying cases, neither have the severity of the cases diminished. The governance of these services are clearly lacking.

CASE STUDY 2: THE IMPACT OF PUBLIC OPINION, AN AUSTRALIAN CASE

In Australia, the murder of Trinity Bates in Queensland, Australia in February 2010 saw much Internet actively, including Facebook pages being set up. Some were tribute sites to mourn the loss of a child, others were hate sites set up by web vigilantes against the man accused of the murder. The Queensland Premier sent an open letter to Facebook's CEO asking "what it will do to block the 'sickening' hijacking of Internet memorials?" (Herald Sun, 2010). Whilst the Queensland Premier was concerned mainly about the users posting Internet pornography and other inappropriate material on the memorial sites, of as much concern was the ethical issue surrounding the use of Facebook to vilify and prejudge the accused defendant. The man charged with the murder has been named in the mainstream press, but the vigilantes went further, posting much more personal information, such as addresses and information about the defendant's family members. Facebook answered the letter by releasing a statement from its US based director of communications and public policy. Defending Facebook's monitoring systems, the response stated that users could draw attention to offensive content by clicking on a "report" button beneath any post on the SNS. This answer has done little to placate people who feel their grief has been compounded by the actions of a few; they fail to understand why there is a lack of control and limited monitoring taking place on many SNSs (The Australian, 2010a).

The comments on the vigilante sites may have major consequences for legal trials and could lead to them being aborted. This could mean that jury selection could be put at risk because the process of innocence until proven guilty could be compromised. In terms of the Trinity Bates example, how could someone have a fair trial in Queensland, when public opinion has already found a person guilty?'' (The Australian, 2010b). It appears that governments are struggling to deal with new media and are playing catch up with methods of dealing with the legal issues that arise from SNS use in these situations. This incident has clearly highlighted the lack of security and monitoring on SNSs, but also the ethical issues that emerge when free speech on which such sites are based collide with legal pejoratives. The fact that such software could severely impact our judicial system, a fundamental core of society, means that this is an issue of great importance to all societies and requires higher regulation. Facebook currently has a low user to staff ratio with only 1000 staff across the world, therefore there are simply not enough resources to manage all the information that has been uploaded and posted in real time (The Australian, 2010b).

The solution to this situation is complicated. One option may be to employ more staff and put structures and boundaries in place to clearly define what is considered unacceptable Facebook behaviour. In doing this, however, we are then fundamentally changing the core of Facebook and allowing a third party (government or public opinion) to decide what is, or is not, acceptable to society (Leitch & Warren, 2011). A more successful long term strategy would be to improve education and self regulation of such sites, but success is dependent upon the reliance of most people to act in a responsible manner and set their own rules and boundaries. As a result of the Trinity Bates case, the Australian Federal Government announced that they will create an online ombudsman to deal with concerns regarding SNSs and inappropriate content (The Australian, 2010c). The plan was later abandoned.

The sheer number of people using SNS makes it difficult to monitor misuse, both for law enforcement officials and site administrators. Tim Sparapani (Facebook's Director of Public Policy) estimates that Facebook users spend 18 billion minutes on the site each day. "We have 400 million active users and a tiny, tiny staff. We need to find novel ways to handle that kind of crushing amount of activity. It's the burden of being so immensely popular," (Time Magazine, 2010).

Some victim advocates believe that, as well as offenders losing civil liberties when they are found guilty of a crime, they should also lose their "cyberliberties" (Time Magazine, 2010). Each SNS is dealing with these issues in different ways and governments are strategizing to put into place policy and law to minimise the risks. Facebook currently bans people who have been convicted of sexually based offences but has no specific policy for those convicted of other sorts of crimes; "policing" this policy is, not surprisingly, difficult, and therefore, a number of countries and states have been required to bring about their own legislation. The US state of Illinois, has made it illegal for sex offenders to use SNS, and if found doing so can be charged with a felony offence. In the UK, however, plans to do something similar have been thwarted as it was believed these plans breach human rights law (Doward, 2009). The issue arose when it was revealed that the police would be asked to share sex offenders' details and email addresses with SNS administrators. These types of policies do not deal with the "average" cyber bully who may not have a criminal record. In the same way, identifying and prosecuting traditional bullying behaviour in schools and workplaces is challenging when we add in the electronic means of delivery, the 500 million users of SNS, along with the veil of anonymity, and the "right to free speech, the expectation that cyber bullying can be reduced in the near future is unlikely.

It is further demoralising that the US Federal Communications Decency Act clearly states that, "web sites aren't responsible for harassment by users" (Davis, 2009) and therefore cannot be held legally liable. This fact does little to calm the users who are becoming increasingly frustrated with the lack of concern regarding personal privacy and security from abuse and bullying.

CONCLUSION

In conclusion, the security and privacy threats that exist within the general Internet community also relate to SNSs. In many cases these risks are greater due to the sheer number of SNS users as well as the fact that users place their trust in safeguarding personal information in their friends' hands. As the number of SNS users and third party applications increase, so will the security risks.

The chapter focuses on two case studies, one relates to the USA and one to Australia. In both of these cases the ability not to resolve the ethical dimensions resulted in the cases becoming escalating to major incidents. The impact of SNS and the Internet has brought great benefits to society. The problem is, it has brought negative issues as well, with many of the negative issues mirroring the physical world, in particular the issue of cyber bullying or the smearing of good causes. This chapter has highlighted the weakness of SNS providers to protect against these issues; this weakness could be due to limited governance models or the ability of SNS providers to react in real time to incidents.

FUTURE RESEARCH DIRECTION

The future research direction will be focused on analysing future ethical situations in relation to social media and learning lessons from those ethical situations. This analysis would help to inform the contributed debate about the global social impact of social media.

REFERENCES

American Broadcasting Company (ABC). (2010a). *'Jessi Slaughter' says death threats won't stop her from posting videos on the internet.* Retrieved from: http://abcnews.go.com/GMA/Technology/jessi-slaughter-viral-tweens-violent-online-rant-spurs/story?id=11224731

American Broadcasting Company (ABC). (2010b). *Do kids need more privacy protection on social networks?* Retrieved from: http://abcnews.go.com/WN/social-networking-privacy-kids-protected-online-world-news/story?id=11831552

BBC. (2009). *Facebook gives users more control of privacy.* Retrieved from: http://news.bbc.co.uk/2/hi/technology/8404284.stm

BBC. (2010). *Facebook unveils 'groups' feature and user controls.* Retrieved from: http://www.bbc.com/news/technology-11486427

BBC. (2011a). *Facebook profile access 'leaked' claims Symantec.* Retrieved from: http://www.bbc.com/news/technology-13358293

BBC. (2011b). *Four on trial accused of using Facebook during riots.* Retrieved from: http://www.bbc.co.uk/news/uk-england-lancashire-15382412

BBC. (2012a). *Worm steals 45,000 Facebook passwords.* Retrieved from: http://www.bbc.com/news/technology-16426824

BBC. (2012b). *Facebook has more than 83 million illegitimate accounts.* Retrieved from: http://www.bbc.com/news/technology-19093078

Cassidy, W., Jackson, M., & Brown, K. N. (2009). Sticks and stones can break my bones but how can pixels hurt me? Students' experiences with cyberbullying. *School Psychology International*, *30*(4), 383–404. doi:10.1177/0143034309106948

CBS. (2010). *'Jessi Slaughter' YouTube cyberbully case: 11-year-old tells GMA she didn't want it to go this far.* Retrieved from: http://www.cbsnews.com/8301-504083_162-20011349-504083.html

4 . Chan. (2012). *Rules*. Retrieved from http://www.4chan.org/rules

Davis, W. (2009). *Facebook harassment suit could spur cyberbullying laws.* Retrieved from: http://www.mediapost.com/publications/index.cfm?fa=Articles.showArticle&art_aid=114854

Doward, J. (2009). Bid to block pedophiles from Facebook fails. *The Guardian.* Retrieved from: http://www.theguardian.com/technology/2009/nov/08/facebook-sex-offenders-law

Facebook. (2014). *Statistics*. Retrieved from: http://newsroom.fb.com/company-info

Farquhar, P. (2010). *Jessi Slaughter and the 4chan trolls - The case for censoring the internet.* Retrieved from: http://www.news.com.au/technology/jessi-slaughter-and-the-4chan-trolls-the-case-for-censoring-the-internet/story-e6frfro0-1225894369199#ixzz1lHbLxHqO [

Goldie, L. (2008). Facebook to discuss security with ICO after data leak. *New Media Age.* Retrieved from: http://www.nma.co.uk/news/facebook-to-discuss-security-with-ico-after-private-data-leak/38591.article.

Herald Sun. (2010). *Governments powerless to stop Facebook vandalism, says IT expert.* Retrieved from: http://www.heraldsun.com.au/.../governments-powerless-to-stop-facebook-vandalism-says-itexpert/story-e6frf7jx-1225834291255

Jones, S., Millermaier, S., Goya-Martinez, M., & Schuler, J. (2008). Whose space is MySpace? A content analysis of MySpace profiles. *First Monday*, *13*(9). doi:10.5210/fm.v13i9.2202

Krishnamurthy, B., & Wills, C. (2009). On the leakage of personally identifiable information via online social networks. In *Proceedings of 1st ACM Workshop on Online Social Networks*. Barcelona, Spain: ACM. doi:10.1145/1592665.1592668

Leitch, S., & Warren, M. (2011). The ethics of security of personal information upon Facebook. In ICT ethics and security in the 21st century: New developments and applications (pp. 46-65). IGI Global.

Leitch, S., & Warren, M. (2012). Cyber-bulling and vigilantism: Should social media services be held to account. In *Proceedings of Sixth Australian Institute of Computer Ethics Conference*. Melbourne, Australia: Academic Press.

Mathieu, S. E. (2011). *Misogyny on the web: Comparing negative reader comments made to men and women who publish political commentary online*. (Thesis: Master of Arts). University of Missouri, Columbia, MO.

McCarthy, C. (2008). You, there: Step back from the webcam. *Cnet News*. Retrieved from: http://news.cnet.com/8301-13577_3-9853908-36.html

Mishna, F., Khoury-Kassabri, M., Gadalla, T., & Daciuk, J. (2011). Risk factors for involvement in cyber bullying: Victims, bullies and bully–victims. *Children and Youth Services Review, 34*(1), 63–70. doi:10.1016/j.childyouth.2011.08.032

Moor, P., Heuvelman, A., & Verleur, R. (2010). Flaming on YouTube. *Computers in Human Behavior, 26*(6), 1536–1546. doi:10.1016/j.chb.2010.05.023

New York Times. (2008). *How to use social networking sites for marketing and PR*. Retrieved from: http://www.nytimes.com/allbusiness/AB11702023_primary.html

Olweus, D. (1993). *Bullying in schools: What we know and what we can do*. Oxford, UK: Blackwell Publishers.

Olweus, D. (1999). Sweden. In P. K. Smith, Y. Morita, J. Junger-Tas, D. Olweus, R. Catalano, & P. Slee (Eds.), *The nature of school bullying: A cross-national perspective* (pp. 7–27). London: Routledge.

Seendahera, V., Warren, M., & Leitch, S. (2011). A Study into how Australian banks use social media. In *Proceedings of PACIS '11*. Brisbane, Australia: Academic Press.

Smith, P. K., Mahdavi, J., Carvalho, M., Fisher, S., Russell, S., & Tippett, N. (2008). Cyberbullying: Its nature and impact in secondary school pupils. *Journal of Child Psychology and Psychiatry, and Allied Disciplines, 49*(4), 376–385. doi:10.1111/j.1469-7610.2007.01846.x PMID:18363945

Smith, P. K., Mahdavi, J., Carvalho, M., & Tippett, N. (2006). *An investigation into cyberbullying and its forms, awareness and impact and the relationship between age and gender in cyberbullying*. Research Report, University of London. Retrieved from: http://www.antibullyingalliance.org.uk/downloads/pdf/cyberbullyingreportfinal230106.pdf

Socialman. (2009). *Allowing staff to use Orkut? Better take care*. Social Unwire India. Retrieved from: http://www.social.unwireindia.com/2009/07/allowing-staff-to-use-orkut-better-take-cover

The Australian. (2010a). *Bligh hits out at sick net sites*. Retrieved from: http://www.theaustralian.com.au/politics/state-politics/bligh-hits-out-at-sick-net-sites/story-e6frgczx-1225834063831

The Australian. (2010b). *Facebook vandal complaints futile*. Retrieved from: http://www.theaustralian.com.au/australian-it/facebook-vandal-complaints-futile/story-e6frgakx-1225834303404

The Australian. (2010c). *Online ombudsman for Facebook woes*. Retrieved from: http://www.theaustralian.com.au/australian-it/online-ombudsman-for-facebook-woes/story-e6fr-gakx-1225834756343

Time Magazine. (2010). *How prisoners harass their victims using Facebook*, Retrieved from: http://www.time.com/time/business/article/0,8599,1964916,00.html#ixzz0gb2oD8Ge

Vijayan, J. (2009). *Social networking sites leaking personal information to third parties*. Retrieved from: http://www.networkworld.com/news/2009/092409-social-networking-sites-leaking-personal.html

Warren, M., & Leitch, S. (2014). *Be safe, be social*. IDG Communications.

Wehmhoener, K. (2010). *Social norm or social harm: An exploratory study of internet vigilantism*. (Masters Thesis). Iowa State University.

Whitney, I., & Smith, P. K. (1993). A survey of the nature and extent of bullying in junior/middle and secondary schools. *Educational Research*, *35*(1), 3–25. doi:10.1080/0013188930350101

Whitney, L. (2009). *Employers grappling with social network use*. Retrieved from: http://news.cnet.com/8301-10797_3-10360849-235.html

Willard, N. (2005). *Educators guide to cyberbullying and cyber threats*. Centre for Safe and Responsible Internet Use. Retrieved from: http://www.csriuorg/cyberbully/docs/cbcteducator.pdf.

Wilton, C., & Campbell, M. A. (2011). An exploration of the reasons why adolescents engage in traditional and cyber bullying. *Journal of Educational Sciences and Psychology*, *1*(2), 101–109.

Wolke, D. (2010). Bullying: Facts and processes. *Worcester Medicine*, *74*(4), 13–15.

ADDITIONAL READING

Kamel, N., Boulos, M., & Wheeler, S. (2007). The emerging Web 2.0 social software: An enabling suite of sociable technologies in health and health care education. *Journal of Health Information and Libraries*, *24*(1), 2–23. doi:10.1111/j.1471-1842.2007.00701.x PMID:17331140

Kaplan, A. M., & Haenlein, M. (2010). Users of the world, unite! The challenges and opportunities of Social Media. *Business Horizons*, *53*(1), 59–68. doi:10.1016/j.bushor.2009.09.003

Pallegedara, D., Warren, M., & Mather, D. (2013) Ethical Aspects of Controlling Information Disclosure on Social Networking Sites, *Proceedings of the 7th Australian Computer Ethics Conference*, Melbourne, Australia.

KEY TERMS AND DEFINITIONS

Facebook: Online system to allow exchange of information between agreed parties.

Internet: An interconnected system of networks that connects computers around the world via the TCP/IP protocol.

Risk: The possibility of suffering harm or loss; danger.

Security: Something that gives or assures safety, such as measures adopted by a government to prevent espionage, sabotage or attack, or measures adopted, as by a business or homeowner, to prevent a crime.

SNS: Social Networking Site.

Social Networking: A term to describe websites that allow people to join a social network and exchange information with their online friends.

Threat: An indication of impending danger or harm.

Web 1.0: Web pages from earlier Web applications, the information is static.

Web 2.0: Web pages from current Web applications, the information is dynamic and interactive.

Section 4
Detection Techniques

Chapter 16
Guidance for Selecting Data Collection Mechanisms for Intrusion Detection

Ulf Larson
Ericsson AB, Sweden

Erland Jonsson
Chalmers University of Technology, Sweden

Stefan Lindskog
Karlstad University, Sweden

ABSTRACT

This chapter aims at providing a clear and concise picture of data collection for intrusion detection. It provides a detailed explanation of generic data collection mechanism components and the interaction with the environment, from initial triggering to output of log data records. Taxonomies of mechanism characteristics and deployment considerations are provided and discussed. Furthermore, guidelines and hints for mechanism selection and deployment are provided. Finally, this chapter presents a set of strategies for determining what data to collect, and it also discusses some of the challenges in the field. An appendix providing a classification of 50 studied mechanisms is also provided. This chapter aims at assisting intrusion detection system developers, designers, and operators in selecting mechanisms for resource-efficient data collection.

INTRODUCTION

Collection and analysis of audit data is a critical component for intrusion detection. Previous research efforts (Almgren et al., 2007; Axelsson et al., 1998; Kuperman, 2004; Lundin Barse & Jonsson, 2004; Price, 1997; Zamboni, 2001) have concluded that by carefully selecting and configuring data collection mechanisms, it is possible to obtain better and more accurate analysis results. However, data is required to be correct and to be delivered in a timely fashion. The data should also be sparse to reduce the amount of resources used to collect and store it. Since production of audit data

DOI: 10.4018/978-1-4666-7381-6.ch016

directly depends on the deployed data collection mechanisms, adequate mechanism knowledge is thus a critical asset for intrusion detection system (IDS) developers, designers, and operators.

This chapter consists of a theoretical part that introduces the basic concepts of data collection, and a practical part where guidelines and hints for mechanism selection are discussed. The theoretical part discusses the basics of data collection from several perspectives. The components and operation of a generic IDS is described followed by an in-depth discussion of the components and operation of a generic data collection mechanism. Then, two taxonomies are presented, discussing mechanism characteristics and deployment considerations, respectively. Thereafter, the practical part discusses operational considerations and outlines a deployment strategy. Finally, future challenges are discussed, followed by some concluding remarks and an appendix providing a classification of 50 studied data collection mechanisms and techniques.

Both the appendix and the guidelines can be used when selecting mechanisms. They can also assist when a specific type of data collection is desired. For example, it is easy to find out what mechanisms collect samples for execution profiling, and what mechanisms that can be reconfigured without the need for restart. This is a valuable source of information that removes the need to browse multiple manual pages and white papers to find the desired mechanism. Furthermore, by using the selection guidelines, we can obtain a more resource efficient data collection and obtain a more accurate data analysis.

RELATED WORK

Anderson (1980) proposed to use data collection and analysis as a means of monitoring computer systems for detection of different types of intruders. Denning (1986) proposed An Intrusion-Detection Model and pointed out specific log information that

is useful for intrusion detection. Price (1997) then derived the audit data needs of a number of misuse detection systems and investigated how well conventional operating systems (OSs) collection mechanisms met these needs. It was clear from her report that the collection mechanisms lacked useful content. Axelsson et al. (1998) investigated the impact on detection by carefully selecting a set of system calls as input to the detector. Their paper showed that the detection rate improved when a selected set of data was collected. Wagner & Soto (2002) further showed that if insufficient data is recorded, an attack might well be treated as normal behavior.

Kuperman (2004) investigated in his PhD thesis the log data needs of four different types of computer monitoring systems and showed that when log data was carefully selected, the detection rate was improved. Killourhy et al. (2004) discussed the impact of attack manifestations on the ability to detect attacks. Attack manifestations are information items that are not present during normal execution and can thus be the key to reveal attacks. Furthermore, Almgren et al. (2007) investigated what impact the use of different log sources had on detection of web server attacks. It was concluded that the properties of the log sources affect the detection capability. Finally, taxonomies regarding data collection mechanisms in general have also been proposed (Albari, 2008; Delgado et al., 2004; Larus, 1993; Schroeder, 1995). Fessi et al. (2010), discusses a network based IDS, and also provides a comparison of different types of IDS.

Log data requirements for security logging have also been proposed in several whitepapers and reports from renowned industry-centered research institutes. The SANS consensus project (SANS, 2006) proposes several log sources, such as network data, OS data and applications. Furthermore, the SANS top 20 critical security controls (SANS, 2013) discusses maintenance, monitoring, and analysis of audit logs. In National Institute of Standards and Technology (2013), a set of guidelines for security log management was released. The guidelines discuss infrastructure, planning, and operations management. They also discuss various log sources, including security software, OSs, and applications.

In the most recent years, application logging has become more important since more applications are published on the Internet. As such, they are exposed to a wider range of threats and must thus be properly protected. Chuvakin & Peterson (2010) discuss logging strategies and what should be collected for web connected applications. Maggi et al. (2009) has addressed the need of carefully selecting log items due to the concept drift often found in dynamic applications. Furthermore, web applications normally communicate with databases, which in turn have received more focus in the latter years (Jin et al., 2007; Mathew et al., 2010).

The industry has focused much attention on COTS-products for solving data collection, analysis, and intrusion detection. This type of systems is known as Security Information and Event Management Systems (SIEM). To provide a comprehensive overview of current SIEM solutions and vendors, Gartner group (2014) publishes an annual survey and evaluation of important stakeholders in the SIEM field. A

list of core elements of successful deployment of log management and SIEM systems is provided by Swift (2010). These elements include defining the scope of the log coverage, log all relevant events centrally, and review logs in a timely fashion.

Several standards and frameworks have been developed to assist organizations in meeting regulatory compliance requirements and developing and implementing a sound information security strategy. These include PCI Security Standards Council (2013), FISMA (2002), and ISO/IEC (2013).

DATA COLLECTION FOR INFORMATION SECURITY

Data collection has a vital role in information security in general and it serves as input to a large set of controls and activities. An overview and taxonomy of anti-intrusion techniques is provided by Halme et al. (1995). This taxonomy inspired the model in Figure 1 that illustrates the following techniques and their relation to data collection.

Figure 1. Protective techniques for mitigation of possible threats against system resources (Adapted from Larson (2009)).

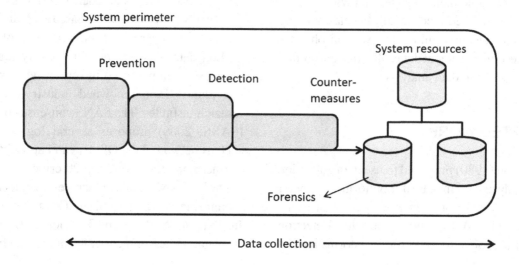

- **Prevention:** Prevention includes access control, identification and authentication, and the use of firewalls to filter illegitimate traffic. The goal is to strengthen the system to minimize the potential for intrusion.
- **Detection:** Detection is used to detect and issue alarms about possible intrusions, i.e., situations that either match a specific malicious signature or that deviate from what is considered normal.
- **Countermeasures:** Countermeasures add a reactive ability for the system to take action when an intrusion attempt is being made. Disabling accounts, killing running processes or increasing data collection are examples of possible countermeasures.
- **Forensics:** Forensics attempt to find digital evidence after an intrusion or attack has been confirmed. They are used for backtracking criminals and making a reconstruction of the events that have occurred.

Data collection is an important activity for all techniques above. For prevention, it is used for recording, e.g., firewall alerts and for detection, it provides input data to the IDS. Countermeasures use collected data to determine which accounts to disable and which processes to kill. Forensics use logs for trace back, event reconstruction, and discovery of digital evidence.

Furthermore, Bishop (1989) and Price (1997) also discuss several use cases where logging is important. In addition to detection, these use cases include:

- **Maintaining Individual Accountability:** The activity of individual users or processes can be monitored. The sense of being monitored may deter potential insiders from attempting to circumvent policy controls.
- **Reconstructing Events:** Event reconstruction is an activity that is heavily used in the area of computer forensics to backtrack criminal activity and collect evidence.

Event reconstruction is also used for identifying and removing system vulnerabilities.
- **Problem Monitoring:** Monitoring is used to uncover software and hardware problems. It is used for debugging and optimization, and to discover disk and network failures.

Finally, regulatory compliance is an important driver for data collection and subsequent auditing. Regulatory compliance describes how an organization adheres to laws, regulations, guidelines and specifications. Notable compliance laws and regulations include the Payment Card Industry (PCI) Security Standards Council (2013) and the Federal Information Security Management Act (FISMA) (2002).

DATA COLLECTION FOR INTRUSION DETECTION

IDSs play a vital role in the protection of computer systems. Intrusion detection is also a field where data collection is of utmost importance and the foundation for all subsequent analysis and response activity. IDSs are heavily dependent on data collection since detection decisions are based on and guided by the collected data. In this section, we provide a generic model of an IDS, a general data collection scenario, and a description of a log record.

Components of a Generic IDS

A model of a generic IDS inspired by Lundin Barse (2004) is shown in Figure 2. The data collection mechanism collects statistics or events related to system use and performance from the target system, e.g., a host or a network. The data collection mechanism uses its data collection configuration to decide what data should be collected. The data collection configuration may for example be a configuration rule for, e.g., tcpdump (2010), or an entry in the httpd.conf file for, e.g., the Apache web server.

Figure 2. Components of a generic IDS, including the data collection mechanism and a response mechanism (Adapted from Lundin Barse (2004)).

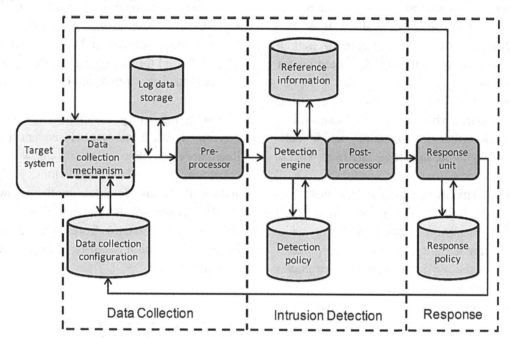

When the data collection mechanism has collected the data, it is then sent to an output device, e.g., a log data storage such as a disk drive. The data it then converted by the pre-processor from the native format to the format expected by the detection engine. The detection engine uses a detection algorithm to perform intrusion detection. It also uses one or more databases containing reference information, e.g., signatures. The analysis engine also uses a detection policy that determines how data should be interpreted by the detection engine. For example, the detection policy can state that connections made from IP-address 192.168.0.1 are malicious.

After processing, the detection engine outputs the results. The post-processor formats the output data and may also perform correlation of data from different detection engines. Finally, if a response unit is attached to the IDS it decides how to act on the output from the post-processor based on the response policy.

A General Data Collection Scenario

This section outlines a typical data collection scenario and describes the components involved. An operational scenario for a data collection mechanism can be illustrated as in Figure 3.

In the figure, there are six components which are described as follows: The executing process is a running application or system program which executes a sequence of machine instructions. The log trigger is a set of machine instructions contained within the executing process. These instructions are also known as instrumentation code, i.e., machine instructions which are not necessary for execution, but rather for notification. The log control is a set of machine instructions that are located in the executing process, or as a separate process. The latter case is shown in Figure 3. The combination of the log trigger and log control is denoted as the data collection mechanism. The data target is an addressable memory area

Figure 3. The interaction between a data collection mechanism and its environment (Larson et al., 2008a). (© 2008, IEEE. Used with permission.).

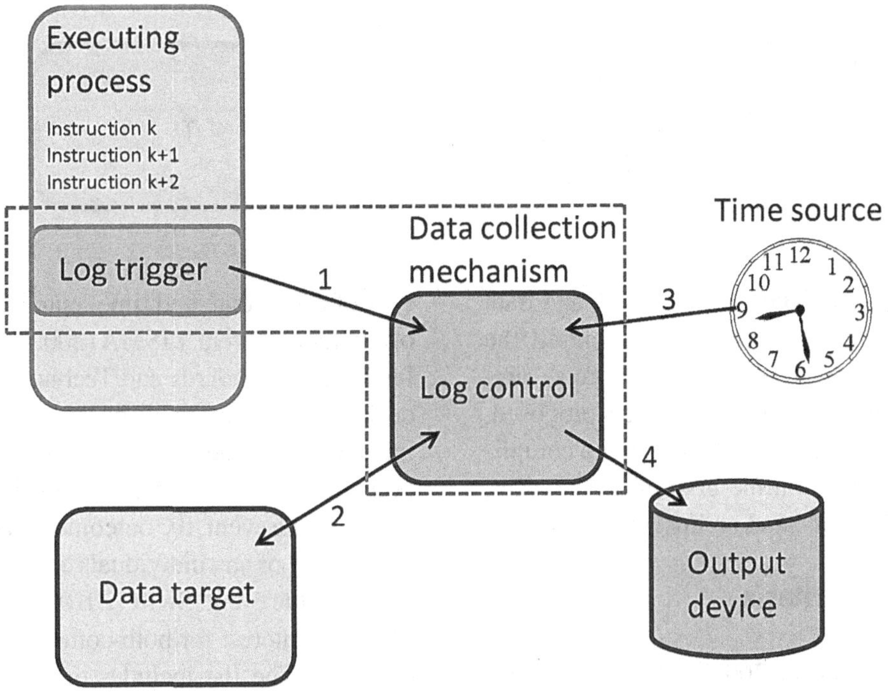

The Log Record

The log record is the result of a data collection operation. A conceptual model of a log record is illustrated in Figure 4.

The log record contains one or more attributes (A_i) for describing the event that caused the triggering of the data collection. It also contains a time stamp (T). Some mechanisms also provide statistics regarding the total number of occurred events of a certain type over a predefined time.

within the system, and either internal or external to the executing process. The time source is the entity providing time. Finally, the output device is a device to which the collected data is sent for display, storage, or further processing. Referring to Figure 2, the output device is located between the data collection mechanism and the preprocessing entities.

During execution, the CPU executes the machine instructions located inside the executing process. When the instruction flow reaches the Log trigger, the log control is notified (arrow 1). The log control collects the content of one or more data target memory areas (arrow 2), and appends a time stamp from the time source (arrow 3). The combination of the collected data and the time stamp now constitutes a log data record, which is sent to the output device (arrow 4). When the log control has concluded its operation, it awaits the next alert from the log trigger.

DETERMINING WHAT DATA TO COLLECT

Before collecting data, it must be determined what data should be collected. The rates at which events are produced in modern computer systems readily yield all exhaustive data collection strategies infeasible. Thus, disks would rapidly be filled

Figure 4. A log record consists of a set of attributes (A_i) and a time stamp (T)

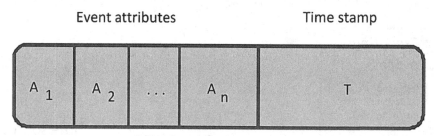

with log data and IDS pre-processors and data collection mechanisms would consume all the available computing resources. Therefore, several more elaborate strategies have been proposed, notably based on established criteria, on compliance requirements, on the goal of the attacker, on identified threats, and on information theory.

Established Criteria

The Common Criteria (2005) states several audit requirements that must be met by a system. It states that each audit record should contain date and time of an event, the type of event, the identity of the subject responsible for generating event, and finally, the outcome, i.e., success or failure. A similar criterion includes *A Guide to Understanding Audit in Trusted Systems* (National Computer Security Center, 1988). This guide contains several important security goals that an audit mechanism should fulfill and an in-depth discussion regarding auditable events and auditable information. ISO/IEC (2013) states several log events that should be collected, including user ids (subject), result/outcome, files accessed (objects), dates and times, and system activities.

Regulatory Compliance

The PCI Security Standards Council (2013) states that actors must track and monitor all access to network resources and cardholder data. In particular, the following data is necessary to collect: subject (user identification), object (resource, asset),

type of event, date and time, outcome/result and origination of event. FISMA (2002) uses National Institute of Standards and Technology (2013) to declare events that should be logged. These events include what type of event occurred, when the event occurred, where the event occurred, the source of the event, the outcome of the event, and the identity of any individuals or subjects associated with the event. Swift (2010) presents a set of events of interest for both compliance and audit purposes. The list includes event sources such as centralized authentication servers, switches, routers, and hosts.

Goal-Oriented Logging

Bishop et al. (1996) proposes a goal-oriented approach to data collection. This approach suggests that a clear goal, and good knowledge of what target information is important, strongly improves the analysis and data collection. Bishop therefore models a security policy and determines which actions can cause a violation of the policy. These actions are translated into auditable events which can be observed. Bishop's goal oriented approach to logging was further explored by Peisert (2007) in his PhD thesis.

Threat Modeling

Denning (1986) took possible threats into consideration and attempted to identify data that could reveal these threats. Furthermore, threat and attack analyses can reveal events, or manifestations that must be collected. This method has been further explored by, e.g., Axelsson et al. (1998). Along the same line, Kuperman (2004) investigated and determined the log data needs of four types of computer monitoring systems. The log data was then represented as subsets of system calls and used as templates for data collection for the four systems.

Information-Theoretic Approaches

Lee et al. (1997) and Lee & Xiang (2001) applied an information-theoretic approach to anomaly detection. Several measures was used to estimate, e.g., information gain and information cost from using different combinations of information. They used for example different combinations of system calls and the system object accessed by the system call and estimated which combination was the most accurate and least costly.

A TAXONOMY OF MECHANISM CHARACTERISTICS

The taxonomy presented in this section is derived from previously published work by Larson et al. (2008a). The taxonomy uses the following two dimensions: realization and behavior to describe mechanism characteristics. The following subsections are structured in a manner where a description of the term is provided, followed by a brief discussion regarding the relation to and usefulness for intrusion detection. Figure 5 shows the taxonomy tree.

Realization

The realization of a data collection mechanism consists of two parts: the point in time the log trigger is inserted and the level of granularity of the log trigger. The two main categories in this dimension are thus: time of introduction of log trigger and granularity of log trigger.

Figure 5. A taxonomy of mechanism characteristics; the two dimensions realization and behavior are illustrated as branches in the tree.

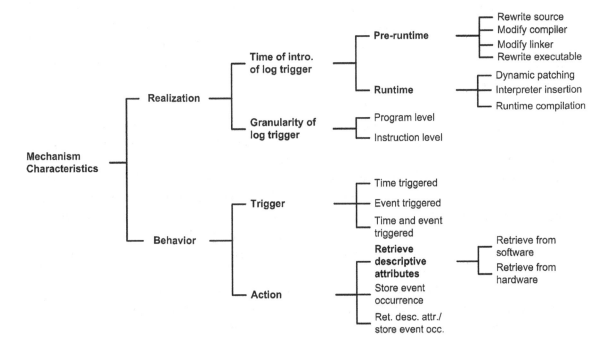

Time of Introduction of Log Trigger

Time of introduction of the log trigger represents the time at which the log trigger is introduced into the executing process. The log control is assumed to be introduced either before or at the same time as the log trigger. This category consists of two possible times of introduction: pre-runtime and runtime.

Pre-Runtime

The log trigger is inserted into the executing process at any time before the corresponding program is loaded into the main memory by the loader. This can be accomplished in one of the following ways: rewrite source program, modify compiler, modify linker, or rewrite executable. These methods are described below.

- **Rewrite Source:** Rewriting source programs means that an existing source file is modified by either manual or application based insertion of program language statements. Manual insertion is the most versatile way of inserting code. This approach allows for insertion of arbitrary statements and constructs conforming to the rules of the used programming language. It is used for inserting arbitrary log messages. An application based insertion depends on a preprocessing entity to perform a source-to-source transformation technique. The source rewriting approach only allows additions to the affected source file.
- **Modify Compiler:** Modification of the compiler means that the compiler itself is enhanced with an ability to insert log triggering into the source file during compile or assembly time. This requires access to the compiler source.
- **Modify Linker:** Since the linker is responsible for combining multiple object files including files residing in libraries, access

to all code in the final linked executable is granted during this step. This also removes the need for having pre-configured libraries, either compiled or assembled with a modified compiler/assembler.

- **Rewrite Executable:** Rewriting executables is done by inserting the log triggering directly into the complete executable binary file. This technique is also known as patching or static instrumentation of binary code. The rewriting takes place before the execution starts.
- **Discussion:** A mechanism that is inserted before runtime requires that the monitored asset is permanently rewritten. This inevitably introduces a delay and possible downtime for the asset or the system. Thus, a busy web server should not use pre-runtime insertion of mechanisms. Pre-runtime can be useful for reflecting a long-term constant monitoring policy. It provides a deterministic processing overhead, e.g., the same code is executed each time. It is useful for policies stating, e.g., that each login attempt should be recorded. An example of a pre-runtime inserted mechanism is the UNIX *syslog* (Garfinkel & Spafford, 1996) facility which consists of function calls for transmitting data to the *syslog* daemon.

Runtime

Inserting the log trigger at runtime means that the executing process is modified in its running state. This can be accomplished either by a runtime linker or loader process or by a dedicated log process which is external to the executing process. Runtime insertion of a log trigger can be performed by dynamic patching, interpreter insertion, or runtime compilation as further described below.

- **Dynamic Patching:** Dynamic patching can be performed with two different methods. One method is runtime patching which means that the logging control starts the instrumentation target as a child process and then immediately suspends it. Then, the logging control uses the symbol table of the executing process to map addresses against function names and source line numbers. The more information the symbol table provides, the more detailed the patching. The logging control inserts log triggering by introducing illegal instructions that causes interrupts and transfers control to the logging control when encountered. In this way, the logging control gathers information based on the illegal instruction interrupts.

Another method is for the logging control to attach itself to an already running process. In this way, the logging control can register itself as the parent of the executing process at runtime. By being the parent, the logging control can use the same mechanisms as in runtime patching and in addition it can detach from the executing process at any time.

- **Interpreter Insertion:** An interpreter reads the contents of an executable file and translates the contents into proper instructions when the executable is in running state. Contents, for instance unresolved symbols that cannot directly be translated must be appropriately handled to enable translation. The translation process is the basis for dynamic linking of files. Whenever an unresolved symbol is encountered, the appropriate mapping is done and the execution can progress. This method allows for dynamic linking of library functions at load time and it also allows for dynamic loading of library procedures and system modules into a running executable. An interpreter can be instructed to link or load special libraries containing log triggering instead of the normal libraries. The technique of placing a special library between the running executable call and the normal library is called interposition.

- **Runtime Compilation:** Compilation of code is performed at runtime, either from source code or from an intermediate, partially compiled, representation of the source code. Runtime compilation can be done by using one of two methods. The first method is called byte-code compilation and means that the code is compiled when it is needed, i.e., when execution reaches the next instruction, this instruction is compiled and executed. The second method consists of programs that generate source code and both compile the code and run the compiled code at runtime. Both these methods can be used to insert log triggering during compilation.

- **Discussion:** A mechanism that is inserted during runtime, e.g., *strace* (2010), rewrites the asset during execution. The mechanism can thus be enabled and disabled at will and provides an execution overhead only when it is enabled. Runtime inserted mechanisms can be used to enforce a dynamic or adaptive detection policy where monitoring is enabled on-demand. For example, if a network-based IDS indicates the presence of buffer overflow packets, monitoring that is not normally enabled, can be enabled for the web server for a shorter period of time without the need of recompiling and restarting the web server.

Granularity of Log Trigger

The granularity of the log trigger represents the level on which the log trigger is inserted. Two levels of granularity are used: program level and instruction level.

- **Program Level:** A program level trigger is inserted as one or more program level statements in the used programming language. The trigger can operate on the granularity of the used language, e.g., statements, variables, and structures. The developer can benefit from the semantic meaning of higher-level statements which normally is easier to comprehend than a lower counterpart.

- **Discussion:** A log trigger that is inserted on the program level can be used to collect data on program-level events, e.g., the return value of a function or system call. A typical example of a program level trigger is the *syslog* function call. A program level log trigger allows the designer to create tailored log messages and can be used to express events in terms of natural language, e.g., login attempt failed.

- **Instruction Level:** An instruction level trigger has the resolution of the hardware architecture. Architecture level constructs such as hardware registers or single instructions and register data items can thus be resolved. While presenting a more fine-grained resolution, the semantic meaning of the constructs are harder to comprehend. Often, a mapping construct, such as a symbol table, is required to resolve the individual instructions to procedure names, source level line numbers, and variables. An example of a mechanism that inserts instruction level triggers is *Dtrace* (Cantrill et al., 2004).

- **Discussion:** When the log trigger is inserted on instruction level, finer-grained traces or profiles of execution can be performed. Instruction level insertion is needed to gain the sufficient granularity for host-based detection of polymorphic attacks. However, instruction traces tend to grow rapidly and the space required to store the traces is sig-

nificant. Using instruction traces is recommended only for critical applications and should be combined with an adaptive strategy for collecting data.

Behavior

The behavior dimension categorizes possible methods for the log trigger to activate the log control, and what actions the log control performs when it is activated. This dimension has two categories denoted trigger and action.

Trigger

The log trigger causes the log control to initiate a data collection operation. Data collection may be initiated either by the expiration of a timer or the occurrence of an event. In this context we distinguish between three sub-categories: time triggered, event triggered, and time and event triggered.

- **Time Triggered:** A time trigger requires a log trigger which is invoked at regular intervals by, e.g., a hardware clock pulse, or a software timer set by the system.

- **Discussion:** Time triggered (sampling-based) data collection is useful to create execution profiles of many applications without consuming too many resources for collection. This collection can be performed to measure the CPU consumption by different processes. A mechanism supporting time triggered collection is *OProfile* (Levon & Elie, 2009).

- **Event Triggered:** An event trigger requires log trigger instructions that either wrap a specific event or that are placed before or after the event. Every time the specific event is reached, the log trigger is also invoked.

- **Discussion:** Event triggered collection is most commonly used in practice for intrusion detection. Several detection engines operate on event data, e.g., Forrest et al. (1996) and Tan et al. (2002). Event triggering denotes that each time a specific event occurs, corresponding data is recorded. Event triggering is used for misuse-based detection for monitoring access to specific resources, e.g., recording every occurrence of write() to the /etc/passwd file in UNIX or every login attempt. It can also be used for anomaly detection by, e.g., collecting all occurrences of system calls issued by a process or all user commands issued during a login session. An example of an event-based data collection mechanism is *strace*.

- **Time and Event Triggered:** Some data collection mechanisms allow for both time and event triggered invocation of the log control. This category is included for completeness.

Action

The action is the response from the log control when it receives a trigger alert. There are two possible actions. Either to store data for describing the event, or to note that the event has taken place, e.g., storing the occurrence of the event. These two types are denoted retrieve descriptive attributes and store event occurrence. The retrieve descriptive attributes and store event occurrence categories denote a combination of the other two and are included for completeness.

Retrieve Descriptive Attributes

Retrieving descriptive attributes is the process of reading the contents of

1. A software construct residing in main memory, including buffers and variables, or
2. Hardware-based storage mechanisms, such as on-chip CPU general purpose registers,

debug registers, and performance counters. If the desired data is not confined to a specific location, several locations might need to be visited by the log control.

- ○ **Retrieve from Software:** Data retrieved from software is contents of one or more software constructs residing in main memory. This includes program buffers, OS structures, and variables.
- ○ **Retrieve from Hardware:** Data retrieved from hardware is contents of one or more hardware constructs. This includes on-chip general purpose registers, debug registers, and performance counters.
- ○ **Discussion:** Retrieving descriptive attributes is performed when information that describes an event or a state is required. In this case, the mechanism denotes each event with one or more <attribute:value> sets that describe the occurred events. This is useful for detection engine for determining that a user accessed the /etc/passwd file, or that the payload of a network packet contained the string /bin/sh.
- ○ **Store Event Occurrence:** Storing event occurrence refers to the process of storing information regarding the occurrence of a specific event. This can be done by, e.g., incrementing a counter for each time the event is observed. An example is *OProfile*.
- ○ **Discussion:** Storing the occurrence of events is used when constructing histogram charts of issued commands during a login session. This in turn can be used to calculate the correspondence between a known distribution and an unknown user session to reveal masquerading users.

○ **Retrieve Descriptive Attributes and Store Event Occurrence:** Some data collection mechanisms allows for the log control to retrieve data regarding both descriptive attributes and event occurrence information. This category is included in the taxonomy for completeness.

A TAXONOMY OF DEPLOYMENT CONSIDERATIONS

The taxonomy of deployment considerations presented in this section is inspired from previously published work (Larson et al., 2008a; Lundin Barse, 2004; Zamboni, 2001). This taxonomy uses the following five dimensions: collection structure, collection strategy, location relative environment, location relative monitored asset, and log data. The taxonomy of deployment considerations is illustrated in Figure 6. Each of the five dimensions is further described in this chapter.

Collection Structure

When considering deploying an IDS and data collection infrastructure, this can be done in a centralized, decentralized, or distributed manner (Hedbom et al., 1999; Lundin Barse, 2004).

Centralized

A centralized strategy means that the data collection is performed by the same entity that performs the intrusion detection.

- **Discussion:** Since both detection and data collection is performed by the same entity, data and detection policies can be well protected against tampering. However, the system becomes a single point of failure, and correlation becomes difficult.

Figure 6. A taxonomy of deployment considerations containing five dimensions

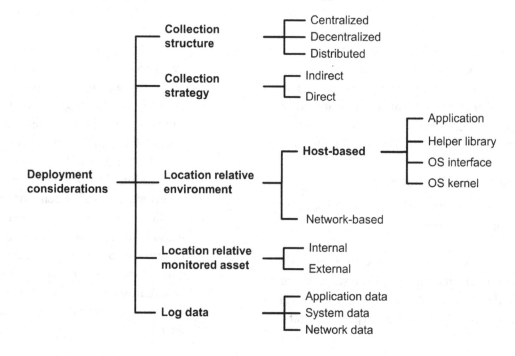

Decentralized

In the decentralized approach, data is collected on several locations, and is thereafter sent to a central location for analysis and detection.

- **Discussion:** With a decentralized strategy, the collected data can be readily correlated at the central location. However, since the collection policy must be transmitted to each node, an attacker can attack the communication channel and modify the policy and the collected data.

Distributed

Finally, with the distributed strategy, both data collection and all or parts of the intrusion detection are distributed.

- **Discussion:** Since data is collected and analyzed at the same location, this strategy has the advantages of the strictly centralized approach, but without being a single point of failure. Data can also be readily correlated. However, the detection and data collection policies must be transmitted and may thus be subject to modification in transit.

Collection Strategy

Collection strategy denotes whether data collection is indirect or direct with respect to a monitored component.

Indirect

When data is collected from an intermediate storage in which the monitored component previously has stored data, the term indirect monitoring is used. An example is when the collection mechanism reads from a log file.

- **Discussion:** Indirect collection is more convenient than direct collection since mechanisms that generate audit trails are readily available. Thus, they must not be produced before they can be used. Moreover, popular mechanisms normally have well developed interfaces and numerous configuration options which provide a diverse operation. However, an attacker may modify the contents of the log file before it is passed to the IDS. Indirect collection mechanisms may also cause mismatches between collected and required data since they do not know what the requirements of the IDS are (Crosbie & Spafford, 1995).

Direct

When data is collected directly from the monitored component, the term direct data collection is used. An example is to read data from a network subsystem data structure.

- **Discussion:** A direct collection strategy means that data can be transported directly to the IDS from the monitored component. The time available to an attacker for modifying the data is thus short. Furthermore, direct data collection can be better tailored to the requirements of the IDS and thus provide exactly the required data. On the downside, direct collection mechanisms must often be specifically developed for each purpose. They must also be carefully implemented to not disturb the operation of the monitored component.

Location Relative Environment

The location of the data collector can be roughly divided into host-based and network-based collectors. These two categories and their subcategories are discussed in this section.

Host-Based

Host-based data collection takes place on a host computer and can be on application, helper library, OS interface, or OS kernel level.

Application

Applications are defined as user programs and system utilities running at user level. Applications are, for example, software based firewalls, database systems and web server and web browser software. Application instrumentation captures execution inside the application's memory space. Each application that needs to be monitored must be individually instrumented.

- **Discussion:** An application level log trigger is tailored to a specific application and can thus be constructed with the specifics of that application in mind. Using an application level trigger, only the relevant behavior can be monitored and thus, irrelevant actions can be left out by simply not inserting triggers for them. An attacker who wants to affect the monitoring also has to affect each application, which makes it more elaborate to disguise attacker actions. However, correlation of events between applications may be somewhat problematic, especially if different designers have been involved. Then, the format of the messages may differ and extensive pre- or post-processing may be required. Furthermore, this requires the presence of a highly accurate time source.

Helper Library

Helper libraries are collections of object files that perform standard operations and provide an easier-to-use interface against the system services. The libraries are linked into the program object file at link time, and the result is the final executable. Helper libraries provide a more general point of instrumentation insertion. They are shared by all applications running on the system and instrumentation inserted into helper libraries is thus common to all applications that use the specific library.

- **Discussion:** Helper libraries are collections of general programming functions. Thus, by inserting log triggers in helper libraries, all programs that use the libraries can be monitored. This allows for constructing complete traces of function calls, even between different helper libraries. This has been used by Kuperman & Spafford (1999). This approach also supports dynamic monitoring through dynamic linking.

OS Interface

The OS interface handles input to and output from the OS kernel. Inserting a data collection mechanism at the OS interface provides a highly general log triggering location and requests from all applications can be captured. The OS interface is implemented through interrupts. Two locations are generally used for interrupt handling: the data structures containing the interrupt descriptors and the system call descriptors. Usually, the interrupt descriptor structure is more general and routes a subset of its calls to the system call structure.

- **Discussion:** All activities that require higher privileges must be issued through the use of well-defined system calls. Thus, this is a good place to monitor security-critical events, such as file read()s, and the use of the network. Many host-based IDS, e.g., *snare* (Intersect Alliance, 2003) operate on system call data since it represents a decent level of granularity. However, it must be noted that the more processes that are monitored, the larger the amount of collected data becomes. Regardless, it is still the most popular source of host-based IDS data.

OS Kernel

The OS kernel handles process and memory management, file systems and I/O communication. Depending on the exact location of the log triggering, higher or lower degree of coverage is possible. Some subsystems perform specific tasks such as file system management, while others perform very general tasks such as process scheduling. Regardless of the subsystem, all requests for service from any caller are captured by the inserted instrumentation. Inserting a data collection mechanism in the core subsystems provides access to process management, main and secondary memory management, file and I/O management as well as network management.

- **Discussion:** OS kernel monitoring allows for monitoring privileged execution and provides system-wide information. By targeting the most general parts of the system, e.g., the process_task structure (Linux Audit Subsystem, 2004), all processes can be uniformly monitored. It is recommended that monitoring of the OS kernel is carefully conducted both with respect to the amount of data produced and the fact that the entire system may crash if monitoring is erroneously performed. Access to hardware constructs such as performance counters is useful program counter sampling for determining where programs spend their time, which, can be used to detect rootkits. Correlation between events is also easier since a uniform representation and a common clock can be used. In an architecture that permits inserting kernel modules, data collection can easily be performed dynamically. Most network monitoring

tools operate in the OS kernel since this provides access to all data packets. The OS kernel is also the place where general purpose audit trail mechanisms, such as the (Linux Audit Subsystem, 2004; Sun Microsystems, 1995) are located. These mechanisms support a wide variety of events and are thus the opposite of application specific mechanisms. This data must be rich enough to promote several types of detection, therefore it is highly necessary that configuration of general purpose mechanisms is carefully performed to prevent being drowned in data.

Network-Based

Network locations include network interface cards on hosts, firewalls and routers, or other network equipment. The main sources of network data are TCP/IP packets and data link layer frames.

Location Relative Monitored Asset

The data collection mechanism can be internal or external to the monitored component.

Internal

An internal data collection mechanism is inserted directly into the code of the monitored component. The data collection is performed directly from inside the component.

- **Discussion:** Internal data collection requires changes to the monitored component. This may or may not be feasible from an availability perspective, and it is advised that the collection mechanism is inserted before the component is deployed. However, mistakes in design or implementation of the mechanism may break the component or require run-time changes, which may lead to downtime. This is dependent on how the mechanism is realized. Internal collection mechanisms minimize the risk that data has been altered before delivery to the IDS and they cannot easily be modified.

External

An external mechanism is implemented in the code that is separate from the monitored component.

- **Discussion:** External data collection mechanisms are less intrusive to the monitored component and do not require any changes. As such, they affect the operation of the asset and the host system less. For example, the UNIX *ps* utility program is an external data collection mechanism since disabling it does not imply that the kernel is correspondingly disabled. However, it is more prone to modification, e.g., by a rootkit, and can be instrumented to hide certain results.

Log Data

The following three categories of log data are covered: application data, system data, and network data.

Application Data

Application data is produced by an application during its execution. Application data includes contents of used data structures and function call traces.

- **Discussion:** Application data can be collected from both within the application itself and from any other location that is invoked during execution. If data from

only a specific application is desired it is more efficient to use a log trigger which triggers on actions performed by that application only. This promotes a low degree of pre-processing and a more accurate and efficient data delivery. If data for a larger set of applications is required, the trigger can be inserted in any other location, i.e., a helper library, the OS interface, or the OS kernel. This may be useful if a uniform representation of several different applications is desired, e.g., for correlation. A frequently used approach to analyze the behavior of applications is inserting a data collection mechanism at the OS interface, i.e., collecting system calls. This provides a uniform representation of all applications, and each application that requires higher privileges during execution must use system calls. Therefore, security relevant behavior can be collected.

System Data

System data is produced by the OS kernel. This data includes resource usage statistics such as CPU activity, number of software and hardware interrupts, and various times. It also includes system events and system structure contents, such as the current system configuration. Finally, it includes data generated by interrupts from software and hardware.

- **Discussion:** Mechanisms that collect system data must be inserted in the OS interface or OS kernel. The kernel operation is normally only invoked by applications through the OS interface. It is therefore not possible to put a log trigger in an application to monitor events occurring in the kernel.

Network Data

Network data is data contained in network protocol stacks, network services, network device drivers or firmware in network interface cards. The data itself is either data packets or data related to handling of data packets such as interface characteristics and counts of sent and received packets. Furthermore, network enabled applications can also be a source of network data.

- **Discussion:** Network data can be collected in both applications and the OS kernel, and all applications that want to use the network resources must use system calls, e.g., send() and receive() to access the network. Most detection systems rely on network data collected by the *libpcap* packet capturing library which provides access to raw network data from the network interface card. The OS kernel contains a network subsystem which parses and distributes packets to listening applications.

OPERATIONAL CONSIDERATIONS

This section discusses a few operational considerations that may arise when deploying a data collection infrastructure. In particular, it is discussed how data collection mechanisms affect the monitored resource and host system. Additionally, a listing of common pitfalls and recommendations to how to avoid the issues is provided.

Impact on Resources

A host-based collection mechanism consumes resources from the host system. In particular, it uses disk space to store collected data and CPU cycles to operate. Furthermore, depending on its realization, it may affect the availability of the monitored components or the host system.

Storage and Performance

When data collection mechanisms are deployed, they will inevitably consume resources of the host system. First, a collection mechanism consumes CPU cycles. Thus, the amount of CPU cycles available for production purposes decreases. Each deployed mechanism imposes a basic performance penalty. Furthermore, an additional penalty is imposed when the mechanism is triggered to collect data. Second, the collected data will occupy disk space. Data that is not directly analyzed must be stored on disk until it can be processed.

- **Recommendation:** Consider the complete data requirement and remember that all mechanisms occupy resources. Try to minimize the number of active mechanisms. Primarily use mechanisms that have low performance penalty when inactive. Make sure that the selected mechanism is tailored to the requirements of the IDS. If the target is a single process, do not use a mechanism which monitors this process only.

Availability

The availability of the monitored component may be affected by the data collection mechanism. For example, a data collection mechanism may need to be taken offline to be reconfigured. Reconfiguration includes patching the mechanism software, changing the output format, or writing more informative log messages. For an internal data collection mechanism, reconfiguration means that the monitored component must be stopped and then restarted. The reconfiguration introduces a collection downtime, which is dependent on how long time the resource is interrupted from its normal operation. A mechanism with a large reconfiguration time may have a small impact on availability if the time between reconfigurations is short.

- **Recommendation:** To avoid availability penalties and downtime, use a mechanism that is introduced during runtime, e.g., *strace* or *Dtrace*. Another option is to use an existing audit subsystem. Most audit subsystems are installed with the OS. These systems support a transparent reconfiguration which does not affect the availability of the monitored components.

Common Pitfalls

In this section we focus on reducing the amount of excess data, i.e., data that is collected but that is not subsequently analyzed by the IDS. This section describes three situations where excess data is produced. For each situation, it also provides a recommendation for how to reduce the amount of excess data.

Example 1: Mechanisms Are Not Tailored to the IDSs

The *mod_log_config* module provides logging facilities for the Apache web server. An IDS uses the access logs created by *mod_log_config* to scan for the "GET /cgi-bin/test-cgi? *" string. In this case, the access log does not have to contain more information than the request string. If the access log contains more information, this information must be filtered by a pre-processor before the IDS can use the data.

- **Recommendation:** Investigate the input data requirement for each IDS and make sure that no more information than what is required by the IDS is collected.

Example 2: Mechanisms Cannot Be Tailored to the IDSs

Consider that an IDS operates on sequences of system call names, as described in, e.g., Forrest et al. (1996). A mechanism such as the Linux audit subsystem readily provides the system call name, but also 15 other attributes, e.g., UID and EUID. These attributes are not used by the IDS and are therefore excess data.

- **Recommendation:** Always consider different mechanisms when collecting data for intrusion detection. There are several mechanisms available and if one mechanism cannot be properly configured, there may be several alternatives. A classification of 50 data collection mechanisms is available in Appendix. These mechanisms have roughly the same characteristics and can thus be used interchangeably.

Example 3: Mechanisms Are Active when They Are Not Needed

Assume that a host connected to the Internet runs a web server that listens to ports 80 and 443. An IDS monitor's ports 80 and 443 in order to detect intrusion attempts against the web server. If the web server is taken offline for maintenance, the IDS is temporarily no longer required and the data collection can be temporarily disabled. However, if packets would still be collected, we have excess data production.

- **Recommendation:** Make sure that data collection mechanisms and IDSs are only active when they are needed. If there is no need for data collection, the collection mechanism should be disabled. A suggestion for how to create an architecture that supports enabling and disabling of data collection mechanisms is presented in Larson et al. (2008b).

DEPLOYMENT STRATEGY

This section provides a four-step strategy for achieving efficient data collection inspired by Wetmore (1993). For each item in the list, a reference to a section in this document is provided. The referenced section contains additional information which is useful when making the decisions.

1. Determine which types of data that should be collected (sections determining what data to collect and a taxonomy of deployment considerations).
2. Determine an appropriate set of IDSs. This item is outside the scope of this chapter, but relevant information can be found in, e.g., (Axelsson, 2000; Debar et al., 1999). Furthermore, an indication of what intrusion detection models are appropriate for specific audit data is discussed by Lee & Xiang (2001).
3. Determine which characteristics are required from the mechanism, taking the desired data and applicable resource restrictions in consideration (sections a taxonomy of mechanisms characteristics, a taxonomy of deployment considerations, and operational considerations).
4. Determine how the data collection framework should be established and deployed (section a taxonomy of deployment considerations).

FUTURE CHALLENGES

Future challenges for data collection with respect to intrusion detection include:

1. Reconfigurable internal collection mechanisms,
2. New data collection mechanisms for security in embedded systems, and
3. Big Data and Internet of Things. These three topics are discussed below.

Internal collection mechanisms (Zamboni, 2001) have several useful characteristics for intrusion detection. For example, they produce little excess data and they are not easily subverted. However, on the downside, the monitored component must be taken offline when the collection mechanism is reconfigured. To mitigate this availability reduction, the mechanisms should be transparent to the monitored component. This strategy is similar to the transparent data collection strategies proposed in Cantrill et al. (2004). These mechanisms only impose a small performance penalty for the monitored component when they are disabled and they do not affect availability. A combination of internal and transparent collection mechanisms would eliminate some of the issues with internal mechanisms. They would then be more useful for detection. Thus, the applicability should therefore be further investigated.

Security in embedded systems is a novel field with respect to security. However, security is highly important since previously and isolated embedded systems and networks are opened up for external communication. Two examples are process control systems and automobile in-vehicle networks. Recent security analyses of a generic in-vehicle network (Nilsson & Larson, 2008a; Nilsson & Larson, 2008b) have shown that the communication protocols and node computers deployed in the network have no protection against most security threats. Furthermore, methods for data collection and intrusion detection are missing. Therefore, research of new methods for data collection and intrusion detection that fits the embedded environment is needed. One such approach is presented by Larson et al. (2008) and is based on specifications of the embedded system.

Another challenge is coping with intrusion detection in the advent of Big Data and Internet of Things. This has been discussed by Ptak (2013). The sheer amount of data that is produced will call for carefully planned strategies for log management. A common problem with intrusion detection is the amount of log data and processing capabilities. As data becomes even larger and is generated from even more different devices, this will remain a problem for the analyst. Some strategies have been proposed, e.g., Logging-as-a-Service (TIBCO, 2014).

CONCLUSION

This chapter has provided a structured overview of how to select data collection mechanisms for intrusion detection. A theoretical part discusses the basics of data collection, provides alternative methods for determining what to collect and discusses pitfalls, deployment considerations and challenges. As such, this part is thus useful for newcomers to the field. Furthermore, a practical part discusses some operational considerations and common pitfalls. It also provides a collection mechanism deployment strategy and a classification of 50 data collection mechanisms and techniques. The practical part is useful for designers and operators who must select, configure, and deploy suitable collection mechanisms for their IDSs.

ACKNOWLEDGMENT

The work at Chalmers University of Technology is financially supported by the Swedish Civil Contingencies Agency (former Swedish Emergency Management Agency). Part of the work at Karlstad University has been carried out within the Compare Business Innovation Centre phase 3 (C-BIC 3) project, funded partly by European Regional Development Fund (ERDF).

REFERENCES

Albari, M. Z. (2005). *A taxonomy of runtime software monitoring systems*. Retrieved August 9, 2008, from http://www.informatik.uni-kiel.de/~wg/Lehre/Seminar-SS05/Mohamed_Ziad_Abari/vortrag-handout4.pdf

Almgren, M., Jonsson, E., & Lindqvist, U. (2007). A comparison of alternative audit sources for web server attack detection. In *Proceedings of the 12th Nordic Workshop on Secure IT systems (NordSec 2007)* (pp. 101–112). Reykjavik, Iceland: Academic Press.

Anderson, J. M., Berc, L. M., Dean, J., Ghemawat, S., Henzinger, M. R., & Leung, S. A. et al. (1997). Continuous profiling: Where have all the cycles gone? *Operating Systems Review*, *31*(5), 1–14. doi:10.1145/269005.266637

Anderson, J. P. (1980). *Computer security threat monitoring and surveillance*. Fort Washington, PA: Anderson Company.

Apache mod_log_config. (2010). *Apache mod_log_config module*. Retrieved November 25, 2010, from http://httpd.apache.org/docs/2.2/mod/mod_log_config.html

Aranya, A., Wright, C. P., & Zadok, E. (2004). Tracefs: A file system to trace them all. In *Proceedings of the 3rd USENIX Conference on File and Storage Technoligies (FAST 2004)* (pp. 129–145). San Francisco, CA: USENIX Association.

Ariel, T., & Miller, B. P. (1999). Fine-grained dynamic instrumentation of commodity operating system kernels. In *Proceedings of the Third Symposium on Operating Systems Design and Implementation (OSDI'99)* (pp. 117–130). New Orleans, LA: Academic Press.

Axelsson, S. (2000). *Instrusion detection systems: A survey and taxonomy* (Technical Report 99-15). Chalmers University of Technology.

Axelsson, S., Lindqvist, U., Gustafson, U., & Jonsson, E. (1998). An approach to UNIX security logging. In *Proceedings of the 21st National Information Systems Security Conference* (pp. 62–75). Arlington, VA: Academic Press.

Baker, M. G., Hartman, J. H., Kupfer, M. D., Shirriff, K. W., & Ousterhout, J. K. (1991). Measurements of a distributed file system. *Operating Systems Review, 25*(5), 198–212. doi:10.1145/121133.121164

Baxter, I. D. (2002). *Branch coverage for arbitrary languages made easy* (Technical report). Semantic Designs. Retrieved November, 2010, from http://www.semdesigns.com/Company/Publications/TestCoverage.pdf

Bishop, M. (1987). Profiling under UNIX by patching. *Software, Practice & Experience, 17*(10), 729–739. doi:10.1002/spe.4380171006

Bishop, M. (1989). A model of security monitoring. In *Proceedings of the Fifth Annual Computer Security Applications Conference* (pp. 46–52). Tucson, AZ: Academic Press.

Bishop, M., Wee, C., & Frank, J. (1996). *Goal-oriented auditing and logging*. Retrieved November, 2010, from http://seclab.cs.ucdavis.edu/papers/tocs-96.pdf

Borg, A., Kessler, R. E., & Wall, D. W. (1990). Generation and analysis of very long address traces. In *Proceedings of the 17th Annual Symposium on Computer Architecture (ISCA-17)* (pp. 270–279). Seattle, WA: ISCA. doi:10.1109/ISCA.1990.134535

Braden, R. T. (1988). A pseudo-machine for packet monitoring and statistics. *Computer Communication Review, 18*(4), 200–209. doi:10.1145/52325.52345

Buck, B., & Hollingsworth, J. K. (2000). An API for runtime code patching. *Journal of High Performance Computing Applications, 14*(4), 317–329. doi:10.1177/109434200001400404

Cantrill, B. M., Shapiro, M. W., & Leventhal, A. H. (2004). Dynamic instrumentation of production systems. In *Proceedings of the Annual Conference on USENIX Annual Technical Conference (ATEC'04)* (pp. 15–28). Boston, MA: USENIX Association.

Chuvakin, A., & Peterson, G. (2010). *How to do application logging right*. Retrieved November 24, 2010, from http://www.computer.org/cms/Computer.org/ComputingNow/homepage/2010/1010/W_SP_ApplicationLogging.pdf

Common Criteria. (2005). *Common criteria for information technology security evaluation: Part 2: Security functional requirements, version 2.3*. Retrieved November 25, 2010, from http://www.commoncriteriaportal.org/files/ccfiles/ccpart2v2.3.pdf

Crosbie, M., & Spafford, E. (1995). Defending a computer system using autonomous agents. In *Proceedings of the 18th National Information Systems Security Conference*. Academic Press.

Curry, T. W. (1994). Profiling and tracing dynamic library usage via interposition. In *Proceedings of the USENIX Summer 1994 Technical Conference (USTC'94)* (pp. 267–2780. Boston, MA: USENIX Association.

Debar, H., Dacier, M., & Wespi, A. (1999). *A revised taxonomy for intrusion-detection systems*. Rüschlikon, Switzerland: IBM Zürich Research Laboratory.

Delgado, N., Gates, A. Q., & Roach, S. (2004). A taxonomy and catalog of runtime software-fault monitoring tools. *IEEE Transactions on Software Engineering, 30*(12), 859–872. doi:10.1109/TSE.2004.91

Denning, D. E. (1986). An intrusion-detection model. In *Proceedings of the 1986 IEEE Symposium on Security and Privacy* (pp. 118–131). Oakland, CA: IEEE.

Dongarra, J., London, K., Moore, S., Mucci, P., & Terpstra, D. (2001). *Using PAPI for hardware performance monitoring on Linux systems.* Paper presented at Conference on Linux Clusters: The HPC Revolution, Urbana, IL, USA.

Etsion, Y., Tsafrir, D., Kirkpatrick, S., & Feitelson, D. (2007). Fine grained kernel logging with Klogger: Experience and insights. In *Proceedings of the 2nd ACM SIGOPS/EuroSys European Conference on Computer Systems 2007* (pp. 259–272). Lisbon, Portugal: ACM. doi:10.1145/1272996.1273023

Eustace, A., & Srivastava, A. (1994). *ATOM: A flexible interface for building high performace program analysis tools.* Palo Alto, CA: DEC Western Research Laboratory.

Federal Information Security Management Act. (2002). *FISMA, P.L. 107-347, Title III, December 17, 2002.* Retrieved March 28, 2014 from http://www.csrc.nist.gov/policies/FISMA-final.pdf

Fessi, B. A., BenAbdallah, S., Hamdi, M., Rekhis, S., & Boudriga, N. (2010). Data collection for information security system. In *Proceedings of the Second International Conference on Engineering Systems Management and Applications (ICESMA 2010).* Sharjah, UAE: Academic Press.

Forrest, S., Hofmeyr, S. A., Somayaji, A., & Longstaff, T. A. (1996). A sense of self for Unix processes. In *Proceedings of the 1996 IEEE Symposium on Research in Security and Privacy* (pp. 120–128). Oakland, CA: IEEE. doi:10.1109/SECPRI.1996.502675

Garfinkel, S., & Spafford, G. (1996). *Practical UNIX and internet security* (2nd ed.). Sebastopol, CA: O'Reilly.

Gartner Group. (2014). *Magic quadrant for security information and event management.* Retrieved March 25, 2014 from https://www.gartner.com/doc/2477018/magic-quadrant-security-informa-tion-event

GDB. (2010). *GDB: The GNU project debugger.* Retrieved November 25, 2010, from http://www.gnu.org/software/gdb/gdb.html

Graham, S. L., Kessler, P. B., & McKusick, M. K. (1984). gprof: A call graph execution profiler. *ACM SIGPLAN Notices, 39*(4), 49–57. doi:10.1145/989393.989401

Halme, L. R., & Bauer, K. R. (1995). AINT misbehaving: A taxonomy of anti-intrusion techniques. In *Proceedings of the 18th National Information Systems Security Conference* (pp. 163-172). Baltimore, MD: Academic Press.

Harrington, D., Presuhn, R., & Wijnen, B. (2002). *RFC 3411: An architecture for describing simple network management protocol (SNMP) management frameworks.* Academic Press.

Hedbom, H., Kvarnström, H., & Jonsson, E. (1999). Security implications of distributed intrusion detection architectures. In *Proceedings of the Fourth Nordic Workshop on Secure IT Systems* (pp. 225–243). Kista, Sweden: Academic Press.

Intersect Alliance. (2003). *Guide to snare for Linux.* Retrieved November 25, 2010, from http://www.intersectalliance.com/resources/Documentation/Guide_to_Snare_for_Linux-3.2.pdf

ISO/IEC (2013). *ISO 27002, information technology – Security techniques – Code of practice for information security controls.* Author.

Itzkowitz, M., Wylie, B. J. N., Aoki, C., & Kosche, N. (2003). Memory profiling using hardware counters. In *Proceedings of the 2003 ACM/IEEE Conference on Supercomputing (SC'03)* (pp. 17–29). Phoenix, AZ: IEEE. doi:10.1145/1048935.1050168

Jin, X., & Osborn, S. L. (2007). Architecture for data collection in database intrusion detection systems. In *Proceedings of the 4th VLDB Workshop on Secure Data Management (SDM 2007).* Vienna, Austria: VLDB. doi:10.1007/978-3-540-75248-6_7

Jin, X., & Osborn, S. L. (2007). Architecture for data collection in database intrusion detection systems. In *Proceedings of the 4th VLDB Workshop on Secure Data Management (SDM 2007)*. Vienna, Austria: VLDB. doi:10.1007/978-3-540-75248-6_7

KAD. (2010). *Handling interrupt descriptor table for fun and profit*. Retrieved November 25, 2010, from http://www.phrack.org/issues.html?issue=59&id=4#article

Kent, K., & Souppaya, M. (2006). *Guide to computer security log management: Recommendations of the National Institute of Standards and Technology (NIST), special publication 800-92*. Retrieved November 24, 2010, from http://csrc.nist.gov/publications/nistpubs/800-92/SP800-92.pdf

Killourhy, K. S., Maxion, R. A., & Tan, K. M. C. (2004). A defense-centric taxonomy based on attack manifestations. In *Proceedings of the International Conference on Dependable Systems and Networks (DSN 2004)* (pp. 102–111). Florence, Italy: IEEE. doi:10.1109/DSN.2004.1311881

Kuperman, B. A. (2004). *A categorization of computer security monitoring systems and the impact on the design of audit sources*. (PhD thesis). Purdue University, West Lafayette, IN.

Kuperman, B. A., & Spafford, E. (1999). *Generation of application level audit data via library interposition: Technical Report CERIAS TR 99-11*. West Lafayette, IN: COAST Laboratory, Purdue University.

Larson, U. E., Jonsson, E., & Lindskog, S. (2008a). A revised taxonomy of data collection mechanisms with a focus on intrusion detection. In *Proceedings of the 3rd IEEE International Conference on Availability, Security, and Reliability (ARES 2008)* (pp. 624–629). Barcelona, Spain: IEEE. doi:10.1109/ARES.2008.38

Larson, U. E., Lindskog, S., Nilsson, D. K., & Jonsson, E. (2008b). Operator-centric and adaptive intrusion detection. In *Proceedings of the Fourth International Conference on Information Assurance and Security (IAS'08)* (pp. 161–166). Naples, Italy: IEEE. doi:10.1109/IAS.2008.42

Larson, U. E., Nilsson, D. K., & Jonsson, E. (2008). An approach to specification-based attack detection for in-vehicle networks. In *Proceedings of the 12th IEEE Intelligent Vehicles Symposium (IV08)*. Eindhoven, the Netherlands: IEEE. doi:10.1109/IVS.2008.4621263

Larus, J. R. (1993). Efficient program tracing. *Computer*, *26*(5), 52–61. doi:10.1109/2.211900

Larus, J. R., & Ball, T. (1994). Rewriting executable files to measure program behavior. *Software, Practice & Experience*, *24*(2), 197–218. doi:10.1002/spe.4380240204

Lee, W., Stolfo, S., & Chan, P. (1997). Learning patterns from Unix process execution traces for intrusion detection. In *AI approaches to fraud detection and risk management* (pp. 50–60). Providence, RI: AAAI Press.

Lee, W., & Xiang, D. (2001). Information-theoretic measures for anomaly detection. In *Proceedings of the 2001 Symposium on Research in Security and Privacy* (pp. 130–143). Oakland, CA: Academic Press.

Levon, J., & Elie, P. (2009). *Oprofile: A system-wide profiler for Linux systems*. Retrieved November 25, 2010, from http://oprofile.sourceforge.net/news/

Linux Audit Subsystem. (2004). *Linux audit subsystem design documentation for kernel 2.6*. Retrieved November 25, 2010, from http://www.uniforum.chi.il.us/slides/HardeningLinux/LAuS-Design.pdf

Love, R. (2005). *Linux kernel development* (2nd ed.). Novell Press.

ltrace. (2002). *ltrace – Default branch*. Retrieved November 25, 2010, from http://freshmeat.net/projects/ltrace/

Luk, C.-K., Cohn, R., Muth, R., Patil, H., Klauser, A., & Lowney, G. et al. (2005). Pin: Building customized program analysis tools with dynamic instrumentation. In *Proceedings of the 2005 ACM SIGPLAN Conference on Programming Language Design and Implementation (PLDI'05)* (pp. 190–200). Chicago, IL: ACM. doi:10.1145/1065010.1065034

Lundin Barse, E. (2004). *Logging for intrusion and fraud detection*. (PhD thesis). Chalmers University of Technology, Göteborg, Sweden.

Lundin Barse, E., & Jonsson, E. (2004). Extracting attack manifestations to determine log data requirements for intrusion detection. In *Proceedings of the 20th Annual Computer Security Applications Conference (ACSAC 2004)* (pp. 158–167). Tucson, AZ: IEEE.

Maggi, F., Robertson, W., Kruegel, C., & Vigna, G. (2009). Protecting a moving target: Addressing web application concept drift. In *Proceedings of the 12th International Symposium on Recent Advances in Intrusion Detection (RAID 2009)*. Saint-Malo, France: RAID. doi:10.1007/978-3-642-04342-0_2

Mathew, S., Petropoulos, M., Ngo, H. Q., & Upadhyaya, S. (2010). A data-centric approach to insider attack detection in database systems. In *Proceedings of the 13th International Symposium on Recent Advances in Intrusion Detection (RAID 2010)*. Ottawa, Canada: Academic Press. doi:10.1007/978-3-642-15512-3_20

McCanne, S., & Jacobson, V. (1993). The BSD packet filter: A new architecture for user-level packet capture. In *Proceedings of the USENIX Winter 1993 Conference (USENIX'93)* (pp. 259–270). San Diego, CA: USENIX Association.

McKusick, M. K., Bostic, K., Karels, M. J., & Quarterman, J. S. (1996). *The design and implementation of the 4.4BSD operating system*. Boston, MA: Addison-Wesley.

Mogul, J. C., Rashid, R. F., & Acetta, M. J. (1987). The packet filter: An efficient mechanism for user-level network code. *Operating Systems Review*, *21*(5), 39–51. doi:10.1145/37499.37505

Moore, R. J. (2001). A universal dynamic trace for Linux and other operating systems. In *Proceedings of the FREENIX Track: 2001 USENIX Annual Technical Conference* (pp. 297–308). Boston, MA: USENIX Association.

National Computer Security Center. (1988). *A guide to understanding audit in trusted systems* (Technical Report NCSC-TG-001). National Computer Security Center (NCSC).

National Institute of Standards and Technology. (2013). *NIST special publication 800-53, security and privacy controls for federal information systems and organizations*. Retrieved March 25, 2014 from http://nvlpubs.nist.gov/nistpubs/SpecialPublications/NIST.SP.800-53r4.pdf

Nilsson, D. K., & Larson, U. E. (2008a). Conducting forensic investigations of cyber attacks on automobile in-vehicle networks. In *Proceedings of the First ACM International Conference on Forensic Applications and Techniques in Telecommunications, Information and Multimedia (e-Forensics 2008)* (pp. 1–6). Adelaide, Australia: ACM. doi:10.4108/e-forensics.2008.32

Nilsson, D. K., & Larson, U. E. (2008b). Simulated attacks on CAN-buses: Vehicle virus. In *Proceedings of the Fifth IASTED Asian Conference on Communication Systems and Networks (AsiaCSN 2008)* (pp. 66–72). Langkawi, Malaysia: IASTED.

Ousterhout, J. K., Costa, H. D., Harrison, D., Kunze, J. A., Kupfer, M., & Thompson, J. G. (1985). A trace-driven analysis of the UNIX 4.2 BSD file system. *Operating Systems Review, 19*(5), 15–24. doi:10.1145/323627.323631

Panchamukhi, P. S. (2004). *Kernel debugging with Kprobes*. Retrieved November 25, 2010, from http://www.ibm.com/developerworks/linux/library/l-kprobes.html

PCI Security Standards Council. (2013). *PCI DSS requirements and security assessment procedures v 3.0*. Retrieved March 25, 2014 from https://www.pcisecuritystandards.org/documents/PCI_DSS_v3.pdf

Peisert, S. P. (2007). *A model of forensic analysis using goal-oriented logging*. (PhD thesis). University of California, San Diego, CA.

Price, K. E. (1997). *Host-based misuse detection and conventional operating systems' audit data collection*. (Master's thesis). Purdue University, West Lafayette, IN.

Ptak, R. (2013). *What is happening to log files?* Retrieved March 26, 2014 from http://www.eventtracker.com/newsletters/what-is-happening-to-log-files-the-internet-of-things-big-data-analytics-security-visualization-oh-my/

Punti, G., Gil, M., Martorell, X., & Navarro, N. (2002). *gtrace: Function call and memory access traces of dynamically linked programs in ia-32 and ia-64 linux* (Technical Report UPC-DAC-2002-51). Polytechnic University of Catalonia, Barcelona, Spain.

Risso, F., & Degioanni, L. (2001). An architecture for high performance network analysis. In *Proceedings of the Sixth IEEE Symposium on Computers and Communications (ISCC'01)*. Hammamet, Tunisia: IEEE. doi:10.1109/ISCC.2001.935450

Rubini, A., & Corbet, J. (2001). *Linux device drivers* (2nd ed.). Sebastopol, CA: O'Reilly.

Russinovich, M., & Cogswell, B. (2010). *Process monitor*. Retrieved November 25, 2010, from http://technet.micrsoft.com/en-us/sysinternals/bb896645.aspx

Russinovich, M. E., & Solomon, D. A. (2005). *Microsoft Windows internals* (4th ed.). Microsoft Press.

SANS. (2006). *SANS consensus project information system audit logging requirements*. Retrieved November 24, 2010, from http://www.sans.org/resources/policies/info_sys_audit.pdf

SANS. (2013). *SANS top 20 critical security controls – Maintenance, monitoring, and analysis of audit logs*. Retrieved March 24, 2014, from http://www.sans.org/critical-security-controls/control/14

Schroeder, B. A. (1995). On-line monitoring: A tutorial. *Computer, 28*(6), 72–78. doi:10.1109/2.386988

Smith, M. D. (1991). *Tracing with pixie* (Technical Report CSL-TR-91-497). Stanford University.

strace. (2010). *strace – Default branch*. Retrieved November 25, 2010, from http://sourceforge.net/projects/strace

Sun Microsystems. (1988). *SunOS reference manual*. The Network Interface Tap.

Sun Microsystems. (1995). SunSHIELD basic security module guide. Mountain View, CA: Author.

Swift, D. (2010). *Successful SIEM and log management strategies for audit and compliance*. Retrieved March 28, 2014 from https://www.sans.org/reading-room/whitepapers/auditing/successful-siem-log-management-strategies-audit-compliance-33528 syscalltrack. (2010). *syscalltrack*. Retrieved November 25, 2010, from http://syscalltrack. sourceforge.net

Tan, K. M. C., Killourhy, K. S., & Maxion, R. A. (2002). Undermining an anomaly-based intrusion detection system using common exploits. In *Proceedings of the 5th International Symposium on Recent Advances in Intrusion Detection* (pp. 54–73). Zurich, Switzerland: Springer-Verlag. doi:10.1007/3-540-36084-0_4

tcpdump. (2010). *tcpdump/libpcap*. Retrieved November 25, 2010, from http://www.tcpdump.org

TIBCO. (2014). *How to centralize your logs with logging as a service: Solving logging challenges in the face of big data*. Retrieved March 26, 2014 from http://www.tibco.com/multimedia/solution-brief-logging-as-a-service_tcm8-19872.pdf

Vogels, W. (2000). File system usage in Windows NT 4.0. *Operating Systems Review, 34*(2), 17–18. doi:10.1145/346152.346177

Wagner, D., & Soto, P. (2002). Mimicry attacks on host-based intrusion detection systems. In *Proceedings of 9th ACM Conference on Computer and Communications Security* (pp. 255–264). Washington, DC: ACM. doi:10.1145/586143.586145

Wall, D. W. (1989). *Link-time code modification: Technical report research report 89/17*. Palo Alto, CA: DEC Western Research Laboratory.

Wetmore, B. R. (1993). *Paradigms for the reduction of audit trails*. (Master's thesis). University of California Davis, Davis, CA.

Yaghmour, K., & Dagenais, M. R. (2000). Measuring and characterizing system behavior using kernel-level event logging. In *Proceedings of the Annual Conference on USENIX Annual Technical Conference (ATEC'00)*. San Diego, CA: USENIX Association.

Zamboni, D. (2001). *Using internal sensors for computer intrusion detection*. (PhD thesis). Purdue University, West Lafayette, IN.

Zhang, X., Wang, Z., Gloy, N., Chen, J. B., & Smith, M. D. (1997). System support for automatic profiling and optimization. In *Proceedings of the Sixteenth ACM Symposium on Operating Systems Principles (SOSP'97)* (pp. 15–26). New York, NY: ACM. doi:10.1145/268998.266640

Zhou, S., Costa, H. D., & Smith, A. J. (1985). *A file system tracing package for Berkeley UNIX: Technical report*. Berkeley, CA: University of California at Berkeley.

ADDITIONAL READING

Amoroso, E. (1999). Intrusion Detection: An Introduction to Internet Surveillance, Correlation, Trace Back, Traps, and Response. Sparta, NJ, USA: Intrusion.Net Books.

Anderson, R. J. (2008). *Security Engineering: A Guide to Building Dependable Distributed Systems* (2nd ed.). New York, NY, USA: JohnWiley & Sons.

Axelsson, S. (2000). The base-rate fallacy and the difficulty of intrusion detection. [TISSEC]. *ACM Transactions on Information and System Security, 3*(3), 186–205. doi:10.1145/357830.357849

Axelsson, S. (2004). Visualising intrusions: Watching the webserver. In *Proceedings of the 19th IFIP International Information Security Conference (SEC2004)*, (pp. 259–274). Tolouse, France: Springer.

Cheswick, W. R., Bellovin, S. M., & Rubin, A. D. (2003). *Firewalls and Internet Security: Repelling the Wily Hacker* (2nd ed.). Upper Saddle River, NJ, USA: Addison Wesley.

Cheung, S., Dutertre, B., Fong, M., Lindqvist, U., Skinner, K., & Valdes, A. (2007). Using model-based intrusion detection for SCADA networks. In *Proceedings of the SCADA Security Scientific Symposium*, Miami, FL, USA.

CIDF. (2010). Common Intrusion Detection Framework. Retrieved November 25, 2010, from http://gost.isi.edu/cidf/

Durst, R., Champion, T., Witten, B., Miller, E., & Spagnuolo, L. (1999). Testing and evaluating computer intrusion detection systems. *Communications of the ACM, 42*(7), 53–61. doi:10.1145/306549.306571

Erbacher, R. F. (2004). Analysis and management of intrusion data collection. In *Proceedings of the 2004 International Conference on Security and Management (SAM'04)*, (pp. 179–185). Las Vegas, NV, USA.

Erbacher, R. F., & Augustine, B. (2002). Intrusion detection data: Collection and analysis. In *Proceedings of the 2002 International Conference on Security and Management (SAM'02)*, (pp. 3–9). Las Vegas, NV, USA.

Fisch, E. A., White, G. B., & Pooch, U. W. (1994). The design of an audit trail analysis tool. In *Proceedings of the 10th Annual Computer Security Applications Conference (ACSAC 1994)*, (pp.126–132). Orlando, FL, USA. doi:10.1109/CSAC.1994.367314

Gollmann, D. (2006). *Computer Security* (2nd ed.). West Sussex, England: John Wiley & Sons.

Jaquith, A. (2007). *Security Metrics: Replacing Fear, Uncertainty, and Doubt.* Upper Saddle River, NJ, USA: Addison Wesley.

Kemmerer, R. A., & Vigna, G. (2002). Intrusion detection: A brief history and overview. *Computer, 35*(4), 27–30. doi:10.1109/MC.2002.1012428

Kurose, J. F., & Ross, K. W. (2009). *Computer Networking: A Top-Down Approach Featuring the Internet* (5th ed.). Upper Saddle River, NJ, USA: Addison-Wesley.

Larson, U. E. (2009). *On Adapting Data Collection to Intrusion Detection.* PhD thesis, Chalmers University of Technology, Göteborg, Sweden.

Larson, U. E., Lundin Barse, E., & Jonsson, E. (2005). METAL: A tool for extracting attack manifestations. In *Proceedings of the Second Conference on Detection of Intrusions and Malware, and Vulnerability Assessment (DIMVA 2005)*, volume 3548 of Lecture Notes in Computer Science *(LNCS)*, (pp. 85–102). Vienna, Austria: Springer-Verlag. doi:10.1007/11506881_6

Lindqvist, U. (1999). *On the Fundamentals of Analysis and Detection of Computer Misuse.* PhD thesis, Chalmers University of Technology, Göteborg, Sweden.

McHugh, J. (2000). Testing intrusion detection systems: A critique of the 1998 and 1999 DARPA intrusion detection system evaluations as performed by Lincoln Laboratory. [TISSEC]. *ACM Transactions on Information and System Security, 3*(4), 262–294. doi:10.1145/382912.382923

Pfleeger, C. P., & Pfleeger, S. L. (2006). *Security in Computing* (4th ed.). Upper Saddle River, NJ, USA: Prentice Hall.

Ragsdale, D., Carver, C., Humphries, J., & Pooch, U. (2000). Adaptation techniques for intrusion detection and intrusion response systems. In *Proceedings of the 2000 IEEE International Conference on Systems, Man, and Cybernetics*, volume 4, (pp. 2344–2349)., Nashville, TN, USA: IEEE. doi:10.1109/ICSMC.2000.884341

Sebring, M. M., Shellhouse, E., Hanna, M., & Whitehurst, R. (1988). Expert systems in intrusion detection: A case study. In *Proceedings of the 11th National Information Systems Security Conference*, (pp.74–81), Arlington, VA, USA.

Silberschatz, A., Galvin, P., & Gagne, G. (2009). *Operating System Concepts* (8th ed.). Hoboken, NY, USA: John Wiley & sons.

Stallings, W., & Brown, L. (2007). *Computer Security: Principles and Practice*. Upper Saddle River, NJ, USA: Prentice Hall.

Vigna, G., Robertson, W., & Balzarotti, D. (2004). Testing network based intrusion detection signatures using mutant exploits. In *Proceedings of the 11th ACM Conference on Computer and Communications Security (CCS 2004)*, (pp. 21–30). Washington D.C., USA: ACM. doi:10.1145/1030083.1030088

KEY TERMS AND DEFINITIONS

Audit Data: A chronological record of system activities.

Data Collection: The process of capturing events in a computer system. The result of a data collection operation is a log record. The term logging is often used as a synonym for data collection.

Intrusion Detection System (IDS): An automated system used to warn operators of intrusions or intrusion attempts. An IDS is implemented in software and/or hardware.

Intrusion Detection: Intrusion detection is the process of identifying attacks or attack attempts. This process could be performed either manually or automatically.

Intrusion: The term intrusion is in this context simply defined as an attack on a computer system, resulting in a breach.

Security Log: A security log stores log record in chronological order. The terms security log and audit trail are often used interchangeably within the security community.

Taxonomy: Taxonomy is the science and practice of classification. Taxonomies are used when categorizing real-life as well as artificial phenomenon and the aim is to make systematic studies easier.

APPENDIX: CLASSIFICATION OF MECHANISMS AND TECHNIQUES FOR DATA COLLECTION

Table 1 provides an overview of 50 classified mechanisms and techniques for data collection. Each row in Table 1 represents the classification of one mechanism. The table contains dimensions from the taxonomies, i.e., log data, location with respect to environment (Location), time of introduction (ToI), granularity of log trigger (Gr), trigger (Tr), and action (Ac). The final column provides a reference to Table 2, which contains additional information.

Table 1. Mechanisms classified according to selected dimensions of the two taxonomies

Log Data	Location	Realization		Behavior		Reference
		ToI	Gr	Tr	Ac	(See Table 2)
Network	OS Kernel	Pre-runtime	Program	Event	Retrieve attributes	1
Network	OS Kernel	Pre-runtime	Program	Event	Occurrence	2
System	OS Kernel	Pre-runtime	Program	Time	Occurrence	3
System	OS Kernel	Runtime	Program	Time	Occurrence	4
System	OS Kernel	Pre-runtime	Instruction	Event	Retrieve attributes	5
System	OS Kernel	Pre-runtime	Instruction	Event	Retrieve attributes/Occurrence	6
System	OS Interface	Pre-runtime	Instruction	Event	Retrieve attributes/Occurrence	7
System	OS Interface	Pre-runtime	Program	Event	Retrieve attributes	8
System	OS Kernel	Pre-runtime	Program	Event	Retrieve attributes	9
System	OS Kernel	Runtime	Program	Event	Retrieve attributes	10
System	OS Kernel	Pre-runtime	Program	Event/Time	Retrieve attributes/Occurrence	11
Application	Application	Pre-runtime	Instruction	Event	Retrieve attributes/Occurrence	12
Application	Application	Pre-runtime	Program	Event	Occurrence	13
Application	Application	Runtime	Instruction	Event	Retrieve attributes/Occurrence	14
Application	Application	Runtime	Instruction	Event	Occurrence	15
Application	Helper library	Runtime	Program	Event	Retrieve attributes/Occurrence	16
Application	Application	Pre-runtime	Instruction	Event/Time	Retrieve attributes/Occurrence	17
Application	OS Kernel	Pre-runtime	Program	Time	Occurrence	18
Application	Application	Pre-runtime	Program	Event	Retrieve attributes	19
Application	OS Kernel	Runtime	Program	Time	Occurrence	20
System/ Application	OS Kernel	Runtime	Instruction	Event	Retrieve attributes/Occurrence	21
System/ Application	OS Kernel	Pre-runtime	Program	Time	Occurrence	22
System/ Application	OS Kernel	Pre-runtime	Program	Event/Time	Retrieve attributes/Occurrence	23
System/ Application	OS Kernel	Runtime	Instruction	Event/Time	Retrieve attributes/Occurrence	24

continued on following page

Table 1. Continued

Log Data	Location	Realization		Behavior		Reference
		ToI	Gr	Tr	Ac	(See Table 2)
System/ Application	OS Kernel	Pre-runtime	Program	Event	Retrieve attributes	25
System/ Application	OS Interface	Pre-runtime	Program	Event	Retrieve attributes	26
System/ Application	OS Kernel	Pre-runtime	Program	Event	Retrieve attributes/Occurrence	27
System/ Application	OS Kernel	Pre-runtime	Program	Event	Retrieve attributes	28

Table 2. Translation for the references in Table 1

Reference	Source of Information
1	(McCanne & Jacobson, 1993; Mogul et al., 1987; Risso & Degioanni, 2001; Sun Microsystems, 1988; tcpdump, 2010)
2	(Braden, 1988; Harrington et al., 2002; Rubini & Corbet, 2001)
3	(McKusick et al., 1996)
4	(Itzkowitz et al., 2003)
5	(Panchamukhi, 2010)
6	(Etsion et al., 2007; Moore, 2001)
7	Ousterhout et al. (1985), Zhou et al. (1985)
8	(kad, 2010)
9	(Love, 2005)
10	(Aranya et al., 2004; Russinovich & Cogswell, 2010)
11	(Baker et al., 1991; Vogels, 2000)
12	(Borg et al., 1990; Eustace & Srivastava, 1994; Larus & Ball, 1994; Smith, 1991; Wall, 1989)
13	(Baxter,2001)
14	(Buck & Hollingsworth, 2000; gdb, 2010; ltrace, 2010; Luk et al., 2005; Punti et al., 2002; strace, 2010)
15	(Bishop, 1987)
16	(Curry, 1994; Kuperman & Spafford, 1999)
17	(Graham et al., 1984)
18	(Zhang et al., 1997)
19	(Apache mod_log_config, 2010; Garfinkel & Spafford, 1996)
20	(Anderson et al., 1997)
21	(Ariel & Miller, 1999)
22	(Levon & Elie, 2010)
23	(Dongarra et al., 2001)
24	(Cantrill et al., 2004)
25	(Russinovich & Solomon, 2005)
26	(syscalltrack, 2010)
27	(Yaghmour & Dagenais, 2000)
28	(Linux Audit Subsystem, 2010; Sun Microsystems,1995)

Chapter 17
An Auto-Reclosing-Based Intrusion Detection Technique for Enterprise Networks

Nana K. Ampah
Jacobs Engineering Group, USA

Cajetan M. Akujuobi
Prairie View A&M University, USA

ABSTRACT

Designing, planning, and managing telecommunication, industrial control, and enterprise networks with special emphasis on effectiveness, efficiency, and reliability without considering security planning, management, and constraints have made them vulnerable. They have become more vulnerable due to their recent connectivity to open networks with the intention of establishing decentralized management and remote control. Existing Intrusion Prevention and Detection Systems (IPS and IDS) do not guarantee absolute security. The new IDS, which employs both signature-based and anomaly detection as its analysis strategies, will be able to detect both known and unknown attacks and further isolate them. Auto-reclosing techniques used on long rural power lines and multi-resolution techniques were used in developing this IDS, which will help update existing IPSs. It should effectively block Distributed Denial of Service attack (DDoS) based on SNY-flood attacks and help eliminate four out of the five major limitations of existing IDSs and IPSs.

INTRODUCTION

Enterprise networks are the main targets for hackers or intruders due to the fact that most financial transactions take place online and the networks also handle vast amounts of data and other resources (Satti & Garner, 2001). Handling transactions online is on the increase every day because it makes life easier for both the customers as well as the enterprises offering services (Jou et al., 2000; Yau & Xinyu Zhang, 1999; Ko, 2003; Tront & Marchany, 2004). Enterprise networks also have lots of bandwidth, which is very attractive to hackers because they take advantage of that by using those networks as launching pads to attack others (Tront & Marchany, 2004; Janakiraman,

DOI: 10.4018/978-1-4666-7381-6.ch017

Waldvogel, & Qi Zhang, 2003). It therefore becomes very difficult for the IDSs and IPSs at the receiving end to detect and prevent the attacks or hackers, since the packet header information will indicate legitimate senders. This is the main reason why most IPSs are easily bypassed by hackers (Tront & Marchany, 2004; Paulson, 2002; Weber, 1999). Intrusion prevention, which is a proactive technique, prevents the attacks from entering the network. Unfortunately, some of the attacks still bypass the intrusion prevention systems. Intrusion detection on the other hand, detects attacks only after they have entered the network.

Although attacks are generally assumed to emanate from outside a given network, the most dangerous attacks actually emanate from the network itself. Those are really difficult to detect since most users of the network are assumed to be trusted people. The situation has necessitated drastic research work in the area of network security, especially in the development of intrusion detection and prevention systems intended to detect and prevent all possible attacks on a given network (Akujuobi & Ampah, 2007; Akujuobi, Ampah, & Sadiku, 2007). These IDSs use either anomaly or signature-based detection techniques. Anomaly detection techniques detect both known and unknown attacks, but signature-based detection techniques detect only known attacks. The main approaches of anomaly detection techniques are statistical, predictive pattern generation, neural networks, and sequence matching and learning (Palnaty, & Rao, 2013; Suthaharan, 2012; Aljarah, & Ludwig, 2013; Strasburg, Basu, & Wong, 2013; Kumar, Hanumanthappa, & Kumar, 2012; Gupta, Pandey, Shukla, Dadhich, Mathur, & Ingle, 2013; Ganapathy, Kulothungan, Yogesh, & Kannan, 2012; Thaseen, & Kumar, 2013; Tomasek, Cajkovsky, & Mados, 2012; Quang Anh Tran, Jiang, & Jiankun Hu, 2012; Sadighian, Zargar, Fernandez, & Lemay, 2013). The main approaches of signature-based detection techniques are expert systems, keystroke

monitoring, model-based, state transition analysis, and pattern matching (Mahdinia, Berenjkoob, & Vatankhah, 2013; Barhate, & Jaidhar, 2013; Mechtri, Tolba, & Ghanemi, 2012; Thaseen, & Kumar, 2013; Kumar, & Hanumanthappa, 2013; Biermann, Cloete, & Venter, 2001). There is no existing IDS or IPS that can detect or prevent all intrusions. For example, configuring a firewall to be 100% foolproof compromises the very service provided by the network. The use of conventional encryption algorithms and system level security techniques have helped to some extent, but not to the levels expected (Fadia, 2006; Leinwand & Conroy, 1996; Stallings, 2003). The following are the five limitations associated with existing IDSs (Satti & Garner, 2001):

1. **Use of Central Analyzer:** Whenever the central analyzer is attacked by an intruder the whole system will be without protection, so it becomes a single point of failure (Janakiraman, Waldvogel, & Qi Zhang, 2003);

2. **Limited Scalability:** Processing all data at a central point limits the size of the entire network that can be monitored and controlled at a time. Data collection in a distributed fashion also causes excessive traffic in the network (Kayacik, Zincir-Heywood, & Heywood, 2004);

3. **Effectiveness:** The ability of existing IDSs/IPSs to detect and prevent intrusion is still not clearly established because of high false positive and false negative rates (Chunmei, Mingchu, Jianbo, & Jizhou, 2004);

4. **Efficiency:** Quantifying resources like time, power, bandwidth, and storage used by existing IDSs will be a critical success factor (Khoshgoftaar & Abushadi, 2004); and

5. **Security:** Securing the security data itself from intruders is also a very important limitation to existing IDSs.

It is still an open problem to develop IDSs and IPSs to detect and prevent SNY-flood attacks, Distributed Denial of Service (DDoS) attacks based on SYN-flood attacks, and also eliminate some or all of the limitations of existing IDSs. Although many IDS and IPS techniques have been proposed for securing networks from attacks, problems with SYN-flood attacks and DDoS attacks based on SYN-flood attacks have not been resolved (Ganapathy, Kulothungan, Yogesh, & Kannan, 2012). Also, there is no research work that has attempted to solve the above problems nor have there been attempts to eliminate the majority or all of the five major problems of existing IDSs. Most research works solved only one or two of the major problems. Our approach will resolve the above problems through the following steps:

1. Design an IDS technique based on a well-established model (i.e., auto-reclosing), which specifically targets SYN-flood attacks and DDoS attacks based on SYN-flood attacks; and
2. Transmit all security data from the network directly to the central detection point for analysis instead of transmitting them through the network itself.

Step one aims at solving the problems with effectiveness of existing IDSs. Step two aims at solving the problems with efficiency (i.e., saving bandwidth), security (i.e., securing security data from intruders), and limited scalability (i.e., reducing traffic in the network). These are the objectives of our approach.

BACKGROUND

The following major approaches are used to manage network security problems:

1. Intrusion Detection (traditional); and
2. Intrusion Prevention (proactive).

The basic techniques used by the two approaches are as follows:

1. **Signature Based Detection System:** Attack patterns are considered as signatures;
2. **Anomaly Detection System:** Anything unusual is considered as suspect;
3. **Distributed Intrusion Detection System:** Data is collected and analyzed in a distributed fashion; and
4. **Centralized Intrusion Detection System:** Data is collected in a distributed fashion but analyzed centrally.

The use of intrusion detection and prevention techniques in addition to other authentication techniques has become very necessary in managing enterprise network security. A layer approach is often used since there is no single technique that guarantees absolute security against all attacks on a given network. Very strong authentication techniques will also help prevent attacks from within the network. Depending on where the IDS software is installed, it can be referred to as network based intrusion detection system (NIDS) or host based intrusion detection system (HIDS). NIDS ensures preventive control of a given system, whiles HIDS ensures detective control. The following are some existing NIDS: Internet Security Systems Real Secure, Network Security Wizard Dragon IDS, Symantec Net Prowler, Cisco Systems Net Ranger, Network Flight Recorder Intrusion, Detection Appliance, Network Ice Black Ice Defender, CyberSafe Centrax, and Snort. The following are some existing HIDS: Internet Security Systems Real Secure, Symantec Intruder Alert, CyberSafe Centrax, and Tripwire.

Securing information on data networks and the networks themselves have become very difficult tasks considering the diverse types and number of intrusions being recorded daily. There is a lot of ongoing research work in the area of data network security management to develop techniques to combat intruders because of the financial losses incurred by enterprises due to activities of intruders (Palnaty, & Rao, 2013;

Paez & Torres, 2009; Jing-Wen, Mei-Juan, Ling-Fang, & Shi-Ru, 2009; Kui, 2009; Lixia, Dan, & Hongyu, 2009; Momenzadeh, Javadi, & Dezfouli, 2009; Jing, HouKuan, ShengFeng, & Xiang, 2009; Ihn-Han & Olariu, 2009; Cannady, 2009; Changxin & Ke, 2009; Wei, Xiangliang, Gombault, & Knapskog, 2009). This effort should seriously include securing networks also, and that is exactly what this IDS proves to do. Research work in network security can be categorized into three major areas: intrusion detection systems only; intrusion prevention systems only; and combined intrusion detection and intrusion prevention systems.

INTRUSION DETECTION SYSTEMS

Intrusion detection, which is a traditional technique, detects attacks only after they have entered the network. An attack signature technique based on the processing power of general purpose graphic cards was developed in (Mahdinia, Berenjkoob, & Vatankhah, 2013). It seems to be more effective than FPGAs in terms of speed, scalability, flexibility, ease of programming and price. It can also enhance Snort's speed of detection. Jaccords Coefficient Similarity was used to achieve a high detection rate and significantly low false positive and negative alarms in (Palnaty & Rao, 2013). It looked promising after it was tested with a KD-DCUP99 data set. An ellipsoid-based technique was proposed in (Suthaharan, 2012) to fix problems in normal and intrusion attacks data. It was tested with KDDCUP99 and NSL-KDD data sets revealing very interesting results. An automated Digital Forensic Technique, which captures the state of the system after sending an alert message to the administrator was introduced in (Barhate & Jaidhar, 2013). Damage to the system can be proved in court using the captured image. A MapReduce methodology based on a particle swarm optimization clustering algorithm was proposed in (Aljarah & Ludwig, 2013). Test results established high

scalability for the technique. A Semantic Model of Automated Intrusion Detection Systems was developed in (Strasburg, Basu, & Wong, 2013).

It was combined with existing Intrusion Detection and Response Systems to ensure automated tuning, cross-system correlation and response selection. A decision tree algorithm based on a classification model for misuse and anomaly attack detection was proposed in (Kumar, Hanumanthappa, & Kumar, 2012). The efficient detection of malicious network activities by adaptive and cognitive intrusion detection systems, based on computational intelligent techniques was introduced in (Gupta, Pandey, Shukla, Dadhich, Mathur, & Ingle, 2013). A novel three-tier architecture for designing intelligent intrusion detection systems was proposed for wireless network. An intrusion detection systems, which have the following features: flexibility, distribution and cooperation, autonomy, lightweight, reactivity and fault tolerance was designed for mobile ad hoc networks (MANETs) in (Mechtri, Tolba & Ghanemi, 2012). An intrusion detection system an attribute selection algorithm, classifier and architecture was presented for ad hoc networks in (Ganapathy, Kulothungan, Yogesh, & Kannan, 2012). Removal of redundant attributes for decision making on intrusions was ensured by the attribute selective method. Test results produced higher detection rates and reduced false alarm rate. Tests with KDD'99 Cup data set was successful. Shortcomings of Snort NIDS due to high-speed and heavy traffic leading to dropping of packets were discussed in (Bulajoule, James, & Pannu, 2013).

This fact was demonstrated using an experimental real network. A parallel NIDS technology was suggested as a means of reducing dropping of packets. The fact that wireless sensor networks are susceptible to various attacks and have limited memory, battery life and computational power was highlighted in (Darra & Katsikas, 2013). To identify the attack detection capabilities of relevant intrusion detection approaches, a review of types of attacks against wireless network and the relevant intrusion detection approaches was presented. An evaluation of different tree based classification algorithms, which classify network events in intrusion detection systems was introduced in (Thaseen & Kumar, 2013). Test results confirmed that Random Tree emerged as the best algorithm with the highest degree of accuracy and reduced false alarm rate. The experiments were conducted on NSL-KDD 99 data set. Hadoop, an open source computing platform of MapReduce and a distributed file system, can efficiently enhance the throughput and scalability of IDS Log analysis as described in (Kumar & Hanumanthappa, 2013). The proposed intrusion detection system in (Tomasek, Cajkovsky, & Mados, 2012) is based on general system behavior and evaluates the behavior of the observed system. It works at low level system observation to enable it expose malicious codes from user perspective. The overview of different intrusions in Cloud Computing was provided in (Mehmood, Habiba, Shibli, & Masood, 2013).

Cloud based intrusion detection systems were analyzed with respect to their type, positioning, detection time, detection technique, data source and attacks they can detect. An intrusion detection systems equipped with multiple detection methods was recommended as the best choice to cope with security challenges in the clouds. Snort, Tcpdump and Network Flight Recorder, which are the most famous Network Intrusion Detection System, are very vital for ensuring network security (Vanathi & Gunasekaran, 2012). They also provide a defensive layer to monitor network traffic for pre-defined suspicious activity. The above NIDS were examined and contrasted. An improved Block-Based Neural Network (BBNN) based IDS was compared to four major schemes of Support Vector Machine (SVM) and Naïve Bayes algorithm in (Quang, Jiang, & Jiankun, 2012). The improved BBNN outperformed the four algorithms on the basis of classification and detection. The false alarm rate was reduced to 5.14% and the genuine detection rate was maintained at 99.92%. A semantic-based contex-aware alert fusion for distributed Intrusion Detection Systems was highlighted in (Sadighian, Zargar, Fernandez, & Lemay, 2013). It incorporates contextual information with the goal of leveraging the benefits of multi-sensor detection while reducing false positives. Results obtained after illustration and evaluation of the system using DARPA 2000, confirmed a reduction in false positives and also achieving the same detection rate as Snort and ISS RealSecure.

The analysis of IDSs in terms of advantages and disadvantages was done in (Vokorokos, Kleinova, & Latka, 2006). This study was purely theoretical and it was proposed to consider different types of IDSs based on attack types, and whether attacks are directed towards a whole network, a sub network or a host. It will finally consider at the implementation stage, the important criterion for determining which layers of the ISO/OSI model will be covered by the IDSs including their ranges of operation. The importance of an automated intrusion response and further proposal on a dynamic intrusion response known as Gnipper vaccine was highlighted in (Zhaoyu & Uppala, 2006). This is a countermeasure, which uses dynamic agents to mitigate denial of service attacks. Although the approach provided an efficient and effective response to an intrusion with very little overhead, future work in this effort will focus on developing an efficient "trust model." A pattern matching NIDS, which consists of four modules: collection module, analysis module, response module and attack rule library was developed in (Zhou, Liu, & Zhang, 2006).

The system is based on Common Intrusion Detection Framework (CIDF) architecture and mature intrusion detection technology. Although efficient and effective, the system has to include anomaly detection in the future. An intrusion detection engine based on neural networks combined with a protection method, also based on watermarking techniques, was presented in (Mitrokotsa, Komninos, & Douligeris, 2007). This engine exploits two research areas, that is, visual representation and watermarking, which have not been used in mobile ad hoc network (MANET) in the past. The advantages of eSOM and visual representation in achieving intrusion detection were demonstrated. The use of the proposed engine with various routing protocols, for detecting various types of attacks and testing real MANET in the future was emphasized. An approach to combat threats from worms, insiders, and attackers with a toehold was discussed in (Weaver, Paxson, & Sommer, 2007). This was done by exploiting the VLAN capabilities of modern switches to enforce that all LAN communications must traverse and meet the approval of an intrusion detection monitor that operates separately from the switch. Two benefits were realized here: deployment and operation in today's enterprise networks without requiring replacement of existing infrastructure, and the use of highly flexible, commodity PCs for LAN monitoring, rather than algorithms embedded in difficult-to-reprogram custom hardware. Further work is required in the development of a mechanism capable of processing WAN traffic and not only LAN traffic as described here.

A novel feature classification scheme for features that can be extracted by sniffing the network was introduced in (Onut & Ghorbani, 2006). It further gives a better understanding for real-time features that can be extracted from packets in order to detect intrusions. Preliminary results are promising for mapping the network features into the network attack domain. Future work will introduce statistical analysis of subsets of features versus specific attacks and attack categories in order to determine the necessary set of features to be analyzed by an IDS/IPS. Research into the question as to whether one can detect attacks without keeping per-flow state was initiated in (Ramana, Singh, & Varghese, 2007). It suggests that a tradeoff between performance and completeness may not be as Draconian as is commonly thought. Some progress has been made for bandwidth-based and partial completion DoS attacks, and scan-based

attacks including worms, but the general problem still remains very difficult. Further work is needed concerning issues of "behavioral aliasing" and "spoofing" in such scalable solutions. An introduction to new evasion methods, presentation of test results for confirming attack outcomes based on server responses, and proposal of a methodology for confirming response validity were discussed in (Chaboya, Raines, Baldwin, & Mullins, 2006). These methods must be implemented as either analyst guidance or preferably in a NIDS plug-in or similar software solution. Also, these methods lead to the development of payload-size and shell-code-matching filters for Snort. Future work looks promising in reducing both the analyst workload and the risk from evasion attacks.

A framework for internet banking security using multi-layered, feed-forward artificial neural networks was outlined in (Bignell, 2006). Anomaly detection techniques applied for transaction authentication and intrusion detection within internet banking security architectures were utilized. This comprehensive fraud detection model via networks technology has the potential to significantly limit present level of financial fraud experienced with existing fraud prevention techniques. A prototype for this neural network will be developed to quantitatively validate the effectiveness of this machine learning technique. An innovative approach to the design and implementation of a VoIP specific honeypot was presented in (Nassar, State, & Festor, 2007). Simulation results from using this Session Initiation Protocol (SIP) specific honeypot look promising in relation to the effectiveness of the information gathering tools and the correctness of the inference engine deductions. Attempts to reduce false positive rates generated by cooperative Intrusion Detection Systems (IDSs) in MANETs were discussed in (Otrok, Debbabi, Assi, & Bhattacharya, 2007). This was done by analyzing the intrusion detected by mobile nodes within a cooperative game theoretic framework. Simulation results provided better results compared to existing methods.

An Incident Response Support System (IRSS) that correlates past and present events in order to classify attacks was introduced in (Capuzzi, Spalazzi, & Pagliarecci, 2006). This also serves as a preliminary report on a system to support the incident response activities of a security administrator. So far, a prototype has been implemented, but a massive set of experiments in order to evaluate the effectiveness of this system is underway. Plans to investigate new similarity metrics (for response retrieval) and more sophisticated adaptation algorithm will be dealt with in the future. A suit of detection techniques to identify fraudulent usage of mobile telecommunications services by exploiting regularities demonstrated in users' behaviors was presented in (Sun, Xiao, & Wang). This leads to the creation of an end user's profile for anomaly detection in wireless networks.

The intrusion detection problem is formulated as a multi-feature two-class pattern classification problem, which applies Bayes Decision Rule to the collected data. Both algorithms can achieve good performance depending on the input parameters as indicated by results from simulation studies. More features need to be considered in the future so as to make the system more general and robust. A fully automated technique for detecting, preventing and reporting SQL Injection Attacks (SQLIAs) incidents was discussed in (Muthuprasanna, Ke, & Kothari, 2006). Preliminary evaluation results of a prototype developed against various performance metrics affecting web server performance was also provided. Solutions for these critical security issues in web applications ensure easy transition towards next generation web services.

INTRUSION PREVENTION SYSTEMS

Intrusion prevention, which is a proactive technique, prevents the attacks from entering the network. Unfortunately, some of the attacks still bypass the intrusion prevention systems. A simple methodology for testing dynamic intrusion-prevention systems for McAfee Entercept version 5.0 and the Cisco Security Agent version 4.5 was developed in (Labbe, Rowe, & Fulp, 2006). Although test results showed that neither of the products stood up to their required effectiveness, the Cisco product did better. This test even supports the fact that effectiveness is one of the major problems of existing IDSs and IPSs. A multiple joint prevention technique of information security in Storage Area Networks (SAN) environment was presented in (Zheng-De, Zhi-Guo, Dong, & Fei-Teng, 2006). Although this technique can greatly improve the ability of preventing intrusion, issues with misreporting of intrusion prevention in IDS and filch of information in SAN need to be considered in future. A novel pattern-matching algorithm, which uses ternary content addressable memory (TCAM) and capable of matching multiple patterns in a single operation was considered in (Weinberg, Tzur-David, Dolev, & Anker, 2006). This system is compatible with Snort's rules syntax, which is the de facto standard for intrusion prevention systems. This Network Intrusion Prevention System (NIPS) presents several advantages over existing NIPS devices.

The necessary and sufficient conditions for the application of Byzantine agreement protocol to the intrusion detection problem were investigated in (Colon Osorio, 2007). This was done by developing a secure architecture and fault-resilient engine (SAFE), which is capable of tolerating such problems. This IPS eliminates some of the common shortcomings of existing IPSs. Both the implementation and evaluation stages are complete and require extra research work in relation to masquerading, distribution and protection of sensitive data, scalability and implementation issues. The link between concepts of the immune system in relation to the Danger Theory and components of operating system (such as application processes and sockets) was investigated in (Krizhanovsky & Marasanov, 2007). Although it is expected to develop intrusion prevention systems out of this link, more work needs to be done for this to be achieved. A framework for protecting against buffer overflow attacks, the oldest and most pervasive attack technique was introduced and discussed in (Piromsopa & Enbody, 2006a). It was used to create an effective, hardware, buffer overflow prevention tool. A formal argument made here was that "a necessary condition for preventing buffer-overflow attacks is the prevention of the integrity of addresses across domains." A further description of how the above statement supports a variety of successful hardware-based methods to prevent buffer overflow attacks was given.

Arbitrary copy, a type of buffer-overflow attack that is capable of bypassing most buffer-overflow solutions was introduced in (Piromsopa & Enbody, 2006b)]. Work is still ongoing to extend Secure Bit, which is one of the most promising buffer-overflow protection techniques, to protect against buffer-overflow of non-control data. A better solution for Information Security management by designing Preventive Information Security Management (PrISM) aimed at developing and deploying an indigenous Information Security Management System (ISMS) with intrusion prevention capabilities was proposed in (Anwar, Zafar, & Ahmed, 2007). This solution is based on reverse engineering of Open Source Security Information Management (OSSIM) system. A new strategy for dealing with the impossible path execution (IPE) and mimicry attack in the N-gram base Host Intrusion Detection System (HIDS) model was introduced in (Bruschi, Cavallaro, & Lanzi, 2007). This is also a novel defensive technique, represented by the obfuscator module, which works in a transparent way and low overhead of 5.9% with the higher accuracy than the state of the art HIDS. Future work will consider using the obfuscator module in order to reduce the false rate and to detect other kinds of IPE attacks.

COMBINED INTRUSION DETECTION AND PREVENTION SYSEMS

Combined intrusion detection and prevention systems take advantage of both the traditional and proactive approaches with the aim of eliminating some of the limitations of both systems. The use of active traffic splitters on the traffic with the goal of reducing the load on sensors, thereby improving performance in the detection and prevention of intrusion was presented in (Xinidis, Charitakis, Antonatos, Anagnostakis, & Markatos, 2006). Some improvements were made in terms of sensor performance for each of the methods used. The overall cost of the approach was also reasonable. An intelligent agent based intrusion detection and prevention system for mobile ad hoc networks was studied in (Sampathkumar, Bose, Anand, & Kannan, 2007). Although the developed system worked efficiently and detected intrusion at multiple levels, namely, user and packet levels, there is the chance of improving the efficiency in terms of time reduction and effectiveness in terms of increased prediction rate of the system by using training with more instances. A Session Initiation Protocol (SIP) intrusion detection and prevention architecture was implemented as an extension of the very popular open-source software Snort in (Niccolini, Garroppo, Giordano, Risi, & Ventura, 2006). The results indicated that the quality of service experienced by clients did not decrease, hence signaling a good basis for further development of more advanced VoIP IDS/IPS solutions. The effective detection of both known and unknown attacks by means of unified real-time analysis of network traffic introduced by ESIDE-DEPIAN based on Bayesian Belief Networks concepts was established in (Bringas, 2007). This is referred to as a unified Intrusion Detection paradigm.

An application-based intrusion detection and intrusion prevention (ID/IP) system coupled with data mining and mobile agent technologies was introduced in (Yee, Rao, & Radha, 2006). This hybrid system, consisting of a core engine with data sensor, detector, configuration device and alert and response device as its main components, uses both signature-based and anomaly based mechanisms in detecting and preventing intrusions. It further uses data mining and mobile agent technologies in providing a real-time adaptive and responsive ID and IP systems. An examination of integrated multiple intrusion detection sensors, which seek to minimize the number of incorrect-alarms was designed and implemented in (Beheshti & Wasniowski, 2007). The system was implemented using Open Software whenever possible such as Snort, Honeypot, MySQL, etc. This information fusion based intrusion detection and prevention model, which is a prototype, needs to include database design allowing for more efficient data fusion from multiple sensors.

Proactive screening of the health of a corporate network and performing first aid by systematically monitoring vital signs of mobile devices within the network was outlined in (Ransbottom & Jacoby, 2006). Some of the vital signs to be used to detect and prevent system intrusion were registry content changes, active processes, open ports, power usage thresholds, and power signatures. This system provides a comprehensive overall assessment of a network, which leads to building broader immunities to help maintain the health of any enterprise network. A security model to protect IP Multimedia Subsystem (IMS) Service Delivery Platform (SDP) from different time independent attacks, e.g., SQL injection and media flow attacks was developed in (Sher & Magedanz, 2007). This is an Intrusion Detection and Prevention (IDP) system for detecting and preventing message tempering and media flow attacks for IMS Service Delivery. The performance results at Open IMS Tested Fraunhofer show the processing delay of the IDP as very small. In the next section, we discuss a unified approach to network information security which is the main focus of this chapter.

THE INTRUSION DETECTION SYSTEM TECHNIQUE

The intrusion detection system (IDS) technique is an approach that is based on auto-reclosing technique employed on long rural electrical lines and generally targets SYN-flood attacks and distributed denial of service attacks based on SYN-Flood attacks. It makes use of parameters like packet interarrival time and packet arrival rate to block suspicious attacks on data networks. This IDS will identify new attacks and further help update existing IPSs. It will also eliminate most of the five major shortcomings of existing IDSs and IPSs. Traditionally, most IPSs and IDSs depend on packet header information for prevention and detection respectively, but this approach additionally considers using quantitative parameters such as packet arrival rate and time interval between packets.

Monitoring such parameters can lead to signature-based detection or/and anomaly detection. Monitoring port probes or packets that look at specific virtual ports that all computers have when connected to the internet, will help detect hackers trying to link up with Back Orifice software running on computers they want to take control of. If the parameters captured match values of known attacks, then, signature-based detection should be flagged (Anjum, Subhadrabandhu, Sarkar, & Shetty, 2004; Guan, Liu Da-Xin, & Cui Bin-Ge, 2004). On the other hand, a sudden surge in traffic on a certain port for no apparent reason indicates a network anomaly, therefore anomaly detection should be flagged (Guan, Liu Da-Xin, & Cui Bin-Ge, 2004).

In addition to logging information about attacks and issuing alerts that an attack has occurred, this technique will further block or log off all sources of attack. Information about new or unknown attacks gathered by this IDS will be used to reprogram firewalls or generally used to update the list of known attacks already existing in the IPSs (Nadkarni & Mishra, 2004; Schmoyer, Yu Xi Lim, & Owen, 2004).

DENIAL OF SERVICE ATTACKS

There are so many dangerous types of attacks commonly used by attackers of data networks. It has been established, that, the most dangerous and commonly used attacks are denial of service (DoS) attacks. A denial of service attack is an attack that blocks large parts of the memory of the target system, such that it can no longer serve its users. This situation leads to crashing, rebooting or denial of services to legitimate users. Almost every server experiences DoS attacks at a given time during its operations. Some of the popular DoS attacks are Ping of death, Teardrop, SYN-flood, Land, Smurf, UDP-flood, Distributed DoS, and Modem-disconnect attacks. Although a well-configured firewall is an effective countermeasure against nearly all DoS attacks, it also affects normal network traffic. There are existing countermeasures to protect data networks and systems from all the DoS attacks with the exception of SYN-flood attacks and Distributed DoS attacks based on SYN-flood attacks. SYN-flood attacks basically flood the target system with connection requests from spoofed source addresses making it very difficult or impossible to trace the origin of the attacks.

In an attempt to establish full connections with all the requests, the memory of the target gets used up and prevented from serving legitimate users. It exploits the three-way handshake process that takes place any time two systems across the network initiate a TCP/IP connection. The client should send a SYN packet to the host, then, the host should reply with a SYN packet and acknowledge the client's packet by sending an ACK packet (i.e., SYN/ACK packet), and finally the client should send an ACK packet to acknowledge the SYN/ACK packet sent by the host (i.e.,, ACK/SYN/ACK packet). A TCP/IP connection is established only after the above three steps are completed.

Under SYN-flood attacks, all SYN/ACK packets from the targeted host are sent into the void, since all the SYN packets are sent from invalid source IP addresses. While the targeted host waits in vain for the ACK/SYN/ACK packets from the client (i.e., attacker in this case), additional SYN packets or connection requests queue up behind the first set of requests. These repeated cycles of requests use up all the memory of the targeted host, preventing it from answering requests from legitimate clients. TCP/IP protocol enables the targeted host to free part of its used up memory by discarding queued up connection requests after a time out period. But the attacker sends the connection requests from the spoofed addresses faster than the earlier connection requests can be timed out, thereby continuously using up the target host's memory. This means, the packet arrival rate will rapidly increase or the packet interarrival time will rapidly decrease for subsequent connection requests. These were the two parameters used as threshold values for detection in the automated IDS technique discussed in this chapter.

Although there is no single reliable countermeasure to protect a host from SYN-flood attacks, the following steps can be taken to minimize the risk of damage caused by them: reducing the "timed out" period (this can lead to disconnecting legitimate clients); increasing acceptable number of connection requests by the host (this leads to additional memory and system resources consumption); installing vendor-specific updates and patches (this can be time consuming and not always guaranteed); using firewall (this can lead to blocking legitimate clients).

Distributed DoS (DDoS) attacks have proved to be the most dangerous DoS attack because unlike SYN-flood attacks, they leave no trails behind after disabling large networks, thereby making it impossible to trace the attackers. They are even more dangerous than viruses and worms. A DDoS attack is basically the execution of any other DoS attack in a distributed fashion. The attacker takes full control of a less secured network of about 50 computers and installs DDoS attack tools on each of them. The attacker will then launch the DDoS attack from the 50 computers on the real target system with a single command line instruction. This raises the ratio of number of attackers to number of targets from 1:1 to 50:1, thereby making it more effective than all other DoS attacks. A combination of countermeasures is used to counter DDoS attacks, since there is no single existing reliable countermeasure. This was the main reason why the IDS technique discussed in this chapter was developed based on automated detection (Fadia, 2006).

METHOD OF APPROACH

As described above, additional SYN packets or connection requests are sent faster than the earlier connection requests can be timed out during SYN-flood attacks. This situation leads to an increase in packet arrival rate at the targeted host or node. Our method of approach is to detect these changes in packet arrival rate, classify them as anomalies and further block their sources. Detection and blocking of the additional SYN packets will be based on auto-reclosing technique.

MODELING TECHNIQUE

This is an automated IDS technique based on the mechanisms of auto-switches or auto-reclosers used extensively on long rural power lines. An auto-recloser prevents unnecessary disconnection of a long rural power line from the entire grid due to an over-current caused by a fault (e.g., short circuit) anywhere along that particular line. It differentiates between transient (temporal) and permanent faults, thereby managing outage time efficiently (Gans, 1996; Shepherd, Lane, & Steward, 1990). This technique reduces outage time thereby reducing revenue losses. The operations of a typical auto-recloser can be described as follows:

1. A short circuit occurs on any portion of the power line being protected;
2. Auto-recloser signals circuit breaker to open in order to block fault current from flowing through the power line;
3. Auto-recloser again signals circuit breaker to close after a set time (i.e., dead time);
4. If short circuit is cleared (i.e., transient fault), then, circuit breaker remains closed. This is referred to as successful reclosure; and
5. If short circuit persists (i.e., permanent fault), then, auto-recloser again signals circuit breaker to open, but lock out permanently until fault is cleared. This is referred to as unsuccessful reclosure (Luxenburger & Schegner, 2004).

The application of such mechanisms in data networks will not only reduce outage time and revenue losses, but also help reduce high false positive and false negative rates in existing IDSs/IPSs. The main task here was to look for a parameter, which could help achieve the above stated goals. The auto-recloser uses current levels as threshold values for detecting a fault, but this new approach used packet arrival rate and/or packet interarrival time to detect an intrusion. (Please refer to the previous section for further details).

All models for the simulation studies based on our algorithm were developed with the help of Optimized Network Engineering Tools (OPNET) 14.0. OPNET is the most widely used platform by the communications industry for network packet analysis. This software is based on Proto C (i.e., a special version of C language for OPNET), C, and C++ languages (Dale, Weems, & Headington, 2002). The simulation studies involved two stages: blocking analysis and sensitivity analysis. Blocking analysis investigated the possibility of blocking packet streams temporarily or permanently and further determined the effectiveness of its implementation. Sensitivity analysis investigated the sensitivity of the developed IDS technique.

The following were the assumptions made for this model during the blocking analysis:

1. The packet interarrival time for normal packets was assumed to be 40 seconds (i.e., the packet arrival rate was assumed to be 0.025 packet per second); and
2. The packet interarrival time for attack packets was assumed to be 1 second (i.e., the packet arrival rate was assumed to be 1 packet per second).

Please note that the interarrival time, which is simulation time and not real time, was chosen based on the total simulation time of 1,000s just for the sake of clarity. In reality, it was in the order of a few microseconds (i.e., around 40 μs for normal packets and 1 μs for attack packets). This means that the packet arrival rates were also very high (i.e., around 25,000 packets per second for normal packets and 1,000,000 packets per second for attack packets or 50kbps and 2Mbps respectively, since each packet consists of 2 bits). Figure 1 describes the algorithm for the automated IDS technique. The IDS temporarily blocked the packet stream (i.e., the packet stream with an increased packet arrival rate or decreased interarrival time) such that, information about the attack packet could be analyzed and decisions made quickly. The automated IDS technique was modeled around a major node, where the node itself was classified as the central IDS node (i.e., IDSC) and each of the connecting or surrounding nodes was referred to as the peripheral IDS node (i.e., IDSP). Figure 2 shows the network model of the automated IDS technique and details of a typical connection between two IDSPs (i.e., IDSP1 and IDSP3) across the IDSC.

The algorithm in Figure 1 can be described further with the help of Figure 2. For example, a stream of packets is created or generated with a particular packet arrival rate at IDSP1 and assigned a destination address such that it is forwarded by IDSC to IDSP3 in Figure 2. Figure 2 also shows

details of the links between IDSP1, IDSC, IDSP3 and their respective packet generators (PG), receivers (RP, R1 and R3), and transmitters (TP, T1 and T3). The role of the IDSC is to ensure packets are sent to the right destination. Various statistics like end-to-end delay, throughput, utilization and queuing delay are captured from the packets at IDSP3 before they are destroyed. When the packet arrival rate is increased, partial blocking or/and full blocking are effected at IDSP1 and the above statistics are recaptured and compared to the previous ones for further analysis. The auto-reclosing set in during and also after the analysis.

1. The packet interarrival time for attack packets was assumed to be 1, 10, 20, 30, 40, 50, and 100 seconds (i.e., the packet arrival rate was assumed to be 1, 0.1, 0.05, 0.033, 0.025, 0,02, 0.01 packet per second). Please note also that these are all simulation times and not real times.

Figure 3 shows an overview of the implementation scheme for the automated IDS technique. The implementation steps will be presented at the end of this chapter.

Only two IDSC nodes can be efficiently implemented for this sample network. Each IDSC node is linked to four IDSP nodes for detection. Please note that LAN 1 does not form part of the IDS nodes because it is not linked directly to any of the chosen central IDS nodes. All security data from the IDSC and IDSP nodes will be directly transmitted to the central detection point for analysis. This is done using multiresolution techniques.

RESULTS FROM THE SIMULATION STUDIES

Three scenarios were considered during the initial part of the first stage of the simulation studies. Scenario 1 did not implement the automated IDS technique, that is, packet arrival rate or packet interarrival time remained the same throughout the simulation. Scenario 2 implemented the automated IDS technique partially, that is, packet

Figure 1. Algorithm for the developed automated IDS technique

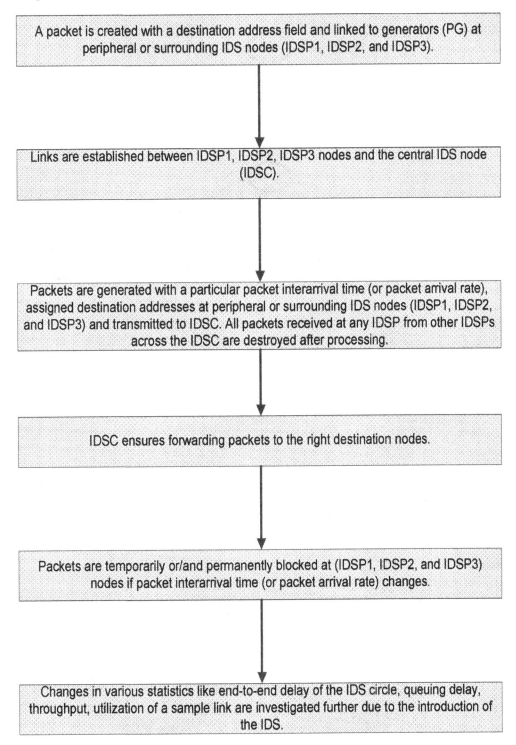

Figure 2. Network model of the automated IDS technique and a typical connection between two IDS peripheral nodes

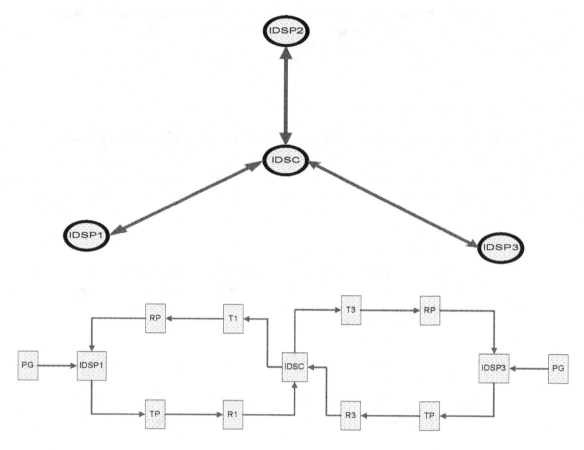

Figure 3. Overview of implementation scheme for the automated IDS

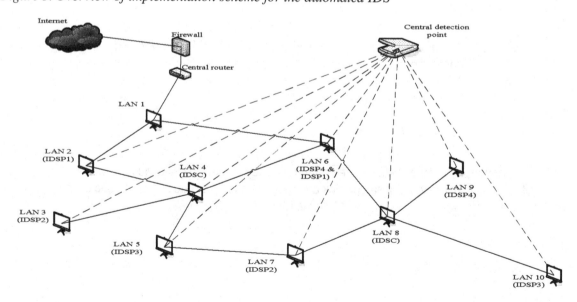

arrival rate or packet interarrival time changed, but the automated IDS technique only blocked the next interrupt of the packet stream (i.e., only one interrupt was blocked). Blocking the packet stream temporarily will give the central detection point time to analyze information about the attack or intrusion and subsequently take decisions. Scenario 3 implemented the automated IDS technique permanently, that is, packet arrival rate or packet interarrival time changed, but the automated IDS technique blocked the packet stream indefinitely.

Initial Results

This subsection presents the initial results obtained from the first stage of the simulation studies. Please note that the same models were used for all the three scenarios and all times were simulation times and not real times. All the network performance statistics obtained from the simulation studies were averages. The packet interarrival time and packet arrival rate for normal packets used in all the three scenarios were assumed to be 10 seconds and 0.1 packet per second, respectively. The packet arrival rate for attack packets used for blocking in scenarios 2 and 3 was 0.025 packets per second. Please note also that although the packet arrival

rate of the attack packets was far less than that for the normal packets, the main test at this stage was to verify whether blocking could be effected whenever the packet arrival rate was changed. The simulation speed and duration were set at 21 events per second and 1000 seconds respectively for both stages of the simulation studies.

A comparison of network performance statistics (in averages) like end-to-end delay from one IDSP to the other IDSP across the IDSC, queuing delay, throughput, and utilization of one of the links (in the IDS circle) obtained from all three scenarios is presented here. Please note that the end-to-end and queuing delays relate to only the IDSC and its surrounding IDSPs (i.e., in the IDS circle). Those delays will form part of the global ETE Delay of the entire system or network to be determined at the central detection point. Table 1 summarizes all the obtained performance statistics (averages) from the three scenarios.

ETE delay increased from 0.279s to 40.4s after the automated IDS was used temporarily, but it didn't exist when used permanently. Queuing delay (from IDSP to IDSC) did not change after the automated IDS was used temporarily, and it didn't exist when used permanently.

Table 1. Comparison of scenarios

	Scenario 1: No Blocking	Scenario 2: Temporal Blocking	Scenario 3: Permanent Blocking
ETE Delay in seconds	0.279	40.4	Did not exist
Queuing delay in seconds (From IDSP to IDSC)	0.119	0.119	Did not exist
Queuing delay in seconds (From IDSC to IDSP)	0.129	0.13	Did not exist
Throughput in bits/second (From IDSP to IDSC)	101	93	0
Throughput in bits/second (From IDSC to IDSP)	80	85	0
Utilization in percent (From IDSP to IDSC)	113	104	0
Utilization in percent (From IDSC to IDSP)	90	94	0

Queuing delay (from IDSC to IDSP) changed slightly after the automated IDS was used temporarily, but it didn't exist when used permanently. Throughput (from IDSP to IDSC) dropped from 101bps to 93bps after the automated IDS was used temporarily, but fell to zero when used permanently. Throughput (from IDSC to IDSP) rose from 80bps to 85bps after the automated IDS was used temporarily, but fell to zero when used permanently. Utilization (from IDSP to IDSC) dropped from 113% to 104% after the automated IDS was used temporarily, but fell to zero when used permanently.

Please note that utilization values greater or equal to 100% imply growth in the queue size at the node as time increases. Utilization (from IDSC to IDSP) rose from 90% to 94% after the automated IDS was used temporarily, but fell to zero when used permanently. Throughput and utilization generally dropped in the direction of IDSP towards IDSC and increased in the direction of IDSC towards IDSP because packets were only blocked at the IDSP nodes but not at the IDSC nodes, in favor of traffic flow in the direction of IDSC towards IDSP after removing the temporal block. The packet stream was blocked for about 80 simulation seconds (i.e., far less than 1 second in real time) in scenario 2.

Further Results

This subsection presents results obtained from the rest of the first stage and the second stage of the simulation studies. Only the possibility of blocking packet streams temporarily or permanently due to changes in the packet inter-arrival time or packet arrival rate has been investigated so far. That proved to be possible from the initial results obtained. The following were investigated here:

Blocking Analysis

1. To determine the required type(s) and sequence of blocking;

2. To determine the required number of blockings; and
3. To determine the duration of each blocking.

Sensitivity Analysis

1. To determine how the performance of this IDS relates to packet arrival rate or packet interarrival time; and
2. To discuss how the performance of this IDS technique will be linked to the following metrics:
   a. False positive rate (FPR);
   b. False negative rate (FNR); and
   c. Crossover error rate (CER).

BLOCKING ANALYSIS

Six scenarios were considered under this analysis as follows:

1. No blocking;
2. One partial blocking;
3. Two or more successive partial blockings;
4. One full blocking;
5. Two or more successive full blockings; and
6. One successive partial and full blocking.

Please note that the packet interarrival time used for normal packets was 40 seconds (i.e., the packet arrival rate was 0.025 packets per second). Also, the packet interarrival time used for attack packets was 1 second (i.e., the packet arrival rate was 1 packet per second). Both average and instantaneous statistics were considered for better clarification at this stage. Only throughput and end-to-end delay statistics were used for the rest of this analysis due to space. Table 2 summarizes results from all the six scenarios.

Table 2. Blocking analysis, all scenarios

Packet Inter-Arrival Time (Seconds)	Packet Arrival Rate (Packets/Second)	Packet Arrival Rate (Bits/Second)	Throughput (Average) (Bits/Second)	Throughput (Instantaneous) (Bits/Second)	Time Interval Between Successive Packets (Seconds)	End-To-End Delay (Seconds)
No Blocking						
1	1	2	1010	1040	0	0.265
40	0.025	0.05	26	104/0	20	0.25
One Partial Blocking						
1	1	2	510	515	0	0 - 0.248
40	0.025	0.05	13	104/0	65	0 - 0.24
Two or More Successive Partial Blockings						
1	1	2	510	515	0	0 - 0.248
40	0.025	0.05	13	104/0	65	0 - 0.24
One Full Blocking						
1	1	2	2	104/0	0	0
40	0.025	0.05	2	104/0	0	0
Two or More Successive Full Blockings						
1	1	2	2	104/0	0	0
40	0.025	0.05	2	104/0	0	0
One Successive Partial and Full Blocking						
1	1	2	2	104/0	0	0
40	0.025	0.05	2	104/0	0	0

Scenario 1 (Without Blocking)

- **Attack Packet:** The average throughput was almost the same as the instantaneous throughput because there were no time intervals between successive packets. The end-to-end delay was virtually constant.
- **Normal Packet:** The average throughput was far less than the instantaneous throughput because of the presence of time intervals (or dips to zero) between successive packets. The end-to-end delay was virtually constant.

Scenario 2 (With One Partial Blocking)

- **Attack Packet:** The average throughput was almost the same as the instantaneous throughput because there were no time intervals between successive packets. The end-to-end delay increased steadily from 0s to 0.248s.
- **Normal Packets:** The average throughput was far less than the instantaneous throughput because of the presence of larger time intervals (or dips to zero) between successive packets. The end-to-end delay increased steadily from 0 s to 0.24s.

Please note that the time intervals between successive packets increased from 20s (i.e., in scenario 1) to 65s because an interrupt or a packet stream was blocked partially. This difference of 40s equals to the duration of one spike cycle (i.e., when there was no blocking: scenario 1) and depicts that a packet stream or an interrupt was blocked within that period. The number of spikes decreased by about half from 25 (i.e., in scenario 1) to 13 due to the blocking. The average throughput also dropped from 26 (1010) bps to 13 (510) bps as a result of the partial blocking. Please note that the numbers in parenthesis relate to normal packets.

- **Comparison:** The average throughput values in this scenario decreased by about half compared to those of scenario 1. Only the instantaneous throughput of the attack packets was reduced by about half. The instantaneous throughput for the normal packets remained the same.

Scenario 3 (With Two or More Successive Partial Blockings)

All results were the same as obtained in scenario 2.

Scenario 4 (With One Full Blocking)

- **Attack Packet:** Instantaneous throughput spiked once initially to 104bps and dropped sharply to 0bps throughout. This was why the average throughput remained at 2bps and not 0 bps. The packet stream was blocked permanently, so time interval between successive packets and end-to-end delay did not exist.
- **Normal Packets:** The situation was the same as in the case of attack packets. Comparison: Please note that the average throughput values in this scenario dropped from 1010bps in scenario 1 to virtually 0bps because the packet stream was blocked fully. The instantaneous throughput of the attack packets

dropped to the level for the normal packet in scenario 1. The instantaneous throughput for the normal packets remained the same.

Scenario 5 (With Two or More Successive Full Blockings)

All results were the same as obtained in scenario 4.

Scenario 6 (With One Successive Partial and Full Blocking)

All results were the same as obtained in scenario 4.

RECOMMENDATIONS

Two partial blockings and one full blocking are recommended based on the above study. This is how the new IDS will make use of the auto-reclosing technique. Auto-reclosers installed on power lines temporarily isolate the power lines twice and move into a state of lockout permanently until the fault on the line is cleared by a fault team. The outage time between the two isolations is roughly 0.3333s. Considering the high packet rate in communications networks (i.e., 100Mbps) compared to the frequency of power systems (i.e., 60 Hz), the recommended blocking time should be in microseconds and must also be less than the lower end-to-end delay in scenario 1 (i.e., without blocking). Please note that the values of end-to-end delay for the entire simulation studies need to be divided by thousand in order to get closer to the real delays. The recommended time between blockings was therefore 250 µs. Please note that end-to-end delay at any stage of the entire simulation studies referred to the time for a packet to travel from one IDSP to the other and not the global end-to-end delay of the entire network. This outage time value should be less than the time out period of the three-way handshake process required for establishing a TCP/IP connection between two nodes within a particular network.

SENSITIVITY ANALYSIS

This subsection investigated and discussed how the performance of this IDS technique is linked to false positive rate (FPR), false negative rate (FNR), and crossover error rate (CER). Any or a combination of the above metrics can be used to determine the performances of IDSs. The same setup was used at this stage as before but this time, the packet interarrival time for attack packets was varied from 1s up to 100s in order to establish the sensitivity of the IDS technique in relation to packet arrival rate or packet interarrival time. The statistics collected were end-to-end delay, time interval between successive packets, average throughput, and instantaneous throughput. Three scenarios were considered at this stage: no blocking, one partial blocking, and one full blocking. Table 3 summarizes the results from all three scenarios.

Table 3. Sensitivity analysis, all scenarios

Packet Inter-Arrival Time (Seconds)	Packet Arrival Rate (Packets/ Second)	Packet Arrival Rate (Bits/ Second)	Throughput (Average) (Bits/Second)		Throughput (Instantaneous) (Bits/ Second)		Time Interval Between Successive Packets (Seconds)		End-To-End Delay (Seconds)
No Blocking									
1	1	2	1040		1040		0		0.265
10	0.1	0.2	104		104		0		0.26
20	0.05	0.1	52		104		2		0.255
30	0.033	0.67	34		104		10		0.25
40	0.025	0.05	26		104		20		0.25
50	0.02	0.04	21		104		35		0.25
100	0.01	0.02	11		104		80		0.249
One Partial Blocking									
1	1	2	510		515		0		0 - 0.248
10	0.1	0.2	51		0		0		0 - 0.245
20	0.05	0.1	26		0		20		0 - 0.24
30	0.033	0.67	17		0		40		0 - 0.24
40	0.025	0.05	13		0		65		0 - 0.24
50	0.02	0.04	11		0		80		0 - 0.225
100	0.01	0.02	5		0		180		0 - 0.2
One Full Blocking									
1	1	2	2		0		0		0
10	0.1	0.2	2		0		0		0
20	0.05	0.1	2		0		0		0
30	0.033	0.67	2		0		0		0
40	0.025	0.05	2		0		0		0
50	0.02	0.04	2		0		0		0
100	0.01	0.02	2		0		0		0

Scenario 1 (Without Blocking)

- **Discussion:** There was a general increase in time interval between successive packets as packet arrival rate decreased. Average throughput also decreased as the packet arrival rate decreased. The instantaneous throughput generally remained constant at 104bps apart from the high initial value of 1040bps when packet interarrival time was 1s. The end-to-end delay virtually remained constant throughout.

Scenario 2 (With One Partial Blocking)

- **Discussion:** The effect of partial blocking reduced with increasing packet arrival rate as indicated by the time interval between successive packets (i.e., increasing from 0s to 180s). Instantaneous throughput followed the same trend as in scenario 1 (i.e., drastic decrease from 515bps to 0bps).

Scenario 3 (With One Full Blocking)

- **Discussion:** All the above four statistics did not exist. The average throughput will be 0bps in reality as described in scenario 4 under blocking analysis. It was around 2bps just because of the initial spike. Figures 4 to 7 depict the graphs of the four chosen statistics against packet inter-arrival time/packet arrival rate for all the three scenarios. Figures 4 to 6 supported the fact that this IDS technique was very sensitive when the packet arrival rate was 0.2bps and lower (i.e., because both the instantaneous and average throughput values dropped quickly to 0bps in

this case and at the same time, the time interval between successive packets increased drastically) as compared to when the packet arrival rate was above 0.2bps (i.e., because both the instantaneous and average throughput values dropped steadily and not quickly to 0bps in this case and at the same time, the time interval between successive packets remained constant at around 0s). It is clear from Figure 7 that the end-to-end delay was virtually constant for scenarios 1 and 2, but didn't exist for scenario 3. This outcome will also help determine the range of packet arrival rate within which this IDS can be implemented.

A detailed sensitivity analysis requires testing this IDS technique by introducing attacks to a particular node in a real network (i.e., during the implementation stage). Some of the metrics that can be used to assess the performance of an IDS technique due to changes in sensitivity are false positive rate (FPR), false negative rate (FNR), and crossover error rate (CER). The sensitivity of the IDS will be varied by varying the range of the threshold values of the IDS. FPR is the frequency with which the IDS reports malicious activity in error. It generally increases as the sensitivity increases. FNR is the frequency with which the IDS fails to raise an alarm when a malicious activity actually occurs. It generally decreases as the sensitivity increases. CER is the frequency value at which FPR is equal to FNR. If it is required to achieve a balance between FPR and FNR, then the best choice must be the IDS with the lowest CER. If it is required to detect every single attack, then the best choice will be the IDS with the lowest FNR or highest FPR. Please note that this choice may lead to an increase in administrative overhead associated with the FPR.

Figure 4. Instantaneous throughput for all 3 scenarios

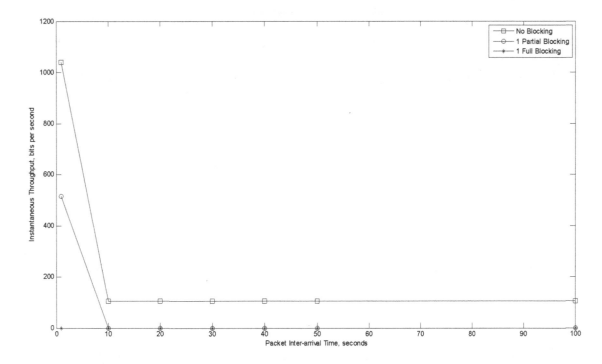

Figure 5. Average throughput for all 3 scenarios

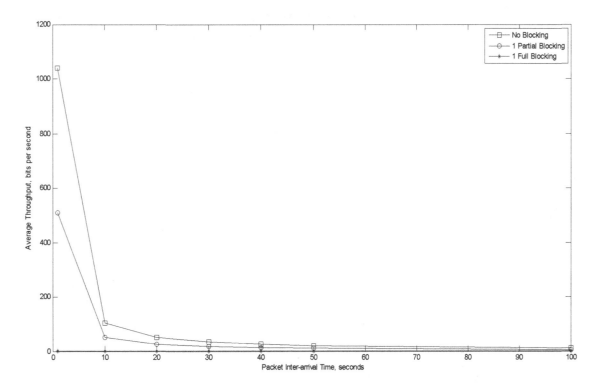

Figure 6. Time interval between successive packets for all 3 scenarios

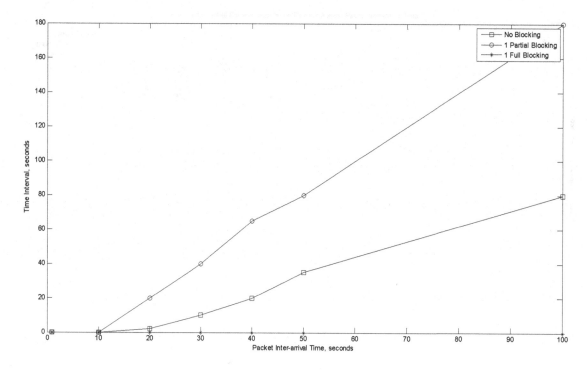

Figure 7. End-to-end delay for all 3 scenarios

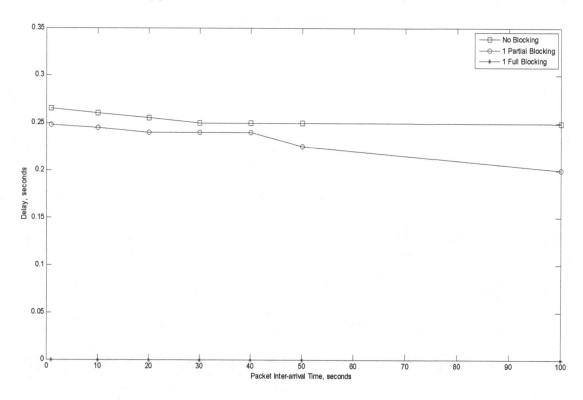

MULTIRESOLUTION TECHNIQUES

A multiresolution technique is an application of wavelet transform, which decomposes an image and reconstructs it after transmission, with the aim of reproducing the exact image. The decomposition (or decimation) process involves convolving data samples from the image with low pass and high pass wavelet coefficients (i.e., h0 and h1, respectively). This process is also known as sampling. The reconstruction (or interpolation) process involves convolving the received data after decomposition and transmission with the transformed (i.e., reflection in the line y = x or 180° rotation about the origin) low pass and high pass wavelet coefficients. This process is also known as upper-sampling. The high pass portion of the multiresolution technique eliminates any noise associated with the two major processes. The low pass portion of the technique, which contains no noise, is therefore projected further. It contains much of the energy content of the original data samples. Data received from the two portions of the technique are finally summed up to reproduce the original image.

Only the signal processing applications of wavelets was taken advantage of in this research work. In the field of signal analysis, the methods of wavelet transform have wide applications because of their unique merit. One of the important applications is multiresolution technique, which was used to decompose, transmit and reconstruct signals or data from the enterprise network to a Central Detection Point for further analysis. Multiresolution technique simultaneously represents segments of an image or data by multiple scales and further consists of two very important concepts, that is, dilation and translation.

Multiresolution Haar transform, which is a multiresolution technique using Haar wavelets coefficients, produces detail information of segments from an image or data as described in (Yung-Da & Paulik, 1996). Transmission of traffic from the network nodes to the central detection point for the technique developed in this research work was done using a one-dimensional, two-stage multiresolution technique. Haar Wavelets was applied here. The effectiveness of multiresolution Haar transform was also taken advantage of in (Piscaglia & Maccq, 1996).

FUTURE RESEARCH DIRECTIONS

Further investigation should be done in the following areas to enhance this automated IDS technique: modeling the automated IDS such that a generator can generate a packet stream with variable interarrival times; and repeating the simulation for increasing simulation run times and analyzing the outcome.

IMPLEMENTATION OF IDS TECHNIQUE

Implementation of this IDS technique involves two major parts: "set-up inside the network" and "set-up at the central detection point." The following should be the steps under the "set-up inside the network" part:

1. Group all the nodes in the network into various IDS circles (i.e.,, each IDS circle consists of one central IDS or IDSC and all the peripheral IDSs or IDSPs linked to it);
2. Install a detector (i.e., software on a computer) at each IDSP for determining the packet arrival rate etc. at that node; and
3. Install a transmitter at each IDSP for sending the packet arrival rate data etc. to the central detection point by multiresolution techniques.

The following should be the steps under the "set-up at the central detection point" part:

1. Install OPNET 14.0 at the central detection point (i.e., software on a computer);
2. Replicate the actual network in OPNET 14.0 at the central detection point with reference to Figure 3 or the actual implementation scheme for the IDS;
3. Install a receiver at the central detection point to receive the packet arrival rate data etc. from the network (i.e., at the end of the multiresolution techniques);
4. Furnish the replica of the actual network developed in OPNET with the packet arrival rate data etc. of all the IDSP nodes; and
5. Carry out all the steps discussed under the simulation studies above.

CONCLUSION

It was clear from the discussions under this IDS technique that although the packet stream was blocked temporarily, the average performance statistics did not change that much from the scenario without the automated IDS. Zero values obtained for all statistics from scenario 3 of the first stage of the simulation studies explained the fact that the packet stream was really blocked, thereby preventing the attack packets (i.e., packets with arrival rate of 1 packet per second) from getting to their target destinations. This automated IDS was very effective because it instantly prevented the attack packets from leaving the IDSP node as shown in the results obtained from scenario 2 (i.e., All performance statistics before time t = 80 seconds were zero). The implementation scheme makes the automated IDS technique efficient because bandwidth will be saved for normal network activities by transmitting security data separately. This indicates that this IDS technique also guaranteed security for the security data itself. This implies that four out of the five limitations of existing IDSs/IPSs have so far been eliminated by this technique.

CONTRIBUTION

Results obtained so far from this IDS technique look promising. They seek to eliminate the following limitations: limited scalability (i.e., partly by reducing traffic in the network); efficiency (i.e., saving bandwidth for network operation); and security (i.e., securing security data) because security data was sent directly to the central detection point using multiresolution techniques; effectiveness (i.e., reducing false positive and false negative rates) because of the use of auto-reclosing technique. They also seek to show how the IDS counters DDoS attacks based on SYN-flood attacks or distributed attacks in general and also SYN-flood attacks in particular.

REFERENCES

Akujuobi, C. M., & Ampah, N. K. (2007). Enterprise network intrusion detection and prevention system. In *Proceedings of Society of Photographic Instrumentation Engineers Defense and Security Symposium* (Vol. 6538, pp. 1-12). Academic Press.

Akujuobi, C. M., Ampah, N. K., & Sadiku, M. N. O. (2007). An intrusion detection technique based on change in Hurst parameter with application to network security. *International Journal of Computer Science and Network Security*, 5(7), 55–64.

Aljarah, I., & Ludwig, S. A. (2013). MapReduce intrusion detection system based on a particle swarm optimization clustering algorithm. In *IEEE Congress on Evolutionary Computation (CEC)* (pp. 955-962). IEEE. doi:10.1109/CEC.2013.6557670

Amanullah, M. T. O., Kalam, A., & Zayegh, H. (2005). Network security vulnerabilities in SCADA and EMS. In Proceedings of Transmission and Distribution Conference and Exhibition: Asia and Pacific (pp. 1-6). Academic Press.

Ampah, N. K., & Akujuobi, C. M. (2012). Protecting enterprise networks: An intrusion detection technique based on auto-reclosing. In P. Kabiri (Ed.), *Privacy, intrusion detection and response: Technologies for protecting networks* (pp. 40–76). IGI Global. doi:10.4018/978-1-60960-836-1.ch002

Anjum, F., Subhadrabandhu, D., Sarkar, S., & Shetty, R. (2004). *On optimal placement of intrusion detection modules in sensor networks.* BroadNets. doi:10.1109/BROADNETS.2004.52

Anwar, M. M., Zafar, M. F., & Ahmed, Z. (2007). A proposed preventive information security system. In *Proceedings of International Conference on Electrical Engineering* (pp. 1-6). Academic Press.

Barhate, K., & Jaidhar, C. (2013). Automated digital forensic technique with intrusion detection systems. In *Proceedings of IEEE 3rd International Advance Computing Conference (IACC)* (pp. 185-189). IEEE.

Beheshti, M., & Wasniowski, R. A. (2007). Data fusion support for intrusion detection and prevention. In *Proceedings of International Conference on Information Technology* (pp. 966-966). Academic Press. doi:10.1109/ITNG.2007.62

Biermann, E., Cloete, E., & Venter, L. M. (2001). A comparison of intrusion detection systems. *Computers & Security*, 8(20), 676–683. doi:10.1016/S0167-4048(01)00806-9

Bignell, K. B. (2006). Authentication in the internet banking environment: Towards developing a strategy for fraud detection. In *Proceedings of International Conference on Internet Survaillance and Protection* (pp. 23-23). Academic Press. doi:10.1109/ICISP.2006.3

Bridis, T., & Sullivan, E. (2007). *US video shows hacker hit on power grid.* Associated Press Writers. Retrieved September, 27, 2007, from http://www.physorg.com/news110104929.html

Bringas, P. G. (2007). Intensive use of Bayesian belief network for the unified, flexible and adaptable analysis of misuses and anomalies in network intrusion detection and prevention systems. In *Proceedings of International Conference on Database and Expert Systems Applications* (pp. 365-371). Academic Press. doi:10.1109/DEXA.2007.38

Bruschi, D., Cavallaro, L., & Lanzi, A. (2007). An effective technique for preventing mimicry and impossible paths execution attacks. In *Proceedings of International Conference on Performance, Computing, and Communications* (pp. 418-425). Academic Press.

Bulajoul, W., James, A., & Pannu, M. (2013). Network intrusion detection systems in high-speed traffic in computer networks. In *Proceedings of IEEE 10th International Conference on e-Business Engineering (ICEBE)* (pp. 168-175). IEEE.

Cannady, J. (2009). Distributed detection of attacks in mobile ad hoc networks using learning vector quantization. In *Proceedings of Third International Conference on Network and System Security* (pp. 571–574). Academic Press. doi:10.1109/NSS.2009.99

Capuzzi, G., Spalazzi, L., & Pagliarecci, F. (2006). IRSS: Incident response support system. In *Proceedings of International Symposium on Collaborative Technologies and Systems* (pp. 81-88). Academic Press. doi:10.1109/CTS.2006.55

Car, J., & Jakupovic, G. (2005). SCADA system security as a part of overall security of deregulated energy management system. In *Proceedings of International Conference on Computer as a Tool* (pp. 338-341). Academic Press. doi:10.1109/EURCON.2005.1629930

Chaboya, D. J., Raines, R. A., Baldwin, R. O., & Mullins, B. E. (2006). Network intrusion detection: Automated and manual methods prone to attacks and evasion. *Security and Privacy Magazine*, 6(4), 36–43. doi:10.1109/MSP.2006.159

Changxin, S., & Ke, M. (2009). Design of intrusion detection system based on data mining algorithm. In *Proceedings of International Conference on Signal Processing Systems* (pp. 370–373). Academic Press.

Chunmei, Y., Mingchu, L., Jianbo, M., & Jizhou, S. (2004). Honeypot and scan detection in intrusion detection system. In *Proceedings of Canadian Conference on Electrical and Computer Engineering* (pp. 1107–1110). Academic Press. doi:10.1109/CCECE.2004.1345313

Colon Osorio, F. C. (2007). Using Byzantine agreement in the design of IPS systems. In *Proceedings of International Conference on Performance, Computing, and Communications* (pp. 528-537). Academic Press.

Dagle, J. E., Windergren, S. E., & Johnson, J. M. (2002, January). *Enhancing the security of supervisory control and data acquisition (SCADA) systems: The lifeblood of modern energy infrastructure.* Paper presented at the Power Engineering Society Winter Meeting, New York, NY. doi:10.1109/PESW.2002.985079

Dale, N., Weems, C., & Headington, M. (2002). *Programming and problem solving with C.* Sudbury, MA: Jones and Bartlett.

Darra, E., & Katsikas, S. K. (2013). Attack detection capabilities of intrusion detection systems for wireless sensor networks. In *Proceedings of Fourth International Conference on Information, Intelligence, Systems and Applications (IISA)* (pp. 1-7). Academic Press. doi:10.1109/IISA.2013.6623718

Fadia, A. (2006). *Network security: A hacker's perspective.* Boston: Thomson Course Technology.

Farris, J. J., & Nicol, D. M. (2004). Evaluation of secure peer-to-peer overlay routing for survivable SCADA systems. In Proceedings of 2004 Winter Simulation Conference (pp. 308-317). Academic Press.

Ganapathy, S., Kulothungan, K., Yogesh, P., & Kannan, A. (2012). An intelligent intrusion detection system for ad hoc networks. In Proceedings of IET Chennai 3rd International on Sustainable Energy and Intelligent Systems (SEISCON 2012) (pp. 1-5). IET.

Gans, M. (1996). Development of a pole-mounted RTU for use on rural power lines. In *Proceedings of Power System Control and Management Conference* (pp. 103–107). Academic Press. doi:10.1049/cp:19960245

Guan, J., Liu, D.-X., & Cui, B.-G. (2004). An intrusion learning approach for building intrusion detection models using genetic algorithms. In *Proceedings of World Congress on Intelligent Control and Automation* (pp. 4339–4342). Academic Press. doi:10.1109/WCICA.2004.1342332

Gupta, A., Pandey, O. J., Shukla, M., Dadhich, A., Mathur, S., & Ingle, A. (2013). Computational intelligence based intrusion detection systems for wireless communication and pervasive computing networks. In *Proceedings of IEEE International Conference on Computational Intelligence and Computing Research (ICCIC)* (pp. 1-7). IEEE. doi:10.1109/ICCIC.2013.6724156

Haji, F., Lindsay, L., & Song, S. (2005). Practical security strategy for SCADA automation systems and networks. In *Proceedings of Canadian Conference on Electrical and Computer Engineering* (pp. 172-178). Academic Press. doi:10.1109/CCECE.2005.1556903

Ihn-Han, B., & Olariu, S. (2009). A weighted-dissimilarity-based anomaly detection method for mobile wireless networks. In *Proceedings of International Conference on Computational Science and Engineering* (pp. 29–34). Academic Press.

Janakiraman, R., Waldvogel, M., & Qi, Z. (2003). Indra: A peer-to-peer approach to network intrusion detection and prevention. In *Proceedings of International Workshops on Enabling Technologies: Infrastructures for Collaborative Enterprises* (pp. 226-231). Academic Press.

Jing, Z., HouKuan, H., ShengFeng, T., & Xiang, Z. (2009). Applications of HMM in protocol anomaly detection. In *Proceedings of International Joint Conference on Computational Sciences and Optimization* (pp. 347–349). Academic Press.

Jing-Wen, T., Mei-Juan, G., Ling-Fang, H., & Shi-Ru, Z. (2009). Community intrusion detection system based on wavelet neural network. In *Proceedings of International Conference on Machine Learning and Cybernetics* (vol. 2, pp. 1026–1030). Academic Press.

Jou, Y. F., Gong, F., Sargor, C., Wu, S., Wu, S. F., Chang, H. C., & Wang, F. (2000). Design and implementation of a scalable intrusion detection system for the protection of network infrastructure. *Defense Advanced Research Projects Agency Information Survivability Conference and Exposition*, *2*, 69–83.

Kayacik, H. G., Zincir-Heywood, A. N., & Heywood, M. I. (2004). On dataset biases in a learning system with minimum a priori information for intrusion detection. In *Proceedings of Communication Networks and Services Research Conference* (pp. 181–189). Academic Press. doi:10.1109/DNSR.2004.1344727

Khoshgoftaar, T. M., & Abushadi, M. E. (2004). Resource-sensitive intrusion detection models for network traffic. In *Proceedings of High Assurance Systems Engineering Symposium* (pp. 249–258). Academic Press.

Ko, C. (2003). System health and intrusion monitoring (SHIM): Project summary. *Defense Advanced Research Projects Agency Information Survivability Conference and Exposition*, *2*, 202–207. doi:10.1109/DISCEX.2003.1194966

Krizhanovsky, A., & Marasanov, A. (2007). An approach for adaptive intrusion prevention based on the danger. In *Proceedings of 2nd International Conference on Availability, Reliability and Security* (pp. 1135-1142). Academic Press. doi:10.1109/ARES.2007.36

Kui, Z. (2009). A danger model based anomaly detection method for wireless sensor networks. In *Proceedings of Second International Symposium on Knowledge Acquisition and Modeling* (pp. 11–14). Academic Press.

Kumar, M., & Hanumanthappa, M. (2013). Scalable intrusion detection systems log analysis using cloud computing infrastructure. In *Proceedings of IEEE International Conference on Computational Intelligence and Computing Research (ICCIC)* (pp. 1-4). IEEE. doi:10.1109/ICCIC.2013.6724158

Kumar, M., Hanumanthappa, M., & Kumar, T. V. S. (2012). Intrusion detection system using decision tree algorithm. In *Proceedings of IEEE 14th International Conference on Communication Technology (ICCT)* (pp. 629-634). IEEE.

Labbe, K. G., Rowe, N. G., & Fulp, J. D. (2006). A methodology for evaluation of host-based intrusion prevention systems and its application. In *Proceedings of Information Assurance Workshop* (pp. 378-379). Academic Press. doi:10.1109/IAW.2006.1652120

Leinwand, A., & Conroy, K. F. (1996). *Network management: A practical perspective*. New York, NY: Addison-Wesley.

Lixia, X., Dan, Z., & Hongyu, Y. (2009). Research on SVM based network intrusion detection classification. In *Proceedings of Sixth International Conference on Fuzzy Systems and Knowledge Discovery* (pp. 362–366). Academic Press.

Luxenburger, R., & Schegner, P. (2004). A new intelligent auto-reclosing method considering the current transformer saturation. In *Proceedings of Eight International Conference on Developments in Power Systems Protection* (vol. 2, pp. 583-586). Academic Press. doi:10.1049/cp:20040191

Mahdinia, P., Berenjkoob, M., & Vatankhah, H. (2013). Attack signature matching using graphics processors in high-performance intrusion detection systems. In *Proceedings of 21st Iranian Conference on Electrical Engineering (ICEE)* (pp. 1-7). Academic Press. doi:10.1109/IranianCEE.2013.6599567

McMillan, R. (2008). CIA says hackers pulled plug on power grid. *IDG News Service*. Retrieved January 19, 2008, from http://www.networkworld.com

Mechtri, L., Tolba, F. D., & Ghanemi, S. (2012). MASID: Multi-agent system for intrusion detection in MANET. In *Proceedings of Ninth International Conference on Information Technology: New Generations (ITNG)* (pp. 65-70). Academic Press. doi:10.1109/ITNG.2012.18

Mehmood, Y., Habiba, U., Shibli, M. A., & Masood, R. (2013). Intrusion detection system in cloud computing: Challenges and opportunities. In *Proceedings of 2nd National Conference on Information Assurance (NCIA)* (pp. 59-66). NCIA. doi:10.1109/NCIA.2013.6725325

Mitrokotsa, A., Komninos, N., & Douligeris, C. (2007). Intrusion detection with neural networks and watermarking techniques for MANET. In *Proceedings of International Conference on Pervasive Services* (pp. 966-966). Academic Press. doi:10.1109/PERSER.2007.4283901

Momenzadeh, A., Javadi, H. H. S., & Dezfouli, M. A. (2009). Design an efficient system for intrusion detection via evolutionary fuzzy system. In *Proceedings of 11th International Conference on Computer Modeling and Simulation* (pp. 89–94). Academic Press. doi:10.1109/UKSIM.2009.57

Motta Pires, P. S., & Oliveira, L. A. H. G. (2006). Security aspect of SCADA and corporate network interconnection: An overview. In *Proceedings of International Conference on Dependability of Computer Systems* (pp. 127-134). Academic Press. doi:10.1109/DEPCOS-RELCOMEX.2006.46

Muthuprasanna, M., Ke, W., & Kothari, S. (2006). Eliminating SQL injection attacks – A transport defense mechanism. In *Proceedings of 8th International Symposium on Web Site Evolution* (pp. 22-23). Academic Press.

Nadkarni, K., & Mishra, A. (2004). A novel intrusion detection approach for wireless ad hoc networks. In *Proceedings of Wireless Communications and Networking Conference* (pp. 831–836). Academic Press. doi:10.1109/WCNC.2004.1311294

Nassar, M., State, R., & Festor, O. (2007). VoIP honeypot architecture. In *Proceedings of International Symposium on Integrated Network Management* (pp. 109-118). Academic Press.

Niccolini, S., Garroppo, R. G., Giordano, S., Risi, G., & Ventura, S. (2006). SIP intrusion detection and prevention: Recommendation and prototype recommendation. In *Proceedings of 1st Workshop on VoIP Management and Security* (pp. 47-52). Academic Press.

Onut, I. V., & Ghorbani, A. A. (2006). Toward a feature classification scheme for network intrusion detection. In *Proceedings of 4th Annual Communication and Networks and Service Research Conference* (p. 8). Academic Press. doi:10.1109/CNSR.2006.53

Otrok, H., Debbabi, M., Assi, C., & Bhattacharya, P. (2007). A cooperative approach for analyzing intrusion in mobile ad hoc networks. In *Proceedings of 27th International Conference on Distributing Computing Systems Workshops* (pp. 86-86). Academic Press. doi:10.1109/ICDCSW.2007.91

Paez, R., & Torres, M. (2009). Laocoonte: An agent based intrusion detection system. In *Proceedings of International Symposium on Collaborative Technologies and System* (pp. 217–224). Academic Press. doi:10.1109/CTS.2009.5067484

Palnaty, R. P., & Rao, A. (2013). JCADS: Semi-supervised clustering algorithm for network anomaly intrusion detection systems. In *Proceedings of 15th International Conference on Advanced Computing Technologies (ICACT)* (pp. 1-5). Academic Press. doi:10.1109/ICACT.2013.6710498

Paulson, L. D. (2002). Stopping intruders outside the gates. *Computer, 11*(35), 20–22. doi:10.1109/MC.2002.1046967

Piromsopa, K., & Enbody, R. J. (2006). Buffer-overflow protection: The theory. In *Proceedings of International Conference on Electro/information Technology* (pp. 454-458). Academic Press.

Piromsopa, K., & Enbody, R. J. (2006). Arbitrary copy: Buffer-overflow protections. In *Proceedings of International Conference on Electro/information Technology* (pp. 580-584). Academic Press.

Piscaglia, P., & Maccq, B. (1996). Multiresolution lossless compression scheme. In *Proceedings of International Conference on Image Processing* (vol. 1, pp. 69-72). Academic Press. doi:10.1109/ICIP.1996.559435

Pollet, J. (2002). Developing a solid SCADA security strategy. In *Proceedings of 2nd International Society of Automation Sensors for Industry Conference* (pp. 148-156). Academic Press.

Ramana, R. K., Singh, S., & Varghese, G. (2007). On scalable attack detection in the network. *Association for Computing Machinery Transactions on Networking, 1*(15), 31–44.

Ransbottom, J. S., & Jacoby, G. A. (2006). Monitoring mobile device vitals for effective reporting. In *Proceedings of Military Communication Conference* (pp. 1-7). Academic Press. doi:10.1109/MILCOM.2006.302338

Sadighian, A., Zargar, S. T., Fernandez, J. M., & Lemay, A. (2013). Semantic-based context-aware alert fusion for distributed intrusion detection systems. In *Proceedings of International Conference on Risks and Security of Internet and Systems (CRiSIS)* (pp. 1-6). Academic Press. doi:10.1109/CRiSIS.2013.6766352

Sampathkumar, V., Bose, S., Anand, K., & Kannan, A. (2007). An intelligent agent based approach for intrusion detection and prevention in ad hoc networks. In *Proceedings of International Conference on Signal Processing Communications and Networking* (pp. 534-536). Academic Press.

Satti, M. M., & Garner, B. J. (2001). Information security on internet enterprise managed intrusion detection system (EMIDS). In *Proceedings of International Multitopic Conference* (pp. 234-238). Academic Press. doi:10.1109/INMIC.2001.995343

Schmoyer, T. R., Lim, Y. X., & Owen, H. L. (2004). Wireless intrusion detection and response: a classic study using main-in-the-middle attack. In *Proceedings of Wireless Communications and Networking Conference* (pp. 883–888). Academic Press. doi:10.1109/WCNC.2004.1311303

Shepherd, A. D., Lane, S. E., & Steward, J. S. (1990). A new microprocessor relay for overhead line SCADA application. In *Proceedings of Distribution Switchgear Conference* (pp. 100–103). Academic Press.

Sher, M., & Magedanz, T. (2007). Protecting IP multimedia subsystem (IMS) server delivery platform from time independent attacks. In *Proceedings of 3rd International Symposium on Information Assurance and Security* (pp. 171-176). Academic Press. doi:10.1109/ISIAS.2007.4299770

Stallings, W. (2003). *Cryptography and network security: Principles and practices*. Pearson Education, Inc.

Strasburg, C., Basu, S., & Wong, J. S. (2013). S-MAIDS: A semantic model for automated tuning, correlation, and response selection in intrusion detection systems. In *Proceedings of IEEE 37th Annual Computer Software and Applications Conference (COMPSAC)* (pp. 319-328). IEEE.

Sun, B., Xiao, Y., & Wang, R. (2007). Detection of fraudulent usage in wireless networks. *Transactions on Vehicular Technology, 6*(56), 3912–3923. doi:10.1109/TVT.2007.901875

Suthaharan, S. (2012). An iterative ellipsoid-based anomaly detection technique for intrusion detection systems. In *Proceedings of IEEE Southeastcon* (pp. 1-6). IEEE. doi:10.1109/SECon.2012.6196956

Thaseen, S., & Kumar, C. A. (2013). An analysis of supervised tree based classifiers for intrusion detection system. In *Proceedings of International Conference on Pattern Recognition, Informatics and Mobile Engineering (PRIME)* (pp. 294-299). Academic Press. doi:10.1109/ICPRIME.2013.6496489

Tomasek, M., Cajkovsky, M., & Mados, B. (2012). Intrusion detection system based on system behavior. In *Proceedings of IEEE 10th International Symposium on Applied Machine Intelligence and Informatics (SAMI)* (pp. 271-275). IEEE.

Tran, Q. A., Jiang, F., & Hu, J. (2012). A real-time NetFlow-based intrusion detection system with improved BBNN and high-frequency field programmable gate arrays. In *Proceedings of IEEE 11th International Conference on Trust, Security and Privacy in Computing and Communications (TrustCom)* (pp. 201-208). IEEE.

Tront, J. G., & Marchany, R. C. (2004). Internet security: Intrusion detection and prevention. In *Proceedings of 37th Annual Hawaii International Conference on System Sciences* (pp. 188-188). Academic Press.

Tsang, C-H., & Kwong, S. (2005). Multi-agent detection system in industrial network using ant colony clustering approach and unsupervised feature extraction. In *Proceedings of International Conference on Industrial Technology* (pp. 51–56). Academic Press.

Vanathi, R., & Gunasekaran, S. (2012). Comparison of network intrusion detection systems in cloud computing environment. In *Proceedings of International Conference on Computer Communication and Informatics (ICCCI)* (pp. 1-6). Academic Press. doi:10.1109/ICCCI.2012.6158820

Vokorokos, L., Kleinova, A., & Latka, O. (2006). Network security on the intrusion detection system level. In *Proceedings of International Conference on Intelligent Engineering Systems* (pp. 534-536). Academic Press. doi:10.1109/INES.2006.1689382

Weaver, N., Paxson, V., & Sommer, R. (2007). *Work in progress: Bro-LAN pervasive network inspection and control for LAN traffic* (pp. 1–2). Securecomm and Workshops.

Weber, W. (1999). Firewall basics. In *Proceedings of 4th International Conference on Telecommunications in Modern Satellite, Cable and Broadcasting Services* (vol. 1, pp. 300-305). Academic Press.

Wei, W., Xiangliang, Z., Gombault, S., & Knapskog, S. J. (2009). Attribute normalization in network intrusion detection. In *Proceedings of 10th International Symposium on Pervasive Systems, Algorithms, and Networks* (pp. 448–453). Academic Press.

Weinberg, Y., Tzur-David, S., Dolev, D., & Anker, T. (2006). High performance string matching algorithm for a network intrusion prevention system. In *Proceedings of Workshop on High Performance Switching and Routing* (p. 7). Academic Press.

Xinidis, K., Charitakis, I., Antonatos, S., Anagnostakis, K. G., & Markatos, E. P. (2006). An active splitter architecture for intrusion detection and prevention. *Transactions on Dependable and Secure Computing*, *1*(3), 31–44. doi:10.1109/TDSC.2006.6

Yau, S. S., & Zhang, X. (1999). Computer networks intrusion detection, assessment and prevention based on security dependency relation. In *Proceedings of Computer Software and Applications Conference* (pp. 86–91). Academic Press. doi:10.1109/CMPSAC.1999.812681

Yee, C. G., Rao, G. V. S., & Radha, K. (2006). A hybrid approach to intrusion detection and prevention business intelligent applications. In *Proceedings of International Symposium on Communications and Information Technologies* (pp. 847-850). Academic Press. doi:10.1109/ISCIT.2006.339856

Yung-Da, W., & Paulik, M. J. (1996). A discrete wavelet model for target recognition. In *Proceedings of 39th Midwest Symposium on Circuit and Systems* (vol. 2, pp. 835-838). Academic Press. doi:10.1109/MWSCAS.1996.588044

Zhaoyu, L., & Uppala, R. (2006). A dynamic countermeasure method for large-scale network attacks. In *Proceedings of International Symposium on Dependable, Autonomic and Secure Computing* (pp. 163-170). Academic Press.

Zheng-De, Z., Zhi-Guo, L., Dong, Z., & Fei-Teng, J. (2006). Study on joint prevention technique of information security in SUN. In *Proceedings of International Conference on Machine Learning and Cybernetics* (pp. 2823-2827). Academic Press.

Zhou, C., Liu, Y., & Zhang, H. (2006). A pattern matching based network intrusion detection system. In *Proceedings of 9th International Conference on Control, Automation, Robotics and Vision* (pp. 1-4). Academic Press.

ADDITIONAL READING

Erramilli, A., Roughan, M., Veitch, D., & Willinger, W. (2002). Self-similar traffic and network dynamics. *Proceedings of the Institute of Electronics and Electrical Engineers*, *5*(90), 800–819. doi:10.1109/JPROC.2002.1015008

Garcia, R. C., Sadiku, M. N. O., & Cannady, J. D. (2002). WAID: wavelet analysis intrusion detection. *Midwest Symposium on Circuits and Systems:* Vol. 3 (pp. 688–691).

Graps, A. (1995). An introduction to wavelets. *Computing in Science & Engineering*, *2*(2), 50–61. doi:10.1109/99.388960

Kay, S. M. (1993). *Fundamentals of Statistical Signal Processing - Estimation Theory*. Upper River Saddle, New Jersey: Prentice Hall.

Nash, D. A., & Ragsdale, D. J. (2001). Simulation of self-similarity in network utilization patterns as a precursor to automated testing of intrusion detection systems. *Transactions on Systems, Man and Cybernetics, Part A: Systems and Humans*, *4*(31), 327–331. doi:10.1109/3468.935051

Qinghua, S., & Xiongjian, L. (2003). The fractal feature of telecommunication network. *International Conference on Communication Technology:* Vol. 1 (pp. 77–80).

Shibin, S., & Ng, J. K.-Y., & Tang Bihai. (2004). Some results on the self-similarity property in communication networks. *Transactions on Communications*, *10*(52), 1636–1642.

Ziemer, R. E., & Tranter, W. H. (5). (2002). Principles of Communications: Systems, Modulation and Noise. Wiley.

KEY TERMS AND DEFINITIONS

Anomaly Detection: An approach which considers any unusual pattern as an anomaly and therefore an attack. It helps in detecting both known and unknown attacks.

Auto-Reclosing: A technique which protects sections of electrical power systems from transient and permanent faults through the isolation of faulted parts from the rest of the electrical network. It prevents unnecessary disconnection of a long rural power line from the entire grid due to an over-current caused by a fault anywhere along that particular line.

Centralized Intrusion Detection: An intrusion detection technique, whereby data is collected in a distributed fashion, but analyzed centrally.

Denial of Service Attack: An attempt to block large parts of the memory of a target system, such that it can no longer serve its users. This situation leads to crashing, rebooting or denial of services to legitimate users.

Distributed Intrusion Detection: An intrusion detection technique, whereby data is collected and analyzed in a distributed fashion.

Distributed SYN-Flood Attack: A SYN-flood attack implemented in a distributed fashion. This is one of the most dangerous distributed denial of service attacks known.

Intrusion Detection: A traditional technique which detects actions that attempt to compromise the confidentiality and integrity of a resource in information security. It is used only after an attack has already entered a given system.

Intrusion Prevention: A proactive technique which detects actions that attempt to compromise the confidentiality and integrity of a resource in information security. This is used to prevent an attack from entering a given system.

Signature Based Detection: An approach which considers attack patterns as signatures and further compares signatures of known attacks to incoming attacks for detection. It helps in detecting only known attacks.

SYN-Flood Attack: An attempt to flood a target system with connection requests from spoofed source addresses making it very difficult or impossible to trace the origin of the attacks. This is one of the most dangerous denial of service attacks known.

Chapter 18

A Dynamic Subspace Anomaly Detection Method Using Generic Algorithm for Streaming Network Data

Ji Zhang

University of Southern Queensland, Australia

ABSTRACT

A great deal of research attention has been paid to data mining on data streams in recent years. In this chapter, the authors carry out a case study of anomaly detection in large and high-dimensional network connection data streams using Stream Projected Outlier deTector (SPOT) that is proposed in Zhang et al. (2009) to detect anomalies from data streams using subspace analysis. SPOT is deployed on 1999 KDD CUP anomaly detection application. Innovative approaches for training data generation, anomaly classification, false positive reduction, and adoptive detection subspace generation are proposed in this chapter as well. Experimental results demonstrate that SPOT is effective and efficient in detecting anomalies from network data streams and outperforms existing anomaly detection methods.

INTRODUCTION

Great research efforts have been taken by researchers in recent years to study discovery of useful patterns from data streams. One important category of such data streams are the streams collected over the network. Analyzing these network data streams is quite critical in unveiling suspicious patterns that may indicate network intrusions. An intrusion into a computer network can compromise the stability and security of the network, leading to possible loss of privacy, information and revenue (Zhong et al. 2004). To safeguard network security, there are two major classes of approaches for detecting anomalies that may represent the manifestations of intrusions: misuse-based detection (or signature-based detection) and anomaly-based detection.

DOI: 10.4018/978-1-4666-7381-6.ch018

As far as data format representation is concerned, data streams collected in network environments can be typically, but not necessarily, modeled as continuously arriving high-dimensional connection oriented records. Each record contains a number of varied features to measure the quantitative behaviors of the network traffic. Such data representation is used in the 1999 KDD CUP anomaly detection application. In high-dimensional space, anomalies are embedded in some lower-dimensional subspaces (spaces consisting of a subset of attributes). These anomalies are termed projected anomalies in the high-dimensional space context. The underlying reason for this phenomenon is the Curse of Dimensionality. The increase in dimensionality will make data to be equally distant from each other. Consequently, the difference of data points' outlier-ness will become increasingly weak and thus undistinguishable. Only in moderate or low dimensional subspaces can significant outlier-ness of data be observed. This is the major motivation for detecting outliers in subspaces.

We can formulate the problem of detecting projected anomalies from high-dimensional data streams as follows: given a data stream D with ϕ-dimensional data points, each data point pi = {pi1, pi2, . . ., piϕ} in D will be labeled as either a projected anomaly if it is found abnormal in one or more subspaces. Otherwise, it will be flagged as a regular data. If pi is a projected anomaly, its associated outlying subspace(s) will be presented as well in the result.

Unfortunately, the existing outlier/anomaly detection techniques are mostly limited in identifying anomalies embedded in subspaces. Most are only capable of detecting anomalies in relatively low dimensional and static data sets (stored in databases without frequent changes) (Breuning et al., 2000; Knorr et al., 1998; Knorr et al., 1999; Ramaswamy et al, 2000; Tang et al., 2002). Recently, there are some emerging work in dealing with outlier detection either in high-dimensional data or data streams. However, there have not been

any substantial research work so far for exploring the intersection of these two active research areas. For those methods in projected outlier detection in high-dimensional space (Aggarwal et al., 2001; Aggarwal et al., 2005; Boudjeloud et al., 2005; Zhu et al., 2005; Zhang et al., 2006; Guha et al., 2009), their measurements used for evaluating points' outlier-ness are not incrementally updatable and many of the methods involve multiple scans of data, making them incapable of handling fast data streams. The techniques for tackling outlier detection in data streams (Aggarwal, 2005; Palpanas et al, 2003;, Zhang et al., 2010) rely on full data space to detect outliers and thus the projected outliers cannot be discovered by these techniques.

To detect anomalies from high-dimensional data streams, a new technique, called Stream Projected Outlier deTector (SPOT), is proposed (Zhang et al, 2009). It utilizes a novel subspace analysis method to detect anomalies hidden in the subspaces of the full data space. In this paper, efforts are taken to carry out a real-life case study of SPOT to test its practical applicability. We apply in 1999 KDD CUP anomaly detection application. We have also tackled several important issues, including training data generation, anomaly categorization using outlying subspaces analysis and false positive reduction, for a successful deployment of SPOT in the case study. Experimental evaluates reveals that SPOT is efficient in this application for detecting anomalies.

OVERVIEW OF SPOT

Before the case study is carried out, it is worthwhile presenting a short description of SPOT. SPOT performs anomaly detection into two stages: the learning and detection stages. SPOT can further support two types of learning, namely offline learning and online learning. In the offline learning, Sparse Subspace Template (SST) is constructed using either the unlabeled training data (e.g., some available historic data) and/

or the labeled anomaly examples provided by domain experts. SST is a set of subspaces that feature higher data sparsity/outlier-ness than other subspaces. SST consists of three groups of subspaces, i.e., Fixed SST Subspaces (FS), Unsupervised SST Subspaces (US) and Supervised SST Subspaces (SS), where FS is a compulsory component of SST while US and SS are optional components. SST casts light on where projected anomalies are likely to be found in the high-dimensional space. SST is mainly constructed in an unsupervised manner where no labeled examples are required. However, it is possible to use the labeled anomaly exemplars to further improve SST. As such, SPOT is very flexible and is able to cater for different practical applications that may or may not have available labeled exemplars.

When SST is ready, SPOT enters the detection stage and starts to screen projected anomalies from constantly arriving data. The incoming data will be first used to update the data synopsis in each subspace of SST. This data will then be labeled as an anomaly if the values of the data synopsis are lower than some pre-specified thresholds. The detected anomalies are archived in the so-called Outlier Repository. Finally, all or only a specified number of the top anomalies in Outlier Repository will be returned to users when the detection stage is finished.

During the detection stage, SPOT can perform online training periodically. The online training involves updating SST with new sparse subspaces SPOT finds based on the current data characteristics and the newly detected anomalies. Online training improves SPOT's adaptability to dynamics of data streams. A system overview of SPOT is presented in Figure 1. Interested reader can refer to (Zhang et al. 2009) for more details on SPOT.

Figure 1. An overview of SPOT

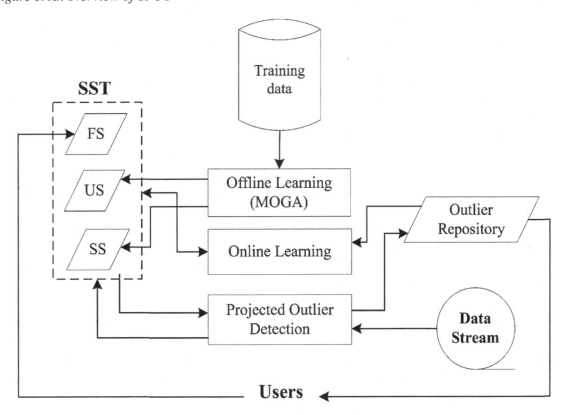

Genetic Algorithm Design for SPOT

In many real-world applications, multiple, often conflicting, objectives arise naturally. Genetic algorithms possess some ideal characteristics for dealing with these optimization problems, making them widely used search strategies for multiobjective optimization for a long time. GAs base on their working mechanisms on the fundamental idea of Darwinian evolution, that is, resources are limited in nature, which leads to a competition amongst the species. In this competition process, all the species will undergo a selection mechanism, in which only the fittest will be able to survive. As such, the fitter individuals stand a higher chance to mate each other, producing even better individuals. In the evolution, variation occasionally occur through the means of mutation. This improves the amount of diversity among the species, and contributes to a greater fitness improvement. GAs have been proven as general, robust and powerful search mechanism. They are particularly suitable for tackling complicate optimization/search problems that features 1) Multiple conflicting objectives; and 2) Intractably large and highly complex search spaces.

In the offline learning stage of SPOT, we employ Multi-Objective Genetic Algorithm (MOGA) to search for subspaces whose RD, IRSD and IkRD objectives can be minimized in construction of SST. MOGA conducts search of good subspaces through a number of generations each of which has a population containing a specific number of individuals (i.e., subspaces). The subspaces in the first generation are typically generated randomly, while the subspaces in the subsequent generations are generated by applying search operators such as crossover and mutation on those subspaces in their preceding generation. In a multi-objective minimization problem, subspaces in the population of each generation can be positioned on different trade-off surfaces in the objective function space. The subspaces located on a surface closer to the origin is better than the one far from the origin. The superiority (or inferiority) of the subspaces on the same surface are not distinguishable. The surface where the optimal subspaces are located is called *Pareto Front*. The goal of MOGA is to gradually produce an increasing number of optimal subspaces, located in the Pareto Front, from non-optimal subspaces as evolution proceeds. MOGA provides a good general framework for dealing with multiobjective search problems. However, we still need to perform ad-hoc design of MOGA in SPOT for outlying subspace search, including individual representation, objective functions, fitness function, selection scheme and elitism.

- **Individual Representation:** In SPOT, all individuals are represented by binary strings with fixed and equal length which is equal to the number of dimensions of the dataset. Each bit in the individual will take on the value of "0" and "1", respectively, indicating whether or not its corresponding dimension is selected for a particular subspace.

- **Objective Functions:** The objective function of subspace s w.r.t data point p is the data sparsity (measured by RD, IRSD, IkRD) of the cell c in s where p belongs to.

- **Selection Scheme:** Pareto-based selection scheme is used to select fitter solutions in each step of evolution. It is a stochastic selection method where the selection probability of a subspace is proportional to its fitness value.

- **Elitism:** Elitism is the effort to address the problem of losing those potentially good solutions during the optimization process because of the randomness of MOGA. If no special measures are taken, MOGA cannot guarantee the individuals obtained in a newer generation always outperform those in the older one. In SPOT, we use the elitism method that directly copies the best or a few best subspaces in the population of one generation to the next one, in an attempt to achieve a constantly improving population of subspaces.

CASE STUDY DESCRIPTION

The data streams in KDD-CUP'99 anomaly detection application contains a wide variety of intrusions simulated in a military network environment. Each instance in this data stream is a vector of extracted feature values from a connection record obtained from the raw network data gathered during the simulated intrusions. The TCP packets were assembled into connection records using the Bro program modified for use with MADAM/ID. Each connection was labeled as either normal or as exactly one specific kind of attack. All labels are assumed to be correct. The attacks will be considered as anomalies in our study.

There are a total of four categories for the simulated attacks in this study:

- **DoS:** Denial of Service (e.g., a syn flood);
- **R2L:** Unauthorized access from a remote machine (e.g., password guessing);
- **U2R:** Unauthorized access to superuser or root functions (e.g., a buffer overflow attack);
- **Probing:** Surveillance and other probing for vulnerabilities (e.g., port scanning).

There are 42 features for this data stream. In addition, labeled training and test data sets are available in this application. They are the data collected in the first seven weeks of the DARPA experiments.

In this case study, identifying only anomalies from data streams is not sufficient. Given the inherently varying behaviors of different categories of anomalies, it is desirable that the anomalies

we detect could be further categorized into one of known anomaly subtypes for a better understanding of their nature and characteristics. In this application, anomalous network connections may be manifestations of anomalies that can be divided into as many as 4 different classes. Different classes of attacks may distinguish themselves by anomalous connection behaviors exhibiting in different subspaces. Our task is to, by means of their different connection behaviors in outlying subspaces revealed by SPOT, classify anomalous connection records into one of the known attack classes (or the false-positive class).

Network Anomaly Detection using SPOT

When applying on KDD-CUP'99 anomaly Detection data stream, SPOT takes three major steps in its learning stage to detect anomalies, which are presented below:

Step 1: SST is first generated. As a large number of labeled sample anomalies are available in this application, SST will contain SS besides FS and US. Supervised learning is performed to generate SS in SST. Since the sample anomalies have been assigned varied class labels, we can perform MOGA on all the sample anomalies belonging to the same class to produce the SS for that particular class, and the final SS in SST contains SS s for the four different classes. That is, $SST = FS \cup US \cup SS(OD)$, where OD is whole set of label anomaly samples in the data set. $SS(OD)$ is computed as $SS(OD) = \cup_{i=1}^{4} SS(OD_i)$, where OD_i is the set containing the anomaly samples that belong to the ith attack class.

Step 2: Once we have obtained SST, we need to generate PCS for each subspace in SST to detect anomalies from the data set. Because normal samples are available in the train-

Figure 2. Generating single training data set for obtaining SS

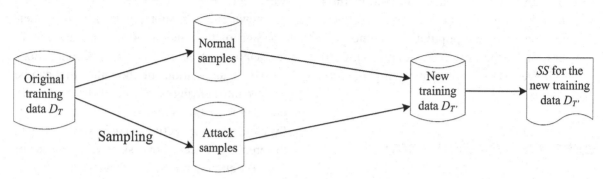

ing data set, thus it is possible for us to use only the normal samples, rather than the whole training data, to construct PCS. This ensures that PCS is constructed in a way to better reflect the normal behavior of data in the application.

Step 3: All the sample anomalies in the training data will be evaluated in SST to find their outlying subspaces. Please note that, when we are evaluating each anomaly, we only retrieve, but do not update, the PCS of the cell it falls into. This is because the total number of anomaly samples is far larger than that of normal samples. Updating PCS using anomaly samples will therefore bias it towards anomalies, which will disable the ability of SPOT to accurately identify anomalies thereafter. When outlying subspaces of all anomaly samples are found, signature subspace lookup table will be built. Signature subspace lookup table records the outlying subspaces of anomalies that are used to categorize anomalies. We will discuss it later on in this subsection.

Training Data Generation

A major obstacle impeding the direct application of SPOT and other anomaly-based detectors is the high proportion of attack instances in this training data set; over 90% of the samples in this training data are attacks. Normal data be-

havior is needed in identifying anomalies from the data stream. As such, we need to construct new training data sets based on the original one to meet the distribution assumption that the number of normal connections is much larger than the number of attack connections.

In order to do this, all the normal instances are selected from the original training data set and uses sampling technique to sample the attack samples (Cui, 2002) (see Figure 2). In this way, a new training data satisfying the distribution assumption is obtained. In this new training data set, normal connections are dominating the whole data set with 98% of the samples being normal connections while the number of samples for the four attack classes combined amounts to 2%.

Nevertheless, since only a small number of attack instances are sampled, the new training data set may not be comprehensive enough for capturing sufficient attack instances to generate accurate profiles for different attack classes. Another major limitation of the approach is that the training data set contains anomaly samples of different classes. Samples of one class may become noises for another class in the training. To minimize the effect of noises, it would be desired that the training data set contain only anomaly samples that belong to the same class. MOGA can be applied to cleaner training data sets to find outlying subspaces that are more relevant to different classes.

Figure 3. Generating multiple training data sets for obtaining SS

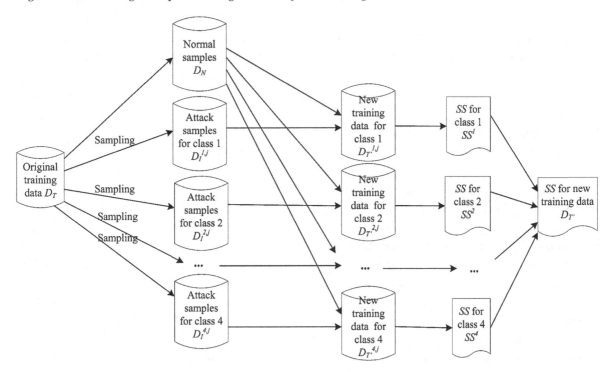

To curb the inherent drawbacks of the single training data set generation method, we adopt a strategy to generate multiple training data sets in order to meet the learning needs of SPOT, as presented in Figure 3. The basic idea of this strategy is that, for each anomaly class, multiple training data sets are generated and MOGA will be applied on each of them to produce for each class.

Mathematically, let D_T be the original training data set available. D_T consists of two parts, the normal and anomaly samples, denoted by D_N and D_I, respectively. D_T can be expressed as

$$D_T = D_N \cup D_I \quad (1)$$

where D_I consists of anomaly instances of up to four different classes, so we have

$$D_I = \cup_{i=1}^{4} D_I^i \quad (2)$$

In our work, we generate multiple new training data sets with replacement from D_I^i for each class $i \in [1,4]$, each such training data set can be expressed as

$$D_{T'}^{i,j} = D_N \cup D_I^{i,j} \quad (3)$$

where j is the number of data sets generated from D_I^i. The data distribution in each new training data set for different classes satisfies the requirement that the normal data dominate the whole training data set. By applying MOGA on $D_{T'}^{i,j}$, we can obtain SS for class i, denoted as SS^i, as

$$SS^i = \cup_j MOGA(D_{T'}^{i,j}). \quad (4)$$

The complete SS is simply the union of SS^i for $i \in [1,4]$ as

$$SS = \cup_i SS^i . \qquad (5)$$

By including FS and US, the complete SST is finally constructed as

$$SST = FS \cup US \cup SS . \qquad (6)$$

Redundant Outlying Subspace Removal

SPOT is able to find outlying subspaces for data in the stream. However, we may obtain a large number of resulting outlying subspaces even for a single data in the stream. Amongst these outlying subspaces, there are some dominating outlying subspaces that contribute to the outlierness of anomalies. Other outlying subspaces are considered as redundant ones. To facilitate the analysis of anomalies, we need to extract the dominating outlying subspaces for anomalies from their outlying subspaces detected by SPOT.

- **Definition 1, Dominating Subspace:** Let s and s' be two subspaces in the set of outlying subspaces of an anomaly o. If $s \subset s'$, then we call s a dominating subspace over s'. Here $s \subset s'$ (i.e., s is a proper subset of s') if for each dimension $d \in s$, we have $d \in s'$ and $\exists d \in s'$ that $d \notin s$.

In a space lattice where the low order subspaces are positioned in the bottom while the high order subspaces are put on the top, there exists a boundary between dominating outlying subspaces and non- dominating outlying subspace/non-outlying subspaces. In our work, we term this line as 'Outlying Subspace Front.' Next, we present the definition of Outlying Subspace Front of an anomaly.

- **Definition 2, Outlying Subspace Front:** Let OS(o) denote the set of outlying subspaces of an anomaly o. The Outlying Subspace Front of o is defined as the set of all its dominating subspaces in OS(o), *i.e.*, OSF (o) = {s, where s is a dominating subspace in OS(o)}

OSF has the following attributes:

- A subspace in OSF cannot dominate (or be dominated by) any other subspaces in OSF. They are all partial ordered subspaces;
- OSF is a subset of the corresponding OS and each subspace in OS will be dominated by one or a few subspaces in OSF;
- OSF is able to capture the subspaces that are truly contributing to the outlier-ness of anomalies. The existence of a large number of non-dominated (redundant) subspaces may adversely bias the weights of the underlying contributing subspaces in the classification analysis of anomalies.

Figure 4 presents an example of outlying subspaces of an anomaly and its corresponding Outlying Sub- space Front. The algorithm for finding OSF for an anomaly o is presented in Figure 5.

Anomaly Classification

Anomaly classification mainly involves categorizing detected anomalies into one of known anomaly classes or the class of false positive. We derive categorization functionality and incorporate it into SPOT for achieving this objective.

To achieve anomaly categorization, we generate signature subspaces for each anomaly class. The signature subspaces for a target class are those subspaces that can be used to identify anomalies for this particular class. To generate signature subspaces for a particular class, we collect the

Figure 4. Example of outlying subspaces and its corresponding Outlying Subspace Front (OSF) for an anomaly

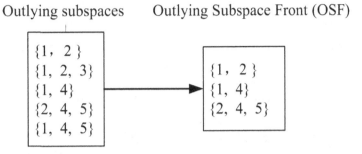

Figure 5. Algorithm for finding Outlying Subspace Front

Algorithm Find-OSF

Input: OS (o).

Output: OSF(o).

1. Set OSF(o) as an empty set;

2. Sort subspaces in OS(o) in an ascending order based on their dimensions;

3. FOR each existing subspace s in sorted OS(o) DO {

4. Add s to OSF(o);

5. Delete s from OS(o);

6. For each existing subspaces s' in sorted OS(o) DO
7. IF s is a subset of s' THEN delete s' from OS(o);}

subspaces in OSF of those anomalies falling to this class and use them as the signature subspaces of this class. Mathematically speaking, the set of signature subspaces of class c is defined as

$$Signature(c) = \{s: \exists o \text{ belonging to } c, s \in OSF(o)\}. \tag{7}$$

Within a class, different signature subspaces have varying weights to indicate their capability in correctly identifying anomalies for this class. The weighting scheme is necessary in the similarity measure used in the categorization process.

The weight of a signature subspace s with respect to a class represents the discriminating ability of s towards c. The higher the weight is, the stronger the discriminating power of this subspace is in identifying the instances of class c. Because OSF is by nature a bag of subspaces, we thus borrow the idea of tf-idf (term frequency-inverse document frequency) weighting method, a commonly used technique in the domain of information retrieval and text mining, to measure the weight of signature subspaces for each class. The tf-idf weight is a statistical measure used to evaluate how important a term is to a document in a collection or corpus. The importance increases proportionally to the number of times a term appears in the document but is offset by the frequency of the term in the whole corpus.

Term Frequency (tf)

The term frequency (tf) for a class is simply the number of times a given signature subspace appears in that class. This count is normalized to give a measure of importance for the signature subspace within the class. The normalization is performed to prevent a bias towards class with larger number of signature subspaces that may feature a higher term frequency regardless of the actual importance of those subspaces in the class. The tf for subspace s_i in class c_j is defined as

$$tf_{i,j} = \frac{N(s_i, c_j)}{N(c_j)} \tag{8}$$

where $N(s_i, c_j)$ denotes the number of occurrences of signature subspace s_i in class c_j and $N(c_j)$ is the number of occurrences of all signature subspaces in class c_j.

Inverse Document Frequency (idf)

The inverse document frequency (idf) is a measure of the general importance of the term. The idf for signature subspace s_i in class c_j is defined as the inverse of percentage of the classes that contained s_i. Normally, the logarithmic form of this ratio is used for scaling purpose, i.e.,

$$idf_{i,j} = log \frac{|C|}{|\{c_j, \text{ where } s_i \in c_j\}|} \tag{9}$$

where $|C|$ corresponds to the total number of classes and $|\{c_j, \text{ where } s_i \in c_j\}|$ is the number of classes that contain s_i.

Finally, the tf-idf weight of signature subspace si with regard to class cj is the product of $tf_{i,j}$ and $idf_{i,j}$, i.e.,

$$w_{s_i,c_j} = tfidf_{i,j} = tf_{i,j} \times idf_{i,j} \tag{10}$$

Similarity Measure

Similarity measure needs to be properly defined before the anomalies can be classified. The similarity between an anomaly o and class c is defined as their average inner product, which is the normalized sum of weight products of the outlying subspaces of o and the signature subspaces of class c, i.e.,

$$Sim(o,c) = \frac{o \cdot c}{|OSF(o)|} \tag{11}$$

where $|OS(o)|$ denotes the number of outlying subspaces of o. Let $w_{o,s}$ be the binary vector of o and $w_{c,s}$ be the weight vector of class c. Normally, we assign $w_{o,s} = 0$ if subspace s does not appear in OS(o), so the above similarity measurement can be written as

$$Sim(o,c) = \frac{\sum_{s \in Q} w_{s,o} \cdot w_{s,c}}{|OSF(o)|}. \tag{12}$$

Signature Subspace Lookup Table

In order to compute the similarity between anomalies and classes efficiently, we need to have a mechanism to realize fast retrieval of tf-idf information for a give signature subspace. To this end, we construct a signature subspace lookup table to store all the signature subspaces, occurring in different classes, for efficient retrieval. Also, to render it suitable for handling data stream, we incorporate time stamp information to imple-

Table 1. The time-decayed signature subspace lookup table

	c_1	c_2	...	c_m
s_1	$N(s_1, c_1), T(s_1, c_1)$	$N(s_1, c_2), T(s_1, c_2)$	...	$N(s_1, c_m), T(s_1, c_m)$
s_2	$N(s_2, c_1), T(s_2, c_1)$	$N(s_2, c_2), T(s_2, c_2)$	...	$N(s_2, c_m), T(s_2, c_m)$
...	...	...	...	...
s_n	$N(s_n, c_1), T(s_n, c_1)$	$N(s_n, c_2), T(s_n, c_2)$	...	$N(s_n, c_m), T(s_n, c_m)$

ment time model in this table. We term this table the time-decayed signature subspace lookup *table*, which is defined as shown in Table 1.

- **Definition 3, Time-Decayed Signature Subspace Lookup Table:** Given the set of classes C and the signature subspaces for all the classes in C, the time-decayed signature subspace lookup table is a $(|S|+1) \times |C|$ table, where |S| and |C| are the total number of signature subspaces and classes, respectively. C consists of the attack and false-positive classes. The entry of $a_{i,j}, 1 \leq i \leq |s|, 1 \leq j \leq |C|$ is a pair of $< N(s_i, c_j), T(s_i, c_j) >$, corresponding respectively to the count of s_i in c_j and the time stamp when this entry was last updated. The entry of $a_{|s|+1,j}, 1 \leq j \leq |C|$ is also a pair in the format of $< N(c_j), T(c_j) >$, recording the total number of signature subspaces in c_j and the time stamp when this entry was last updated.

An example of the time-decayed signature subspace lookup table is given in Table 1. It is worthwhile noting that, in time-decayed signature subspace lookup table, T (s_i, c_j) needs to be updated every time when an anomaly that has outlying subspace s_i is classified into class c_j, and T (c_j) needs to be updated when an anomaly is classified into c_j, regardless of its outlying subspaces.

Based upon the signature subspace lookup table, it will be very efficient to compute td-idf of each signature subspace. First, $tf_{i,j}$ can be computed as follows.

$$tf_{i,j} = \frac{weight(T', T(s_i, c_j)) * N(s_i, c_j)}{weight(T', T(c_j)) * N(c_j)} \quad (13)$$

where T' is the time stamp when the data that has outlying subspace s_i is processed. The information of $N(s_i, c_j)$ and $N(c_j)$ can be directly retrieved for computation from the signature subspace lookup table. The weight coefficients are defined as

$$weight(T', T(s_i, c_j)) = e^{-\frac{\alpha(T' - T(s_i, c_j))}{\Delta t}} \quad (14)$$

$$weight(T', T(c_j)) = e^{-\frac{\alpha(T' - T(c_j))}{\Delta t}} \quad (15)$$

$idf_{i,j}$ can be computed as

$$idf_{i,j} = log \frac{|C|}{|c, \text{ where } s_i \in c \text{ at } T'|} \quad (16)$$

where $|c, \text{ where } s \in c \text{ at } T'|$ denotes the number of classes that contain s at time T'. This only involves counting from the lookup table the classes that contains s_i.

The time-decayed signature subspace lookup table is constructed in the training stage of SPOT using the labeled training data. To do so, we need to register signature subspaces of different classes into this lookup table. Specifically, for each anomaly o found in the labeled training data with its Outlying Subspace Front $OSF(o)$, class label c and time stamp T', we need to register all the subspaces of $OSF(o)$ into the lookup table. This mainly involves initializing and/or updating the counts and time stamps for classes and signature subspaces in the lookup table. Varying updating schemes are used in the following two cases

1. If $s_i \in OSF(o)$ has already existed in the signature subspace lookup table, then we update class count $N(c)$ and time stamp $T(c)$ of class c as

$$N(c) = weight(T', T(c)) * N(c) + 1 \qquad (17)$$

$$T(c) = T' \qquad (18)$$

and update subspace count $N(s, c)$ and time stamp $T(s, c)$ as

$$N(s, c) = weight(T', T(s, c)) * N(s, c) + 1 \qquad (19)$$

$$T(s, c) = T' \qquad (20)$$

2. If $s \in OSF(o)$ does not exist in the signature subspace lookup table, then we will update class count $N(c)$ and time stamp $T(c)$ of class c as

$$N(c) = weight(T', T(c)) * N(c) + 1 \qquad (21)$$

$$T(c) = T' \qquad (22)$$

and initialize subspace count $N(s, c)$ and time stamp $T(s, c)$ as

$$N(s, c) = 1 \qquad (23)$$

$$T(s, c) = T' \qquad (24)$$

For each class $c' \neq c$, we perform the following initialization:

$$N(s, c') = 0 \qquad (25)$$

$$T(s, c') = \text{Null (null time stamp)} \qquad (26)$$

When constructed, the signature subspace lookup table can be used to classify anomalies in the data stream. Each anomaly is classified into one or more possible attack classes or the false-positive class based on the class membership probabilities of the anomaly. The class membership probability of an anomaly o with respect to class $c_i \in C$ is computed as

$$pr(o, c_i) = \frac{sim(o, c_i)}{\sum_i sim(o, c_i)} \times 100\%, \text{ where } c_i \in C \qquad (27)$$

The higher the probability for a class is, the high chance that the anomaly falls into this class.

An anomaly o can be classified into a class c_i if $pr(o, c_i) \geq \tau$, where τ is the similarity threshold. As s result, under a given τ, it is possible that an anomaly o is classified into a few, instead of one, classes if their similarities are high enough. The set of classes that o may fall into, denoted as $class(o)$, is defined as

$$class(o) = \{c_i, \text{ where } pr(o, c_i) \geq \tau, c_i \in C\}. \qquad (28)$$

For each anomaly, we can further sort its membership classes based on the respective membership probabilities in a descending order. This facilitates users to pick up the top k ($k \in [1, |C|]$) most likely attack class(es) of the anomaly for further investigation.

After the classification of o is finished, we need to update the counts and time stamps for classes and signature subspaces in the lookup table. Such updates reflect the concept drift as the lookup table is updated accordingly in response to the data dynamics by adjusting the weights of signature subspace in the lookup table. A promising characteristic of signature subspace lookup table is that it can be updated incrementally, enabling the update of lookup table to be performed very efficiently in the detection process. For each detected anomaly, the steps of class membership probability computation, class classification and signature subspace lookup table updating are performed in an on-the-fly manner.

Handle False Positives

False positives, also called false alarms, are those anomalies that are erroneously detected as the attacks by the system. Even though they are benign in nature and not harmful as compared to real attacks, false positives consume a fair amount of human effort spent on investigating them whatsoever and thus making it almost impossible for security officers to really concentrate only on the real attacks. Generally, among all the anomalies detected, up to 90% of them may be false positives. It is much desirable to quickly screen out these false positives in order to allow closer attention to be paid towards the real harmful attacks.

The situation we are facing in the KDD-CUP'99 anomaly detection application is that there are no avail- able false-positive exemplars in the training data set. Therefore, unlike the attack classes, it is not easy to directly create the signature subspaces for the false-positive class. However,

there are a fair amount of normal samples in the training data set. If any of them are found abnormal, *i.e.*, they have some outlying subspaces, then they will be considered as false positives. These false positives from the training data provide the basis for constructing the signature subspace for the false-positive class. Consequently, like other attack classes, the construction of signature subspaces of false-positive class can be started as early as in the learning stage of SPOT.

The set of signature subspaces of the false-positive class starts from an empty set. In the learning stage of SPOT, a normal data in the training data set will be considered as a false positive if it is found abnormal in some subspaces. Formally, a data point p is a false positive if we have

$$OS(p) = \varnothing \text{ and label}(p) = \text{normal}. \quad (29)$$

The moment a data point p is identified as a false positive, the subspaces in its OSF will be properly registered into the current signature subspace lookup table. Ideally, the similarity between false positives and the false-positive class should be significantly higher than their similarities to other attack classes. However, this may not be true in the early stage due to the immatureness of the signature subspaces of the false-positive class. As an increasing number of false positives are continuously registered, the signature subspaces of the false-positive class will keep on growing. As a result, we will witness an continuously improved classification accuracy of false positives. We keep trace of the goodness of the signature subspaces we have constructed thus far at any time of the learning process. As a rule of thumb, the growing stage could be continued until the moment when satisfactory detection accuracy, say 90%, is achieved for false-positive class.

If the training data fail to establish a signature subspace lookup table for achieving a satisfactory classification accuracy, the construction of signature subspaces for the false-positive class will be continued to the detection stage of SPOT. Since the examination of false positives by domain experts during the detection stage is rather time-consuming, if it is not completely impossible, we thus employ an alternative automatic approximation method to expand the set of signature subspaces for the false-positive class. The basic idea for this automatic approach is that we collect the anomalies detected by SPOT and label those anomalies as false positives whose probability for falling into any known attack class is lower than a corresponding probability threshold. Given that the overwhelming majority of anomalies detected by SPOT are false positives, it is reasonable to consider all these anomalies that cannot be categorized into any attack classes as false-positives without significantly compromising its detection accuracy. This could save a lot of human efforts taken in anomaly examination.

When labeled samples are absent, we cannot rely on the detection rate to properly pinpoint the transition from the growing stage to the later mature stage. Alternatively, we depend on the changes in the membership probabilities of anomalies with regard to the false-positive class. The higher the membership probability is, the better identification is achieved for the false positives. Such membership probability value is relatively low at the beginning due to the immatureness of the signature subspaces of the false-positive class. When this set grows as time evolves, we gradually obtain a better detection performance of false positives and the similarity value will be increased. When the similarity value starts to converge (reaching a plateau stage), then we can consider the set of signature subspaces of the false-positive class to be mature. Figure 6 shows the change of the membership probabilities of anomalies with respect to the false-positive class. Please note that, after the set of signature subspace has reached the mature stage, we are in a better position to identify anomalies. One such example will be the 93th anomaly shown in Figure 6 that has remarkably low probability with respect to false-positive class compared to other anomalies. It is probably an attack instance, though its exact attack class is unknown by solely reading this figure.

Adaptively Update SST through Relevance Feedback

By incorporating relevance feedback, SST is no longer a static set of subspaces that SPOT needs to explore. Instead, SPOT can dynamically update/refine SST in order to cater for concept drifts of the network data that it is processing. Being able to adjust to the dynamics of network data is particularly necessary for the scenario that the network data arrives continuously. Concept drift is an important characteristic of Big Data which is more likely to contain data whose distribution/characteristic changes abruptly. The originality of this approach is to incorporate human feedbacks to improve the detection accuracy of SPOT. Also, this approach will help reduce the size of SST which is able to contribute to the efficiency of SPOT as well. This approach is applicable for the scenario when human intervention and feedback is possible which produces true positives and true negatives for anomaly detection. In practice, the human feedback can be carried out in either an online or a off-line fashion and may affect all the 3 subsets of SST.

The basic idea of this relevance feedback approach is that we assign a weight of 1 to each of the subspaces in SST after redundancy has been removed. The weights of the subspaces in SST are increased if they are the outlying subspaces of the true positives, while their weights are decreased if they are the outlying subspaces of the false positives. Every time after a specific number of (i.e. a batch of) network data are processed, the subspaces in SST whose weight are lower than a weight threshold are pruned from SST, and the new subspaces whose weights are higher than the threshold are added into SST. In this way, we end up with a dynamic SST which can reveal which subspaces are more important in accurately detecting true positives and reduce false positives. Please note that

Figure 6. Change of the member probabilities of anomalies with regard to the false-positive class

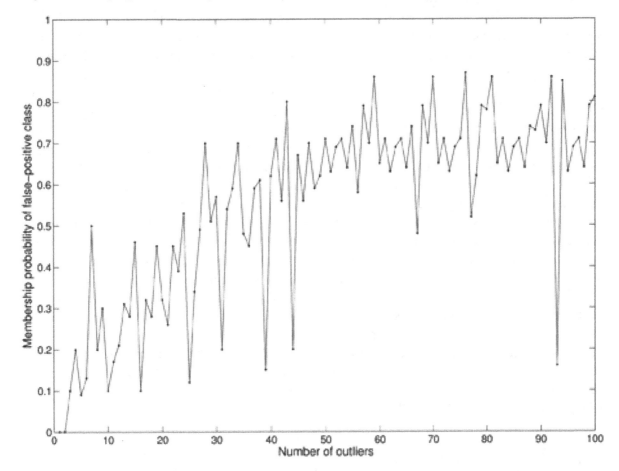

1. The weights of subspaces are normalized in order to facilitate the specification of the value for the weight threshold;
2. The weights of all the subspaces in SST are reset to 1 in order to keep them current with regard to the current batch of data; and
3. The size of the data batch that determines the frequency of SST update should be larger than 30 in order to make the update warranted by concept drifts with statistically significance.

Please note that a concept drift does not necessarily lead to a change of the SST. This is because that, even though the overall characteristics/distribution of the data in the dat set suddenly changes, there may be no or little impact on anomaly detec-

tion. In this sense, our approach is advantageous as it is highly targeted to task of anomaly detection when dealing with concept drifts - SST is only updated when there is a significant impact on anomaly detection resulting from concept drifts. This is a major difference between our method and other concept drift detection methods that are primarily based upon metric distance or density calculation.

EXPERIMENTAL EVALUATION

In this section, we will conduct experimental evaluation on SPOT in 1999 KDD anomaly detection application in terms of its effectiveness and efficiency.

Effectiveness Study Results

We will first report the results of experimental evaluation on the effectiveness of SPOT in 1999 KDD CUP anomaly detection application.

Effect of Number of Training Data Sets

When applying SPOT to KDD-CUP'99 anomaly detection application, we need to generate multiple training data sets for each attack classes for training purpose. This is to sample an enough amount of attack instances and at the same time satisfy the distribution requirement regarding normal and attack instances in each training data set. In this experiment, we investigate the effect of the number of training data sets generated for each class on the detection performance of SPOT. Recall that, due to the size limitation, each training data set is only able to contain a small portion of the labeled anomaly exemplars from the original training data set. Therefore, it

is expected that, as the number of training data set for each class is increased, the detection accuracy will be enhanced accordingly and finally a kind of convergence phenomenon is expected to be observed. In this experiment, we evaluate the true positive rate and false positive rate of SPOT under varying number of training data sets. The result is presented in Figure 7. Besides the curve of true positive rate, two additional curves corresponding respectively to the cases of using and not using the false positive reduction are also presented for the false positive rate in the figure. We can see that, as the number of training data set increases, the true positive rate is indeed improved. However, a larger number of training data set tend to result in a higher false positive rate. Fortunately, we observe a noticeably lower false positive rate for SPOT thanks to the false positive categorization we introduced in SPOT to automatically screen out false positives through the anomaly categorization process.

Figure 7. Effect of number of training data sets for each attack class

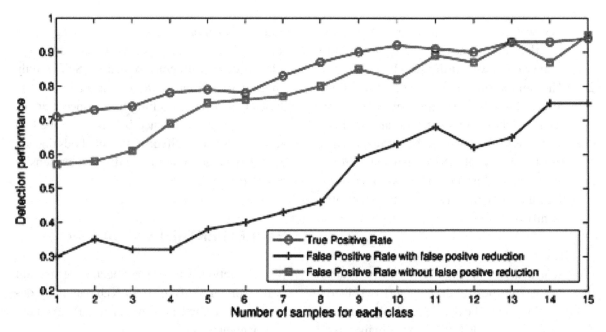

Table 2. Analysis on the redundant outlying subspaces of anomalies

Datasets	5.0	4.0	3.0	2.0	1.0
SD1	54%	62%	62%	64%	69%
RD1	49%	52%	59%	68%	70%
RD2	57%	61%	69%	70%	73%
RD4	55%	56%	57%	60%	66%

Table 3. Comparison of the manual and automatic methods for identifying false positives

	0.5	0.6	0.7	0.8	0.9
Difference of signature subspaces generated	23.5%	7.6%	13.7%	17.8%	28.5%
Accuracy in classifying false positives	87.2%	92.3%	88.5%	83.4%	72.1%

Redundant Outlying Subspace Removal

We also investigate the existence of redundant outlying subspaces of anomalies. We first study the percent- age of anomalies that have redundant outlying subspaces in KDD-CUP'99 anomaly detection data stream and other data sets. We can see from Table 2 that the majority of anomalies have redundant subspaces. We also study the Redundancy Ratio for these data sets. Here, the Redundancy Ratio (RR) of a data set D is defined as the ratio of the number of outlying subspaces (OS) of anomalies against the size of their outlying subspace front (OSF), i.e.

$$RR(D) = \frac{\sum |OS(o)|}{\sum |OSF(o)|}, \text{ for } o \text{ being an anomaly in } D.$$

As also shown in Table 2, from the whole data set's perspective, the Redundancy Ratio of its outlying subspace set is between 49% and 73%, indicating a fairly high Redundancy Ratio for different data sets. As a result, using Outlying Subspace Front would help reduce the number of outlying subspaces by from 49% to 73%. Another important observation is that the values of these two measures are increased when the outlier-ness threshold goes down. This is because that, as the outlier-ness threshold become smaller, more subspaces will become outlying subspaces and they are likely to be dominated by some of their lower dimensional counterparts.

Signature Subspace Analysis

We are also interested in studying the diversity of signature subspaces of the false-positive class, as compared with those of the attack classes. We record the number of strong unique signature subspaces for different classes (including the false-positive class) as the number of data we evaluated increases. In this experiment, the strong signature subspaces we select are those signature subspaces whose tf-idf weight is 5 times higher than the average weight level. This definition of strong signature subspaces is of course subjective. We plot the results in Figure 8. Interestingly, we find that the number of unique strong signature subspaces for the false-positive class is significantly higher than any other attack classes by a factor of three or four. This means that the strong signature subspaces for the false-positive class is far more diverse than those of the attack classes. This finding offers an important insight to us when we are creating the set of signature subspaces of the false-positive class. We need to collect a relatively large pool of signature subspaces in the detection process to achieve an accurate detection of false positives.

Figure 8. Number of strong signature subspaces for each attack class under varying number of data being processed

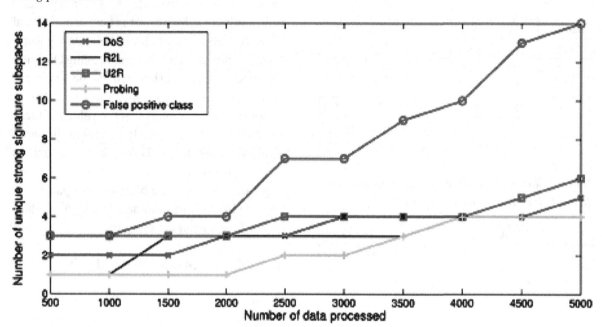

Comparative Study

Comparative study is also performed to investigate the detection accuracy and false positive rate between SPOT and other existing anomaly detection methods.

Competitive Methods

Since there is little research conducted in projected anomaly detection for high dimensional data streams, we cannot find the techniques tackling exactly the same problem as SPOT does for comparison. However, there are some related existing approaches for detecting anomalies from data streams that we can compare SPOT with. These methods can be broadly categorized as methods using histogram, Kernel density function, distance-based function and clustering analysis, respectively.

Histogram and Kernel density function are amongst the most commonly used statistical techniques in anomaly/intrusion detection. Histograms

are created for each dimension of the data stream. The density (i.e., number of data points) falling into each bin of the histogram are recorded. The outlier-ness of a data point is computed feature-wise for multi-variate data as

$$outlier\_ness(p) = \sum_{f \in F} w_f \times (1 - p_f) / \mid F \mid$$

(31)

where p_f is the probability that feature f takes the value of p, p_f is calculated as the ratio of the density of the bin p belongs to against the total number of points arriving thus far. w_f is the weight assigned to feature f . For simplicity, w_f is set equal for all the attributes in the data stream. All attributes are considered in calculating the outlier-ness of data points of the stream in the histogram method. IF I denotes the total number of features in the data set. In this histogram-based anomaly detection method, a data point is an anomaly if its outlier- ness is above a threshold. Kernel density function models local data distribution in a single or multiple dimensions of space. One of the representative methods using Kernel function is proposed for detecting anomalies from sensor network (Palpanas et al., 2003). A point is detected as an anomaly if the number of values that have fallen into its neighborhood (delimited by a sphere of radius r) is less than an application-specific threshold. The number of values in the neighborhood can be computed by the Kernel density function. To facilitate the comparison, the functionalities of this Kernel function based method for dealing with distributed nodes are ignored. Anomaly detection from data stream is performed only in a single-node mode for this method. A major recent distance-based method for data stream is called 'Incremental LOF' (Pokrajac et al., 2007). It is a variant of LOF method tailored for coping with frequent data updates (insertions and deletions) for dynamic databases. Clustering analysis can also be used to detect anomalies from those data that are located far apart from the data clusters. HPStream (Aggarwal et al., 2004) is the representative method for finding subspace clusters in high-dimensional data streams. In our experiments, a minor modification is needed to enable HPStream to detect anomalies. A data will be labeled abnormal if it is far apart from the so-called limiting radius of all the clusters. Here, the limiting radius of a cluster is typically a few times of the average radius of the data points in the cluster. We test four different possible sets of dimensions associated with each cluster, *i.e.*, 1, 2, 3 and 4, respectively. The exact number of dimension for a cluster is chosen from these four configurations such that the best F -measure can be achieved. This specification ensures that all the subspaces explored in HPStream are included in the 4-dimensional space lattice.

Effectiveness Measures

Appropriate performance metrics are needed in evaluating the detection performance of SPOT and other competitive detection methods. In the KDD-CUP'99 anomaly detection application, we will use detection rate (or called true positive rate)

and false positive rate for performance evaluation. These two metrics are the most commonly used ones in detection systems. Detection rate refers to the percentage of hits (correctly identified anomalies) in the whole set of anomalies existing in the data set and false positive rate represents the percentage of erroneously labeled anomalies in the whole set of normal data.

Based on detection rate and false positive rate, Receiver Operating Characteristic (ROC) analysis is usually used. ROC is a commonly used technique for performance evaluation of detection methods by plotting its detection rate and false positive rate in the same ROC space. In a ROC curve, the detection rate is plotted in function of the false positive rate for different cut-offs. The closer the ROC curve of a method is from the left-upper corner in ROC space, the better the detection performance of this method will be.

Comparative Study Results

In this subsection, we will report the results of comparing the effectiveness of SPOT with other existing anomaly detection methods, including histogram method, Kernel function method, Incremental LOF and HPStream in KDD-CUP'99 anomaly detection application. ROC analysis is used in this comparative study. To conduct ROC analysis, we need to know in advance the true positives (anomalies) and true negatives (normal data). This is possible in KDD-CUP'99 anomaly detection application as labeled test data are available. As we know, any detection method can easily achieve a 100% detection rate by simply labeling all the connections as anomalies. However, this strategy will result in an extremely high false positive rate. Likewise, one can obtain a 0% false positive rate by claiming all the connections as normal, but this will lead to 0% true positive rate. Therefore, we need to consider these two rates simultaneously. In Figure 9, we plot the ROC curves for SPOT and other four competitive methods. We can see from this figure that

Figure 9. ROC curves of different methods

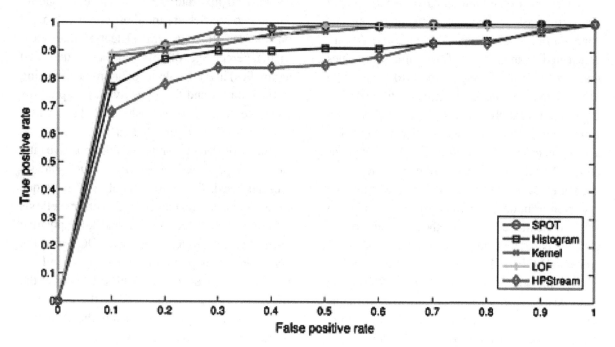

the ROC curves of SPOT, Incremental LOF and Kernel function method progress much closer to the upper-left corner of the plot than the curves of histogram method and HPStream, indicating that SPOT, Incremental LOF and Kernel function method generally achieve a better detection performance. A closer examination of the figure suggests that Incremental LOF and Kernel function method perform better than SPOT when the false positive rate is relatively low (i.e., in the early stage of the ROC curves). However, SPOT starts to outperform Incremental LOF and Kernel function method as the false positive rate further increases. The false positive categorization that SPOT is equipped with enables it to identify false positives in an automated fashion while other competitive methods cannot. This helps SPOT to significantly reduce false positives and achieves a lower false positive rate under the same detection rate (or achieves a higher detection rate under the same false positive rate).

CONCLUSION

In this paper, we investigate anomaly detection problem in large and high-dimensional network data streams. By applying SPOT, we carry out a detailed case study using 1999 KDD CUP anomaly detection data stream. As the major contributions, several important issues, including training data generation, anomaly categorization using outlying subspaces analysis and false positive reduction, have been tackled in this paper for rendering SPOT applicable in this study. The experimental evaluations show that SPOT is not only more effective in detecting anomalies hidden in the subspaces of high-dimensional data streams but also produces a significantly lower level of false positives than the existing anomaly detection methods. Moreover, SPOT is efficient and scalable to large and high-dimensional data streams.

ACKNOWLEDGMENT

The author would like to thank Dr. Qigang Gao from Dalhousie University Canada, Dr. Hai Wang from St. Mary's University, Canada, Dr. Qing Liu and Dr. Kai Xu from CSIRO ICT Centre Australia, for their contribution to the development of SPOT.

REFERENCES

Aggarwal, C. C., & Yu, P. S. (2001). Outlier detection in high dimensional data. In *Proceedings of SIGMOD Conference* (pp. 37-46). Santa Barbara, CA: ACM.

Aggarwal, C. C., Han, J., Wang, J., & Yu, P. S. (2004). A framework for projected clustering of high dimensional data streams. In *Proceedings of International Conference on Very Large Data Base (VLDB)* (pp. 852-863). Toronto, Canada: Academic Press. doi:10.1016/B978-012088469-8/50075-9

Aggarwal, C. C., & Yu, P. S. (2005). An effective and efficient algorithm for high-dimensional outlier detection. *The VLDB Journal*, *14*(2), 211–221. doi:10.1007/s00778-004-0125-5

Boudjeloud, L., & Poulet, F. (2005). Visual interactive evolutionary algorithm for high dimensional data clustering and outlier detection. In *Proc. of 9th Pacific-Asia Conference on Advances in Knowledge Discovery and Data Mining (PAKDD)* (pp.426-431). Hanoi, Vietnam: Academic Press. doi:10.1007/11430919_50

Breuning, M., Kriegel, H.-P., Ng, R., & Sander, J. (2000). LOF: Identifying density-based local outliers. In *Proceedings of SIGMOD Conference* (pp 93-104). Dallas, TX: ACM.

Cui, H. (2002). *Online outlier detection over data streams*. (Master thesis). Simon Fraser University.

Guha, A., Krishnamurthi, S., & Jim, T. (2009). Using static analysis for ajax intrusion detection. In *Proceedings of International World Wide Web Conferences (WWW)* (pp. 561-570). Madrid, Spain: Academic Press.

Knorr, E. M., & Ng, R. T. (1998). Algorithms for mining distance-based outliers in large dataset. In *Proceedings of International Conference on Very Large Data Base (VLDB)* (pp. 392-403). New York, NY: VLDB.

Knorr, E. M., & Ng, R. T. (1999). Finding intentional knowledge of distance-based outliers. In *Proceedings of International Conference on Very Large Data Base (VLDB)* (pp. 211-222). Edinburgh, UK: VLDB.

Palpanas, T., Papadopoulos, D., Kalogeraki, V., & Gunopulos, D. (2003). Distributed deviation detection in sensor networks. *SIGMOD Record*, *32*(4), 77–82. doi:10.1145/959060.959074

Pokrajac, D., Lazarevic, A., & Latecki, L. (2007). Incremental local outlier detection for data streams. In Proceedings of IEEE Symposiums on Computational Intelligence and Data Mining (CIDM'07) (pp. 504-515). Honolulu, HI: IEEE.

Ramaswamy, S., Rastogi, R., & Kyuseok, S. (2000). Efficient algorithms for mining outliers from large data sets. In *Proceedings of SIGMOD Conference* (pp. 427-438). Dallas, TX: ACM. doi:10.1145/342009.335437

Tang, J., Chen, Z., Fu, A., & Cheung, D. W. (2002). Enhancing effectiveness of outlier detections for low density patterns. In *Proceedings of Pacific-Asia Conference on Knowledge Discovery and Data Mining (PAKDD)*. Taipei, Taiwan: Academic Press. doi:10.1007/3-540-47887-6_53

Zhang, J., Gao, Q., & Wang, H. (2006). A novel method for detecting outlying subspaces in high- dimensional databases using genetic algorithm. In *Proceedings of IEEE International Conference on Data Mining* (pp. 731-740). Hong Kong, China: IEEE. doi:10.1109/ICDM.2006.6

Zhang, J., Gao, Q., Wang, H., Liu, Q., & Xu, X. (2009). Detecting projected outliers in high-dimensional data streams. In *Proceedings of International Conference on Database and Expert Systems Applications* (pp. 629-644). Academic Press. doi:10.1007/978-3-642-03573-9_53

Zhang, J., Gao, Q., Wang, H., & Wang, H. (2010). *Detecting anomalies from high-dimensional wireless net- work data streams: A case study.* Springer Publishing.

Zhang, J., & Wang, H. (2006). Detecting outlying subspaces for high-dimensional data: The new task, algorithms and performance. *Knowledge and Information Systems*, *10*(3), 333–355. doi:10.1007/s10115-006-0020-z

Zhong, S., Khoshgoftaar, T. M., & Nath, S. V. (2005). A clustering approach to wireless network intrusion detection. In *Proceedings of IEEE International Conference on Tools with Artificial Intelligence (ICTAI)* (pp. 190-196). IEEE.

Zhu, C., Kitagawa, H., & Faloutsos, C. (2005). Example-based robust outlier detection in high dimensional datasets. In *Proceedings of IEEE International Conference on Data Mining* (pp. 829-832). IEEE.

Zhu, C., Kitagawa, H., Papadimitriou, S., & Faloutsos, C. (2004). OBE: Outlier by example. In *Proceedings of Pacific-Asia Conference on Knowledge Discovery and Data Mining (PAKDD)* (pp. 222-234). PAKDD.

ADDITIONAL READING

Aggarwal, C. C. (2005). On Abnormality Detection in Spuriously Populated Data Streams. *SIAM Conference on Data Mining*, Newport Beach, CA. doi:10.1137/1.9781611972757.8

Aggarwal, C. C., Han, J., Wang, J., & Yu, P. S. (2003). A Framework for Clustering Evolving Data Streams. *International Conference on Very Large Data Base (VLDB)*, (pp. 81-92). Berlin, Germany. doi:10.1016/B978-012722442-8/50016-1

Angiulli, F., & Pizzuti, C. (2002). Fast Outlier Detection in High Dimensional Spaces. *European Conference on Principles of Data Mining and Knowledge Discovery (PKDD)*, Helsinki, Finland, (pp. 15-26). doi:10.1007/3-540-45681-3_2

Barbara, D. (2002). Requirements for Clustering Data Streams. [ACM Press.]. *ACM SIGKDD Explorations Newsletter*, *3*(2), 23–27. doi:10.1145/507515.507519

Eskin, E., Arnold, A., Prerau, M., Portnoy L., & Stolfo, S. (2002). A Geometric Framework for Unsupervised Anomaly Detection: Detecting Intrusions in Unlabeled Data. *Applications of Data Mining in Computer Security*.

Guttman, A. (1984). R-trees: a Dynamic Index Structure for Spatial Searching, *SIGMOD Conference*, (pp. 47-57). Boston, Massachusetts. doi:10.1145/602264.602266

Han, J., & Kamber, M. (2000). *Data Mining: Concepts and Techniques*. Morgan Kaufman Publishers.

Zhang, J., Lou, M., Ling, T. W., & Wang, H. (2004). HOS-Miner: A System for Detecting Outlying Subspaces of High-dimensional Data. *International Conference on Very Large Data Base (VLDB)*, (pp. 1265-1268). Toronto, Canada.

KEY TERMS AND DEFINITIONS

Anomaly Classification: The classification process of the anomies into one or more known categories/classes.

Anomaly Detection: The process for detecting those data that are considered as inconsistent, abnormal when compared with the majority of the data in the databases or population.

Data Streams: A set of continuously arriving data generated from different application such as telecommunications, network, sensor networks, etc.

False Positive: The data that are detected the ones that satisfy a certain hypothesis but does not actually the case.

Genetic Algorithms: A search heuristic that mimics the process of natural evolution. This heuristic is routinely used to generate useful solutions to optimization and search problems.

ROC: The analysis of the relationship between the true positive fraction of test results and the false positive fraction for a diagnostic procedure that can take on multiple values.

Subspaces: Data spaces that only contain a partial set of the attributes of the data under study.

Chapter 19
Detecting Botnet Traffic from a Single Host

Sebastián García
Universidad Nacional del Centro (UNICEN University), Argentina & Czech Technical University (CTU University), Czech Republic.

Alejandro Zunino
Universidad Nacional del Centro (UNICEN University), Argentina

Marcelo Campo
Universidad Nacional del Centro (UNICEN University), Argentina

ABSTRACT

The detection of bots and botnets in the network may be improved if the analysis is done on the traffic of one bot alone. While a botnet may be detected by correlating the behavior of several bots in a large amount of traffic, one bot alone can be detected by analyzing its unique trends in less traffic. The algorithms to differentiate the traffic of one bot from the normal traffic of one computer may take advantage of these differences. The authors propose to detect bots in the network by analyzing the relationships between flow features in a time window. The technique is based on the Expectation-Maximization clustering algorithm. To verify the method they designed test-beds and obtained a dataset of six different captures. The results are encouraging, showing a true positive error rate of 99.08% with a false positive error rate of 0.7%.

INTRODUCTION

In the last decade botnets have evolved from being used as a personal activity platform to becoming a financially aimed structure controlled by malicious groups (Wilson, 2007). We consider a botnet as a network of remotely controlled, compromised computers, used for malicious purposes. The hosts in a botnet are called 'Bots' and the owner

of a botnet is called 'Botmaster'. Botnets have become the technological backbone of a growing community of malicious activities (Clinton, 2008), from small DDoS (Distributed Denial of Service attacks) to worldwide spam campaigns. They still remain as the most significant threat to the Internet today.

The first attempts to control a malicious programs remotely first appeared in late 1999. Since then the primary goal of the owners has been to

DOI: 10.4018/978-1-4666-7381-6.ch019

obtain financial gain. This forced the development of several botnet detection technologies trying to cope with the attacks, but botnets resisted besiege security measures resting on the infection of home based computers, circumventing security methods (Stone-Gross, Cova, Cavallaro, Gilbert, Szydlowski, Kemmerer, Kruegel & Vigna, 2009), encryption algorithms and anti-reverse engineering techniques. Although the IRC (Internet Chat Relay) protocol has been the most used command and control (C&C) channel in the last decade, nowadays the trend is towards decentralized networks, such as P2P (Peer to Peer) (Yan, Eidenbenz & Nago, 2009) (Kang, Zhang, Li & Li, 2009).

A wide diversity of methods had been proposed to detect botnets. In the survey presented by Garcia, Zunino and Campo (2013) there is a basic classification of these network-based detection methods. It shows that there is still a large amount of signature-based methods and protocol-dependant feature analysis. While these techniques may work under certain conditions, they are usually not enough to capture new botnets that significantly deviate from those signatures. More important, the survey shows a growing amount of algorithms making use of the behavior of the botnets. These techniques are more dynamic and therefore have a better chance to detect new behavior.

Since a real and large network usually generate a huge amount of diverse traffic, instead of detecting a botnet, some proposals focused only on detecting a single infected host. The survey shows that there are some proposals in this area, because it may be easier to differentiate a single bot from a single normal computer.

Our proposal is based on the idea of detecting a single bot by means of its network-based behavior. The benefits of analyzing the traffic of one bot, compared to analyzing a network, are that there is considerably less traffic to process and that the traffic may tend to be more homogeneous. On the other hand, the disadvantages are that less traffic

may mean less behavior available to detect the bot and that to capture the traffic of one host we usually need the authorization of the owner.

The detection model that is proposed in this paper was created after a thorough analysis of the most inherent characteristics of the behavior of the bot. This analysis showed that the most typical characteristics of the bot are maliciousness (attacking and infecting, sending SPAM, DDoS, etc.) and being remotely managed. During some botnet life cycle phases, a single bot computer usually generates high network flow rates within very short time periods (Gu, 2008), for example, during Spam sending, DDoS attacks, network scanning and botnet distribution. Therefore, we focus on the relationship between the amount of IP addresses and ports in a time window. We hypothesize that our group of features can be used to detect the traffic of a single bot.

Our proposal first separates the bots' flows into time windows, then it extracts some aggregated features and then it applies a clustering algorithm (Baeza-Yates, 1999) to detect the bot. With this method it is possible to detect bots using encrypted traffic, without using static details of the protocols and within the first stages of infection.

The validation of the method was done by capturing a real dataset that contains labeled botnet traffic and labeled non-botnet traffic. This dataset allowed us to achieve a verified and more robust algorithm. For verification purposes the dataset was made public and can be downloaded from the website http://mcfp.felk.cvut.cz. This site is the Malware Capture Facility Project were more botnets are being captured, labeled and published (Garcia, 2013).

The contributions of our proposal are:

- It separates the aggregated network flows in time windows using behavioral features.
- It clusters instances using the Expectation-Maximization algorithm.
- It evaluates the algorithm with botnet, non-botnet and manual attacks labeled data.

The rest of the chapter is organized as follows: Section Background describes previous work in the area; Section Detection Method shows details about our approach; Section Dataset shows how network data has been obtained; Section Validation explains corroboration procedures; Section Experiments and Results describe each experiments and presents the corresponding results; Section Error Metrics shows the performance of the algorithm; Section Conclusions presents our conclusions and finally Section Future Research Directions refers to future work we are planning.

Background

The past years has been marked by several improvements in the area of botnet detection methods. The survey done by Garcia et. al. (2013) analyzed thirteen botnet detection proposals based on network traffic. The survey discusses some areas were the detection proposals could improve, such as the description of the experiments for verification, the creation of better datasets that include normal data, the publication of all the results and error metrics, and the discussion of the meaning of the results.

A good paper about how important it is to correctly design an experiment was presented by Rossow et. al. (2012). The paper discusses the common pitfalls in designing a dataset and which of its aspects should be considered. It accounts for the few amounts of papers that use normal traffic on their captures and how this can bias the results. Another important discussion is about the need to discus more the reasons for the errors found in the experiments. They remark the importance of knowing the traffic on the experiments.

Some approaches have been proposed to detect botnets in recent years using network features, including the study of anomalous DNS (Domain Name System) usage (Villamarin-Salomon & Brustoloni, 2008), IRC protocol analysis (Mazzariello, 2008) and P2P network features (Kang et al., 2009) among others (Shahrestani, Ramadass &

Feily, 2009) (Zhu, Lu, Chen, Fu, Roberts & Han, 2008) (Rieck et. al., 2011) (Saad et. al., 2011), but the variability of botnets and their rapid mutation have forced researchers from different security domains to consider the analysis of behavioral patterns as a solid foundation for botnet detection.

A recent analysis about the detection of botnets based on traffic flow analysis and time intervals was done by Zhao et. al. (2013). This paper uses NetFlows for analyzing the traffic, and thus have the advantage of being able to get flows from a large amount of devices. The paper proposes a group of thirteen features to be analyzed for detection, and then evaluates a group of machine learning algorithms on them. The dataset used was a mixture of botnet and normal traffic. They concluded that their decision tree classifier was able to successfully detect botnets in their experiments.

Particularly, network behavior detection has been studied from different perspectives: traffic classification based on flow characteristics (Strayer, Lapsely, Walsh & Livadas, 2007), protocol analysis based on temporal-frequent features (Lu, Tavallaee, Rammidi & Ghorbani, 2009) and network analysis based on spatial-temporal correlation (Gu, 2008), where activity response crowds on IRC botnets are grouped together by destination IP address-port pairs and time windows.

The analysis of the behavior of bots, based on protocol-dependent features, has proved to be successful only under certain conditions. There seems to be three main problems with behavioral protocol-dependant approaches. First, only a subset of botnets can be detected analyzing protocol dependent characteristics, e.g., analyzing IRC messages behavior is not enough to detect P2P botnets. Second, new unseen botnets are unlikely to be detected if a new protocol is used. Finally, botmasters can change their current malware protocol characteristics used to detect their botnet (Stinson & Mitchell, 2008).

Addressing the aforementioned problems, botnets invariants were sought in order to detect them independently of protocol changes and implementation details. Botnet correlation have been proposed (Gu, Perdisci, Zhang & Lee, 2008) among other techniques (Liu, Chan, Yan & Zhang, 2008), based on the fact that every bot in a botnet normally act at the same time. However, synchronization has not been deeply studied, and temporal correlation approaches have been found to be evadable under certain circumstances (Chen, Chen & Wang, 2009), for example, proposing a time delay in bot responses before applying commands.

Our feature set was selected based on a previous work of the best network features for intrusion detection (Onut & Ghorbani, 2007). This paper defines a time window based detection schema, where some features related to the number of TCP connections are used. We extended some of the ideas in this paper to the botnet detection problem. Furthermore, the detection of botnets using groups of source IP address and groups of destination IP address was also proposed by Li et. al. (Li, Goyal, & Chen, 2007). The paper uses a honeypot to analyze this *Sips/Dip* relationship.

DETECTION METHOD

Our detection methodology is focused on detecting bots and not botnets. These are two quite different problems. Bots may be detected by the distinguishable behavior of one host; while botnets may be detected by the traffic correlations between several bots. Our method aims at detecting the behavior of the bot by applying machine learning algorithms on real data.

The first step of our methodology consists in capturing and labeling real network data. These real captures are the ground truth-data and they are very important to verify the method. The data is stored into pcap formatted files. The next Section describes this process in detail.

The second step consists in processing the pcap captures files and separating the TCP flows. A tool called tcptrace (Shawn, 2010) was used to find out every TCP flow, including its start time and network characteristics.

The third step of our approach involves dividing the TCP flows in one-second time windows, allowing us to monitor and identify bots behavior. Each time window contains aggregated information about every TCP flow. In the fourth step, for every TCP flow in each time window, we compute the amount of unique source IP addresses (referred hereafter as *sips*), unique destination IP addresses (referred hereafter as *dips*) and unique destination ports (referred hereafter as *dports*). These features had been successfully used before to detect manual network attacks (Onut & Ghorbani, 2007). Although we are focusing on detecting only one host, the aggregation of source IP addresses has two advantages. First, it allow us to compare this approach with a botnet detection approach, and second, it allow us to deal with the rest of the source IP addresses in a single computer like multicast addresses, broadcast and IPv6. A time window can then be represented by a four dimensional vector containing the Window Id, amount of unique source IP addresses in that time window, amount of unique destination IP addresses in that time windows and amount of unique destination TCP ports in that time window. An example vector should look like this: [23, 1, 10, 1].

The fourth step involves clustering these vectors by first using the EM (Expectation-Maximization) algorithm (Dempster, Laird & Rubin, 1977) and then forming clusters according to the likelihood. The Expectation-maximization algorithms is a method for finding the maximum likelihood estimates of parameters in statistical models with incomplete data, and has been used successfully before in traffic flow analysis for characterizing communication connectivity patterns (Chen, Li & Cao, 2009), botnet detection (Masud, Gao, Khan, Han, & Thuraisingham, 2008) and spam detection (Zhang, 2009).

The EM algorithm works with a density function $p(x|\Theta)$ that is defined by a set of parameters Θ. It also works with a known dataset $X=\{x1, ..., xn\}$, of size N, extracted from this distribution. The resulting density for the samples can be seen in Equation (1).

$$p(X \mid \Theta) = \prod_{i=1}^{N} p(x_i \mid \Theta) = L\left(\Theta \mid X\right). \tag{1}$$

This function L is called the likelihood of the parameters given the known data. The likelihood is a function of the parameters Θ where the known data X is fixed. In the maximum likelihood problem, represented by Equation (2), the goal is to find the Θ parameter that maximizes L.

$$\Theta' = \arg\max_{\Theta} L\left(\Theta \mid X\right). \tag{2}$$

The EM algorithm is a technique to solve the maximum likelihood problem. In our proposal, the windows vectors are the known data, coming from different statistical distributions (computers). The amount of distributions and the correspondence between vectors and distributions are the hidden variables to be found. Each botnet generates packets given a unique statistical distribution with unknown parameters Θ and our goal is to maximize the a-posteriori probability of these parameters given the known data (vectors) in the presence of hidden data.

The intuition of the EM algorithm is to alternate between estimating the unknowns Θ and the hidden variables. The idea is to start with a guess of these parameters Θ and to determine for each vector which underlying distribution is more likely to have generated the observed data (using the current parameters estimates). Then, assume these guessed assignments to be correct and apply the regular maximum likelihood estimation procedure to get next Θ. The procedure iterates until convergence to a local maximum. The algorithm computes the models parameters and assigns the cluster number with highest probability to each window vector (McGregor, Hall, Lorier & Brunskill, 2004).

The EM algorithm provides a simple, easy-to-implement and efficient tool for learning the parameters of a model. We used the Weka's (Hall, Frank, Holmes, Pfahringer, Reutemann & Witten, 2009) implementation of this algorithm because of the independence assumption of the attributes in the model, making it suitable for our purposes.

DATASET

Our proposed algorithm was verified using a dataset that consist of six traffic captures that were taken using three different test-beds networks. Each capture was designed to have a different botnet or normal behavior. Three of these captures have botnet traffic and three of them have non-botnet traffic. Two of the non-botnet traffic captures have normal traffic from non-infected computers and the last non-botnet traffic capture corresponds to a manual port scanning activity. The packets were captured using the tcpdump tool (Lawrence Berkeley National Labs, 2010). Table 1 summarizes their main features.

First Botnet Capture

The first botnet capture is called Botnet1 and it was obtained by executing a variant of the Virut.n malware (MD5 d60e538e721c30a0ea-946404330f324a). The execution was done in one computer using the first test-bed network. This test-bed was composed of a Linux computer running VirtualBox (Watson, Jon. 2008) with a Microsoft Windows XP SP3 virtual machine (VM). The VM was connected to the Internet through a home DSL router and only the network packets from the VM were captured. This test-bed was created because current botnets usually target this type of home computers, looking for its high bandwidth and personal sensitive information (Corrons, PandaLabs, 2010), (Nazario, 2006).

Table 1. Details of the labeled dataset

Name	Duration	Unique Flows	Family	C&C Protocol	Hosts
Botnet1	11h:12m:29s	37,389	Virut	IRC C&C	1 bot
Botnet2	00h:20m:37s	21,124	Agobot	HTTP C&C. DGA. Fast-Flux	10 bots, 12 normal
Botnet3	10h:11m:33s	34,117	Rbot	IRC C&C	1 bot
Non-botnet1	00h:02m:38s	45,148	-	-	1 host scanning a network.
Non-botnet2	03h:28m:14s	5,251	-	-	37 normal
Non-botnet3	04h:19m:36s	12,017	-	-	1 normal

The malware in the Botnet1 capture sent 37,389 TCP flows during a little more than eleven hours. Its most important actions were to use an IRC command and control channel (C&C) and to perform a horizontal port scan in the local network looking for Microsoft Windows shared resources (port 445/TCP in particular). The sequence of actions was: first, it connected to an IRC server in s.unicat.org, port 2081/TCP. Second, the IRC servers sent the command "adv.start asn 100 5 0 -r -s". Third, it scanned the Class B network where the bot is connected (even if it's not a Class B network), looking for ports 445/TCP. The malware did not find an open port and did not make any other action. Figure 1 shows the traffic pattern of this capture as it was generated by the tcpflow[1] tool. It can be seen that the scanning of Windows resources has always the same pattern, suggesting an automatic behavior.

Second Botnet Capture

The second botnet capture is called Botnet2 and it was obtained by executing a variant of the Agobot malware (MD5 53077cd8545c1c2588a-caed3d8818180) on ten computers using the second test-bed. This test-bed consisted in a University campus sub-network of twenty two non-virtualized Microsoft Windows hosts. We make sure that the non-infected machines were producing normal traffic by manually analyzing them one by one. The Botnet2 was the only capture that was taken using this test-bed.

The twenty two hosts in the Botnet2 capture sent 21,124 TCP flows during twenty minutes. From these flows, 4,453 corresponded to normal flows and 16,671 to botnet flows. The normal actions included the download of binaries from the web, updates using the NTP protocol, NetBIOS protocol, SMB protocol and DNS. No users were using the normal computers during the capture.

Figure 1. Traffic pattern of the botnet1 capture

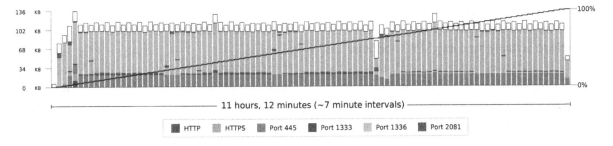

Figure 2. Traffic pattern of the botnet2 capture

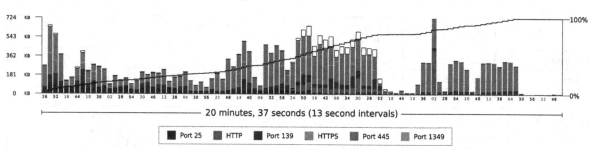

Regarding the ten infected computers, their most common characteristics were to use a DGA (Domain Generation Algorithm) to find out domain names; that all the domain names in the DGA resolved to the same group of seven IP addresses; and that the Command and Control (C&C) channel was non-encrypted HTTP. It total, the ten bots contacted 131 different domain names in the DGA.

The infected IP addresses were 192.168.1.9, 192.168.1.91, 192.168.1.239, 192.168.1.242, 192.168.1.71, 192.168.1.236, 192.168.1.238, 192.168.1.242, 192.168.1.243, 192.168.1.245 and 192.168.1.247. Each of them showed a slightly different sequence of actions, but the most common were: First to connect to www.msn.com. Second, to resolve some domain names, e.g: yssze.info, lvbylqtwg.org, ifyjbbuqo.cn, pwgqiecd.info. Third, to connect to the port 80/TCP of some hosts and ask for a web page such as "GET /search?q=6". The numbers in the parameter were: 1, 21, 3, 4, 5 and 6. Most of the time this web server did not answer or give a "404 Not Found" answer, but from time to time it answered a web page having only the following line <title> 0x0a0b0c0d0e-0f0xwwddooppwddwd0909ssww </title>. The title was always the same.

Five of the bots also tried to send SPAM to several mail servers; however most of them were not able to actually send any SPAM because the source IP addresses was blacklisted. In total the bots were able to send 121 SPAM messages from 2,003 attempts. Figure 2 shows the traffic pattern of this capture as it was generated by the tcpflow

tool. This pattern is not uniform because there were other computers in the network. However, the SPAM traffic and the HTTP connections can be seen clearly.

Third Botnet Capture

The third botnet capture is called Botnet3, and it was obtained by executing a malware of the 'Rbot' family. It is a real IRC-controlled malware with the capabilities to scan ports, make DDoS attacks, crack passwords, capture keystrokes and control the computer remotely. The capture was done in the first test-bed by only infecting one computer. This bot sent 34,117 flows.

The actions done by the bot were: it connected to the port 2,081/TCP of the s.unicat.org host, then it started scanning the port 445/TCP in the local Class B network and from time to time it received commands such as ".adv.start asn 100 3 0 -r -s". Figure 3 shows the traffic pattern of this capture as it was generated by the tcpflow tool. It can be seen how the port 2,081/TCP was used by the IRC server and how the main activity of the bot was to scan Windows shared resources on port 445/TCP.

First Non-Botnet Capture

The first non-botnet capture is called Non-botnet1 and was obtained by capturing the traffic of only one computer connected to the third test-bed network. The third test-bed consisted in a network

Figure 3. Traffic pattern of the botnet3 capture

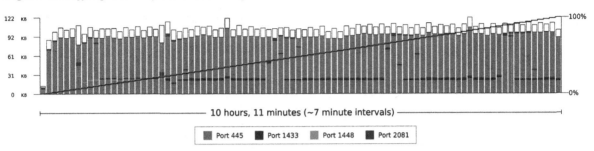

of thirty seven normal computers working in a University Campus, including the one making the manual port scan. The traffic was captured on the computer performing the scan and it only includes the packets going to and from that computer. The goal of this capture was to perform a port scan with the nmap (Lyon G.,2009) tool. Port scanning is one of the most common network attacks and also one of the most common network administrator's tasks. This capture is meant to verify the differentiation between botnet activity and other types of attacks. We performed a TCP SYN (-sS) scan of the top 1,000 default nmap's ports of all the Class C network without changing the default timing values of nmap. The version of nmap was 5.35DC18. Figure 4 shows the traffic pattern of this capture as it was generated by the tcpflow tool.

Second Non-Botnet Capture

The second non-botnet capture is called Non-botnet2 and was obtained using the third test-bed. In this case the traffic includes all the packets of the thirty seven normal computers. We verify the normality of this capture by manually inspecting the traffic and by analyzing it with the Snort NIDS (Roesch, 1999) The traffic include users sending SMTP mails, connecting to the web using an HTTP proxy, accessing web sites with AJAX updates, web mails, edonkey and torrent protocols, operating systems updates and several of the Google web tools. It is a good measure of normality since the users are well known. Figure 5 shows the traffic pattern of this capture as it was generated by the tcpflow tool.

Third Non-Botnet Capture

The third non-botnet capture is called Non-botnet3 and it was obtained using the third test-bed. It is the same computer that the Non-botnet1 capture, but it is only acting normally. The traffic only includes the packets going to and from this computer. The normal actions consisted of access to gmail, google docs, yahoo, and several more web sites; an update of the Kubuntu operating system and Firefox extensions and several automatic actions like ARP packets and DNS requests. Figure 6 shows the traffic pattern of this capture as it was generated by the tcpflow tool.

DATA PROCESSING

The processing of the captured data is a fundamental part of the research analysis and the preparation of the dataset. It helps determine which characteristics should be taken into account and used in the algorithms. The first phase of our processing was the extraction of TCP flows from the captured pcap files using the tcptrace tool[2]. This tool generates a text file with the characteristics of every TCP flow.

The second processing phase consisted in the extraction of certain features from the TCP flows. It was performed using our own tool called *tcptrace-reader.py*. As a result of this phase, a text file is generated with the following information per flow: start timestamp in epoch time format, source IP address in decimal format, destination

433

Figure 4. Traffic pattern of the Non-botnet1 capture

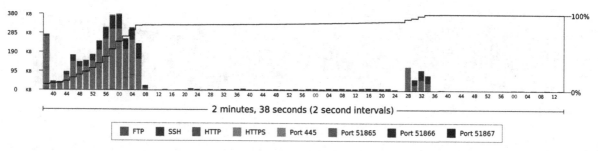

Figure 5. Traffic pattern of the non-botnet2 capture

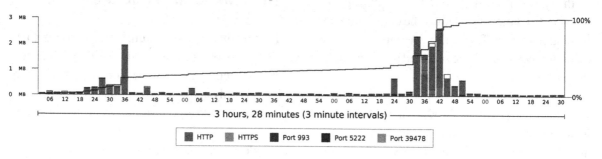

Figure 6. Traffic pattern of the non-botnet3 capture

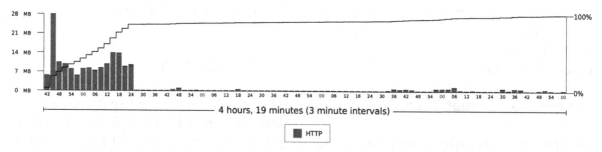

IP address in decimal format and destination port. Each one of these lines containing the three features is called an instance. In this phase we also assign to each instance the labels 'botnet' or 'non-botnet' based on our knowledge of the traffic.

In the third phase, we use the tcptrace-reader. py tool to perform the time window aggregation of instances. The data on each time window is aggregated into a vector. All the vectors are outputted in ARFF (Attribute-Relation File Format) format. The third phase also generates a text file with the relationship between instances and vectors for future back reference. Later on, when our algorithm assigns a certain vector in the ARFF file to a cluster, we need to know which IP addresses were included on it.

The fourth phase clusters the vectors in the ARFF file using the EM algorithm in the WEKA toolset. After the clustering, WEKA outputs a new ARFF file that includes the clusters assignments to each vector.

In the fifth phase we compute the percentage of botnet and non-botnet instances in each cluster. This is done using our own tool called *analysis. sh*. For each cluster in the complete ARFF file, this tool retrieves every vector on it and for each vector it retrieves every instance on it with its label. We can then compute how many botnets and non-botnets instances were assigned to each cluster.

Validation

On each phase of our work a special validation was conducted to prove the practical soundness of our method. First, all the virtual machines were clean because we installed the operating systems from scratch, we scanned it with antivirus products and we analyzed its traffic both with the Snort NIDS (Network Intrusion Detection System) (Roesch, 1999) and by hand. Second, the binaries were verified as malware using the VirusTotal (Hispasec, 2010) service and the EUREKA! automated Malware Binary Analysis Service (Yegneswaran, Saidi, Porras, Sharif, Mark & President, 2008). Finally, a manual traffic analysis was done to verify that there was malware activity on captures Botnet1, Botnet2 and Botnet3.

The validation in the third step was conducted by checking the values inside a time window, e.g., a one-hour capture must have almost 3,600 one-second windows. Time windows with a high amount of flows were verified manually.

The clustering step was verified with the labeled data. Trustworthy botnet and non-botnet experiments were performed, building an accurate cluster compare base. Once available, this information allowed interpretation of the resulting clusters and experiments improvement. The labeling was performed by manually analyzing every flow using Wireshark (Wireshark, 2010).

Finally, an experimental validation was conducted on the hypothesis about the bot behavior detection methodology. Our hypothesis, based on the time window and network load concept proved in (Gu, 2008), states that bots can be detected analyzing the correlation of the time window *timestamp*, the amount of unique source IP addresses within the time window, the amount of unique destination IP addresses within the time window and the amount of unique destination ports within the time window. For example, finding 1 *sips*, 20 *dips* and 1 *dports* within a one second time frame might mean that we have detected a bot looking for vulnerabilities. This last validation step generated the results on next section.

EXPERIMENTS AND RESULTS

Several experiments were conducted to verify our detection method. To obtain a proper verification, the experiments should be carried out using the most real dataset available. A real dataset has normal traffic, unknown traffic and botnet traffic. The six captures in our dataset, as previously described, have this type of traffic, but not in one single capture. Therefore, we decided to merge the captures and obtain a better dataset.

The criteria to select which pair of captures should be merged had two steps. In the first step we selected the captures based on how much they represent its own class. Captures with more non-botnet traffic were preferred and botnets with more traffic rates were preferred. In the second step we merge both captures by superimposing the traffic and not by concatenation. We assumed that superimposed traffic is more difficult to differentiate and therefore more real. When non-botnet and botnet traffic is not superimposed but only concatenated, the separation of both classes may be straight forward. Consequently, the traffic of the two selected captures was completely merged by inserting the shorter traffic into the larger traffic. This was done by concatenating the tcptrace text files of both captures and modifying the start times. This approach proved easier than modifying and mixing the pcap files directly.

Table 2. Results for the first experiment; a merge of non-botnet1 and botnet2 captures

Cluster Number	Botnet Flows	Non-Botnet Flows	% Botnet	% Non-Botnet
0	2,128	0	100%	0%
1	7,129	0	100%	0%
2	5,633	0	100%	0%
3	0	7,971	0%	100%
4	480	0	100%	0%
5	240	0	100%	0%
6	3,322	0	100%	0%
7	2,192	0	100%	0%
8	0	37,177	0%	100%

Fourth experiments were designed and conducted to verify our method and each of them uses a different merged pair of captures. Next Subsections describe each of them, and the last Subsection discusses the results.

First Experiment

One of the most common phases in every network attack is the port scanning activity, which generates high traffic rates. Our first experiment aims at comparing the traffic from a non-botnet port scanning with the traffic of a botnet. For this experiment we merged the Non-botnet1 capture, consisting in an nmap port scan, with the Botnet2 capture, consisting in ten bots in a network.

The results of our algorithm on this merged capture are shown in Table 2, where it can be seen that the higher traffic rate of the port scan results in a very clear separation. This experiment suggests that botnet traffic and network scans have different network behaviors.

Second Experiment

On the second experiment we worked with the merged traffic of the Rbot malware in Botnet3 capture and the non-infected computer of Non-botnet3 capture. Results are shown in Table 3. For this particular merge, we assumed that a non-infected computer behaves almost identically during fourteen days of office work, so we copied the original four-hours of the non-infected capture twenty times. Each copy starts in a different day at the same hour. We finally obtained 19,443 non-botnet flows from September 13th to October 2th and 34,118 botnets flows from September 14th to September 15th, resulting in a more balanced experiment. This experiment differentiates between 19 days of low rate non-botnet traffic and ten hours of a high rate bot burst in the middle of it.

Third Experiment

On the third experiment we merged three hours of non-botnet traffic from the computer in Non-botnet2 capture, with ten hours of the IRC-based bot traffic in Botnet3 capture. This resulted in a more unbalanced dataset. The non-botnet capture was modified to start on September 15th, in the middle of botnet traffic. The results are shown in Table 4.

Fourth Experiment

On the fourth experiment we merged the traffic of the infected computer in the Botnet3 capture with the traffic of a network of non-infected computers from the Non-botnet3 capture. The five hour non-botnet capture was modified to start on September

Table 3. Results for the second experiment; a merge of non-botnet3 and botnet3 captures

Cluster Number	Botnet Flows	Non-Botnet Flows	Botnet %	Non-Botnet %
0	14,433	24	99.83%	0.16%
1	1,517	18,721	7.49%	92.50%
2	3,539	14	99.60%	0.39%
3	14,629	684	95.53%	4.46%

Table 4. Results for the third experiment; a merge of non-botnet2 and botnet3 captures

Cluster Number	Botnet Flows	Non-Botnet Flows	Botnet %	Non-Botnet %
0	2,147	1,358	61.25%	38.74%
1	3,539	12	99.66%	0.33%
2	14,469	81	99.44%	0.55%
3	13,963	66	99.52%	0.47%

Table 5. Results for the fourth experiment; a merge of non-botnet3 and botnet3 captures

Cluster Number	Botnet Flows	Non-Botnet Flows	Botnet %	Non-Botnet %
0	2,147	916	70.09%	29.90%
1	13,918	22	99.84%	0.15%
2	3,539	14	99.60%	0.39%
3	14,469	25	99.82%	0.17%
4	45	0	100%	0%

15th, in the middle of the ten-hour botnet traffic. The non-botnet traffic was composed of more than 40 office computers with a low traffic rate, resulting in a more realistic setup. The results are shown in Table 5.

DISCUSSION ABOUT THE EXPERIMENTS

Our detection method is designed to differentiate bot traffic from non-botnet traffic. However, the non-botnet traffic may include normal traffic as well as manual or automatic attacks. The four experiments seem to show that it may be possible to make this differentiation.

From the experiments we can conclude that automatic port scans tend to have high traffic rates, bots tend to have medium traffic rates (Yen & Lee, 2009) and our normal traffic tends to have low traffic rates. The normal rates depend on the traffic captured, but our experiments confirmed this relationship.

Apart from the raw numbers from the clustering, it is important to analyze the balance of the dataset (Rossow et. al., 2012). If we have a balanced

Table 6. Evaluation of the errors by IP address

Experiment Number	Error Type	IP Address	Actually Is	# Detected as Non-Botnet	# Detected as Botnet	Error %
2	FP	10.1.1.1	Non-botnet	10,570	180	1.67%
2	FP	192.168.2.79	Non-botnet	18,697	542	2.81%
3	FP	10.1.1.1	Non-botnet	466	1	0.21%
3	FP	192.168.2.71	Non-botnet	5	1	16.66%
3	FP	192.168.2.74	Non-botnet	783	89	10.20%
3	FP	192.168.2.76	Non-botnet	235	31	11.65%
4	FP	192.168.2.79	Non-botnet	910	60	6.18%
2	FN	192.168.3.104	Botnet	1,103	15,978	6.45%
3	FN	192.168.3.104	Botnet	1,563	15,518	9.15%
4	FN	192.168.3.104	Botnet	1,563	15,518	9.15%

data set (the number of samples in botnet and non-botnet classes is almost equal), the classifier error rates could be correctly interpreted, because each instance belongs to one class with 50% probability. If we have an unbalanced data set (the number of samples in different classes varies greatly) the error rate of a classical statistics classifier may not represent the true effectiveness of the classifier. In real environments the traffic is usually unbalanced, and that is why we performed these experiments to evaluate this situation. Some studies even had to modify the EM clustering method to deal with unbalanced data sets (Wu, 1995).

Error Metrics

With the results from the experiments there is enough information to compute the error metrics. The error metrics can be defined in different ways, and each way may lead to different interpretations. Therefore, we first define how we are going to compute the errors.

The definition we used is the classic flow-by-flow comparison. From this point of view, a False Positives is accounted each time a non-botnet flow is detected as botnet, a False Negatives is accounted each time a botnet flow is detected as non-botnet, a True Positive is accounted each time a botnet flow is detected as botnet and a True Negative is accounted each time a non-botnet flow is detected as non-botnet. This is the most simple and classic point of view.

We first consider the analysis of the false positives and false negatives regarding each IP address in all the experiments. Table 6 summarizes this information. The values for each IP address were computed against the total number of times its flows where detected as botnet or non-botnet. The first experiment is not included in this table because its goal was to prove that the botnet traffic and the port scannings could be successfully separated.

Starting with the second experiment, Table 6 shows that the False Positives are reasonably low. There is only one False Negative, where one botnet IP address is detected as non-botnet 6.45% of the time. A detailed manual analysis showed that the non-botnet label was assigned to this botnet when a single flow per second was generated. This is an example of a botnet behaving like a non-botnet computer. From a practical point of view, the IP address generating the False Negatives was the network web proxy, and therefore it may be white-listed by the administrator to obtain better error rates. We did not white-list any IP address.

The third experiment has, in comparison, a higher False Positive error rate. An analysis of these errors showed that both the botnet and non-botnet computers were clustered together because they generated several connections at the same time. This situation is not uncommon and we are already analyzing it for our future work.

The fourth experiment shows an increment in False Negatives and False Positive values. This may be caused by the few amounts of instances in the dataset. The worst case is a 6.18% False Positive.

From the analysis of Table 6 we conclude that the most challenging problem is to classify a non-botnet computer traffic that behaves like a botnet as non-botnet.

From the data presented in Table 6, a confusion matrix was created to help understand the meanings of these values. A confusion matrix is an analysis tool commonly used in supervised learning, where the rows represents how each instance was detected and the columns represent what each instance actually was. From this matrix we can compute the False Positive Rate (FPR), the False Negative Rate (FNR), the True Positive Rate (TPR) and the True Negative Rate (TNR). The confusion matrix is shown in Table 7.

Table 7. Confusion flow matrix

Detected		Actual		
		Botnet	**Non-Botnet**	
Botnet		TP=98,125	FP=904	0.91%
Non-Botnet		FN=4,229	TN=21,033	16.74%
		4.13%	4.12%	

The FPR is the proportion of non-botnet flows that were detected as botnet (904 in Table 7) among all the tests performed. Our algorithm achieved a FPR = 0.7% for all the experiments. The FNR is the proportion of botnet flows that were detected as non-botnet (4,229 in Table 7) among all the tests performed. Our algorithm achieved a FNR = 3.4% for all our experiments. The TPR is the proportion of botnet flows that were detected as botnet (98,125 in Table 7) among all the tests performed. Our algorithm achieved a TPR=99.08%. The TNR is the proportion of non-botnets that were detected as non-botnets (21,033 in Table 7) amount all the tests performed. Our algorithm achieved a TNR=83.25%.

Figure 7. Error analysis

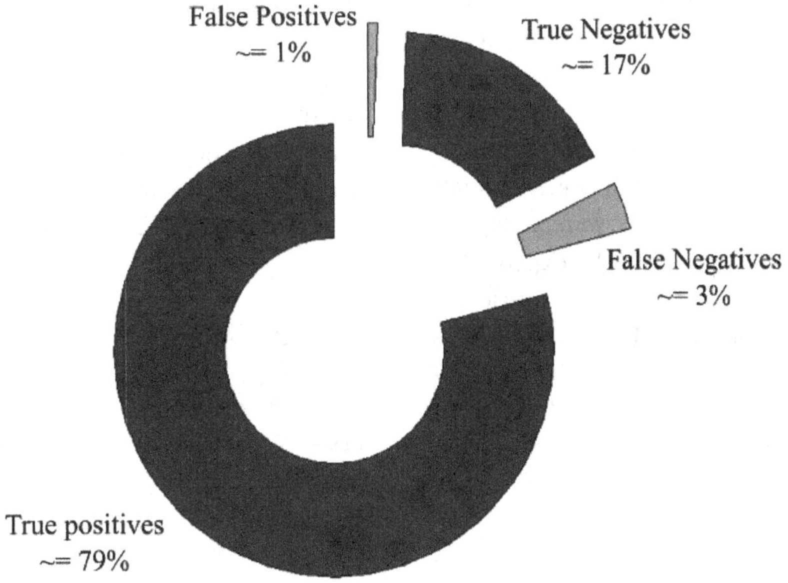

False Positives ~= 1%

True Negatives ~= 17%

False Negatives ~= 3%

True positives ~= 79%

Other type of conclusions can be extracted from Table 7. For example, the proportion of non-botnet flows that were detected as botnet among the presumed botnets is 0.91% . That is, from the total amount of infection alerts that the network administrator receives from our algorithm, only 0.91% were not infected.

Another conclusion is that the proportion of botnet flows that were detected as non-botnet among the presumed non-botnet computers is 16.74%. This is the proportion of infected flows that the administrator will not see. Note that we are analyzing flows and not IP addresses.

According to Table 7, a real life usage of this algorithm in a network may result in 4.13% of the bots not being detected and 4.12% of our internal users being bothered by the administrator trying to clean their non-infected computers.

A graphical analysis of the confusion matrix can be seen in Figure 7. It shows the approximate percentages and the relationship between errors and true detections.

CONCLUSION

In this paper we presented a new approach for detecting bots in the network. We focused on individual bots and not botnets because of the unique characteristics that can be used to detect the bots traffic. Our method clusters the behaviors of the bots using the Expectation-Maximization algorithm.

To validate and study the behaviors of the bots we designed several test-beds and created a dataset of six captures. These captures were generated by real botnets and were labeled by experts. We captured bot and botnet traffic, normal traffic and an automatic port scan attack. Our algorithm was able to differentiate them by using the relationship between the unique source IP addresses, the unique destination IP addresses and the unique destination ports within a time windows.

We conclude that despite our limitations, the results achieved are encouraging, showing that bots can be differentiated from non-botnet traffic with a FPR of 0.7% and a FNR of 3.4%.

FUTURE RESEARCH DIRECTIONS

Several improvements are planned for future research. First, we are going to include UDP (User Datagram Protocol) traffic in our captures, because plenty of botnet traffic is performed using this protocol. Most notably, DNS queries that take up to 40% of the total traffic. Another improvement will be to analyze the total amount of transferred bytes within a single flow, in order to capture long lived botnet connections with their C&C server. In the clustering area, we are currently working on analyzing cluster assignments to synthesize classification rules that later allows us to automatically classify clusters. In the network capture area, several one-week long non-botnet and botnet captures are planned. Finally an important improvement will be done in the dataset production and processing, creating a methodology for flow capture, publication, labeling, comparison and verification.

ACKNOWLEDGMENT

We thank the editor and anonymous reviewers for their helpful comments and suggestions to improve the quality of this paper. This work was supported by the project of the Czech Ministry of Interior No. VG20122014079.

REFERENCES

Baeza-Yates, R. A., & Riberiro-Neto, B. A. (1999). *Modern information retrieval*. Boston, MA: ACM-Press / Addison-Wesley Longman Publishing Co., Inc.

Chen, A., Li, L., & Cao, J. (2009). Tracking cardinality distributions in network traffic. In *Proceedings of IEEE 28th Conference on Computer Comunications (INFOCOM 2009)* (pp. 819-827). IEEE. doi:10.1109/INFCOM.2009.5061991

Chen, Z., Chen, C., & Wang, Q. (2009). Delay-tolerant botnets. In *Proceedings of 18th International Conference on Computer Communications and Networks (ICCCN 2009)* (pp. 1-6). Academic Press.

Corrons, L. (PandaLabs). (2010). *Mariposa botnet*. Retrieved August 17, 2010, from http://pandalabs. pandasecurity.com/mariposa-botnet/

Dempster, A. P., Laird, N. M., & Rubin, D. B. (1977). Maximum likelihood from incomplete data via the em algorithm. *Journal of the Royal Statistical Society. Series B. Methodological, 39*(1), 1–38.

García, S. (2013). *Malware capture facility project*. Retrieved April 13, 2014, from https://mcfp. felk.cvut.cz/

Garcia, S., Zunino, A., & Campo, M. (2013). Survey on network-based botnet detection methods. In *Security and communication networks*. John Wiley & Sons, Ltd.

Gu, G. (2008). *Correlation-based botnet detection in enterprise networks.* (Doctoral dissertation). Georgia Institute of Technology.

Gu, G., Perdisci, R., Zhang, J., & Lee, W. (2008). BotMiner: Clustering analysis of network traffic for protocol-and structure-independent botnet detection. In *Proceedings of the 17th Conference on Security Symposium* (pp. 139-154). Berkeley, CA: USENIX Association.

Gu, G., Zhang, J., & Lee, W. (2008). BotSniffer: Detecting botnet command and control channels in network traffic. In *Proceedings of the 15th Network and Distributed System Security Symposium (NDSS)*. San Diego, CA: Academic Press.

Ha, D., Yan, G., Eidenbenz, S., & Ngo, H. (2009). On the effectiveness of structural detection and defense against p2p-based botnets. In *Proceedings of IEEE/IFIP International Conference on Dependable Systems & Networks (DSN '09)* (pp. 297-306). IEEE.

Hall, M., Frank, E., Holmes, G., Pfahringer, B., Reutemann, P., & Witten, H. I. (2009). The weka data mining software: An update. *ACM SIGKDD Explorations Newsletter, 11*(1), 10–18. doi:10.1145/1656274.1656278

Kang, J., Zhang, J.-Y., Li, Q., & Li, Z. (2009). Detecting new p2p botnet with multi-chart cusum. In *Proceedings of the International Conference on Networks Security, Wireless Communications and Trusted Computing (NSWCTC '09)* (vol. 1, pp. 688-691). Academic Press.

LBNL. (2010). *TCPDUMP & LiBPCAP*. Retrieved March 30, 2010, from http://www.tcpdump.org/

Li, Z., Goyal, A., & Chen, Y. (2007). Honeynet-based botnet scan traffic analysis. Botnet Detection, 36, 25–44.

Liu, L., Chen, S., Yan, G., & Zhang, Z. (2008). Execution-based bot-like malware detection. [LNCS]. *Proceedings of Information Security, 5222,* 97–113.

Lu, W., Tavallaee, M., Rammidi, G., & Ghorbani, A. A. (2009). Botcop: An online botnet traffic classifier. In *Proceedings of 7th Annual Communication Networks and Services Research Conference (CNSR '09)* (pp. 70-77). Academic Press. doi:10.1109/CNSR.2009.21

Lyon, G. F. (2009). *NMAP network scanning: The official NMAP project guide to network discovery and security scanning*. Insecure.

Masud, M. M., Gao, J., Khan, L., Han, J., & Thuraisingham, B. (2008). A practical approach to classify evolving data streams: Training with limited amount of labeled data. In *Proceedings of 8th IEEE International Conference on Data Mining (ICDM '08)* (pp. 929–934). IEEE. doi:10.1109/ICDM.2008.152

Mazzariello, C. (2008). Irc traffic analysis for botnet detection. In *Proceedings of 4th International Conference on Information Assurance and Security (ISIAS '08)* (pp. 318-323). ISIAS.

McGregor, A., Hall, M., Lorier, P., & Brunskill, J. (2004). Flow clustering using machine learning techniques. In *Proceedings of Passive and Active Network Measurement (LNCS)* (pp. 205–214). Berlin, Germany: Springer-Verlag.

Mielke, C., & Chen, H. (2008). Botnets, and the cybercriminal underground. In *Proceedings of IEEE International Conference on Intelligence and Security Informatics (ISI 2008)* (pp. 206-211). IEEE. doi:10.1109/ISI.2008.4565058

Nazario, J. (2006). *Botnet tracking: Tools, techniques, and lessons learned (Tech. Rep.)*. Chemsford, MA: Arbor Networks.

Onut, I. V., & Ghorbani, A. A. (2007). A feature classification scheme for network intrusion detection. *International Journal of Network Security, 5,* 1–15.

Rieck, K., Trinius, P., Willems, C., & Holz, T. (2011). Automatic analysis of malware behavior using machine learning. *Journal of Computer Security, 19*(4), 639–668.

Roesch, M. (1999). Snort-lightweight intrusion detection for networks. In *Proceedings of 13th Systems Administration Conference (LISA '99)* (pp. 229-238). Academic Press.

Rossow, C., Dietrich, C. J., Grier, C., Kreibich, C., Paxson, V., Pohlmann, N., & Steen, M. (2012). Prudent practices for designing malware experiments: Status quo and outlook. In *Proceedings of 2012 IEEE Symposium on Security and Privacy* (pp. 65-79). IEEE. doi:10.1109/SP.2012.14

Saad, S., Traore, I., Ghorbani, A., Sayed, B., Zhao, D., Lu, W., & Hakimian, P. (2011). Detecting P2P botnets through network behavior analysis and machine learning. In *Proceedings of Privacy, Security and Trust (PST), 2011 Ninth Annual International Conference on* (pp. 174 – 180). Montreal, Canada: IEEE.

Shahrestani, A., Ramadass, S., & Feily, M. (2009). A survey of botnet and botnet detection. In *Proceedings of 3rd International Conference on Emerging Security Information, Systems and Technologies (SECURWARE '09)* (pp. 268-273). Academic Press.

Shawn, O. (2010). *Tcptrace*. Retrieved March 30, 2010, from http://www.tcptrace.org/

Sistemas, H. (2010). *Virus total*. Retrieved March 30, 2010, from http://www.virustotal.com/es/

SSAC. (2008). *SSAC advisory on fast flux hosting and DNS* (Tech. Rep.). ICANN Security and Stability Advisory Committee. Retrieved on March 10, 2008, from http://www.icann.org/en/committees/security/ssac-documents.htm

Stinson, E., & Mitchell, J. (2008). Towards systematic evaluation of the evadability of bot/botnet detection methods. In *Proceedings of the 2nd Conference on USENIX Workshop on Offensive Technologies (WOOT '08)* (pp. 1-9). Berkeley, CA: USENIX Association.

Stone-Gross, B., Cova, M., Cavallaro, L., Gilbert, B., Szydlowski, M., Kemmerer, R., & Vigna, G. (2009). Your botnet is my botnet: Analysis of a botnet takeover. In *Proceedings of the 16th ACM Conference on Computer and Communications Security (CCS '09)* (pp. 635-647). New York, NY: ACM. doi:10.1145/1653662.1653738

Strayer, W., Lapsely, D., Walsh, R., & Livadas, C. (2007). Botnet detection based on network behavior. *Advances in Information Security, 36,* 1–24.

Villamarin-Salomon, R., & Brustoloni, J. (2008). Identifying botnets using anomaly detection techniques applied to dns traffic. In *Proceedings of the 5th IEEE Consumer Communications and Networking Conference (CCNC 2008)* (pp. 476–481). IEEE. doi:10.1109/ccnc08.2007.112

Watson, J. (2008). Virtualbox: Bits and bytes masquerading as machines. *Linux Journal, 2008,* 166.

Wilson, C. (2007). *Botnets, cybercrime, and cyberterrorism: Vulnerabilities and policy issues for congress (Tech. Rep.)*. Washington, DC: Library of Congress Congressional Research Service.

Wireshark. (2010). *Wireshark: The world's foremost network protocol analyzer*. Retrieved March 30, 2010, from http://www.wireshark.org/

Wu, J. M. (1995). *Maximum likelihood estimation in the random coefficient regression model via the EM algorithm*. (PhD Thesis). Texas Tech University, Lubbock, TX.

Yegneswaran, V., Saidi, H., Porras, P., Sharif, M., Mark, W., & President, V. (2008). Eureka: A framework for enabling static analysis on malware (Tech. Rep.). Atlanta, GA: Georgia Institute of Technology.

Yen, S.-J., & Lee, Y. (2009). Cluster-based under-sampling approaches for imbalanced data distributions. *Expert Systems with Applications*, *36*(3), 5718–5727. doi:10.1016/j.eswa.2008.06.108

Zhang, L. (2009). *A sublexical unit based hash model approach for SPAM detection*. (PhD Thesis). University of Texas, San Antonio, TX.

Zhao, D., Traore, I., Sayed, B., Lu, W., Saad, S., Ghorbani, A., & Garant, D. (2013). Botnet detection based on traffic behavior analysis and flow intervals. *Computers & Security*, *39*, 2–16. doi:10.1016/j.cose.2013.04.007

Zhu, Z., Lu, G., Chen, Y., Fu, Z., Roberts, P., & Han, K. (2008). Botnet research survey. In Proceedings of 32nd Annual IEEE International Computer Software and Applications (COMPSAC'08) (pp. 967-972). IEEE.

ADDITIONAL READING

Akiyama, M., Kawamoto, T., Shimamura, M., Yokoyama, T., Kadobayashi, Y., & Yamaguchi, S. (2007). A proposal of metrics for botnet detection based on its cooperative behavior. In International Symposium on Applications and the Internet Workshops. SAINT Workshops, (pp. 82-82). IEEE Computer Society.

Bächer, P., Holz, T., Kötter, M., & Wicherski, G. (2008). *Know your enemy: Tracking botnets*. Retrieved March 17, 2010, from http://www.honeynet.org/papers/bots/

Barford, P., & Blodgett, M. (2007). Toward botnet mesocosms. In Proceedings of the first Workshop on *Hot Topics in Understanding Botnets, HotBots'07*, (pp. 6-6), Berkeley, CA, USA. USENIX Association.

Barford, P., & Yegneswaran, V. (2006). An Inside Look at Botnets. In *Special Workshop on Malware Detection*, Advances in Information Security, Springer Verlag.

Bayer, U., Comparetti, P., Hlauschek, C., Kruegel, C., & Kirda, E. (2009). Scalable, Behavior-Based Malware Clustering. In *Network and Distributed System Security Symposium* (NDSS).

Binkley, J. R., & Singh, S. (2006). An algorithm for anomaly-based botnet detection. In Proceedings of the 2nd conference on *Steps to Reducing Unwanted Traffic on the Internet*, SRUTI'06, (pp. 7-7), Berkeley, CA, USA. USENIX Association.

Caglayan, A., Toothaker, M., Drapaeau, D., Burke, D., & Eaton, G. (2009). Behavioral analysis of fast flux service networks. In Proceedings of the 5th Annual Workshop on *Cyber Security and Information Intelligence Research, CSIIRW '09*, (pp. 1-4), New York, NY: ACM.

Castle, I., & Buckley, E. (2008). The automatic discovery, identification and measurement of botnets. In Second International Conference on *Emerging Security Information, Systems and Technologies*, SECURWARE '08. (pp. 127-132).

Casullo, G. A., Fink, S. A., Jaime, J. M., & Tami, L. R. (2009). Webbotnets, la amenaza fantasma. In Proceedings of the *38 JAIIO, WSegI '09*, Buenos Aires, Argentina.

Chang, S., Zhang, L., Guan, Y., & Daniels, T. (2009). A framework for p2p botnets. In *WRI International Conference* on Communications and Mobile Computing. *CMC '09*, volume 3, (pp. 594-599).

Christodorescu, M., Jha, S., & Kruegel, C. (2008). Mining specifications of malicious behavior. In Proceedings of the *1st conference on India software engineering conference, ISEC '08,* (pp. 5-14), Hyderabad, India. ACM Press New York, NY: ACM.

Christodorescu, M., & Rubin, S. (2007). Can cooperative intrusion detectors challenge the base-rate fallacy? In US, S., (Ed), Malware Detection, Advances in Information Security, (pp. 193-209). Springer US.

Cooke, E., Jahanian, F., & McPherson, D. (2005). The Zombie Roundup: Understanding, Detecting, and Disrupting Botnets. In *Proceedings of the Steps to Reducing Unwanted Traffic on the Internet Workshop, SRUTI'05*, (pp. 6-6). USENIX Association.

Dagon, D., Gu, G., Zou, C., Grizzard, J., Dwivedi, S., Lee, W., & Lipton, R. (2007). A Taxonomy of Botnet Structures. In *IEEE Computer Security Applications Conference. ACSAC 2007.*

Dittrich, D. & Dietrich, S. (2007). Command and control structures in malware: From Handler/Agent to P2P. *USENIX*, 32(6).

Duan, Z. (2006). Behavioral characteristics of spammers and their network reachability properties. In Proceedings of *IEEE International Conference on Communications, ICC 2007, (pp 164-171)*.

Erbacher, R., Cutler, A., Banerjee, P., & Marshall, J. (2008). A Multi-Layered Approach to Botnet Detection. In Proceedings of the *2008 World congress in computer science, computer engineering and applied computing, The 2008 International Conference on Security and Management.*

Erman, J., Arlitt, M., & Mahanti, A. (2006). Traffic classification using clustering algorithms. In *Proceedings of the 2006 SIGCOMM workshop on Mining network data, MineNet '06* (pp. 281–286). New York, NY, USA: ACM.

Gao, Y., Zhao, Y., Schweller, R., Venkataraman, S., Chen, Y., Song, D., & Kao, M.-Y. (2007). Detecting stealthy spreaders using online outdegree histograms. In Proceedings of the *Fifteenth IEEE International Workshop on Quality of Service,* (pp. 145-153).

Gu, G., Sharif, M., Qin, X., Dagon, D., Lee, W., & Riley, G. (2004). Worm Detection, Early Warning and Response Based on Local Victim Information. In *Proceedings of the Annual Computer Security Applications Conference,* (pp. 136-145).

Husna, H., Phithakkitnukoon, S., Palla, S., & Dantu, R. (2008). Behavior analysis of spam botnets. In Proceedings of the *3rd International Conference on Communication Systems Software and Middleware and Workshops, 2008. COMSWARE 2008.* (pp. 246-253).

Jacob, G., Debar, H., & Filiol, E. (2008). Behavioral detection of malware: From a survey towards an established taxonomy. *Journal in Computer Virology*, 4(3), 251–266.

Kiayias, A., Neumann, J., Walluck, D., & Mc-Cusker, O. (2009). A combined fusion and data mining framework for the detection of botnets. In Proceedings of the *Conference For Homeland Security*. CATCH '09. Cybersecurity Applications & Technology, (pp. 273-284).

Kugisaki, Y., Kasahara, Y., Hori, Y., & Sakurai, K. (2007). Bot detection based on traffic analysis. In Proceeding of the *2007 International Conference on Intelligent Pervasive Computing. IPC.* (pp. 303-306).

Lim, S., & Jones, A. (2008). Network anomaly detection system: The state of art of network behaviour analysis. In Proceedings of the *International Conference on Convergence and Hybrid Information Technology. ICHIT '08* (pp. 459-465).

Lu, W., & Ghorbani, A. (2008). Detecting IRC Botnets on Network Application Communities. In *Fifth Annual Research Exposition* (pp. 57–57). Fredericton, New Brunswick, Canada: Faculty of Computer Science UNB.

Passerini, E., Paleari, R., Martignoni, L., & Bruschi, D. (2008). Fluxor: Detecting and monitoring fast-flux service networks. In Detection of Intrusions and Malware, and Vulnerability Assessment, Lecture Notes in Computer Science, (pp. 186-206). Springer Berlin / Heidelberg.

Strayer, W. T., Walsh, R., Livadas, C., & Lapsley, D. (2006). Detecting botnets with tight command and control. In Proceedings of *the 31st IEEE Conference on Local Computer Networks*, LCN, (pp. 15-16).

Sung, A., & Mukkamala, S. (2003). Identifying important features for intrusion detection using support vector machines and neural networks. In Proceedings of the *Symposium on Applications and the Internet, 2003.* (pp. 209-216).

Wang, B., Li, Z., Tu, H., Hu, Z., & Hu, J. (2009). Actively measuring bots in peer-to-peer networks. In Proceedings of the *International Conference on Networks Security, Wireless Communications and Trusted Computing. NSWCTC '09*, volume 1, (pp. 603-607).

Wang, P., Wu, L., Aslam, B., & Zou, C. (2009). A systematic study on peer-to-peer botnets. In Proceedings of *18th International Conference on Computer Communications and Networks. ICCCN 2009.* (pp. 1-8).

Yu, J., Li, Z., Hu, J., Liu, F., & Zhou, L. (2009a). Structural robustness in peer to peer botnets. In Proceedings of the *International Conference on Networks Security, Wireless Communications and Trusted Computing, NSWCTC '09*, volume 2, (pp. 860-863).

Yu, J., Li, Z., Hu, J., Liu, F., & Zhou, L. (2009b). Using simulation to characterize topology of peer to peer botnets. In Proceedings of the *International Conference on Computer Modeling and Simulation, ICCMS '09.*, (pp. 78-83).

KEY TERMS AND DEFINITIONS

Bot: Infected computer, member of a botnet.

Botnet: Coordinated group of infected computers externally managed by an attacker.

Command and Control (C&C) Server: These are the servers used by the botmaster to communicate and remotely control bots. Bots report back to these servers periodically.

Dips: Amount of unique destination IP address seen in a time frame.

Dports: Amount of unique destination ports seen in a time frame.

Network Behavior: Group of periodic patterns extracted from different network characteristics.

Sips: Amount of unique source IP address seen in a time frame.

Time Frame: Period of time a network administrator is willing to wait to have the information about a computer.

Time Window: Period of time in which TCP flows characteristics are aggregated. This information is stored in a four dimensional vector.

ENDNOTES

[1]   http://www.circlemud.org/jelson/software/tcpflow/.

[2]   http://www.tcptrace.org/.

Compilation of References

1999/93/EC – Directive. (1999). *1999/93/EC of the European Parliament and of the Council of 13, December 1999 on a Community Framework for Electronic Signature – 1999*. Author.

4. Chan. (2012). *Rules*. Retrieved from http://www.4chan.org/rules

Abu-Nimeh, S., & Mead, N. R. (2009). Privacy risk assessment in privacy requirements engineering. In *Proceedings of Requirements Engineering and Law (RELAW)2009 Second International Workshop* (pp. 17-18). Hoboken, NJ: IEEE.

Abu-Nimeh, S., & Mead, N. R. (2010). *Combining privacy and security risk assessment in security quality requirements engineering*. Paper presented at the 2010 Association for the Advancement of Artificial Intelligence (AAAI) Spring Symposium Series, Intelligent Information Privacy Management, Palo Alto, CA.

Abu-Nimeh, S., Miyazaki, S., & Mead, N. R. (2009). Integrating privacy requirements into security requirements engineering.In*Proceedings of the Twenty-First International Conference on Software Engineering and Knowledge Engineering* (pp. 542–547). Skokie: Knowledge Systems Institute Graduate School.

Access: One. (2014). Retrieved online on 4/12/2014 from http://pirean.com/access-one/

Acquisti, A. (2002). Protecting privacy with economic: Economic incentives for preventive technologies in ubiquitous computing environment. In *Proceedings of Workshop on Socially-Informed Design of Privacy-Enhancing Solutions in Ubiquitous Computing*. Ubicomp.

Active Authentication. (n.d.). Retrieved March 12, 2014, from http://www.darpa.mil/Our_Work/I2O/Programs/Active_Authentication.aspx

Adams, A., & Sasse, M. (1999). Users are not the enemy. *Communications of the ACM, 42*(12), 41–46. doi:10.1145/322796.322806

Adams, A., & Sasse, M. A. (2001). Privacy in multimedia communications: Protecting users, not just data. In *People and computers XV-Interaction without frontiers* (pp. 49–64). London: Springer. doi:10.1007/978-1-4471-0353-0_4

Aegis Identity Software. (2014). Retrieved online on 4/12/2014 from http://aegisidentity.com/identity-software/products/tridenthe/

Agaku, I. T., Adisa, A. O., Ayo-Yusuf, O. A., & Connolly, G. N. (2014). Concern about security and privacy, and perceived control over collection and use of health information are related to withholding of health information from health care providers. *US National Library of Medicine, National Institutes of Health*. Retrieved from http://www.ncbi.nlm.nih.gov/pubmed/23975624/

Aggarwal, C. C., & Yu, P. S. (2001). Outlier detection in high dimensional data. In *Proceedings ofSIGMOD Conference* (pp. 37-46). Santa Barbara, CA: ACM.

Aggarwal, C. C., Han, J., Wang, J., & Yu, P. S. (2004). A framework for projected clustering of high dimensional data streams. In *Proceedings ofInternational Conference on Very Large Data Base (VLDB)* (pp. 852-863). Toronto, Canada: Academic Press. doi:10.1016/B978-012088469-8/50075-9

Aggarwal, C. C., & Yu, P. S. (2005). An effective and efficient algorithm for high-dimensional outlier detection. *The VLDB Journal, 14*(2), 211–221. doi:10.1007/s00778-004-0125-5

Akao, Y. (1990). *Quality function deployment, integrating customer requirements into product design.* Cambridge, MA: Productivity Press.

Akujuobi, C. M., & Ampah, N. K. (2007). Enterprise network intrusion detection and prevention system. In *Proceedings of Society of Photographic Instrumentation Engineers Defense and Security Symposium* (Vol. 6538, pp. 1-12). Academic Press.

Akujuobi, C. M., Ampah, N. K., & Sadiku, M. N. O. (2007). An intrusion detection technique based on change in Hurst parameter with application to network security. *International Journal of Computer Science and Network Security, 5*(7), 55–64.

Albari, M. Z. (2005). *A taxonomy of runtime software monitoring systems.* Retrieved August 9, 2008, from http://www.informatik.uni-kiel.de/~wg/Lehre/Seminar-SS05/Mohamed_Ziad_Abari/vortrag-handout4.pdf

Alchian, A., & Allen, W. R. (1983). *Exchange and production, competition, coordination & control* (3rd ed.; p. 184). Belmont, CA: Wadsworth Publishing Co.

Alder, G. S., Noel, T. W., & Ambrose, M. L. (2006). Clarifying the effects of internet monitoring on job attitudes: The mediating role of employee trust. *Information & Management, 43*(7), 894–903. doi:10.1016/j.im.2006.08.008

Aldhizer, G. III, Juras, P., & Martin, D. (2008). Using automated identity and access management controls. *The CPA Journal, 78*(9), 66–71.

Aljarah, I., & Ludwig, S. A. (2013). MapReduce intrusion detection system based on a particle swarm optimization clustering algorithm. In *IEEE Congress on Evolutionary Computation (CEC)* (pp. 955-962). IEEE. doi:10.1109/CEC.2013.6557670

Alkhalifah, A., & D'Ambra, J. (2012). The role of identity management systems in enhancing protection of user privacy, cyber security, cyber warfare and digital forensic. In *Proceedings of 2012 International Conference.* SyberSec.

Allan, A., Perkins, E., Carpenter, P., & Wagner, R. (2008). What is identity 2.0? Key issues for identity and access management, 2008. *Gartner Research Report*, ID Number: G00157012.

Almgren, M., Jonsson, E., & Lindqvist, U. (2007). A comparison of alternative audit sources for web server attack detection. In *Proceedings of the 12th Nordic Workshop on Secure IT systems (NordSec 2007)* (pp. 101–112). Reykjavik, Iceland: Academic Press.

Almuairfi, S., Veeraraghavan, P., & Chilamkurti, N. (2011). *IPAS: Implicit password authentication system.* Paper presented at the Advanced Information Networking and Applications (WAINA), New York, NY.

Alotaibi, S. J., & Mike, W. (2012). Security, user experience, acceptability attributes for the integration of physical and virtual identity access management systems. In *Proceedings of International Conference on Information Society (i-Society 2012).* Academic Press.

Alsaleh, M., & Adams, C. (2006). Enhancing consumer privacy in the liberty alliance identity federation and web servies frameworks. In *Proceedings of the 6th International conference on Privacy Enhancing Technologies (PET'06).* Springer-Verlag. doi:10.1007/11957454_4

AMA Survey. (2001). *Workplace monitoring and surveillance* [online]. Retrieved November 8, 2014, from http://www.amanet.org/research/pdfs/ems_short2001.pdf

AMA Survey. (2003). *Email rules, policies and practices survey* [online]. Retrieved November 10, 2014, from http://www.amanet.org/research/pdfs/email_policies_practices.pdf

AMA Survey. (2005). *Electronic monitoring and surveillance survey* [online]. Retrieved November 10, 2014, from http://www.amanet.org/research/pdfs/ems_summary05.pdf

Amanullah, M. T. O., Kalam, A., & Zayegh, H. (2005). Network security vulnerabilities in SCADA and EMS. In Proceedings of Transmission and Distribution Conference and Exhibition: Asia and Pacific (pp. 1-6). Academic Press.

American Broadcasting Company (ABC). (2010a). *'Jessi Slaughter' says death threats won't stop her from posting videos on the internet.* Retrieved from: http://abcnews.go.com/GMA/Technology/jessi-slaughter-viral-tweens-violent-online-rant-spurs/story?id=11224731

American Broadcasting Company (ABC). (2010b). *Do kids need more privacy protection on social networks?* Retrieved from: http://abcnews.go.com/WN/social-networking-privacy-kids-protected-online-world-news/story?id=11831552

Ampah, N. K., & Akujuobi, C. M. (2012). Protecting enterprise networks: An intrusion detection technique based on auto-reclosing. In P. Kabiri (Ed.), *Privacy, intrusion detection and response: Technologies for protecting networks* (pp. 40–76). IGI Global. doi:10.4018/978-1-60960-836-1.ch002

Analytics, I. D. (2007). *Data breach harm analysis from ID analytics uncovers new patterns of misuse arising from breaches of identity data.* Retrieved November 12, 2009, from http://www.idanalytics.com/news_and_events/20071107.html

Anderson, D., & Murphy, C. (2012). The charter of fundamental rights. In A. Biondi, P. Eeckhout, & S. Ripley (Eds.), *EU law after Lisbon* (pp. 155–179). Oxford, UK: Oxford University Press.

Anderson, J. M., Berc, L. M., Dean, J., Ghemawat, S., Henzinger, M. R., & Leung, S. A. et al. (1997). Continuous profiling: Where have all the cycles gone? *Operating Systems Review*, *31*(5), 1–14. doi:10.1145/269005.266637

Anderson, J. P. (1980). *Computer security threat monitoring and surveillance.* Fort Washington, PA: Anderson Company.

Anderson, R. (2006). *Security engineering: A guide to building dependable distributed systems* (2nd ed.). Cambridge, UK: Wiley.

Andrews, L. W. (2004). *Passwords reveal your personality.* Retrieved March 13, 2007, from http://cms.psychology-today.com/articles/pto- 20020101-000006.html

Anjum, F., Subhadrabandhu, D., Sarkar, S., & Shetty, R. (2004). *On optimal placement of intrusion detection modules in sensor networks.* BroadNets. doi:10.1109/BROADNETS.2004.52

Anwar, M. M., Zafar, M. F., & Ahmed, Z. (2007). A proposed preventive information security system. In *Proceedings of International Conference on Electrical Engineering* (pp. 1-6). Academic Press.

Apache mod_log_config. (2010). *Apache mod_log_config module.* Retrieved November 25, 2010, from http://httpd.apache.org/docs/2.2/mod/mod_log_config.html

APWG. (2013). Anti-phishing working group. *Global Phishing Survey.* Retrieved 1st August, 2012 from http://docs.apwg.org/reports/APWG_GlobalPhishingSurvey_1H2013.pdf

Aranya, A., Wright, C. P., & Zadok, E. (2004). Tracefs: A file system to trace them all. In *Proceedings of the 3rd USENIX Conference on File and Storage Technoligies (FAST 2004)* (pp. 129–145). San Francisco, CA: USENIX Association.

Ardichivili, A., Page, V., & Wentling, T. (2003). Motivation and barriers to participation in virtual knowledge-sharing communities of practice. *Journal of Knowledge Management*, *7*(1), 64–77. doi:10.1108/13673270310463626

Ariel, T., & Miller, B. P. (1999). Fine-grained dynamic instrumentation of commodity operating system kernels. In *Proceedings of the Third Symposium on Operating Systems Design and Implementation (OSDI'99)* (pp. 117–130). New Orleans, LA: Academic Press.

Armour, F., & Miller, G. (2000). *Advanced use case modeling: Software systems.* Boston, MA: Addison-Wesley Professional.

Armstrong, A., &, J. (1996). The real value of on-line communities. *Harvard Business Review*, *74*(3), 134–141.

Arnold, T. (2000). *Internet identity theft: A tragedy for victims* (White Paper). SIIA.

Article 29 Data Protection Working Party. (2007). *Opinion 4/2007 on the concept of personal data.* Retrieved February 28, 2014, from http://www.droit-technologie.org/upload/actuality/doc/1063-1.pdf

Artzner, P., Delbaen, F., Eber, J. M., & Heath, D. (2001). Coherent measures of risk. *Mathematical Finance*, *9*(3), 203–228. doi:10.1111/1467-9965.00068

Ashford, W. (2014, March). State surveillance keeping a third of firms from the cloud. *Computer Weekly.* Retrieved from http://www.computerweekly.com/news/2240217011/State-surveillance-keeping-a-third-of-firms-from-the-cloud

Attrition.org. (2009). Retrieved from 3rd March, 2013 from Attrition.org http://attrition.org/security/dataloss.html

Australian Law Reform Commission (ALRC). (2014). *Health information privacy.* Retrieved May 1, 2014 from http://www.alrc.gov.au/publications/3-overview-current-law/health- information-privacy#_ftnref20

Authentication Techniques. (2006, January 10). Retrieved 3rd April, 2010 from www.sheshunoff.com: http://www.sheshunoff.com/ideanet/index.php?itemid=204&catid=4

Authentication. (2007, June 4). Retrieved 3rd April, 2010 from www.searchsecurity.techtarget.com

Axelsson, S. (2000). *Instrusion detection systems: A survey and taxonomy* (Technical Report 99-15). Chalmers University of Technology.

Axelsson, S., Lindqvist, U., Gustafson, U., & Jonsson, E. (1998). An approach to UNIX security logging. In *Proceedings of the 21st National Information Systems Security Conference* (pp. 62–75). Arlington, VA: Academic Press.

Baeza-Yates, R. A., & Riberiro-Neto, B. A. (1999). *Modern information retrieval.* Boston, MA: ACM-Press / Addison-Wesley Longman Publishing Co., Inc.

Baier, A. (1986). Trust and antitrust. *Ethics, 96*(2), 231–260. doi:10.1086/292745

Baker, M. G., Hartman, J. H., Kupfer, M. D., Shirriff, K. W., & Ousterhout, J. K. (1991). Measurements of a distributed file system. *Operating Systems Review, 25*(5), 198–212. doi:10.1145/121133.121164

Balasubramaniam, S., Lewis, G. A., Morris, E., Simanta, S., & Smith, D. B. (2009). Identity management and its impact on federation in a system-of-systems context. In *Proceedings of 3rd Annual IEEE International Systems Conference.* IEEE.

Barhate, K., & Jaidhar, C. (2013). Automated digital forensic technique with intrusion detection systems. In *Proceedings of IEEE 3rd International Advance Computing Conference (IACC)* (pp. 185-189). IEEE.

Barrett-Howard, E., & Tyler, T. R. (1986). Procedural justice as a criterion in allocation decisions. *Journal of Personality and Social Psychology, 50*(2), 296–304. doi:10.1037/0022-3514.50.2.296 PMID:3746613

Basel Committee. (2001). *Operational risk.* Supporting Document to the New Basel Capital Accord on Banking Supervision (May 31).

Baskerville, R. (1993). Information systems security design methods: Implications for information systems development. *ACM Computing Surveys, 25*(4), 375–414. doi:10.1145/162124.162127

Battle of the Clouds. (2009, October 15). *The Economist.* Retrieved from http://www.economist.com/node/14644393

Bauer, L., Cranor, L. F., Reiter, M. K., & Vaniea, K. (2007). Lessons learned from the deployment of a smartphone-based access-control system. In *Proceedings of the 3rd Symposium on Usable Privacy and Security* (pp. 64-75). ACM.

Baxter, I. D. (2002). *Branch coverage for arbitrary languages made easy* (Technical report). Semantic Designs. Retrieved November, 2010, from http://www.semdesigns.com/Company/Publications/TestCoverage.pdf

BBC. (2009). *Facebook gives users more control of privacy.* Retrieved from: http://news.bbc.co.uk/2/hi/technology/8404284.stm

BBC. (2010). *Facebook unveils 'groups' feature and user controls.* Retrieved from: http://www.bbc.com/news/technology-11486427

BBC. (2011a). *Facebook profile access 'leaked' claims Symantec.* Retrieved from: http://www.bbc.com/news/technology-13358293

BBC. (2011b). *Four on trial accused of using Facebook during riots.* Retrieved from: http://www.bbc.co.uk/news/uk-england-lancashire-15382412

BBC. (2012a). *Worm steals 45,000 Facebook passwords.* Retrieved from: http://www.bbc.com/news/technology-16426824

BBC. (2012b). *Facebook has more than 83 million illegitimate accounts.* Retrieved from: http://www.bbc.com/news/technology-19093078

Beheshti, M., & Wasniowski, R. A. (2007). Data fusion support for intrusion detection and prevention. In *Proceedings of International Conference on Information Technology* (pp. 966-966). Academic Press. doi:10.1109/ITNG.2007.62

Bélanger, F., & Crossler, R. E. (2011). Privacy in the digital age: A review of information privacy research in information systems. *Management Information Systems Quarterly*, *35*(4), 1017–A36.

Bella, S. D., Peretz, I., & Aronoff, N. (2003). Time course of melody recognition: A gating paradigm study. *Perception & Psychophysics*, *65*(7), 1019–1028. doi:10.3758/BF03194831 PMID:14674630

Ben-Asher, N., Kirschnick, N., Sieger, H., Meyer, J., Ben-Oved, A., & Möller, S. (2011). On the need for different security methods on mobile phones. In *Proceedings of the 13th International Conference on Human Computer Interaction with Mobile Devices and Services*. Academic Press.

Bennet, M. (2010, November). Negotiating cloud computing agreements. *Law Technology News*. Retrieved from http://www.lawtechnologynews.com/id=120244602592 8?slreturn=20140923072606

Berman, P. (2012). From Laeken to Lisbon: The origins and negotiation of the Lisbon Treaty. In A. Biondi, P. Eeckhout, & S. Ripley (Eds.), *EU law after Lisbon* (pp. 3–39). Oxford, UK: Oxford University Press. doi:10.1093/acprof:oso/9780199644322.003.0001

Besson, M., Faïta, F., Bonnel, A.-M., & Requin, J. (2002). Singing in the brain: Independence of music and tunes. *Psychological Science*, *9*(6), 494–498. doi:10.1111/1467-9280.00091

Bhattacharyya, J. (2004). Theorizing community development. *Journal of the Community Development Society*, *34*(2), 5–34. doi:10.1080/15575330409490110

Bianchi, A., Oakley, I., Kostakos, V., & Kwon, D. S. (2011). The phone lock: Audio and haptic shoulder-surfing resistant PIN entry methods for mobile devices. In *Proceedings of the Fifth International Conference on Tangible, Embedded, and Embodied Interaction* (pp. 197-200). Madeira, Portugal: Academic Press. doi:10.1145/1935701.1935740

Biddle, R., Mannan, M., van Oorschot, P. C., & Whalen, T. (2011). User study, analysis, and usable security of passwords based on digital objects. *IEEE Transactions on Information Forensics and Security*, *6*(3), 970–979.

Biermann, E., Cloete, E., & Venter, L. M. (2001). A comparison of intrusion detection systems. *Computers & Security*, *8*(20), 676–683. doi:10.1016/S0167-4048(01)00806-9

Bies, R. J., & Moag, J. F. (1986). Interactional justice: Communication criteria of fairness. *Research on Negotiations in Organisations*, *1*, 43–55.

Bigand, E., & Poulin-Charronnat, B. (2006). Are we "experienced listeners"? A review of the musical capacities that do not depend on formal musical training. *Cognition*, *100*(1), 100–130. doi:10.1016/j.cognition.2005.11.007 PMID:16412412

Bignell, K. B. (2006). Authentication in the internet banking environment: Towards developing a strategy for fraud detection. In *Proceedings ofInternational Conference on Internet Survaillance and Protection* (pp. 23-23). Academic Press. doi:10.1109/ICISP.2006.3

Bijwe, A., & Mead, N. R. (2010). *Adapting the SQUARE process for privacy requirements engineering* (CMU/SEI-2010-TN-022). Retrieved July 8, 2014, from the Software Engineering Institute, Carnegie Mellon University website: http://resources.sei.cmu.edu/library/asset-view.cfm?AssetID=9357

Bishop, M. (1989). A model of security monitoring. In *Proceedings of the Fifth Annual Computer Security Applications Conference* (pp. 46–52). Tucson, AZ: Academic Press.

Bishop, M., Wee, C., & Frank, J. (1996). *Goal-oriented auditing and logging*. Retrieved November, 2010, from http://seclab.cs.ucdavis.edu/papers/tocs-96.pdf

Bishop, M. (1987). Profiling under UNIX by patching. *Software, Practice & Experience*, *17*(10), 729–739. doi:10.1002/spe.4380171006

Bishop, M., & Klein, D. V. (1995). Improving system security via proactive password checking. *Computers & Security*, *14*(3), 233–249. doi:10.1016/0167-4048(95)00003-Q

BITS. (2003, April). *Fraud prevention strategies for internet banking*. Retrieved 3rd April, 2010 from http://www.bits.org/downloads/Publications%20Page /mointernetwp.pdf

BOA. (2014). *Bank of America SiteKey*. Retrieved 6th June 2013 from https://www.bankofamerica.com/privacy/online-mobile-banking-privacy/SiteKey.go

Boehmer, W. (2008). Appraisal of the effectiveness and efficiency of an information security management system based on ISO 27001. In *Proceedings, Second International Conference on Emerging Security Information, Systems and Technologies (SECUWARE 2008)*. IEEE Computer Society. doi:10.1109/SECURWARE.2008.7

Boehmer, W. (2009a). Cost-benefit trade-off analysis of an ISMS based on ISO 27001. In *Proceedings of ARES Conference: The International Dependability Conference*. IEEE Computer Society.

Boehmer, W. (2009b). Survivability and business continuity management system according to BS 25999. In *Proceedings, Third International Conference on Emerging Security Information, Systems and Technologies (SECUWARE '09)*. IEEE Computer Society. doi:10.1109/SECURWARE.2009.29

Boehmer, W. (2009c). Performance, survivability and cost aspects of business continuity processes according to BS25999. *International Journal on Advances in Security*, 2(4). Retrieved from http://www.iariajournals.org/security/

Boehmer, W. (2010a). Toward an objective function for an information security management system. In *Proceedings, Third IEEE International Symposium on Trust, Security and Privacy for Emerging Applications (TSP-2010)*. IEEE Computer Society.

Boehmer, W. (2010b). Analysis of strongly and weakly coupled management systems in information security. In *Proceedings, Fourth International Conference on Emerging Security Information, Systems, and Technologies (SECURWARE 2010)*. IEEE Computer Society. doi:10.1109/SECURWARE.2010.26

Boehmer, W. (2014). (in preparation). Application and formal description of discrete and event driven feedback systems in the IT/Inf. *Security*.

Bonneau, J., Herley, C., van Oorschot, P. C., & Stajano, F. (2012). The quest to replace passwords: A framework for comparative evaluation of web authentication schemes. In *Proceedings of IEEE Symposium on Security and Privacy* (pp. 553 – 567). IEEE. doi:10.1109/SP.2012.44

Boos, K. H., & Schulte-Mattler, H. (2001). Basel II: Methoden zur quantifizierung operationeller risiken. *Die Bank*, 8, 549–553.

Borg, A., Kessler, R. E., & Wall, D. W. (1990). Generation and analysis of very long address traces. In *Proceedings of the 17th Annual Symposium on Computer Architecture (ISCA-17)* (pp. 270–279). Seattle, WA: ISCA. doi:10.1109/ISCA.1990.134535

Boudjeloud, L., & Poulet, F. (2005). Visual interactive evolutionary algorithm for high dimensional data clustering and outlier detection. In *Proc. of 9th Pacific-Asia Conference on Advances in Knowledge Discovery and Data Mining (PAKDD)* (pp.426-431). Hanoi, Vietnam: Academic Press. doi:10.1007/11430919_50

Boyle, J. (1997). *Foucault in cyberspace: Surveillance, sovereignty, and hard-wired censors*. Retrieved February 28, 2014, from http://www.law.duke.edu/boylesite/foucault.htm

Braden, R. T. (1988). A pseudo-machine for packet monitoring and statistics. *Computer Communication Review*, 18(4), 200–209. doi:10.1145/52325.52345

Brandon, D. P., & Hollingshead, A. B. (2007). Characterizing online groups. In A. N. Joinson, K. Y. A. McKenna, T. Postmes, & U. D. Reips (Eds.), *The Oxford handbook of Internet psychology* (pp. 105–119). Oxford, UK: Oxford University Press.

Braz, C., & Robert, J.-M. (2006). Security and usability: the case of the user authentication methods. In *Proceedings of the 18th International Conference of the Association Francophone d'Interaction Homme-Machine* (pp. 199 – 203). ACM. doi:10.1145/1132736.1132768

Brenkert, G. (1998). Trust, business and business ethics: An introduction. *Business Ethics Quarterly*, 8(2), 195–203. doi:10.5840/beq19988219

Breuning, M., Kriegel, H.-P., Ng, R., & Sander, J. (2000). LOF: Identifying density-based local outliers. In *Proceedings of SIGMOD Conference* (pp 93-104). Dallas, TX: ACM.

Breyer, P. (2005). Telecommunications data retention and human rights: The compatibility of blanket traffic data retention with the ECHR. *European Law Journal*, 11(3), 365–375. doi:10.1111/j.1468-0386.2005.00264.x

Bridis, T., & Sullivan, E. (2007). *US video shows hacker hit on power grid.* Associated Press Writers. Retrieved September, 27, 2007, from http://www.physorg.com/news110104929.html

Bringas, P. G. (2007). Intensive use of Bayesian belief network for the unified, flexible and adaptable analysis of misuses and anomalies in network intrusion detection and prevention systems. In *Proceedings ofInternational Conference on Database and Expert Systems Applications* (pp. 365-371). Academic Press. doi:10.1109/DEXA.2007.38

British Broadcasting Corporation. (2014). *Care.data: How did it go so wrong?* Retrieved February 21, 2014 from http://www.bbc.co.uk/news/health-26259101

Brostoff, S., & Sasse, M. A. (2000). Are passfaces more usable than passwords? a field trial investigation. In S. McDonald, (Ed.), *People and computers XIV - Usability or else!Proceedings of HCI 2000* (pp. 405-424). Springer. doi:10.1007/978-1-4471-0515-2_27

Brostoff, S., & Sasse, M. A. (2001). *Safe and sound: A safety-critical approach to security.* Paper presented at the New Security Paradigms Workshop 2001, Cloudcroft, NM. doi:10.1145/508176.508178

Bruschi, D., Cavallaro, L., & Lanzi, A. (2007). An effective technique for preventing mimicry and impossible paths execution attacks. In *Proceedings ofInternational Conference on Performance, Computing, and Communications* (pp. 418-425). Academic Press.

Buchan, N. R., Croson, R., & Solnick, S. J. (2008). Trust and gender: An examination of behavior, biases, and beliefs in the investment game. *Journal of Economic Behavior & Organization*, 68(3-4), 466–476. doi:10.1016/j.jebo.2007.10.006

Buck, B., & Hollingsworth, J. K. (2000). An API for runtime code patching. *Journal of High Performance Computing Applications*, 14(4), 317–329. doi:10.1177/109434200001400404

Buell, A. D., & Sandhu, R. (2003). Identity management. *IEEE Internet Computing*, 7(6), 26–28. doi:10.1109/MIC.2003.1250580

Bulajoul, W., James, A., & Pannu, M. (2013). Network intrusion detection systems in high-speed traffic in computer networks. In *Proceedings of IEEE 10th International Conference on e-Business Engineering (ICEBE)* (pp. 168-175). IEEE.

Bunnell, J., Podd, J., Henderson, R., Napier, R., & Kennedy-Moffat, J. (1997). Cognitive, associative, and conventional passwords: Recall and guessing rates. *Computers & Security*, 16(7), 645–657. doi:10.1016/S0167-4048(97)00008-4

Burauskas, G., & Aldama, J. I. (2008). *Trust in virtual community.* (Unpublished master thesis). Lund University, Lund, Sweden.

Bureau of Consumer Protection. (2014). *Complying with COPPA: Frequently asked questions.* Retrieved April 30, 2013 from http://www.business.ftc.gov/documents/0493-Complying-with-COPPA-Frequently-Asked-Questions

Bureau of Consumer Protection. (2014B). *Federal trade commission enforcement of the U.S.- EU and U.S.-Swiss safe harbor frameworks.* Retrieved April 30, 2013 from http://www.business.ftc.gov/documents/0494-federal-trade-commission-enforcement-us-eu-and-us-swiss-safe-harbor-frameworks

Burnett, M., & Kleiman, D. (2006). *Perfect passwords, selection, protection, authentication.* Syngress.

Bygrave, L. A. (2003). Digital rights management and privacy. In E. Becker, W. Buhse, D. Günnewig, & N. Rump (Eds.), *Digital rights management: Technological, economic, legal and political aspects* (pp. 418–446). New York: Springer. doi:10.1007/10941270_27

Byron, B. (2003, August 1). *The need for authentication & authorization.* Retrieved on 3rd April, 2010 from http://www.redbooks.ibm.com/abstracts/tips0266.html?Open

CA. (2012). *Guidelines for the issuance and management of extended validation certificates.* Retrieved from www.cabforum.org

Cabinet Office. (2008). *The data handling procedure in government: Final report, June 2008.* Retrieved from http://www.cesg.gov.uk/products_services/iatp/documents/data_handling_review.pdf

Cahill, C. P., Martin, J., Phegade, V., Rajan, A., & Pagano, M. W. (2011). Client-based authentication technology: User-centric authentication using secure containers. In *Proceedings of the 7th ACM Workshop on Digital Identity Management*. Chicago: ACM. doi:10.1145/2046642.2046659

Campbell, P. L., & Stamp, J. E. (2004). *A classification scheme for risk assessment methods* (SAND2004-4233). Retrieved July 8, 2014, from the Sandia National Laboratories website: http://prod.sandia.gov/techlib/access-control.cgi/2004/044233.pdf

Cannady, J. (2009). Distributed detection of attacks in mobile ad hoc networks using learning vector quantization. In *Proceedings of Third International Conference on Network and System Security* (pp. 571–574). Academic Press. doi:10.1109/NSS.2009.99

Canotilho, J. G., & Moreira, V. (2007). *Constituição da República Portuguesa Anotada*. Coimbra: Coimbra Editora.

Cantor, S., & Kemp, J. (2005). *Liberty ID-FF protocols and schema specification*. Technical Report for Liberty Alliance Project, version: 1.2- errata-v3.0; 2004-2005.

Cantrill, B. M., Shapiro, M. W., & Leventhal, A. H. (2004). Dynamic instrumentation of production systems. In *Proceedings of the Annual Conference on USENIX Annual Technical Conference (ATEC'04)* (pp. 15–28). Boston, MA: USENIX Association.

Cao, Y., & Yang, L. (2010). A survey of identity management technology. In *Proceedings of 2010 IEEE International Conference on Information Theory and Information Security (ICITIS)*. IEEE.

Capra, F. (1984). *The turning point: Science, society, and the rising culture*. Bantam.

Capra, F. (1996). *The web of life: A new scientific understanding of living systems* (1st ed.). Anchor Books/Doubleday.

Capuzzi, G., Spalazzi, L., & Pagliarecci, F. (2006). IRSS: Incident response support system. In *Proceedings of International Symposium on Collaborative Technologies and Systems* (pp. 81-88). Academic Press. doi:10.1109/CTS.2006.55

Car, J., & Jakupovic, G. (2005). SCADA system security as a part of overall security of deregulated energy management system. In *Proceedings of International Conference on Computer as a Tool* (pp. 338-341). Academic Press. doi:10.1109/EURCON.2005.1629930

Casassa, M., Bramhall, P., Gittler, M., Pato, J., & Rees, O. (2002). Identity management: A key e-business enabler. Paper presented at SSGR2002s, L'Aquila, Italy.

Cassidy, W., Jackson, M., & Brown, K. N. (2009). Sticks and stones can break my bones but how can pixels hurt me? Students' experiences with cyberbullying. *School Psychology International*, *30*(4), 383–404. doi:10.1177/0143034309106948

Castelfranchi, C., & Tan, Y. H. (2001). *Trust and deception in virtual societies*. Dordrecht, The Netherlands: Kluwer Academic Publishers. doi:10.1007/978-94-017-3614-5

Castro, C. S. (2005). O direito à autodeterminação informativa e os novos desafios gerados pelo direito à liberdade e à segurança no pós 11 de Setembro. In *Estudos em homenagem ao Conselheiro José Manuel Cardoso da Costa, II*. Coimbra: Coimbra Editora.

Castro, C. S. (2006). *Protecção de dados pessoais na Internet*. Coimbra, Portugal: Almedina.

CA Technologies. (2014). Retrieved online on 4/12/2014 from http://www.ca.com/us/products/detail/ca-cloudminder-identity-management/details.aspx

CBS. (2010). *'Jessi Slaughter' YouTube cyberbully case: 11-year-old tells GMA she didn't want it to go this far*. Retrieved from: http://www.cbsnews.com/8301-504083_162-20011349-504083.html

Centrify Corporation. (n.d.). Retrieved from http://www.centrify.com/blogs/tomkemp/privilege_management_made_easy.asp

CEPIS. (2007, October 27). *Authentication approach for online banking*. Retrieved 3rd April, 2010 from http://www.cepis.org/files/cepis/20090901104203_Authentication%20approaches%20for%20.pdf

CERT Division of the Carnegie Mellon University Software Engineering Institute. (2011). *SQUARE for privacy (P-SQUARE)* [tool]. Retrieved July 8, 2014, from http://www.cert.org/cybersecurity-engineering/products-services/p-square-tool.cfm

CERT. (2009). *Insider threat research.* Retrieved December 1, 2009 from http://www.cert.org/insider_threat

Chaboya, D. J., Raines, R. A., Baldwin, R. O., & Mullins, B. E. (2006). Network intrusion detection: Automated and manual methods prone to attacks and evasion. *Security and Privacy Magazine, 6*(4), 36–43. doi:10.1109/MSP.2006.159

Chadwick, D. W., Inman, G. L., Siu, K. W., & Ferdous, M. S. (2011). Leveraging social networks to gain access to organizational resources. In *Proceedings of the 7th ACM Workshop on Digital Identity Management.* ACM. doi:10.1145/2046642.2046653

Chamberlin, E. (1965). The theory of monopolistic competition: A re-orientation of the theory of value (8th ed.). Harvard University Press.

Changxin, S., & Ke, M. (2009). Design of intrusion detection system based on data mining algorithm. In *Proceedings of International Conference on Signal Processing Systems* (pp. 370–373). Academic Press.

Chan, P. K., Fan, W., Prodromidis, A. L., & Stolfo, S. J. (1999). Distributed data mining in credit card fraud detection, data mining. *IEEE Intelligent Systems & their Applications, 14*(6), 67–74.

Chappell, D. (2006, April). *Introducing Windows CardSpace.* Retrieved from http://msdn.microsoft.com/en-us/library/Aa480189

Chen, Z., Chen, C., & Wang, Q. (2009). Delay-tolerant botnets. In *Proceedings of 18th International Conference on Computer Communications and Networks (ICCCN 2009)* (pp. 1-6). Academic Press.

Chen, A., Li, L., & Cao, J. (2009). Tracking cardinality distributions in network traffic. In *Proceedings of IEEE 28th Conference on Computer Comunications (INFOCOM 2009)* (pp. 819-827). IEEE. doi:10.1109/INFCOM.2009.5061991

Chen, C., Mitchell, C. J., & Tang, S. (2011). SSL/TLS session-aware user authentication using a GAA bootstrapped key information security theory and practice. In *Security and privacy of mobile devices in wireless communication* (pp. 54–68). Springer.

Chen, R. C., Chen, T. S., & Lin, C. C. (2006). A new binary support vector system for increasing detection rate of credit card fraud. *International Journal of Pattern Recognition, 20*(2), 227–239. doi:10.1142/S0218001406004624

Chen, S. C., & Dhillon, G. S. (2003). Interpreting dimensions of consumer in e-commerce. *Information Technology Management, 4*(2-3), 303–318. doi:10.1023/A:1022962631249

Chiasera, A., Casati, F., Daniel, F., & Velegrakis, Y. (2008). Engineering privacy requirements in business intelligence applications. In *Secure data management* (pp. 219–228). Berlin: Springer-Verlag. doi:10.1007/978-3-540-85259-9_15

Chiasson, S., van Oorschot, P. C., & Biddle, R. (2008). Lecture notes in computer science: Vol. 4734: Graphical password authentication using cued click points. Springer.

Chiu, C., Hsu, M., & Wang, E. (2006). Understanding knowledge sharing in virtual communities: An integration of social capital and social cognitive theories. *Decision Support Systems, 42*(3), 1872–1888. doi:10.1016/j.dss.2006.04.001

Chopra, K., & Wallace, W. A. (2003). Trust in electronic environments. In *Proceedings of the 36th Annual Hawaii international Conference on System Sciences.* IEEE Computer Society. doi:10.1109/HICSS.2003.1174902

Christenson, J., Fendley, K., & Robinson, J. (1994). Community development. In J. Christenson & J. Robinson (Eds.), *Community development in perspective* (pp. 3–25). Ames, IA: Iowa State University.

Chunmei, Y., Mingchu, L., Jianbo, M., & Jizhou, S. (2004). Honeypot and scan detection in intrusion detection system. In *Proceedings of Canadian Conference on Electrical and Computer Engineering* (pp. 1107–1110). Academic Press. doi:10.1109/CCECE.2004.1345313

Chuvakin, A., & Peterson, G. (2010). *How to do application logging right.* Retrieved November 24, 2010, from http://www.computer.org/cms/Computer.org/ComputingNow/homepage/2010/1010/W_SP_ApplicationLogging.pdf

Clark, D. D., & Wilson, D. R. (1987). A comparison of commercial and military computer security policies. In *Proceedings of the 1987 IEEE Symposium on Research in Security and Privacy (SP'87)*. Oakland, CA: IEEE Press.

Clark, C. (1996). The answer to the machine is in the machine. In P. Bernt Hugenholtz (Ed.), *The future of copyright in a digital environment*. The Hague, The Netherlands: Kluwer Law International.

Clarke, R. A. (1988). Information technology and dataveillance. *Communications of the ACM, 31*(5), 498–512. doi:10.1145/42411.42413

Clarkson, E., Clawson, J., Lyons, K., & Starner, T. (2005). An empirical study of typing rates on mini-QWERTY keyboards. In CHI'05 extended abstracts on Human factors in computing systems (pp. 1288-1291). ACM. doi:10.1145/1056808.1056898

Clinch, J. (2009). *ITIL V3 and Information security*. Retrieved November 03, 2010 from www.best-management-practice.com/gempdf/ITILV3_and_Information_Security_White_Paper_May09.pdf

CNIL. (2005, October 18). *Délibération no. 2005-235*. Retrieved March 27, 2010, from http://www.legifrance.gouv.fr/affichCnil.do?oldAction=rechExpCnilandid=CNILTEXT000017652059andfastReqId=137369379andfastPos=1

Coates, D., Adams, J., Dattilo, G., & Turner, M. (2000). *Identity theft and the Internet*. Colorado University.

Cohen, J. (2003). DRM and privacy. *Berkeley Technological Law Journal, 18*, 575-617. Retrieved February 28, 2014, from http://ssrn.com/abstract=372741

Cohen-Charash, Y., & Spector, P. E. (2001). The role of justice in organizations: A meta-analysis. *Organizational Behavior and Human Decision Processes, 86*(2), 278–321. doi:10.1006/obhd.2001.2958

Cohen, J. (1996). A right to read anonymously: A closer look at 'copyright management' in cyberspace. *Connecticut Law Review, 28*, 981–1039.

Cohen, J. (1997). Some reflections on copyright management systems and laws designed to protect them. *Berkeley Technology Law Journal, 12*, 161–190.

Colon Osorio, F. C. (2007). Using Byzantine agreement in the design of IPS systems. In *Proceedings of International Conference on Performance, Computing, and Communications* (pp. 528-537). Academic Press.

Commission for the Protection of Privacy. (n.d.). *Binding corporate rules*. Retrieved from http://www.privacycommission.be/en/transfers-outside-the-eu-without-adequate-protection/bcr

Common Criteria. (2005). *Common criteria for information technology security evaluation: Part 2: Security functional requirements, version 2.3*. Retrieved November 25, 2010, from http://www.commoncriteriaportal.org/files/ccfiles/ccpart2v2.3.pdf

Concise Oxford dictionary of current english. (1996). Oxford University Press.

Connolly, P. (2000, September 29). *Single signon dangles prospect of lower help desk costs*. Retrieved march 21, 2009, from infoworld: http://www.infoworld.com/articles/es/xml/00/10/02/001002esnsso.html

Connolly, R. (2008). Trust and the virtual environment: Research and methodological considerations. *International Journal of Networking and Virtual Organisation, 5*(3/4), 259–274. doi:10.1504/IJNVO.2008.018823

Connolly, R., & Bannister, F. (2007). Consumer trust in Internet shopping in Ireland: Towards the development of a more effective trust measurement instrument. *Journal of Information Technology, 22*(2), 102–118. doi:10.1057/palgrave.jit.2000071

Constant, D., Sproull, L., & Kiesler, S. (1996). The kindness of strangers: The usefulness of electronic weak ties for technical advice. *Organization Science, 7*(2), 119–135. doi:10.1287/orsc.7.2.119

Control, A. (2010). *Authentication, authorization and access control*. Retrieved 3rd April, 2010 from http://eregie.premier-ministre.gouv.fr/manual/howto/auth.html

Conway, N., & Briner, R. B. (2002). Full-time versus part-time employees: Understanding the links between work status, the psychological contract and attitudes. *Journal of Vocational Behavior, 61*(2), 279–301. doi:10.1006/jvbe.2001.1857

Conway, W., Maxwell, W. L., & Morgan, H. L. (1972). On the implementation of security measures in information systems. *Communications of the ACM, 15*(4), 211–220. doi:10.1145/361284.361287

Corrons, L. (PandaLabs). (2010). *Mariposa botnet.* Retrieved August 17, 2010, from http://pandalabs.pandasecurity.com/mariposa-botnet/

Coughlan, T., van der Linden, J., & Adams, A. (2012). Local connections: Designing technologies for discovery and creativity within the community. *Interaction, 19*(1), 18–22.

Court of Justice of the European Communities. (2007). *Opinion of advocate General Kokott* [CJEC Case C-275/06]. Author.

Courtney, R. (1977). Security risk analysis in electronic data processing. In *Proceedings of the NatLonal Computer Conference 46.* AFIPS.

Coventry, L., De Angeli, A., & Johnson, G. (2003). Usability and biometric verification at the ATM interface. In *Proceedings of the SIGCHI Conference on Human Factors in Computing Systems* (pp. 153-160). ACM Press. doi:10.1145/642611.642639

Craver, C. B. (2006). Privacy issues affecting employers, employees and labour organizations. *Louisiana Law Review, 66,* 1057–1078.

Cremona, M. (2012). The two (or three) treaty solution: The new treaty structure of the EU. In A. Biondi, P. Eeckhout, & S. Ripley (Eds.), *EU law after Lisbon* (pp. 40–61). Oxford, UK: Oxford University Press. doi:10.1093/acprof:oso/9780199644322.003.0002

Crosbie, M., & Spafford, E. (1995). Defending a computer system using autonomous agents. In *Proceedings of the 18th National Information Systems Security Conference.* Academic Press.

Crowder, R. G., Serafine, M. L., & Repp, B. (1986). Physical interaction and association by contiguity in memory for the words and melodies of songs. *Memory & Cognition, 18*(5), 469–476. doi:10.3758/BF03198480 PMID:2233260

Cser, A., & Penn, J. (2008). *Identity management market forecast: 2007 to 2014.* Forrester Research Report. Retrieved on 4/18/2014 from http://www.securelyyoursllc.com/files/Identity%20Management%20Market%20Forecast%202007%20To%202014.pdf

Cui, H. (2002). *Online outlier detection over data streams.* (Master thesis). Simon Fraser University.

Cullinane, N., & Dundon, T. (2006). The psychological contract: A critical review. *International Journal of Management Reviews, 8*(2), 113–129. doi:10.1111/j.1468-2370.2006.00123.x

Curry, T. W. (1994). Profiling and tracing dynamic library usage via interposition. In *Proceedings of the USENIX Summer 1994 Technical Conference (USTC'94)* (pp. 267–2780. Boston, MA: USENIX Association.

CyberArk Software Inc. (2014). Retrieved online on 4/12/2014 from http://www.cyberark.com/product-etail/application-identity-manager-features

D'Urso, S. C. (2006). Who's watching us at work? Toward a structural-perceptual model of electronic monitoring and surveillance in organisations. *Communication Theory, 16*(3), 281–303. doi:10.1111/j.1468-2885.2006.00271.x

Da Veiga, A., & Eloff, J. H. P. (2007). An information security governance framework. *Information Systems Management, 24*(4), 361–372. doi:10.1080/10580530701586136

Daft, R. L. (2000). Management (5th ed.). The Dryden Press.

Dagle, J. E., Windergren, S. E., & Johnson, J. M. (2002, January). *Enhancing the security of supervisory control and data acquisition (SCADA) systems: The lifeblood of modern energy infrastructure.* Paper presented at the Power Engineering Society Winter Meeting, New York, NY. doi:10.1109/PESW.2002.985079

Dale, N., Weems, C., & Headington, M. (2002). *Programming and problem solving with C.* Sudbury, MA: Jones and Bartlett.

Darra, E., & Katsikas, S. K. (2013). Attack detection capabilities of intrusion detection systems for wireless sensor networks. In *Proceedings of Fourth International Conference on Information, Intelligence, Systems and Applications (IISA)* (pp. 1-7). Academic Press. doi:10.1109/IISA.2013.6623718

Data Breaches. (n.d.). *A source of chronic pain*. Retrieved August 15, 2013 from http://www.experian.com/blogs/data-breach/2013/05/01/medical-data-breaches-a-source-of-chronic-pain

Davenport, T. H. (2005). *Thinking for a living, how to get better performance and results from knowledge workers*. Boston, MA: Harvard Business School Press.

Davis, W. (2009). *Facebook harassment suit could spur cyberbullying laws*. Retrieved from: http://www.mediapost.com/publications/index.cfm?fa=Articles.showArticle&art_aid=114854

Davis, D., Monrose, F., & Reiter, M. K. (2004). On user choice in graphical password schemes. In *Proceedings of the 13th Conference on USENIX Security Symposium* (p. 11). Berkeley, CA: USENIX Association.

De Hert, P., & Gutwirth, S. (2006). Privacy, data protection and law enforcement: Opacity of the individual and transparency of power. In E. Claes, A. Duff, & S. Gutwirth (Eds.), *Privacy and the criminal law* (pp. 61–104). Oxford, UK: Intersentia.

De Hert, P., & Papakonstantinou, V. (2009). The data protection framework decision of 27 November 2008 regarding police and judicial cooperation in criminal matters – A modest achievement however not the improvement some have hoped for. *Computer Law & Security Report*, 25(5), 403–414. doi:10.1016/j.clsr.2009.07.008

De Laat, P. B. (2005). Trusting virtual trust. *Ethics and Information Technology*, 7(3), 167–180. doi:10.1007/s10676-006-0002-6

de Souza, C. S., Nicolaci-da-Costa, A. M., da Silva, E. J., & Prates, R. O. (2004). Compulsory institutionalisation: Investigating the paradox of computer-supported informal social processes. *Interacting with Computers*, 16(4), 635–656. doi:10.1016/j.intcom.2004.07.003

Debar, H., Dacier, M., & Wespi, A. (1999). *A revised taxonomy for intrusion-detection systems*. Rüschlikon, Switzerland: IBM Zürich Research Laboratory.

Dehnart, A. (1999). *Digital neighborhoods*. Retrieved January 12, 2010, from http://www.andydehnart.com/writing/articles/digital_neighborhoods

Delgado, N., Gates, A. Q., & Roach, S. (2004). A taxonomy and catalog of runtime software-fault monitoring tools. *IEEE Transactions on Software Engineering*, 30(12), 859–872. doi:10.1109/TSE.2004.91

Deming, W. E. (1986). *Out of the crisis*. Cambridge, MA: MIT Press.

Dempster, A. P., Laird, N. M., & Rubin, D. B. (1977). Maximum likelihood from incomplete data via the em algorithm. *Journal of the Royal Statistical Society. Series B. Methodological*, 39(1), 1–38.

Denning, D. E. (1986). An intrusion-detection model. In *Proceedings of the 1986 IEEE Symposium on Security and Privacy* (pp. 118–131). Oakland, CA: IEEE.

Department of Defense. (1985). *Password management guideline*. Retrieved September 3, 2004, from http://www.alw.nih.gov/Security/FIRST/papers/password/dodpwman.txt

Dhillon, G., & Backhouse, J. (2000). Technical opinion: Information system security management in the new millennium. *Communication of the European ACM*, 43(7), 125–128. doi:10.1145/341852.341877

di Pietro, L., & Pantano, E. (2013). Social network influences on young tourists: An exploratory analysis of determinants of the purchasing intention. *Journal of Direct Data and Digital Marketing Practice*, 15(1), 4–19. doi:10.1057/dddmp.2013.33

Dibben, M. R., Morris, S. E., & Lean, M. E. J. (2000). Situational trust and co-operative partnerships between physicians and their patients: A theoretical explanation transferable from business practice. *QJM*, 93(1), 55–61. doi:10.1093/qjmed/93.1.55 PMID:10623783

Dinev, T. (2014). Why would we care about privacy? *European Journal of Information Systems*, 23(2), 97–102. doi:10.1057/ejis.2014.1

Dinev, T., Xu, H., Smith, J. H., & Hart, P. (2013). Information privacy and correlates: An empirical attempt to bridge and distinguish privacy-related concepts. *European Journal of Information Systems*, 22(3), 295–316. doi:10.1057/ejis.2012.23

Directive 95/46/EC 1995. (n.d.). Directive 95/46/EC of the European Parliament and of the Council of 24 October 1995 on the protection of individuals with regard to the processing of personal data and on the free movement of such data. Retrieved from http://eur-lex.europa.eu/LexUriServ/LexUriServ.do?uri=CELEX:31995L0046:en

Directive H. T. M. L. 2002/58/EC. (2002). *Protection of privacy to electronic communications*. Retrieved from http://eur-lex.europa.eu/LexUriServ/LexUriServ.do?uri=CELEX:32002L0058:EN:HTML

Dirks, K. T., & Ferrin, D. L. (2001). The role of trust in organizational settings. *Organization Science*, 12(4), 450–467. doi:10.1287/orsc.12.4.450.10640

Donath, J. (1998). Identity and deception in the virtual community. In M. Smith & P. Kollock (Eds.), *Communities in cyberspace* (pp. 29–59). London: Rutledge.

Dongarra, J., London, K., Moore, S., Mucci, P., & Terpstra, D. (2001). *Using PAPI for hardware performance monitoring on Linux systems*. Paper presented at Conference on Linux Clusters: The HPC Revolution, Urbana, IL, USA.

Dougan, M. (2007). The Treaty of Lisbon 2007: Winning minds, not hearts. *Common Market Law Review*, 45, 617–703.

Doward, J. (2009). Bid to block pedophiles from Facebook fails. *The Guardian*. Retrieved from: http://www.theguardian.com/technology/2009/nov/08/facebook-sex-offenders-law

Doyle, J. D. (2012). *Building it up and tearing it down: a three-study examination of trust, trust building, and the effects of erroneous messaging in the blogosphere*. (Doctoral dissertation). Retrieved from https://curve.carleton.ca/theses/31281

Dunn, J., & Schweitzer, M. (2005). Feeling and believing: The influence of emotion on trust. *Journal of Personality and Social Psychology*, 88(5), 736–748. doi:10.1037/0022-3514.88.5.736 PMID:15898872

Educause. (2010). *Privacy risks assessment*. Retrieved from http://www.educause.edu/node/645/tid/30444?time=1281348515

Egelman, S., Sotirakopoulos, A., Muslukhov, I., Beznosov, Z., & Herley, C. (2013). Does my password go up to eleven? The impact of password meters on password selection. In *Proceedings of the SIGCHI Conference on Human Factors in Computing Systems* (pp. 2379-2388). ACM. doi:10.1145/2470654.2481329

El Maliki, T., & Seigneur, J.-M. (2007). A survey of user-centric identity management technol ogies. In *Proceedings of Emerging Security Information, Systems, and Technologies, 2007*. Academic Press.

Electronic Privacy Information Center. (n.d.). *Data retention*. Retrieved May 19, 2014, from http://epic.org/privacy/intl/data_retention.html

Elgesem, D. (1999). The structure of rights in directive 95/46/EC on the protection of individuals with regard to the processing of personal data and the free movement of such data. *Ethics and Information Technology*, 1(4), 283–293. doi:10.1023/A:1010076422893

Elo, J. H. P., & Elo, M. (2003). Information security management: a new paradigm. In *Proceedings, 2003 Annual Research Conference of the South African Institute of Computer Scientists and Information Technologists on Enablement through Technology (SAICSIT '03)*. South African Institute for Computer Scientists and Information Technologists.

Emory Health Care. (n.d.). Retrieved August 4, 2013 from http://healthitsecurity.com/2013/07/23/healthcare-data-breaches-reviewing-the-ramifications/

Engelbert, P. (2009). *5 keys to a successful identity and access management implementation*. A CA white paper. Retrieved on 4/18/2014 from http://www.ca.com/files/whitepapers/iam_services_implementation_whitepaper.pdf

Etsion, Y., Tsafrir, D., Kirkpatrick, S., & Feitelson, D. (2007). Fine grained kernel logging with Klogger: Experience and insights. In *Proceedings of the 2nd ACM SIGOPS/EuroSys European Conference on Computer Systems 2007* (pp. 259–272). Lisbon, Portugal: ACM. doi:10.1145/1272996.1273023

European Comission. (2013). *European Commission calls on the U.S. to restore trust in EU-U.S. data flows.* [Press Release]. Retrieved from http://europa.eu/rapid/press-release_IP-13-1166_en.htm

European Commission. (2010). *Opinion 1/2010 on the concepts of "controller" and "processor".* Retrieved from http://ec.europa.eu/justice/policies/privacy/docs/wpdocs/2010/wp169_en.pdf

European Commission. (2012). *COM (2012)529 - Unleashing the Potential of cloud computing in Europe.* Retrieved from http://eur-lex.europa.eu/LexUriServ/LexUriServ.do?uri=COM:2012:0529:FIN:EN:PDF

European Parliament. (2014). *Report on US NSA surveillance programme, surveillance bodies in various member states and their impact on EU citizens' fundamental rights and on transatlantic cooperation in justice and home affairs (2013/2188(INI)).* Retrieved from http://www.europarl.europa.eu/sides/getDoc.do?type=REPORT&reference=A7-2014-0139&language=EN

European Privacy Association. (2009). *New challenges for privacy: Advanced technologies, effective legal frameworks and active responsibility.* Retrieved from http://ec.europa.eu/justice/news/consulting_public/0003/contributions/organisations/european_privacy_association_en.pdf

European Union Agency for Network and Information Security (ENISA). (2013). *Threat landscape 2013, Overview of current and emerging cyber-threats.* Retrieved December 24, 2013 from http://www.enisa.europa.eu/activities/risk-management/evolving-threat-environment/enisa-threat-landscape-2013-overview-of-current-and-emerging-cyber-threats

European Union Defines Cloud Computing. (2010). *Information Age.* Retrieved on from http://www.information-age.com/technology/data-centre-and-it-infrastructure/1147048/european-union-defines-cloud-computing

Eustace, A., & Srivastava, A. (1994). *ATOM: A flexible interface for building high performace program analysis tools.* Palo Alto, CA: DEC Western Research Laboratory.

Evans, L. (2007). Monitoring technology in the American workplace: Would adopting English privacy standards better balance employee privacy and productivity? *California Law Review, 95,* 1115–1149.

Evidian. (2014). Retrieved online on 4/12/2014 from Retrieved from http://www.evidian.com/pdf/fl-iamanager-en.pdf

Experian: A World of Insight. (n.d.). *Data breach resolution.* Retrieved August 13, 2013 from http://www.experian.com/blogs/data-breach/2013/05/01/medical-data-breaches-a-source-of-chronic-pain%E2%80%8E

Facebook. (2014). *Statistics.* Retrieved from: http://newsroom.fb.com/company-info

Fadia, A. (2006). *Network security: A hacker's perspective.* Boston: Thomson Course Technology.

Farquhar, P. (2010). *Jessi Slaughter and the 4chan trolls - The case for censoring the internet.* Retrieved from: http://www.news.com.au/technology/jessi-slaughter-and-the-4chan-trolls-the-case-for-censoring-the-internet/story-e6frfro0-1225894369199#ixzz1lHbLxHqO [

Farris, J. J., & Nicol, D. M. (2004). Evaluation of secure peer-to-peer overlay routing for survivable SCADA systems. In Proceedings of 2004 Winter Simulation Conference (pp. 308-317). Academic Press.

Fatima, A. (2011). E-banking security issues--Is there a solution in biometrics? *Journal of Internet Banking & Commerce, 16*(2), 1–9.

Featherman, M. S., & Pavlou, P. A. (2003). Predicting e-services adoption: A perceived risk facets perspective. *International Journal of Human-Computer Studies, 59*(4), 451–474. doi:10.1016/S1071-5819(03)00111-3

Federal Information Security Management Act. (2002). *FISMA, P.L. 107-347, Title III, December 17, 2002.* Retrieved March 28, 2014 from http://www.csrc.nist.gov/policies/FISMA-final.pdf

Federal Trade Commission. (2007, November 27). *FTC releases survey of identity theft in the U.S. study shows 8.3 million victims in 2005.* Retrieved March 12, 2014, from Federal Trade Commission: http://www.ftc.gov/news-events/press-releases/2007/11/ftc-releases-survey-identity-theft-usstudy-shows-83-million

Federal Trade Commission. (2010, March 9). *LifeLock will pay $12 million to settle charges by the FTC and 35 states that identify theft prevention and data security claims were false.* Retrieved March 7, 2014, from Federal Trade Commission: http://www.ftc.gov/news-events/press-releases/2010/03/lifelock-will-pay-12-million-settle-charges-ftc-35-states

Federal Trade Commission. (2012, July). *How to keep your personal information secure.* Retrieved March 12, 2014, from Federal Trade Commission: http://www.consumer.ftc.gov/articles/0272-how-keep-your-personal-information-secure

Ferraiolo, D. F., Kuhn, R. D., & Chandramouli, R. (2003). Role-based access control. Artech House Computer Security Series.

Ferrajoli, L. (2001). Fundamental rights. *International Journal for the Semiotics of Law, 14*(1), 1–33. doi:10.1023/A:1011290509568

Fessi, B. A., BenAbdallah, S., Hamdi, M., Rekhis, S., & Boudriga, N. (2010). Data collection for information security system. In *Proceedings of the Second International Conference on Engineering Systems Management and Applications (ICESMA 2010).* Sharjah, UAE: Academic Press.

Festinger, L., Pepitone, A., & Newcomb, T. (1952). Some consequences of deindividuation in a group. *Journal of Abnormal and Social Psychology, 47*(2, Suppl), 382–389. doi:10.1037/h0057906 PMID:14937978

Flaherty, D. H. (2000). Privacy impact assessments: An essential tool for data protection. *Privacy Law & Policy Reporter, 7*(5), 85–90.

Florencio, D., & Herley, C. (2007). A large-scale study of web password habits. In *Proceedings of the 16th International Conference on World Wide Web* (pp. 657-666). ACM. doi:10.1145/1242572.1242661

Forget, A., Chiasson, S., & Biddle, R. (2007). Helping users create better passwords: Is this the right approach? In *Proceedings of the Third Symposium on Usable Privacy and Security* (pp. 151-152). ACM. doi:10.1145/1280680.1280703

Forrest, S., Hofmeyr, S. A., Somayaji, A., & Longstaff, T. A. (1996). A sense of self for Unix processes. In *Proceedings of the 1996 IEEE Symposium on Research in Security and Privacy* (pp. 120–128). Oakland, CA: IEEE. doi:10.1109/SECPRI.1996.502675

Foucault, M. (1977). *Discipline and Punish: The Birth of the Prison* (A. Sheridan, Trans.). New York: Pantheon Books.

Francia, G. A., & Ciganek, A. (2010). Global information security regulations, case studies and cultural issues. In M. E. Whitman & H. J. Mattord (Eds.), Readings and cases in the management of information security, volume II: Legal and ethical issues in information security management. Course Technology.

Francia, G. A., & Hutchinson, F. (2012). Regulatory and policy compliance with regard to identity theft prevention,detection, and response. In T.-S. Chou (Ed.), *Information assurance and security technologies for risk assessment and threat management: Advances* (pp. 292–322). IGI Global Pub. doi:10.4018/978-1-61350-507-6.ch012

Fried, C. (1968). Privacy. *The Yale Law Journal, 77*(3), 475–493. doi:10.2307/794941

Furnell, S. M., Dowland, P. S., Illingworth, H. M., & Reynolds, P. L. (2000). Authentication and supervision: A survey of user attitudes. *Computers & Security, 19*(6), 529–539. doi:10.1016/S0167-4048(00)06027-2

Gaedke, M., Meinecke, J., & Nussbaumer, M. (2005). A modeling approach to federated identity and access management. In *Proceedings of International World Wide Web Conference.* Academic Press. doi:10.1145/1062745.1062916

Gakovic, A., & Tetrick, L. E. (2003). Psychological contract breach as a source of strain for employees. *Journal of Business and Psychology, 18*(2), 235–246. doi:10.1023/A:1027301232116

Gambetta, D. (1988). Can we trust trust? In D. Gambetta (Ed.), *Trust: Making and breaking cooperative relationships* (pp. 213–237). New York: Basil Blackwell.

Ganapathy, S., Kulothungan, K., Yogesh, P., & Kannan, A. (2012). An intelligent intrusion detection system for ad hoc networks. In Proceedings of IET Chennai 3rd International on Sustainable Energy and Intelligent Systems (SEISCON 2012) (pp. 1-5). IET.

Gans, M. (1996). Development of a pole-mounted RTU for use on rural power lines. In *Proceedings of Power System Control and Management Conference* (pp. 103–107). Academic Press. doi:10.1049/cp:19960245

García, S. (2013). *Malware capture facility project.* Retrieved April 13, 2014, from https://mcfp.felk.cvut.cz/

Garcia, F. J. (2005). Bodil Lindqvist: A Swedish churchgoer's violation of the European Union's Data Protection Directive should be a warning to U.S. legislators. *Fordham Intellectual Property, Media, and Entertainment Law Journal, 15,* 1204–1243.

Garcia, S., Zunino, A., & Campo, M. (2013). Survey on network-based botnet detection methods. In *Security and communication networks.* John Wiley & Sons, Ltd.

Garfinkel, S., & Spafford, G. (1996). *Practical UNIX and internet security* (2nd ed.). Sebastopol, CA: O'Reilly.

Gartner Group. (2014). *Magic quadrant for security information and event management.* Retrieved March 25, 2014 from https://www.gartner.com/doc/2477018/magic-quadrant-security-information-event

Gaw, S., & Felten, E. W. (2006). Password management strategies for online accounts. In *Proceedings of the Second Symposium on Usable Privacy and Security* (pp. 44-55). ACM. doi:10.1145/1143120.1143127

GDB. (2010). *GDB: The GNU project debugger.* Retrieved November 25, 2010, from http://www.gnu.org/software/gdb/gdb.html

Gefen, D. (2000). E-commerce: The role of familiarity and trust. *Omega: The International Journal of Management Science, 28*(6), 725–737. doi:10.1016/S0305-0483(00)00021-9

Gefen, D., Karahanna, E., & Straub, D. W. (2003). Trust and TAM in online shopping. *Management Information Systems Quarterly, 27*(1), 51–83.

Gefen, D., & Straub, D. W. (2004). Consumer trust in B2C e-commerce and the importance of social presence: Experiments in e-products and e-services. *Omega: The International Journal of Management Science, 32*(6), 407–424. doi:10.1016/j.omega.2004.01.006

Geiger, C. (2010). The future of copyright in Europe: Striking a fair balance between protection and access to information. *Intellectual Property Quarterly, 1,* 1–14.

Gervais, D. J., & Hyndman, D. J. (2012). Cloud control: Copyright, global memes and privacy. *Journal on Telecommunications & High Technology Law, 10,* 53–92. Retrieved from http://ssrn.com/abstract=372741

Ghosh, A. P. (1998). *E-commerce security – Weak links, best defences.* John Wiley and Sons, Inc.

Giacometti, R., Rachev, S., Chernobai, A., & Bertocchi, M. (2008). Aggregation issues in operational risk. *Journal of Operational Risk, 3*(3).

Gibson, M., Conrad, M., & Maple, C. (2010). Infinite alphabet passwords: A unified model for a class of authentication systems. In S. K. Katsikas & P. Samarati (Eds.), SECRYPT (pp. 94–99). SciTePress.

Gibson, M., Renaud, K., Conrad, M., & Maple, C. (2009). Musipass: Authenticating me softly with "my" song. In *NSPW'09: New security paradigms workshop* (pp. 85–100). New York, NY: ACM. doi:10.1145/1719030.1719043

Gibson, M., Renaud, K., Conrad, M., & Maple, C. (2012). Music is the key: Using our enduring memory for songs to help users log on. In M. Gupta, J. Walp, & R. Sharman (Eds.), *Strategic and practical approaches for information security governance: Technologies and applied solutions.* IGI Global. doi:10.4018/978-1-4666-0197-0.ch008

Giffin, K. (1967). The contribution of studies of source credibility to a theory of interpersonal trust in the communication process. *Psychological Bulletin, 68*(2), 104–120. doi:10.1037/h0024833 PMID:6065581

Gilbert, F. (2012, July). Article 29 working party cloud computing opinion: Blow to safe harbor? *TechTarget.* Retrieved from http://searchcloudsecurity.techtarget.com/tip/Article-29-Working-Party-cloud-computing-opinion-Blow-to-Safe-Harbor

Glasser, U., & Mona, V. (2008). Identity management architecture. In *Proceedings of IEEE International Conference on Intelligence and Security Informatics*. IEEE.

Godfrey, B. (2001). *Electronic work monitoring: An ethical model*. Australian Computer Society.

Goel, V. (2014, January 29). *Big profit at Facebook as it tilts to mobile*. Retrieved March 15, 2014, from The New York Times Company: http://www.nytimes.com/2014/01/30/technology/rise-in-mobile-ads-pushes-up-revenue- and-profit-at-facebook.html

Goemans, C., & Dumortier, J. (2003). Enforcement issues - Mandatory retention of traffic data in the EU: Possible impact on privacy and on-line anonymity. In C. Nicoll, J. E. J. Prins, & M. J. M. Van Dellen (Eds.), *Digital anonymity and the law: Tensions and dimensions* (pp. 161–183). The Hague, The Netherlands: T.M.C. Asser Press. doi:10.1007/978-90-6704-579-7_8

Goldie, L. (2008). Facebook to discuss security with ICO after data leak. *New Media Age*. Retrieved from: http://www.nma.co.uk/news/facebook-to-discuss-security-with-ico-after-private-data-leak/38591.article.

Google Press Center. (2006). Conversation with Eric Schmidt hosted by Danny Sullivan. *Search Engine Strategies Conference*. Retrieved from http://www.google.com/press/podium/ses2006.html

Google Terms of Service. (n.d.). Retrieved from http://www.google.com/apps/intl/en/terms/user_terms.htm

Google. (2014). *Google safe browsing*. Retrieved from http:///www.google.com/chrome/intl/ko/more/security.html

Gorniak, S., Ikonomou, D., Saragiotis, S., Askoxylakis, I., Belimpasakis, P., Bencsath, B., … Vishik, C. (2010, April). Report priorities for research on current and emerging network technologies. *Enisa*. Retrieved from https://www.enisa.europa.eu/activities/identity-and-trust/library/deliverables/procent

Gostin, L. O. (2000). *Public health law: Power, duty, restraint*. Berkeley, CA: University of California Press.

Govier, T. (1997). *Social trust and human communities*. Montreal, Canada: McGill-Queen's University Press.

Grabner-Kräuter, S., Kaluscha, E. A., & Fladnitzer, M. (2006). Perspectives of online trust and similar constructs: A conceptual clarification. In *Proceedings of the 8th International Conference on Electronic Commerce: the New E-Commerce: Innovations for Conquering Current Barriers, Obstacles and Limitations to Conducting Successful Business on the Internet*. ACM. doi:10.1145/1151454.1151496

Grady, D. (2010). *Study finds no progress in safety at hospitals*. Retrieved from http://www.nytimes.com/2010/11/25/health/research/25patient.html?_r=0

Gragg, D. (2007). *A multi-level defense against social engineering*. SANS. Retrieved July 1, 2009, from http://www.sans.org/reading_room/whitepapers/engineering/920.php

Graham, S. L., Kessler, P. B., & McKusick, M. K. (1984). gprof: A call graph execution profiler. *ACM SIGPLAN Notices*, *39*(4), 49–57. doi:10.1145/989393.989401

Grandison, T., & Sloman, M. (2000). A survey of trust in internet applications. *IEEE Communications Surveys and Tutorials*, *3*(4), 2–16. doi:10.1109/COMST.2000.5340804

Granovetter, M. S. (1985). Economic action and social structure: The problem of embeddedness. *American Journal of Sociology*, *91*(3), 481–510. doi:10.1086/228311

Great Britain Office of Government Commerce (OGC). (2007). *Service design (SD): ITIL*. London: The Stationery Office.

Gruteser, M., & Grunwald, D. (2004). A methodological assessment of location privacy risks in wireless hotspot networks in security in pervasive computing. *Lecture Notes in Computer Science*, (2802), 113–142.

GTISC. (2013). *Emerging cyber threats report 2014*. The Georgia Tech Information Security Center and Georgia Tech Research Institute. Retrieved from http://www.gtsecuritysummit.com/2014Report.pdf

Gu, G. (2008). *Correlation-based botnet detection in enterprise networks*. (Doctoral dissertation). Georgia Institute of Technology.

Gu, G., Zhang, J., & Lee, W. (2008). BotSniffer: Detecting botnet command and control channels in network traffic. In *Proceedings of the 15th Network and Distributed System Security Symposium (NDSS)*. San Diego, CA: Academic Press.

Guan, J., Liu, D.-X., & Cui, B.-G. (2004). An intrusion learning approach for building intrusion detection models using genetic algorithms. In *Proceedings of World Congress on Intelligent Control and Automation* (pp. 4339–4342). Academic Press. doi:10.1109/WCICA.2004.1342332

Guest, D. (2004). The psychology of the employment relationship: An analysis based on the psychological contract. *Applied Psychology*, *53*(4), 541–555. doi:10.1111/j.1464-0597.2004.00187.x

Gu, G., Perdisci, R., Zhang, J., & Lee, W. (2008). BotMiner: Clustering analysis of network traffic for protocol-and structure-independent botnet detection. In *Proceedings of the 17th Conference on Security Symposium* (pp. 139-154). Berkeley, CA: USENIX Association.

Guha, A., Krishnamurthi, S., & Jim, T. (2009). Using static analysis for ajax intrusion detection. In *Proceedings of International World Wide Web Conferences (WWW)* (pp. 561-570). Madrid, Spain: Academic Press.

Guidance, D. (2014). *Belgium: Decree fully transposes data retention directive*. Retrieved May 1, 2014 from http://www.dataguidance.com/dataguidance_privacy_this_week.asp?id=2128

Guild, E., & Carrera, S. (2010). The European Union's area of freedom, security and justice ten years on. In E. Guild, S. Carrera, & A. Eggenschwiler (Eds.), *The area of freedom, security and justice ten years on: Successes and future challenges under the Stockholm Programme* (pp. 1–12). CEPS.

Gunson, N., Marshall, D., Morton, H., & Jack, M. (2011). User perceptions of security and usability of single-factor and two-factor authentication in automated telephone banking. *Computers & Security*, *30*(4), 208–220. doi:10.1016/j.cose.2010.12.001

Gupta, A., Pandey, O. J., Shukla, M., Dadhich, A., Mathur, S., & Ingle, A. (2013). Computational intelligence based intrusion detection systems for wireless communication and pervasive computing networks. In *Proceedings of IEEE International Conference on Computational Intelligence and Computing Research (ICCIC)* (pp. 1-7). IEEE. doi:10.1109/ICCIC.2013.6724156

Gupta, M., & Sharman, R. (2008a). Security-efficient identity management using service provisioning (markup language). In Handbook of research on information security and assurance (pp. 83-90). Hershey, PA: IGI Global.

Gupta, M., & Sharman, R. (2008c). Emerging frameworks in user-focused identity management. In Handbook of research on enterprise systems (pp 362-377). Hershey, PA: IGI Global.

Gupta, M., & Sharman, R. (2010). Activity governance for managing risks in role design for SSO systems. *Journal of Information Assurance and Security, 5*(6).

Gupta, M., Lee, J., & Rao, H. R. (2008). Implications of FFIEC guidance on authentication in electronic banking. In Handbook of research on information security and assurance. Hershey, PA: IGI Global.

Gupta, M., Rao, H. R., & Upadhyaya, S. (2004, July-September). Electronic banking and information assurance issues: Survey and synthesis. *Journal of Organizational and End User Computing, 16*(3), 1–21. doi:10.4018/joeuc.2004070101

Gupta, M., & Sharman, R. (2008b, December). Dimensions of identity federation: A case study in financial services. *Journal of Information Assurance and Security, 3*(4), 244–256.

Ha, D., Yan, G., Eidenbenz, S., & Ngo, H. (2009). On the effectiveness of structural detection and defense against p2p-based botnets. In *Proceedings of IEEE/IFIP International Conference on Dependable Systems & Networks (DSN '09)* (pp. 297-306). IEEE.

Hagel Abdul-Rahman, A., & Hailes, S. (2000). Support trust in virtual communities. In *Proceedings of the 33rd Hawaii International on System Science* (pp. 1769-1777). IEEE.

Haimes, Y. Y. (2004). *Risk modeling, assessment, and management* (Vol. 40). Hoboken, NJ: John Wiley & Sons. doi:10.1002/0471723908

Haji, F., Lindsay, L., & Song, S. (2005). Practical security strategy for SCADA automation systems and networks. In *Proceedings of Canadian Conference on Electrical and Computer Engineering* (pp. 172-178). Academic Press. doi:10.1109/CCECE.2005.1556903

Hall, M., Frank, E., Holmes, G., Pfahringer, B., Reutemann, P., & Witten, H. I. (2009). The weka data mining software: An update. *ACM SIGKDD Explorations Newsletter, 11*(1), 10–18. doi:10.1145/1656274.1656278

Halme, L. R., & Bauer, K. R. (1995). AINT misbehaving: A taxonomy of anti-intrusion techniques. In *Proceedings of the 18th National Information Systems Security Conference* (pp. 163-172). Baltimore, MD: Academic Press.

Hardin, R. (1992). The street-level epistemology of trust. *Analyse & Kritik, 14*, 152–176.

Hardt, D. (2012). *The OAuth 2.0 authorization framework.* RFC 6749, IETF; October 2012.

Harrell, E., & Langton, L. (2013). *Victims of identity theft, 2012.* U.S. Department of Justice, Bureau of Justice Statistics, December, 2013, NCJ 243779. Retrieved April 30, 2014, from http://www.bjs.gov/content/pub/pdf/vit12.pdf

Harrington, D., Presuhn, R., & Wijnen, B. (2002). *RFC 3411: An architecture for describing simple network management protocol (SNMP) management frameworks.* Academic Press.

Harris Poll. (2003). *Harris interactive* [online]. Retrieved November 10, 2014, from http://www.harrisinteractive.com/harris_poll/index.asp?PID=365

Harris, E. A., Perlroth, N., & Popper, N. (2014, January 24). *Neiman Marcus data breach worse than first said.* Retrieved March 15, 2014, from The New York Times Company: http://www.nytimes.com/2014/01/24/business/neiman-marcus-breach-affected-1-1- million-cards.html?_r=1

Hasan, R., & Yurcik, W. (2006). A statistical analysis of disclosed storage security breaches. In *Proceedings of 2nd International Workshop on Storage Security and Survivability* (StorageSS '06). Academic Press. doi:10.1145/1179559.1179561

Hasan, M., Prajapati, N., & Vohara, S. (2010). Case study on social engineering techniques for persuasion. *GRAPH-HOC, 2*(2), 17–23. doi:10.5121/jgraphoc.2010.2202

Hauenstein, N. M. A., McGonigle, T., & Flinder, S. W. (2001). A meta-analysis of the relationship between procedural justice and distributive justice: Implications for justice research. *Employee Responsibilities and Rights Journal, 13*(1), 39–56. doi:10.1023/A:1014482124497

Haythornthwaite, C. (2005). Social networks and internet connectivity effects. *Information Communication and Society, 8*(2), 125–147. doi:10.1080/13691180500146185

Heckle, R. R., & Holden, S. H. (2006). Analytical tools for privacy risks: Assessing efficacy on vote verification technologies. In *Symposium on Usable Privacy and Security.* Pittsburgh, PA: Carnegie Mellon University. Retrieved July 8, 2014, from the Carnegie Mellon University website: http://cups.cs.cmu.edu/soups/2006/posters/heckle-poster_abstract.pdf

Hedbom, H., Kvarnström, H., & Jonsson, E. (1999). Security implications of distributed intrusion detection architectures. In *Proceedings of the Fourth Nordic Workshop on Secure IT Systems* (pp. 225–243). Kista, Sweden: Academic Press.

Helberger, N., & Hugenholtz, P. B. (2007). No place like home for making a copy: Private copying in European copyright law and consumer law. *Berkeley Technology Law Journal, 22*, 1061–1098.

Helne, C. A. (2005). Predicting workplace deviance from the interaction between organizational justice and personality. *Journal of Managerial Issues, 17*(2), 247–263.

Herald Sun. (2010). *Governments powerless to stop Facebook vandalism, says IT expert.* Retrieved from: http://www.heraldsun.com.au/.../governments-powerless-to-stop-facebook-vandalism-says-itexpert/story-e6frf7jx-1225834291255

Hercheui, M. D. (2011). A literature review of virtual communities. *Information Communication and Society, 14*(1), 1–23. doi:10.1080/13691181003663593

Herley, C. (2009). So long and no thanks for the externalities: The rational rejection of security advice by users. In *NSPW'09: New security paradigms workshop* (pp. 133–144). New York, NY: ACM. doi:10.1145/1719030.1719050

Herley, C., & Oorschot, P. C. V. (2012). A research agenda acknowledging the persistence of passwords. *IEEE Security and Privacy, 10*(1), 28–36. doi:10.1109/MSP.2011.150

Herring, S. C. (2002). Computer mediated communication on the internet. *Annual Review of Information Science & Technology*, *36*(1), 109–168. doi:10.1002/aris.1440360104

HI TECH Act. (2010). *Health information technology for economic and clinical health act: Subtitle A, SEC 3000, definitions, 2009.* Retrieved from http://www.healthit.gov/sites/default/files/hitech_act_excerpt_from_arra_with_index.pdf

HID Global's 4TRESS Authentication Appliance. (n.d.). Retrieved from http://www.hidglobal.com/sites/hidglobal.com/files/resource_files/identity-assurance-4tress-authentication-appliance-ds-en.pdf

Hijmans, H., & Scirocco, A. (2009). Shortcomings in EU data protection in the third and the second pillars: Can the Lisbon Treaty be expected to help? *Common Market Law Review*, *46*, 1485–1525.

Hilligoss, B., & Rieh, S. Y. (2008). Developing a unifying framework of credibility assessment: Construct, heuristics, and interaction in context. *Information Processing & Management*, *44*(4), 1467–1484. doi:10.1016/j.ipm.2007.10.001

Hiltz, S. R., & Turoff, M. (1978). *The network nation: Human communication via computer.* Reading, MA: Addison-Wesley.

HIPAA. (2006). *Saint Louis University institutional review board: HIPPA TIP sheet.* Retrieved from www.slu.edu/Documents/provost/irb/hipaa_tip_sheet.doc

Hirsch, F., Philpott, R., & Maler, E. (2005). *Security and privacy considerations for the OASIS security assertion markup language (SAML) v2.0.* Technical report, OASIS; March 2005.

Hirsch, L. E. (2007). Weaponizing classical music: Crime prevention and symbolic power in the age of repetition. *Journal of Popular Music Studies*, *19*(4), 342–358. doi:10.1111/j.1533-1598.2007.00132.x

Hitachi ID Systems Inc. (2014). Retrieved online on 4/12/2014 from User Provisioning Best Practices.

HMG IA Standard No. 6. (2009). *Protecting personal data and managing information risk.* Cabinet Office, CESG National Technical Authority for Information Assurance, Issue 1.2.

Hoffman, R. R., Lee, J. D., Woods, D. D., Shadbolt, N., Miler, J., & Bradshaw, J. M. (2009). The dynamics of trust in cyberdomain. *IEEE Intelligent Systems*, *24*(6), 5–11. doi:10.1109/MIS.2009.124

Hofstede, G. (1980). *Culture's consequences: International differences in work-related values.* Newbury Park, CA: Sage.

Hoonakker, P., Bornoe, N., & Carayon, P. (2009). Password authentication from a human factors perspective: Results of a survey among end-users. In *Proceedings of the Human Factors and Ergonomics Society Annual Meeting* (Vol. 53, No. 6, pp. 459-463). SAGE Publications. doi:10.1177/154193120905300605

Ho, S. Y., & Chau, P. Y. K. (2013). The effects of location personalization on integrity trust and integrity distrust in mobile merchants. *International Journal of Electronic Commerce*, *17*(4), 39–71. doi:10.2753/JEC1086-4415170402

Hunter, B. (2002). Learning in the virtual community depends upon changes in local communities. In K. A. Renninger & W. Shumar (Eds.), *Building virtual communities: Learning and change in cyberspace* (pp. 96–126). Cambridge, UK: Cambridge University Press. doi:10.1017/CBO9780511606373.009

Hunt, S. D., & Morgan, R. M. (1994). Relationship marketing in the era of network competition. *Marketing Management*, *3*(1), 18–28.

Hutchinson, D., & Warren, M. (2003). Security for internet banking: A framework. *Logistics, Information, &. Management*, *16*(1), 64–73.

IBM. (2006). *Stopping insider attacks: How organizations can protect their sensitive information* [online]. Retrieved November 10, 2014, from http://www-935.ibm.com/services/us/imc/pdf/gsw00316-usen-00-insider-threats-wp.pdf

IBM Tivoli. (n.d.). Retrieved on 2/2/2011 from http://www.rv-nrw.de/content/koop/tim/identity-mgr_43.pdf

Identity Theft Assistance Center. (2013). Retrieved March 7, 2014, from http://www.identitytheftassistance.org/pageview.php?cateid=47#childIDfraudReport

Ihn-Han, B., & Olariu, S. (2009). A weighted-dissimilarity-based anomaly detection method for mobile wireless networks. In *Proceedings ofInternational Conference on Computational Science and Engineering* (pp. 29–34). Academic Press.

Imprivata. (n.d.). *Benefits of single sign on*. Retrieved March 22, 2009, from Imprivata: http://www.imprivata.com/contentmgr/showdetails.php ?id=1170

INCITS. (2014). Retrieved online on 4/12/2014 from https://standards.incits.org/a/public/group/cs1

Information Commissioner's Office. (2009). *Privacy impact assessment: Handbook version 2.0. appendix 1 – PIA screening process*. Retrieved from http://www.ico.gov.uk/upload/documents/pia_handbook_html_v2/html/3-app1.html

Ingalsbe, J. A., Kunimatsu, L., Baeten, T., & Mead, N. R. (2008). Threat modeling: Diving into the deep end. *IEEE Software*, 25(1), 28–34. doi:10.1109/MS.2008.25

Inglesant, P. G., & Sasse, M. A. (2010). The true cost of unusable password policies: password use in the wild. In *Proceedings of the 28th International Conference on Human Factors in Computing Systems (CHI '10)* (pp. 383-392). ACM. doi:10.1145/1753326.1753384

Inness, J. (1996). *Privacy, intimacy and isolation*. Oxford, UK: Oxford University Press. doi:10.1093/0195104609.001.0001

Intelegen, Inc. (2008). *Human memory*. Retrieved December 1, 2009, from http://brain.web-us.com/memory/human_memory.htm

International Association of Privacy Professionals (IAPP). (2014). *Mexico federal data protection act*. Retrieved May 01, 2014 from https://www.privacyassociation.org/media/pdf/knowledge_center/Mexico_Federal_Data_Protection_Act_July2010.pdf

International Standard Organization (ISO). (2008). *ISO 9001:2008, quality management systems Requirements*. Geneva, Switzerland: ISO.

International Standard Organization (ISO). (2009). *ISO/IEC 27004:2009, information technology, security techniques, information security management measurement*. Geneva, Switzerland: ISO.

International Standard Organization (ISO). (2013a). *ISO survey of certifications 2012*. Retrieved March 15, 2014 from http://www.iso.org/iso/home/standards/certification/iso-survey.html

International Standard Organization (ISO). (2013b). *ISO/IEC 27001:2013, information technology, security techniques, information security management systems requirements*. Geneva, Switzerland: ISO.

Intersect Alliance. (2003). *Guide to snare for Linux*. Retrieved November 25, 2010, from http://www.intersectalliance.com/resources/Documentation/Guide_to_Snare_for_Linux-3.2.pdf

Introna, L. D. (2001). Workplace surveillance, privacy and distributive justice. In Readings in CyberEthics. Sudbury, MA: Jones and Barlett Publishers.

Introna, L.D. (1996). Privacy and the computer: Why we need privacy in the information society. *Ethicomp e-Journal, 1*.

ISO. (n.d.). Retrieved from http://www.iso.org/iso/iso_catalogue/catalogue_tc/catalogue_tc_browse.htm?commid=45306

ISO/IEC (2013). *ISO 27002, information technology – Security techniques – Code of practice for information security controls*. Author.

IT Governance Institute. (2006). *Information security governance: Guidance for boards of directors and executive management*. IT Governance Institute.

IT Governance Institute. (2007). *COBIT® 4.1: Framework, control objectives, management guidelines, maturity models*. Rolling Meadows, IL: IT Governance Institute.

Itzkowitz, M., Wylie, B. J. N., Aoki, C., & Kosche, N. (2003). Memory profiling using hardware counters. In *Proceedings of the 2003 ACM/IEEE Conference on Supercomputing (SC'03)* (pp. 17–29). Phoenix, AZ: IEEE. doi:10.1145/1048935.1050168

Iyer, G., Soberman, D., & Villas-Boas, J. M. (2003, May). *The targeting of advertising*. Retrieved March 15, 2014, from http://groups.haas.berkeley.edu/marketing/PAPERS/VILLAS/tgtadv1_apr03.pdf

Jackson, M. (2005, January 10). Music to deter yobs by. *BBC News Magazine*. Retrieved December 12, 2010 from http://news.bbc.co.uk/1/hi/magazine/4154711.stm

Jackson, T., Dawson, R., & Wilson, D. (2001). *The cost of email interruption*. Loughborough University Institutional Repository: Item 2134/495 [online]. Retrieved November 10, 2014, from http://km.lboro.ac.uk/iii/pdf/JOSIT%202001.pdf

Jain, A., Bolle, R., & Pankanti, S. (Eds.). (1998). Biometrics: Personal identification in networked society. Dordrecht, The Netherlands: Kluwer.

Jain, A. K., Ross, A., & Pankanti, S. (2006). Biometrics: A tool for information security. *IEEE Transactions of Information Forensics and Security, 1*(2), 125–143. doi:10.1109/TIFS.2006.873653

Jakobsson, M., & Akavipat, R. (2012). Rethinking passwords to adapt to constrained keyboards. In *Proc. IEEE MoST*. IEEE.

Janakiraman, R., Waldvogel, M., & Qi, Z. (2003). Indra: A peer-to-peer approach to network intrusion detection and prevention. In *Proceedings of International Workshops on Enabling Technologies: Infrastructures for Collaborative Enterprises* (pp. 226-231). Academic Press.

Jaquith, A. (2007). *Security metrics, replacing fear, unceartainty, and doubt*. Addison Wesley.

Jarvenpaa, S. L., & Leidner, D. E. (1998). Communication and trust in global virtual teams. *Journal of Computer-Mediated Communication, 3*(4). Retrieved from http://jcmc.indiana.edu/vol3/issue4/jarvenpaa.html

Jarvenpaa, S. L., Shaw, T. R., & Staples, D. S. (2004). Toward contextualized theories of trust: The role of trust in global virtual teams. *Information Systems Research, 15*(3), 250–267. doi:10.1287/isre.1040.0028

Jarvenpaa, S. L., Tractinsky, N., & Vitale, M. (2000). Consumer trust in an internet store. *Information Technology Management, 1*(1-2), 45–71. doi:10.1023/A:1019104520776

Jaszi, P. (1998). *Intellectual property legislative update: Copyright, paracopyright, and pseudo-copyright*. Paper presented at the Association of Research Libraries Conference: The Future Network: Transforming Learning and Scholarship, Eugene, OR. Retrieved February 28, 2014, from http://old.arl.org/resources/pubs/mmproceedings/132mmjaszi~print.shtml

Jefferey, K., & Neidecker-Lutz, B. (Eds.). (2010). Expert group report: The future of cloud computing. *European Commission: Information Society and Media*. Retrieved from http://cordis.europa.eu/fp7/ict/ssai/docs/cloud-report-final.pdf

Jensen, J. (2012). Federated identity management challenges. In *Proceedings of 2012 Seventh International Conference on Availability, Reliability and Security (ARES)*. Academic Press. doi:10.1109/ARES.2012.68

Jeong, E., & Jang, S. (2011). Restaurant experiences triggering positive electronic word of mouth (eWOM) motivations. *International Journal of Hospitality Management, 30*(2), 356–366. doi:10.1016/j.ijhm.2010.08.005

Jing, Z., HouKuan, H., ShengFeng, T., & Xiang, Z. (2009). Applications of HMM in protocol anomaly detection. In *Proceedings of International Joint Conference on Computational Sciences and Optimization* (pp. 347–349). Academic Press.

Jing-Wen, T., Mei-Juan, G., Ling-Fang, H., & Shi-Ru, Z. (2009). Community intrusion detection system based on wavelet neural network. In *Proceedings of International Conference on Machine Learning and Cybernetics* (vol. 2, pp. 1026 – 1030). Academic Press.

Jin, X., & Osborn, S. L. (2007). Architecture for data collection in database intrusion detection systems. In *Proceedings of the 4th VLDB Workshop on Secure Data Management (SDM 2007)*. Vienna, Austria: VLDB. doi:10.1007/978-3-540-75248-6_7

Johnson, M. E., & Goetz, E. (2007). Embedding information security into the organization. *IEEE Security and Privacy, 5*(May/June), 16–24. doi:10.1109/MSP.2007.59

Jonassen, D. H., Peck, K. L., & Wilson, B. G. (1999). *Learning with technology: A constructivist perspective.* Upper Saddle River, NJ: Merrill.

Jones, S., Millermaier, S., Goya-Martinez, M., & Schuler, J. (2008). Whose space is MySpace? A content analysis of MySpace profiles. *First Monday, 13*(9). doi:10.5210/fm.v13i9.2202

Jøsang, A. (1996). The right type of trust for distributed systems. In *Proceedings of the 1996 Workshop on New Security Paradigms.* Academic Press. doi:10.1145/304851.304877

Jøsang, A., & Pope, S. (n.d.). User centric identity management. *CRC for Enterprise Distributed Systems Technology* (DSTC Pty Ltd). The University of Queensland.

Jøsang, A., Al Zomai, M., & Suriadi, S. (2007). Usability and privacy in identity management architectures. In *Proceedings of the Australasian Information Security Workshop 2007.* Ballarat, Australia: Academic Press.

Jou, Y. F., Gong, F., Sargor, C., Wu, S., Wu, S. F., Chang, H. C., & Wang, F. (2000). Design and implementation of a scalable intrusion detection system for the protection of network infrastructure. *Defense Advanced Research Projects Agency Information Survivability Conference and Exposition, 2,* 69–83.

Judgement of the Court in Digital Rights Ireland. (2014). *InfoCuria - Case-law of the Court of Justice.* Retrieved from http://curia.europa.eu/juris/document/document.jsf;jsessionid=9ea7d0f130d686ae333e76e448e28720eb03f4442ff1.e34KaxiLc3eQc40LaxqMbN4OaNiLe0?text=&docid=150642&pageIndex=0&doclang=en&mode=req&dir=&occ=first&part=1&cid=30149

KAD. (2010). *Handling interrupt descriptor table for fun and profit.* Retrieved November 25, 2010, from http://www.phrack.org/issues.html?issue=59&id=4#article

Kahneman, D., & Tversky, A. (1979). Prospect theory: An analysis of decisions under risk. *Econometrica, 47*(2), 313–327. doi:10.2307/1914185

Kahneman, D., & Tversky, A. (2000). *Choices, values, and frames.* Cambridge University Press.

Kaifa-Gbanti, M. (2010). *Surveillance models in the security state & fair criminal trial.* Athens, Greece: Nomiki Vivliothiki. (in Greek)

Kanaley, R. (2001). Login error trouble keeping track of all your sign-ons? Here's a place to keep your electronic keys, but you better remember the password. *San Jose Mercury News,* p. 3G.

Kanawattanachai, P., & Yoo, Y. (2007). The impact of knowledge coordination on virtual team performance over time. *Management Information Systems Quarterly, 31*(4), 783–808.

Kang, J., Zhang, J.-Y., Li, Q., & Li, Z. (2009). Detecting new p2p botnet with multi-chart cusum. In *Proceedings of the International Conference on Networks Security, Wireless Communications and Trusted Computing (NSWCTC '09)* (vol. 1, pp. 688-691). Academic Press.

Kaplan, R. S., & Norton, D. P. (1996). *The balanced scorecard: Translating strategy into action* (reprinted ed.). Boston, MA: Harvard Business School Press.

Kark, K. (2010). *Twelve recommendations for your 2011 security strategy.* Forrester Research Report. Retrieved on 4/18/2014 from http://www.forrester.com/Twelve+Recommendations+For+Your+2011+Security+Strategy/fulltext/-/E-RES57684

Karlsson, J. (1996). Software requirements prioritizing. *Requirements Engineering, 1996,* 110–116.

Karole, A., Saxena, N., & Christin, N. (2010). A comparative usability evaluation of traditional password managers. In *Proceedings of the 13th International Conference on Information Security and Cryptology* (pp. 233-251). Springer-Verlag.

Katyal, S. (2004). The new surveillance. *Case Western Reserve Law Review, 54,* 297–386.

Kay, R. (2005, April 4). *Biometric authentication.* Retrieved 3rd April 2010 from http://www.computerworld.com/s/article/100772/Biometric_Authentication?taxonomyId=17&pageNumber=1

Kayacik, H. G., Zincir-Heywood, A. N., & Heywood, M. I. (2004). On dataset biases in a learning system with minimum a priori information for intrusion detection. In *Proceedings of Communication Networks and Services Research Conference* (pp. 181–189). Academic Press. doi:10.1109/DNSR.2004.1344727

Kelton, K., Fleischmann, K. R., & Wallace, W. A. (2008). Trust in digital information. *Journal of the American Society for Information Science and Technology, 59*(3), 363–374. doi:10.1002/asi.20722

Kent, K., & Souppaya, M. (2006). *Guide to computer security log management: Recommendations of the National Institute of Standards and Technology (NIST), special publication 800-92*. Retrieved November 24, 2010, from http://csrc.nist.gov/publications/nistpubs/800-92/SP800-92.pdf

Khan, I. (2009). Cloud computing set to go mainstream. *Outsourcing, 13*, 30–31.

Khodyakov, D. (2007). Trust as a process: A three-dimensional approach. *Sociology, 41*(1), 115–132. doi:10.1177/0038038507072285

Khoshgoftaar, T. M., & Abushadi, M. E. (2004). Resource-sensitive intrusion detection models for network traffic. In *Proceedings of High Assurance Systems Engineering Symposium* (pp. 249–258). Academic Press.

Kiesler, S. (1986). Thinking ahead: The hidden messages in computer networks. *Harvard Business Review*, (January-February), 46–60.

Kietzmann, J. H., Hermkens, K., McCarthy, I. P., & Silvestre, B. S. (2011). Social media? Get serious! Understanding the functional building blocks of social media. *Business Horizons, 54*(3), 241–251. doi:10.1016/j.bushor.2011.01.005

Killourhy, K. S., Maxion, R. A., & Tan, K. M. C. (2004). A defense-centric taxonomy based on attack manifestations. In *Proceedings of the International Conference on Dependable Systems and Networks (DSN 2004)* (pp. 102–111). Florence, Italy: IEEE. doi:10.1109/DSN.2004.1311881

Kim, D. J. (2008). Self-perception-based versus transference-based trust determinants in computer-mediated transactions: A cross-cultural comparison study. *Journal of Management Information Systems, 24*(4), 13–45. doi:10.2753/MIS0742-1222240401

Klein, P. G. (2009). Risk, uncertainty, and economic organization. In J. G. Hülsmann & S. Kinsella (Eds.), *Property, freedom, & society: Essays in honor of Hans-Hermann Hoppe* (pp. 325-338). Auburn, AL: Ludwig von Mises Institute. Retrieved on May 1st, 2010, from web site: http://mises.org/daily/3779

Kleyman, B. (2013). *Healthcare data breaches: Reviewing the ramifications*. Retrieved August 13, 2013, from http://healthitsecurity.com/2013/07/23/healthcare-data-breaches-reviewing-the-ramifications/

Knight, F. H. (1921). *Risk, uncertainty, and profit*. New York: Kelley and Millman, Inc.

Knight, R., & Pretty, D. (1996). *The impact of catastrophes on shareholder value*. Oxford, UK: Templeton College, Oxford University.

Knorr, E. M., & Ng, R. T. (1998). Algorithms for mining distance-based outliers in large dataset. In *Proceedings of International Conference on Very Large Data Base (VLDB)* (pp. 392-403). New York, NY: VLDB.

Knorr, E. M., & Ng, R. T. (1999). Finding intentional knowledge of distance-based outliers. In *Proceedings of International Conference on Very Large Data Base (VLDB)* (pp. 211-222). Edinburgh, UK: VLDB.

Ko, C. (2003). System health and intrusion monitoring (SHIM): Project summary. *Defense Advanced Research Projects Agency Information Survivability Conference and Exposition, 2*, 202–207. doi:10.1109/DISCEX.2003.1194966

Kollock, P. (1999). The production of trust in online markets. In E. J. Lawler, M. Macy, S. Thyne, & H. A. Walker (Eds.), *Advanced in group process* (vol. 16, pp. 99–123). Greenwich, CT: JAI Press.

Komanduri, S., & Hutchings, D. (2008). Order and entropy in picture passwords. In *Proceedings of Graphics Interface*. Academic Press.

Komanduri, S., Shay, R., Kelley, P. G., Mazurek, M. L., Bauer, L., & Christin, N. et al. (2011). Of passwords and people: Measuring the effect of password-composition policies. In *Proceedings of ACM CHI Conference on Human Factors in Computing Systems* (pp. 2595 – 2604). ACM.

Kosta, E. (2013). The way to Luxemburg: National court decisions on the compatibility of the data retention directive with the rights to privacy and data protection. *SCRIPT-ed*, *10*(3), 339–363. doi:10.2966/scrip.100313.339

Kramer, M. L., Wayne, S. J., Liden, R. C., & Sparrowe, R. T. (2005). The role of job security in understanding the relationship between employee's perceptions of temporary workers and employee performance. *The Journal of Applied Psychology*, *90*(2), 389–398. doi:10.1037/0021-9010.90.2.389 PMID:15769247

Kramer, R. M. (1999). Trust and distrust in organizations: Emerging perspectives, enduring questions. *Annual Review of Psychology*, *50*(1), 569–598. doi:10.1146/annurev.psych.50.1.569 PMID:15012464

Krishnamurthy, B., & Wills, C. (2009). On the leakage of personally identifiable information via online social networks. In *Proceedings of 1st ACM Workshop on Online Social Networks*. Barcelona, Spain: ACM. doi:10.1145/1592665.1592668

Krizhanovsky, A., & Marasanov, A. (2007). An approach for adaptive intrusion prevention based on the danger. In *Proceedings of 2nd International Conference on Availability, Reliability and Security* (pp. 1135-1142). Academic Press. doi:10.1109/ARES.2007.36

Kroft, S. (2014, March 9). *The data brokers: Selling your personal information*. Retrieved March 15, 2014, from http://www.cbsnews.com/news/the-data-brokers-selling-your-personal-information/

Kühn, H., Karagiannis, D., & Junginger, S. (1996) *Metamodellierung in dem BPMS-Analysewerkzeug ADONIS, Konferenz Informatik '96*. Uni Klagenfurt.

Kui, Z. (2009). A danger model based anomaly detection method for wireless sensor networks. In *Proceedings of Second International Symposium on Knowledge Acquisition and Modeling* (pp. 11–14). Academic Press.

Kumar, M., & Hanumanthappa, M. (2013). Scalable intrusion detection systems log analysis using cloud computing infrastructure. In *Proceedings of IEEE International Conference on Computational Intelligence and Computing Research (ICCIC)* (pp. 1-4). IEEE. doi:10.1109/ICCIC.2013.6724158

Kumar, M., Hanumanthappa, M., & Kumar, T. V. S. (2012). Intrusion detection system using decision tree algorithm. In *Proceedings of IEEE 14th International Conference on Communication Technology (ICCT)* (pp. 629-634). IEEE.

Kuo, C., Romanosky, S., & Cranor, L. F. (2006). Human selection of mnemonic phrase-based passwords. In *Proceedings of the Second Symposium on Usable Privacy and Security* (pp. 67–78). ACM. doi:10.1145/1143120.1143129

Kuperman, B. A. (2004). *A categorization of computer security monitoring systems and the impact on the design of audit sources*. (PhD thesis). Purdue University, West Lafayette, IN.

Kuperman, B. A., & Spafford, E. (1999). *Generation of application level audit data via library interposition: Technical Report CERIAS TR 99-11*. West Lafayette, IN: COAST Laboratory, Purdue University.

Labbe, K. G., Rowe, N. G., & Fulp, J. D. (2006). A methodology for evaluation of host-based intrusion prevention systems and its application. In *Proceedings of Information Assurance Workshop* (pp. 378-379). Academic Press. doi:10.1109/IAW.2006.1652120

Laio, K. H., & Chueh, H. E. (2012). An evaluation model of information security management of medical staff. *International Journal of Innovation*, *8*(11), 7865–7873.

Lane, F. S. (2003). *The naked employee: How technology is compromising workplace privacy.* New York: AMA-COM, American Management Association.

Larson, U. E., Jonsson, E., & Lindskog, S. (2008a). A revised taxonomy of data collection mechanisms with a focus on intrusion detection. In *Proceedings of the 3rd IEEE International Conference on Availability, Security, and Reliability (ARES 2008)* (pp. 624–629). Barcelona, Spain: IEEE. doi:10.1109/ARES.2008.38

Larson, U. E., Lindskog, S., Nilsson, D. K., & Jonsson, E. (2008b). Operator-centric and adaptive intrusion detection. In *Proceedings of the Fourth International Conference on Information Assurance and Security (IAS'08)* (pp. 161–166). Naples, Italy: IEEE. doi:10.1109/IAS.2008.42

Larson, U. E., Nilsson, D. K., & Jonsson, E. (2008). An approach to specification-based attack detection for in-vehicle networks. In *Proceedings of the 12th IEEE Intelligent Vehicles Symposium (IV08)*. Eindhoven, the Netherlands: IEEE. doi:10.1109/IVS.2008.4621263

Larus, J. R. (1993). Efficient program tracing. *Computer, 26*(5), 52–61. doi:10.1109/2.211900

Larus, J. R., & Ball, T. (1994). Rewriting executable files to measure program behavior. *Software, Practice & Experience, 24*(2), 197–218. doi:10.1002/spe.4380240204

Laudon, K. C., & Laudon, J. P. (2001). *Essentials of management information systems: Organisation and technology in the networked enterprise* (4th ed.). Prentice Hall.

Laudon, K. C., & Laudon, J. P. (2002). *Management information systems: Managing the digital firm* (7th ed.). Prentice Hall International.

Laudon, K. C., & Traver, C. G. (2010). *E-commerce 2010 – Business, technology, society* (6th ed.). Boston: Pearson.

Lazarsfeld, P., & Field, H. (1946). *The people look at radio.* Chapel Hill, NC: University of North Carolina Press.

LBNL. (2010). *TCPDUMP & LiBPCAP.* Retrieved March 30, 2010, from http://www.tcpdump.org/

Lea, M., & Spears, R. (1991). Computer-mediated communication, de-individuation and group decision-making. *International Journal of Man-Machine Studies, 34*(2), 283–301. doi:10.1016/0020-7373(91)90045-9

LeDoux, J. E. (1992). Emotion as memory: Anatomical systems underlying indelible neural traces. In S. Christianson (Ed.), *Handbook of emotion and memory: Theory and research* (pp. 269–288). Hillsdale, NJ: Erlbaum.

Lee, S. (2003). An introduction to identity management systems. *SANS Institute InfoSec Reading Room.* Retrieved online on 4/12/2014 http://sans.org/reading_room/whitepapers/authentication/introduction-identity-management_852

Lee, W., & Xiang, D. (2001). Information-theoretic measures for anomaly detection. In *Proceedings of the 2001 Symposium on Research in Security and Privacy* (pp. 130–143). Oakland, CA: Academic Press.

Lee, S., & Zhai, S. (2009). The performance of touch screen soft buttons. In *Proceedings of the SIGCHI Conference on Human Factors in Computing Systems* (pp. 309-318). ACM. doi:10.1145/1518701.1518750

Lee, W., Stolfo, S., & Chan, P. (1997). Learning patterns from Unix process execution traces for intrusion detection. In *AI approaches to fraud detection and risk management* (pp. 50–60). Providence, RI: AAAI Press.

Legal Information Institute (LII). (2014). *TOPN: Children's online privacy protection act of 1998.* Retrieved April 30, 2014, from http://www.law.cornell.edu/topn/childrens_online_privacy_protection_act_of_1998

Leimer, H. W. (1990). *Vernetztes denken im bankmanagement.* Gabler Verlag. doi:10.1007/978-3-322-91058-5

Leinwand, A., & Conroy, K. F. (1996). *Network management: A practical perspective.* New York, NY: Addison-Wesley.

Leippold, M., & Vanini, P. (2003). *The quantification of operational risk.* Available at SSRN: http://ssrn.com/abstract=481742 or doi:10.2139/ssrn.481742

Leitch, S., & Warren, M. (2011). The ethics of security of personal information upon Facebook. In ICT ethics and security in the 21st century: New developments and applications (pp. 46-65). IGI Global.

Leitch, S., & Warren, M. (2012). Cyber-bulling and vigilantism: Should social media services be held to account. In *Proceedings of Sixth Australian Institute of Computer Ethics Conference.* Melbourne, Australia: Academic Press.

Lemire, L., & Rouillard, C. (2005). An empirical exploration of the psychological contract violation and individual behaviour. *Journal of Managerial Psychology,* *20*(2), 150–163. doi:10.1108/02683940510579786

Lesk, M. (2013). Electronic medical records: Confidential, care and epidemiology. *IEEE Security & Privacy, Building Dependability, Reliability and Trust, 6*(11).

Lessig, L. (2006). *Code 2.0.* New York: Basic Books.

Lester, S. W., Claire, E., & Kickull, J. (2001). Psychological contracts in the 21st century: What employees values most and how well organizations are responding to these expectations. *Human Resource Planning, 24,* 10–21.

Levi, M., & Burrows, M. (2008). Measuring the impact of fraud in the UK: A conceptual and empirical journey. *The British Journal of Criminology, 48*(3), 293–318. doi:10.1093/bjc/azn001

Levon, J., & Elie, P. (2009). *Oprofile: A system-wide profiler for Linux systems.* Retrieved November 25, 2010, from http://oprofile.sourceforge.net/news/

Lewicki, R. J., & Bunker, B. B. (1996). Developing and maintaining trust in work relationships. In R. M. Kramer & T. R. Tyler (Eds.), *Trust in organization: Frontiers of theory and research* (pp. 114–139). Thousand Oaks, CA: Sage. doi:10.4135/9781452243610.n7

Lewicki, R. J., McAllister, D. J., & Bies, R. J. (1998). Trust and distrust: New relationships and realities. *Academy of Management Review, 23*(3), 438–458.

Lewicki, R. J., & Wiethoff, C. (2000). Trust, trust development, and trust repair. In M. Deutsch & P. T. Coleman (Eds.), *The handbook of conflict resolution: Theory and practice* (pp. 86–107). San Francisco, CA: Jossey-Bass.

Lewis, J. D. (1999). *Trusted partner: How companies build mutual trust and win together.* New York: Simon & Schuter.

Lewis, J. D., & Weigert, A. J. (1985). Trust as a social reality. *Social Forces, 63*(4), 967–985. doi:10.1093/sf/63.4.967

Leyden, T. (2009, October). A brief history of cloud computing. *Sys-Con Media.* Retrieved from https://tleyden.sys-con.com/node/1150011

Li, Z., Goyal, A., & Chen, Y. (2007). Honeynet-based botnet scan traffic analysis. Botnet Detection, 36, 25–44.

Liang, W., & Wang, W. (2005). *A quatitative study of authentication & QoS in wirless IP network.* Retrieved 8th April, 2010 from http://www.ece.ncsu.edu/netwis/papers/05LW-INFOCOM

Liddell, J., Renaud, K. V., & De Angeli, A. (2003). *Authenticating users using a combination of sound and images.* Paper presented at British Computer Society, Bath, UK.

Lieberman Software. (2014). Retrieved online on 4/12/2014 from http://www.liebsoft.com/Enterprise_Random_Password_Manager/

Linden, M., & Vilpola, I. (2005). An empirical study on the usability of logout in a single sign-on system. In *Proceedings of the 1st International Conference in Information Security Practice and Experience* (LNCS), (vol. 3439, pp. 243-254). Springer-Verlag. doi:10.1007/978-3-540-31979-5_21

Lindup, K. R. (1995). A new model for information security policies. *Computers & Security, 14*(8), 691–695. doi:10.1016/0167-4048(96)81709-3

Links, C. H. (2008). *IAM success tips: Identity and access management success strategies.* CreateSpace Independent Publishing Platform.

Linux Audit Subsystem. (2004). *Linux audit subsystem design documentation for kernel 2.6.* Retrieved November 25, 2010, from http://www.uniforum.chi.il.us/slides/HardeningLinux/LAuS-Design.pdf

Lipnack, J., & Stamps, J. (1997). *Virtual teams.* New York: John Wiley and Sons, Inc.

Liu, S. (2004, February). *Authentication in ASP.NET web servers.* Retrieved from 3rd March 2010 from http://progtutorials.tripod.com/Authen.htm

Liu, L., Chen, S., Yan, G., & Zhang, Z. (2008). Execution-based bot-like malware detection.[LNCS]. *Proceedings of Information Security, 5222,* 97–113.

Lixia, X., Dan, Z., & Hongyu, Y. (2009). Research on SVM based network intrusion detection classification. In *Proceedings of Sixth International Conference on Fuzzy Systems and Knowledge Discovery* (pp. 362–366). Academic Press.

Lobosco, K. (2014, March 14). *Target details risks from giant data breach.* Retrieved March 15, 2014, from Cable News Network: http://money.cnn.com/2014/03/14/news/companies/target-breach/

Logan, D. (2009). Hype cycle for legal and regulatory information governance. *Gartner.* Retrieved from http://www.gartner.com/DisplayDocument?doc_cd=208630&ref=g_rss

Louis Harris Poll. (1999). Available from http://www.natlconsumersleague.org/FNLSUM1.PDF

Love, R. (2005). *Linux kernel development* (2nd ed.). Novell Press.

ltrace. (2002). *ltrace – Default branch.* Retrieved November 25, 2010, from http://freshmeat.net/projects/ltrace/

Lu, W., Tavallaee, M., Rammidi, G., & Ghorbani, A. A. (2009). Botcop: An online botnet traffic classifier. In *Proceedings of 7th Annual Communication Networks and Services Research Conference (CNSR '09)* (pp. 70-77). Academic Press. doi:10.1109/CNSR.2009.21

Lucero, J., & Wallerstein, N. (2013). Trust in community–academic research partnerships: Increasing the consciousness of conflict and trust development. In J. Oetzel & S. Ting-Toomey (Eds.), *The SAGE handbook of conflict communication* (2nd ed.; pp. 537–563). Thousand Oaks, CA: SAGE Publications. doi:10.4135/9781452281988.n23

Luhmann, N. (1979). *Trust and power.* Toronto: John Wiley.

Luhmann, N. (1988). Familiarity, confidence, trust: Problems and alternatives. In D. Gamebetta (Ed.), *Trust: Marking and breaking cooperative relations* (pp. 94–107). New York: Basil Blackwell.

Luk, C.-K., Cohn, R., Muth, R., Patil, H., Klauser, A., & Lowney, G. et al. (2005). Pin: Building customized program analysis tools with dynamic instrumentation. In *Proceedings of the 2005 ACM SIGPLAN Conference on Programming Language Design and Implementation (PLDI'05)* (pp. 190–200). Chicago, IL: ACM. doi:10.1145/1065010.1065034

Lund, M. S., Solhaug, B., & Stølen, K. (2011). *Model-driven risk analysis: The CORAS approach.* Springer.

Lundin Barse, E. (2004). *Logging for intrusion and fraud detection.* (PhD thesis). Chalmers University of Technology, Göteborg, Sweden.

Lundin Barse, E., & Jonsson, E. (2004). Extracting attack manifestations to determine log data requirements for intrusion detection. In *Proceedings of the 20th Annual Computer Security Applications Conference (ACSAC 2004)* (pp. 158–167). Tucson, AZ: IEEE.

Luxenburger, R., & Schegner, P. (2004). A new intelligent auto-reclosing method considering the current transformer saturation. In *Proceedings of Eight International Conference on Developments in Power Systems Protection* (vol. 2, pp. 583-586). Academic Press. doi:10.1049/cp:20040191

Lu, Y., Zhao, L., & Wang, B. (2008). Exploring factors affecting trust and purchase behavior in virtual communities. In *Proceedings of IEEE Symposium on Advanced Management of Information for Globalized Enterprises.* IEEE. doi:10.1109/AMIGE.2008.ECP.11

Lu, Y., Zhao, L., & Wang, B. (2009). (in press). From virtual community members to C2C e-commerce buyers: Trust in virtual communities and its effect on consumers' purchase intention. *Electronic Commerce Research and Applications.* doi:10.1016/j.elerap.2009.07.003

Lynch, C. (2001). When documents deceive: Trust and provenance as new factors for information retrieval in a tangled web. *Journal of the American Society for Information and Technology, 52*(1), 12–17. doi:10.1002/1532-2890(2000)52:1<12::AID-ASI1062>3.0.CO;2-V

Lyon, G. F. (2009). *NMAP network scanning: The official NMAP project guide to network discovery and security scanning.* Insecure.

Magalhaes, R. M. (2001, November 19). *Understanding ISA's different types of authentication.* Retrieved 3rd April 2010 from www.isaserver.org/tutorials/Understanding_ISAs_different_Authentication_types.html

Maggi, F., Robertson, W., Kruegel, C., & Vigna, G. (2009). Protecting a moving target: Addressing web application concept drift. In *Proceedings of the 12th International Symposium on Recent Advances in Intrusion Detection (RAID 2009).* Saint-Malo, France: RAID. doi:10.1007/978-3-642-04342-0_2

Mahdinia, P., Berenjkoob, M., & Vatankhah, H. (2013). Attack signature matching using graphics processors in high-performance intrusion detection systems. In *Proceedings of 21st Iranian Conference on Electrical Engineering (ICEE)* (pp. 1-7). Academic Press. doi:10.1109/IranianCEE.2013.6599567

Mangum, M. (2011). Explaining political trust among African Americans: Examining demographic, media, and social capital and social networks effects. *The Social Science Journal*, *48*(4), 589–596. doi:10.1016/j.soscij.2011.03.002

Mann, P. S., & Sharma, M. (2012). Social engineering: A partial technical attack. *International Journal of Computer Science Issues*, *9*(2), 557–559.

Markert, B. K. (2002). *Comparison of three online privacy seal programs*. Bethesda, MD: SANS Institute. Retrieved July 8, 2014, from http://www.sans.org/reading-room/whitepapers/privacy/comparison-online-privacy-seal-programs-685

Marlinspike, M. (2009). *New tricks for defeating SSL in practice, Blackhat*. Retrieved 21st April, 2011 from https://www.blackhat.com/presentations/bh-dc-09/Marlinspike/BlackHat-DC-09-Marlinspike-Defeating-SSL.pdf

Marx, G., & Sherizen, S. (1991). Monitoring on the job: How to protect privacy as well as property. In Computers in the human context: Information technology, productivity, and people. Cambridge, MA: MIT Press.

Massey, A. K., Otto, P. N., & Anton, A. I. (2009). Prioritizing legal requirements. In *Proceedings of Requirements Engineering and Law (RELAW) 2009 Second International Workshop* (pp. 27–32). Hoboken, NJ: IEEE.

Masud, M. M., Gao, J., Khan, L., Han, J., & Thuraisingham, B. (2008). A practical approach to classify evolving data streams: Training with limited amount of labeled data. In *Proceedings of 8th IEEE International Conference on Data Mining (ICDM '08)* (pp. 929–934). IEEE. doi:10.1109/ICDM.2008.152

Mathew, S., Petropoulos, M., Ngo, H. Q., & Upadhyaya, S. (2010). A data-centric approach to insider attack detection in database systems. In *Proceedings of the 13th International Symposium on Recent Advances in Intrusion Detection (RAID 2010)*. Ottawa, Canada: Academic Press. doi:10.1007/978-3-642-15512-3_20

Mathieu, S. E. (2011). *Misogyny on the web: Comparing negative reader comments made to men and women who publish political commentary online.* (Thesis: Master of Arts). University of Missouri, Columbia, MO.

Matulevicius, R., Mayer, N., Mouratidis, H., Dubois, E., Heymans, P., & Genon, N. (2008). Adapting secure tropos for security risk management in the early phases of information systems development. In *Proceedings of CAiSE* (pp. 541–555). CAiSE. doi:10.1007/978-3-540-69534-9_40

Matzat, U. (2004). The social embeddedness of academic online groups in offline networks as a norm generating structure: An empirical test of the Coleman model on norm emergence. *Computational & Mathematical Organization Theory*, *10*(3), 205–226. doi:10.1023/B:CMOT.0000045369.98848.71

Mayer, R. C., Davis, J. D., & Schoorman, F. D. (1995). An integrative model of organisational trust. *Academy of Management Review*, *20*(3), 709–734.

Mazzariello, C. (2008). Irc traffic analysis for botnet detection. In *Proceedings of 4th International Conference on Information Assurance and Security (ISIAS '08)* (pp. 318-323). ISIAS.

McAlearney, S. (2008, August 7). TJX data breach: Ignore cost lessons and weep. *CIO Magazine*.

McAlister, D. J. (1995). Affect- and cognition-based trust as foundations for interpersonal cooperation in organizations. *Academy of Management Review*, *38*(1), 24–59. doi:10.2307/256727

McCanne, S., & Jacobson, V. (1993). The BSD packet filter: A new architecture for user-level packet capture. In *Proceedings of the USENIX Winter 1993 Conference (USENIX'93)* (pp. 259–270). San Diego, CA: USENIX Association.

McCarthy, C. (2008). You, there: Step back from the webcam. *Cnet News*. Retrieved from: http://news.cnet.com/8301-13577_3-9853908-36.html

McEvily, B., Radzevick, J., & Weber, R. A. (2012). Whom do you trust and how much does it cost? An experiment on the measurment of trust. *Games and Economic Behavior*, *74*(1), 285–298. doi:10.1016/j.geb.2011.06.011

McEvily, B., & Tortoriello, M. (2011). Measuring trust in organisational research: Review and recommendations. *Journal of Trust Research, 1*(1), 23–63. doi:10.1080/215 15581.2011.552424

McGraw, D. (2013). Privacy and security as enabler, not barrier, to responsible health data uses. *IEEE Security & Privacy, Building Dependability, Reliability, and Trust, 6*(11).

McGregor, A., Hall, M., Lorier, P., & Brunskill, J. (2004). Flow clustering using machine learning techniques. In *Proceedings of Passive and Active Network Measurement (LNCS)* (pp. 205–214). Berlin, Germany: Springer-Verlag.

McKnight, D. H., & Chervany, N. L. (1996). *The meanings of trust* (Technical Report 94004). Carlson School of Management, University of Minnesota. Retrieved on February 1st, 2010, from http://misrc.umn.edu/wpaper/WorkingPapers/9604.pdf

McKnight, D. H., & Chervany, N. L. (2001). Conceptualizing trust: A typology and e-commerce customer relationships model. In *Proceedings of Hawaii International Conference on System Sciences.* IEEE Computer Society. doi:10.1109/HICSS.2001.927053

McKnight, D. H., & Chervany, N. L. (2002). What trust means in e-commerce customer relationships: An interdisciplinary conceptual typology. *International Journal of Electronic Commerce, 6*(2), 35–59.

McKnight, D. H., & Chervany, N. L. (2006). Distrust and trust in B2C e-commerce: Do they differ? In *Proceedings of the Eighth International Conference on Electronic Commerce* (pp. 482-491). Fredericton, Canada: Association for Computing Machinery. doi:10.1145/1151454.1151527

McKnight, D. H., Cummings, L. L., & Chervany, N. L. (1998). Initial trust formation in new organizational relationships. *Academy of Management Review, 23*(3), 473–490.

McKusick, M. K., Bostic, K., Karels, M. J., & Quarterman, J. S. (1996). *The design and implementation of the 4.4BSD operating system.* Boston, MA: Addison-Wesley.

McMillan, R. (2008). CIA says hackers pulled plug on power grid. *IDG News Service.* Retrieved January 19, 2008, from http://www.networkworld.com

McParland, C., & Connolly, R. (2009). *The role of dataveillance in the organsiation: Some emerging trends.* Paper presented at the Irish Academy of Management Conference, Galway, Ireland.

Mead, N. R., & Morales, J. A. (in press). *Using malware analysis to improve security requirements on future systems.* Paper to be presented at the Evolving Security and Privacy Requirements Engineering (ESPRE) Workshop, International Requirements Engineering Conference (RE) 2014, Karlskrona, Sweden. doi:10.1109/ESPRE.2014.6890526

Mead, N. R., Hough, E., & Stehney, T. (2005). *Security quality requirements engineering* (CMU/SEI-2005-TR-009). Retrieved July 8, 2014, from the Software Engineering Institute, Carnegie Mellon University website: http://resources.sei.cmu.edu/library/asset-view.cfm?AssetID=7657

Meadows, D. H. (2008). Thinking in systems: A primer. Chelsea Green Publishing Company.

Mechtri, L., Tolba, F. D., & Ghanemi, S. (2012). MASID: Multi-agent system for intrusion detection in MANET. In *Proceedings of Ninth International Conference on Information Technology: New Generations (ITNG)* (pp. 65-70). Academic Press. doi:10.1109/ITNG.2012.18

Medlin, B. D., & Cazier, J. A. (2007). An empirical investigation: Health care employee passwords and their crack times in relationship to HIPAA security standards. *International Journal of Healthcare Information Systems and Informatics, 2*(3), 39–48. doi:10.4018/jhisi.2007070104

Mehmood, Y., Habiba, U., Shibli, M. A., & Masood, R. (2013). Intrusion detection system in cloud computing: Challenges and opportunities. In *Proceedings of 2nd National Conference on Information Assurance (NCIA)* (pp. 59-66). NCIA. doi:10.1109/NCIA.2013.6725325

Mélen, M., & Deliége, I. (1995). Extraction of cues or underlying harmonic structure: Which guides recognition of familiar melodies? *The European Journal of Cognitive Psychology, 7*(1), 81–106. doi:10.1080/09541449508520159

Mell, P., & Grance, T. (2009). *The NIST definition of cloud computing.* National Institute of Standards and Technology. Retrieved from http://www.nist.gov/itl/cloud/upload/cloud-def-v15.pdf

Mell, Peter, & Grance. (2009). *The NIST definition of cloud computing*. National Institute of Standards and Technology, Information Technology Laboratory. Retrieved February 28, 2014, from http://www.nist.gov/itl/cloud/upload/cloud-def-v15.pdf

Mendori, T., Kubouchi, M., Okada, M., & Shimizu, A. (2002). Password input interface for primary school children. In *Proceedings of the International Conference on Computers in Education (ICCE02)*. Auckland, New Zealand: IEEE Computer Society. doi:10.1109/CIE.2002.1186069

Merriam-Webster, Incorporated. (2014). Retrieved February 28, 2014, from Merriam- Webster.com: www.merriam-webster.com

Mickle, M. (2012). *Top ten security breaches in 2012*. Retrieved July 21, 2013, from http://www.healthcarefinancenews.com/news/top-10-data-security-breaches-2012

Microsoft. (2014). Retrieved online on 4/12/2014 from file:///C:/Users/Reema/Dropbox/Sem%202/IDM%20Chapter/FIM_datasheet_MSForeFront.pdf

Mielke, C., & Chen, H. (2008). Botnets, and the cybercriminal underground. In *Proceedings of IEEE International Conference on Intelligence and Security Informatics (ISI 2008)* (pp. 206-211). IEEE. doi:10.1109/ISI.2008.4565058

Miller, P. (2008, August). Everywhere I look I see clouds. *ZDNET*. Retrieved from http://www.zdnet.com/blog/semantic-web/everywhere-i-look-i-see-clouds/179

Miller, R. M. (1988). Market automation: Self-regulation in a distributed environment. *ACM SIGGROUP Bulletin, 9*(2–3), 299–308. doi:10.1145/966861.45443

Misener, D. (2014, January 21). *Google's Nest deal highlights privacy-policy issues: Dan Misener*. Retrieved March 15, 2014, from http://www.cbc.ca/news/technology/google-s-nest-deal-highlights-privacy-policy-issues-dan-misener-1.2504839

Mishna, F., Khoury-Kassabri, M., Gadalla, T., & Daciuk, J. (2011). Risk factors for involvement in cyber bullying: Victims, bullies and bully–victims. *Children and Youth Services Review, 34*(1), 63–70. doi:10.1016/j.childyouth.2011.08.032

Mishna, F., Saini, M., & Solomon, S. (2009). Ongoing and online: Children and youth's perceptions of cyber bullying. *Children and Youth Services Review, 31*(12), 1222–1228. doi:10.1016/j.childyouth.2009.05.004

Mitchell, A., & Zigurs, I. (2009). Trust in virtual teams: Solved or still a mystery? *The Data Base for Advances in Information Systems, 40*(3), 61–83. doi:10.1145/1592401.1592407

Mitrano, T., Kirby, D. R., & Maltz, L. (2005). *What does privacy have to do with it?* Paper presented at the Security Professionals Conference, St. Louis, MO.

Mitrokotsa, A., Komninos, N., & Douligeris, C. (2007). Intrusion detection with neural networks and watermarking techniques for MANET. In *Proceedings of International Conference on Pervasive Services* (pp. 966-966). Academic Press. doi:10.1109/PERSER.2007.4283901

Miyata, T., Koga, Y., Madsen, P., & Adachi, S. (2006, January). A survey on identity management protocols and standards. *IEICE Transactions on Information and Systems, E89-D*(1), 112–123. doi:10.1093/ietisy/e89-d.1.112

Miyazaki, S., Mead, N., & Zhan, J. (2008). Computer-aided privacy requirements elicitation technique. In *Proceedings of Asia-Pacific Services Computing Conference* (pp. 367-372). Hoboken, NJ: IEEE.

Mogul, J. C., Rashid, R. F., & Acetta, M. J. (1987). The packet filter: An efficient mechanism for user-level network code. *Operating Systems Review, 21*(5), 39–51. doi:10.1145/37499.37505

Momenzadeh, A., Javadi, H. H. S., & Dezfouli, M. A. (2009). Design an efficient system for intrusion detection via evolutionary fuzzy system. In *Proceedings of 11th International Conference on Computer Modeling and Simulation* (pp. 89–94). Academic Press. doi:10.1109/UKSIM.2009.57

Monaco, B., & Riordan, J. (1987). *The platinum rainbow... How to make it big in the music business*. Sherman Oaks, CA: Omnibus Books.

Mont, M. C., Bramhall, P., Gittler, M., Pato, J., & Rees, O. (2000). *Identity management: A key e-business enabler*. Retrieved from hpl.hp.com

Moore, R. J. (2001). A universal dynamic trace for Linux and other operating systems. In *Proceedings of the FREENIX Track: 2001 USENIX Annual Technical Conference* (pp. 297–308). Boston, MA: USENIX Association.

Moor, P., Heuvelman, A., & Verleur, R. (2010). Flaming on YouTube. *Computers in Human Behavior, 26*(6), 1536–1546. doi:10.1016/j.chb.2010.05.023

Morrison, E. W., & Robinson, S. (1997). When employees feel betrayed: A model of how psychological contract violation develops. *Academy of Management Review, 22*, 226–256.

Morris, R., & Thomson, K. (1979). Password security: A case history. *Communications of the ACM, 22*(11), 594–597. doi:10.1145/359168.359172

Mossholder, K. W., Bennett, N., Kemery, E. R., & Wesolowski, M. A. (1998). Relationships between bases of power and work reactions: The mediational role of procedural justice. *Journal of Management, 24*(4), 533–552. doi:10.1016/S0149-2063(99)80072-5

Motta Pires, P. S., & Oliveira, L. A. H. G. (2006). Security aspect of SCADA and corporate network interconnection: An overview. In *Proceedings of International Conference on Dependability of Computer Systems* (pp. 127-134). Academic Press. doi:10.1109/DEPCOS-RELCOMEX.2006.46

Mowbray, M. (2009). *The fog over the Grimpen Mire: Cloud computing and the law*. HP Laboratory. Retrieved from http://www.hpl.hp.com/techreports/2009/HPL-2009-99.pdf

Mowshowitz, A. (1997). Virtual organization - Introduction to the special section. *Communications of the ACM, 40*(9), 30–37. doi:10.1145/260750.260759

Mozilla. (2014). *Phishing protection: Design documentation, Mozila Wiki*. Retrieved from https://wiki.mozilla.org/Phishing_Protection:_Design_Documentation

MS-Live. (2010). *Home - Windows Live*. Retrieved online from http://home.live.com

Murnighan, J. K., Malhotra, D., & Weber, J. M. (2004). Paradoxes of trust: Empirical and theoretical departures from a traditional model. In R. M. Kramer & K. S. Cook (Eds.), *Trust and distrust in organizations: Emerging perspectives, enduring questions* (pp. 293–326). New York: Russell Sage Foundation.

Mustafic, T., Messerman, A., Camtepe, S. A., Schmidt, A. D., & Albayrak, S. (2011). Behavioral biometrics for persistent single sign-on. In *Proceedings of the 7th ACM Workshop on Digital Identity Management*. ACM. doi:10.1145/2046642.2046658

Muthuprasanna, M., Ke, W., & Kothari, S. (2006). Eliminating SQL injection attacks – A transport defense mechanism. In *Proceedings of 8th International Symposium on Web Site Evolution* (pp. 22-23). Academic Press.

Nadkarni, K., & Mishra, A. (2004). A novel intrusion detection approach for wireless ad hoc networks. In *Proceedings of Wireless Communications and Networking Conference* (pp. 831–836). Academic Press. doi:10.1109/WCNC.2004.1311294

Nassar, M., State, R., & Festor, O. (2007). VoIP honeypot architecture. In *Proceedings of International Symposium on Integrated Network Management* (pp. 109-118). Academic Press.

Nass, C., & Brave, S. (2005). *Wired for speech*. Cambridge, MA: MIT Press.

National Computer Security Center. (1988). *A guide to understanding audit in trusted systems* (Technical Report NCSC-TG-001). National Computer Security Center (NCSC).

National Institute of Standards and Technology (NIST). (2008). *Performance measurement guide for information security, NIST special publication 800-55 revision 1*. Retrieved January 28, 2010 from http://csrc.nist.gov/publications/nistpubs/800-55-Rev1/SP800-55-rev1.pdf

National Institute of Standards and Technology. (2013). *NIST special publication 800-53, security and privacy controls for federal information systems and organizations*. Retrieved March 25, 2014 from http://nvlpubs.nist.gov/nistpubs/SpecialPublications/NIST.SP.800-53r4.pdf

Nazario, J. (2006). *Botnet tracking: Tools, techniques, and lessons learned (Tech. Rep.)*. Chemsford, MA: Arbor Networks.

NetIQ Identity Management. (2014). Retrieved online on 4/12/2014 from https://www.netiq.com/solutions/identity-access- management/

New York Times. (2008). *How to use social networking sites for marketing and PR*. Retrieved from: http://www.nytimes.com/allbusiness/AB11702023_primary.html

NHS Database. (2014). *NHS bosses accused of 'climate of fear' over care data*. Retrieved from http://www.telegraph.co.uk/journalists/laura-donnelly/10628950/NHS-bosses-accused-of-climate-of-fear-over-care.data.html

Niccolini, S., Garroppo, R. G., Giordano, S., Risi, G., & Ventura, S. (2006). SIP intrusion detection and prevention: Recommendation and prototype recommendation. In *Proceedings of1st Workshop on VoIP Management and Security* (pp. 47-52). Academic Press.

Nilsson, D. K., & Larson, U. E. (2008b). Simulated attacks on CAN-buses: Vehicle virus. In *Proceedings of the Fifth IASTED Asian Conference on Communication Systems and Networks (AsiaCSN 2008)* (pp. 66–72). Langkawi, Malaysia: IASTED.

Nilsson, D. K., & Larson, U. E. (2008a). Conducting forensic investigations of cyber attacks on automobile in-vehicle networks. In *Proceedings of the First ACM International Conference on Forensic Applications and Techniques in Telecommunications, Information and Multimedia (e-Forensics 2008)* (pp. 1–6). Adelaide, Australia: ACM. doi:10.4108/e-forensics.2008.32

Nip, J. Y. M. (2004). The relationship between online and offline communities: The case of the Queer Sisters. *Media Culture & Society, 26*(3), 409–428. doi:10.1177/0163443704042262

Nixon Peabody. (2009). *Health law alert*. Retrieved November 15, 2009, from http://www.nixonpeabody.com/publications_detail3.asp?ID=2621

Noble, J. (2013, September 11). *U.S. debates security vs privacy 12 years after 9/11*. Retrieved March 10, 2014, from USA Today: http://www.usatoday.com/story/news/nation/2013/09/10/us-debates-security-vs-privacy-12-years-after-911/2796399/

Nooteboom, B. (2002). *Trust: Forms, foundations, functions, failures and figures*. Cheltenham, UK: Edward Elgar. doi:10.4337/9781781950883

Nord, G. D., McCubbins, T. F., & Horn Nord, J. (2006). Email monitoring in the workplace: Privacy, legislation, and surveillance software. *Communications of the ACM, 49*(8), 73–77.

Normalini, M. K., & Ramayah, T. (2012). Biometrics technologies implementation in internet banking reduce security issues? In *Proceedings of International Congress on Interdisciplinary Business and Social Sciences 2012 (ICIBSoS 2012)* (vol. 65, pp. 364–369). Academic Press. doi:10.1016/j.sbspro.2012.11.135

Nusbaum, E. C., & Silvia, P. J. (2010). Shivers and timbres: Personality and the experience of chills from music. *Social Psychological & Personality Science*, (October), 2010.

O'Gorman, L. (2003, December). Comparing passwords, tokens, and biometrics for user authentication. *Proceedings of the IEEE, 91*(12), 2019–2040. doi:10.1109/JPROC.2003.819605

OASIS. (2014a). Retrieved online on 4/12/2014 from http://docs.oasis-open.org/ws-sx/ws-securitypolicy/v1.3/errata01/os/ws-securitypolicy-1.3-errata01-os-complete.pdf

OCC. (1999, October). *Internet banking*. Retrieved 3rd April, 2010 from http://www.occ.treas.gov/handbook/intbank.pdf

OECD & Microsoft Corporation. (2000). *OECD privacy statement generator*. Retrieved April 25, 2009, from http://www2.oecd.org/pwv3/

Office of the National Coordinator for Health Information Technology. (2010). *Strategic health IT advanced research projects (SHARP)*. Retrieved from http://www.healthit.gov/policy-researchers-implementers/strategic-health-it-advanced-research-projects-sharp

Ofuonye, E., Beatty, P., Reay, I., Dick, S., & Miller, J. (2008). How do we build trust into ecommerce web sites? *IEEE Software, 25*(5), 7–9. doi:10.1109/MS.2008.136

Olweus, D. (1993). *Bullying in schools: What we know and what we can do*. Oxford, UK: Blackwell Publishers.

Olweus, D. (1999). Sweden. In P. K. Smith, Y. Morita, J. Junger-Tas, D. Olweus, R. Catalano, & P. Slee (Eds.), *The nature of school bullying: A cross-national perspective* (pp. 7–27). London: Routledge.

OneLogin. (2014). Retrieved online on 4/12/2014 from http://www.onelogin.com/product/

Online Banking. (2010). Retrieved 3rd April, 2010, from http://www.investorglossary.com/online-banking.htm

Onut, I. V., & Ghorbani, A. A. (2006). Toward a feature classification scheme for network intrusion detection. In *Proceedings of 4th Annual Communication and Networks and Service Research Conference* (p. 8). Academic Press. doi:10.1109/CNSR.2006.53

Onut, I. V., & Ghorbani, A. A. (2007). A feature classification scheme for network intrusion detection. *International Journal of Network Security, 5*, 1–15.

Onwubiko, C. (2011). Challenges to managing privacy impact assessment of personal identifiable data. In Information assurance and security technologies for risk assessment and threat management: Advances. Hershey, PA: IGI Global.

Oracle-IDM. (n.d.). Retrieved from http://www.oracle.com/technetwork/middleware/id-mgmt/overview/index.html?ssSourceSiteId=opn

Organization for Economic Co-operation and Development (OECD). (2004). *Principles of corporate governance.* Retrieved November 03, 2010 from http://www.oecd.org/dataoecd/32/18/31557724.pdf

Ostwald, M. J. (1997). Virtual urban futures. In D. Holmes (Ed.), *Virtual politics: Identity & community in cyberspace* (pp. 125–144). London: Sage.

Otrok, H., Debbabi, M., Assi, C., & Bhattacharya, P. (2007). A cooperative approach for analyzing intrusion in mobile ad hoc networks. In *Proceedings of 27th International Conference on Distributing Computing Systems Workshops* (pp. 86-86). Academic Press. doi:10.1109/ICDCSW.2007.91

Ousterhout, J. K., Costa, H. D., Harrison, D., Kunze, J. A., Kupfer, M., & Thompson, J. G. (1985). A trace-driven analysis of the UNIX 4.2 BSD file system. *Operating Systems Review, 19*(5), 15–24. doi:10.1145/323627.323631

Owston, R. (1998). *Making the link: Teacher professional development on the internet.* Portsmouth, NH: Heinemann.

Paez, R., & Torres, M. (2009). Laocoonte: An agent based intrusion detection system. In *Proceedings of International Symposium on Collaborative Technologies and System* (pp. 217–224). Academic Press. doi:10.1109/CTS.2009.5067484

Paivio, A. (1983). The empirical case for dual coding. In J. Yuille (Ed.), *Imagery, memory and cognition: Essays in honour of Allan Paivio* (pp. 307–322). Hillsdale, NJ: Erlbaum.

Paivio, A., & Csapo, K. (1973). Picture superiority in free recall: Imagery or dual coding? *Cognitive Psychology, 5*(2), 176–206. doi:10.1016/0010-0285(73)90032-7

Palmer, A. R. (1996). Waltzing with asymmetry. *Bioscience, 46*(7), 518–532. doi:10.2307/1312930

Palnaty, R. P., & Rao, A. (2013). JCADS: Semi-supervised clustering algorithm for network anomaly intrusion detection systems. In *Proceedings of 15th International Conference on Advanced Computing Technologies (ICACT)* (pp. 1-5). Academic Press. doi:10.1109/ICACT.2013.6710498

Palpanas, T., Papadopoulos, D., Kalogeraki, V., & Gunopulos, D. (2003). Distributed deviation detection in sensor networks. *SIGMOD Record, 32*(4), 77–82. doi:10.1145/959060.959074

Panchamukhi, P. S. (2004). *Kernel debugging with Kprobes.* Retrieved November 25, 2010, from http://www.ibm.com/developerworks/linux/library/l-kprobes.html

Paquette, A., Painter, F., & Jackson, J. L. (2011). Management and risk assessment of wireless medical devices in the hospital. *Biomedical Instrumentation & Technology, 45*(3), 243–248. doi:10.2345/0899-8205-45.3.243 PMID:21639775

Parker, R. B. (1974). A definition of privacy. *Rutgers Law Review, 27*(1), 275.

Paulson, L. D. (2002). Stopping intruders outside the gates. *Computer, 11*(35), 20–22. doi:10.1109/MC.2002.1046967

Pavlou, P. A. (2003). Consumer acceptance of electronic commerce: Integrating trust and risk with the technology acceptance model. *International Journal of Electronic Commerce, 7*(3), 69–103.

Pavlou, P. A. (2011). State of the information privacy literature: Where are we now and where should we go? *Management Information Systems Quarterly, 35*(4), 977–988.

PCI Security Standards Council. (2013). *PCI DSS requirements and security assessment procedures v 3.0.* Retrieved March 25, 2014 from https://www.pcisecuritystandards. org/documents/PCI_DSS_v3.pdf

Peers, S. (2011). *EU justice and home affairs law.* Oxford, UK: Oxford University Press.

Peirce, T. (2009). RFID privacy & security. *IEEE International Conference on Communications, ICC, 24,* 11-15

Peisert, S. P. (2007). *A model of forensic analysis using goal-oriented logging.* (PhD thesis). University of California, San Diego, CA.

Penn, J. (2002). *IT trends 2002: Directories and directory-enabled applications.* GIGA Report.

Peretz, I., Radeau, M., & Arguin, M. (2004). Two-way interactions between music and language: Evidence from priming recognition of tune and lyrics in familiar songs. *Memory & Cognition, 32*(1), 142–152. doi:10.3758/ BF03195827 PMID:15078051

Petrie, H., & Kheir, O. (2007). The relationship between accessibility and usability of websites. In *Proceedings of the SIGCHI Conference on Human Factors in Computing Systems* (pp. 397-406). ACM. doi:10.1145/1240624.1240688

Pfleeger, C. P., & Pfleeger, S. L. (2007). *Security in computing* (4th ed.). Prentice Hall.

Pfleeger, S. L., & Pfleeger, C. P. (2009). Harmonizing privacy with security principles and practices. *IBM Journal of Research and Development, 53*(2), 273–289. doi:10.1147/JRD.2009.5429048

Piromsopa, K., & Enbody, R. J. (2006). Arbitrary copy: Buffer-overflow protections. In *Proceedings of International Conference on Electro/information Technology* (pp. 580-584). Academic Press.

Piromsopa, K., & Enbody, R. J. (2006). Buffer-overflow protection: The theory. In *Proceedings of International Conference on Electro/information Technology* (pp. 454-458). Academic Press.

Piscaglia, P., & Maccq, B. (1996). Multiresolution lossless compression scheme. In *Proceedings of International Conference on Image Processing* (vol. 1, pp. 69-72). Academic Press. doi:10.1109/ICIP.1996.559435

Podio, F. L., & Dunn, J. S. (2001). *Biometric authentication technology.* Retrieved 3rd April, 2010, from http:// www.itl.nist.gov/div893/biometrics/Biometricsfromthe-movies.pdf

Pokrajac, D., Lazarevic, A., & Latecki, L. (2007). Incremental local outlier detection for data streams. In Proceedings of IEEE Symposiums on Computational Intelligence and Data Mining (CIDM'07) (pp. 504-515). Honolulu, HI: IEEE.

Pollet, J. (2002). Developing a solid SCADA security strategy. In *Proceedings of 2nd International Society of Automation Sensors for Industry Conference* (pp. 148-156). Academic Press.

Pond, R., Podd, J., Bunnell, J., & Henderson, R. (2000). Word association computer passwords: The effect of formulation techniques on recall and guessing rates. *Computers & Security, 19*(7), 645–656. doi:10.1016/ S0167-4048(00)07023-1

Porter, A., Votta, L., & Basili, V. (1995). Comparing detection methods for software requirements inspections: A replicated experiment. *IEEE Transactions on Software Engineering, 21*(6), 563–575. doi:10.1109/32.391380

Porter, C. E. (2004). A typology of virtual communities: A multi-disciplinary foundation for future research. *Journal of Computer-Mediated Communication, 10*(1). Retrieved from http://jcmc.indiana.edu/vol10/issue1/porter.html

Prakhaber, P. R. (2000). Who owns the online consumer? *Journal of Consumer Marketing, 17*(2), 158–171. doi:10.1108/07363760010317213

PRC. (2009). *A chronology of data breaches reported since the choicepoint incident (list).* Privacy Rights Clearinghouse. Retrieved January 24th 2010 from http://www. privacyrights.org/ar/ChronDataBreaches.htm

Price, K. E. (1997). *Host-based misuse detection and conventional operating systems' audit data collection.* (Master's thesis). Purdue University, West Lafayette, IN.

PricewaterhouseCoopers LLP. (2010). *Information security breaches survey 2010, technical report.* Retrieved July 13, 2010 from http://www.pwc.co.uk/pdf/isbs_survey_2010_technical_report.pdf

PricewaterhouseCoopers LLP. (2013). *Defending yesterday, key findings from the global state of information security survey 2014.* Retrieved December 25, 2013 from http://www.pwc.com/gx/en/consulting-services/information-security-survey/download.jhtml

Privacy by Design. (2014). *We must strongly protect privacy in electronic health records.* Retrieved from http://www.privacybydesign.ca/index.php/must-strongly-protect-privacy-electronic-health-records/

Ptak, R. (2013). *What is happening to log files?* Retrieved March 26, 2014 from http://www.eventtracker.com/newsletters/what-is-happening-to-log-files-the-internet-of-things-big-data-analytics-security-visualization-oh-my/

Pucella, R., & Weissman, V. (2004). Foundations of software science and computation structures. *Lecture Notes in Computer Science, 2987,* 453–467.

Punti, G., Gil, M., Martorell, X., & Navarro, N. (2002). *gtrace: Function call and memory access traces of dynamically linked programs in ia-32 and ia-64 linux* (Technical Report UPC-DAC-2002-51). Polytechnic University of Catalonia, Barcelona, Spain.

Putnam, R. (1993). *Making democracy work: Civic tradition in modern Italy.* Princeton, NJ: Princeton University Press.

Putnam, R. (2000). *Bowling alone: The collapse and revival of American community.* New York: Simon and Schuster. doi:10.1145/358916.361990

Radack, S. (2010). Guide to protecting personally identifiable information (PII). *NIST ITL Security Bulletin.* Retrieved from http://csrc.nist.gov/publications/nistbul/april-2010_guide-protecting-pii.pdf

Radin, P. (2006). "To me, it's my life": Medical communication, trust, and activism in cyberspace. *Social Science & Medicine, 62*(3), 591–601. doi:10.1016/j.socscimed.2005.06.022 PMID:16039031

Rai, S., Bresz, F., Renshaw, T., Rozek, J., & White, T. (2007). *Global Technology Audit Guide: Identity and Access Management.* The Institute of Internal Auditors.

Ramana, R. K., Singh, S., & Varghese, G. (2007). On scalable attack detection in the network. *Association for Computing Machinery Transactions on Networking, 1*(15), 31–44.

Ramaswamy, S., Rastogi, R., & Kyuseok, S. (2000). Efficient algorithms for mining outliers from large data sets. In *Proceedings of SIGMOD Conference* (pp. 427-438). Dallas, TX: ACM. doi:10.1145/342009.335437

Ransbottom, J. S., & Jacoby, G. A. (2006). Monitoring mobile device vitals for effective reporting. In *Proceedings of Military Communication Conference* (pp. 1-7). Academic Press. doi:10.1109/MILCOM.2006.302338

Rauhofer, J. (2006). Just because you're paranoid, doesn't mean they're not after you: Legislative developments in relation to the mandatory retention of communications data in the European Union. SCRIPT-ed, 322-343.

Rawlins, B. (2009). *Irrational trust.* Retrieved on May 1st, 2010, from http://www.instituteforpr.org/essential_knowledge/detail/irrational_trust_rawlins

Reiman, J. (1976). Privacy, intimacy, and personhood. *Philosophy & Public Affairs, 6,* 26–44.

Reinmann-Rothmeier, G. (2002). Mediendidaktik und wissensmanagement. *MedienPädagogik, 2*(2), 1-27. Retrieved August 18, 2006 from www.medienpaed.com/02-2/reinmann1.pdf

Renaud, K. (2009, February). On user involvement in production of images used in visual authentication. *Journal of Visual Languages and Computing, 20*(1), 1–15. doi:10.1016/j.jvlc.2008.04.001

Renaud, K., & De Angeli, A. (2009). Visual passwords: Cure-all or snake-oil? *Communications of the ACM, 52*(12), 135–140. doi:10.1145/1610252.1610287

Renaud, K., & Ramsay, J. (2007). Now what was that password again? A more flexible way of identifying and authenticating our seniors. *Behaviour & Information Technology, 26*(4), 309–322. doi:10.1080/01449290601173770

Rentfrow, P. J., & Gosling, S. D. (2003). The do re mi's of everyday life: The structure and personality correlates of music preferences. *Journal of Personality and Social Psychology, 84*(6), 1236–1256. doi:10.1037/0022-3514.84.6.1236 PMID:12793587

Restoring Trust in EU-US Data Flows - Frequently Asked Questions. (2013, November 27). Retrieved from http://europa.eu/rapid/press-release_MEMO-13-1059_en.htm

Reymann, P. (2008). *Aligning people, processes, and technology for effective risk management*. Retrieved on 4/18/2014 from: http://www.theiia.org/intAuditor/itaudit/archives/2008/january/aligning-people-processes-andtechnology-for-effective-risk-management

Rheingold, H. (1993). *The virtual community: Homesteading on the electronic frontier*. Reading, MA: Addison-Wesley.

Ridings, C. M., & Gefen, D. (2004). Virtual community attraction: Why people hang out online. *Journal of Computer-Mediated Communication, 10*(1). Retrieved from http://jcmc.indiana.edu/vol10/issue1/ridings_gefen.html

Ridings, C. M., Gefen, D., & Arinze, B. (2002). Some antecedents and effects of trust in virtual communities. *The Journal of Strategic Information Systems, 11*(3-4), 271–295. doi:10.1016/S0963-8687(02)00021-5

Rieck, K., Trinius, P., Willems, C., & Holz, T. (2011). Automatic analysis of malware behavior using machine learning. *Journal of Computer Security, 19*(4), 639–668.

Rieh, S. Y., & Danielson, D. R. (2007). Credibility: A multidisciplinary framework. *Annual Review of Information Science & Technology, 41*(1), 307–364. doi:10.1002/aris.2007.1440410114

Risso, F., & Degioanni, L. (2001). An architecture for high performance network analysis. In *Proceedings of the Sixth IEEE Symposium on Computers and Communications (ISCC'01)*. Hammamet, Tunisia: IEEE. doi:10.1109/ISCC.2001.935450

Riva, O., Qin, C., Strauss, K., & Lymberopoulos, D. (2012). Progressive authentication: Deciding when to authenticate on mobile phones. In *Proceedings of the 21st USENIX Security Symposium*. USENIX.

Robinson, S. L., & Rousseau, D. M. (1994). Violating the psychological contract: Not the exception but the norm. *Journal of Organizational Behavior, 15*(3), 245–259. doi:10.1002/job.4030150306

Rochet, J—C., & Tirole, J. (2003). Platform competition in two–sided markets. *Journal of the European Economic Association, 1*(4), 990–1029.

Roesch, M. (1999). Snort-lightweight intrusion detection for networks. In *Proceedings of 13th Systems Administration Conference (LISA '99)* (pp. 229-238). Academic Press.

Rogaway, P. (2004). *Nonce-based symmetric encryption*. International Association for Cryptologic Research. Retrieved from: http://www.pewinternet.org/fact-sheets/mobile- technology-fact-sheet/

Rosenberg, M. J. (2001). *E-learning: Strategies for delivering knowledge in the digital age*. New York, NY: McGraw-Hill.

Rosen, J. (2012). The right to be forgotten. *Stanford Law Review Online, 64*, 88–92.

Rossow, C., Dietrich, C. J., Grier, C., Kreibich, C., Paxson, V., Pohlmann, N., & Steen, M. (2012). Prudent practices for designing malware experiments: Status quo and outlook. In *Proceedings of 2012 IEEE Symposium on Security and Privacy* (pp. 65-79). IEEE. doi:10.1109/SP.2012.14

Rousseau, D., Sitkin, S., Burt, R., & Camerer, C. (1998). Not so different after all: A cross-discipline view of trust. *Academy of Management Review, 23*(3), 393–404. doi:10.5465/AMR.1998.926617

Rousseau, D., & Tijoriwala, S. (1998). Assessing psychological contracts: Issues, alternatives and measures. *Journal of Organizational Behavior, 19*(S1), 679–696. doi:10.1002/(SICI)1099-1379(1998)19:1+<679::AID-JOB971>3.0.CO;2-N

Rouvroy, A., & Poullet, Y. (2008). The right to informational self-determination and the value of self-development: Reassessing the importance of privacy for democracy. In *Reinventing Data Protection: Proceedings of the International Conference*. Berlin: Springer.

Rouvroy, A., & Poullet, Y. (2009). The right to informational self-determination and the value of self-development: reassessing the importance of privacy for democracy. In S. Gutwirth et al. (Eds.), *Reinventing data protection?* (pp. 45–76). Dordrecht, The Netherlands: Springer. doi:10.1007/978-1-4020-9498-9_2

Rubini, A., & Corbet, J. (2001). *Linux device drivers* (2nd ed.). Sebastopol, CA: O'Reilly.

Russer, M. (2010, June). *Maximize profits through hyper-targeted Facebook ads.* Retrieved March 15, 2014, from http://realtormag.realtor.org/technology/mr-internet/article/2010/06/maximize-profits-through-hyper-targeted-facebook-ads

Russinovich, M., & Cogswell, B. (2010). *Process monitor.* Retrieved November 25, 2010, from http://technet.micrsoft.com/en-us/sysinternals/bb896645.aspx

Russinovich, M. E., & Solomon, D. A. (2005). *Microsoft Windows internals* (4th ed.). Microsoft Press.

Russo, P. (2012). *The antecedents, objects, and consequents of user trust in location-based social networks* (Doctroal dissertation). Available from ProQuest Dissertations and Theses database. (UMI No. 3518792).

Rust, R. T., Kannan, P. K., & Peng, N. (2002). The customer economics of internet privacy. *Journal of the Academy of Marketing Science*, *30*(4), 455–464. doi:10.1177/009207002236917

Saad, S., Traore, I., Ghorbani, A., Sayed, B., Zhao, D., Lu, W., & Hakimian, P. (2011). Detecting P2P botnets through network behavior analysis and machine learning. In *Proceedings of Privacy, Security and Trust (PST), 2011 Ninth Annual International Conference on* (pp. 174–180). Montreal, Canada: IEEE.

Sabzevar, A. P., & Stavrou, A. (2008). Universal multi-factor authentication using graphical passwords. In *Proceedings of IEEE International Conference on Signal Image Technology and Internet Based Systems.* IEEE. doi:10.1109/SITIS.2008.92

Sadighian, A., Zargar, S. T., Fernandez, J. M., & Lemay, A. (2013). Semantic-based context-aware alert fusion for distributed intrusion detection systems. In *Proceedings of International Conference on Risks and Security of Internet and Systems (CRiSIS)* (pp. 1-6). Academic Press. doi:10.1109/CRiSIS.2013.6766352

Safire, W. (2002). The great unwatched. *New York Times.* Retrieved November 10, 2014, from http://query.nytimes.com/gst/fullpage.html?res=9A03E7DB1E3FF93BA257 51C0A9649C8B63

Saint-Germain, R. (2005). Information security management best practice based on ISO/IEC 17799. *Information Management Journal*, *39*(4), 60–66.

Salehl, M. S., Alrabiah, A., & Bakry, S. H. (2007). Using ISO 17799: 2005 information security management: A stope view with six sigma approach. *International Journal of Network Management*, *7*(1), 85–97. doi:10.1002/nem.616

Salomon, K. D., Cassat, P. C., & Thibeau, B. E. (2003, March 20). *IT security for higher education: A legal perspective.* Retrieved September 22, 2010, from http://net.educause.edu/ir/library/pdf/CSD2746.pdf

Sampathkumar, V., Bose, S., Anand, K., & Kannan, A. (2007). An intelligent agent based approach for intrusion detection and prevention in ad hoc networks. In *Proceedings of International Conference on Signal Processing Communications and Networking* (pp. 534-536). Academic Press.

SANS. (2006). *SANS consensus project information system audit logging requirements.* Retrieved November 24, 2010, from http://www.sans.org/resources/policies/info_sys_audit.pdf

SANS. (2013). *SANS top 20 critical security controls – Maintenance, monitoring, and analysis of audit logs.* Retrieved March 24, 2014, from http://www.sans.org/critical-security-controls/control/14

Sapolsky, R. (2005). Stressed out memories. *Scientific American Mind*, *14*(5), 28.

Sarker, S., Valacich, J. S., & Sarker, S. (2003). Virtual team trust: Instrument development and validation. *Information Resources Management Journal*, *16*(2), 35–55. doi:10.4018/irmj.2003040103

Satti, M. M., & Garner, B. J. (2001). Information security on internet enterprise managed intrusion detection system (EMIDS). In *Proceedings of International Multitopic Conference* (pp. 234-238). Academic Press. doi:10.1109/INMIC.2001.995343

Savage, C. (2013, December 16). Judge questions legality of N.S.A. phone records. *The New York Times.* Retrieved March 2, 2014, from http://www.nytimes.com/2013/12/17/us/politics/federal-judge-rules-against-nsa-phone-data-program.html?pagewanted=1&_r=2

Saydjari, O. S. (2006). Is risk a good security metric? in *Proceedings of the 2nd ACM Workshop on Quality of Protection, QoP '06* (pp. 59–60). ACM. doi:10.1145/1179494.1179508

Schechter, S., Herley, C., & Mitzenmacher, M. (2010). Popularity is everything: A new approach to protecting passwords from statistical guessing attacks. In *Proceedings of the 5th USENIX Workshop on Hot Topics in Security*. USENIX Association.

Scheer, A.-W. (2001) *ARIS-modellierungs-methoden, metamodelle, anwendungen.* Springer.

Scherer, K. R., & Zentner, M. R. (2001). Emotional effects of music: Production rules. In Music and emotion: Theory and research (pp. 361–392). Oxford, UK: Oxford University Press.

Schmidt, A., Kölbl, T., Wagner, S., & Strassmeier, W. (2004). Enabling access to computers for people with poor reading skills. In *Proceedings of 8th ERCIM Workshop on User Interfaces for All* (LNCS), (Vol. 3196, pp. 96–115). Vienna, Austria: Springer. doi:10.1007/978-3-540-30111-0_8

Schmoyer, T. R., Lim, Y. X., & Owen, H. L. (2004). Wireless intrusion detection and response: a classic study using main-in-the-middle attack. In *Proceedings of Wireless Communications and Networking Conference* (pp. 883 – 888). Academic Press. doi:10.1109/WCNC.2004.1311303

Schoorman, F. D., Mayer, R. C., & Davis, J. H. (2007). An integrative model of organizational trust: Past, present and future. *Academy of Management Review, 32*(2), 344–354. doi:10.5465/AMR.2007.24348410

Schroeder, B. A. (1995). On-line monitoring: A tutorial. *Computer, 28*(6), 72–78. doi:10.1109/2.386988

Seendahera, V., Warren, M., & Leitch, S. (2011). A Study into how Australian banks use social media. In *Proceedings of PACIS '11*. Brisbane, Australia: Academic Press.

Selmi, M. (2006). Privacy for the working class: Public work and private lives. *Louisiana Law Review, 66,* 1035–1056.

Senge, P. (2003). Taking personal change seriously: The impact of organizational learning on management practice. *The Academy of Management Executive, 17*(2), 47–50. doi:10.5465/AME.2003.10025191

Serino, C., Furner, C. P., & Smatt, C. M. (2005). Making it personal: How personalization affects trust over time. In *Proceedings of the Hawaii International Conference on System Sciences (ICIS)*. Waikoloa, HI: IEEE. doi:10.1109/HICSS.2005.398

Sewall, M. A., & Sarel, D. (1986). Characteristics of radio commercials and their recall effectiveness. *Journal of Marketing, 50*(1), 52–60. doi:10.2307/1251278

Shahrestani, A., Ramadass, S., & Feily, M. (2009). A survey of botnet and botnet detection. In *Proceedings of 3rd International Conference on Emerging Security Information, Systems and Technologies (SECURWARE '09)* (pp. 268-273). Academic Press.

Shane, D. (2010). *Zurich insurance hit with record data loss fine.* Retrieved from http://www.information-age.com/channels/security-and-continuity/news/1277718/zurich-insurance-hit-with-record-data-loss-fine.thtml

Shankar, V., Urban, G. L., & Sultan, F. (2002). Online trust: A stakeholder perspective, concepts, implications, and future directions. *The Journal of Strategic Information Systems, 11*(3-4), 325–344. doi:10.1016/S0963-8687(02)00022-7

Shannon, C. (1948). A mathematical theory of communication. *Bell System Technical Journal,* 379-423, 623-656.

Shannon, C. (1948). A mathematical theory of communication. *The Bell System Technical Journal, 27,* 379-423.

Shapiro, S. P. (1987). The social control of impersonal trust. *American Journal of Sociology, 93*(3), 623–658. doi:10.1086/228791

Shawn, O. (2010). *Tcptrace.* Retrieved March 30, 2010, from http://www.tcptrace.org/

Shepherd, A. D., Lane, S. E., & Steward, J. S. (1990). A new microprocessor relay for overhead line SCADA application. In *Proceedings of Distribution Switchgear Conference* (pp. 100–103). Academic Press.

Sheppard, B. H., & Sherman, D. M. (1998). The grammars of trust: A model and general implications. *Academy of Management Review, 23*(3), 422–437.

Sher, M., & Magedanz, T. (2007). Protecting IP multimedia subsystem (IMS) server delivery platform from time independent attacks. In *Proceedings of 3rd International Symposium on Information Assurance and Security* (pp. 171-176). Academic Press. doi:10.1109/ISIAS.2007.4299770

Shewhart, W. A. (1939, reprint 1986). Statistical method from the viewpoint of quality control. Dover Publications.

Shewhart, W. A. (1980). *Economic control of quality of manufactured product*. American Society for Quality Control.

Shibboleth. (2014). Retrieved online on 4/12/2014 from https://shibboleth.net/about/

Short, J., Williams, E., & Christie, B. (1976). *The social psychology of telecommunications*. New York, NY: John Wiley.

SHRM. (2005). *Workplace privacy – Poll findings: A study by the society for human resource management and careerjournal.com, January 2005*. Author.

Siciliano, R. (2014, January 27). *Stolen identities are cheap on the darknet*. Retrieved March 10, 2014, from http://bestidtheftcompanys.com/2014/stolen-identities-are-cheap-on-the-darknet

Siegrist, M., Cvetkovich, G. T., & Gutscher, H. (2001). Shared values, social trust, and the perception of geographic cancer clusters. *Risk Analysis, 21*(6), 1047–1054. doi:10.1111/0272-4332.216173 PMID:11824680

Simpson, R. L. (2002). Chicago. *Nursing Management, 33*(12), 46–48. doi:10.1097/00006247-200212000-00017 PMID:12488639

Sindre, G., & Opdahl, A. L. (2000). Eliciting security requirements by misuse cases. In *Proceedings of the 37th International Conference on Technology of Object-Oriented Languages* (pp. 120-131). Los Alamitos, CA: IEEE Computer Society.

Singh, K. (2012). Can mobile learn from the web. In *Proceedings of IEEE Computer Society Security and Privacy Workshops, WPSP '12*. IEEE.

Sistemas, H. (2010). *Virus total*. Retrieved March 30, 2010, from http://www.virustotal.com/es/

Sitkin, S. B., & Roth, N. L. (1993). Explaining the limited effectiveness of legalistic remedies for trust/distrust. *Organization Science, 4*(3), 367–392. doi:10.1287/orsc.4.3.367

Small, A., Stern, Y., Tang, M., & Mayeux, R. (1999). Selective decline in memory function among healthy elderly. *Neurology, 52*(7), 1392–1396. doi:10.1212/WNL.52.7.1392 PMID:10227623

Smith, M. D. (1991). *Tracing with pixie* (Technical Report CSL-TR-91-497). Stanford University.

Smith, P. K., Mahdavi, J., Carvalho, M., & Tippett, N. (2006). *An investigation into cyberbullying and its forms, awareness and impact and the relationship between age and gender in cyberbullying*. Research Report, University of London. Retrieved from: http://www.antibullyingalliance.org.uk/downloads/pdf/cyberbullyingreportfinal230106.pdf

Smith, A. B. (1932). The pleasures of recognition. *Music & Letters, 13*(1), 80–84. doi:10.1093/ml/XIII.1.80

Smith, H. J., Dinev, T., & Xu, H. (2011). Information privacy research: An interdisciplinary review. *Management Information Systems Quarterly, 35*(4), 980–A27.

Smith, P. K., Mahdavi, J., Carvalho, M., Fisher, S., Russell, S., & Tippett, N. (2008). Cyberbullying: Its nature and impact in secondary school pupils. *Journal of Child Psychology and Psychiatry, and Allied Disciplines, 49*(4), 376–385. doi:10.1111/j.1469-7610.2007.01846.x PMID:18363945

Smojver, S. (2011). Selection of information security risk management method using analytic hierarchy process (ahp). In *Proceedings of Central European Conference on Information and Intelligent Systems*. Academic Press.

Socialman. (2009). *Allowing staff to use Orkut? Better take care*. Social Unwire India. Retrieved from: http://www.social.unwireindia.com/2009/07/allowing-staff-to-use-orkut-better-take-cover

Solms, B., & Solms, R. (2005). From information security to ... business security? *Computers & Security, 24*(4), 271–273. doi:10.1016/j.cose.2005.04.004

Solove, D. (2008). *Understanding privacy*. Boston: Harvard University Press.

So, M. W. C., & Sculli, D. (2002). The role of trust, quality, value and risk in conducting e-business. *Industrial Management & Data Systems, 102*(9), 503–512. doi:10.1108/02635570210450181

Song, J., & Kim, Y. J. (2006). Social influence process in the acceptance of a virtual community service. *Information Systems Frontiers, 8*(3), 241–252. doi:10.1007/s10796-006-8782-0

South Carolina Department of Health and Human Services. (n.d.). Retrieved August 5, 2013, from http://healthitsecurity.com/2013/07/23/healthcare-data-breaches-reviewing-the-ramifications/

Sowa, S., Tsinas, L., & Gabriel, R. (2009). BORinformation security - Business ORiented management of information security. In M. E. Johnson (Ed.), *Managing information risk and the economics of security* (pp. 81–97). New York, NY: Springer; doi:10.1007/978-0-387-09762-6_4

Spafford, E. (1992). Observing reusable password choices. In *Proceedings of 3rd USENIX Security Symposium* (pp. 299-312). Berkeley, CA: USENIX Association.

Spears, R., & Lea, M. (1992). Social influence and the influence of the 'social' in computer mediated communication. In M. Lea (Ed.), *Contexts of computer-mediated communication* (pp. 30–65). Hemel Hempstead, UK: Harvester Wheatsheaf.

Spears, R., Lea, M., Corneliessen, R. A., Postemes, T., & Ter Harr, W. (2002). Computer-mediated communication as a channel for social resistance: The strategic side of SIDE. *Small Group Research, 33*(5), 555–574. doi:10.1177/104649602237170

Sproull, L., & Faraj, S. (1997). Atheism, sex and databases: The net as a social technology. In S. Kiesler (Ed.), *Culture of the internet* (pp. 35–51). Mahwah, NJ: Lawrence Erlbaum Associates.

Sproull, L., & Kiesler, S. (1991). Computers, networks and work. *Scientific American*, (September), 84–91.

SSAC. (2008). *SSAC advisory on fast flux hosting and DNS* (Tech. Rep.). ICANN Security and Stability Advisory Committee. Retrieved on March 10, 2008, from http://www.icann.org/en/committees/security/ssac-documents.htm

SSH Communications Security. (2014). Retrieved on 04/17/2014 from http://www.ssh.com/resources/datasheets/3-universal-ssh-key-manager

Stabb, S., Bhargava, B., Lilien, L., Rosenthal, A., Winslett, M., & Sloman, M. (2004). The pudding of trust. *IEEE Intelligent Systems, 19*(5), 74–88. doi:10.1109/MIS.2004.52

Stallings, W. (2003). *Cryptography and network security: Principles and practices*. Pearson Education, Inc.

Stanford Hospital. (n.d.). Retrieved August 3, 2013, from http://www.nytimes.com/2011/09/09/us/09breach.html?pagewanted=all&_r=0

Stanton, J. M. (2000a). Reactions to employee performance monitoring: Framework, review, and research directions. *Human Performance, 13*(1), 85–113. doi:10.1207/S15327043HUP1301_4

Stanton, J. M. (2000b). Traditional and electronic monitoring from an organizational justice perspective. *Journal of Business and Psychology, 15*(1), 129–147. doi:10.1023/A:1007775020214

Stanton, J. M., & Barnes-Farrell, J. L. (1996). Effects of electronic performance-monitoring on personal control, satisfaction and performance. *The Journal of Applied Psychology, 81*(6), 738–745. doi:10.1037/0021-9010.81.6.738

Stanton, J. M., Stam, K. R., Mastrangelo, P., & Jolton, J. (2005). Analysis of end user security behaviors. *Computers & Security, 24*(2), 124–133. doi:10.1016/j.cose.2004.07.001

Statistics Canada. (2008). *Privacy impact assessment*. Retrieved July 8, 2014, from http://www.statcan.gc.ca/about-apercu/pia-efrvp/gloss-eng.htm

Stepanikova, I., Mollborn, S., Cook, K. S., Thom, D. H., & Kramer, R. M. (2006). Patients' race, ethnicity, language, and trust in a physician. *Journal of Health and Social Behavior, 47*(4), 390–405. doi:10.1177/002214650604700406 PMID:17240927

Stinson, E., & Mitchell, J. (2008). Towards systematic evaluation of the evadability of bot/botnet detection methods. In *Proceedings of the 2nd Conference on USENIX Workshop on Offensive Technologies (WOOT '08)* (pp. 1-9). Berkeley, CA: USENIX Association.

Stoll, M. (2007). Managementsysteme und prozessorientiertes wissensmanagement. In N. Gronau (Ed.), *Proc. 4th Conference on Professional Knowledge Management – Experiences and Visions* (vol. 1, pp. 433-434). Berlin: Gito Verlag.

Stoll, M. (2008). E-learning promotes information security. In M. Iskander (Ed.), *Innovative techniques in instruction technology, e-learning, e-assessment, and education*. Dordrecht, The Netherlands: Springer; doi:10.1007/978-1-4020-8739-4_54

Stoll, M., & Breu, R. (2013). Information security measurement roles and responsibilities. In T. Sobh & K. Elleithy (Eds.), *Emerging trends in computing, informatics, systems sciences, and engineering* (pp. 11–23). Springer. doi:10.1007/978-1-4614-3558-7_2

Stoneburner, G., Goguen, A., & Feringa, A. (2002). *Risk management guide for information technology systems* (NIST Special Publication 800-30). Retrieved July 8, 2014, from http://csrc.nist.gov/publications/nistpubs/800-30/sp800-30.pdf

Stone-Gross, B., Cova, M., Cavallaro, L., Gilbert, B., Szydlowski, M., Kemmerer, R., & Vigna, G. (2009). Your botnet is my botnet: Analysis of a botnet takeover. In *Proceedings of the 16th ACM Conference on Computer and Communications Security (CCS '09)* (pp. 635-647). New York, NY: ACM. doi:10.1145/1653662.1653738

strace. (2010). *strace – Default branch*. Retrieved November 25, 2010, from http://sourceforge.net/projects/strace

Strasburg, C., Basu, S., & Wong, J. S. (2013). S-MAIDS: A semantic model for automated tuning, correlation, and response selection in intrusion detection systems. In *Proceedings of IEEE 37th Annual Computer Software and Applications Conference (COMPSAC)* (pp. 319-328). IEEE.

Strayer, W., Lapsely, D., Walsh, R., & Livadas, C. (2007). Botnet detection based on network behavior. *Advances in Information Security, 36*, 1–24.

Stroh, S., Acker, O., & Kunar, A. (2009, June). *Why cloud computing is gaining strength in the IT marketplace*. Retrieved from http://www.strategy-business.com/article/li00131?gko=c331a

Strouble, D., Schechtman, G., & Alsop, A. S. (2009). Productivity and usability effects of using a two-factor security system. In *Proceedings of the Southern Association for Information Systems Conference* (pp. 195-201). Academic Press.

Strowel, A. (2009). Internet piracy as a wake-up call for copyright law makers – Is the ''graduated response'' a good reply? *World Intellectual Property Organization Journal, 1*, 75–86.

Sullivan, B. (2013, July 6). *Privacy vs. security: 'False choice' poisons debate on NSA leaks*. Retrieved March 7, 2014, from http://www.nbcnews.com/business/consumer/privacy-vs-security-false-choice-poisons-debate-nsa-leaks-f6C10536226

Sun Microsystems. (1988). *SunOS reference manual*. The Network Interface Tap.

Sun Microsystems. (1995). SunSHIELD basic security module guide. Mountain View, CA: Author.

Sun, S.-T., Boshmaf, Y., Hawkey, K., & Beznosov, K. (2010). A billion keys, but few locks: The crisis of web single sign-on. In Proceedings of the 2010 Workshop on New Security Paradigms. Academic Press. doi:10.1145/1900546.1900556

Sun, B., Xiao, Y., & Wang, R. (2007). Detection of fraudulent usage in wireless networks. *Transactions on Vehicular Technology, 6*(56), 3912–3923. doi:10.1109/TVT.2007.901875

Suoranta, S., Tontti, A., Ruuskanen, J., & Aura, T. (2013). Logout in single sign on systems. In Policies and research in identity management: Third IFIP WG 11.6 working conference. London: Springer.

Suthaharan, S. (2012). An iterative ellipsoid-based anomaly detection technique for intrusion detection systems. In *Proceedings of IEEE Southeastcon* (pp. 1-6). IEEE. doi:10.1109/SECon.2012.6196956

Sutton, G., & Griffen, M. (2004). Integrating expectations, experiences and psychological contract violations: A longitudinal study of new professionals. *Journal of Occupational and Organizational Psychology*, 77(4), 493–514. doi:10.1348/0963179042596487

Swift, D. (2010). *Successful SIEM and log management strategies for audit and compliance*. Retrieved March 28, 2014 from https://www.sans.org/reading-room/whitepapers/auditing/successful-siem-log-management-strategies-audit-compliance-33528

Swinth, K. R., & Blascovich, J. (2002). Perceiving and responding to others: Human-human and human-computer social interaction in collaborative virtual environments. In *Proceedings of the 5th Annual International Workshop on PRESENCE*. Porto, Portugal: Academic Press.

syscalltrack. (2010). *syscalltrack*. Retrieved November 25, 2010, from http://syscalltrack.sourceforge.net

Tajfel, H., & Turner, J. C. (1986). *The social identity of intergroup relations*. Chicago: Nelson-Hall.

Takeda, Y., Kondo, S., Kitayama, Y., Torato, M., & Motegi, T. (2006). Avoidance of performance bottlenecks caused by HTTP redirect in identity management protocols. In *Proceedings of the Second ACM Workshop on Digital Identity Management*. ACM. doi:10.1145/1179529.1179535

Takeuchi, H., & Nonaka, I. (2004). *Hitotsubashi on knowledge management*. Singapore: John Wiley & Sons.

Talbot, D. (2013, September 16). *Encrypted heartbeats keep hackers from medical implants*. Retrieved March 12, 2014, from MIT Technology Review: http://www.technologyreview.com/news/519266/encrypted-heartbeats-keep-hackers- from-medical-implants/

Tang, J., Chen, Z., Fu, A., & Cheung, D. W. (2002). Enhancing effectiveness of outlier detections for low density patterns. In *Proceedings of Pacific-Asia Conference on Knowledge Discovery and Data Mining (PAKDD)*. Taipei, Taiwan: Academic Press. doi:10.1007/3-540-47887-6_53

Tan, K. M. C., Killourhy, K. S., & Maxion, R. A. (2002). Undermining an anomaly-based intrusion detection system using common exploits. In *Proceedings of the 5th International Symposium on Recent Advances in Intrusion Detection* (pp. 54–73). Zurich, Switzerland: Springer-Verlag. doi:10.1007/3-540-36084-0_4

Taubenberger, S., Jürjens, J., Yu, Y., & Nuseibeh, B. (2011). Problem analysis of traditional IT-security risk assessment methods – An experience report from the insurance and auditing domain. In *Proceedings of SEC* (pp. 259–270). SEC.

Tavani, H. T. (2004). *Ethics and technology: ethical issues in an age of information and communication technology* (International Edition). John Wiley and Sons.

tcpdump. (2010). *tcpdump/libpcap*. Retrieved November 25, 2010, from http://www.tcpdump.org

Tehan, R. (2005, December 16). *Personal data security breaches: Context and incident summaries*. Congressional Research Service Report for Congress.

Thaseen, S., & Kumar, C. A. (2013). An analysis of supervised tree based classifiers for intrusion detection system. In *Proceedings of International Conference on Pattern Recognition, Informatics and Mobile Engineering (PRIME)* (pp. 294-299). Academic Press. doi:10.1109/ICPRIME.2013.6496489

The Australian. (2010a). *Bligh hits out at sick net sites*. Retrieved from: http://www.theaustralian.com.au/politics/state-politics/bligh-hits-out-at-sick-net-sites/story-e6frgczx-1225834063831

The Australian. (2010b). *Facebook vandal complaints futile*. Retrieved from: http://www.theaustralian.com.au/australian-it/facebook-vandal-complaints-futile/story-e6frgakx-1225834303404

The Australian. (2010c). *Online ombudsman for Facebook woes*. Retrieved from: http://www.theaustralian.com.au/australian-it/online-ombudsman-for-facebook-woes/story-e6frgakx-1225834756343

Thigpen, S. (2005, July 17). *Banking authentication methods*. Retrieved 3rd April, 2010 from http://www.infosecwriters.com/text_resources/pdf/ Authentication_Methods_For_Banking.pdf

Thompson, S. T. (2006). Helping the hacker? Library information, security, and social engineering. *Information Technology and Libraries*, 25(4), 222–226.

Thornburgh, T. (2004). Social engineering: The dark art. In *Proceedings of the 1st Annual Conference on Information Security Curriculum Development*. Kennesaw State University.

Thorpe, J., & van Oorschot, P. C. (2007). Human-seeded attacks and exploiting hot-spots in graphical passwords. In *Proceedings of the 16th Conference on USENIX Security Symposium*. Berkeley, CA: USENIX Association.

TIBCO. (2014). *How to centralize your logs with logging as a service: Solving logging challenges in the face of big data*. Retrieved March 26, 2014 from http://www.tibco.com/multimedia/solution-brief-logging-as-a-service_tcm8-19872.pdf

Time Magazine. (2010). *How prisoners harass their victims using Facebook*, Retrieved from: http://www.time.com/time/business/article/0,8599,1964916,00.html#ixzz0gb2oD8Ge

Tiwari, A., Sanyal, S., Abraham, A., Knapskog, S. J., & Sanyal, S. (2011). A multi-factor security protocol for wireless payment-secure web authentication using mobile devices. In *Proceedings of IADIS International Conference on Applied Computing*. IADIS.

Tomasek, M., Cajkovsky, M., & Mados, B. (2012). Intrusion detection system based on system behavior. In *Proceedings of IEEE 10th International Symposium on Applied Machine Intelligence and Informatics (SAMI)* (pp. 271-275). IEEE.

Tomlinson, E. C., & Mayer, R. C. (2009). The role of causal attribution dimensions in trust repair. *Academy of Management Review*, *34*(1), 85–104. doi:10.5465/AMR.2009.35713291

Tracy, K. (2008). Identity management systems. *IEEE Potentials*, (November/December), 2008.

Tran, Q. A., Jiang, F., & Hu, J. (2012). A real-time NetFlow-based intrusion detection system with improved BBNN and high-frequency field programmable gate arrays. In *Proceedings of IEEE 11th International Conference on Trust, Security and Privacy in Computing and Communications (TrustCom)* (pp. 201-208). IEEE.

Transparency Report. (n.d.) Retrieved from http://www.google.com/transparencyreport/userdatarequests/

Tront, J. G., & Marchany, R. C. (2004). Internet security: Intrusion detection and prevention. In *Proceedings of 37th Annual Hawaii International Conference on System Sciences* (pp. 188-188). Academic Press.

Tsai, C., Chen, C., & Zhuang, D. (2012). Trusted m-banking verification scheme based on a combination of OTP and biometrics. *Journal of Convergence*, *3*(3), 23–30.

Tsang, C-H., & Kwong, S. (2005). Multi-agent detection system in industrial network using ant colony clustering approach and unsupervised feature extraction. In *Proceedings of International Conference on Industrial Technology* (pp. 51–56). Academic Press.

Tsiftsoglou, A., & Flogaitis, S. (2011). *Transposing the data retention directive in Greece: Lessons from Karlsruhe*. Academic Press.

Tulving, E. (1974). Cue-dependent forgetting. *American Scientist*, *62*, 74–82.

Turban, E., King, D., Lee, J., Liang, T. P., & Turban, D. (2010). *Electronic commerce 2010: A managerial perspective* (6th ed.). Boston: Pearson.

Turban, E., Leidner, D., McClean, E., & Wetherbe, J. (2006). *Information technology for management – Transforming organisations in the digital economy* (5th ed.). John Wiley & Sons Inc.

Turel, O., Yuan, Y., & Connelly, C. E. (2008). In justice we trust: Predicting user acceptance of e-customer services. *Journal of Management Information Systems*, *24*(4), 123–151. doi:10.2753/MIS0742-1222240405

Turow, J., Feldman, L., & Metlzer, K. (2005). *Open to exploitation: American shoppers online and offline*. A Report from the Annenberg Public Policy Centre of the University of Pennsylvania, June 2005.

Tyler, T. R., & Lind, E. A. (1992). A relational model of authority in group. *Advances in Experimental Social Psychology*, *25*, 115–192. doi:10.1016/S0065-2601(08)60283-X

Tzanou, M. (2011). Data protection in EU law: An analysis of the EU legal framework and the ECJ jurisprudence. In C. Akrivopoulou & A. Psygkas (Eds.), *Personal data privacy and protection in a surveillance era: Technologies and practices* (pp. 273–297). Hershey, PA: IGI Global. doi:10.4018/978-1-60960-083-9.ch016

Tzanou, M. (2013). Data protection as a fundamental right next to privacy? 'Reconstructing' a not so new right. *International Data Privacy Law*, *3*(2), 88–99. doi:10.1093/idpl/ipt004

Tzanou, M. (2013). Is data protection the same as privacy? An analysis of telecommunications' metadata retention measures. *Journal of Internet Law, 17*(3), 20–33.

U.S. Government Printing Office Public Law 111-5. (2009). *American Recovery and reinvestment act of 2009.* Retrieved April 24, 2014 from http://www.gpo.gov/fdsys/pkg/PLAW-111publ5/pdf/PLAW-111publ5.pdf

UK Copyright Service. (n.d.). *Factsheet P-01: UK copyright law.* Retrieved December 12, 2010 from http://www.copyrightservice.co.uk/copyright/p01_uk_copyright_law

United States Computer Emergency Readiness Team. (2008). *Privacy impact assessment for EINSTEIN 2.* United States Department of Homeland Security. Retrieved July 8, 2014, from https://www.dhs.gov/xlibrary/assets/privacy/privacy_pia_einstein2.pdf

Ur, B., Kelley, P. G., Komanduri, S., Lee, J., Maass, M., & Mazurek, M. L. … Shay, L.F. (n.d.). *How does your password measure up? The effect of strength meters on password creation.* Carnegie Mellon University. Retrieved March 2, 2014, from https://www.ece.cmu.edu/~lbauer/papers/2012/usenix2012-meters.pdf

US Copyright Office. (n.d.). *Fair use.* Retrieved December 12, 2010 from http://www.copyright.gov/fls/fl102.html

US Department of Health and Human Services. (2009). *Protecting the privacy of patients' health information.* Retrieved November 12, 2009, from http://www.hhs.gov/news/facts/privacy.html

US-CERT. (2008). *Privacy impact assessment EINSTEIN program.* Department of Homeland Security, National Cyber Security Division, United States. Retrieved from http://www.dhs.gov/xlibrary/assets/privacy/privacy_pia_einstein2.pdf

Utah Department of Health. (n.d.). Retrieved August 2, 2013, from http://healthitsecurity.com/2013/07/23/healthcare-data-breaches-reviewing-the-ramifications/

Utimaco. (2009). *Health IT data breaches: No harm, no foul.* Retrieved November 12, 2009, from http://compliance.utimaco.com/na/tag/hitech-act

van der Meyden, R. (1996). The dynamic logic of permission. *J. Log. Comput., 6*(3), 465–479. doi:10.1093/logcom/6.3.465

Vanacker, B., & Heider, D. (2012). Ethical harm in virtual communities. *Convergence (London), 18*(1), 71–84. doi:10.1177/1354856511419916

Vanathi, R., & Gunasekaran, S. (2012). Comparison of network intrusion detection systems in cloud computing environment. In *Proceedings of International Conference on Computer Communication and Informatics (ICCCI)* (pp. 1-6). Academic Press. doi:10.1109/ICCCI.2012.6158820

Vance, A. (2010). If your password is 123456, just make it hackme. *New York Times.* Retrieved 15th March, 2010 from http://www.nytimes.com/2010/01/21/technology/21password.html

Venkatraman, S., & Delpachitra, I. (2008). Biometrics in banking security: A case study. *Information Management & Computer Security, 16*(4), 415–430. doi:10.1108/09685220810908813

Veracode. (2014). *Sony PSN breach infographic.* Retrieved March 15, 2014, from http://www.veracode.com/sony-psn-breach-infographic

Verrecchia, P., & Weiss, D. M. (2013). *Privacy vs. security.* Retrieved March 2, 2014, from York College of Pennsylvania: http://www.ycp.edu/offices-and-services/advancement/communications/york-college-magazine/fall-2013/privacy-vs.-security/

ViewDS Identity Solutions. (2014). Retrieved online on 4/12/2014 from http://www.viewds.com/images/pdf/AccessSentinel.pdf

Vijayan, J. (2009). *Social networking sites leaking personal information to third parties.* Retrieved from: http://www.networkworld.com/news/2009/092409-social-networking-sites-leaking-personal.html

Villamarin-Salomon, R., & Brustoloni, J. (2008). Identifying botnets using anomaly detection techniques applied to dns traffic. In *Proceedings of the 5th IEEE Consumer Communications and Networking Conference (CCNC 2008)* (pp. 476–481). IEEE. doi:10.1109/ccnc08.2007.112

Vogels, W. (2000). File system usage in Windows NT 4.0. *Operating Systems Review*, *34*(2), 17–18. doi:10.1145/346152.346177

Vokorokos, L., Kleinova, A., & Latka, O. (2006). Network security on the intrusion detection system level. In *Proceedings ofInternational Conference on Intelligent Engineering Systems* (pp. 534-536). Academic Press. doi:10.1109/INES.2006.1689382

von Solms, S. H., & Solms, R. v. (2009). *Information security governance*. New York, NY: Springer. doi:10.1007/978-0-387-79984-1

Wagner, D., & Soto, P. (2002). Mimicry attacks on host-based intrusion detection systems. In *Proceedings of9th ACM Conference on Computer and Communications Security* (pp. 255–264). Washington, DC: ACM. doi:10.1145/586143.586145

Wall, D. W. (1989). *Link-time code modification: Technical report research report 89/17*. Palo Alto, CA: DEC Western Research Laboratory.

Wang, H., Lee, M. K. O., & Wang, C. (1998). Consumer privacy concerns about internet marketing. *Communications of the ACM*, *41*(3), 63–70. doi:10.1145/272287.272299

Ward, K. J. (1999). The cyber-ethnographic and the emergence of the virtually new community. *Journal of Information Technology*, *14*(1), 95–105. doi:10.1080/026839699344773

Warkentin, M., & Willison, R. (2009). Behavioral and policy issues in information systems security: The insider threat. *European Journal of Information Systems*, *18*(2), 101–105. doi:10.1057/ejis.2009.12

Warren, M., & Leitch, S. (2014). *Be safe, be social*. IDG Communications.

Warren, S. D., & Brandeis, L. D. (1890). Right to privacy. *Harvard Law Review*, *4*(5), 193–220. doi:10.2307/1321160

Wasko, M. M., & Faraj, S. (2000). "It is what one does": Why people participate and help others in electronic communities of practice. *The Journal of Strategic Information Systems*, *9*(2-3), 155–173. doi:10.1016/S0963-8687(00)00045-7

Watson, J. (2008). Virtualbox: Bits and bytes masquerading as machines. *Linux Journal*, *2008*, 166.

Weaver, N., Paxson, V., & Sommer, R. (2007). *Work in progress: Bro-LAN pervasive network inspection and control for LAN traffic* (pp. 1–2). Securecomm and Workshops.

Weber, W. (1999). Firewall basics. In *Proceedings of 4th International Conference on Telecommunications in Modern Satellite, Cable and Broadcasting Services* (vol. 1, pp. 300-305). Academic Press.

Weber, J. M., Malhotra, D., & Murnighan, J. K. (2005). Normal acts of irrational trust, motivated attributions, and the process of trust development. In B. M. Staw & R. M. Kramer (Eds.), *Research in organizational behavior* (pp. 75–102). Elsevier.

Wehmhoener, K. (2010). *Social norm or social harm: An exploratory study of internet vigilantism*. (Masters Thesis). Iowa State University.

Wei, W., Xiangliang, Z., Gombault, S., & Knapskog, S. J. (2009). Attribute normalization in network intrusion detection. In *Proceedings of10th International Symposium on Pervasive Systems, Algorithms, and Networks* (pp. 448–453). Academic Press.

Weigold, T. K. (2006, March/April). *Secure internet banking and authentication*. Retrieved 3rd April 2010 from http://www.zurich.ibm.com/pdf/csc/SecureInternetBanking Authentication.pdf

Weinberg, Y., Tzur-David, S., Dolev, D., & Anker, T. (2006). High performance string matching algorithm for a network intrusion prevention system. In *Proceedings ofWorkshop on High Performance Switching and Routing* (p. 7). Academic Press.

Weiss, R., & De Luca, A. (2008). Passshapes: Utilizing stroke based authentication to increase password memorability. In *Proceedings of the 5th Nordic Conference on Human-Computer Interaction*. Academic Press. doi:10.1145/1463160.1463202

Welcome to AWPHD: Keeping Quality Care Local. (2013). Retrieved August 20, 2013, from http://www.awphd.org/presentations/.../Model%20Password%20Policy.doc

Wellman, B., & Gulia, M. (1999). Net surfers don't ride alone. In B. Wellman (Ed.), *Networks in the global village* (pp. 331–366). Boulder, CO: Westview Press.

Wells, W. D., Burnett, J., & Moriarty, S. (1989). *Advertising: Principles and practice*. Prentice Hall.

Wen, H. J., Schwieger, D., & Gershuny, P. (2007). Internet usage monitoring in the workplace: Its legal challenges and implementation strategies. *Information Systems Management*, 24(2), 185–196. doi:10.1080/10580530701221072

Werner, S., & Hoover, C. (2012). *Cognitive approaches to password memorability – The possible role of story-based passwords*. Retrieved March 2, 2014, from http://pro.sagepub.com/content/56/1/1243

Werra, J. (2001). Le régime juridique des mesures techniques de protection des oeuvres selon les Traités de l'OMPI, le Digital Millennium Copyright Act, les Directives Européennes et d'autres legislations (Japon, Australie). *Revue Internationale du Droit d'Auteur*, 189, 66–213.

Westin, A. (1970). *Privacy and freedom*. New York: Atheneum.

Wetmore, B. R. (1993). *Paradigms for the reduction of audit trails*. (Master's thesis). University of California Davis, Davis, CA.

Whitney, L. (2009). *Employers grappling with social network use*. Retrieved from: http://news.cnet.com/8301-10797_3-10360849-235.html

Whitney, I., & Smith, P. K. (1993). A survey of the nature and extent of bullying in junior/middle and secondary schools. *Educational Research*, 35(1), 3–25. doi:10.1080/0013188930350101

Whittaker, S., Isaacs, E., & O'day, V. (1997). Widening the net: Workshop report on the theory and practice of physical and network communities. *SIGCHI Bulletin*, 18(1), 27–32. doi:10.1145/264853.264867

Wiedenbeck, S., Waters, J., Birget, J., Brodskiy, A., & Memon, N. (2005, July). PassPoints: Design and longitudinal evaluation of a graphical password system. *International Journal of Human-Computer Studies*, 63(1-2), 102–127. doi:10.1016/j.ijhcs.2005.04.010

Wiedenbeck, S., Waters, J., Sobrado, L., & Birget, J.-C. (2006). Design and evaluation of a shoulder-surfing resistant graphical password scheme. In *Proceedings of the Working Conference on Advanced Visual Interfaces* (pp. 177-184). ACM. doi:10.1145/1133265.1133303

Wiesmaier, A., Fischer, M., Karatsiolis, E. G., & Lippert, M. (2004). *Proceedings of the 2005 International Conference on Security and Management*. Retrieved from arxiv.org/pdf/cs.CR/0410025

Willard, N. (2005). *Educators guide to cyber-bullying and cyber threats*. Centre for Safe and Responsible Internet Use. Retrieved from: http://www.csriuorg/cyberbully/docs/cbcteducator.pdf.

Williamson, G. D. (2006). Enhanced authentication in online banking. *Journal of Economic Crime Management*, 42(2).

Williamson, O. E. (1993). Calculativeness, trust, and economic organization. *The Journal of Law & Economics*, 36(S1), 453–486. doi:10.1086/467284

Wilms, F. (2003). Systemorientierte unternehmensfhrung von KMUs. In *Management von KMU und grndungsunternehmen* (pp. 3–26). Deutscher Universtätsverlag Wiesbaden.

Wilson, B., & Ryder, M. (1996). Dynamic learning communities: An alternative to designed instruction. In M. Simonson (Ed.), *Proceedings of selected research and development presentations* (pp. 800-809). Washington, DC: Association for Educational Communications and Technology. Retrieved on January 20, 2010, from http://carbon.ucdenver.edu/~mryder/dlc.html

Wilson, C. (2007). *Botnets, cybercrime, and cyberterrorism: Vulnerabilities and policy issues for congress (Tech. Rep.)*. Washington, DC: Library of Congress Congressional Research Service.

Wilson, P. (1983). *Second-hand knowledge: An inquiry into cognitive authority*. Westport, CT: Greenwood Press.

Wilton, C., & Campbell, M. A. (2011). An exploration of the reasons why adolescents engage in traditional and cyber bullying. *Journal of Educational Sciences and Psychology*, 1(2), 101–109.

Wimberly, H., & Liebrock, L. M. (2011). Using fingerprint authentication to reduce system security: An empirical study. In *Proceedings of IEEE Symposium on Security and Privacy* (pp. 32–46). IEEE. doi:10.1109/SP.2011.35

Wireshark. (2010). *Wireshark: The world's foremost network protocol analyzer*. Retrieved March 30, 2010, from http://www.wireshark.org/

Wobbrock, J. O. (2009, October). Tapsongs: Tapping rhythm-based passwords on a single binary sensor. In *Proceedings of the 22nd Annual ACM Symposium on User Interface Software and Technology* (pp. 93-96). ACM. doi:10.1145/1622176.1622194

Wolak, J., Finkelhor, D., & Mitchell, K. J. (2004). Internet-initiated sex crimes against minors: Implications for prevention based on findings from a national study. *The Journal of Adolescent Health*, 35(5), 424–433. doi:10.1016/j.jadohealth.2004.05.006 PMID:15488437

Wolke, D. (2010). Bullying: Facts and processes. *Worcester Medicine*, 74(4), 13–15.

Wood, P. (2005, September). Implementing identity management security - An ethical hacker's view. *Network Security*, 2005(9), 12–15. doi:10.1016/S1353-4858(05)70282-8

Worchel, P. (1979). Trust and distrust. In W. G. Austin & P. Worchel (Eds.), *Social psychology of intergroup relations* (pp. 174–187). Monterey, CA: Broks/Cole.

Wu, J. M. (1995). *Maximum likelihood estimation in the random coefficient regression model via the EM algorithm*. (PhD Thesis). Texas Tech University, Lubbock, TX.

Wu, J. J., & Tsang, A. S. L. (2008). "Factors affecting members" trust belief and behaviour intention in virtual communities. *Behaviour & Information Technology*, 27(2), 115–125. doi:10.1080/01449290600961910

Xi, K., Ahmad, T., Han, F., & Hu, J. (2011). A fingerprint based bio-cryptographic security protocol designed for client/server authentication in mobile computing environment. *Security and Communication Networks*, 4(5), 487–499. doi:10.1002/sec.225

Xinidis, K., Charitakis, I., Antonatos, S., Anagnostakis, K. G., & Markatos, E. P. (2006). An active splitter architecture for intrusion detection and prevention. *Transactions on Dependable and Secure Computing*, 1(3), 31–44. doi:10.1109/TDSC.2006.6

Yaghmour, K., & Dagenais, M. R. (2000). Measuring and characterizing system behavior using kernel-level event logging. In *Proceedings of the Annual Conference on USENIX Annual Technical Conference (ATEC'00)*. San Diego, CA: USENIX Association.

Yang, Y.-J. (1997). *The security of electronic banking*. Retrieved 3rd April, 2010, from http://csrc.nist.gov/nissc/1997/proceedings/041.pdf

Yan, J., Blackwell, A., Anderson, R., & Grant, A. (2004). Password memorability and security: Empirical results. *IEEE Security and Privacy*, 2(5), 25–31. doi:10.1109/MSP.2004.81

Yan, Z. (2009). Limited knowledge and limited resources: Children's and adolescents' understanding of the internet. *Journal of Applied Developmental Psychology*, 30(2), 103–115. doi:10.1016/j.appdev.2008.10.012

Yan, Z., Dong, Y., Niemi, V., & Yu, G. (2013). Exploring trust of mobile applications based on user behaviors: An empirical study. *Journal of Applied Social Psychology*, 43(3), 467–686. doi:10.1111/j.1559-1816.2013.01044.x

Yau, S. S., & Zhang, X. (1999). Computer networks intrusion detection, assessment and prevention based on security dependency relation. In *Proceedings of Computer Software and Applications Conference* (pp. 86–91). Academic Press. doi:10.1109/CMPSAC.1999.812681

Yee, C. G., Rao, G. V. S., & Radha, K. (2006). A hybrid approach to intrusion detection and prevention business intelligent applications. In *Proceedings of International Symposium on Communications and Information Technologies* (pp. 847-850). Academic Press. doi:10.1109/ISCIT.2006.339856

Yegneswaran, V., Saidi, H., Porras, P., Sharif, M., Mark, W., & President, V. (2008). Eureka: A framework for enabling static analysis on malware (Tech. Rep.). Atlanta, GA: Georgia Institute of Technology.

Yen, S.-J., & Lee, Y. (2009). Cluster-based under-sampling approaches for imbalanced data distributions. *Expert Systems with Applications, 36*(3), 5718–5727. doi:10.1016/j.eswa.2008.06.108

Yung-Da, W., & Paulik, M. J. (1996). A discrete wavelet model for target recognition. In *Proceedings of 39th Midwest Symposium on Circuit and Systems* (vol. 2, pp. 835-838). Academic Press. doi:10.1109/MWSCAS.1996.588044

Zamboni, D. (2001). *Using internal sensors for computer intrusion detection.* (PhD thesis). Purdue University, West Lafayette, IN.

Zave, P. (1997). Classification of research efforts in requirements engineering. *ACM Computing Surveys, 29*(4), 315–321. doi:10.1145/267580.267581

Zezschwitz, E., De Luca, A., & Hussmann, H. (2013). Survival of the shortest: A retrospective analysis of influencing factors on password composition. In *Proceedings of Human-Computer Interaction.* Academic Press.

Zhang, J., Gao, Q., & Wang, H. (2006). A novel method for detecting outlying subspaces in high- dimensional databases using genetic algorithm. In *Proceedings of IEEE International Conference on Data Mining* (pp. 731-740). Hong Kong, China: IEEE. doi:10.1109/ICDM.2006.6

Zhang, J., Gao, Q., Wang, H., Liu, Q., & Xu, X. (2009). Detecting projected outliers in high-dimensional data streams. In *Proceedings of International Conference on Database and Expert Systems Applications* (pp. 629-644). Academic Press. doi:10.1007/978-3-642-03573-9_53

Zhang, L. (2009). *A sublexical unit based hash model approach for SPAM detection.* (PhD Thesis). University of Texas, San Antonio, TX.

Zhang, J., Gao, Q., Wang, H., & Wang, H. (2010). *Detecting anomalies from high-dimensional wireless net- work data streams: A case study.* Springer Publishing.

Zhang, J., & Wang, H. (2006). Detecting outlying subspaces for high-dimensional data: The new task, algorithms and performance. *Knowledge and Information Systems, 10*(3), 333–355. doi:10.1007/s10115-006-0020-z

Zhang, X., Wang, Z., Gloy, N., Chen, J. B., & Smith, M. D. (1997). System support for automatic profiling and optimization. In *Proceedings of the Sixteenth ACM Symposium on Operating Systems Principles (SOSP'97)* (pp. 15–26). New York, NY: ACM. doi:10.1145/268998.266640

Zhao, D., Traore, I., Sayed, B., Lu, W., Saad, S., Ghorbani, A., & Garant, D. (2013). Botnet detection based on traffic behavior analysis and flow intervals. *Computers & Security, 39*, 2–16. doi:10.1016/j.cose.2013.04.007

Zhao, L., Lu, Y., Wang, B., Chau, P., & Zhang, L. (2012). Cultivating the sense of belonging and motivating user participation in virtual communities: A social capital perspective. *International Journal of Information Management, 32*(6), 574–588. doi:10.1016/j.ijinfomgt.2012.02.006

Zhaoyu, L., & Uppala, R. (2006). A dynamic countermeasure method for large-scale network attacks. In *Proceedings of International Symposium on Dependable, Autonomic and Secure Computing* (pp. 163-170). Academic Press.

Zheng-De, Z., Zhi-Guo, L., Dong, Z., & Fei-Teng, J. (2006). Study on joint prevention technique of information security in SUN. In *Proceedings of International Conference on Machine Learning and Cybernetics* (pp. 2823-2827). Academic Press.

Zhong, S., Khoshgoftaar, T. M., & Nath, S. V. (2005). A clustering approach to wireless network intrusion detection. In *Proceedings of IEEE International Conference on Tools with Artificial Intelligence (ICTAI)* (pp. 190-196). IEEE.

Zhou, C., Liu, Y., & Zhang, H. (2006). A pattern matching based network intrusion detection system. In *Proceedings of 9th International Conference on Control, Automation, Robotics and Vision* (pp. 1-4). Academic Press.

Zhou, S., Costa, H. D., & Smith, A. J. (1985). *A file system tracing package for Berkeley UNIX: Technical report.* Berkeley, CA: University of California at Berkeley.

Zhou, T. (2011). An empirical examination of intial trust in mobile banking. *Internet Research, 21*(5), 527–540. doi:10.1108/10662241111176353

Zhou, T. (2012). Understanding users' initial trust in mobile banking: An elaboration likelihood perspective. *Computers in Human Behavior*, 28(4), 1518–1525. doi:10.1016/j.chb.2012.03.021

Zhu, C., Kitagawa, H., & Faloutsos, C. (2005). Example-based robust outlier detection in high dimensional datasets. In *Proceedings of IEEE International Conference on Data Mining* (pp. 829-832). IEEE.

Zhu, C., Kitagawa, H., Papadimitriou, S., & Faloutsos, C. (2004). OBE: Outlier by example. In *Proceedings of Pacific-Asia Conference on Knowledge Discovery and Data Mining (PAKDD)* (pp. 222-234). PAKDD.

Zhu, Z., Lu, G., Chen, Y., Fu, Z., Roberts, P., & Han, K. (2008). Botnet research survey. In Proceedings of 32nd Annual IEEE International Computer Software and Applications (COMPSAC'08) (pp. 967-972). IEEE.

Zucker, L. G. (1986). Production of trust: Institutional sources of economic structure. In B. M. Staw & L. L. Cummings (Eds.), *Research in organizational behavior* (pp. 53–111). Greenwich, CT: JAI Press.

Zweig, D., & Webster, J. (2002). Where is the line between benign and invasive? An examination of psychological barriers to the acceptance of awareness monitoring system. *Journal of Organizational Behavior*, 23(5), 605–633. doi:10.1002/job.157

About the Contributors

Manish Gupta is Vice President in Information Security Department at M&T Bank. He is also Adjunct Assistant Professor at State University of New York at Buffalo, NY. He has more than 15 years of experience in information systems, security policies, and technologies. He has edited or co-edited 7 books in the area of information security and assurance. He received PhD in Management Science and Systems in 2011 and an MBA in Information Systems and Finance in 2003, both from State University of New York at Buffalo, NY. He received his Bachelor's degree in Mechanical Engineering from Institute of Engineering and Technology, Lucknow, India, in 1998. He has authored or co-authored more than 60 research articles in leading journals, conference proceedings, and books. His research has received best paper awards. He serves in editorial boards of more than a dozen international journals and has served in program committees of several international conferences. He holds several professional designations including CISSP, CISA, CISM, CRISC, CFE, CIW Security Analyst, and PMP.

* * *

Saeed Abu-Nimeh is the Founder and CEO of Seclytics Inc. He holds a PhD in Computer Science from Southern Methodist University. Prior to founding Seclytics, he was a Distinguished Scientist at PayPal Inc. His research interests include Threat Intelligence and Machine Learning.

Cajetan M. Akujuobi Dean, College of Science, Mathematics, Technology, and Engineering, Alabama State University, provides vision, leadership, and advocacy for the college, its programs, faculty, and staff in the Departments of Biological Sciences, Mathematics and Computer Science, Physical Sciences, Technology, and Engineering. Prior to joining Alabama State University, Akujuobi was a fully tenured professor of electrical and computer engineering and the founding director of the multi-million dollar Center of Excellence for Communications Systems Technology Research at Prairie View A&M University (PVAMU). During a 12-year span at PVAMU, Akujuobi was instrumental in helping to secure research awards in excess of $15 million. He also was one of the founding directors of the Broadband (High-Speed Network) Communication Systems Program, Analog and Mixed Signal Program (AMSP), the DSP Solutions Programs, and the founding Director of the Communication Control Research Programs at PVAMU. His research areas also include wavelet and wavelet transform applications, information security, signal/image/video processing, communication systems, and forensic imaging systems. Akujuobi has held various positions in academia and industry for the past 30 years. He also has written more than 100 journal and peer-reviewed publications and co-authored a book, *Introduction to Broadband Communication Systems*. He is listed in *Who's Who in Science and Engineering, Who's Who* *in the World, Who's Who in America, Who's Who in American Education,* and *Who's Who in Industry & Finance.* Akujuobi received an OND in Electrical and Electronics Engineering from the Institute of Management and Technology, BS in Electrical and Electronics Engineering, Southern University, MS in Electrical and Electronics Engineering, Tuskegee University, MBA, Hampton University, and the PhD in Electrical Engineering, George Mason University.

Nana K. Ampah currently works with Jacobs Engineering Group, Houston, Texas, as an Electrical Engineer. He worked with the Electricity Company of Ghana for 8 years as a Project Engineer on World Bank-funded urban/rural electrification projects, specializing in the design, construction, commissioning, and management of projects. He also worked with Skanska Jensen International as a Materials Coordinator (Consultant) on similar projects in 1997. He is a member of IEEE, Ghana Institute of Engineers, and Ghana Institute of Management and Public Administration (GIMPA) Alumni Association. He graduated from Prairie View A&M University, Prairie View, Texas, with a PhDEE and an MSEE in Telecommunications and Signal Processing in 2008 and 2004, respectively. He also graduated from Kiev Polytechnic Institute (KPI) in Kiev, Ukraine, in 1993 with an MSEE in Power Systems and Networks. He also has a Post-Graduate Certificate in Urban Management from GIMPA, 2001.

Reema Bhatt has a Master's degree in Management Information Systems with a specialization in IS Audit and IT Risk Management. Having an inclination towards the domain of information security, she is an avid reader of texts on trending technologies. She enjoys writing and considers it as a way of disseminating knowledge.

Wolfgang Boehmer holds a PhD in Applied Physics from the University of Hamburg (Germany), and he is a research scientist and lecturer in Information Security, Computer Science Department, Security Engineering Group, from the Technische Universitaet Darmstadt (Germany). His research interests include security management systems, control systems, risk analysis, applied Game Theory in the field of security in large and small enterprises, Business Continuity Management Systems (BCMS), and mobile networks.

Marcelo Campo received a PhD degree in Computer Science from the Universidade Federal do Rio Grande do Sul, Porto Alegre, Brazil, in 1997, and the Systems Engineer degree from the UNICEN, in 1988. He is an Associate Professor at UNICEN and Head of the ISISTAN Research Institute. He is also a research fellow of the CONICET. His research interests include intelligent-aided software engineering, software architecture and frameworks, agent technology, and software visualization.

Joseph A. Cazier, PhD, is the Associate Dean for Graduate Programs and Research and Professor of Computer Information Systems at Appalachian State University. His work focuses on ethical applications of information systems and analytics. His research has appeared in *Information & Management, Communications of the Association for Information Systems, International Journal of Social Ecology and Sustainable Development* (IJSESD), *International Journal of Management, Information Systems Frontiers,* and others. Dr. Cazier received his PhD from the W. P. Carey School of Business at Arizona State University.

Regina Connolly is an Associate Professor in Information Systems at Dublin City University Business School, Dublin, Ireland. She was conferred with a PhD in Information Systems from Trinity College Dublin. Her research interests include eCommerce trust and privacy issues, website service quality evaluation, eGovernment, and IT value evaluation in the public sector. Dr. Connolly has served on the expert eCommerce advisory group for Dublin Chamber of Commerce, which has advised national government on eCommerce strategic planning.

Marc Conrad currently works for the Faculty of Creative Arts, Technology, and Science, at the University of Bedfordshire as a Principal Lecturer in Computer Science. Being educated as a Mathematician, where he received his PhD, his research interests are now in areas as diverse as Virtual Worlds, Algebraic Number Theory, Software Engineering, Project Management, Trust, Security, and Art. Together with his colleague, Tim French, he developed a lightweight mathematical model of trust propagation that identifies how much experience matters to establish trust (the answer is 30% experience and 70% hearsay). Marc Conrad is also the inventor of a framework to evaluate virtual worlds. His personal Web site is http://perisic.com/marc.

Xavier P. Francia received his BS in Nuclear and Radiological Engineering in May 2012 from Georgia Institute of Technology in Atlanta, GA, and his MS in Computer Systems and Software Design with Information Assurance concentration from Jacksonville State University in April 2014. His research interests include network vulnerability and penetration testing, industrial control system security, performance monitoring and data analytics, change and patch management, and modeling and simulation. He has published in information security areas of change and patch management, control system protocols, and embedded system authentication.

Guillermo A. Francia, III, received his BS in Mechanical Engineering degree from Mapua Tech in 1978. His PhD in Computer Science is from New Mexico Tech. Before joining Jacksonville State University (JSU), he was the chairman of the Computer Science Department at Kansas Wesleyan University. Dr. Francia is a recipient of numerous grants. His projects have been funded by prestigious institutions such as the National Science Foundation, Eisenhower Foundation, Department of Education, Department of Defense, and Microsoft Corporation. Dr. Francia served as a Fulbright scholar to Malta in 2007. He has published articles and book chapters on numerous subjects such as Computer Security, Digital Forensics, Regulatory Compliance, Educational Technology, Expert Systems, Computer Networking, Software Testing, and Parallel Processing. Currently, Dr. Francia is a Professor of Computer Science and the Director of the Center for Information Security and Assurance at JSU.

Sebastián García is currently finishing his PhD at the UNICEN University in Argentina (ISISTAN Institute) and working as a researcher in the Agents Technology Group of Czech Technical University in Czech Republic. Some of his recent projects focus on using machine learning to detect botnets behavior on large networks, on modelling the different behaviors of botnets, and on capturing real botnet traffic. What he enjoys the most is to teach and research. He has been teaching and working on penetration testing and computer security for some time. His current interests are on network-based botnet behavior detection, machine learning, penetration testing, honeypots, malware detection, keystroke dynamics, bluetooth analysis, intruder detection, and network analysis. He also enjoys looking at real malware traffic.

Marcia Gibson is a lecturer in Computer Science and Technology at the University of Bedfordshire, where she also completed her PhD in Computer Security. Her research interests include authentication systems, cyberstalking and privacy and security in smart cities. She teaches Computer Security and HCI and is an associate of the UK's National Centre for Cyberstalking Research.

Frances S. Hutchinson is a computer science professional from Jacksonville, FL. She graduated magna cum laude from Jacksonville State University in 2010 with a bachelor's degree in Computer Science. In 2012, she attained a Masters in Computer Science with a focus on information security and a 4.0 GPA. During her time in college, Frances attained two certifications from the Committee on National Security Systems and the National Security Agency, and she also assisted in the creation of an internal security compliance checklist website and identity theft prevention policy for university personnel. She is currently a full time software developer.

Erland Jonsson (1946) is Professor of Computer Security and past head of the Department of Computer Engineering at Chalmers University of Technology, Göteborg, Sweden. He has worked for the ERICSSON Company for almost 20 years. His present research interests include intrusion detection, security modeling, and security metrics. He has supervised over 10 PhD students in these areas. He is or was a member of a number of scientific advisory boards and program or steering committees of a large number of conferences. He is a major promoter of the security areas in the Nordic countries. Among other things, he started NordSec, a Nordic conference and forum for security research and development, and was one of the initiators of SWITS, the Swedish IT Security network for PhD students. Lately, he has been active in establishing a Security Arena in Lindholmen Science Park and URBSEC, the Urban Safety and Societal Security Research Center.

Sylvia Mercado Kierkegaard is a leading international authority in computer law. Her articles are widely published in top international journals and books. Her research is frequently cited and covers a wide range of topics, including comparative contract law, alternative dispute resolution, intellectual property rights, EU law, privacy, electronic commerce, cybersecurity, computer law, and data protection. She has authored, edited, and published books and over 2000 articles. She is the President of the International Association of IT Lawyers (IAITL). She is a Professor at the Communications University of China, Professor-Research Fellow at ILaws (UK), University of Southampton, Adjunct Professor at Xi'an Jiaotong University, among others. Sylvia Kierkegaard serves as Chairman of the Organizing Committee of the IAITL legal conference. She is a also member of the academic staff, and Professor at CyberSecurity Research – EPSRC/GCHQ Academic Centre of Excellence, one of the eight UK universities conducting world-class research in the field of cyber security. She is a frequent keynote speaker, invited expert, and panelist of various international workshops organised by international institutions, judiciary, EU, television, and government bodies. She is listed as a policy expert at the Media Policy Project, London School of Economics and Political Science database of individual experts, and is a member of the Policy and Scientific Committee of the European Privacy Association. Sylvia Kierkegaard is also a fellow at the UN African Center for Cyberlaw and Cybercrime Prevention, consultant for the Data Protection SDN, BHD Malaysia, and a member of the Advisory Board, World Council for Law Firms and Justice. She is the editor-in-chief of the *Journal of International Commercial Law and Technology, International Journal of Private Law,* and *International Journal of Public Law and Policy.* She is in the editorial board of over 25 international journals. She has served as an expert adviser and member of various Study Groups and Committees for the EU and the Council of Europe that draft policies and proposals for legislative and regulatory policies on international level as well as international associations. She is an advisor to numerous organisations and government bodies. She is also the IAITL delegation head/representative to the World Intellectual Property Organization (WIPO) and the International Telecommunication Union (ITU-T).

Ulf Larson (1975) holds a PhD in Computer Security from Chalmers University of Technology, Göteborg, Sweden. Ulf works at Ericsson as a System Manager focusing on telecom and node security. He initiates and drives changes in processes and implementations within the security area and also assists in risk and vulnerability assessments. Ulf is also the founder and one of the chapter leaders for OWASP Göteborg. His research interests include data collection, intrusion detection, secure application development, and robustness testing.

Shona Leitch is the Director, Undergraduate Programs, College of Business, RMIT, and previously the Course Director, Bachelor of Commerce and Bachelor of Management, at Deakin University. She has a PhD in Educational Systems Analysis and Design focusing on the design and user acceptance of online learning systems. Her research focus has been in teaching and learning area with a specific focus on the use of technology to support innovative education. She also publishes in her discipline area of privacy and ethics. Shona is a reviewer for a number of journals and conferences within her discipline area. She obtained (as part of a team) an Office for Learning and Teaching Grant of $206,000 in 2013 to develop an assessment framework for ePortfolios in business education.

Stefan Lindskog (1967) received his Licentiate and PhD degrees in Computer Engineering from Chalmers University of Technology, Göteborg, Sweden, in 2000 and 2005, respectively. In 2008, he received the Docent degree in Computer Science at Karlstad University, Sweden. He joined the Department of Computer Science at Karlstad University in 1990, where he is currently a full professor. His research focus is the design of tunable and adaptable security services and security and performance analysis of security services and protocols. He has authored/coauthored 1 textbook, 8 book chapters, and over 50 journal and conference papers.

Carsten Maple is a Professor of Cyber Systems Engineering at the University of Warwick. He works with organisations in key sectors such as manufacturing, healthcare, and financial services, addressing the challenges presented by today's global cyber environment. He was previously Professor of Applicable Computing and Pro Vice Chancellor (Research and Enterprise) at the University of Bedfordshire. He has published over 200 peer-reviewed papers and is co-author of the "UK Security Breach Investigations Report 2010" and "Cyberstalking in the UK," a report supported by the Crown Prosecution Service and Network for Surviving Stalking. His research has attracted millions of pounds in funding and has been widely reported through the media. He has given evidence to government committees on issues of anonymity and child safety online. He works with various departments such as the Association of Chief Police Officers, the College of Policing, Interpol, and the Equality and Human Rights Commission.

Nancy R. Mead is a Fellow and Principal Researcher at the Software Engineering Institute (SEI). Mead is also an Adjunct Professor of Software Engineering at Carnegie Mellon University. She is currently involved in the study of security requirements engineering and the development of software assurance curricula. Mead has more than 150 publications and invited presentations, and has a biographical citation in *Who's Who in America*. She is a Fellow of the Institute of Electrical and Electronic Engineers, Inc. (IEEE) and a Distinguished Member of the Association for Computing Machinery (ACM). Dr. Mead received her PhD in Mathematics from the Polytechnic Institute of New York, and received a BA and an MS in Mathematics from New York University.

B. Dawn Medlin is currently serving as a Professor in the Department of Computer Information Systems in the John A. Walker College of Business at Appalachian State University in Boone, North Carolina. Her teaching and research activities have been primarily in the area of security and privacy issues as well as e-commerce. She has published in journals such as *The Journal of Information Systems Security, Information Systems Security, International Journal of Electronic Marketing and Retailing*, and the *International Journal of Healthcare Information Systems and Informatics*. Additionally, she has taught at the Université d'Angers in France, Addis Ababa University in Ethiopia, and the National Chung Cheng University, Taiwan. Most recently, Dr. Medlin received the Walker College of Business Research Award for 2013-14.

Vidya Mulukutla is a graduate student at University at Buffalo, SUNY, where she specializes in Information Systems with a keen interest in topics of Information Assurance. Prior to this, she was a management consultant in a Big 4 consulting firm. She holds a Post Graduate Diploma in Business Management with a specialization in Finance and Marketing. She has working experience in the financial services industry.

Cyril Onwubiko is a leading information security expert and founder of Research Series in London, UK, where he leads on intelligence and security assurance, cyber security, and situational awareness in computer network defense. Prior to Research Series, he was an information security consultant at British Telecommunications, CLAS Consultant at Cable & Wireless Worldwide, and a security analyst at COLT Telecommunications. He holds a PhD degree in Computer Network Security from Kingston University, London, UK. Dr. Onwubiko has authored several books, including *Security Frameworks for Attack Detection in Computer Networks, Concepts in Numerical Methods, Situational Awareness in Computer Network Defense: Principles, Methods, and Applications*, and has published over 30 academic articles in reputable journals, conference proceedings, and edited books. He is a senior member of the IEEE, member of the Institute of Information Security Professionals (IISP), Senior member of the CESG Certified Professional (in Security Architecture & SIRA), and CESG Listed Advisor Scheme (CLAS).

Eun Park is an Associate Professor in the School of Information Studies at McGill University, Montreal, Quebec, Canada. Her research interests include electronic records systems, digital content management, digital preservation, metadata, authenticity and authentication, and social aspects of information technology.

Pedro Pina is a lawyer and a law teacher in the Oliveira do Hospital School of Technology and Management at the Polytechnic Institute of Coimbra. He holds a law degree from the University of Coimbra Law School and a post-graduation in Territorial Development, Urbanism, and Environmental Law from the Territorial Development, Urbanism, and Environmental Law Studies Center (CEDOUA) at the University of Coimbra Law School. He holds a Master degree in Procedural Law Studies from the University of Coimbra Law School and is currently a PhD student in the Doctoral Programme "Law, Justice, and Citizenship in the Twenty First Century" from the University of Coimbra Law School and Economics School.

H. R. Rao graduated from Krannert Graduate School of Management at Purdue University. His interests are in the areas of management information systems, decision support systems, e-business, emergency response management systems, and information assurance. He has chaired sessions at international conferences and presented numerous papers. He also has co-edited four books of which one is on Information Assurance in Financial Services. He has authored or co-authored more than 175 technical papers, of which more than 100 are published in archival journals.

Karen Renaud is a Scottish Computer Scientist and Senior Lecturer at the University of Glasgow. She was educated at the Universities of Pretoria, South Africa, and Glasgow. She has made contributions in the fields of usable security, technology adoption, email usage, electronic voting, and design patterns, and works with research collaborators in Germany, Canada, the US, South Africa, and the UK.

Raj Sharman is an Associate Professor in the Management Science and Systems Department of the State University of New York at Buffalo. His expertise is in the areas of Information Assurance and the development of Biologically Inspired Computer Security Models, Disaster Preparedness and Response Management, Patient Safety, and Health Care Systems. He has published widely in national and international journals and is the recipient of several grants from university and external agencies, including the National Science Foundation. He received his PhD in Computer Science and a Master of Science degree in Industrial Engineering from the Louisiana State University. He received his Bachelors degree in Engineering and Masters Degree in Management from the Indian Institute of Technology, Bombay, India.

Margareth Stoll passed her PhD degree in Technical Sciences at the Vienna University of Technology (Austria) and worked for several years as collaborator, lecturer, and consultant for different small, medium, and great-sized organizations in Austria, Germany, and Italy. Further, she is certified auditor for ISO 9001 quality management, ISO 27001 information security management, and ISO/IEC 20000-1 IT service management. After some years as project leader of scientific projects and scientific assistant at the University of Innsbruck, funded by the Tyrolean Future Foundation, she returned to industry. Her main research topics are holistic, interdisciplinary management systems for sustainable organizational development. She integrates most different research disciplines, such as strategic management, controlling, business process management, project management, IT management, information security management, quality management, knowledge management, and organizational learning.

Maria Tzanou is a Lecturer in Law at Keele Law School, UK. Maria holds a PhD in Law from the European University Institute (Florence, Italy), an LLM in Comparative, European, and International Law from the EUI, a Master II in "Specialized Public Law" from the Universities of Athens and Bordeaux IV, an LLM in European Law from the University of Cambridge, and an LLB from the University of Athens. Maria's research interests lie in EU privacy and data protection law, constitutional and human rights law, and counter-terrorism. She has published several articles on data protection in peer-reviewed journals and edited books and co-authored three reports for the EU Fundamental Rights Agency (FRA).

M. J. Warren is a Professor of Information Systems at Deakin University, Australia. Professor Warren is a researcher in the areas of Information Security, Computer Ethics, and Cyber Security. He has authored and co-authored over 300 books, book chapters, journal papers, and conference papers. He has received numerous grants and awards from national and international funding bodies, such as Australian Research Council (ARC), Engineering Physical Sciences Research Council (EPSRC) in the United Kingdom, National Research Foundation (NRF) in South Africa and the European Union. Professor Warren gained his PhD in Information Security Risk Analysis from the University of Plymouth, United Kingdom, and he has taught in Australia, Finland, Hong Kong, and the United Kingdom.

Ji Zhang is currently a Senior Lecturer in the Department of Mathematics and Computing, University of Southern Queensland (USQ), Australia. His research interests are Knowledge Discovery and Data Mining (KDD), Databases, Information Privacy, and Security. He was a Post-Doctoral Research Fellow in CSIRO ICT Center at Hobart, Australia, from 2008-2009. He received his degree of PhD from the Faculty of Computer Science at Dalhousie University, Canada, in 2008, degree of MSc from Department of Computer Science at National University of Singapore in 2002, and degree of BE from Department of Information Management and Information Systems at the Southeast University, China, in 2000. He has published over 70 papers in major peer-reviewed papers in major international journals and conferences.

Qing Zou is a PhD candidate in the School of Information Studies at McGill University. His research interests are metadata, ontology, knowledge organization systems, archival description, and knowledge representation.

Alejandro Zunino is an adjunct professor at UNICEN and member of ISISTAN and CONICET. His research areas include grid computing, service-oriented computing, Semantic Web services, and mobile agents. Zunino has a PhD in Computer Science from UNICEN.

Index

T

V

W